CW01338167

LOVE LOST
IN TRANSLATION

Homosexuality and the Bible

K. Renato Lings

Order this book online at www.trafford.com
or email orders@trafford.com

Most Trafford titles are also available at major online book retailers.

© Copyright 2013 K. Renato Lings.
All rights reserved. No part of this publication may be reproduced, stored in a retrieval system, or transmitted, in any form or by any means, electronic, mechanical, photocopying, recording, or otherwise, without the written prior permission of the author.

Printed in the United States of America.

ISBN: 978-1-4669-8790-6 (sc)
ISBN: 978-1-4669-8789-0 (hc)
ISBN: 978-1-4669-8791-3 (e)

Library of Congress Control Number: 2013906335

Cover image: *Scriptorium Monk at Work (from Lacroix)*

Trafford rev. 06/04/2013

Trafford PUBLISHING   www.trafford.com

North America & international
toll-free: 1 888 232 4444 (USA & Canada)
phone: 250 383 6864 ♦ fax: 812 355 4082

CONTENTS

ABBREVIATIONS	xix
SPELLING AND STYLE	xxi
ACKNOWLEDGEMENTS	xxiii
INTRODUCTION	xxv
Does the Bible Deal with Homosexuality?	xxv
A Cultural Gap	xxvii
A Problematic Consensus	xxx
The Bible in History	xxxiii
Asceticism, Language, and Exegesis	xxxiv
Sola Scriptura	xxxvi
Interpreting Ancient Texts	xxxviii
Formal or Dynamic?	xl
Relevant Bible Texts	xliv
Conclusion	xlv

PART ONE
Creation, Sex, and Knowing

1. BEGINNINGS	3
Introduction	3
Creation in the Christian Tradition	4
Non-Christian Perspectives on Creation	6
Feminist Perspectives	10
Sexuality and Gender	14
Genesis in Greek and Hebrew	18
Singular, Dual, and Plural	20
Groundling, Man, or Adam?	24
Translating ADAM	26
Rib or Side?	29
Who Invented the 'Rib'?	33
One Flesh	36

    Original Nakedness   39
    Conclusion   41

2. THE LANGUAGE OF SEX   **44**
    Introduction   44
    Come/Go In   45
    Lie Down   49
    Two Complementary Verbs   52
    Translating BŌ and EL   53
    Paraphrasing BŌ and EL   57
    Precision and Imprecision   59
    Translating SHAKHAV   62
    Secondary Verbs   66
    Sexual Violence   67
    Translating Sexual Transgression   70
    Illicit Sex   73
    Sex in a Nutshell   76
    Conclusion   78

3. TO KNOW IN THE BIBLICAL SENSE   **79**
    Introduction   79
    To Know in the Biblical Sense   82
    Knowing and Descendants   85
    The Meaning of Formal YADA'   88
    Significant Repetition and Grammar   90
    I Have Known Him   93
    Let Me Know   94
    Let Us Know Them   97
    Knowing a Husband   99
    He Did Not Know   103
    He Did Not Know Her Again   106
    Non-Sexual Knowing   108
    When Know Is Enquire   109
    Inconsistent Knowing   112
    Sex and Knowing   113
    Conclusion   117

PART TWO
Curse and Prohibitions

4. NOAH'S NAKEDNESS — 123
   Introduction — 123
   Interpreting Ham and Noah — 124
   A Garden and a Vineyard — 127
   Translating Noah's Drunkenness — 129
   Translating Ham's Reactions — 132
   Was Noah Castrated? — 135
   Was Noah Raped? — 137
   An Act of Incest? — 140
   Seeing a Naked Man — 143
   Ham and His Brothers — 146
   Curse and Blessing — 149
   Conclusion — 153

5. CONSECRATED — 155
   Introduction — 155
   A Mysterious Group of People — 156
   QADESH: A Matter of Debate — 158
   Hebrew Holiness — 160
   QADESH According to the Versions — 162
   A Vertical View — 164
   A Horizontal View — 166
   QEDESHĪM According to the Versions — 167
   Holiness or Depravity? — 171
   Consecrated — 172
   What Does a QEDESHAH Do? — 175
   The Veiled Woman — 177
   Prostitutes and Priestesses — 180
   The Price of a Dog — 184
   Translating 'Dog' — 186
   Trade, Prostitutes, and Dogs — 191
   Conclusion — 193

6. WITH A MALE   **195**
    Introduction   195
    Restricted Bisexuality   197
    Translating Leviticus 18.22   199
    'As With' Inserted   202
    Male/Man, Woman/Wife   206
    Lyings or Beds   209
    Abomination   213
    Early Interpretations of Leviticus 18.22   216
    Leviticus and Tradition   219
    Continuing Debate   222
    Unresolved Issues   225
    Incest, Part One   229
    Incest, Part Two   232
    Translating MISHKEVEY ISHSHAH   234
    Turn It and Turn It   236
    Conclusion   237

PART THREE
Sodom and Gomorrah

7. SODOM IN THE BIBLE   **241**
    Introduction   241
    The Story   242
    A Text in Genesis   246
    Sodom in the Hebrew Bible   248
    Sodom and Polytheism   255
    Hebrew Texts Mentioning Sodom   256
    Isaiah and Ezekiel on Sodom   258
    Sodom in the Apocrypha   263
    Sodom in the Second Testament   266
    Sodom in Jude   268
    Translating 'Other Flesh'   271
    Sodom as Immorality   276
    Lot in the Bible   278
    Conclusion   280

8. SODOM YESTERDAY — 282
Introduction — 282
Sodom in Pseudepigraphy — 283
Sodom in Philo and Josephus — 284
Sodom in the Early Church — 288
Sodom in the Fourth Century — 291
Sodomite and Sodomitic Vice — 294
The Invention of Sodomy — 297
Amplifying Sodomy — 300
Renaissance and Reformation — 303
Sodom According to Martin Luther — 306
The Triumph of Sodomy — 309
Sodomy in Literature — 312
Sodom in Judaism — 314
The Ambiguous World of Lot — 319
Conclusion — 322

9. SODOM TODAY — 325
Introduction — 325
Gagnon: A Traditional Reading — 326
Sodom as Humiliation — 327
Lot: Villain or Hero? — 330
Lot as Dirty Old Man — 332
The Ambiguity of Lot — 334
Standing Sodom on Its Head — 336
The Challenge of Postcolonialism — 338
Rediscovering Biblical Sodom — 343
Tradition and Innovation — 345
The Collectiveness of Sodom — 348
Can the Sodomites Know God? — 351
Reassessing 'Know' — 354
Conclusion — 356

10. TRANSLATING SODOM — 358
Introduction — 358
Any Homoeroticism in Sodom? — 359

All the People	364
To Come Upon Two Women	369
Come, Lie Down, and Know	372
YADA‛ in Sodom	376
'Know' in the Septuagint	377
To Know in the Greek Sense	380
'Know' in the Vulgate	381
Two Classical Versions	383
'Know' According to Martin Luther	385
'Know' in the King James Version	387
'Know' in Today's English Versions	389
Unknowing Versions	390
Choose, Find Out, or Rape?	394
YADA‛ in Twelve Versions	396
Conclusion	397

11. THE VICTIM OF SODOM 400

Introduction	400
Lot's Uncle	401
Abraham's Nephew	403
A Problematic Marriage	406
As the Good in Your Eyes, Part One	409
As the Good in Your Eyes, Part Two	414
Women and Children in the Buffer Zone	417
Lot's Dilemma	421
Loyalty and Non-Aggression	424
A Resident Alien	427
Sodom as a Legal Treatise	430
Outcry	434
Come Forward or Stand Back?	436
Conclusion	440

PART FOUR
Politics, Polemics, and Passions

12. THE OUTRAGE AT GIBEAH — 445
Introduction — 445
The Story — 447
Gibeah Yesterday — 450
A Text of Terror — 451
Gibeah after Trible — 453
Gibeah, Sodom, and Jericho — 456
Gibeah as Politics — 459
'Know' According to the Translators — 460
Sexual Violence in Gibeah and Beyond — 464
'Know' in a Violent Setting — 465
To Humiliate a Woman — 467
Having Fun at Someone's Expense — 470
The Good in Your Eyes — 475
Differences between Gibeah and Sodom — 477
Literary Allusions — 480
Conclusion — 484

13. SOFTIES AND MALE-LIERS — 486
Introduction — 486
Paul's Vices — 488
Softies — 490
Early Translations of *Malakoi* — 493
Translating *Malakoi* Today — 496
From Softness to Male Prostitution — 499
Male-Liers — 501
Early Translations of *Arsenokoitai* — 506
Translating *Arsenokoitai* Today — 508
Inconsistent Translators — 511
Paul's Concerns — 514
Conclusion — 519

14. BEYOND NATURE — 521
- Introduction — 521
- Interpreting Romans 1 — 523
- Past vs. Present, Part One — 526
- Past vs. Present, Part Two — 531
- Past vs. Present, Part Three — 536
- Idolatrous Females — 538
- Natural vs. Unnatural — 541
- Translating *Para Physin* — 543
- Idolatrous Males — 546
- Text and Context — 550
- Paul and Wisdom — 552
- Passions and Idolatry — 557
- Paul's Addressees — 560
- Conclusion — 563

PART FIVE
The Language of Love

15. LOVE LOST IN TRANSLATION — 569
- Introduction — 569
- Love in the First Testament — 571
- Ruth and Naomi — 573
- Translating Ruth's Commitment — 576
- A Blessed Relationship — 579
- David and Jonathan — 583
- Saul's Love for David — 585
- You Were Dear to Me — 588
- Faithful Love — 590
- Love in the Second Testament — 593
- Physical Intimacy — 596
- The Beloved Disciple — 600
- Translating the Beloved Disciple — 604
- Simon Peter's Commitment — 607
- Love Lost in Translation — 610
- Conclusion — 614

CONCLUSION

APPENDICES

APPENDIX 1 — 625
Sodom in Islam — 625
APPENDIX 2 — 629
Knowing in Babylonia — 629

GLOSSARIES

HEBREW GLOSSARY — 645
GREEK GLOSSARY — 650
LATIN GLOSSARY — 654

BIBLIOGRAPHY — 657
SCRIPTURE REFERENCE INDEX — 699
NAME INDEX — 723
AUTHOR INDEX — 731

TABLES

1	Divine Plurals and Singulars in Gen. 1	22
2	Human Plurals and Singulars in Gen. 1	23
3	English Versions of the Bible	27
4	Translating ADAM and HA-ADAM	28
5	Translating Hebrew TSELA‘	31
6	BŌ as Sexual Agent	48
7	SHAKHAV in Sexual Contexts	52
8	Sex in Genesis	53
9	Translating BŌ & EL	54
10	Literalness of Twelve Versions	59
11	Consistency and Inconsistency	60
12	Renderings of SHAKHAV & Preposition	63
13	Translating Sexual Debasement in Gen. 34.2	70
14	Verbs Denoting Sex in Genesis	76
15	A Text in Genesis with YADA‘	91
16	Forms of YADA‘ in Genesis 18–19	92
17	Two Significant Cohortatives	98
18	Translating YADA‘ in Gen. 38.26	107
19	Translating YADA‘ in Gen. 39.6 & 39.8	110
20	Translations of YADA‘ in Genesis 38–39	112
21	Sex, Knowing and Intimacy in Genesis 38 & 39	116
22	Translating Noah's Drunkenness	130
23	Translating Ham's Reactions	133
24	Behaviour of Ham and His Brothers	147
25	QADOSH According to the Versions	161
26	Translating QADESH and QEDESHĪM	162
27	Translating QEDESHĪM	168
28	Comparing QEDESHAH and QADESH	173
29	Translating QEDESHAH / QEDESHŌTH	176
30	ZONAH and QEDESHAH in Hosea 4.14	180
31	Translating MECHĪR KELEV	187

32	Translating Lev. 18.22	200
33	Translating TO'EVAH HĪ	213
34	Hypotheses about Lev. 18.22	228
35	Destruction and Desolation	249
36	Pride and Arrogance	250
37	Apostasy and Idolatry	252
38	Corruption and Oppression	254
39	Sodom in the Hebrew Bible	257
40	Sodom in the Apocrypha	264
41	Sodom in the Second Testament	268
42	Translating Reference to Sodom in Jude	272
43	Translating SHAKHAV in Gen. 19.4	361
44	Translating BŌ & EL in Gen. 19.5	362
45	Translating 'From Boy to Old Man'	365
46	Translating 'From Small to Great'	366
47	Translating BŌ & 'AL in Gen. 19.31	370
48	Translating SHAKHAV, BŌ and YADA'	374
49	YADA' in the Hebrew Text of Sodom	376
50	YADA' in the Verbal Paradigm	377
51	'Know' in Sodom According to the LXX	378
52	'Know' in Sodom According to the Vulgate	382
53	'Know' According to the MT and Two Classical Versions	384
54	'Know' in Sodom According to Luther	386
55	'Know' in Sodom According to the KJV	388
56	YADA' in Gen. 18–19 According to English Versions	389
57	YADA' in Twelve Versions (Genesis 18–19)	396
58	From 'Good' to 'Abuse': Two Interpretations	413
59	As the Good in Your Eyes	414
60	Legal/Judicial Language of Genesis 18–19	432
61	Translating NAGASH	438
62	Translating 'Know' in Judges 19	461
63	Translating 'ANAH	468
64	Translating 'ALAL	471
65	Translating Two Verbs of Violence	474

66	'The Good in Your Eyes' (Judges 19.24)	476
67	Differences between Gibeah and Sodom	478
68	Micah-Dan and Gibeah	480
69	Literary Allusions in Judges 19–21	482
70	Translating *malakos* and *malakoi*	496
71	Translating *arsenokoitai*	509
72	Translating 'Their Females'	539
73	Translating *para physin* in Romans	544
74	Translating 'Males' & 'Their Error' in Rom. 1.27	546
75	The Book of Wisdom in Romans 1	554
76	Translating DAVAQ, 'Cling'	577
77	Saul Loved Him Greatly	586
78	David's Feelings for Jonathan	589
79	Translating 'On Jesus' Chest' in John 13	598
80	Jesus Loving Lazarus (John 11)	604
81	Simon Peter Loving Jesus (Greek)	608
82	Translating Simon Peter Loving Jesus	609
83	Translating *agapaō* and *phileō* in John 21.15-17	611
84	Translation Issues in Twelve Versions	618
85	Marriage and Sex in the Laws of Hammurabi	640

ABBREVIATIONS

AD	Anno Domini
BCE	Before the Common Era
BDB	Brown, Driver, and Briggs
CCB	Christian Community Bible
CE	Common Era
DBHE	*Diccionario bíblico hebreo-español* (Alonso Schökel)
D-R	Douay-Rheims Version
FFM	Friberg, Friberg and Miller: *Analytical Lexicon*
FT	First Testament (Hebrew Bible, Old Testament)
HB	Hebrew Bible (First Testament, Old Testament)
HCSB	Holman Christian Standard Bible
JM	James Moffatt, *The Bible: A New Translation*
JPS	Jewish Publication Society
LEB	Lexham English Bible
LGBTI	Lesbian, gay, bisexual, transgender, and intersex
L&S	Liddell and Scott, *A Greek-English Lexicon*
LXX	Septuagint
MT	Masoretic Text (Hebrew Bible)
NAB	New American Bible
NCV	New Century Version
NIV	New International Version
NJB	New Jerusalem Bible
NT	New Testament (Second Testament)
NKJV	New King James Bible
NLT	New Living Translation
NRSV	New Revised Standard Version
NWT	New World Translation
OD	Oxford Dictionaries
OT	Old Testament (First Testament, Hebrew Bible)
REB	Revised English Bible
SR	Significant repetition
ST	Second Testament (New Testament)

SPELLING AND STYLE

Most Bible quotations in this book are taken from the New Revised Standard Version (NRSV). Whenever this or other sources are not stated explicitly, translations are mine.

I have used British spelling norms, e.g. *centre, defence, enquire, favour, practice* (noun) and *practise* (verb). Likewise, British style rules apply, including single quotation marks ('rib') and no comma following *i.e.*

Greek words in this book are transliterated, with long vowels such as η and ω represented as *ē* and *ō*, respectively: *agapē* ('love'), *paredōken* ('he handed over').

To transcribe Hebrew words, I have chosen simplified spelling:

- Representation of the consonant א (*alef*) is omitted in words such as *adam* ('groundling' or 'Adam'), *bō* ('come') and *Elohim* ('God').
- The guttural consonant ע (*'ayin*) is reproduced by means of the graph ʻ as in *ʻasah* ('do'), *toʻevah* ('abomination'), and *yadaʻ* ('know').
- The consonant ו (*waw*) is written *w* as in *Chawwah*, 'Eve', while *v* represents the consonant ב (*beth*) positioned immediately after a vowel sound, e.g. *davaq*, 'cling', *toʻevah*, 'abomination', and *ahav*, 'love'.
- The Hebrew consonant ח (*chet*) is pronounced with a guttural sound as *ch* in Scottish *loch* and German *Bach*. The transcription is *ch*: *Chawwah*, 'Eve', *mechīr*, 'price', and *laqach*, 'take'.

ACKNOWLEDGEMENTS

For the many different ways in which they have offered practical and moral support, I wish to express my gratitude to Heather Barfoot, EABS Postgraduate Seminar in Hamburg 2012, Thomas D. Hanks, Ole Kongsdal, Philip Law, Samarth Joel Ram, Johannes Sørensen, Juan Stam, Jørgen Thiesen, Alfredo Vallejo, and Ignacio Villares. I am indebted to the following for providing high-quality proofreading at different stages of this book: Stephen Barton, Christina Beardsley, Mary Benefiel Dunn, Tom Flanagan, John-Francis Friendship, Sara Hubner, Hilary Johnson, Iain McDonald, Catherine McNamara, Sophie MacKenzie, Rebecca Rosewarne, Marian Taylor, Damian Wedge, and Ian Woods. A very special thank you goes to Clare Hamon who graciously volunteered to proofread the whole book twice.

CONTACT

Any mistakes that may have slipped into the final edition of this study are my responsibility. Readers are kindly invited to send corrections and constructive criticism to biblioglot@gmail.com. I thank everyone in advance.

INTRODUCTION

The classical Christian tradition . . . concerning sexual morality is a product of the patristic, not the biblical age.

— Joseph Monti [1]

Does the Bible Deal with Homosexuality?

Before analysing a subject such as 'homosexuality and the Bible', the first question to address should be whether or not these two terms are compatible. They certainly originated from very different historical eras and contexts. The word *Biblia* has ancient Greek roots and literally means 'books'. Over time, *Biblia* became singular in several languages and equivalent to the English word 'Bible'. The various biblical writings were composed in three different languages. A very small part of the First Testament (FT)[2] was penned in Aramaic, but the vast majority of its pages were written in Biblical Hebrew.[3] For this reason, the term 'Hebrew Bible' (HB) is justifiable. The language of the Second Testament (ST) is Greek. The HB was assembled into a single volume more than 2000 years ago and the ST about 1800 years ago.

---

[1] Monti 1995: 27.
[2] Harry James Cargas (1989: 125) urges Christian theologians to abandon the terms 'Old Testament' and 'New Testament'. Following the example of *The Queer Bible Commentary* (2006), I use 'First Testament' as a synonym of 'Hebrew Bible' and 'Second Testament' rather than 'New Testament'.
[3] Biblical Hebrew is sometimes known as Classical Hebrew; cf. Sáenz-Badillos 1993: 52; Groom 2003: 3.

The word 'homosexual' was coined in the nineteenth century. It was first used in 1869 by Karl-Maria Benkert, a Hungarian journalist living in Germany.[4] During the twentieth century the term was adopted by sexologists and became one of three major 'sexual orientations': heterosexual, homosexual, and bisexual. Given the risk of historical and conceptual confusion when such a modern word is imported into a biblical context, it should be clearly defined. According to the *Oxford Dictionary* (OD), a 'homosexual' is 'a person who is sexually attracted to people of their own sex'.[5] However, Bernadette Brooten (1996: 8) has observed that the word 'homosexual' in English often has masculine connotations. Occasionally it is used in a pejorative sense.

In the entire Bible, there is not a single term that translates as 'homosexual'. For all such reasons, whenever ancient cultures are studied, including those mentioned in the books of the Bible, it is wise to use flexible terminology with little or no traditional bias. According to Brooten, such a term is 'homoerotic'. There may be some support for this point in the *OD*. It defines the adjective 'homoerotic' as 'concerning or arousing sexual desire centred on a person of the same sex'. Martti Nissinen (1998: 17) has reached a similar conclusion. By homoeroticism, he refers to

> all erotic-sexual encounters and experiences of people with persons of the same sex, whether the person is regarded as homosexual or not. This concept encompasses also bisexual behaviour as long as it occurs in an erotic contact with a person of the same sex.

---

[4] In Hungarian, the name is Károly Mária Kertbeny.
[5] oxforddictionaries.com/view/entry/m_en_gb0384640#m_en_gb0384640 (2012).

Anthony Heacock (2011: 3) offers this definition:

> Homoerotic describes the erotic bonding of men with men (as well as women with women) that manifests itself in various sexual acts.

Heacock acknowledges the distinctly sexual focus of his description. I intend to reuse and redefine this formulation by making it shorter and wider. In my own personal dictionary, the word would appear as follows:

> Homoerotic describes erotic bonding of men with men and women with women. It may or may not manifest itself in sexual acts.

In the light of this reflection, I choose to go along with Brooten, Nissinen, and Heacock, opting for the term homoerotic.[6]

A Cultural Gap

A rigorous historical examination of the evolution of Christian thinking about sex reveals that the origin of some key elements is not, strictly speaking, biblical. Yet despite the cultural gap between the world of the Bible and the twenty-first century, it is widely believed that some passages of the Bible address the phenomenon currently called homosexuality. It is often stated that the biblical writers condemn all manifestations of same-sex intimacy

---

[6] Some scholars, including Rebecca Alpert (2006: 61), use the adjective 'translesbigay' in reference to a wider group extending beyond 'homoerotic' to include transgender persons. Currently several different acronyms are in use: LGBT, LGBTI and LGBTIQ. LGBT stands for 'lesbian, gay, bisexual and transgender', while the letters 'I' and 'Q' represent 'intersexual' and 'queer', respectively.

among human beings (Heacock 2011: 2, 90). A representative work is *The Bible and Homosexual Practice* by Robert Gagnon (2001). On one occasion Gagnon admits a hypothesis: *'If same-sex intercourse is indeed sin'* (p. 28, his emphasis). However, he very soon makes up his mind as doubt turns into absolute certainty. He is convinced that scripture and church tradition, as he understands them, are unequivocally opposed to homoeroticism (pp. 29, 341, 432-8). Gagnon strives to present the whole Bible as an infallible law book with a pervasive stance on the subject 'across the Testaments and accepted for nearly two millennia of the church's existence' (pp. 28-9).

Among the 'traditional sexual values' discussed by Gagnon, one finds 'sexual holiness' (p. 26). In his opinion, all biblical writers disapprove of 'sinful behaviour' because God 'loves the entire world but does not tolerate sin'. Gagnon defines what he calls homosexual behaviour as sin because it has 'negative health effects'. Moreover, he considers it to be 'destructive to individuals and/or society' as well as 'contrary to God's will' (pp. 26-7). Indeed, for Gagnon 'homosexual practice' includes such negative side effects and societal ills as health risks (particularly AIDS), rampant promiscuity, sadomasochism, domestic violence, and murder (p. 30).[7] Gagnon's position is clearly indebted to a long church tradition (p. 29), causing some of his main

---

[7] Apparently Gagnon is ready to accuse anyone who does not share his arguments of having misunderstood the biblical material. He takes the view that 'the burden of proof is entirely on those who would assert otherwise' (2001: 29, 78). At first sight, Gagnon's bibliography looks impressive, but the index of modern authors contains a series of names whose academic profile is at best insignificant and, in several cases, questionable. Gagnon adheres to the controversial ex-gay movement, which proposes 'curing' gay people of their homoerotic feelings by means of psychotherapy based on so-called Christian principles (pp. 420-9). Furthermore, Gagnon avoids tentative working hypotheses. Throughout this work, the

points about homoerotic relationships to be very close to the essence of official Roman Catholic doctrine (Jordan 2000: 7).

Given such scholarly and popular insistence, further clarification is needed. Since there is no direct way in which one can consult ancient writers, the only possible access to their thinking is through available literature. The difficulty here is that modern readers are frequently inclined to impose contemporary concepts (and not just sexual ones) on cultures that existed in the past (Brenner 1997: 28). Thus, Hilary Lipka (2006: 7) has detected a clear tendency to believe that current sexual notions are universally valid, applicable to all periods everywhere. Lipka warns that very few norms or values can be classified as intercultural or universal (2006: 2–5). The problem becomes particularly acute when the literary and social environment under exploration is remote from our own era and geographical location (p. 4).

Likewise, various scholars underline the multiple discrepancies between current sexual vocabularies and the concepts commonly used in the ancient world (Alter 1996: xxx; Brenner 1997: 151, 177). For example, Alan Cadwallader (2012: 56-7) observes how sexuality in the Hellenistic period (ca. 300 BCE to ca. 300 CE) was understood in close connection with notions of property and a hierarchy of gender relations. Similarly, for Anthony Heacock (2011: 4), contemporary notions of sexuality, including homosexuality, are far removed from the rigid hierarchical views on gender and sexual expression that were prevalent in antiquity. Ancient Greece rated masculinity highly whereas femininity represented a lower, weak, or incomplete stage of personal development (Cranny-Francis, Waring, Stavropoulos & Kirkby 2003: 2). As noted by Haddox (2010: 4), 'becoming

---

complete self-assuredness with which he trusts his personal criteria and intuition often causes his conclusions to be predictable.

like women' has been a frequent metaphor used by men to represent loss of social prestige and power.

In the past this has had a bearing on male sexuality, including same-sex relationships. In ancient Mesopotamia, sexual intimacy among men of equal status is described as acceptable in the saga of Enkidu and Gilgamesh (Vanggaard 1969: 108), while the relationship of Achilles and Patroclus is a famous example from ancient Greece (Boswell 1980: 25 n. 44). However, from several parts of the world there are literary references to men with male lovers who struggled not to be perceived as feminized. In pre-Christian Scandinavian literature, this issue is interwoven with notions of honour and shame (Vanggaard 1969: 70–4). In certain cultures, the characteristic pattern was pederasty. It would entail a considerable age-gap between the two partners inasmuch as one would be a mature man and the other a teenage boy. The older man would typically be well-positioned socially and economically while his younger male lover could be either free-born or a slave. Considerable diversity existed in antiquity with regard to forms of pederasty (Boswell 1980: 28–30; Carden 2006: 24). Such variations concerning same-sex relationships in ancient times should be borne in mind when the Bible is approached.

A Problematic Consensus

In recent years, a growing number of scholars have suggested that current beliefs about homoeroticism in the Bible do not have a solid scriptural basis (Jordan 1997; Long 2006; Lings 2011; Sharpe 2011). A major factor to be reckoned with is the presence of a long church tradition. Two thousand years of theological reflection have created a pre-established bias, which affects modern readers of biblical passages dealing with sexual issues. Many church fathers took inspiration from certain dualist aspects of Greek philosophy, particularly Neo-Platonism with its emphasis on concepts such as intellect, soul, nature, and salvation (Boswell 1980: 128-9; Gaca 2003: 1-2). A very large part of what today's Roman Catholic and Protestant theologians have to say on eroticism derives from theological treatises written by sexually chaste and/or celibate male clergy, often middle aged or elderly and given to misogyny (Brown 1990: 484). The magnitude of this historical legacy is such that no Christians today can declare themselves free from prejudice when it comes to interpreting biblical reflections of human sexuality.

When dealing with the fierce controversy over the Bible and homosexuality, which has rocked the entire Christian world for several decades, it is intriguing to note that no great differences are found in terms of exegesis. Leviticus 18.22 is an example of a text to which most debaters seem to apply the same analytical methodology (cf. chapter 5). Discrepancies among scholars arise in the hermeneutical conclusions they derive from these texts. Without excessively simplifying the panorama, two opposed theological schools may be said to exist. One school argues that the Bible condemns unequivocally any expression of a homoerotic nature. For this reason, it is deemed crucial that believers should reject this phenomenon in all its manifestations, including recent lesbian and gay civil rights movements (Gagnon 2001: 30 n. 3, 35, 483). At the other extreme of the spectrum, one finds debaters who suggest that scriptural statements on this issue echo specific social and cultural contexts of the ancient world, which do not apply to people today (Stuart 2003: 105). According to the latter approach, it is legitimate to disregard the biblical prohibitions and emphasize the inclusive message proclaimed by the Christian Gospel (Helminiak 2000: 72-3; Stuart 2003: 18-19).

The ideological schools mentioned here have been in conflict for years. This writer has been greatly surprised to discover that something essential is missing from the current debate: few detailed academic analyses have been carried out of the literary and semantic aspects of the most controversial texts. This raises questions about the credibility of traditional exegesis. In order to find a way out of the current theological deadlock, I propose to introduce a different methodology, bypassing medieval tradition. Specifically the pronounced ascetic and misogynistic preoccupations of the post-biblical era should be sidelined. There is an urgent need to take a fresh look at the texts based on their biblical contexts and original languages in order to appreciate their literary, cultural, and theological richness.

A number of fresh questions have to be asked of the texts. To gauge the depth of the biblical material, a substantial amount of curiosity is not just an advantage but a necessity. If scholars from different backgrounds and disciplines are consulted, the variety of hypotheses that they formulate is likely to stimulate research efforts, which in turn lead to fresh insights.[8] The biblical passages generally contain fascinating information unrelated to the sphere of sexuality. I therefore postulate that scripture is not concerned about the manifestations that many today may choose to call homoerotic. Over the pages of this book, I perform two operations: (1) explore the material offered by the Bible by means of a detailed scrutiny of the nuances of the original languages, (2) compare my findings with twelve contemporary English versions of the Bible. As they communicate the biblical messages to Christian readers today, these versions are crucial. Millions of people around

---

[8] Cf. Miller (2010: 43): 'People from all situations of life are needed in the task of Bible exegesis. Your situation affects the questions you ask of the text, and questions that do not get asked also do not get answered.'

the world base their views on same-sex relationships on the specific wording chosen by the Bible versions they habitually use.

The Bible in History

It is impossible to determine the exact time of composition of most books included in the Bible. While historians disagree, it is generally thought that most sacred Hebrew writings were written well before the third century BCE. Given the archaic nature of the language, the earliest books seem to date back to at least the sixth century BCE (Sáenz-Badillos 1993: 52). With the rise of the empire of Alexander the Great in the fourth century BCE, Hellenistic culture spread across vast areas of the ancient world, including Palestine. Greek became the lingua franca in all the recently occupied territories, and many Jewish communities in different parts of the empire adopted Greek (Rajak 1983: 8). Even before the conquests of Alexander, Greek language and culture were a constant presence in Jewish life (1983: 2, 7, 8). A growing number of Jews had difficulty in understanding Biblical Hebrew, so a translation of scripture into the vernacular of the diaspora was needed. Early versions of the Septuagint appeared in Alexandria around the year 200 BCE.

With the advent of the Roman Empire, the entire Mediterranean basin became acquainted with another new language, Latin. This added to the already impressive linguistic diversity of the ancient world. At the time in which the ministry of Jesus began—the first century CE—no fewer than five languages coexisted in Palestine: (1) Biblical Hebrew, used in synagogues for liturgical purposes; (2) Late Hebrew, spoken by some rabbis and their followers, primarily in Judea; (3) Aramaic, the common language of the majority used in daily communication and in many synagogues to explain the meaning of biblical texts; (4) Greek, the literary language of this period; and (5) the administrative Latin introduced by the Roman occupation.

From the very start, the influence of the Septuagint, also known as LXX, on Christian thinking was immense. In the early church, the prestige of the LXX was such that it completely superseded the original HB (Metzger 2001: 18). Many believers today ignore the fact that all the writers who contributed to the Second Testament read the Septuagint and used it whenever they wanted to quote the First Testament (Caird 1980: 122). In other words, Christian writers soon adopted the habit of neglecting the Hebrew language (Loader 2004: 127).[9] As Christianity spread across the Roman Empire, the imperial language became increasingly important in the life of the church. In the fourth century, all scriptural books were translated into Latin. Jerome's *Vulgate* appeared towards the year 400 CE. The prestige of this seminal work is based on the translator's fame and the time of publication. Within the Western Catholic Church, the Vulgate grew in importance until the sixteenth century, when it became identified as the official Catholic Bible, a privilege it held until the 1960s. Thus, the word 'Vulgate' became synonymous with 'Bible' (Long 2001: 121-3). For well over a millennium, it provided the exclusive framework for biblical interpretation, with significant repercussions in Christian theology (Jordan 1997: 31).

Asceticism, Language, and Exegesis

One of the noteworthy phenomena of early Christianity was the growth of a general fear of erotic instincts coupled with

---

[9] Today's Orthodox churches still venerate the LXX as their official version of the First Testament (Metzger 2001: 20).

a widespread preoccupation with the desires of the human body. In some Christian circles, the perceived evil nature of worldly worries was of grave concern. The believers wanted to break the chains that tied them to the material world, and in their view, this included reproduction. One radical approach extensively adopted was to abstain deliberately from having children (Brown 1990: 481). Following the rise of the Christian church to official status in the fourth century, a dual or ambivalent approach to human sexuality gradually took hold. Some prominent theologians thought that an active sex life was acceptable within marriage in order to ensure reproduction (Stuart & Thatcher 1997: 18). In other cases, however, there was a growing tendency to exalt the *pure* life in the form of asceticism and celibacy. This became a movement that invited the entire caste of priests, monks, and nuns to fight against their erotic instincts and renounce all bodily pleasures.

The repressive climate prevalent in church circles needed to be justified ideologically. This was achieved by turning to the supreme source of religious and literary inspiration, the Bible, initially the LXX and subsequently the Vulgate. An outstanding example of the issues just described is provided by Augustine of Hippo (354–430 CE). This church father made use of the incipient ideas on original sin expressed by Paul in Romans 5.12, elevating the concept to the status of doctrine (Stuart & Thatcher 1997: 18–19; McGrath 1998: 82). If one takes Augustine's interpretation of the so-called fall of Adam and Eve as narrated in Genesis and then compares it with Jewish commentaries on the same story, a remarkable fact is discovered: Judaism lacks the notion of the basic sinfulness or indelible contamination of humankind. According to rabbinic tradition, the events of Genesis 3 do not correspond to some concept of 'original sin' but rather express the process of development of human consciousness from childhood and puberty to mature adulthood (Bechtel 1993: 84–6; Magonet 2004: 124–5).

Another noteworthy example is the concept of sodomy. This is applied to homoerotic relationships for the first time in the eleventh century in a work written in Latin by the Italian monk Peter Damian. By contrast, the notion of sodomy is absent from the Jewish horizon. Instead, medieval Judaism coined the Hebrew term *middat Sedom*, 'the yardstick of Sodom', which denotes cruelty and indifference to the needs of fellow citizens (Greenberg 2004: 71). In other words, the lessons drawn from Sodom by Jewish theologians have to do with inhospitality and hardheartedness, rather than sexual behaviour.

Sola Scriptura

For centuries no one questioned the faults and failures of the Vulgate. Alister McGrath (1998: 123) observes how a series of mistakes appeared in the Latin text over time despite its canonical status. The errors were detected as soon as Renaissance scholars obtained access to the biblical texts in the original languages. This endeavour was facilitated by the publication of the Hebrew Bible in 1488 and subsequently the Second Testament in Greek (1512). From then on the credibility of the Vulgate was considerably undermined (Flood 2001: 48). In the early sixteenth century, the idea that Christian theology should not be founded on translation errors began to take hold and had a considerable impact on the Protestant reformers (2001: 49). As may be deduced from the motto *sola scriptura* ('scripture only'), the Reformation proposed to return to the written sources in the original languages. The stated aim of the reformers was to distance themselves from Catholic tradition and the Vulgate (Metzger 2001: 9).

However, while the linguists of the Renaissance were capable of discovering and correcting a number of transcription errors in various editions of the LXX and the Vulgate, other problems were left intact. Such is the case of the unconvincing renderings in these versions of the Hebrew verb *yada'*, 'know', especially in the story of Sodom and Gomorrah, which are still being imitated today (cf. chapter 10). Clearly the reformers did not succeed in liberating themselves from several repressive aspects of traditional hermeneutics in sexual matters. Thus, in most Protestant circles, restrictive medieval approaches to sex have remained stable until the twenty-first century, especially in regard to homoerotic relationships.

A few years ago, a survey was conducted in the United States on views and attitudes among young non-believers (Kinnaman & Lyons, 2007). When asked to express their personal impressions of Christians in the United States, the majority said that they found Christians to be (a) anti-gay, (b) intolerant, and (c) hypocritical. This survey succinctly reflects how the current negative attitude towards homo- and bisexuality inherited from medieval theology is perceived by non-Christians. In a number of cases, this perception is accurate. In some churches today, the rejection of homoerotic relationships ranks as fundamental doctrine, having virtually become the touchstone of Christian orthodoxy (Brooten 1996: 194; Stuart 2003: 105). It is maintained that a homosexual person cannot be a Christian and Christians cannot be gay, and according to this view, monogamous heterosexuality and/or sexual abstinence are the only lifestyles capable of leading believers to salvation (Kraus 2011: 30). This theological standpoint is often defended with such energy that it may practically be classified as a significant, post-biblical extension of the ancient Ten Commandments. A hypothetical eleventh commandment seems to say, 'You shall not have homoerotic relationships.'

In some cases, the intransigence of the anti-gay imperative is justified by affirming (echoing the words of several medieval theologians) that homo- and bisexual impulses are instigated by the devil (Damian 1982: 60; Jordan 1997: 55-7). The anti-gay postulate in Christian thought today is buttressed by a large number of versions of the Bible as well as by commentaries and dictionaries. Almost universally, they make it clear that the Bible prohibits all aspects of homoeroticism. The core texts are found in both testaments: the opening chapters of Genesis, the story of Sodom and Gomorrah (Gen. 18 & 19), Leviticus 18.22 (& 20.13), the drama of Judges 19, and some Pauline letters in the ST (Rom. 1.26-27; 1 Cor. 6.9; 1 Tim. 1.10).

Interpreting Ancient Texts

All ancient texts present challenges to translators. This is true of every single text frequently quoted in connection with the Bible/homosexuality controversy. All such passages contain opaque elements, many of which make it difficult for translators to reach agreement on essential details. This basic difficulty explains why versions often differ. It raises the question of how biblical interpretation is to be carried out by people who do not read Classical Hebrew or Hellenistic Greek. The distance in time and culture separating today's scholars from the text they are studying is such that 'most ancient texts do not have clear meanings readily discernible by us today' (Cotterell & Turner 1989: 43). The huge gap between our culture and the worlds in which the biblical writings were born is 'perhaps unbridgeable' (Jasper 1998: 24). This situation affects everyone born in post-biblical times, including the great Jewish exegetes of the Middle Ages. While they were scrutinizing the biblical text in the original Hebrew (unlike Christian commentators who relied on the Latin Vulgate), they wrote in Medieval Hebrew (Alter 1992: 142). Derived from the Late Hebrew of the Hellenistic era, this language diverged considerably from the classical norms (Sáenz-Badillos 1993: 211–19 ff).[10]

Inevitably, all modern Bible interpreters, including translators, commentators, religious ministers, and readers face a series of obstacles and risks unknown to ancient speakers of Hebrew and Greek familiar with the scriptures. For translators, the situation becomes particularly challenging if they do not receive proper training. Undoubtedly theology and biblical studies provide useful academic tools, but these are not always sufficient. Above all, they do not equip the translator with adequate linguistic methodology, which is indispensable for anyone wishing to analyse texts from the ancient cultures of the Middle East. Peter Cotterell and Max Turner (1989: 9) summarize the problem:

> Unfortunately our system of higher education seems designed to keep the disciplines of biblical studies and linguistics isolated from each other, and few theologians have been exposed even to those aspects of linguistics which are of most relevance to them.

While biblical language is rife with complexity, it is possible that even greater obstacles to modern exegesis are found outside the texts. Lyn Bechtel (1998: 108) invites exegetes to reflect on their personal attitudes and assumptions and finds that many biblical scholars inadvertently allow their modern world view to determine their reading or translation of the text. Richard Holloway (1999: 49, 83) offers a similar word of caution:

---

[10] This is so much the case that those exegetes whose knowledge of Hebrew is limited to the biblical texts find it very difficult to understand the Medieval Hebrew used in the works of Rashi, Maimonides, and others (Alter 1992: 140).

> We probably read more into the Bible than we get out of it . . . What we bring to scripture . . . is as important as what we get from it.

No Bible reader is free from bringing assumptions to the book. Robert Alter (1992: 131) argues that interpreters ineluctably betray ancient texts by translating them into their own conceptual frameworks. He adds a warning (p. 132):

> No comment on a text is ever innocent . . . every act of exegesis or even of ostensibly simple glossing is a means of intervening in the text, asserting power over it and over those who would use it.

Formal or Dynamic?

> If you wish to influence the masses, a simple translation is always best. Critical translations vying with the original really are only of use for conversations the learned conduct among themselves.[11]

Thus, Johann Wolfgang von Goethe in the early nineteenth century. He was commenting on the 'simple' or 'popular' language adopted by Martin Luther for his famous sixteenth-century German version of the Bible. Judging from a series of modern versions, Goethe's argument still holds even if it tends to be phrased somewhat less polemically; many Bible editors today hold the concept of simple language as their ideal.[12] What exactly, then, is a 'simple'

---

[11] For the original German see *Goethe Handbuch*, Bd. 4/2, 1998: 1071. The above English quotation is taken from Long 2001: 130.

[12] The introduction to the *New Light Bible* (1998) is representative: 'Above all, the Bible is meant to be understood. Scholars have

translation of the Bible? The answer is much less evident than it may seem at first sight.

Two different trends or schools operate in the field of Bible translation. The literal translation method is sometimes called formal equivalence while the other is known as dynamic equivalence. The formal school sets out to achieve a high level of accuracy or fidelity vis-à-vis the original text, whereas the dynamic approach aims to produce a readable, accessible text (Thomas 2000: 89–90). Generally speaking, the dynamic method does away with ambiguous interpretations (p. 169). Translators are invited to choose among various options and to take the risk of a high level of subjectivity (p. 180). This phenomenon occurs frequently in obscure Bible passages (p. 177 n. 54). The tension between these two approaches has been recognized and discussed for a good number of years, and no Bible translator avoids dealing with the issue.

Most recent Bible editions have adopted the dynamic equivalence approach. The current tendency stands in intriguing contrast to early Christian translations, which to a large extent followed formal criteria (2000: 184). One of the risk factors involved in the dynamic method is underestimating the importance of the cultural, historical, and religious issues of the biblical era. At the same time, the dynamic method may be excessively prone to reflecting contemporary concerns that were never present in the minds of HB and ST narrators (pp. 107, 188). Any modification, including that of minor, apparently insignificant nuances, is capable of distorting the basic meaning of a text. The history

---

worked hard over the years to keep producing new and clearer translations. They have tried to put the original Hebrew and Greek Bible into words that today's readers can readily understand . . . The New Light Bible puts the words of the Bible as accurately as possible into the kind of easy-to-read style of the original authors.'

of Bible translation is awash with controversies caused by religious, theological, or political differences. An oft-quoted example is the debate surrounding the Hebrew word ʿalmah in Isaiah 7.14. Strictly speaking, the meaning of ʿalmah is 'young woman' (BDB p. 761; DBHE p. 569). However, a long hermeneutical tradition in Christianity interprets ʿalmah as 'virgin'. In this manner, a prophetic link is established between the Isaiah passage and the Gospel of Matthew (1.22). At times the controversies surrounding ʿalmah have been heated.[13]

It is characteristic of dynamic equivalence that it tends to place little importance on the literary style of the original text and on the long historical processes reflected in it (Long 2001: 210). That said, this method should not be entirely discarded. Perhaps the greatest purpose of dynamic equivalence is in introducing the Bible to youthful audiences. In addition, in some situations it may be a necessary supplement to other translation methods. This is often the case in difficult texts where an entirely literal procedure may yield poor results. One such example is Leviticus 18.22 (cf. chapter 6). Furthermore, it is a great advantage for curious Bible readers to have access to a wide range of versions, an observation made by Augustine of Hippo (354-430) in his work *De doctrina christiana*. At the same time, this church father writing in Latin warned his readers against taking all versions at face value. The important thing was to be 'discerning' (Long 2001: 3, 174).

Robert Thomas (2000) highlights the temptation which presents itself to anyone who wishes to produce a 'simple' version: the possibility of transferring to the text one's own personal views by subtle means. In this context, he asks a critical question (pp. 189-90):

---

[13] Thuesen 1999: 4, 10-11, 13-14, 94-6, 125, 143, 147, 154, etc.

> But if a translator goes one step further and intentionally incorporates his personal interpretations when he could have left many passages with the same ambiguity as the original, has he done right by those who will use his translation?

As the present book will demonstrate, this question is highly relevant in connection with a number of texts thought to deal with homoeroticism, including the story of Sodom and Gomorrah. If one wishes to avoid the risk of distorting the narrative logic of a given passage, the safest procedure is, in Thomas's view, to reproduce the original words and sentences following a strictly literal procedure (p. 100). Free translations that make room for considerable flexibility are of little help to those readers who wish to become better acquainted with the text (p. 190 n. 109). All keen Bible readers should have access to several literal or critical translations because they are vital for intensive Bible study (p. 101).

Contradictions between different academic approaches today come to the surface if the English versions of the Bible are compared attentively. The solutions proposed by the translators often differ considerably. This is to be expected because the ancient texts are loaded with allusions, nuances, ambiguities, and opacity. Biblical prose is highly sophisticated literature with multiple layers, which does not lend itself to simple, clear, and unequivocal translation procedures. David Jasper (1998: 30) comments that, in contrast to the minute detail characterizing descriptions in Homer, biblical narrative employs a bare minimum of literary tools. This includes leaving a series of gaps and omissions, all of which cause 'frictionality'; i.e. irritating qualities that drive us to 'scratch' and reread. The technique goes hand in hand with the extraordinary poetic quality of the language, and at times what the texts leave out is just as important as what they include (Whitelam 1998: 41).

In summary, if one is to produce an honest and faithful rendering of the Bible, the aim should be to create an essential reflection of the original in every way. Such an approach involves sharing with future readers all the difficulties and enigmatic aspects that are present in the text. This requires respect, curiosity, attention to detail, patience, and perseverance on the part of translators.

Relevant Bible Texts

The Bible includes a number of texts of great importance to the subject of this book. Each of these passages reveals multiple literary, historical, cultural, and social aspects worth scrutinizing. However, owing to limitations of time and space, only the most emblematic and polemical texts have been selected. The bulk of the present book is dedicated to a semantic and literary exegesis of various texts in the HB while a few chapters focus on texts in the ST. The following have been selected:

- The creation and lives of the first human beings (Gen. 1–4)
- Sexual language in the HB
- The importance of biblical 'knowing'
- Noah's nakedness (Gen. 9.18–27)
- The consecrated ones (Deut. 23.17–18)
- The Levitical prohibition (Lev. 18.22 and 20.13)
- Sodom and Gomorrah (Gen. 18–19)
- The outrage at Gibeah (Judg. 19–20)
- Three letters attributed to Paul (Rom. 1, 1 Cor. 6, and 1 Tim. 1).

In each case, I will reflect on the question, What is this text about? Numerous subtle translation problems in current English versions of the Bible invite a hermeneutical suspicion. Which versions are accurate, and which are driven by ideological concerns? In this regard, I am in agreement with the hermeneutics of suspicion defined and applied by feminist and queer theologians (Perdue 2005: 105-9; Bohache 2006: 488). In addition, what appears to be a literal translation may sometimes be the result of a particular hermeneutical process (Musskopf 2008: 5; Miller 2010: 6). Adding to this panorama of suspicion is the fact that a number of English translations of the Bible seem to be biased whenever they are dealing with perceived homoeroticism (Jordan 1997: 36).

In the light of the often bilious history of Christianity in this respect, I am formulating a new hypothesis: what if the original messages carried by these biblical texts are unrelated to homoeroticism as we know it? The exploration that occurs in the present book will often take readers to unexpected places. Along the way, it will become clear that if one is to discover traces of homoeroticism or bisexuality in the Bible, the search should include a study of the language employed by the biblical narrators to describe sex in general, including the phenomenon known today as heterosexuality. Other texts that are important in connection with homoeroticism in the Bible are studied in chapter 15:

- The book of Ruth: two women called Ruth and Naomi
- Samuel 1 and 2: two men called David and Jonathan
- The Gospel of John: the Beloved Disciple
- John 21: the meaning of 'love'.

Conclusion

Ever since the days of antiquity, a number of cultural, literary, historical, and theological factors have influenced our way of reading scripture. With regard to human sexuality, a considerable proportion of biblical interpretation carried out today is strongly indebted to the main theological currents of the Patristic era and the Middle Ages. Among the key factors that motivate the present work, the following should be highlighted: (a) the suspicion that some textual problems in the original texts were never sufficiently understood; (b) the intuition that traditional translations of such passages may be incomplete or misleading; (c) the astonishing literary, theological, and human richness contained in the Hebrew Bible and the Second Testament; (d) the theological void into which the Christian majority has relegated believers who identify as lesbian, gay, bisexual, and transgender; and (e) the desire to build hermeneutical bridges enabling all readers to approach the biblical texts with an attitude of curiosity and respect.

In practical terms, this book pursues five main objectives:

(1) To study the common vocabulary dealing with sexual relationships in the Bible
(2) To analyse a number of frequently quoted texts in order to verify whether or not they are relevant to a discussion of the place of homoeroticism and bisexuality in the Bible
(3) To examine the approaches to translation adopted by twelve contemporary English versions of the Bible and to assess their level of accuracy
(4) To be open to the possibility that the texts explored may contain aspects of theological and cultural interest beyond the realm of sex, which have been largely ignored by contemporary scholarship
(5) To study the language of love describing same-sex relationships in the Bible.

PART ONE

Creation, Sex, and Knowing

1

BEGINNINGS

He called them 'groundling' on the day of their creation.

—Genesis 5.2

Introduction

It is often said that the Bible is 'very clear' in regard to homoerotic relationships (Gagnon 2001: 26-8). Yet current literature on the subject provides little insight into some biblical themes that are crucial for understanding the basic issues involved. In particular, two subjects are under-researched: (1) sexual language in the Bible and (2) the biblical meaning of the verb 'to know'. Since information on these is scarce and has to be sought in a variety of academic sources, chapters 2 and 3 are dedicated to these subjects. Furthermore, while the creation story in the book of Genesis is widely discussed, relatively few scholars focus directly on the importance on this text for anyone wishing to gauge biblical approaches to homoeroticism. For these reasons, the present book's part 1 starts with a chapter on creation.

Many readers are likely to ask whether the opening pages of the book of Genesis have anything to do with homoerotic relationships. Lesbian, gay, bisexual, and transgender people rarely think of the biblical creation story in relation to the various orientations inherent in human sexuality as they are understood today. However, the circles most hostile to awarding civil rights to the so-called sexual minorities often search this part of the Bible for arguments (Stone 2000: 59; Kraus 2011: 29). Characteristically, they will say 'God created man male and female'. This means, in their view, that it is the divinely ordained destiny and duty of all human beings to marry heterosexually and produce children (Nissinen 1998: 135).

The popularity and pervasiveness of this approach motivates me to undertake an in-depth analysis of the original Hebrew narrative. The first half of this chapter consists of an extensive literature review for the purpose of gleaning insights from contemporary scholars on this pivotal part of the Hebrew Bible (HB). A wide range of innovative approaches are available from Jewish, feminist, and queer theologians. Their research is documenting how rich the creation story is in biological, psychological, and social insights and the extent to which it excels in symbolic, mythological language. All of this poses major challenges to translators and biblical interpreters in general, which is why I pay special attention to translation issues. The second half of the chapter explores the Hebrew text of Genesis 1–4 in order to gauge the meaning of key words such as 'God', 'Adam', 'male', and 'female', which play a prominent role in Genesis 1. Subsequently, 'rib' and 'one flesh' occur in Genesis 2, while the concept of 'sexual desire' appears in Genesis 3. Marriage and childbirth enter the picture in Genesis 4. The language associated with sexual intercourse makes its first appearance in Genesis 6 (cf. this book's chapter 2).

Creation in the Christian Tradition

According to traditional Christian theology, the book of Genesis explains that God created the first human beings as male and female (1.27). This apparently precise statement makes it clear that the masculine/feminine duality exists due to an act of divine will and that humans should respect it at all times. Thus, Robert Gagnon (2001) argues that the differentiation between the sexes is inherent in being created in the image of God. In addition, this is the way in which procreation is ensured (pp. 57–8, 61). In terms of anatomy, male and female bodies were made to be joined (p. 365). Therefore, the complementarity of the sexes naturally excludes any intimate union between two people of the same sex (p. 156). According to Gagnon, the female is not there in the opening verses of Genesis 2. When the first 'man' feels lonely, God asks him to choose a 'helpmeet' from among the animals (cf. Gen. 2.19). However, the experiment does not produce a satisfactory outcome and this causes the Creator to decide on surgery. During the operation, a 'rib' is removed from the man (cf. 2.21). From this bone, the Creator shapes a woman and presents her to the man. The latter receives the new arrival with delight, accepting her as companion.

On the basis of this passage, Gagnon infers that man and woman were created to complement each other (2001: 60). Marriage is the institution that enables successive generations to reassemble what was divided on that day of separation (p. 194). In Gagnon's view, this is the significance of the phrase 'become one flesh' in Genesis 2.24 (p. 61). He concludes that intimate same-sex relationships do not match the criteria established by Genesis. He applies the same argument to Jesus's statements on divorce in the Gospel of Mark 10.2–12, interpreting Jesus's words as an absolute ratification of Gagnon's own approach to the subject (2001: 193).

According to other traditional readings of Genesis 2, the arrival of woman in the Garden of Eden occurs after the man has been there for a while. The story has caused Christian tradition to posit that God is male and has conferred superiority on the human male vis-à-vis woman (Svartvik 2006: 225). In other words, for many Christian thinkers the story of the rib operation and subsequent events justify the subordination of women (Bechtel 1993: 77; Meyers 1993: 129). It is important to point out that this way of reasoning is indebted to the letters of Paul, e.g. 1 Corinthians.[14] Prominent advocates of biblical interpretation from the perspective of male superiority among the fathers and doctors of the Christian church include John Chrysostom (García Estébanez 1992: 85, 95), Thomas Aquinas (p. 79), and Augustine of Hippo (p. 97-8). In this context, it is important to recall that the early church—including the authors of the Second Testament (ST)—did not study the Hebrew Bible in the original language but rather in Greek translation (LXX). Subsequently the Latin Vulgate became normative for the medieval church. This situation continued for 1500 years. In other words, the vast majority of Christian theologians would discuss the creation story as presented in Greek and Latin translations without consulting the Hebrew original. The many centuries of Christian misogyny continued into the Protestant Reformation and beyond—clearly expressed in the writings of, for instance, Calvin and Luther (Milne 1993: 150). Given the long, pervasive influence of this approach to the initial chapters of Genesis, the continued presence in modern theology of misogynous elements is hardly surprising (Stuart & Thatcher 1997: 151-5).

Non-Christian Perspectives on Creation

For centuries, Jewish interpretations of the creation story have diverged considerably from Christian approaches. It

---

[14] Cf. 1 Cor. 11.8-9 (NRSV): 'Indeed, man was not made from woman, but woman from man. Neither was man created for the sake of woman, but woman for the sake of man.'

is significant that Jewish commentators never abandoned their studies of the HB in the original language. This section summarizes contemporary interpretations of the Hebrew text offered by Jewish and non-Jewish scholars with concerns and methodologies rarely found in mainstream Christian theology.

According to Everett Fox (1995: 18), the opening events in Genesis have been subjected to multiple interpretations. Perhaps the psychological approach is among the most original and creative. The Eden story offers 'a vision of childhood and of the transition to the contradictions and pain of adolescence and adulthood'. Adam and Eve begin their lives as children, in all senses of the word. Once they have broken the rules by eating the forbidden fruit, their actions betray bewilderment as they are unable to cope with important, newfound insights. Their banishment from the garden leads them into awareness of the great difficulties, including death, which all human beings have to face: 'Knowledge and mortality are inextricably linked'. This may be a tragic discovery, but it is also essential for life on Planet Earth. The way in which the rebellion against the rules established by God is narrated in Genesis 3 stresses the element of choice, a major facet of human existence (1995: 18).

Robert Alter (1996: 3) observes that in some parts of the HB, the noun *ruach*, 'breath', 'wind', or 'spirit' (Gen. 1.2) describes 'an eagle fluttering over its young and so might have a connotation of parturition or nurture as well as rapid back-and-forth movement'. In Genesis 1.26, Alter disagrees with those who translate *adam* as 'man' because it is 'a generic term for human beings', which does not automatically suggest maleness. Similarly, Alter points out that 'him' in this verse is 'grammatically but not anatomically masculine' (p. 5). One Hebrew phrase that is 'notoriously difficult to translate' is *ʽezer kenegdō* (Gen. 2.18). The second term literally means 'alongside him' or 'opposite him', but ʿezer is more than just 'help' or 'helper'. In fact, ʿezer connotes 'active intervention on behalf of someone'. For the context of Genesis 2, Alter proposes the translation 'a sustainer beside him' (p. 9).

According to Gordon and Rendsburg (1997: 36), 'the knowledge of good and evil' is a much misunderstood phrase. In antiquity, it was used as the literary device known as merism.[15] In the Genesis context, the phrase means 'everything'. By eating the magic fruit of the Tree of Knowledge, the man and the woman gain 'knowledge that up to that time had been the monopoly of divinity'. Prior to that moment, they had virtually been living like animals unashamed of their nudity. The new knowledge includes a sense of decency. If the story is examined objectively, one realizes that both woman and man grow intellectually. The new insight available to them enables them to move to a higher level. Indeed, the so-called fall of man is no such thing. It would be more appropriate to speak of the 'rise of man halfway to divinity' (p. 37). Similarly, in Thomas Brodie's view (2001: 101), 'the story of the Fall is not primarily about a distant historical event but about an inner process' that is 'deeper than history'. In actual fact, the idea of a fall does not appear until Genesis 4.6–7 where God asks Cain why his face is 'fallen'. The word introduces a double meaning in reference to Cain's state of mind as well as to the crime he has just committed (2001: 153).

---

[15] In rhetoric, a *merism* is a figure of speech by which a single thing is referred to by a conventional phrase that enumerates several of its parts, or which lists several synonyms for the same thing. Merisms figure in a number of familiar English expressions. When we say that someone *searched high and low*, it means that they searched thoroughly or everywhere (cf. dictionary.cambridge.org, 2012). Similarly, the merism 'heaven and earth' in Gen. 1.1 represents the whole universe (Gordon & Rendsburg 1997: 36).

For her part, Lyn Bechtel (1993) questions the well-known 'fall' of Adam and Eve and the alleged biblical basis of 'original sin' (pp. 78-9). Such pessimistic concepts leading to resignation are not found elsewhere in the HB. Indeed, they are the product of the Hellenistic era, which is a time of major cultural transformation. From a sociological point of view, the crucial shift from group-oriented societies to predominantly individual-oriented societies is particularly noteworthy (p. 80). The language employed by the Hebrew narrator is characterized by mythological imagery full of symbolism (p. 81). An important concept is 'shame' (Gen. 2.25; 3.7). Bechtel interprets it as a psychological phenomenon that appears naturally during the formative years in which human beings mature from early childhood and adolescence into adulthood (p. 84).

For Samuel Terrien (1985), the creation narrative was told from the very beginning as 'a pungent description of every man and every woman'. In this sense, the story is a 'true' myth, i.e. 'a parable of the human situation' (p. 8). It reveals 'the perennial temptation of human beings in every age' to acquire infinite knowledge in order to become like God. The initial loneliness of the groundling has to do with the human condition: 'True life is not individual but corporate and social' (p. 9). Unlike many Christian commentators, Terrien argues that the Hebrew narrator is far from being anti-feminist. Instead, the storyteller was 'a theologian who unabashedly admired womanhood' (p. 9). The solemn verb used in Genesis 2.22 to describe the creation of the woman is *banah*, which means 'build' (1985: 12). In the HB, this word appears frequently in relation to works of architecture (cf. Gen. 4.17; 8.20; 11.4-8). The Hebrew term *'ezer* denotes that the woman is not a simple 'helper'. Rather, her important role vis-à-vis the man is comparable to the way in which God delivers the oppressed Israelites (1985: 10-11). Thus, the woman delivers the man from 'the distress of his solitude' (p. 11; cf. Wenham 1987: 70).

For Rabbi Jonathan Magonet (2004) and his faith community, the Eden story illustrates the impossibility for human beings to linger indefinitely in a paradise-like state. The narrator seems to say that the appropriate place for us to live is the earth. We are formed by both earth and breath (spirit) and thus possess a close link to the earth. With our Creator, we share the ability to shape, mould, and create (p. 121). The mention of death in Genesis 2.17 is not intended as a threat but rather a statement of fact (p. 122). According to Magonet, many Christian interpretations of this text are influenced by the arbitrary fragmentation of the biblical text into separate chapters that occurred during the Middle Ages (p. 123). The dialogue between the serpent and Eve represents a psychological process whereby the woman grows in awareness of the world around her and of the forces governing it. She is taking the first steps toward another level of existence, which leads to the independence inherent in adulthood (p. 124). Only by leaving behind the innocence of childhood do we humans become able to absorb the knowledge of good and bad, that is, of the facts of life. In other words, to become responsible adults we need to achieve a state of psychological maturity. This entails learning to take decisions and to foresee their consequences for our lives on Planet Earth. In the Rabbinic view, the eating of the fruit and the subsequent expulsion from Eden 'was ultimately a great liberation' for it gave the first human beings 'the chance to grow up' (p. 132).

Feminist Perspectives

In recent decades, feminist scholars have produced a number of critical essays inviting readers to rethink their understanding of the creation story by considering elements that have been overlooked for centuries. Like Jewish and HB scholars in general, they tend to highlight significant elements in the Hebrew text. Luise Schottroff (1993) focuses on the gender of the important noun *ruach*, which occurs in Genesis 1.2. Grammatically female, the word means 'breath', 'wind' or 'spirit'. Schottroff quotes Martin Buber for whom *ruach* represents a giant mother-bird hovering above the waters (1993: 24).[16] According to Schottroff, the biblical narrator conceives of the Creator as a three-dimensional being: a conscientious craftsman, a mother-bird, and a sovereign king (p. 26).

Adrien Janis Bledstein (1993) underlines the fact that in Genesis 3, the woman is not the object of a curse. Rather, the word 'cursed' is applied to the serpent and to the earth (p. 142). For Bledstein, the word *elohīm* spoken by the serpent in Genesis 3.5 is plural meaning 'gods' (as opposed to the proper noun *Elohīm*, 'God'): 'you will be like gods, knowing good and evil'. On a different note, the 'desire' of woman for her man (Gen. 3.16) reflects the Hebrew term *teshuqah*, which is often translated as 'urge' or 'lust'. However, for Bledstein the word is multifaceted and may be interpreted as an adjective in the sense of 'desirable' or 'attractive' (p. 143). In this context, Bledstein is struck by the curious parallel to sin's 'desire' for Cain in 4.7. She understands the latter passage to mean (p. 144): 'It [sin] is powerfully attractive to you, but you can rule over it'. If a similar approach is adopted for Genesis 3.16, *teshuqah* becomes part of a warning: 'you are powerfully attractive to your husband, but he can rule over you'. Bledstein continues (p. 144),

> her erotic allure is powerful. But beware, she is cautioned, her man has the capacity—not the

---

[16] According to Hamilton (1990: 115), in ancient Ugaritic texts, the relevant verb is associated with eagles.

> license nor the authority—to dominate her. Cain is admonished that he is able to master his arousal toward sinful action.

For Carol Meyers (1993: 120), the biblical writings are characterized by enormous complexity. The above-mentioned notion of the 'fall' attributed to Genesis 3 is, in Meyers's view, extra-biblical (pp. 126–7). When it comes to the social status of women in the hill country of Palestine approximately three thousand years ago, Meyers applies sociological methodology to the Hebrew text. She observes the frequent occurrences of the verb *akhal*, 'eat', which to her denote a persistent concern for food. In other words, subsistence was a key issue for the people of Palestine (p. 128). Meyers wonders what it means that man will 'rule' over woman in Genesis 3.16. In her analysis, both man and woman are meant to share the toil and labour required to produce the daily bread. According to Meyers, if man is ordered to 'predominate' it means that his efforts in agriculture are destined to be greater than the contribution of woman. This is so because she has the additional responsibility of childbirth and childcare (p. 134).

Ilana Pardes (1993) notes that the creation of the world is the first in a string of mythological stories in Genesis, all of which show creation as an ongoing process (p. 173). It is important to note that in Genesis 4 Eve is the one who names her children (pp. 174–5). In Genesis 4.1, it is astonishing that Eve virtually presents herself as God's partner as she exclaims that she has created a human being *with* the deity (1993: 178–9). From a literary viewpoint, Eve responds in this manner to the occasions when she was named by Adam in Genesis 2.23 and 3.20 (1993: 182). At the same time, she claims the privilege of being the primordial mother, which was assigned to her in Genesis 3.20 (p. 185). In this sense, the first feminist reader of the creation story is Eve herself

(p. 189). Generally speaking, the HB may be infused with patriarchal or male-centred ideology, but Eve's assertiveness reveals the presence of a female counterpoise (p. 188).

Mary Phil Korsak (1993) has paid attention to several Hebrew terms in Genesis, which are often mistranslated. The existence of a long tradition within Christianity does not guarantee that it rests on solid exegesis. An example worth considering is found in Genesis 2.21 where the famous 'rib' is no such thing. In reality, the Hebrew text speaks of the first human being's *side* (p. 225). This is so because 'the groundling, *adam*, appears as a plural being, made in the image of a plural God' (p. 229). According to Genesis, only after the spectacular surgical division of the original *adam* into two separate individuals does it make sense to speak of the existence of man and woman (p. 230). The Hebrew word *chawwah* (Eve) makes a connection between Eve's name and the concept of 'life'. In fact, her name recalls 'the mysterious tree that is described as standing in the middle of the Garden of Eden' (p. 232).

Diane Sharon (1998) observes that, from the very beginning, the original *adam* contains within himself 'the female aspect that is later literally split off from his body' (p. 78). After being divided into two separate beings in the form of man and woman, they become co-protagonists of the story. Initially only the solitary *adam* is warned by God not to eat from the tree of life (Gen. 2.17), but obviously the woman feels that she is under the same prohibition (3.3). This becomes clear in her conversation with the serpent, which treats the woman as representative of the human couple by addressing her with the plural pronoun 'you'. She responds accordingly by answering with the plural 'we' (1998: 78–9). Man and woman together represent 'the hero who is tested and fails' (p. 71). Fundamentally the relationship between Adam and Eve is egalitarian. It is their common destiny as a couple to share the very hard work that is inextricably linked to life on earth (p. 79).

Sexuality and Gender

For discussions of homoeroticism and the Bible, questions of sexuality and gender are paramount. Michael Vasey (1995) notes that the homophobic tradition in the Christian church builds its biblical interpretation on two weak foundations: (1) an inadequate analysis of human sexuality, including the cultural complexity of homosexuality, and (2) an idyllic vision of modern family life imposed on scripture. Vasey finds it simplistic 'to see the story of Adam and Eve as providing a biblical mandate for the isolated nuclear family of Western culture' (p. 115). The modern domestic ideal is not confirmed by the events described in Genesis or by any other portion of scripture (p. 116).

Ronald Simkins (1998: 33–4) argues that, in the light of the multiple cultural differences found around the world, any discussion of gender and sex should start by analysing and clearly defining the cultural space in which they are being played out. This includes the culture of ancient Israel according to the biblical writings (p. 35). Even the current distinction between 'gender' and 'sex' is a cultural construct (p. 37). The desire to know good and evil, i.e. to acquire knowledge of the universe, is 'what distinguishes the human couple from all the other creatures that Yahweh created from the arable land'. Indeed, 'the human couple become creators like God' (p. 47). While it is true that in Eden both are punished for their actions, neither the woman nor the man is cursed (p. 48). Moreover, it is only by leaving Eden that the first humans can dedicate themselves to the purpose for which they were created according to Genesis 2.5, 8, and 15, namely, agriculture, horticulture, and gardening (1998: 50).

For his part, Ken Stone (2000: 60-2) critiques some points made by Protestant theologian Karl Barth (1886–1968) in his influential *Church Dogmatics*. Barth raises the spectre of 'the malady called homosexuality', which he classifies as a 'physical, psychological and social sickness'. Barth emphatically tells his readers that the 'togetherness of man and woman' is an essential ingredient of our humanity (2000: 61). Stone questions the logic of Barth's argument by pointing out that the commandment of procreation (Gen. 1.28) does not necessarily require heterosexuality (2000: 60). When the woman is told in Genesis 3.16 that her 'desire' will be directed toward her husband, this may well be interpreted as a punishment for what she did (2000: 63). For Stone, the biblical creation account as it now stands 'is riven with tensions and contradictions', not to mention 'problems of logic' that require a considerable intellectual effort on the part of interpreters (p. 65). One such contradiction relates to the loneliness of the original *adam*. When this becomes manifest in Genesis 2.18 it is clear that the animals are insufficient to fill the psychological and social void. Curiously, God's search on *adam*'s behalf implies a tacit recognition that God alone is not sufficient company for a single human being (2000: 67).

David Carr (2003: 18) finds that the human being created in Genesis 1.27—by being both male and female—physically reflects the divine body. In other words, the human body is not an impediment to the life of the spirit. Instead, the Bible begins with 'an affirmation of male and female sexual bodies as signs of the divine'. Significantly Genesis 1.28 makes it clear that the Creator is especially happy with this work. The text ends in 1.31 by saying, 'It was indeed *very* good' (p. 20). Contrary to popular wisdom, humans do not project their own image onto the divine. Instead they were made 'in the image and likeness that God already had' (p. 21). If the human body is 'a mark of our connection to God' (p. 22), human sexuality is also 'a reflection of divinity' (p.

23). In short, if 'male and female bodies are both godlike and sexual', there is no contradiction between bodily sensuality and the divine. The humans of Genesis 1 are made 'in the image of an erotic God' (p. 24).

According to Carr, the difference between Genesis 1 and 2 is to be sought in their perspectives. The creative process of Genesis 1 unfolds on a cosmic level while the focus of Genesis 2 narrows to the Garden of Eden (2003: 27). Generally speaking, the picture of sexuality presented by Genesis 2 is not centred on reproduction or fertility. Rather, it emphasizes the intimacy of 'two embodied creatures whom God has so carefully made for shared work as equals'. Of particular relevance for discussions on homoeroticism in Genesis, Carr approaches this text as a vision of non-reproductive, joyful sexuality between partners who may be male–female, male–male, or female–female (p. 32). The issue of having children is not highlighted. Instead, 'humans were created for erotic connection with one another' (p. 33).

Gareth Moore (2003) highlights the subject of companionship as a centrepiece of Genesis 2. After God has created the animals, the *adam* is invited to choose from among them. However, no animal seems to be the right partner. As a result of a major operation woman emerges, and only then the *adam* feels entirely happy (p. 139). In Moore's view the message of this story is significant for all humans as we look for life companions. We need someone by our side with whom we find fulfilment. The *adam* is not ordered to find any partner in particular but is allowed to make his own choice (p. 140). This should come as no surprise (p. 141):

> for that is just the sort of thing a companion is. A companion, in the sense of companionship which is in view in this text, is somebody you actually *want* to be with and to share your life with.

Consequently, Moore argues that human beings should not blindly accept the kind of partner that our social, political, or religious environment thinks is right for us. If the heterosexual option does not fill us with joy, to embark on it would be a serious moral and theological error. Indeed, such a step would be tantamount to a form of 'adamism' because it would turn us into mistaken followers of Adam. Moore reminds his readers that Christians are not called to imitate Adam, but Christ (2003: 144), the Saviour who provides us with life in abundance (John 10.10). Therefore, a lesbian woman and a gay man should choose a partner that will fill them with delight because only in this manner will they proceed according to the overriding message of Genesis 2 (2003: 143).

Michael Carden (2006) is reminded of Plato's philosophical work *Symposium* in which Aristophanes shares a creation story. According to this Greek myth, the Olympic gods created three sexes, namely, male, female, and hermaphrodite (p. 28). In the context of Genesis, Jewish tradition has recognized the androgynous nature of the first *adam* (pp. 26, 28). The rabbis were aware that not all human beings are born with distinct female or male characteristics, i.e. a number of intermediate types exist. Given the dualistic gender ideology of our time, Western culture finds it difficult to accommodate intersex conditions. Therefore, if the sex of a newborn baby is not in evidence from the beginning, surgical interventions are common to assign the 'appropriate' gender. Carden argues that this is tantamount to taking away the child's right of choice (p. 27). As he observes the couple formed by Adam and Eve in Genesis, Carden finds that the woman is stronger and more responsible than the man. Speaking and acting with confidence, she takes centre stage (2006: 29). Indeed, for Carden the woman is presented as the 'crown of creation' (p. 30). By contrast, the man in Genesis 3 is passive and refuses to take responsibility for his actions.

He blames not only the woman but even the Creator for having placed her by his side (2006: 29).

Genesis in Greek and Hebrew

In order to appreciate the points made by the ancient narrator(s) in the opening chapters of Genesis, a discussion of language and style is paramount. William Loader (2004) has analysed the relationship between the Greek vocabulary of the Septuagint (LXX) and the way in which the authors of the ST and Philo deal with human sexuality. With a series of examples, Loader demonstrates how the Greek terms of the LXX repeatedly provide nuances that are not present in the Hebrew original. For instance, the LXX translator was unable to reproduce the pun in Genesis 1.25-27 between *adam*, 'groundling', and *adamah*, 'ground', which in the Hebrew is crucial (2004: 30, 34). Unlike the original, the LXX suggests the subordination of woman to man (pp. 35-6). Another pivotal term discussed by Loader is 'one flesh' in Genesis 2.24 (2004: 91). He notes that the vision presented by Paul in 1 Corinthians 6 is indebted to the Greek of the LXX where Paul focuses on the effects of sexual intercourse in creating 'one body'. The notion of *sarx* ('flesh') in Greek often denotes sexual impulses, whereas the corresponding term *basar* of the Hebrew original in this passage refers to the creation of kinship (2004: 41-2).[17]

If Christianity's traditional misogyny is not based on the Hebrew text of Genesis but rather on its translation into Greek, this should make us ponder the power of language. No matter how 'faithful' translations are aimed to be they cannot always reproduce every single nuance and ambiguity of the original text. At the same time, a translation is often

---

[17] Cf. Lev. 18.6; Wenham 1987: 71. See also section 'One Flesh' below.

capable of evoking ideas and allusions that are not present in the *Vorlage* (source text) owing to cultural and conceptual differences between the two languages. In other words, the longevity of Christian tradition in the sexual realm is arguably not the outcome of any alleged infallibility but rather seems to be the product of lengthy theological inertia perpetuated by authoritarian ideologies since the days of the early church, partly based on some letters attributed to Paul.

As noted above, the biblical interpretations imposed by early Christian theologians and cemented during the Middle Ages are certainly not the only ones available. In numerous cases, they are less than convincing because they leave a series of textual complexities and subtleties in the Hebrew unresolved (Alter 1992: 5). The richness of the original narratives attests to the level of sophistication attained by the anonymous authors and editors of Genesis. Undoubtedly here is a powerful work of art put together by inspired people with a remarkable level of literary education and communication skills. This is clearly a literary, psychological, and theological gem (Brodie 2001: 34, 101, 106). In the experience of numerous scholars, the most rewarding approach to Genesis is to adopt an attitude of humility vis-à-vis the extraordinary elegance and profound mysticism inherent in the Classical Hebrew text. Surprising treasures are hidden there.

The stories included in the Pentateuch are so multifaceted that they outclass the narrow interpretive paradigms that traditional scholarship has striven to apply. As Walter Brueggemann (1997: 42) points out, the HB constantly challenges readers:

> It is material that insists on being taken seriously, and it refuses to be reduced or domesticated into a settled coherence. This refusal may not be simply a literary one but a theological one,

> pertaining to its central Subject. The restless character of the text that refuses excessive closure . . . is reflective of the One who is its main Character, who also refuses tameness and systematization.

In other words, for Brueggemann, it is of the very essence of the Bible to let its pages reflect facets of the divine, which, in its inscrutable greatness, will never allow itself to be grasped entirely by the human mind. This also affects Yhwh, Hebrew name of the God of Israel, which first appears in Genesis 2.4 in conjunction with *Elohīm*, 'God', as Yhwh Elohīm, whereby readers are made aware that the two names refer to the same deity. Sometimes known as the Tetragrammaton (in Greek: 'four letters'), by far the most popular rendition of Yhwh among English translators is 'the Lord'. This adequately translates the actual *reading* of Yhwh, which in the rabbinic tradition is pronounced *adonāy*, 'my lord', because the divine name is considered too holy to be uttered (Browning 2009: 353). As regards spelling, the capitalization of the four letters of Lord imitates Yhwh, setting the word apart from the ordinary usage of 'lord'. However, it does not reflect the extraordinary ambiguity of the Hebrew in which Yhwh is spelled one way and pronounced in an entirely different manner for religious reasons.[18]

Singular, Dual, and Plural

Following on from the above literature review, the second half of this chapter discusses textual analysis and translation issues. The opening chapters of Genesis contain several remarkable

---

[18] Known as *qere perpetuum*, this tradition was not noted but handed down orally from generation to generation (Groom 2003: 24). Another euphemism for Yhwh, regularly used among Orthodox Jews, is *Ha-Shem*, literally, 'The Name' (Fox 1995 p. *xxix*).

allusions to the nature of the Creator of the universe. Indeed, an extraordinary ambivalence emerges when the name *Elohīm*, 'God', is analysed. In Genesis 1.26-29, the narrator several times lets Elohim the Creator use plural forms of verbs and pronouns saying (emphasis added), 'let *us* make' (*na'aseh*) a groundling 'in *our* image' (*betsalmenū*). Intriguingly, the narrator explains that the divine being 'created', using third person singular (*wayyivrā*, 1.27). Despite its highly unusual character from a grammatical point of view, nothing in this passage implies that an error has been made. The literary style of Genesis 1 is too polished for any such hypothesis to be realistic. It seems far more likely that the spectacular oscillation between plural and singular is part of the way in which the divine is approached. Even the word *Elohīm*, usually translated as 'God', is nominally plural. The Hebrew termination-*īm* belongs formally to the plural of masculine nouns, and in some cases, it denotes the dual number of either gender.[19] Therefore, in theory the noun *elohīm* (lower case) should be translated as 'gods'. However, if a plural was meant, the corresponding verb would also take a plural form, and this is not the case in this text. All verbs attached to *Elohīm* (upper case) invariably occur in the third person singular.

In other words, from a strictly formal point of view, the divine force acting in Genesis appears to possess some plural or dual aspects on the one hand, and on the other, this very same being acts as a single entity as reflected in the relevant Hebrew verbs (Grelot 2006: 11). Put differently, the biblical narrators create and/or resolve this grammatical tension in a consistent manner by accompanying the formally plural noun *Elohīm* with singular verbs. This invites theological reflection. Clearly the narrator(s) of Genesis approach(es) the

---

[19] For certain Hebrew nouns such as *yad*, 'hand', the termination for the dual number is *-ayim*. Thus, *yadayim* usually means 'two hands' or 'both hands' (Weingreen 1959: 38).

divine sphere with the utmost respect. They are conscious of the inability of human imagination to encompass the universal driving force in its fullness. In fact, the text of Genesis is suggesting that the Creator transcends the well-known categories of singular and plural that humans apply to all created things.

Table 1 shows the coexisting plurals and singulars in textual references to the divine in Genesis 1.26–29 (emphasis added).

Table 1
Divine Plurals and Singulars in Gen. 1

Verse	Divine Plurals	Divine Singulars
1.26	Elohīm	God
		and *he* said
	Let *us* make	
	in *our* image	
	after *our* likeness	
1.27	Elohīm	*he* created
		in *his* image
1.28	Elohīm	*he* blessed
		he said
1.29	Elohīm	*he* said
		I give (*I* have given)

A brief examination of twelve contemporary English versions of the Bible (cf. table 3) shows that in this passage, they all translate *Elohīm* as 'God', a word which in English is perceived as singular. As a result, what is missing from the translations is the creative theological tension in the Hebrew text on several levels: (a) between the nominally plural name of *Elohīm* and the singular aspect of 'in *his* image'; (b) between the first person plural of 'let *us* make in *our* image' and the first person singular of '*I* give'; and (c) between the name *Elohīm* and a whole series of verbs in the third person singular. Clearly much of this creative tension is lost in translation.[20]

In the original narrative, the juxtaposition of divine plurals and singulars does not stand alone. Particularly intriguing is the fact that the first human creature reflects exactly the same grammatical and literary complexity. Created from the *adamah* (feminine gender), the *adam* is referred to in both singular and plural (or dual) terms. If *adamah* equals 'soil', 'earth' or 'ground', the literal meaning of *adam* is 'earthling' or 'groundling' (Korsak 1993: 228; McKeown 2008: 31). Table 2 presents a picture of the way in which the Hebrew narrator has provided the first human being with singular and plural characteristics (emphasis added).

Table 2
Human Plurals and Singulars in Gen. 1

Verse	Human Plurals	Human Singulars
1.26		a groundling (*adam*)
	they shall rule	
1.27		the groundling (*ha-adam*)
		he created *him* (or *it*)
	he created *them*	
1.28	Elohīm blessed *them*	
	Elohīm said to *them*	
1.29	I give *you*	
	they shall be for *you*	

---

[20] An exception is Mary Phil Korsak (1993: 1–7) who consistently uses the name 'Elohim'.

In most languages, it is highly unusual to combine a singular noun such as 'groundling' with the plural pronoun 'them'. Even more striking is the occurrence of 'him', singular, in 1.27 followed immediately by 'them', plural, in the very same verse. By using such an extraordinary literary technique, the narrator is clearly stretching one's imagination and challenging readers and hearers to ponder the mystery of the origins of human existence. James Miller (2010: 12) argues that the main physical characteristics of the groundling directly reflect the image and likeness of the Creator. Similarly, 'the God of the Bible has a body, which looks human, and this is why our bodies have their shape'.

Groundling, Man, or Adam?

All English versions of the Bible tell us that the first human creature on earth is 'male and female' (Gen. 1.27). In some cases, they say that the first human creatures on earth are male and female, i.e. they picture not one but two individuals created together. The rendering 'male and female' is correct (Hebrew *zakhar uneqevah*). That said, this aspect as well as other nuances of the Hebrew text are well worth paying attention to. It is important to highlight that the initial being is not a 'man' in the usual sense of 'male person'. Traditionally the English word 'man' is ambivalent because it has both the generic sense of 'human being' and the more specific meaning 'male person'. Now, Hebrew texts generally refer to a human male as *īsh* as in Genesis 2.23. In 1.27, however, the word *īsh* is absent. Instead one finds *adam*, 'groundling', whose association with *adamah*, 'ground', is obvious.

Moreover, a detailed analysis of the Hebrew language reveals another crucial detail. The gender of the recently created *adam* is not in evidence (Alter 1996: 5). In fact, the narrative suggests considerable ambivalence by describing the *adam* as male *and* female. At first readers are told that God created 'him' or 'it' (singular) only to learn immediately that 'male and female he created *them*' (plural or dual number). The presence of the pronoun *them* intimates that this *adam* has a dual nature from the start. Stated differently, several factors indicate that this new individual is characterized by lack of gender differentiation. In all probability the phenomenon might be described by using terms such as bisexuality, hermaphroditism, or intersex condition (Carden 2006: 26-7; cf. Loader 2004: 30).

As noted above, in Genesis 1.26, God uses plural concepts saying, 'Let *us* make a groundling in *our* image and in *our* likeness' (emphasis added). On the basis of this wording, the narrator is suggesting that the remarkable duality of the Creator—singular and plural, male and female—is reflected in the groundling (Carmichael 2010: 40). If 1.27 literally says, 'in God's image he created *him*, male and female he created *them*' (emphasis added), the first human being is also dual having female and male components as well as singular and plural traits (Korsak 1993: 229). This leads to an astonishing insight: the original plan of *Elohīm* is not to create two separate beings but one (Greenberg 2004: 49; Carmichael 2010: 8-9).[21]

Curiously, these observations make it possible to build bridges from Genesis toward other cultures and ways of thinking. Indeed, in antiquity it was not unusual to depict certain deities with two faces. Such was the case of Janus, the Roman god of time, beginnings, transitions, and endings. One of his faces observed the past, and the other face looked

---

[21] A number of translators and commentators have interpreted 'male and female' from a traditional perspective. For instance, the CCB suggests in a footnote (p. 6) that the image of God is reflected in the human couple of man and woman.

to the future (Johnston 1990: 25, 59). Another remarkable example was Hekate (Hecate), the ancient Greek goddess of liminal places, especially crossroads (1990: 23). She would be depicted with two or three heads, at other times with two or three conjoined bodies (1990: 59–60).[22] Thus, the ancient representations of Janus and Hekate would draw attention to unusual physical phenomena in the human race, including conjoined twins.

Moreover, the inherent duality in the human race suggested by Genesis 1.26–27 has been studied and described by modern psychology. A pioneer in this field was Swiss psychoanalyst C. G. Jung (McCarson 2002). Similarly, in biology it is a well-known fact that for several weeks following the moment of conception, the human embryo turning into foetus is androgynous, that is, no distinctive trait of either sex is detectable.[23] Despite these facts, for a very long time Western culture and medical science have felt uncomfortable about babies born with little or no visible gender differentiation or with a combination of male and female features. The current term is 'intersex conditions' (Cornwall 2009: 7–8).

Translating ADAM

The *Oxford Dictionary* defines the word 'translate' as 'express the sense of words or text in another language' (OD).[24] For the purposes of the present book, the following thirteen English versions of the Bible have been selected, all of which were published in the twentieth century. The number of versions consulted will be twelve throughout. Table 3 lists

---

[22] www.theoi.com/Khthonios/Hekate.html (2012).
[23] www.gender.org.uk/about/04embryo/46_mterr.htm (2012).
[24] oxforddictionaries.com/view/entry/m_en_gb0877790#m_en_gb0877790 (2011).

thirteen because the JPS is examined in connection with the Hebrew Bible and the LEB takes its place wherever Second Testament texts are discussed.

Table 3
English Versions of the Bible

Acronyms	Versions
CCB	*The Christian Community Bible*
HCSB	*Holman Christian Standard Bible*
JM	*The Bible: A New Translation / James Moffatt*
JPS	*Jewish Publication Society*
LEB	*Lexham English Bible*
NCV	*New Century Version*
NIV	*New International Version*
NJB	*New Jerusalem Bible*
NKJV	*New King James Version*
NLT	*New Living Translation*
NRSV	*New Revised Standard Version*
NWT	*New World Translation*
REB	*Revised English Bible*

In order to gauge the quality of the twelve versions with respect to their approaches to the Hebrew Bible, it may be helpful to choose two initial, simple tools for verifying their basic accuracy. These tools are (1) determining the degree of faithfulness or literalness vis-à-vis the original text, (2) focusing on the degree of consistency with which a given Hebrew word or phrase is rendered into English.

Undoubtedly one of the trickiest Hebrew words in Genesis 1 and 2 is *adam*. In this context, it is time to see how twelve English versions approach the two initial occurrences of the term. The first is *adam*, indefinite singular (1.26), the second being *ha-adam*, definite singular (1.27), as shown in table 4.

Table 4
Translating ADAM and HA-ADAM

Version	Gen. 1.26 ADAM	Gen. 1.27 HA-ADAM
CCB	man	man
HCSB	man	man
JM	man	man
JPS	man	man
NCV	human beings	human beings
NIV	mankind	mankind
NJB	man	man
NKJV	man	man
NLT	human beings*	human beings**
	*Or *man*; Hebrew *adam*	**Or *the man*; Hebrew *ha-adam*
NRSV	humankind*	humankind*
	*Heb *adam*	
NWT	a man	the man
REB	human beings	human beings

In table 4, the most popular choice for both *adam* and *ha-adam* is 'man' (six versions). While the generic simplicity of the word may seem appealing, this rendering presents several disadvantages vis-à-vis the Hebrew. First, in English there is no obvious semantic connection between 'man' and 'earth'. Second, 'man' has a masculine bias (Alter 1996: 5). Third, by saying simply 'man' in both 1.26 and 1.27, these versions make no distinction between indefinite and definite singular. In the latter context, the NWT is more precise, saying 'a man' (1.26) and 'the man' (1.27). The NIV has attempted to overcome the gender bias of 'man' by using the more generic 'mankind'. Still, 'mankind' is encumbered with most of the disadvantages attached to the shorter 'man'. The NRSV has taken a further step in the right direction by suggesting 'humankind'. On account of the added footnote, readers are made aware of the occurrence of *adam* in the Hebrew. Yet the English 'humankind' does not reflect the earthy quality of the Hebrew term and fails to differentiate between *adam* and *ha-adam*.

Three versions make the unexpected move of turning the singular terms *adam* and *ha-adam* into plural concepts by saying 'human beings' (NCV, NLT, REB). The NLT wisely adds footnotes alerting readers to the fact that the Hebrew terms are singular. However, for the reasons given above 'man' is not a very fortunate choice. In these English versions, the option 'human beings' falls short on three counts: (1) there is no trace of earthiness; (2) it is plural where the original is singular; and (3) unlike the Hebrew original, the presence of 'human beings' implies that the 'male and female' are to be seen as two individuals.

In summary, of the twelve versions represented in table 4, none has achieved full concordance with the meaning of Hebrew *adam* and *ha-adam*. One version not included in the survey is that of Mary Phil Korsak (1993: 4–7), which consistently (in my view successfully) uses the literal term 'groundling' (*adam*) and 'the groundling' (*ha-adam*).

Rib or Side?

Genesis 2 redevelops the central theme of 1.26–27, i.e. the creation of humanity, including the mysterious coexistence of male/female components as well as singular/plural ones. The perspective has shifted from the cosmic level in Genesis 1 to the more detailed aspects of life in the Garden of Eden (Carr 2003: 27). Having observed the fundamental loneliness of the groundling, the Creator decides to perform an operation by removing one of his sides (*tselaʿ*) in order to transform this half into a woman (2.21–22). As already noted, this makes good sense because, before undergoing such life-changing surgery, the first human being is not a fully fledged male but rather an *adam*, a 'groundling' of dual gender.

The Hebrew wording is transparent enough and should not pose any major problem of exegesis. Nevertheless, according to Christian tradition the part that is removed is a 'rib'. On this basis, theologians have argued for centuries that woman is a complementary being whose life only finds fulfilment if she is under the care of a man. The vast majority of English versions of the Bible have modified the text accordingly. This is confusing since the Hebrew word for 'rib' is ʿ*ala*ʿ as attested by Daniel 7.5. As noted, the noun *tselaʿ* means 'side'.[25] In this sense, it occurs in detailed descriptions of objects such as arks (Exod. 25.12) as well as rooms and buildings (Exod. 26.20, 26). Applied to landscapes, *tselaʿ* translates as 'hillside' or 'mountainside' (2 Sam. 16.13). In the light of these facts, it would be logical for the English versions to mention the groundling's 'side' in Genesis 2.22 (Korsak 1993: 225; McKeown 2008: 34).

Table 5 shows the approaches to *tselaʿ* adopted by the twelve English versions in three different contexts.

---

[25] Terrien 1985: 12; Hamilton 1990: 178; Korsak 1993: 7; Fox 1995: 20 n. 21; Greenberg 2004: 48; Carden 2006: 28.

Table 5
Translating Hebrew TSELA(

Version	Gen. 2.21–22	Exod. 25.12	2 Sam. 16.13
CCB	rib	side	hillside
HCSB	rib	side	ridge of the hill
JM	rib	side	side of the hill
JPS	rib	side wall	slope of the hill
NCV	rib	side	hillside
NIV	rib* *or part of the man's side	side	hillside
NJB	rib	side	mountainside
NKJV	rib	side	hillside
NLT	rib* *or a part of the man's side	side	hillside
NRSV	rib	side	hillside
NWT	rib	side	side of the mountain
REB	rib	side	ridge of the hill

Read vertically, the first column clearly reveals that all versions are firmly in agreement with church tradition. In a single biblical text, Genesis 2.21–22, consensus dictates that *tsela(* should be translated as 'rib'. Only two versions concede in footnotes that there may be an alternative rendering in the form of '(a) part of the man's side' (NIV, NLT). By inserting the word 'side', they acknowledge the presence of *tsela(*. However, these versions are not prepared to go all the way. Literally they only go *part* of the way. By cautiously mentioning a 'part' of the side, they do not disturb the current consensus but simply choose a different way of expressing the well-established idea of 'rib'.

Likewise, the second column is a model of uniformity. In this case, however, there is no hint at any rib. Due to an accurate rendering of *tselaʿ*, all versions have achieved commendable clarity. Indeed, Exodus 25.10–15 offers a detailed description of the ark of the covenant of which *tselaʿ* represents one side. Among the versions in table 5, the only variation is provided by the JPS suggesting 'side wall'. This does not change the overall picture even though there seems to be no particular need for adding the word 'wall'. The ark is made of acacia wood (Exod. 25.10) and fitted with four rings of gold arranged by twos on opposite *sides* (25.12–15).

The third column presents more diversity than the rest. The Hebrew phrase in 2 Samuel 16.13 is *betselaʿ ha-har*, 'on the side of the hill' (or 'side of the mountain'). Nine versions rightly propose 'hillside', 'mountainside', or similar. Two versions offer the variation 'ridge of the hill' (HCSB, REB) while the JPS opts for 'slope of the hill'. Certainly 'slope' seems defendable up to a point even though it might be classified as less accurate than 'side'. Even less precise is 'ridge', which may mean a narrow stretch of elevated land but does not contain any allusion to 'side'.

A very different scenario unfolds as soon as a horizontal reading of table 5 is undertaken. While the correspondence between columns 2 and 3 is fairly obvious throughout, there is no link between these and column 1. Obviously all versions have fallen into the same trap. Within this picture of discordance between the columns, a relatively consistent approach is presented by nine versions offering the three options rib/side/hillside (or similar). More difficult to defend is the three-part solution suggested by the JPS: rib/side wall/slope of the hill. In this version, there are no connecting elements. A similar difficulty is incurred by the HCSB and the REB. English nouns such as 'rib', 'side', and 'ridge of the hill' are by no means interchangeable. No one would suspect that the same Hebrew noun *tselaʿ* is being translated. Even if one were to argue that 'rib' occasionally means 'a ridge of rock or land' (OD), this sense certainly does not apply to *tselaʿ* in Genesis 2.21 or Exodus 25.12.

Who Invented the 'Rib'?

In Genesis 2.21-22, it is indeed surprising that all versions choose to speak of a rib despite the fact that they translate *tselaʿ* accurately everywhere else. The problem has been observed by a number of biblical scholars. According to Samuel Terrien (1985: 12), the idea of a rib may well go all the way back to the Greek Septuagint translation. However, this seems unlikely as the LXX rightly renders *tselaʿ* as *pleura*, 'side'. Perhaps more likely is an early rabbinic source:[26]

> Rabbi Joshua (late first–early second century CE) said: 'God deliberated from what member He would create woman, and He reasoned with Himself thus: I must not create her from Adam's head, for she would be a proud person, and hold her head high. If I create her from the eye, then she will wish to pry into all things; if from the ear, she will wish to hear all things; if from the mouth, she will talk much; if from the heart, she will envy people; if from the hand, she will desire to take all things; if from the feet, she will be a gadabout. Therefore I will create her from the member which is hid, that is the rib, which is not even seen when man is naked.

However, other early rabbis seem to have taken a different view. As noted by Robert Gagnon (2001: 60 n. 44), Samuel

---

[26] godswordtowomen.org/lesson%205.htm (2012).

bar Nahman (third century CE) thought of Adam as 'an androgynous being that was sliced in half, down the side'. Among Christian commentators, the 'rib' interpretation of *tselaʕ* may not have been universally accepted until Latin became a major church language. In Jerome's Vulgate version of Genesis the words *costam* and *costis* lend themselves to be understood as either 'side' or 'rib'. Obviously the latter rendering prevailed during the Middle Ages. As demonstrated by today's English versions, it still rules supreme in translations of Genesis 2.

In English, 'rib' and 'side' are not interchangeable. A rib is a bone forming part of the thorax. The *OD* offers several definitions of 'rib'.[27] In anatomy the word refers to a bone in human and animal bodies. In architecture and technology, a rib is a curved piece of metal or wood supporting a structure. For its part, 'side' tends to be used in two ways: (a) it refers to a major section of the body encompassing half of the thorax from the armpit to the hip, and (b) it includes half of the entire body from head to toe. Thus, there is a clear difference between saying 'both ribs' and 'both sides'.

Given that virtually all English Bible translators translate *tselaʕ* correctly in other contexts within the HB, it is remarkable to see how they make an exception in Genesis 2. In fact, the rendering 'rib' turns this occurrence of *tselaʕ* into something unique. It is an astonishing situation for a noun that belongs to the common vocabulary of Classical Hebrew (Hamilton 1990: 178). In defence of the translators, it should be remembered that all professionals need a number of practical tools for performing their work. A translator's daily duties depend to a large extent on specialized dictionaries. In all probability, most Hebrew-English translators regularly use *The Brown-Driver-Briggs Hebrew and English Lexicon*

---

[27] oxforddictionaries.com/definition/rib (2012).

(BDB), which is a standard work. The entry for *tsela*ʿ on p. 854 presents 'rib' as a translation option no fewer than four times and 'side' only twice. Several details in the BDB's approach to *tsela*ʿ are remarkable, including the very first translation options listed, which are 'rib, side' (*sic*). Subsequent renderings include the following:

1. *rib* of man Gn 2.21,22.
2. *rib* of hill, i.e. ridge, or terrace 2 S 16.13.
3. . . .
4. *ribs* of cedar and fir, i.e. *planks, boards* (pl.), of temple wall 1 K 6.15.16, floor v. 15.

Since 'plank' and 'rib' are not interchangeable, the 'ribs' mentioned in option 4 are an unusual metaphor for planks or boards of a temple wall. In these cases it is striking that the BDB has found it necessary to justify the choice of 'rib' and 'ribs' by explaining and clarifying what is meant. In option 2, 'rib' is less than ideal for a simple hillside. Likewise, 'ridge' and 'terrace' seem rather odd in the light of the basic meaning of *tsela*ʿ. Most noteworthy of all is the option suggested for Genesis 2.21-22. Indeed, only 'rib' is listed. Thus, despite its inaccuracy, it is hardly surprising that all the versions surveyed perpetuate Christian tradition on this issue.[28]

In summary, in the original text, there is no other word than *tsela*ʿ indicating the body part that the Creator removes from the groundling. Therefore, the most obvious solution is to translate the word literally as 'side'. Once that is accepted, it becomes clear that the surgery in 2.21 divides the groundling into two parts. One side keeps the name *adam*, which gradually

---

[28] The original edition of the BDB was published in 1906 (p. *xiv*). Bible translations in other languages, including Spanish, present a similar picture. The DBHE lists *tsela*ʿ on p. 638. The first option is *costilla* (rib) applied specifically and exclusively to Gen. 2.21. It is followed by *ladera* (hillside), *tabla* (plank), etc.

evolves into the proper noun Adam, while the part that was removed is shaped into an independent woman. In this manner, two separate sexes emerge. Allowing each half or side of the original groundling to become the other's companion, the operation resolves the problem of human loneliness stated in 2.18.

One Flesh

According to Genesis 2.23, the original groundling reduced to a male being recognizes the woman just introduced to him as his own 'flesh and bones'. For the first time, in Genesis, one finds the Hebrew words *īsh*, 'man', and *ishshah*, 'woman'. On account of their phonetic similarity, the linguistic kinship between these nouns seems obvious. However, this is not in accordance with etymology. Linguists who have studied the evolution of Classical Hebrew have demonstrated that the etymological roots of *īsh* and *ishshah* are different (Korsak 1993: 230). Their separate evolutions surface when the respective plurals are taken into consideration. The plural of *īsh* is *anashīm* while that of *ishshah* is *nashim*. Both plural forms are certainly irregular (Grelot 2006: 88 n. 39). There may be some shared elements in the etymological roots of *ish* and *ishshah*, but they are not necessarily identical (Hamilton 1990: 180).

In the light of these facts, it is advisable to proceed with caution when it comes to interpreting Genesis 2.21–24. The passage may look straightforward at first glance, but in actual fact, the noun *īsh*, 'man', does not appear until 2.23. Up until this point, the narrator has only mentioned the original groundling. If it had been his intention to emphasize beyond any doubt that the male was the original and that the female was created from his rib, the narrator could easily have eliminated any confusion by using the two unequivocal

Hebrew terms *zakhar*, 'male', and *neqevah*, 'female' (Hamilton 1990: 180). On this basis, it might be argued that, above all, the joint appearance of *īsh* and *ishshah* in 2.23 highlights the conceptual kinship between the terms, including the fact that both woman and man were made of the same material (1990: 180). This vision continues to unfold as the narrator inserts a far-reaching statement on the origin of marriage in Genesis 2.24. As a matter of fact, it is a prophecy announcing future events. While the verse mentions 'father and mother', it is not obvious who these parents are. Similarly, readers do not yet know exactly when the man (*īsh*) is going to leave them to cling to his woman (*ishshah*). No formal steps have yet been taken to establish the institution of marriage. This happens in Genesis 4.1 (following the expulsion from the Garden of Eden; cf. chapter 3).

In this context, the phrase 'they become one flesh' is significant. Given the importance of the recent surgery, it would make sense to assume that the text refers to some future reunification of the flesh of the two halves that became disunited. However, in Hebrew the noun *basar*, 'flesh', has different meanings in various parts of the Pentateuch: (a) the organic material of which the human body is made; cf. Genesis 2.21; (b) 'body'; cf. Leviticus 6.3/6.10; (c) 'meat' in the sense of 'food from the animal kingdom'; cf. Genesis 9.4 and Exodus 16.3; and (d) 'family nucleus' or 'kinship'; cf. Genesis 29.14; 37.27; Leviticus 18.6 (Wenham 1987: 71). Thus, *basar* very frequently refers to ties of kinship. The moment that two people establish a new family nucleus through marriage they become 'one flesh'. For their part, the children born to the new couple will belong to both 'fleshes', i.e. the kinship circles of both mother and father (cf. Gen. 29.14; Judg. 9.2). Viewed from a different angle, the form of marriage practised in ancient times seems to belong to the category of contracts or covenants (Hamilton 1990: 181). Specifically, for a man and a woman to become 'one flesh', a formal marital agreement is required (Hugenberger 1994: 163).

Taking all these details into account, it may come as a surprise that so many Christian theologians think that the Hebrew *basar* in Genesis 2.24 is an allusion to sexual union (Nissinen 1998: 99). Undoubtedly, this popular approach is largely based on the Greek term *sarx*, 'flesh'. Unlike *basar*, with its multiple references to anatomy, food, and family ties, *sarx* is used throughout the LXX almost exclusively in the physical realm. By extension, it includes carnal sensuality (Loader 2004: 41–2). In the light of the importance of the LXX for early Christian theology, the Greek connotations of *sarx* are transferred to the Second Testament. Some of the letters of Paul quote Genesis 2.24 verbatim from the LXX as the apostle warns his Christian readers against engaging in sexual relationships with prostitutes. The essence of Paul's argument is precisely that 'the two shall become one flesh' (1 Cor. 6.16). Nevertheless, it should be acknowledged that even in the Pauline Epistles, *sarx* occasionally denotes the idea of kinship suggested by the Hebrew *basar* (Rom. 11.14; cf. Cotterell & Turner 1989: 170).

Returning to the early chapters of Genesis, the Hebrew noun *adam* keeps its original meaning of 'groundling' during several chapters. The narrator regularly alternates between the indefinite *adam* and the definite *ha-adam*, 'the groundling', until the early part of Genesis 5. From this moment on, the definite article *ha* disappears, and Adam becomes the proper name with which all Bible readers are familiar due to its continued use in the Septuagint, the Vulgate, and beyond. For her part, the woman (*ishshah*) is referred to as such until she is given the name *Chawwah* in Genesis 3.20. This original Hebrew word is symbolic due to its nexus with the Hebrew verb *chayyah*, 'to live'. Thus, the narrator expresses the meaning of *Chawwah* as 'the mother of all who live'.

The name 'Eve', which is traditional in English versions of the Bible, has no obvious links to *Chawwah*. For his Greek version, the LXX translator used *Zoē*, 'life', while *Chawwah* became *Hava* in Jerome's Latin Vulgate. However, in the Hellenistic *Koiné* Greek employed by Paul in 2 Corinthians 11.3, the name appears as *Eua*. This seems to be the origin of the modern variants 'Eva' and 'Eve'.

Original Nakedness

According to some scholars, the innocent nudity in which the first man and woman live initially in the Garden of Eden (Gen. 2.25) implies that they enjoy their sexuality 'in freedom' (Terrien 1985: 19). Similarly, David Carr (2003: 32) argues that Genesis 2 provides 'a vision of non-reproductive, joyful sexuality'. However, this approach is questionable. First, this passage contains no verb such as *bō*, 'go in to', or *shakhav*, 'lie down with', both of which connote sexual intercourse (cf. chapter 2). Second, none of the passionately erotic terms and phrases characteristic of the Song of Songs, which celebrates non-reproductive sexuality, is present in the Genesis narrative. Third, the very occurrence in 2.25 of the Hebrew word *ʿarummīm*, 'naked', seems to challenge the hypothesis of an active sexual relationship at this early stage of the first human couple's existence. While man and woman are still in Eden, they live in a state of innocence and ignorance comparable to childhood. In the HB, the concept of nudity often occurs in relation to children who 'do not know good from evil' (Deut. 1.39). This is indeed an essential characteristic of the time in which man and woman refrain from touching the tree of knowledge of good and bad. Under these circumstances, their nudity does not produce any sense of shame.

Furthermore, modern psychology has observed a similar situation in all children who have not yet matured enough to internalize adult social norms (Wenham 1987: 71; Bechtel 1993: 84). One of the messages embedded in the text seems to be that for children, the idea of nudity has no bearing on the way in which they interact with their environment. By contrast, mature, adult persons find it shameful to show their naked bodies in public. Similarly, the concept of sexual desire, *teshuqah*, is not introduced until Genesis 3.16, where the woman is told that her desire shall be for her man. This is mentioned *after* the couple ate the forbidden fruit and in preparation for the earthly scenario outside Eden into which the Creator is sending man and woman who are rapidly approaching adulthood. Thus, sexual desire does not appear in Genesis 3 until humans have become aware of their nakedness. In the biblical narrative, these two phenomena occur in close succession. In addition, it is significant that the awakening of desire precedes marriage, sex, and childbirth, all of which take place in Genesis 4.

From a different perspective, a sensation of shame has no place up until this point in Genesis because these first human creatures have lived in peace and harmony with the Creator and the garden that is their home (Brodie 2001: 149). Only from the moment when the couple feels tempted to try the forbidden fruit do they 'know', i.e. become aware of what they ignored a few moments earlier: the need for protection. Immediately they go on to sew loincloths made of large fig leaves. This new garment has little practical usefulness, but it reflects their bewilderment in the face of the new challenges ahead (Magonet 2004: 126). In the HB, the concept of nudity is often associated with a situation characterized by humiliation or defencelessness. References to nudity have several connotations: (1) to describe poor people; cf. Job 24.7; (2) to provide an image of defenceless prisoners of war taken naked into a life of slavery; cf. Isa. 20.2-4; (3)

as an insult; cf. 2 Samuel 10.4; (4) as a sign of shame; cf. 2 Samuel 10.5; Ezekiel 16.22; (5) to reflect the attractiveness of a naked woman; cf. 2 Samuel 11.2; and (6) to describe the vulnerability of a newborn baby; cf. Job 1.21; Ezekiel 16.6–7 (Hamilton 1990: 181; Magonet 2004: 126).

The state of innocent nudity characteristic of childhood, which is reflected in Genesis 2 and 3, makes the issue of clothing unimportant. However, the moment that these children start acting independently by eating the forbidden fruit, they also become conscious of their nakedness and aware of their awakening sexual impulses. This tends to coincide with the phase in which they are growing strong and mature enough to start working for their daily bread. From this moment on, clothing becomes indispensable. All these aspects are present as the divine parent YHWH Elohīm prepares Adam and Eve for their future joint life as responsible adults on earth by teaching them the importance of hard work (3.17–19) and providing them with appropriate garments (3.21; cf. Magonet 2004: 126; Schneider 2008: 173).[29]

Conclusion

The Hebrew language in the opening chapters of Genesis sheds no direct light on the subject of homoeroticism in the Bible. Indirectly, however, Genesis 2.18–20 presents the idea of freedom of choice granted by the Creator to human beings for us to seek life companions capable of bringing us joy and happiness. To a major degree, the creation story focuses on the mysteries of gender and the awakening of sexual

---

[29] The personal name of the God of Israel appears in this book as YHWH. As noted by Everett Fox (1995 p. *xxix*), the visual effect of YHWH ('the tetragrammaton'; cf. Browning 2009: 353), may be jarring initially, but it has the merit of approximating the Hebrew text as it now stands.

impulses in preparation for adult life. The narrative implies the existence of bisexuality or intersex condition in *ha-adam*, the first 'groundling' created. The popular tendency to quote this part of Genesis as an argument against the acceptance of intimate same-sex relationships has not taken into account the literary complexity of Genesis 1.26–27 and 2.21–22. For example, many Bible readers are unaware that a key word in the Hebrew text of Genesis 2.21–22 is *tsela(*, 'side'. A major problem is caused by a centuries-old tradition encouraging translators to render *tsela(* as 'rib'. Such distortion has no linguistic basis. Since the days of the church fathers, this particular mistranslation has played a crucial part in Christian misogyny.

A similar issue is found in the notion of 'flesh' (Gen. 2.24). Again the semantic and literary analysis carried out in the present chapter has demonstrated the importance for theological reflection of paying attention to the original Hebrew wording and style. In addition to the literal meaning 'flesh', the Hebrew term *basar* denotes 'kinship circle' or 'family nucleus'. The corresponding Greek noun *sarx*, however, tends to evoke 'carnality' and 'carnal knowledge'. The enormous influence of the Greek Septuagint and subsequently of the Latin Vulgate has been highlighted once again. Both versions were crucial for those early theologians who generated some of the core doctrines of Christianity, including 'original sin' and the 'fall' of Adam and Eve, both of which are absent from Judaism.

If the creation story is read in the original Hebrew, it appears to be in harmony with most Jewish, feminist, and queer interpretations. Since the early centuries CE, Jewish scholars have understood the narrative to be a mythological description of human evolution. In their view, it depicts the main phases that characterize the lives of human beings starting with the innocence and ignorance of childhood.

Adolescence brings awareness of our own bodies and invites us to challenge rules and prohibitions. As we move into adulthood, we have to face the facts of life, including becoming independent of our parents, taking responsibility for our actions and working for our daily bread. Finally, the Genesis narrative does not impose rigid commandments or fixed behavioural norms but rather invites human beings of all eras to reflect on the profound mystery of creation and the nature of human life on this planet.

2

THE LANGUAGE OF SEX

*He said, 'Let me come to you'.
She said, 'What will you give me for coming to me?'*

—Genesis 38.16

Introduction

If one wishes to understand how the Hebrew Bible (HB) describes homoerotic relationships, an important preliminary step should then be considered. A practical tool is needed for obtaining a clear vision of the way in which sexual relationships generally are presented in biblical writings. The hypothesis is that the language used to describe heterosexual intercourse is likely to have much in common with the words used in situations depicting homoerotic intimacy. Hence, this second chapter is dedicated to a detailed exploration of the language characterizing sexual incidents in Genesis, a book awash with erotic encounters between men and women. The vocabulary of sex in the HB, including Genesis, is surprisingly rich, varied, and nuanced. The present chapter concentrates primarily on the language reflecting sexual intercourse and situations in which this is requested or suggested. Some words and phrases that occur only sporadically or minimally are mentioned in passing. Once the most typical technical terms have been identified in this chapter (cf. tables 8 & 14), they will then be used in the rest of the book for a thoroughgoing exegesis of the texts commonly assumed to have homoerotic content.

Robert Alter (1996 p. *xxx*) has compared the Hebrew terminology relating to sex with the words used in the English-speaking world today. According to Alter, modern English verbs for sexual intercourse tend to be 'either clinical and technical, or rude, or bawdy, or euphemistic', while none of these descriptions fits the HB. In fact, the Bible is fairly straightforward when it comes to sexual interaction and consistently displays understandable language (Brodie 2001: 192).[30] With these observations in mind, I have selected a number of passages in Genesis with the following characteristics: (1) sexual intercourse takes place, (2) sexual relations are being requested unambiguously, and/or (3) expressions in the text suggest some form of sexual activity or erotic tension.

Come/Go In

Two Hebrew verbs take centre stage when sexual matters are dealt with, namely, *bō* and *shakhav*. In the book of Genesis, the verb *bō* is a very frequent player. Occurring no fewer than 116 times, *bō* usually indicates movement from A to B in the sense of 'come', 'go', 'arrive', or 'enter'. The story of Noah provides illustrative examples. In Genesis 6.13, YHWH declares that 'the end of all flesh *has come*'. In the Hebrew, the point of arrival is indicated by the preposition *el*, 'to' or 'into' as in the phrases 'You shall *go into* the ark' (Gen. 6.18), 'they *went into* the ark' (7.7), and 'they *came to* Noah in the ark' (7.15). Similarly, in the Abraham cycle, one finds *el* joining *bō* in 'you shall *go to* your fathers' (15.15), 'they *arrived at* the place' (22.9), and 'he *went to* the man' (24.30).

In addition to this basic sense of coming and going, *bō* has a sexual meaning. Such is particularly the case when a man

---

[30] Athalya Brenner (1997: 22) takes a different view, classifying all biblical verbs used in the sexual sphere as euphemisms.

'comes to' a woman or 'goes in to' her. In fifteen sexually charged incidents, *bō* combines with the preposition *el*.[31] The first episode in the Bible in which the narrator openly describes the sex life of the protagonists is Genesis 6.1-4. These verses reveal three things about some mythological beings described as 'sons of God': (1) they feel attracted to earthly women, (2) they all 'take' a wife, (3) they impregnate these women by 'going in' to them. The following sexual incident involving *bō* occurs in Genesis 16.2-4. At this stage, Abraham holds his original name Abram, and his wife is Sarai (text abridged, emphasis added):

> And Sarai said to Abram, 'YHWH has kept me from having children. Therefore, I ask you to *go in* to my slave-girl. Perhaps I shall have a son through her'. And Abram listened to Sarai's voice. So . . . Sarai, Abram's wife, took her slave-girl Hagar, the Egyptian, and gave her to her husband Abram as a wife. And he *went in* to Hagar, and she conceived.

The same verb *bō* reappears in Genesis 29 in connection with Jacob's wedding with Rachel. At this time, he has concluded the seven years of service agreed with Laban. In 29.21, Jacob speaks to his uncle requesting his reward (emphasis added):

> And Jacob said to Laban, 'Give me my wife that I may *go in* to her, for my time is completed'.

For his part, Laban celebrates the importance of the occasion by organizing a feast (29.22). According to local tradition, the

---

[31] According to Everett Fox (1995: 33), this is 'the common biblical term for sexual intercourse'. Gordon Wenham (1987: 143) calls it a euphemism. In Hebrew, 'go in to' applies to 'the man entering the woman's tent for the purposes of sex. For Robert Alter (1996: 27), the concept refers to 'the whole act of intercourse, not merely to penetration'.

marriage contract is consummated after bedtime. So Jacob *goes in* to the bride late at night (29.23). Unfortunately he discovers at daybreak that he has been deceived. The young woman sharing his bed is not his beloved Rachel but rather Leah, her elder sister. After promising his uncle to work for seven additional years, Jacob waits for another week in order to *go in* to Rachel (29.30). Similarly, when Rachel plans to have a child through Bilhah, her personal slave, she gives her to Jacob as a wife. He then *goes in* to Bilhah (30.3–4).

The sexual function of *bō* and *el* is obvious in the story of Judah, son of Jacob. Initially Judah marries a Canaanite woman by 'taking' her and subsequently he 'goes in' to her (38.2). The relationship then produces three sons: Er, Onan, and Shelah. A few verses later Er dies, leaving a widow named Tamar. This situation leads to a famous incident involving Onan. From his father Judah, Onan receives this instruction (38.8; emphasis added):

> *Go in* to your brother's wife and perform the brother-in-law duty to her and raise up seed for your brother.

Here is a narrative illustration of the ancient legal arrangement known as levirate marriage (Deut. 25.5–10). It implies that if an Israelite man dies childless, one of his brothers assumes the responsibility of making the widow pregnant. The child born to the widow will be regarded as legal heir to the deceased man.[32] However, in Onan's case, there is an obstacle: he refuses to cooperate. Each time he has to *go in* to Tamar, he rebels by performing *coitus interruptus*. For his disobedience, he is punished by death (38.9–10). Judah promises Tamar that, in a few years' time, he will give

---

[32] Today the levirate marriage custom continues to be practised in some Jewish Orthodox communities (Amit 2010: 218).

his youngest son Shelah to her in levirate marriage. However, as time goes by, Tamar realizes that her father-in-law seems uninterested in making good his promise. Determined not to remain childless, she takes the matter into her own hands. Following the death of Judah's wife, and resorting to unorthodox tactics, Tamar chooses an appropriate moment. As Judah travels to a place called Timnah (38.12), he notices a veiled woman sitting by the roadside at the entrance to Einayim, a small town on the road to Timnah. Thinking she is a prostitute, he approaches her (38.16–18; text abridged, emphasis added):

> He said, 'Let me *come* to you'. He did not know that she was his daughter-in-law. She said, 'And what will you give me for *coming* to me?' He said, 'I will send you a kid from the flock'. She said, 'Give me a pledge until you send it' . . . He gave it to her and *came* to her and she conceived.

It is obvious that both biblical characters understand and use *bō* and *el* with ease. The brevity of the conversation demonstrates that an agreement is reached in a matter of minutes. Table 6 shows the verses in Genesis in which *bō* unequivocally combines with *el* to denote sexual action.

Table 6
BŌ as Sexual Agent

Verb	BŌ & preposition EL
Locations in Genesis	6.4 16.2, 4 29.21, 23, 30 30.3, 4, 16 38.2, 8, 9, 16 (2x), 18
Occurrences	15

Lie Down

The basic meaning of the Hebrew verb *shakhav* is 'lie down', i.e. 'place oneself in a horizontal position'. Occasionally the verb occurs in non-sexual contexts. The story of Sodom offers an example in Genesis 19.4 where it is said that it is almost bedtime in Lot's house; literally, the host and his guests are getting ready to 'lie down'. Later in Genesis, Jacob speaks of the day on which he will 'lie down', in the sense of 'be buried', next to his ancestors (47.30). In addition to this basic sense, *shakhav* is often used to describe sexual intercourse. With regard to the realm of sex in Genesis, *bō* and *shakhav* are equally frequent (Hamilton 1990: 220), occurring fifteen times each. According to Brenner (1997: 29), the agent tends to be male while the woman is receptive or passive. However, exceptions are found in Genesis 19.32–35 where the protagonists are Lot's daughters.

In the HB, *shakhav* denotes sexual intercourse in three situations: (a) between a man and a woman (Gen. 26.10), (b) between two males (Lev. 18.22), or (c) between person and animal (Lev. 18.23). For such purposes, *shakhav* is supported by a preposition, usually ʿ*im* (19.32) or *eth* (Gen. 19.33), both of which mean 'with' (Hamilton 1995: 50 n. 3).[33] The story of Joseph, Jacob's favourite son, has a passage with strong erotic content in which the verbal protagonist is *shakhav*. After being taken to Egypt as a slave, Joseph is sold to Potiphar, a prominent officer at Pharaoh's court. Potiphar soon becomes so impressed with Joseph's administrative skills that he lets him run the entire household. On account of Joseph's good

---

[33] Given the obvious similarity between the preposition *eth* and the particle *eth*, which in some passages acts as an accusative marker in front of Hebrew nouns, pronouns, and proper names, some scholars interpret *eth* as the direct object marker whenever it combines with *shakhav*; cf. Lipka 2006: 186-7.

looks, Potiphar's wife is attracted to him and tries to seduce him (Gen. 39.7-14; text abridged, emphasis added):

> And his master's wife raised her eyes to Joseph and said to him, '*Lie with* me'. But he refused . . . Day after day she insisted . . . but he would not listen to her, to *lie with* her and to be with her . . . One day she grabbed him by his garment, saying, '*Lie with* me'. But he left the garment in her hand and fled and went out . . . She called out to the people of the house, saying, 'He came to me to *lie with* me'.

Similarly, *shakhav* is awarded a crucial role towards the end of the story of Sodom. At this time, Lot's daughters—who were left motherless in Genesis 19.26—are facing the grim prospect of losing their father within the foreseeable future. In addition, the chances of male travellers in this desert region coming to woo them in conformity with established procedures are slim. In fact, they seem to believe that the recent destruction of Sodom and Gomorrah is the end of the world as they know it (19.31). In other words, the girls are more than likely to die childless. Hence, they realize that there is only one way in which they can have children before it is too late (Brenner 1997: 102). Consequently they decide to carry out a pragmatic ruse, which involves using Lot as a sperm donor. The Hebrew word *zerah* literally means 'seed' and is often used in the sense of 'offspring' (Gen. 19.32, 34; Lev. 20.1–3).

In this passage, 19.32–35, *shakhav* is highly active, occurring seven times in rapid succession. Five occurrences are unmistakably sexual. In literary terms, *shakhav* forms a coherent pattern, which is reproduced below (text abridged, emphasis added):

> 'Let us give our father wine to drink and we will *lie with* him that we may give life to offspring by our father'. And that night . . . the elder sister went in and *lay with* her father. And he did not have knowledge in her *lying down* or in her rising. The following day the elder said to the younger, 'Last night I *lay with* my father. This evening we will give him wine again . . . and you go in, *lie with* him . . .' And also that night they gave their father wine . . . and the younger *lay with* him. And he did not have knowledge in her *lying down* or in her rising.

In another dramatic context, *shakhav* appears after Dinah, daughter of Jacob and Leah, has gone out to meet the Canaanite women who live in the area in which her family has settled temporarily. Unfortunately for Dinah, she is seen by a young Canaanite prince named Shechem who stops her, takes her aside, and goes on to have sexual intercourse with her without obtaining permission from her family (Gen. 34.2, 7; text abridged, emphasis added):

> And Shechem saw her, took her and *lay with* her . . . And Jacob's sons, when they learned this they became angry because he [Shechem] had committed an act of folly . . . by *lying with* Jacob's daughter.

Jacob's sons use the noun *nevalah*, 'folly', in the sense of 'criminal folly' or 'outrage' (cf. Judg. 19.23; 20.6). The sexual transgressions recorded in Genesis are not limited to Canaanites. For his part, Reuben, Dinah's elder brother, once committed an act of serious disrespect vis-à-vis his father. He took the liberty of approaching Bilhah, one of Jacob's secondary wives, for sexual intimacy and actually *lay with* her (35.22). Table 7 offers an overview of the presence in Genesis of *shakhav* in sexual contexts.

Table 7
SHAKHAV in Sexual Contexts

Verb	SHAKHAV & preposition ETH or 'IM
Locations in Genesis	19.32, 33, 34 (2x), 35 26.10 30.15, 16 34.2, 7 35.22 39.7, 10, 12, 14
Occurrences	15

It should be noted that in 39.10 *shakhav* is joined by the preposition *etsel*, which means 'next to' or 'beside'.

Two Complementary Verbs

As noted, the verbs *bō* and *shakhav* are often interchangeable in situations involving sexual activity. This fact is clearly demonstrated in an incident occurring between the sisters Leah and Rachel. Both are married to Jacob and compete for his affection (Gen. 30.14-16). One day Reuben, Leah's son, comes home from the fields bringing his mother an aphrodisiac called mandrake. Instantly a situation of barter arises between the two women (text abridged, emphasis added):

> Rachel said to Leah, 'I ask you to give me the mandrakes'. And Leah replied, 'Is it a small matter that you have taken away my husband . . . ?' Rachel said, 'He will *lie with* you tonight if you give me the mandrakes'. And when Jacob came back from the field . . . Leah went out to meet him and said, 'You will *come to* me in exchange

for my son's mandrakes'. And he *lay with* her that night.

Table 8 shows the thirty cases in Genesis where *bō* and *shakhav* describe clear-cut sexual situations and often in complementary ways.

Table 8
Sex in Genesis

Verbs	**BŌ** & preposition **EL**	**SHAKHAV** & preposition **ETH** or **ʿIM**
Locations in Genesis	6.4 16.2, 4 29.21, 23, 30 30.3, 4, 16 38.2, 8, 9, 16 (2x), 18	19.32, 33, 34 (2x), 35 26.10 30.15, 16 34.2, 7; 35.22 39.7, 10, 12, 14
Occurrences	15	15

Table 8 makes it clear that, in a sexual capacity, *bō* and *shakhav* are flexible and equally likely to appear in situations occurring inside and outside of marriage. From this brief overview of Genesis, it may be concluded that in Classical Hebrew, *bō* and *shakhav* are prominent and frequent verbs used to describe, suggest, or request sexual relationships.

Translating BŌ and EL

Having identified two important markers of sexual language in the Hebrew text of Genesis, it is of interest to see how current English versions of the Bible have chosen to translate *bō* and *shakhav*. Below I compare the specific choices made by the versions with respect to these verbs. Characteristically *bō* combined with *el* deals with sex when a man is the acting subject with a woman as recipient. Table 9 divides the various English renderings into two groups: (a) literal, formal, or direct translations; (b) free or dynamic translations that tend to modify, alter, or paraphrase the sense of the Hebrew.

Table 9
Translating BŌ & EL

Version	Literal translations	Free translations
CCB	go to (2), go in to (1)	sleep with (7), lie with (3), [omission] (2)
HCSB	come to (1), go to (1)	sleep with (12), come with (1)
JM	go in to (11), come in to (3)	have intercourse with (1)
JPS	0	cohabit with (7), sleep with (4), consort with (2), join with (2)
NCV	0	have sexual relations with (14), marry (1)
NIV	go to (1)	sleep with (10), make love to (4)
NJB	go to (3), come to (1)	sleep with (9), resort to (1), take (1)
NKJV	go in to (11), come in to (4)	0
NLT	0	sleep with (7), have intercourse with (3), have sex with (2), have sexual relations with (1), marry (2)
NRSV	go in to (12), come in to (3)	0
NWT	0	have relations with (15)
REB	0	Lie with (11), sleep with (2), have intercourse with (1), take (1)

The twelve versions offer a series of different options for translating *bō* in sexual contexts. Among the literal or 'faithful' renderings in the first column one finds: 'come to', 'come in to', 'go to', and 'go in to'. Two versions (NKJV, NRSV) are exclusively in this group as they stick to the basic meaning of *bō* and *el* ('come to' or 'go in to'). Such a literal wording may strike modern ears as unusual, and some readers are likely to consider this a disadvantage. However, it should be pointed out that both versions have the advantage of consistency in their chosen renderings. At the same time, they provide readers with a realistic impression of the original Hebrew style. For its part, JM is predominantly literal (first column) while proposing a non-literal option for Genesis 6.4 ('have intercourse with', second column).

A more mixed approach, which includes one or several of these options but interspersed with non-literal renderings, is taken by four versions (CCB, HCSB, NIV, NJB). As shown in the second column, the emphasis is clearly on the free or 'dynamic' method. In this mixed group, the NJB offers four literal renderings of *bō* (Gen. 16.2, 4; 29.21; 30.16). In nine cases, the option suggested is 'sleep with', which is adequate from several viewpoints. While not being literal but rather euphemistic, this phrase is justified from a semantic point of view given that in modern English 'sleep with' indicates sexual relations. However, it should be pointed out that the proper Hebrew verb for 'sleep' is *yashēn* (Gen. 2.21). Furthermore, on two remaining counts the NJB makes unusual choices. First, this is the only version to suggest that 'the sons of God *resorted to* women' (6.4). Second, in 38.8 the NJB problematically suggests that the *bō* and *el* combination translates as 'take' in '*Take* your brother's wife'. However, the Hebrew verb *laqach*, 'take', is not present here. In addition, in biblical contexts 'take' often means 'marry' (Gen. 6.2; 19.14). Strictly speaking, the relationship between Onan and Tamar is not marital since he is supposed to act as a sperm donor.

The HCSB proposes two literal renderings of *bō* and *el*: 'come to' (6.4) and 'go to' (16.2). The third option 'come with' (Gen. 30.16) is a paraphrase in the sense that *el* does not mean 'with'. In the Hebrew original, Leah is being explicit as she tells Jacob to 'come to' her. In twelve other cases, this nuance is adequately presented in the obvious preference shown by the HCSB for 'sleep with'. As noted, this is justified semantically with the caveat that in Hebrew 'sleep' is *yashēn*. With three literal renderings, the CCB takes a similar approach to *bō* and *el*: 'go to' (6.4; 16.2) and 'go in to' (16.4). The rest are non-literal. On two occasions, the CCB omits any reference to *bō* and *el* (30.4; 38.2). Seven times one finds 'sleep with'. More problematic is 'lie with' in 29.21, 29.23 and 38.8. This option for *bō* and *el* is confusing because 'lie with' in Hebrew is expressed by means of *shakhav* and *eth* or ʿ*im* (see below).

For its part, the NIV introduces a single literal rendering of *bō* in Genesis 6.4 where the 'sons of God' decide to 'go to' human women. However, the meaning of this English rendering is somewhat unclear since the very same sons of God have just married these women by 'taking' them (Hebrew *laqach* in 6.2). Clearly 'go in to' would be a better choice. At any rate, the general solution preferred by the NIV is 'sleep with', a fairly uncomplicated option as noted above. Rather more problematic is the paraphrase 'make love to', which is chosen in four cases. These occurrences of *bō* and *el* describe the initiation of married life (Gen. 29.21, 23, 30; 38.2). From a literary point of view, the main difficulty resides in the gap between the very factual character of the Hebrew 'go in to' and the emotional component in the English 'make love'. The word 'love', Hebrew *ahavah*, is not present in the original text.[34]

---

[34] Elsewhere (Gen. 29.20) *ahavah* refers to Jacob's love for Rachel.

Paraphrasing BŌ and EL

Five versions in table 9 offer no literal options whatsoever. The NWT consistently translates *bō* and *el* as 'have relations with'. While such consistency is laudable, the word 'relations' is ambiguous. It is certainly less direct and more euphemistic than the biblical 'go in to'. Almost as consistent as the NWT is the NCV with fourteen cases of 'have sexual relations with'. The word 'sexual' is helpful as it makes the phrase unambiguous. The disadvantage resides in its somewhat clinical overtones compared with the more down-to-earth nature of the Hebrew.

For its part, the word 'marry' used by the NCV in Genesis 29.21 begs a comment. In that it makes Jacob tell his uncle Laban that he wants to 'marry' Rachel, the NCV is presenting old news. For seven years there has been a deal between the two men (29.18–21). What Jacob is actually saying is that he, after such a long wait, is keen to hold Rachel in his arms. That is why the narrator makes him tell Laban that he wants to 'go in to' her (Hamilton 1995: 261; Alter 1996: 154). Generally speaking, the *bō* and *el* combination indicates physical intimacy inside and outside of marriage (6.4; 16.2-4; 38.16-18). In 38.8, it does not mean 'marry' since Judah is simply telling his son Onan to 'go in to' his widowed sister-in-law Tamar (Hamilton 1995: 435). Classical Hebrew deals with the subject of marriage by means of other terms, including *laqach*, 'take'. It is used of men who take wives (6.2; 11.29; 25.1).[35] Occasionally the verb *yada'*, 'know', is employed in the same sense (4.1, 17; 24.16). Less frequently, women are said to know a husband (19.8).

---

[35] Literary sources from various parts of the Ancient Near East show that, in a number of languages, 'take' denotes 'take in marriage' (Hamilton 1990: 444).

In the case of the NLT, no fewer than five paraphrastic renderings of *bō* and *el* are on offer in the second column: 'sleep with', 'have intercourse with', 'have sex with', 'have sexual relations with', and 'marry'. Viewed separately, four options are fairly adequate while the least accurate is 'marry' (Gen. 29.21). The overall impression left by the NLT is one of relative confusion. Where the Hebrew narrator creates literary continuity by using *bō* and *el* fifteen times, the NLT's variations carry the disadvantage of discontinuity.

The JPS translators suggest four different options for *bō* and *el*: 'sleep with', 'cohabit with', 'consort with', and 'join with'. None is direct or literal. The only straightforward option is 'sleep with' (except for the absence of *yashēn*, 'sleep'). The rest come across as euphemisms with a certain academic flavour. For example, there is a considerable stylistic gap between the 'cohabit with' of the JPS and the plain-sounding 'go in to' in the Hebrew. In addition, cohabitation usually refers to a situation of married life, which only partly seems to be the situation in the case of Abraham and Hagar (Gen. 16.4). Moreover, 'consort with' and 'join with' do not necessarily imply sexual intercourse but may be taken in a social sense.

The REB successfully proposes 'sleep with' on two occasions (30.16; 38.8) and once 'have intercourse with' (6.4). Both renderings are adequate for *bō* and *el*. Unfortunately the remaining options listed are problematic. First, the REB uses 'lie with' eleven times. Clearly this is an error because to 'lie with' someone is expressed in Hebrew by means of *shakhav* ('lie down') joined by '*im* or *eth*. Second, in one case the REB mistranslates *bō* and *el* as 'take'. This happens in Genesis 16.2, where Sarai in the original tells Abram to 'go in to' Hagar. If she were saying 'take', the Hebrew narrator would have used the verb *laqach*. This does not happen until

16.3, where Sarai 'takes' her slave-girl Hagar and gives her to Abram, i.e. she turns Hagar into Abram's concubine.

Precision and Imprecision

Table 9 has shown how the choices of several versions fall at varying distances from the Hebrew wording. At one extreme, there is the literalness of the NKJV and the NRSV and, at the other, the propensity for euphemisms and paraphrase of the JPS and the impreciseness incurred by the REB. Table 10 rearranges the fifteen occurrences of *bō* and *el* in Genesis according to the degrees of literalness or 'faithfulness' achieved by the versions. Each version is tentatively awarded 'points' according to a 15-point scale. In other words, the maximum attainable is 15 points.

Table 10
Literalness of Twelve Versions

Versions	Literalness	Versions	Literalness
NKJV	15	NIV	1
NRSV	15	JPS	0
JM	14	NCV	0
NJB	4	NLT	0
CCB	3	NWT	0
HCSB	2	REB	0

Table 10 is not a convenient litmus test for determining the overall quality of the versions listed. Other criteria would have to be included. What the score does indicate, however, is that nine versions are prepared to create a considerable gap between their 'free' or 'dynamic' renderings and the fairly simple nature of the Hebrew. In the light of the fifteen occurrences of *bō* and *el* in the original text, the ideal for an English version setting out to be faithful and/or accurate would be to aim for a similar level of consistency. This would then imply seeking out an English verb or phrase that could conceivably be used in all fifteen cases and be a worthy match for the original.

From a slightly different perspective, table 11 examines this material to show to what degree the versions actually achieve such an effect. For instance, the number 2 indicated for the NCV shows that two renderings were given for *bō* and *el*. The numbers in parentheses indicate that the renderings suggested represent minor variations or near-duplicity. Thus, the NKJV's two options 'come in to' and 'go in to' may arguably be counted as one.

Table 11
Consistency and Inconsistency

Versions	Options	Versions	Options
NWT	1	HCSB	4 (3)
NKJV	2 (1)	JPS	4
NRSV	2 (1)	REB	4
NCV	2	NJB	5 (3)
JM	3 (2)	CCB	5
NIV	3	NLT	5

Table 11 shows that the NWT is firmly committed to consistency in relation to *bō* and *el*. A fairly similar situation is found in the NKJV and the NRSV. Their choices are compatible variations on the theme of 'come in to' and 'go in to'. The NCV has taken the variation further by saying both 'sleep with' and 'marry'. As previously noted, the latter option is problematic. The three options proposed by James Moffatt (JM) are the plain-sounding 'go in to' and 'come in to' and one case of 'have intercourse with'. The NIV offers 'go to', 'sleep with', and the less appropriate 'make love to'. The four renderings found in the HCSB may be reduced to three taking into account the semantic proximity of 'come to' and 'go to', both of which fall within the basic range of *bō* and *el*. However, such quasi-synonymity does not exist between 'come with' and 'sleep with'.

Semantically speaking, the four options presented by the JPS are not far apart but not entirely interchangeable either: 'cohabit with', 'consort with', 'sleep with', and 'join with'. By comparison, there is some consistency in the eleven occurrences of 'lie with' in the REB but, as noted, this is a mistranslation. 'Sleep with' and 'have intercourse with' are variants on a theme. However, 'take' does not belong in this context. In the NJB, the only attempt at consistency is 'sleep with', with nine occurrences. Other options include 'come to, 'go to', 'resort to', and 'take'. The overall result comes across as inconsistent. For its part, NLT achieves a relative degree of consistency with seven occurrences of 'sleep with'. From a semantic point of view, there is continuity, thanks to 'have intercourse with', 'have sex with', and 'have sexual relations with'. Stylistically, however, there is relative discontinuity.

The one verb that is completely out of place in both NCV and NLT is 'marry'. In theory it may work for a few selected contexts, but in most cases it does not. As noted above, there is no reason for suggesting that *bō* and *el* implies marriage. In the context of 38.16–18, Judah certainly does not want to 'marry' Tamar. In fact, the notion of 'marry' is clearly not present in a great many passages.[36] In the CCB, the seven

---

[36] Gen. 6.4; 16.2, 4; 29.23, 30; 30.16; 38.2, 8, 9, 16 (x2), 18.

occurrences of 'sleep with' provide relative consistency, and semantically they are not incompatible with 'go to' and 'go in to'. However, the remaining occurrences of *bō* and *el* are rendered inconsistently or, in two cases, omitted in translation. The three instances of 'lie with' in the CCB are imprecise since they accord not with *bō* and *el* but rather with the verb *shakhav* (see below).

Translating SHAKHAV

The other important Hebrew verb in the sexual playing field is *shakhav*, 'lie down'. For the fifteen occurrences in the book of Genesis, *shakhav* combines mostly with the preposition '*im* while in six cases the preposition is *eth*, both meaning 'with'. The fact that they alternate in conjunction with *shakhav* shows that these prepositions are virtually interchangeable in sexual contexts. In one case *shakhav* is joined by the preposition *etsel*, which means 'alongside' or 'next to. It appears in 39.10 where Joseph refuses to lie down 'next to' Potiphar's wife. The situation is clearly one of physical intimacy and should be counted in this overview.

The renderings of *shakhav* found in the twelve English versions include 'lie with', 'sleep with', 'come/go to bed with', 'make love to', 'have intercourse with', 'have sexual relations with', 'have sex with', and 'rape'. In table 12, they are divided into two columns according to degrees of literalness or paraphrase.

Table 12
Renderings of SHAKHAV & Preposition

Version	Literal renderings	Free renderings
CCB	Lie with (8)	sleep with (5), come to bed with (1), rape (1)
HCSB	0	sleep with (13), go to bed with (1), rape (1)
JM	Lie with (15)	0
JPS	Lie with (14), lie beside (1)	0
NCV	0	have sexual relations with (13), sleep with (2)
NIV	0	sleep with (11), come/go to bed with (3), rape (1)
NJB	0	sleep with (14), 1 paraphrase
NKJV	Lie with (15)	0
NLT	0	sleep with (6), have intercourse with (3), have sex with (3), rape (3)
NRSV	Lie with (14), lie beside (1)	0
NWT	lie down with (14), lie alongside (1)	0
REB	Lie with (10)	sleep with (2), make love to (2), rape (1)

According to the first column in table 12, the most literal approaches to *shakhav* are taken by the JPS, the NRSV, and the NWT. They all detect and respect the special case of *shakhav* and *etsel* in 39.10. Next are JM and the NKJV, which translate all fifteen occurrences of *shakhav* and preposition as 'lie with', including *shakhav* and *etsel*. There is a considerable difference between these five versions and the ten cases in which the REB rightly suggests 'lie with' and the eight occasions in which the CCB does the same. As for the other versions, no literal renderings are offered.

In the 'free' group, the NJB wisely restricts its range of non-literal options to 'sleep with'. The only exception is found in 39.14. According to the original narrative, Potiphar's wife is saying about Joseph, with unmistakable innuendo, 'He *came to* me to *lie with* me'. By contrast, the NJB goes down a different road: 'He *burst in on* me'. Several problems are noticeable in this paraphrase. First, neither *bō* nor *shakhav* is recognizable on the English side. Second, the NJB has made the unexpected move of collapsing two verbs into one transforming them into 'burst'. Third, in the process, the innuendo is lost. According to the NJB, Potiphar's wife is making a point that seems unrelated to sex. 'He burst in on me' may well be taken as an expression of annoyance caused by a slave who rudely failed to knock at the door before entering.[37] The NCV has chosen two related, modern-sounding renderings of *shakhav* whereas the CCB, the HCSB, and the NIV all offer three different translations. For its part, the NLT raises the number to four. It is joined by the REB as it proposes one literal option ('lie with') along with three non-literal renderings.

If table 12 is read horizontally, six versions give a fairly straightforward impression (JM, JPS, NCV, NKJV, NRSV, NWT). As for the remaining six, the opposite is the case. The surprise move made by the NJB in Genesis 39.14 has been mentioned. Indeed, in addition to various paraphrases

---

[37] According to the *Cambridge Advanced Learner's Dictionary*, 'burst in on sb/sth' is defined as 'to enter a room suddenly and without warning, interrupting the people or activity inside'; cf. dictionaries.cambridge.org (2011).

for *shakhav*, five versions introduce the dramatic rendering 'rape' in one specific case, namely, Genesis 34.2 (CCB, HCSB, NIV, NLT, REB). This is where Hamor's son Shechem lies with Jacob's daughter Dinah. The NLT goes even further by adding two more cases of 'rape'. In 34.7, the word is placed in the mouths of Dinah's brothers. Similarly, in the NLT's version of the story, Potiphar's wife includes this word in her report on the Joseph incident (39.14). In the latter context, the NLT is joined by the REB.

Read vertically, the 'Literal' column in table 12 shows a high degree of uniformity. The second, or non-literal, column presents a mixed picture. As mentioned, one version stands out for its plainness, namely, the NCV. There is no contradiction between 'sleeping with' someone and 'having sexual relations with' them. Thus, the NCV may be classified as relatively successful. However, a close inspection reveals that, in the remaining versions, their free renderings of *shakhav* produce unresolved semantic tensions. For example, the fact that the NLT chooses to extend itself to no fewer than four free translations of *shakhav* raises questions. There is certainly no opposition between 'sleep with', 'have sex with', and 'have intercourse with'. All these options may work well semantically. What is unsettling in the NLT's approach is the presence of the fourth option 'rape'. The NLT applies it to Genesis 34.2 to describe what Shechem does to Dinah (emphasis added): 'He saw her, he seized her and *raped* her'.

The word 'raped' is problematic for at least three reasons. First, *shakhav* always means 'lie down'. The question of whether or not the action happens peacefully or in a context of violence does not change the semantic nature of this verb. Second, Biblical Hebrew is perfectly capable of deploying specific verbs to describe sexual assault, a subject to which I return later. The third reason for questioning the wisdom of the NLT in translating *shakhav* as 'rape' has to do with the issue of incoherence and inconsistency. The NLT has forgotten to cross-check the 'rape' option by tentatively applying it to other occurrences of *shakhav* in Genesis. In a few cases, the rendering might conceivably be appropriate. In 34.7, Dinah's brothers' blood boils as they hear the news of Shechem's rash behaviour. Another situation arises in 39.14 where Potiphar's wife virtually accuses Joseph of sexual assault. However, in few other contexts, the notion of rape would apply. In short, 'lying down with' somebody is not, and cannot be, equivalent to 'raping' them.[38] If sexual violence is the issue, other textual markers are likely to be at play.

Secondary Verbs

In connection with sex and erotic tension in Genesis, an additional number of Hebrew verbs and verbal phrases are active. Characteristically, however, they occur very sporadically and, in most cases, just once. Occasionally the verb *hayah*, 'to be', appears linked to the preposition ʿ*im* ('with'). It may mean 'to be with somebody' in an intimate sense as in the tense interaction between Joseph and Potiphar's wife (Gen. 39.10): 'he would not lie next to her or *be with* her'. Another example is *qarav*, 'approach' ot 'come near' (Brenner 1997: 22–3). In conjunction with the preposition *el* ('to'), *qarav* may express the idea of approaching someone with sexual intent: 'Abimelech had not *approached* her' (Gen. 20.4). Finally, the verb *nagaʿ*, 'touch', is capable of taking on a sexual meaning when the preposition *el* is added: 'I would not let you *touch* her' (20.6).[39]

---

[38] In a hypothetical scenario, it would be absurd for Rachel, when striking a deal with her sister Leah, to say, 'He will *rape* you tonight' (30.15). And it is hard to imagine Potiphar's wife inviting Joseph into her bedroom (39.7, 12) with the words 'Come, *rape* me'.

[39] For the sexual implications of *qarav*, see Hamilton (1995: 61). For a discussion of the sexual side of *nagaʿ*, see Lipka (2006: 137).

In a few cases of special interest for the subject of sex, the verb *tsachaq*, 'laugh', may well have sexual overtones, particularly when it operates in the Hebrew verb form called *piel*. An illustrative example occurs in the life of Isaac and his wife Rebekah. Because of a famine in Palestine, they move to the land of Gerar (Gen. 26.1). Isaac is afraid of the locals and presents Rebekah as his sister (26.7). One day, however, King Abimelech catches him off guard as he is 'having fun with' Rebekah (*tsachaq*, 26.8). The context reveals that the scene is erotically charged. To King Abimelech, this is so obvious that he immediately goes on to rebuke Isaac for not having told the truth (26.9-11). A polemic example of the same verb *tsachaq* (*Piel*) in a sexual context is provided by Potiphar's nameless wife as she unfairly accuses Joseph of 'making fun of' everyone in the house (Gen. 39.14). In this passage, *tsachaq* is joined by the preposition *bĕ* ('in'). Potiphar's wife presents herself as the primary victim alleging that Joseph tried to 'make fun of' her (39.17). In the latter case, the phrase seems to mean 'fool around with'.

Sexual Violence

Peter Cotterell and Max Turner (1989: 253) have observed that biblical narrators are capable of expressing in just a few words a high level of dramatic intensity. This includes a number of incidents involving sexual violence. A crucial story featuring *shakhav* is Genesis 34, which begins when Dinah, daughter of Jacob and Leah, goes out for a walk. As she enters the city of Shechem, she is seen by the crown prince who is also named Shechem. As the young daughter of an isolated immigrant, she is vulnerable, and the situation exposes her to abuse (Alter 1996: 189). In Genesis 34.2, Shechem makes four moves in rapid succession: he 'saw' Dinah (*raah*), he 'took' her (*laqach*), 'lay down' with her (*shakhav*), and 'debased' her (*ʿanah*).⁴⁰ This young man's uninhibited behaviour is risky, and he and his fellow countrymen will pay a very high price for it.

Weston Fields (1997: 137) observes that in the world of the HB, a sexual assault on a defenceless person, whether carried out by one or several local men, is enough to trigger momentous punishment or revenge. This is so because a flagrant crime of this nature is not typified within personal or private law but is seen to affect the entire social structure within which it occurs. The nature of the sexual transgression in Genesis 34.2 is described by means of *ʿanah*, 'oppress', or 'debase'.⁴¹ This significant verb is used in different parts of the HB in the intensive *Piel* form in regard to situations of severe social, religious and cultural oppression. A case in point is the Israelite community suffering under the yoke of slavery in Egypt (Gen. 15.13; Exod. 1.11-12). Another typical example is the poor, mistreated foreigner living among the people of Israel (Exod. 22.21-24; cf. Hanks 1983: 15-17). Similarly, Sarai 'oppresses' Hagar, making her flee into the desert (Gen. 16.6).

Furthermore, *ʿanah* is capable of describing the nature of sexual transgression. The disastrous outcome of Dinah's adventure begs comparison with the moment when Tamar, beautiful daughter of David, becomes a victim of assault (2

---

[40] According to Alter (1996: 189), 'The chain of uninterrupted verbs conveys the precipitousness of the action'; cf. Wenham 1987: 75. Another intriguing feature is the recurring use of *laqach*, 'take'. In 34.2, it denotes physical force while in 34.4 the verb is a request addressed to Shechem's father meaning 'let me *marry* this girl'.

[41] In the simple *Qal* verb pattern, *ʿanah* means 'to be troubled' or 'worried'. When it operates in *Piel*, the verb acquires the active sense of 'oppress', 'mistreat', 'humiliate' or 'debase'; cf. BDB p. 776; DBHE pp. 577-8; Lipka 2006: 253.

Sam. 13).[42] In the latter passage, ʿanah occurs twice. Thus, in 2 Samuel 13.12 Tamar tries to dissuade the rapist, and in 13.14 the actual crime takes place. In addition to the hurt and pain inflicted on Tamar personally, the humiliation she suffers has a sinister, life-changing effect on her social position. Marrying the rapist would have provided Tamar with an honourable way out (Deut. 22.28–29). However, Amnon refuses even to consider a marital settlement (2 Sam. 13.13–17). Because of what happened, Tamar spends the rest of her life in virtual seclusion inside her brother Absalom's house (2 Sam. 13.20). However, Amnon's crime does not go unpunished. Eventually Absalom takes revenge by killing Amnon (2 Sam. 13.28–29).

Another illustrative example of the social shame surrounding the issue of sexual debasement occurs during Absalom's bloody revolt against his father, David. As David hurriedly flees from Jerusalem, he leaves the royal house in the hands of ten concubines (2 Sam. 15.16). When Absalom invades the palace, he is advised to demonstrate his conqueror status by taking possession of the ten women in the sight of his troops (2 Sam. 16.21–22). The unmistakable sexual nature of this act is specified as Absalom 'goes in to' (bō & el) the concubines. Following the defeat and death of Absalom, David regains his throne and palace. He then has a special, isolated room built for these women, in which they live until the day they die without interacting with the rest of the royal household (2 Sam. 20.3). Having been 'debased' by Absalom, the concubines are, in the eyes of their community, considered unfit for performing their previous duties.

Returning to the Dinah/Shechem passage in Genesis 34, the Hebrew narrator describes the sexual action in these

---

[42] This particular Tamar is not to be confused with Tamar, daughter-in-law of Judah (Gen. 38).

terms: 'He *took* her, *lay with* her and *debased* her'. Thus, three elements are distinguishable. Crucially, the illicit or oppressive aspect of the Dinah/Shechem encounter centres upon the verb *'anah* (Lipka 2006: 188-90). The physical act is described by means of 'lying down' (*shakhav*). In and of itself 'lie with' is not an indicator of violence but rather a factual way of stating sexual intercourse (cf. Gen. 30.15-16). The verb 'took' has an element of force as it suggests superiority. In Shechem's case, being the ruler's son, he is in a privileged position (34.2). In addition, he is probably physically stronger than Dinah. At other times, *laqach* simply reflects higher social rank. For example, Sarai has the authority to 'take' her slave-girl Hagar and give her to Abram for him to sleep with (16.3), just as Leah 'takes' Zilpah and gives her to Jacob (30.9). Similarly, Abraham has a right to 'take' Ishmael and all male slaves and circumcise them (17.23).

Translating Sexual Transgression

The twelve English versions have adopted different approaches to the sexual debasement occurring in Genesis 34.2. Their renderings are listed in table 13.

Table 13
Translating Sexual Debasement in Gen. 34.2

Versions	Renderings
CCB	he seized her, raped her and dishonoured her
HCSB	he took her and raped her
JM	he lay with her and dishonoured her
JPS	he took her and lay with her by force
NCV	he took her and forced her to have sexual relations with him
NIV	he took her and raped her

NJB	he seized her and forced her to sleep with him
NKJV	he took her and lay with her, and violated her
NLT	he seized her and raped her
NRSV	he seized her and lay with her by force
NWT	he took her and lay down with her and violated her
REB	he took her, lay with her, and violated her

Five versions represented in table 13 adequately reflect the chain of events laid out in the Hebrew text. Their literal renderings of *ʿanah* are 'violated' (NKJV, NWT, REB) and 'dishonoured' (CCB, JM). Both translation options achieve a high level of correspondence with the Hebrew original. Dinah was indeed violated and dishonoured, and—not to be forgotten in the ancient context—so were the social position and reputation of her father and family. Three versions have opted for the simple paraphrase 'raped' (HCSB, NIV, NLT). In this manner, they conflate two Hebrew verbs—'lie down with' (*shakhav*) and 'debased' (*ʿanah*)—into a single verb. While 'raped' is a familiar word to English-speaking readers, its presence here raises questions. This is because the modern concept of rape does not have a direct equivalent in the HB (Gravett 2004: 279). If brevity were the overarching ideal to be pursued by translators, it might be argued that 'rape' is sufficient. However, given the wider context of Genesis 34, 'rape' only partly covers the oppressive social aspects inherent in *ʿanah* (*Piel*). It barely hints at the severe sociological ramifications of non-marital sex in antiquity, including its potentially lethal consequences (Deut. 22.20-24).

Four versions have adopted a 'dynamic' approach in which the element of force is highlighted. Again in this case, and unlike the three-part action presented by the Hebrew narrator, their methodology leads them to reduce the chain of events to two steps: 'he took/seized her and lay with her by force' (JPS, NRSV), 'he seized her and forced her to sleep with him' (NJB), and 'he took her and forced her to have sexual relations with him' (NCV). In other words, this is another example of how the two Hebrew verbs *shakhav* and *ʿanah* are turned into a one-dimensional paraphrase. Technically speaking *ʿanah* has been confined to the limited space of physical force in a sexual context. What is missing from the equation is the fact that the force aspect has already been suggested by the verb *laqach*, 'he took her', which precedes both *shakhav* and *ʿanah*. In other words, the JPS, NCV, NJB, and NRSV are being repetitious as they focus entirely on Shechem's superior physical strength. A highly significant verb such as *ʿanah* (*Piel*) has been awarded a secondary role. No social or psychological information is added to one's understanding of the incident in which Shechem carries out his impetuous conquest of Dinah. In summary, the downside of all the dynamic approaches is the fact that they either reduce *ʿanah* to be a direct equivalent of the modern term 'rape' or regard it as an indicator of the use of force on a par with *laqach*, 'he took'.

Three versions have preferred 'seized' to 'took' for their translation of *laqach*. In English, 'seize' is a stronger word than 'take'. A similar difference exists in Classical Hebrew between *laqach*, 'take', and *chazaq*, 'seize'.[43] Genesis offers several examples where *chazaq* denotes seizing someone's hand. Because Lot and his family dally in Sodom, the visiting messengers find it necessary to seize them by the hand and lead them to safety outside the city (19.16). As Hagar faces despair in the desert, an angel appears to tell her to seize her son Ishmael's hand and go to a well of water (21.18). In some cases, the occurrence of *chazaq* illustrates a situation of sexual assault (2 Sam. 13.11).

---

[43] In the simple *Qal* verb pattern *chazaq* means 'grow in strength' or 'become invigorated'. Within the *Hiphil* pattern (Causative), *chazaq* acquires the sense of 'make strong', 'take hold of' or 'seize' (BDB pp. 304–5; DBHE pp. 237–9).

However, in a number of cases, *laqach* is sufficient to indicate action in which the subject forcefully uses his or her hands. Three such examples are found in the life of Abraham. In Genesis 17.23, he 'takes' his son Ishmael and all male members of his household and has them all circumcised. In 18.7 he goes to the herd to 'take' a calf to be slaughtered and prepared for a meal, and in 22.10 Abraham reaches out to 'take' the knife to sacrifice his son Isaac. In other words, to translate *laqach* as 'take' in 34.2, as seven versions have done, is adequate. Finally, it is worth pointing out that what characterized Shechem's crime should not be reduced to the physical force he displayed vis-à-vis Dinah. The real problem was the spontaneity and disrespect with which he proceeded. As soon as he saw the girl he failed to ask permission of her parents, 'took' her and 'lay with' her, leaving her and her family 'debased' (Lipka 2006: 188–9; Carmichael 2010: 57).[44]

Illicit Sex

A series of sexual incidents in Genesis commented upon in this chapter have involved the verbal phrase *bō* and *el* while a similar number has featured *shakhav* and *eth* or *'im*. On two occasions, sex is at the heart of commercial transactions of which the narrator provides no moral judgment. Such is the case as the sisters Rachel and Leah negotiate ownership of the mandrakes brought home from the field by Leah's son Reuben. At stake are sleeping rights with Jacob. Both *bō* and

---

[44] In the case of sexual assault of a young virgin in ancient Israel, the rapist or seducer was supposed to marry the girl as stipulated by Deut. 22.28-29. Intriguingly Shechem is more than willing to do just that. If he had been a kinsman of Jacob's, he might indeed have stood a fairly good chance. However, the fact that he is an uncircumcised Canaanite puts Shechem at a disadvantage. According to Carden (2006: 51), the outcome of this episode gives the story 'an added edge of inter-ethnic conflict'.

shakhav play a part in the process (30.15, 16). For his part, Judah the widower negotiates access to the bed of a veiled woman whom he takes to be a prostitute. In this passage, the crucial verb is *bō* and *el* (38.16, 18).

At this point, I want to look briefly at the differences between licit and illicit sexual relationships. With regard to sexual intercourse within formal marriage or cohabitation, *bō* tends to be preferred on twelve occasions.[45] Thus, the *bō* and *el* combination seems to be endowed with a certain 'licit' flavour. However, in one incident the intercourse described occurs in a setting resembling prostitution (Gen. 38.16–18). Of the situations in which *shakhav* is present, many deal with illicit sex. Thus, six passages with *shakhav* at the centre describe incestuous activity,[46] while five cases reflect potential or attempted adultery (Gen. 26.10; 39.7, 10, 12, 14). Two cases imply seduction possibly combined with the use of force and certainly with disregard for social conventions (34.2, 7). In the light of these thirteen instances, it might be argued that *shakhav* and *eth* or *ʿim* is the more likely construction to appear in contexts of illicit sex.

Yet another situation in which sexual activity is categorized as illicit is a woman's adultery. A case in point is the way in which Tamar, widowed daughter-in-law of Judah, has become pregnant. In Genesis 38.24, it is 'reported' (Hebrew root *n-g-d*) to Judah that Tamar has 'played the whore' (NRSV).[47] Other versions suggest that she 'played the harlot' (JPS, NJB, NKJV, NWT), 'played the prostitute' (CCB, REB), 'acted like a prostitute' (NLT), 'has been acting like a prostitute' (HCSB), 'is guilty of acting like a prostitute' (NCV), and 'is guilty of prostitution' (NIV). The

---

[45] Gen. 6.4; 16.2, 4; 29.21, 23, 30; 30.3, 4, 16; 38.2, 8, 9.
[46] 19.32, 33, 34(2x), 35; 35.22.
[47] Lipka (2006: 140 n. 61, 249) proposes the rendering 'she has acted promiscuously'.

longest rendering is 'Tamar had been playing the harlot and was with child by whoredom' (JM). The Hebrew verb translated here is *zanah*, which means 'be unfaithful', 'act adulterously', 'commit fornication' or 'prostitute oneself' (BDB p. 275; DBHE p. 222). Thus, six English versions have translated *zanah* accurately. Strictly speaking, the 'guilty' element suggested by the NCV and the NIV is superfluous. The notion of guilt may be implied in the overall situation but is not inherent in the root meaning of *zanah*. In Classical Hebrew, the concept of 'guilt' is expressed specifically by means of the noun *asham*.[48]

Intimately connected to the verb *zanah* is the noun *zonah*, 'prostitute' or 'whore'. In Genesis, it first occurs in the uncompromising verdict pronounced by Dinah's brothers Simeon and Levi as they justify their recent massacre of the people of Shechem: 'Should our sister *be treated as a prostitute?*' (*kĕzonah 'oseh*, 34.31). In 38.15, *zonah* appears for the second time. This is where Judah assumes that the veiled woman sitting by the roadside is a prostitute. In summary, two Hebrew verbs tend to be active in the realm of illicit sex, namely, *shakhav* and *zanah*. The former may have a female or a male subject as numerous examples in Genesis have shown.[49] As for *zanah*, it primarily requires a female subject (Gen. 38.24; Lev. 21.9; Jer. 3.1). However, in certain contexts, *zanah* may apply to males as where the men of Israel give themselves over to 'whoring' with Moabite women (Num. 25.1).

---

[48] An example in Genesis is the exclamation addressed to Isaac in which King Abimelech reproaches his guest for having lied and exposed him and the men of Gerar to the risk of incurring 'guilt' (26.10; cf. Lipka 2006: 139). The corresponding adjective 'guilty' in Hebrew is *ashēm* with the plural form *ashemīm*. The latter form occurs in Gen. 42.21 where Joseph's brothers are discussing what has gone wrong, realizing they are 'guilty'.

[49] Female subjects: 19.32, 33, 34(2x), 35. In all other contexts, the grammatical subject is male.

In connection with the subject of illicit sex, one may wish to include the Hebrew verb *tamaa* operating in the *Piel* form. In several contexts, *tamaa* refers to the land or a holy place becoming 'defiled' or 'unclean' (Num. 19.20; Deut. 21.23). Similarly, it applies to people (Lev. 11.44; Num. 19.20). Three times in Genesis 34, the narrator notes that Shechem 'defiled' Jacob's daughter Dinah (34.5, 13, 27). In the light of such emphasis, it becomes clear that Jacob and his sons are not only saying that she became a victim of sexual abuse but, significantly, that her reputation and the honour of her family suffered irreparable damage.

Sex in a Nutshell

In this chapter, the book of Genesis has been searched for Hebrew terms associated with the realm of sex. The most frequent verbs are *bō*, 'go in', and *shakhav*, 'lie down', occurring fifteen times each. In addition to these, the narrator occasionally makes use of secondary verbs or verbal phrases to describe different nuances in situations of sexual innuendo, tension or transgression. Table 14 divides the verbs discussed into categories.

Table 14
Verbs Denoting Sex in Genesis

Primary verbs	*bō* & *el*	go in to, come to
	shakhav & ʿ*im* or *eth*	lie down with
Secondary verbs	*shakhav* & *etsel*	lie down next to
	hayah & ʿ*im*	be with
	nagaʿ	touch
	qarav & *el*	go near, approach

	tsachaq & direct object	have fun with
	tsachaq & *bĕ*	make fun of
Superiority	*laqach*	take (use of force)
Oppression	*ʿanah* (Piel)	debase, humiliate
Defilement	*tamaa* (Piel)	defile, make unclean
Prostitution	*zanah*	act as a whore/prostitute
	kĕzonah ʿoseh	be treated as a prostitute

As for the primary verbs, their occurrences in Genesis were presented in table 8. The secondary verbs in table 14 occur just once in sexually charged contexts: *qarav* and *el* (20.4), *nagaʿ* (20.6), *hayah* and *ʿim* (39.10), *shakhav* and *etsel* (39.10), and *tsachaq* (*Piel*), and direct object (26.8) or with the preposition *bĕ* attached (39.14, 17). In the case of *laqach*, it appears occasionally to denote sexual intent on the part of someone with social authority (16.3; 29.23) or such authority combined with superior physical strength (34.2). When it comes to *ʿanah* (*Piel*), this verb expresses a sexual act in which a man debases a female partner (34.2), while *tamaa* (*Piel*) denotes defilement (Num. 19.20). Finally, *zanah* has to do with promiscuity and prostitution (38.24).[50]

---

[50] The verb *ʿalal* (*Hithpael* verb pattern), 'mistreat', occurs in several passages outside Genesis. One such context is sexually charged (Judg. 19.25), and in two other cases, this is clearly a possibility (1 Sam. 31.4; Jer. 38.19). The circumstances surrounding the sexual aspects of *ʿalal* are discussed in this book's chapters 4 and 12.

Conclusion

The HB is well provided with verbs and verbal phrases operating in the realm of sex. The present chapter has identified two primary verbs in Genesis (*bō* and *shakhav*) along with a number of secondary or supplementary verbs. Several major conclusions may be drawn from the word choices made by the twelve English versions of the Bible examined. First, a literal approach to Bible translation is relatively rare. Second, the so-called dynamic approach, which tends to seek variation and often resorts to paraphrase, is very popular. Third, this chapter has detected various imprecise renderings presented by a number of translators who prefer the dynamic approach. Inaccuracies are particularly frequent in cases involving such Hebrew verbs as *bō*, *shakhav*, and *ʿanah*.

Not only do mistranslations occur but also a series of inconsistencies. Very different meanings have been ascribed to the same verb depending on the context. A specific problem in regard to the modern concept of rape should be highlighted. According to several versions, *ʿanah* translates as 'rape'. However, unlike the term 'rape', which in the early twenty-first century describes a man's crime against a victim who is usually female and occasionally male, the ancient context in which *ʿanah* operates calls for somewhat different renderings such as 'oppress', 'debase', or 'humiliate'. Here the social and cultural aspects are emphasized, which include the offended family.

All the verbs studied in this chapter have shown varying degrees of links with the sexual sphere. The terminology identified in this survey as sexual or potentially sexual is likely to be useful for discussing specific texts in the Hebrew Bible commonly thought to have homoerotic content or implications.

3

TO KNOW IN THE BIBLICAL SENSE

*Your father practised justice and righteousness.
Is not this to know me?*

—Jeremiah 22.15–16

Introduction

In the previous chapter, the most common verbs used in the Hebrew Bible for sexual relations were identified. Another important verb in this context is *yada'*, 'to know', which is widely believed to belong in the realm of sex in a number of significant texts. However, it is intriguing that the semantic, literary and legal complexities surrounding *yada'* in the HB have never been examined in any detail. In addition, and contrary to popular assumption, the alleged sexual aspect of *yada'* is under-researched. For this reason, an in-depth analysis is carried out below. The ways in which *yada'* has been translated historically are explored in chapter 10.[51]

All current biblical dictionaries and commentaries assert that *yada'* has sexual connotations. The DBHE argues that this is 'one of the most frequent euphemisms for sexual intercourse' (p. 307).[52] This viewpoint is seconded by

---

[51] Chapter 10 includes a discussion of the plausible Greek origins of the phrase 'to know in the biblical sense'.
[52] In Spanish: *Es uno de los eufemismos más frecuentes del trato o relaciones sexuales.*

Athalya Brenner (1997: 8, 22-3, 29, 137-8) and restated by Meir Malul (2002: 233) who asserts that 'the sexual sense of *yada*ʿ is indisputable'. For his part, Jesper Svartvik (2006: 277) describes *yada*ʿ as 'a technical term' for sexual intercourse in the Bible. This perception of 'know' is so well established that it has become part of common usage, albeit with archaic or humorous overtones. The *Oxford Dictionary* offers the following definition of 'know':

> **3** [*with object*] *archaic* Have sexual intercourse with (someone). [A Hebraism which has passed into modern languages; compare with German *erkennen*, French *connaître*.]

Given the academic insistence on the subject, the purported sexual dimension of *yada*ʿ has become accepted as 'to know in the biblical sense'. In *The Agony of Christianity*, the Spanish writer and philosopher Miguel de Unamuno (1931: 71) uses the expression,

> To know in the biblical sense, where knowledge becomes one with the act of carnal- and spiritual—union, whereby children are begotten, children of flesh and spirit.[53]

Furthermore, within the Hebrew Bible, the BDB (p. 393) has registered 943 occurrences of *yada*ʿ in different contexts while Amira Meir (2012: 56) has located 940 occurrences. For Larry Mitchel (1984: 2), the number is 924. Notwithstanding these discrepancies, *yada*ʿ is obviously a very frequent verb in biblical literature. Meir Malul (2002: 233) argues that *yada*ʿ has sexual connotations in seventeen cases. If one takes the

---

[53] *Conocer en el sentido bíblico, donde el conocimiento se asimila al acto de la unión carnal – y espiritual – por el que se engendra hijos, hijos de carne y de espíritu.*

number 940 as a base, these occurrences would represent 1.8 per cent of the total. In Robert Gagnon's view (2001: 72-4), sixteen cases of *yada(* are to be taken in the sexual sense, which amount to 1.63 per cent. For Derrick S. Bailey (1955: 2-3), the exact number of sexual occurrences is ten (1.01 per cent). He acknowledges, however, that in five additional cases *yada(* combines with the noun *mishkav*, 'bed', to refer to women who have known, or not known, 'the bed of a male'. Adding it all up, the total number of sexual occurrences of *yada(* would, in Bailey's calculation, be fifteen (1.59 per cent), an estimate shared by Ron Pirson (2012: 209). For his part, Gordon Hugenberger (1994: 272) has found fourteen cases of *yada(* in a sexual role (1.48 per cent) while Anthony Heacock (2011: 91) arrives at the number thirteen (1.38 per cent). Furthermore, Martti Nissinen (1998: 46) suggests the sexual occurrences of *yada(* to be 'about a dozen', i.e. 1.27 per cent. At the bottom of the scale, John Boswell (1980: 94), Brian Doyle (1998: 91), and Daniel Helminiak (2000: 45) accept the lower count of ten, or 1.01 per cent, first suggested by Bailey.

In other words, when it comes to determining the scope of the assumed sexual role of *yada(* in the HB, there is no scholarly consensus. Moreover, this overview shows that it is an exaggeration to speak of *yada(* as a very frequent player in the sphere of erotic interaction. Of nearly one thousand occurrences of the verb, the assumed sexual proportion is below two per cent. In addition, even if the purported sense denoting physical intimacy were to be accepted, *yada(* is still a long way behind the verbs *bō* and *shakhav*, which predominate in the sexual realm, particularly in Genesis. Furthermore, several biblical scholars are willing to grant *yada(* a fair amount of ambiguity.[54]

---

[54] Bailey 1955: 3; McNeill 1993: 47; Bechtel 1998b: 117; Doyle 1998: 91-4; Carden 2004: 20.

To Know in the Biblical Sense

Several crucial texts, in which *yada'* plays an important part, are examined below. They include Genesis 1–4 (the creation story), Genesis 18–19 (Sodom and Gomorrah), Genesis 38–39 (Judah and Tamar; Joseph in Egypt), and the Hebrew prophets.

> And the *Adam* knew his woman *Chawwah* who conceived and gave birth to Cain (Gen. 4.1).

In this verse, the BDB (1952: 394) explains that *yada'* means 'to know a person carnally, of sexual intercourse'. Convinced that the verb describes the first instance of sexual intimacy mentioned in scripture, the vast majority of translators and commentators base their exegesis of *yada'* in Genesis 4.1 on this viewpoint.[55] However, other interpretations should not be excluded. It is important to note that Genesis 4.1 is not the earliest occurrence of *yada'*. First, several precedents are found in Genesis 2.9, 2.17 and 3.22 in the form of the noun *da'at*, 'knowledge', which has the same consonantal root as *yada'*, namely, *yd'*. Second, in 3.5, the serpent says that God 'knows' (*yada'*) that if the humans eat from the tree of knowledge, they will become discerning as 'knowers' of good and evil. Third, in the phrase 'know good and bad' (3.5, 22), *yada'* means 'know the things of life'. Fourth, once the forbidden fruit has been tasted, in 3.7, both human beings suddenly 'become aware' (*yada'*) of their naked condition. Fifth, *yada'* occasionally has legal connotations, particularly in solemn or archaic contexts when formal pacts or covenants are established between two parties (4.1; 18.19).

---

[55] Hammershaimb 1957: 16; Jenni and Westermann 1978: 954; Botterwerk and Ringgren 1986: 464; Hamilton 1990: 220; Fox 1995: 25; Alter 1996: 16; Stone 1996: 74–5; Nissinen 1998: 46; Gagnon 2001: 73; Browning 2009: 185; Heacock 2011: 91.

Furthermore, while sexual activity in Genesis is generally denoted by means of *bō* and *shakhav*, neither occurs in the opening chapters. Thus, at this early stage, sex is not an issue. It seems reasonable to interpret the creation narrative as a poetic or mythological illustration of the ways in which social institutions and structures came about (Brodie 2001: 142). In addition, many scholars seem unaware that in antiquity sexual intercourse would occur within well-defined social structures (Hugenberger 1994: 156; Thatcher 1999: 68). The Pentateuch in its entirety shows that people's sex lives were not 'free' to be initiated any time. To be accepted as legitimate, sexual interaction had to unfold in conformity with the legal norms governing the institution of marriage. If such principles were violated, as Shechem did with Dinah in Genesis 34, fierce punishment was likely to be the outcome.[56]

In relation to the meaning of *yadaʿ* in Genesis 4.1, it is important to remember the recent expulsion of the two human beings from the Garden of Eden (3.23-24). Until that moment, the man and the woman have given each other company to overcome loneliness (2.18). However, things change as soon as they are expelled from the garden of their childhood and teens. They have left behind the parental Creator who is both 'father and mother' (2.24). The carefree life in Eden is now a thing of the past, and the couple is no longer in direct communication with their heavenly parent. In this new situation both humans feel a need to establish a reciprocal commitment, which formally recognizes their interdependence. Left to their own devices, they begin to learn to live adult lives, including making responsible decisions (Carr 2003: 46; Magonet 2004: 124-5). This is a time in which the one has to serve the other as helper or sustainer (2.18).

---

[56] Cf. Deut. 22.20-21, 23-24; Judg. 20.12-13; 2 Sam. 13.22, 28-29.

Throughout Genesis, *yadaʿ* regularly describes interaction in which legitimacy plays a major part. Thus, in four cases, it applies to a marriage contract (4.1, 17; 19.8; 24.16). If *yadaʿ* performs a legal function in Genesis 4.1 as a description of the formal initiation of the first marriage (Carmichael 2010: 102), it harks back to the solemn prediction inserted by the narrator in 2.24: 'A man shall leave his father and his mother and join (or 'cling to') his woman'.[57] Significantly, the Hebrew noun *ishshah* means both 'woman' and 'wife' (DBHE p. 93).[58] Thus, the knowing expressed in 4.1 is equivalent to 'formal acknowledgement', i.e. Adam recognizes Eve as *his* woman or wife, fulfilling thereby the standard laid out in Genesis 2.24. Since this move is described as the man 'joining' (Hebrew *davaq*) his wife, it might be argued that in this specific context *davaq* is interchangeable with *yadaʿ*.

Naturally the formalization of a marriage pact subsequently includes consummation. Thus, in Genesis 4.1, it is perfectly logical that Eve becomes pregnant following the moment of 'knowing'. However, the couple's sex life—the second step in the marital process—is not made explicit by means of *bō* or *shakhav*. In other words, consummation is left implicit. Thus, in the world of the HB, it is possible for a man or a woman to 'know' their spouse in a formal sense by virtue

---

[57] It is possible to translate the sentence in the present tense: 'A man leaves his father and his mother and clings to his woman'. By doing so, the man transfers the loyalty previously owed to his parents to the new relationship established with his woman (Hugenberger 1994: 161). Thus, the marriage contract between Adam and Eve in Gen. 4.1 has paradigmatic force, i.e. it is presented as an ideal situation worthy of imitation (1994: 6, 151).

[58] Classical Greek shows a similar situation regarding the noun *gynē*. In everyday language, it meant both 'woman' and 'wife'. In the early third century CE, this phenomenon was observed by Tertullian (Tertullian 1951: 86-7, 142). Analogous usages exist in a number of modern languages, including French (*femme*), German (*Frau*), and Spanish (*mujer*).

of the verb *yada'*. In Genesis 4.1, it is the male who knows the female as he establishes with her a formal contract (as opposed to a simple common-law partnership). Given this context, it makes sense for Eve to exclaim at the birth of her son Cain in 4.1, 'I have acquired a man with Yhwh', because she is indeed being 'fruitful' in accordance with the divine blessing pronounced in Genesis 1.28.[59] At the same time, her relationship with Adam unfolds within the framework of the legitimate marital arrangement stipulated in 2.24.

Analogous situations occur in Genesis 4.17 and 4.19–22. In most cases, the narrator omits the wives' names, stating simply the man's name and that of his first male child (4.18, 26 ff.). From Genesis 5.3 onwards, it is not unusual to mention the birth of daughters, but for the most part, they remain unnamed. In all cases, one observes the absence of concrete allusions to the protagonists' sex lives. What really matters to the narrator are genealogies.

Knowing and Descendants

In all languages, legal terminology tends to become fossilized and many terms from law books sound dated or archaic. The HB is no exception. In solemn, archaic, or mythological settings, *yada'* is often imbued with a legal sense. From a formal point of view, the contract between Adam and Eve mentioned in Genesis 4.1 belongs to this category (Hugenberger 1994: 163). Consequently, it is according to ancient usage to say that Adam 'knew' his woman because at that moment she became his wife. Three English versions of the Bible have indeed done so (JPS, NKJV, NRSV).

---

[59] Calum Carmichael (2010: 2) points out that this blessing should not be taken as a command or duty: 'Duties are laid on persons to help others, but as far as one's own person is concerned, one is free to receive or reject a blessing.'

A parallel situation is found in Genesis 4.17. Here it is Cain, the firstborn son of Adam and Eve, who 'knows' a woman, i.e. he acknowledges her as his wife, after which a child is born. The wording is virtually identical to Genesis 4.1. In these instances, the Hebrew narrator uses an ornate literary style to describe the significant moments in the early existence of human beings on the earth. If Adam and Eve represent the first generation or family bond, the marriage of Cain connoted by *yada'* marks the beginning of the second generation (Carmichael 2010: 101–2). The paradigmatic character of the story suggests that the dignified, formal, and slightly archaic role assigned to *yada'* in this context may be intentional. In these early chapters of the Bible, the term is deployed to highlight the culminating moments of the beginnings of human life.

In the light of such precedents, the appearance of *yada'* at another significant moment in the life of Adam and Eve may at first sight seem surprising (4.25):

> And Adam *knew* his wife again. She gave birth to a son and called him Seth.

It is true that Adam already 'knew' Eve in Genesis 4.1. Since the same verb is employed in 4.25, and Eve becomes pregnant in both cases, many readers are again tempted to think that *yada'* is used in a sexual sense. However, such a simple interpretation ignores the literary refinement of the context. In the case of Abel's birth in Genesis 4.2, the narrator does not speak of any 'knowing'. Likewise, no verb from the sexual realm is mentioned (*bō* or *shakhav*). Stated another way, there is no focus on the moment of Abel's conception or Eve's second pregnancy. What readers are told is that Abel was born within the framework of an established marital relationship. In addition, the Genesis narrator only refers to the sex lives of human couples in specific circumstances.

In most cases, readers are simply informed that people get married and have offspring (Gen. 5 & 10; 25.12-18.). If three children are born to Adam and Eve, it is more than likely that the couple have had sexual relations on a number of occasions, i.e. three times at the very least. Hence, the sexual renderings suggested by most English versions for *yada'* in Genesis 4 are unfortunate. In 4.1 the approaches adopted by nine versions are 'had intercourse with' (CCB, JM, NJB, NWT), 'had sexual relations with' (NCV, NLT), 'knew intimately' (HCSB), 'lay with' (REB), and 'made love to' (NIV), with a similar score for 4.25. Strictly speaking, these renderings leave readers with the erroneous impression that Adam and Eve make love twice, i.e. in 4.1 and 4.25.

From a psychological perspective, the sudden loss of Abel is traumatic for his parents. The tragedy is compounded by the painful exile imposed on Cain (4.16). In this way, Adam and Eve are literally left without children overnight. Being the firstborn son, Cain should have been entrusted with the continuation of the family tree, and there is a brief reference to his descendants in Genesis 4.17-24. However, because of the crime he committed, the link between Cain and his parents is severely weakened, and he ceases to be the ideal ancestor of a major genealogy. Once they have come out of a period of mourning, Adam and Eve decide to renew their initial commitment. The recurrence of *yada'* in Genesis 4.25 undoubtedly matches the logical unfolding of the narrative. The verb formally signals that they start all over again. On this basis, their third son Seth is not simply an addendum to his parents' life story. On the contrary, the birth of Seth confirms and reinforces the formal bond between Adam and Eve. Expressed differently, as crown of the new marital covenant Seth receives the honour of carrying forward the family tree (McKeown 2008: 44). Methuselah (Gen. 5.21-22) and Noah (5.28-30) are among his better known descendants.

The Meaning of Formal YADAʻ

The formal aspects of *yadaʻ* in the HB are reflected in a number of texts in which the deity interacts with human beings. Sometimes the presence of *yadaʻ* adds a solemn, ritual, and perhaps archaic note to the language. In the book of Exodus, Yhwh says to Moses, 'I know you by name and you have found favour in my sight' (Exod. 33.12, 17). In Deuteronomy 34.10, the narrator emphasizes the fact that Yhwh 'knew' Moses face to face. Similarly, in a prayer to the deity, King David refers to the special relationship between him and Yhwh, saying, 'You know your servant' (2 Sam. 7.20). In the prophetic writings, *yadaʻ* appears repeatedly in connection with the concept of covenant, for instance in Ezekiel 16.62 and Hosea 2.20. Speaking to the tribes of Israel, Yhwh declares through the mouth of the prophet Amos (3.2, emphasis added):

> Only you have I *known*
> Among all the families of the earth.

In this passage, it is evident that 'known' means 'acknowledged', or 'recognized'. The words 'known' and 'families' provide direct links to Abraham and his descendants (Gen. 12.3; 18.19; 28.14). Other situations in the HB highlight the bond between Yhwh and his people. The book of Jeremiah offers a number of examples that illustrate how being 'known' by Yhwh involves religious obligations and a firm legal and social commitment. At the very beginning of the book, Jeremiah describes how he himself became a servant of the deity. In Jeremiah 1.5, Yhwh speaks in the first person (italics added):

> Before I had formed you in the womb, I *knew* you,
> And before you were born, I consecrated you.
> I appointed you a prophet to the nations.

Similarly, YHWH explains in Jeremiah 9.24 (italics added):

> And those who boast, let them boast only in this:
> That they understand and *know* me
> That I am YHWH
> I act with kindness, justice and righteousness in
>   the earth
> For in these things I delight.

In this context, the knowing works in both directions, that is, from YHWH towards human beings and vice versa. According to Jeremiah, anyone who keeps the stipulations of the covenant will in practice know YHWH, i.e. they recognize the authority of the deity. In other words, Jeremiah emphasizes that the knowledge of YHWH is intimately connected to the practice of the virtues in which the latter delights such as compassion, mercy, justice and respect for the rights of the poor and vulnerable. Jeremiah provides another example of a person who lived in harmony with divine law, namely, King Josiah of Judah. In Jeremiah 22.15–16, YHWH speaks to Jehoiachim, Josiah's son, referring to his father's commitment (emphasis added):

> Did not your father eat and drink
> And do justice and righteousness?
> Then it was well with him.
> He judged the cause of the poor and needy
> Then it was well.
> Is not this to *know* me?

In this verse, 'know me' not only means 'know my ways' but also 'recognize me as suzerain' (Huffmon 1966: 35–6). At other times, the required knowledge is sadly missing on the human side. In Hosea 8.2, the Israelites claim to 'know' their God, which would imply recognition of YHWH's divine authority and respect for his laws. However, throughout

Hosea 8, the deity demonstrates forcefully that the professed knowing is completely unfounded, as in 8.4: 'They set up offficers, but I did not *know*' (emphasis added).

The solemn covenants that Y<small>HWH</small> establishes in the HB with Abraham, Moses, David, Jeremiah, and others have formal similarities with a number of political treaties dating back to pre-biblical times in the ancient Middle East. Examples abound in the literature of the Hittite, Akkadian, Sumerian, and Ugaritic cultures in which a political suzerain chooses to 'know' somebody. The word denotes the establishment of a formal, binding relationship between a king/lord and a subject/vassal (Huffmon 1966: 31–7; Thatcher 1999: 69). Characteristically, the suzerain is the initiator (Huffmon & Parker 1966: 36–8).[60] As for a divine-human covenant, this is clearly an 'asymmetrical relationship' (Thatcher 1999: 70, 86) based on the theological conviction that God alone takes the initiative (p. 87). In addition, covenants between human beings would usually be witnessed by a god who acts as guarantor of the agreement and adds solemnity to the pledges being made (1 Sam. 20.12–16, 23, 42; cf. Thatcher 1999: 89).

Significant Repetition and Grammar

In the 1930s, German-Jewish theologians Martin Buber and Franz Rosenzweig formulated a literary theory in which the concept of Significant Repetition (SR) is prominent. SR highlights the importance of repeated words and elements in Classical Hebrew prose (Korsak 1993: 223). The repetition of certain key terms is an intentional feature of the artistic pattern woven by a number of biblical writers (Provan 1998:

---

[60] Magonet 2004: 142 defines 'covenant' as a permanent contractual relationship, with mutual responsibilities, and legally binding upon both partners (p. 153). The term also applies to a contractual relationship between husband and wife; cf. Peleg 2005: 179.

200-1). In recent decades, several biblical scholars have found inspiration in the concept of SR, including André Chouraqui (1987), Mary Phil Korsak (1993: 223), Everett Fox (1995 pp. *ix–x, xv–xvi*), and Robert Alter (1996 p. *xxvi*).

According to Sue Groom (2003: 119), it is important for any semantic analysis to define accurately the context in which terms occur and their relative frequency. The story of Sodom and Gomorrah is highly significant from two perspectives: (a) homoeroticism in the Bible and (b) Significant Repetition. Having been mentioned in Genesis 14, the name of Sodom reappears in Genesis 18.16 to recur eight times in close succession. Likewise, in this context, the six occurrences of *yadaʿ* are remarkable. I define the context relevant for *yadaʿ* as the second half of Genesis 18 and the entire chapter of Genesis 19. Table 15 offers an overview of the presence of *yadaʿ* in the text of Sodom and Gomorrah.

Table 15
A Text in Genesis with YADAʿ

Verses	Hebrew	Meaning
18.19	yedaʿetīw	I have *known* him
18.21	edaʿā	Let me *know*
19.5	nedʿā	Let us *know*
19.8	yadʿū	(They) have *known*
19.33	yadaʿ	(He) *knew*
19.35	yadaʿ	(He) *knew*

Table 15 shows the elegant way in which the six occurrences of *yadaʿ* interact by twos in three passages according to what seems to be a deliberate narrative pattern: 18.19 and 18.21, 19.5 and 19.8, and 19.33 and 19.35. One passage is at the beginning of the plot, another in the middle, and the third towards the very end. In this manner, the three passages with *yada'* illustrate two essential factors: (a) the centrality of *yada'* in the Hebrew text of Sodom and Gomorrah; and (b) the literary unity of the story, including the interconnectedness of Genesis 18 and 19 (cf. Cotterell & Turner 1989: 247). Furthermore, in the Hebrew text, *yada'* forms an intriguing grammatical pattern, which is shown in table 16.

Table 16
Forms of YADA' in Genesis 18–19

Verse	Hebrew	Person	Mode
18.19	yeda'etīw	1st singular	Qal
18.21	eda'ā	1st singular	Cohortative
19.5	ned'ā	1st plural	Cohortative
19.8	yad'ū	3rd plural	Qal
19.33	yada'	3rd singular	Qal
19.35	yada'	3rd singular	Qal

Within the structure of SR, a certain systematic distribution of *yada'* is detectable. First, the verb appears three times in the first person and three in the third person. Second, the most frequent verbal mode is *Qal* (four occurrences) supplemented by two occurrences of the infrequent Cohortative. The latter form is an emphatic variant of *Qal* that operates only in the first person (Weingreen 1959: 88). Third, the two final occurrences of *yada'* (Gn. 19.33, 35) are identical, which further highlights the SR aspect. When *yada'* operates in the simple *Qal* form, it is generally translated as 'know'. Hebrew verbs do not respond to the familiar categories of 'present tense' and 'past tense' typical of Indo-European languages. Instead, they are characterized by 'aspect'. Thus, in Hebrew, the aspect of a given verbal action is classified as either completed or uncompleted (Weingreen 1959: 56; Johnstone 1998: 137).

A major characteristic of the Hebrew text of Genesis 18 and 19 is an abundance of formal, legal sounding language (Bruckner 2001: 124–70; van Wolde 2012: 71). If this stylistic aspect is applied to *yadaʿ*, it may yield decisive results for its interpretation. A legal reading of *yadaʿ* enables exegetical progress on two counts: (1) it will become clear that the presence of the verb in the Sodom text is indeed an important case of SR; (2) the juridical nature of the context provides further exegetical elements, which are essential for understanding the entire narrative. The six occurrences of *yadaʿ* in the story of Sodom and Gomorrah are discussed below in order of appearance.

I Have Known Him

The composite *yedaʿetiw*, 'I have known him' (Gen. 18.19), belongs to the completed aspect of *Qal*. In the light of the solemn covenant that Y<small>HWH</small> has established with Abraham in Genesis 15 and 17, the rendering 'I have acknowledged him' or 'I have recognized him' is appropriate (Korsak 1993: 67).[61] Given the law-impregnated character of the Hebrew text, it seems natural to view the occurrence of *yadaʿ* in Genesis 18.19 as an element of ancient legal terminology. The terms used in treaties from the ancient Near East match the steps taken by Y<small>HWH</small> to bring about his covenant with Abraham (Gen. 12.1, 7; 13.14; 15.1, 13; 17.1; 18.1). Furthermore, in 18.19,

---

[61] Amira Meir (2012: 61) cites Bahya ben Asher who interprets *yadaʿ* as 'bestow recognition on someone' in the contexts of Exod. 33.12 and Ps. 144.3.

it is stated that for Abraham to be 'known', he is required to follow 'the way of Yhwh'. The nature of this way is specified in the words 'by doing what is righteous and just'. Other parts of Genesis explain that the way of Yhwh includes faith and devotion (Gen. 12, 13, & 15), obedience (Gen. 14, 17, 21, & 22), humility (Gen. 17 & 18), hospitality and generosity (Gen. 18), and spontaneous solidarity with a family member in crisis (Gen. 14 & 18).

Moreover, for the human party to the treaty to be known by Yhwh implies their accepting the responsibility to teach descendants the importance of the virtues just enumerated (18.19). The compassion for the potentially innocent citizens of Sodom demonstrated by Abraham in the second half of Genesis 18 shows that he fulfils the expectations inherent in the covenant. Another element pertains to the physical sphere, namely, mandatory circumcision (Gen. 17.10–14). For Abraham, the final element attached to divine knowing consists of a rich reward that will last for many centuries: 'All the peoples of the earth will be blessed in him' (Gen. 12.3; 15.1; 17.5–7).

Finally, several passages in Genesis reveal in what ways the blessing will materialize. It implies meeting Yhwh face to face (12.7; 15.1; 17.1; 18.1), being told about the divine plans (Gen. 15 & 18), the ability to intercede for others (18.23–32; 20.17), as well as a series of special favours (Gen. 12–15, 17–19, 21–22, & 24). For the ancient history of Israel and for the whole Bible, the covenant between Yhwh and Abraham is paramount. Because Yhwh himself explains the relationship in a soliloquy (Gen. 18.17–21), this section of Genesis 18 is to be regarded as a centrepiece.

Let Me Know

In the Sodom text, *yada'* reappears very soon after 18.19, namely, in 18.21. The repetition conveys emphasis. In this second case, *yada'* operates in the special mode of the verbal paradigm called Cohortative, a subcategory of *Qal*. In Hebrew, the range of usage of the Cohortative is limited to first person singular and plural. It denotes an uncompleted, emphatic action and is used to highlight the intention, determination, or effort of the speaker (Weingreen 1959: 88). The Cohortative of *yada'* in 18.21 is written *eda'ā* and translates as 'let me know' or 'I want to know'. The speaker is Y<small>HWH</small> expressing desire to go down to Sodom in order to 'know' the origin of the outcry that has come to his attention. The legal terminology in the context reveals that this is not a simple pleasure trip triggered by curiosity but rather a formal inquest (Bovati 1994: 244, 251; Bruckner 2001: 93-5). The sense of *eda'ā* in 18.21 is 'find out', 'investigate', or 'conduct a judicial enquiry' (Hamilton 1995: 15 n. 5; Bruckner 2001: 94, 99). Thus, the deity is undertaking an investigation of alleged events in Sodom (Hamilton 1995: 19-20; Brodie 2001: 249).

Exegetes are fortunate that most dictionaries and commentaries have detected and recognized the presence and meaning of the Cohortative. Most versions indeed translate this correctly as 'I want to know' or 'let me know'. Given the pivotal role of *yada'* in the text of Sodom, below is my literal English rendition of Genesis 18.17-21. Each repeated or parallel element is italicized (text abbreviated).

> *And Y<small>HWH</small> thought*, Shall I hide from Abraham what I am going to *do*? . . . All the nations of the earth shall be blessed through him.
>
> For I have *known* him, so that he may command his sons and his house after him. They shall keep the road of Y<small>HWH</small> by *doing* what is just and right . . .

> *And Y*HWH *said*, The *outcry* of Sodom and Gomorrah, how it has increased! Their sin, how grievous [it is]!
>
> Let me go down and see whether they have *done* altogether according to the *outcry* that has come to me. Let me *know* for certain.

In 18.17, the initial phrase *wa*YHWH *āmār* introduces an unspoken soliloquy on YHWH's part. It lends itself to be rendered 'And YHWH said to himself' or 'thought to himself'.[62] It calls for a comparison with the two previous soliloquies in the story. They occur as first Abraham and then Sarah laugh in disbelief in response to the astonishing announcement of the future birth of Isaac. In 17.17, the Hebrew describes Abraham as 'he laughed saying in his heart'. In 18.12, his wife Sarah responds to the news in a similar manner. Here it is 'Sarah laughed saying inside herself'.[63] What the two have in common is the fact that the thoughts crossing Abraham and Sarah's minds are described in physical terms. Abraham laughed 'in his heart' while Sarah laughed 'in her belly'. In other words, in Genesis the location of inner monologues is perceived as a specific organ or part of the human body. While this is perfectly acceptable for human beings, it would be irreverent in reference to the deity. Heeding Exodus 33.20-23, ancient biblical writers strove to avoid using

---

[62] Frank A. Spina (2005: 178 n. 89) finds that *amar*, 'say', sometimes means 'think'. This is the case in Gen. 18.17 given the inverted word order in the Hebrew. This phenomenon is noted by Sue Groom (2003: 151) who comments that the purpose of variations from the common structure is to change the scene, introduce new characters, or provide background information. She explains that the insertion of background information into a narrative serves to arrest the reader's progress as it either highlights a significant moment or provides a means of distinguishing one subsection of the narrative from what follows or goes before (p. 147).

[63] Literally, 'in her belly' or 'in her entrails'.

anthropomorphic language of God. Hence, the biblical narrator has adopted a reverential approach to the divine soliloquy with no allusion to body parts. The deity's inner monologue is expressed by a subtle syntactic manoeuvre, in which the usual word order of the verb 'said' and the subject 'YHWH' is inverted.[64]

By contrast, in 18.20, the familiar standard phrase *wayyōmær YHWH*, 'And YHWH said', announces direct speech (as in the creation story of Gen. 1). This marks the end of the soliloquy and resumption of the conversation with Abraham. Indeed, the statement in 18.20 and 21 is intended for Abraham's ears, enabling the latter to ponder the news and prepare to share his concerns about the impending destruction of Sodom and Gomorrah (Hamilton 1995: 20). The moral message to ancient Israelite readers and listeners of this passage seems to be that no lawbreaker should be prosecuted without prior investigation of the allegations.[65]

Let Us Know Them

A literal translation of *yadaʿ* offers the advantage of leaving room for fresh interpretations of the text of Genesis 18 and 19. In 19.5 the Cohortative of *yadaʿ* occurs for the second time as the men of Sodom say to Lot, 'Let us *know* them' (*nedʿā*). If this plural version of the Cohortative is taken in its basic,

---

[64] See Alter 1996 p. *xxxi*, who observes that the word order in biblical narrative is very often finely expressive. He also finds biblical syntax to be more flexible than modern English syntax. Alter has found hundreds of instances in Genesis of significant syntactical inversions and, especially, emphatic first positioning of weighted terms (p. *xxxii*).

[65] According to Gordon Wenham (1994: 44), Abraham's being allowed into the secrets of the divine purposes and his subsequent intercession for Sodom show that he is a prophet; cf. Gen. 15 (implicit) and 20.7 (explicit).

grammatical sense, the verb denotes that the crowd thronging the streets around Lot's house is determined to carry out an official enquiry, perhaps in the form of interrogation, in order to establish the nature of the visit to their city of the two strangers. Their massive presence makes it clear that they are keen not to let the visitors escape. The fact that every man in town is there may indicate that King Bera, who plays a major part in Genesis 14, has given orders. While he and his assistants are not mentioned by name in Genesis 19, they are undoubtedly present, a fact that is stated twice. First, the text speaks of all 'the men of Sodom, from boy to old man' (Gen. 19.4). Subsequently, one hears of the same men, 'from small to great' (19.11). In the latter case, 'small' often refers to servants, slaves, or poor people while 'great' frequently denotes rulers.[66] Intriguingly, for the entire chapter of Genesis 19, the narrator has chosen to reduce everyone except Lot and his illegitimate grandchildren (19.37–38) to anonymity.

Table 17 shows the way in which the two Cohortatives of *yada‹* in Genesis 18.21 and 19.5 form a pattern of literary parallels.

Table 17
Two Significant Cohortatives

Gen. 18.21: Let me know	**Gen. 19.5: Let us know**
YHWH investigating Sodom	Sodom investigating the visitors
YHWH responding to the outcry	Sodom responding to suspicions
Mission: to establish facts	Mission: to establish facts
Commissioned: two messengers	Commissioned: all male inhabitants

---

[66] Cf. Lev. 19.15; Deut. 1.17; Job 3.19.

Later in the present chapter, the investigative side of *yada‘* in 18.21 and 19.5 is compared with the roles played by this verb in Genesis 38 and 39.

Knowing a Husband

As Carol Meyers (1988: 38) has pointed out, the HB has no systematic collection of marriage laws. To acquire a realistic impression of the relevant biblical terminology, a number of different texts have to be consulted. While the occurrence of *yada‘* in Genesis 19.8 is frequently commented upon by scholars, the context is little understood.[67]

Having used *yada‘* once in reference to the covenant between Yhwh and Abraham ('I have known him', 18.19) and, subsequently, twice in the enquiring sense denoted by the Cohortative (18.21 and 19.5), the narrator reintroduces the *Qal* form of the verb in 19.8 in the plural *yad‘ū*, 'they have known'. While 'known' in 18.19 means 'acknowledged' or 'recognized', in 19.8, Lot refers to his two minor daughters who 'have not known (acknowledged) a husband'. In other words, they are unmarried. This expression is generally used of nubile girls living in their father's house. A comparable case is that of Jephtha's daughter in Judges 11.39.[68] In both cases, the woman does the knowing or not knowing, i.e. she is the grammatical subject.

Occasionally, however, the grammatical order is reversed. Thus, when Abraham's servant Eliezer meets Rebekah in Genesis 24.15–16, the Hebrew text says of the girl that 'no

---

[67] Most commentators limit themselves to harshly criticizing Lot; cf. chapter 11.
[68] In the first century CE, this tradition is still alive, as shown by the Gospel of Luke 1.34 where Mary, mother of Jesus, explains that she has not 'known' a husband.

husband has known her'. Contrary to what many translators assume, the phrase is not to be taken as an indiscreet disclosure on the narrator's part regarding Rebekah's physical condition or sex life.[69] Rather, readers are presented with a clear, relevant statement of fact, i.e. the girl belongs to a respectable family and is unmarried. This is exactly what Eliezer needs to know in order to fulfil his task of finding a wife for Isaac (Gen. 24.4).

To interpret *yada'* in 19.8, it is important to bear in mind that the Hebrew noun *ish* does not only mean 'man' (Gen. 2.24) but also 'husband' (Gen. 30.15; Num. 5.19–20). Lot's daughters are betrothed to two young men living in Sodom described as Lot's 'sons-in-law' (19.14). The latter term suggests that in antiquity betrothal was, to all intents and purposes, as binding as marriage (Fields 1997: 117 n. 5; Thatcher 2002: 123).[70] Betrothals might last years (Gen. 29:18–21). Because of the formality of the arrangement, Lot is required to inform his sons-in-law before leaving Sodom for good with his entire family (19.12). However, he

---

[69] Several English versions mistakenly turn Rebekah into the grammatical subject: 'a young woman who had not known a man intimately' (HCSB), 'she had never had sexual relations with a man' (NCV), 'a virgin guiltless of intercourse with any man' (REB), 'unmarried, and a virgin' (JM), and 'she was still a virgin' (NLT). Even when the syntax is rendered correctly, with the male party as subject, several versions reduce the situation to a simple matter of virginity: 'a virgin whom no man had known', or similar (JPS, NKJV, NRSV), 'no man had touched her' (NJB), 'no man had ever slept with her' (NIV), 'no man had lain with her' (CCB), and 'no man had had sexual intercourse with her' (NWT). Given the ancient context, the most accurate exegesis would be 'no husband (or 'man') had known her'.

[70] In ST times, women would become betrothed approximately at age twelve. The betrothal ceremony was a legally binding prelude to the marriage contract. According to Tertullian (155–222 CE), the best age for marriage was twelve years for girls and fourteen for boys (Thatcher 2002: 148).

fails to persuade them to go with him. These young men, then, are those who are going to 'take' Lot's daughters (19.14). The Hebrew verb *laqach*, 'take', frequently refers to a man marrying a woman.[71] The word reflects the fact that marriage contracts were established between unequal parties (Thatcher 1999: 68–70). In other words, in marital language, *laqach* is interchangeable with *yada'* when the grammatical subject is male. In Genesis 19.8, when Lot speaks about the girls, he is saying that the 'knowing' has not yet occurred, i.e. the wedding has not taken place. Put differently, the betrothed young people are not yet husbands and wives, and so Lot's daughters are still living with their parents. On the day of marriage, a girl would move to her husband's house (Thatcher 2002: 122).

Just as *yada'* is capable of denoting the formality of the covenant between YHWH and Abraham in 18.19, its role in 19.8 is that of formal language in relation to marriage. In some cases, the language of the marriage contract would be modelled on the covenant between YHWH and the people of Israel (Thatcher 1999: 68). An example is found in Hosea 2.20 (emphasis added):

> I will *take* you for my wife in faithfulness;
> And you shall *know* YHWH.

As mentioned above, the male part either 'takes' or 'knows' a woman/wife while other examples demonstrate that

---

[71] Gen. 4.19; 6.2; 24.3–4, 7, 37–38, 40, 48, 67; 25.1; 28.2; 34.2, 21. The same expression was used in Akkadian, the pre-biblical language of ancient Babylonia; cf. Driver and Miles (eds.) 1952: 246, 248. If the bridegroom 'takes', the one who 'gives' (Hebrew *nathan*) is the monarch or the father of the bride; cf. Gen. 29.19; 34.21; 41.45. Also in this case, there is an Akkadian precedent in the verb *nadánum* (Driver & Miles I, 1952: 323). In Second Testament times, centuries later, the idea of 'taking' is still customary; cf. Joseph 'taking' Mary (Matt. 1.24).

the grammatical subject of 'knowing' may be female. For formal agreements between people, the name of God could be invoked (1 Sam. 20.42; 23.18), while in certain cases the presence of human witnesses was required (Gen. 23.16; Ruth 4.9–11). In Genesis 18.19 and 19.8, the formal nature of *yadaʿ* matches the requirements inherent in contractual language.

These observations make it clear that in Genesis, the act of knowing sometimes denotes the public ceremony in which the bride and bridegroom acknowledge each other in the presence of witnesses. Occasionally, the event is celebrated with a feast (Gen. 29.22). Similarly, according to the traditions of antiquity, any woman who has not yet experienced 'knowing a husband' awaits the day in which a man 'takes' her or in which she is 'given' to him (19.8, 14). As soon as they have 'known' each other, the couple may proceed to consummation, but the physical act is not always specified (4.1, 17). Occasionally *bō* occurs joined by *el* (Gen. 29.23, 30; cf. Hugenberger 1994: 251).

In some cases, the HB uses a longer phrase, which mentions women who 'have not known a husband by lying down with a male' (Num. 31.17; Judg. 21.12). At times the wording may be 'who have not known the bed of a male' (Num. 31.18; Judg. 21.11). The Hebrew noun *mishkav*, 'bed', is related to the verb *shakhav*, 'lie down', while the word for 'male' is *zakhar*. Thus, 'to know a husband' and 'lie down with a male' describe two different situations. The phrases quoted above seem to allude to young women who may or may not be formally married, i.e. their weddings may or may not have been held. What is important to the narrator is to make clear that the women concerned have not yet experienced the act of consummation. In other words, they are still virgins in a technical sense.

He Did Not Know

The fifth and sixth times that *yada'* occurs in the story of Sodom and Gomorrah are in the final episode. Here the verb plays a prominent part in two parallel sentences with identical meanings. Readers are told what happens after the destruction of Sodom and several neighbouring towns. Lot and his two daughters have taken refuge in a remote mountain cave. Because of their isolated lives, the girls decide to become pregnant by using their father as a sperm donor. The ruse consists of plying Lot with wine before the act. Verse 33 reads as follows (emphasis added):

> And to their father they gave wine that evening.
> And the older went in
> And lay down with her father.
> And he did not *know* in her lying down
> Or in her getting up.

The next day, the younger sister repeats the ruse (19.35). The Hebrew wording is almost exactly the same. Using *yada'* for the second time, the narrator emphasizes the fact that Lot does not 'know' what is going on. The entire scene is sexually charged. A major part of the action is carried forward by the verb *shakhav*, 'lie down', whose starring role is highlighted by seven occurrences between 19.32 and 19.35. From this, a significant conclusion may be drawn: *yada'* and *shakhav* operate side by side, and *yada'* is negated. This juxtaposition makes it clear that if Lot did not 'know' while his daughters were having sexual intercourse with him, *yada'* and *shakhav* cannot be synonyms. To say that Lot had sex and did not have sex is absurd. In this way, the Hebrew text shows that *yada'* does not belong to the realm of sex but covers a different aspect.

The book of Genesis offers several additional examples. In Genesis 19.4, *shakhav* refers to bedtime, followed in 19.5 by *yada'* suggesting the beginning of an interrogation. Similarly, in Genesis 39, these verbs operate jointly but fulfil different purposes. In 39.7 Potiphar's wife invites Joseph to share her bed by means of *shakhav*, saying, 'Lie down with me'. Joseph declines the offer, explaining that he does not want to betray his master who does not 'know' how his house is being run (39.8). Here *yada'* means that Potiphar does not inspect, check, or enquire how his slave Joseph manages household affairs because he trusts him.

Returning to the mountain cave, it is essential to point out that the girls carry out their plan without obtaining their father's consent. Therefore, the fact that Lot does not 'know' may have two meanings. First, he is unaware of what is going on. Second, he cannot be held legally responsible for the outcome. His daughters use him as a sperm donor and nothing more. Given the legal implications of *yada'* in other parts of the story, the narrator seems to indicate that Lot's siring of Moab and Ben-Ammi is incidental. The true ancestresses of Moab and Ammon are Lot's unnamed daughters. Just as he did not know what went on at night, Lot will not 'know' his illegitimate offspring. The HB presents a parallel example in Deuteronomy 33.9 mentioning a man who refuses to 'know' his own children, i.e. he fails to acknowledge or recognize them.

In the final part of the story of Sodom, the Hebrew narrator once again showcases his literary mastery. The exact repetition in Genesis 19.35 of the phrase containing *yada'* in Genesis 19.33 makes the girls act almost identically. This literary device produces a ritual, mechanical effect. In 19.33, the older sister 'goes in' to Lot's bed to 'lie down' with him. The simplicity of the language seems to reveal that for her the decision has been taken and there is no turning back. In 19.35, the second text contains a small, but possibly revealing, stylistic variation. The replacement of a single word may suggest that the younger sister is less self-assured. She knows that it is her turn but, when the moment arrives, she does not go straight to Lot's bed. The narrator observes that she first 'gets up' (*qūm*). Perhaps this tiny detail suggests that the younger girl is struggling. She has to make an effort to carry out the adventure awaiting her. Owing to the agreement established with her sister, she goes ahead. But for a moment, she hesitates.

Modern readers tend to find this part of the story difficult. Nonetheless, incest is a harsh reality in many cultures today. A series of surveys conducted in recent decades has documented that the phenomenon of incest occurs regularly all over the Western world. At the same time, however, it is surrounded by social taboos. The literary tone of the Hebrew text in Genesis 19 is neutral and factual. The narrator maintains a balanced approach to his material, presenting it almost like a news report. Furthermore, the whole story is heavily stylized to fit the characteristics of a mythological explanation of the origin of Ammon and Moab, two nations living immediately to the east of biblical Israel across the river Jordan (Gen. 19.37–38).

While the Hebrew text does not express any moral indignation on the narrator's part, nothing in the First Testament indicates that incest was permitted in biblical times. For example, the book of Leviticus lists a long series of prohibitions (Lev. 18 and 20). These texts contain polemical hints as they imply that incestuous relationships were common in the land of Canaan, which included the area of Sodom and Gomorrah. Keeping this in mind, one may detect a political agenda in the final scene of Genesis 19 inasmuch as the text provides an unflattering image of the origins of the Moabites and Ammonites as illegitimate children of

Lot's daughters.[72] By contrast, the Israelites are presented as legitimate descendants of Abraham and Sarah.

He Did Not Know Her Again

As well as this literary and semantic exploration of the role(s) of *yada(* in the text of Sodom and Gomorrah, another intriguing occurrence of the verb in Genesis 38.26 may shed further light on what 'to know in the biblical sense' entails. Towards the end of Genesis 38, Tamar, widowed daughter-in-law of Judah, has finally become pregnant after many years of waiting in vain for a sperm donor. Three months earlier, she disguised herself to avoid detection and cleverly succeeded in seducing her father-in-law (38.16). As soon as her pregnancy becomes apparent, she is arrested on the grounds of alleged infidelity and immorality. She responds by taking the objects that Judah left with her as a pledge and sends them back to him as proof of his fatherhood. Judah instantly recognizes the objects and remembers the unfulfilled promise he once gave to Tamar. Here is a literal translation of 38.26 (emphasis added):

> And Judah identified them, saying, 'She is more righteous than I because I did not give her to my son Selah'. And he did not *know* her again.

In the Hebrew text, 'know' is the familiar *yada(*. However, this verse is difficult to understand because in English knowing is not normally associated with the repeated action implied by the word 'again'. To a modern reader, the meaning of 'he did not know her again' is not self-evident.

---

[72] Another reading of this passage is to see it as an explanation of the original kinship existing between Israelites, Moabites, and Ammonites (Wechsler 2012: 198–9).

The approaches taken by the twelve English versions of the Bible are shown below.

Table 18
Translating YADA‛ in Gen. 38.26

Version	Gen. 38.26
CCB	And he had no further intercourse with her
HCSB	And he did not know her intimately again
JM	So he had no further intercourse with her
JPS	And he was not intimate with her again
NCV	And Judah did not have sexual relations with her again
NIV	And he did not sleep with her again
NJB	He had no further intercourse with her
NKJV	And he never knew her again
NLT	And Judah never slept with Tamar again
NRSV	And he did not lie with her again
NWT	And he had no further intercourse with her after that
REB	He did not have intercourse with her again

The options in table 18 can be arranged as (a) 'he never knew her again' (NKJV); (b) 'he did not know her intimately again' (HCSB); (c) 'he was not intimate with her again' (JPS); (d) 'he did not have intercourse with her again' (REB), 'he had no further intercourse with her' (CCB, JM, NJB, NWT); (e) 'Judah did not have sexual relations with her again' (NCV); (f) 'he did not sleep with her again' (NIV), 'Judah never slept with Tamar again' (NLT); and (g) 'he did not lie with her again' (NRSV). Once again it becomes clear that few Bible translators have taken *yada‛* literally. In table 18, only the NKVJ has done so while the HCSB has added 'intimately', despite the fact that *yada‛* does not necessarily involve intimacy (Gen. 29.5). To different degrees, all other versions have opted for variations on the sexual theme.

In modern English, the sexual connotations of the paraphrase 'have intercourse with' are obvious, and 'sleep with' is even clearer, despite the fact that in Hebrew 'sleep' is expressed by means of the verb *yashēn*. Suggesting 'lie with', the NRSV erroneously makes *yada'* a synonym of *shakhav*. The NCV bluntly proposes 'have sexual relations with', presenting *yada'* as completely interchangeable with *bō* and *shakhav*. Once again, the inaccuracy of these renderings is caused by the pervasive academic hypothesis surrounding *yada'*, according to which ambiguous occurrences of the verb are to be taken in a sexual sense.

Non-Sexual Knowing

So how is *yada'* to be understood in Genesis 38.26? To find an answer, a second question is needed: has any previous 'knowing' taken place between Judah and Tamar? According to Genesis 38, the answer is negative. Some years earlier Judah met an unnamed Canaanite woman whom he decided to 'take', i.e. he married her (38.2). Judah's relationship with Tamar is of a different nature. While he did indeed 'take' her, she was not for himself but rather to be the wife of Judah's eldest son Er (38.6). Thus, Tamar became his daughter-in-law. Up until 38.26 no other relationship between the two is mentioned.

If one takes the word 'intercourse' in the older sense to mean 'social interaction', the five English versions in table 18 that use the word may have a point, at least at first sight. However, even that hypothesis quickly proves unworkable because by Genesis 38.26, Judah has not spoken to Tamar for years. In fact, he himself ordered Tamar to return to her parents' house as a widow (38.11). In other words, the narrator must be using *yada'* in a different sense. Within the cultural horizon of the HB, is it even possible to imagine that Judah did not 'sleep with' or 'lie with' Tamar again as suggested by the NCV, NIV, NLT, and NRSV? Again the answer is that nothing in the text supports this assumption. First, *yada'* and *shakhav* are not interchangeable. Second, the narrator clearly states in 38.16 that it would never have occurred to Judah to sleep with the veiled woman sitting by the roadside if he had known (*yada'*) her identity. Third, Judah did not seek to 'know' Tamar on that occasion because, if he had used the word, it might have sounded like a marriage proposal (cf. Gen. 4.1). He simply asked to 'go in' to her (*bō & el*).

In summary, to say in 38.26 that 'Judah never had sexual relations with Tamar again' is confusing. Nothing indicates that he would have been interested. If the idea were to cross his mind, sleeping with his daughter-in-law would have made him guilty of incest, which carried the death penalty (Lev. 20.12). One of the key points of the Genesis 38 story is that the sexual intercourse that took place between Tamar and Judah was a one-off event. She cleverly tricked her father-in-law for a specific purpose, namely, to have a child. Ultimately Judah was under a legal obligation to ensure that his youngest son Shelah made Tamar pregnant (38.11–14). As this did not happen, her stratagem was well thought out. For all the reasons listed, there must be another way to interpret *yada'* in Genesis 38.26.

When Know Is Enquire

The solution to the puzzle of *yada'* is not far away. A literary analysis shows that chapters 38 and 39 of the book of Genesis are interconnected in several important ways (Spina 2005: 37), including the repeated presence of *yada'* in both.

After becoming steward of Potiphar's household in Egypt, Joseph uses this verb to ward off the amorous advances of Potiphar's wife (39.8). A moment earlier in the text (39.6), it appears in the same sense. Table 19 shows the renderings chosen by the English versions for these occurrences of *yada‛*.

Table 19
Translating YADA‛ in Gen. 39.6 & 39.8

Version	Gen. 39.6	Gen. 39.8
CCB	concern himself with nothing	has no concern about anything
HCSB	he did not concern himself with anything	does not concern himself with anything
JM	not a thing did he trouble himself about	does not trouble himself about anything
JPS	he paid attention to nothing	gives no thought to anything
NCV	and was not concerned about anything	trusts me with everything in his house
NIV	he did not concern himself with anything	does not concern himself with anything
NJB	concerned himself with nothing	does not concern himself with what happens
NKJV	he did not know what he had	does not know what is with me in the house
NLT	he didn't worry about a thing	trusts me with everything in his entire household
NRSV	he had no concern for anything	has no concern about anything
NWT	he did not know what was with him at all	does not know what is with me in the house
REB	and concerned himself with nothing	he leaves the management of his whole house to me

These verses illustrate the amount of trust that Potiphar has invested in Joseph. In fact, the Egyptian official has stopped 'knowing' the affairs of his household. He feels no need to inspect anything because Joseph's administrative skills are more than sufficient to ensure a perfect job. Table 19 shows that all English versions have understood the role of *yada'* in Genesis 39. While two versions (NLT and REB) have paraphrased the text, the overall meaning of the passage is not distorted. Thus, table 19 reflects a rare case of near-unanimity among the translators with generally adequate renderings.

When *yada'* is viewed from this perspective, it becomes clear what the narrator means by saying that Judah stopped 'knowing' Tamar in 38.26. Readers are told that he stopped concerning himself about the affairs of his daughter-in-law. Stated differently, he ceased to interfere in her life, i.e. he left her alone. Consequently, in these passages *yada'* has the sense of 'enquire about' or 'interfere with'. This inquisitive aspect of *yada'* establishes a link to the story of Sodom and Gomorrah. In Genesis 18.21, YHWH announces his intention to 'know' the origin of the outcry that has reached his ears, i.e. he wants to investigate, an aspect highlighted by the additional occurrence of *raah*, 'to see' (van Wolde 2012: 86). Likewise, in 19.5 the inhabitants of Sodom demand the visitors are handed over in order to 'know' them, i.e. to investigate (2012: 92). In this case, one text in Genesis illuminates the contents of another. In the examples analysed here, one may conclude that, semantically speaking, the two Cohortatives of *yada'* in Genesis 18.21 and 19.5 are comparable to the investigative roles adopted by the *Qal* forms of the verb in 38.26, 39.6 and 39.8.

Inconsistent Knowing

The renderings chosen by the versions for *yada'* in Genesis 38 and 39 are listed in table 20. Explicitly sexual wordings are highlighted.

Table 20
Translations of YADA' in Genesis 38–39

Verse	Translations of YADA'	Versions
38.16	Know	CCB, HCSB, JM, JPS, NCV, NJB, NKJV, NRSV, NWT
	Realize	NIV, NLT, REB
38.26	Know	NKJV
	Know *intimately*	HCSB
	Be intimate with	JPS
	Have intercourse with	CCB, JM, NJB, NWT, REB
	Have sexual relations with	NCV
	Sleep with	NIV, NLT
	Lie with	NRSV
39.6	Know	NKJV, NWT
	Concern himself with	CCB, HCSB, NIV, NJB, REB
	Have no concern	NCV, NRSV
	Trouble himself about	JM
	Pay attention to	JPS
	Worry about	NLT
39.8	Know	NKJV, NWT
	Concern himself with	HCSB, NJB
	Have no concern about	CCB, HCSB, NRSV
	Trouble himself about	JM
	Give thought to	JPS
	Trust	NIV, NLT
	Leaves the management	REB

Table 20 shows how the English versions provide more or less literal, semantically accurate renderings of *yada(* in three verses. However, in Genesis 38.26, the preferred approach is predominantly sexual. The main problem showcased by table 20 is literary inconsistency. While the Hebrew narrator uses *yada(* four times to achieve a high level of interconnectedness between the different passages, the only English version to take a similar approach is the NKJV. Many translators have opted for diversity instead of consistency as they resort to liberal paraphrase. For example, the REB has introduced no fewer than four different renderings of *yada(*, including 'realize', 'have intercourse with', 'concern himself with', and 'leave the management to'. While 'realize' and 'concern himself with' make good sense in the relevant contexts, there is no trace of their being interconnected. The overall impression of inconsistency in the REB is aggravated by the confusing presence of 'have intercourse with'. In summary, the latter rendering is in conformity with scholarly and popular tradition ('to know in the biblical sense') but at odds with the surrounding text.

Sex and Knowing

In many cases, English versions of the Bible tend to make unfortunate choices when they deal with sexual matters, or when they assume that is the case. They are particularly prone to offering highly inconsistent renderings of *yada(*. Specifically, many erroneously posit that *yada(* occasionally is interchangeable with *bō* and *shakhav*. Two more passages of the Hebrew Bible provide similar echoes of the formal solemnity of *yada(* applied to the relationship between spouses. In 1 Samuel 1.2, 5–17, the plight of Hannah, afflicted by her childless condition, is described. She earnestly prays to YHWH to grant her a male child and vows to consecrate him to the service of the deity (1.11). Following a time of joint worship, she and her husband embark together on a new phase (1.19-20, emphasis added):

> Elkanah *knew* his wife Hannah, and Y<small>HWH</small> remembered her. After some time Hannah conceived and bore a son. She named him Samuel, for she said, 'I have asked him of Y<small>HWH</small>'.

The use of *yada'* for this context is no coincidence. The entire passage is marked by deep emotion in the form of personal distress (1.7, 10-11, 15-16) and, more importantly, steeped in religious devotion (1.9-12, 15-18). Thus, the language of v. 19 does not reflect a simple act of sexual intercourse, for which more 'trivial' verbs such as *bō* or *shakhav* would be appropriate. Rather, this is a significant moment depicting marital commitment on Elkanah's part. By 'knowing' Hannah, that is, acknowledging her as his spouse and initiating a new phase in his life with her (cf. Adam and Eve in Gen. 4.25), he chooses to become party to the solemn agreement established recently between Hannah and Y<small>HWH</small>.[73]

An additional illustration of the legal role of *yada'* is found in 1 Kings. In David's final years, his blood circulation was insufficient to keep him warm at night (1.1). So a beautiful young girl named Abishag was provided to hold him. The text then says, 'But the king *knew* her not' (1.4, emphasis added). Given the fragile state David was in, this is very

---

[73] Again in this case, many translators have misunderstood the nature of *yada'*. They speak of how Elkanah 'had sexual relations with' (NCV), 'had intercourse with' (NWT, REB), 'slept with' (CCB), 'was intimate with' (HCSB), or 'made love to' (NIV) Hannah. Such renditions are misleading. Elkanah never interrupted his marital intimacy with Hannah because he clearly loved her (1.5, 8), and this is equally inferable from the fact that Hannah was childless (1.2, 5-6). Instead, 1.19 marks a significant new beginning.

unlikely to have sexual connotations. Instead, the fact that David did not 'know' the young girl seems to mean that he did not acknowledge her as his wife.[74] In other words, this arrangement was not of a marital nature, but Abishag was awarded the important task of looking after the king, i.e. to be his private nurse (1.15). This legal subtlety becomes significant soon after David's death in 1 Kings 2, when Solomon's brother Adonijah wants Abishag to be his wife (2.17, 21). Solomon is adamant in his refusal. If he were to give Abishag to Adonijah, he might as well give him the entire kingdom (2.22).[75]

Following this excursus around the HB, it is time to return to Genesis. All of the problems detected above surface again in Genesis 38 and 39 where two sexually charged scenes are played out, one between Judah and Tamar and the other

---

[74] Nonetheless, misunderstandings abound, cf. 'the king was not intimate with her' (JPS), 'had no intimate relations' (CCB), 'did not have intercourse' (JM, NWT, REB), 'did not know her sexually' (NRSV), 'had no sexual relations with her' (NIV), etc. Given David's weak physical state, a purely sexual focus for *yada'* seems disrespectful. With a well-stocked harem, David certainly did not need another wife for sexual purposes. Because her youthful vitality was thought to be beneficial to David's health, Abishag was chosen to nurse the ailing king, her specific task being to keep him warm by holding him (1 Kings 1.2).

[75] Evidently Solomon sees Adonijah as a threat because this brother has been his fiercest rival to the throne (1 Kings 1). Since Abishag never became King David's wife, she was not a widow but technically still a nubile virgin. Her being the most beautiful girl in the land (1.3–4), in addition to her former role as the king's private nurse, would have invested her with the prestige of a princess. Hence, Solomon rejected the request. By giving Abishag to his brother, Solomon would indeed have reinforced Adonijah's claim to the kingship. On account of Adonijah's stunningly good looks (1.6), such a couple would have become formidable contenders for the throne. In ancient Israel, physical beauty was regarded by many as a sign of divine favour. This was in effect one of the criteria for the selection of Saul and David, both of whom became kings of Israel; cf. 1 Sam. 9.2; 16.12. See also Fields 1997: 129 n. 34.

between Potiphar's wife and Joseph. In both passages, *yada'* plays an essential, non-sexual role. For the sake of clarity, the key verbs in these events are shown in table 21.

Table 21
Sex, Knowing and Intimacy in Genesis 38 & 39

Verse	Verb	Translation
38.16	*bō & el*	a. go in to b. have sex with
38.16	*yada'*	know
38.26	*yada'*	enquire about
39.6	*yada'*	enquire about
39.8	*yada'*	enquire about
39.7	*shakhav & 'im*	a. lie down with b. have sex with
39.10	*shakhav & etsel*	lie down beside
39.10	*hayah & 'im*	be with
39.12	*shakhav & 'im*	a. lie down with b. have sex with

While the presence of *bō* and *el* has a sexual sense in 38.16, the same is true of *shakhav* and *'im* in 39.7 and 39.12. In addition, two verbs with prepositions attached denote physical intimacy, namely *shakhav* and *etsel* ('lie down beside') and *hayah* and *'im* ('be with'). Within this textual framework, *yada'* occurs once in the basic sense of 'know' and three times in the related sense of 'enquire' or 'investigate'.

Conclusion

Undoubtedly, the key word in the story of Sodom and Gomorrah is the Hebrew verb *yadaʿ*, 'know'. It is, at the same time, the most ambiguous and least understood. The popular saying 'to know in the biblical sense' is based on a long interpretive tradition. However, the common tendency to ascribe a sexual side to *yadaʿ* is not substantiated by the HB. Whenever sex is unambiguously requested, arranged, or ordained in Genesis, people do not talk of 'knowing' the other person but use other verbs. What has been missing for centuries is a linguistic and literary analysis of *yadaʿ*, particularly its legal aspects. The latter are important because the verb occurs regularly in solemn, archaic contexts when three issues are addressed: (a) covenants, (b) marriage contracts, and (c) enquiries and investigations.

In the text of Sodom and Gomorrah, the six occurrences of *yadaʿ* form a sophisticated literary pattern in which they appear to have legal connotations. In Genesis 18.19, 'known' means 'acknowledged' in reference to the covenant between YHWH and Abraham. The fact that Lot's daughters in 19.8 have not 'known' a husband denotes the absence of formal acknowledgement, i.e. the time for marriage has not yet arrived. This use of *yadaʿ* alludes to the early biblical marriage contracts mentioned in Genesis 4. In 4.1, Adam 'knows' his woman Eve in the sense of 'acknowledges' her as his wife, i.e. their married life begins. The fact that *yadaʿ* is repeated in 4.25 shows that the marriage contract is renewed following the tragic loss of Abel and Cain. Thus, Seth is born within the proper legal framework, which makes him the ideal son and founder of a family tree that will stand for generations.

In Genesis 18.21 YHWH declares his intention to 'know' the origin of the outcry coming out of Sodom. In this context, *yada*ʿ acquires the meaning of 'investigate'. In similar fashion, the men of Sodom demand in 19.5 to 'know' the visitors spending the night at Lot's house, i.e. they want to investigate or interrogate them. When Lot speaks of his two daughters who have not 'known' a husband, he is saying that they are as yet unmarried. Finally, the fact that Lot does not 'know' what goes on in his bed at night may have two implications. On the one hand, he is simply unaware. On the other hand, his lack of knowledge ('acknowledgement') may mean that the daughters took the initiative, and Lot is not legally responsible for the outcome.

Elsewhere *yada*ʿ plays a significant part, particularly in Genesis 38 and 39. A major problem for translators occurs in 38.26 where many erroneously assume that Judah did not have sexual intercourse with Tamar 'again'. Having been tricked (38.16), Judah would never have had sex with her in the first place if he had known the veiled woman's identity. By contrast, all versions translate *yada*ʿ correctly in 39.6 and 39.8 where the verb means 'enquire' or 'inspect'. This echoes the investigative sense of *yada*ʿ in Genesis 18.21 and 19.5. Thus, the narrator assigns two different cognitive meanings to *yada*ʿ, namely, 'know' (38.16) and 'enquire about' (38.26, 39.6 and 39.8).

The phrase 'to know in the biblical sense', allegedly based on *yada*ʿ, has no justification in the HB. For sexual purposes, Classical Hebrew uses the verbs *bō* and *shakhav*. My detailed analysis of the vocabulary of the original text of the story of Sodom and Gomorrah has shown that *yada*ʿ fulfils non-sexual purposes, particularly of a legal nature. Throughout the Hebrew prose, the narrator utilizes *yada*ʿ as a literary building block, very often in the company of either *bō* or *shakhav*, and sometimes of both.

Finally, the discussion of the roles of *yada*ʿ in this chapter has clarified that the biblical texts examined do not contemplate homoerotic relationships. This observation is important since the popular sexual interpretation of the drama of Sodom relies on a particular way of perceiving *yada*ʿ in Genesis 19.5 and 19.8. If this famous biblical legend in reality deals with subjects unrelated to the sexual sphere, an alternative hermeneutics is urgently needed. This issue will be addressed later, including a discussion of the likely Greek origin of the phrase 'to know in the biblical sense' (chapter 10).

PART TWO

Curse and Prohibitions

4

NOAH'S NAKEDNESS

You shall not go up by steps to my altar
Lest your nakedness be uncovered on it.

—Exodus 20.26

Introduction

Chapter 2 provided an exploration of the book of Genesis with a view to identifying sexual language in the Hebrew Bible. The present chapter deals with a biblical text which, according to some scholars, has homoerotic implications. The beginning of the story of Noah and his sons reads as follows (Gen. 9.20–22):

> Noah, a man of the ground, was the first to plant a vineyard. He drank some of the wine and became drunk, and he uncovered himself in his tent. And Ham, father of Canaan, saw the nakedness of his father, and told his two brothers outside.

Because of its condensed style, this enigmatic incident has mystified numerous exegetes in the post-biblical era. Over the centuries many have wondered what exactly happened between Ham and his father (Milgrom 2004: 201). At present, there is no solid consensus when it comes to establishing the nature of Ham's transgression. Several representative hermeneutical schools or approaches are discussed below.

Interpreting Ham and Noah

According to the thirteenth-century Spanish rabbi Nahmanides (Moses ben Nahman, also known as Ramban), this story reflects a situation in which the concepts of honour and shame play a major part. Ham's sin consists in making fun of the highly unusual sight of Noah lying on the floor in a less than dignified posture. In addition, Ham tries to make his brothers join him for a moment's merrymaking at their father's expense. When Noah hears about this later on, he is overpowered by a strong sense of shame caused by a son who acted with disrespect at a time when he ought to have been considerate (Greenberg 2004: 62). Another group of early commentators argue that Ham did more than talk. It is their guess that he penetrated Noah sexually in an attempt to dominate his father. In this context, they quote Joseph, governor of Egypt, who accuses his Israelite brothers of being spies who wish to 'see the country's nakedness', i.e. explore it in order to discover where they may easily penetrate later to take possession of the whole territory (Greenberg 2004: 63). A third approach is adopted by some medieval rabbis who suggest that Ham went even further. In their interpretation, he castrated his father. Such a hypothesis was discussed by different Jewish sources quoted in the thirteenth century by French rabbi Shlomo Yitzhaki, better known as Rashi (2004: 63).

As pointed out by Gordon Wenham (1987: 200), other curious interpretations of the Ham/Noah incident have been proposed over the years. One such approach is to suggest that Ham actually committed incest not with his father but with Noah's wife (Rashkow 1998: 91). In support of this view, some exegetes have quoted the prohibition in Leviticus 18.7, which speaks of 'uncovering the nakedness of your father' equating it with 'the nakedness of your mother'. Whatever the truth of the matter, one of the central elements in the brief drama between Noah and Ham centres upon the concept of nakedness (Gen. 9.22).

In modern times, the discussion about Noah and Ham continues. The different criteria, arguments, and hypotheses recorded in past centuries reemerge in today's academic literature. Gordon and Rendsburg (1997: 40) have posited that where Ham went wrong was in the simple fact that he allowed himself to behold his father's genitals. According to Robert Alter (1996: 40), it may be that such an act was sufficient to violate a terrible ancient taboo (cf. Brodie 2001: 192). That a taboo may be involved is suggested by other passages in the Pentateuch. Emphatically Leviticus 18.6–7 and 20.11, 20–21 prohibit uncovering the 'nakedness' of a kinsman. Furthermore, the book of Exodus (20.26) establishes that Israelite men shall avoid going up by steps to the altar of Y<small>HWH</small> lest their genitals become exposed. For her part, Mary Douglas (2000: 246) is inclined to think that as Ham goes out to his brothers to share the news about the unusual sight inside the tent, he is actually joking about it in public and mocking his father. Brodie (2001: 185) characterizes Ham's behaviour as 'contemptuous'.

What is clear from the text in Genesis 9.24 is the fact that Noah flies into a rage when he learns what his son actually *did*. For Robert Gagnon (2001: 64–6), the passage implies that Ham did not limit himself to staring rudely at his father's genitals; he may have done something much worse (cf. Brenner 1997: 107–8; Nissinen 1998: 52). In Gagnon's view, Ham took advantage of his father's unconscious state and proceeded to penetrate him sexually, whereby the incident somehow exemplifies 'incestuous, homosexual rape' (p. 64; cf. Hanks 2000: 223). Gagnon argues that Ham actively 'uncovers' Noah's nakedness in the sense suggested by Leviticus 18. According to Gagnon, an incestuous relationship begins from the moment when a man 'uncovers the nakedness' of a family member. He speculates that the psychological motivation driving Ham may be the latter's desire to usurp Noah's patriarchal authority and thus become ruler of the entire household (2001: 66–7). At the same time, to Gagnon the incident illustrates what he terms the anti-homosexual prohibition in Leviticus 18.22 (cf. Fields 1997: 117). Theodore Jennings (2005: 86 n. 2) argues that, in addition to committing an act of incest, Ham reverses the roles normally governing relationships in the family: 'The inferior (son) acts upon the father, thereby rendering him passive'.

With respect to the hypothesis of Noah's castration, which started to circulate in the Middle Ages, most scholars today merely refer to it in passing.[76] Regarding incest, David Stewart (2006: 98) partly agrees with Robert Gagnon as he establishes a connection between Genesis 9 and the prohibitions against incest in Leviticus 18. Specifically Stewart argues that Leviticus 18.22 ("With a male you shall not lie . . .") is relevant given that he takes this verse to ban sexual relationships between males. Convinced of the intertextual nexus, Stewart concludes that Genesis 9.22 discusses the issue of incest between son (Ham) and father (Noah).[77] To summarize, the exegetes reviewed here have provided four different interpretations of the drama of Ham and Noah: (1) Ham *saw* Noah's nakedness, (2) Ham cruelly *made fun of* his father, (3) Ham incestuously *raped* Noah, (4) Ham *castrated* his father.

---

[76] Hamilton 1990: 322; Alter 1996: 40; Rashkow 1998: 91; Greenberg 2004: 64; Carden 2006: 32; Stewart 2006: 98.

[77] Stewart (2006: 98) and other exegetes such as Rashkow (1998: 87) and Brodie (2001: 192) find an obvious link between this text and the final part of the story of Sodom and Gomorrah, which describes the acts of heterosexual incest carried out by Lot's daughters (Gen. 19.31–36).

A Garden and a Vineyard

In order to achieve a solid understanding of the Noah/Ham story, a detailed literary scrutiny of the text is likely to yield useful insights. The Bible says virtually nothing about Noah's childhood. His father Lamech hails Noah's birth with an intriguing prophecy saying that the child will bring 'comfort' or 'relief' to his hard-working parents (Gen. 5.29). Noah grows up to be a 'righteous' and 'blameless' adult who, unlike his contemporaries, 'walks with God' (6.8-9). His wife remains nameless throughout (6.18; 7.7, 13; 8.16, 18). Noah raises three sons whose names are recorded as Shem, Ham, and Japheth (6.9-10; 9.18). On three occasions, Ham is highlighted as father of Canaan, ancestor of the Canaanite peoples (9.18, 22; 10.6).

An important part of the Noah story begins when he receives the commission to undertake a great work of engineering and carpentry (6.14-16). The ark enables him to become saviour of the animal kingdom (6.19-20). Once the devastating flood is over, Noah undertakes pioneering farming experiments, which include planting a vineyard (9.20). Subsequently he familiarizes himself with winemaking. In all these processes he acquires skills and knowledge. After taking his exploration of the properties of wine a step too far, Noah loses his adult dignity and ends up half-naked in the middle of his tent. The text makes it clear that his 'nakedness' is exposed (9.21-22). Several commentators and translators suggest that 'nakedness' means 'genitals'.[78]

As pointed out by Thomas Brodie (2001: 192), the fact that Noah tills the ground (*adamah*) and plants a vineyard evokes the task assigned to the original *adam* in Genesis 2.15 and

---

[78] Countryman 1989: 35; Korsak 1993: 35; Gagnon 2001: 66; Lipka 2006: 152 n. 113; Stewart 2006: 98.

Adam in 3.17-19. Noah's excessive intake of wine causes him to expose his genitals, creating another mirror-image flashback to the moment when Adam and Eve have eaten the forbidden fruit and suddenly become aware of their nakedness (3.7). However, Noah's experience forms an intriguing contrast to the adventure in the Garden of Eden. From the moment in which they taste the forbidden fruit, Adam and Eve gain important knowledge of the meaning of the concepts of life and death. This enables them to embark on a growing and maturing process in which they learn to face reality and adjust to adult life on the earth away from their childhood home.

When he tastes a different fruit—the legitimate fruit of the vine, Noah undergoes the opposite process in the sense that he loses his rational, cognitive abilities to descend momentarily into the ignorance and concomitant nakedness brought about by drunkenness (9.21). In his case, the sequence is retrogressive as he returns to a state of unknowing innocence characteristic of early childhood. According to Brodie (2001: 191), these events complement each other to a considerable extent. Clearly the notion of nakedness plays a significant part in both stories: Adam and Eve proceed to cover their genitals while Noah bares his. Taken together, they represent two opposite processes: Noah's temporary, unconscious state is contrasted with the newfound, permanent awareness of the inhabitants of Eden.

Both in the Garden of Eden and in Noah's tent it takes an intrusive visitor to trigger significant events (Brodie 2001: 192). In Eden, the active intervention of the serpent facilitates the acquisition of knowledge (Gen. 3.1-7). In Noah's case, his naked state is witnessed by his son Ham whose next move is to step outside to share the news (9.22). Because the incident is reported subsequently to his father, Ham becomes instrumental in making Noah aware or 'knowledgeable' about some unforeseen consequences of his own actions. Along similar lines, James Miller (2010: 25) finds that, while drunk, 'Noah exposed himself to the very thing from which Adam and Eve sought to protect themselves'. The picture painted by the Hebrew narrator denotes loss of self-control. Another intriguing coincidence pointed out by Miller (p. 25) is the presence in both stories of the verbal root *n-g-d*, 'tell' or 'broadcast', and the idea of clothing or covering (emphasis added):

> God asks Adam, 'Who *told* you that you were naked?' (3.11) and Ham *tells* his brothers that their father was naked (9.22). So God *clothes* Adam and his wife, and Shem and Japheth *cover* their father.

God provides Adam and Eve with adequate clothing as they go into the world (3.21). For their part, as soon as they realize what is going on in Noah's tent, Ham's brothers Shem and Japheth take immediate action, proceeding in silence and with great care, respect, and discretion to cover their father's unprotected body with a garment (9.23). When he wakes up from his drunken stupor and learns (literally 'knows') what has happened, Noah becomes indignant with Ham, cursing his offspring represented by Canaan (9.25–27). By contrast, Shem and Japheth are blessed (9.26–27).

Translating Noah's Drunkenness

To gauge what exactly went on between Ham and his father according to the Hebrew text, I begin by looking first at what Noah did and later try to establish what Ham did. The twelve English versions of the Bible are my starting point. Their renderings of Genesis 9.21 are listed in table 22. Crucial expressions are highlighted.

Table 22
Translating Noah's Drunkenness

Versions	Genesis 9.21
CCB	He drank the wine, became drunk, and *lay uncovered in the middle of his tent.*
HCSB	He drank some of the wine, became drunk, and *uncovered himself inside his tent.*
JM	He drank some of the wine and, becoming drunk, *lay uncovered inside his tent.*
JPS	He drank of the wine and became drunk, and he *uncovered himself within his tent.*
NCV	When he drank wine made from his grapes, he became drunk and *lay naked in his tent.*
NIV	When he drank some of its wine, he became drunk and *lay uncovered inside his tent.*
NJB	He drank some of the wine, and while he was drunk, he *lay uncovered in his tent.*
NKJV	Then he drank of the wine and was drunk, and *became uncovered in his tent.*
NLT	One day he drank some wine he had made, and he became drunk and *lay naked inside his tent.*
NRSV	He drank some of the wine and became drunk, and he *lay uncovered in his tent.*
NWT	And he began drinking of the wine and became intoxicated, and so he *uncovered himself in the midst of his tent.*
REB	He drank so much of the wine that he became drunk and *lay naked inside his tent.*

This passage shows that Noah did three things in close succession: (1) he drank of the wine, (2) he became drunk, (3) he ended up naked inside the tent. Second, all versions agree on (1) and (2). However, there is some opacity with regard to (3). They may all be similar, but the renderings offered by the English translators to describe the naked Noah do not all point in the same direction. Intriguing discrepancies among the versions emerge with respect to the situation surrounding Noah's naked state. According to three versions, Noah went on to 'uncover himself' before falling asleep inside the tent (HCSB, JPS, NWT). He may have been under the influence of alcohol, but somehow the uncovering seems to represent either an act of will or a momentary impulse on Noah's part since he is the grammatical subject.

In the view of another version, however, Noah 'became uncovered' (NKJV). Clearly the passive mode changes the act of uncovering to something involuntary or accidental. In other words, thus far two different visions are suggested: (1) Noah actively uncovers himself, (2) he becomes uncovered by a mere coincidence. Five versions reduce their approach to offering a 'still life' picture showing the final outcome of the intoxication process: Noah 'lay uncovered' (CCB, JM, NIV, NJB, NRSV). Here any reference to the concrete act of uncovering, whether active or passive, is omitted. Finally, three versions take this a step further as they simply state that Noah 'lay naked' (NCV, NLT, REB). With as many as four different approaches to this text, a doubt remains: Are all versions equally valid? Which approach is most in tune with the Hebrew original?

A closer look at the process of uncovering shows that in Genesis 9.21, the crucial Hebrew verb is *galah*, which in the simple *Qal* form means 'uncover' or 'disclose'. In this text, *galah* operates within the verb pattern called *Hithpael*, which carries a reflexive aspect that may be rendered as 'uncover oneself' (Wenham 1987: 199; DBHE p. 159). If this is so, the three versions translating *galah* as 'he uncovered himself' (HCSB, JPS, NWT) would seem to be on track,[79] while the NKJV's proposal 'became uncovered' is less precise. There is nothing seriously wrong with the eight remaining versions. However, by saying 'lay uncovered' and 'lay naked', they omit the important action taking place in 9.21 and focus entirely on the end result.[80]

One more aspect of Noah's stripping act needs highlighting. The Hebrew narrator points out that it takes place *běthōkh ahalō*, 'inside his tent'. In other words, Noah uncovers himself in private, not in public. He may be drunk, but at least he has the presence of mind to go inside the tent as soon as he realizes that he is no longer in control, or perhaps he simply wants to be left in peace. Eight versions successfully emphasize this detail saying, 'inside his tent' (HCSB, JM, NIV, NLT, REB), 'within his tent' (JPS), and 'in the middle/midst of his tent' (CCB, NWT). Four versions are less exact with 'in his tent' (NCV, NJB, NKJV, NRSV), as if the Hebrew preposition were the generic *bě*, 'in', rather than the specific term *běthōkh*, 'inside'.[81]

Translating Ham's Reactions

The main mystery in the Noah/Ham incident emerges when it comes to establishing what exactly Ham did from

---

[79] Several other translators take a similar view of the reflexive aspect of *galah* in the *Hithpael* verb pattern. Mary Phil Korsak says 'uncovered himself' (1993: 35) while Victor Hamilton (1990: 320) and Robert Alter (1996: 40) suggest 'exposed himself'.

[80] Part of the problem is caused by the impreciseness of the BDB p. 163, which for Gen. 9.21 suggests '*was uncovered* (naked)'.

[81] Technically *běthōkh* is a combination of two elements: the preposition *bě*, 'in', and the noun *thawekh*, which means 'middle' or 'centre'. In the construct state as here, placed in front of the noun *ohel*, 'tent', *běthōkh* undergoes a vowel change. So does *ohel*. Thus, the phrase *běthōkh ahalō* literally means 'in the middle of' or 'at the centre of his tent'.

the moment he saw his father's naked state inside the tent. Again it may be useful to start by taking a look at the twelve English versions. Their renderings of Genesis 9.22 are listed in table 23. Crucial details are highlighted.

Table 23
Translating Ham's Reactions

Versions	Genesis 9.22
CCB	When Ham, Canaan's ancestor, *saw his father's nakedness*, he *told* his two brothers *outside* the tent.
HCSB	Ham, the father of Canaan, *saw his father naked* and *told* his two brothers *outside*.
JM	When [Ham the father of Canaan] *saw his father naked*, he *told* his two brothers *outside*.
JPS	Ham, the father of Canaan, *saw his father's nakedness* and *told* his two brothers *outside*.
NCV	Ham, the father of Canaan, *looked at his naked father* and *told* his brothers *outside*.
NIV	Ham, the father of Canaan, *saw his father naked* and *told* his two brothers *outside*.
NJB	Ham, father of Canaan, *saw his father naked* and *told* his two brothers *outside*.
NKJV	And Ham, the father of Canaan, *saw the nakedness of his father*, and *told* his two brothers *outside*.
NLT	Ham, the father of Canaan, *saw that his father was naked* and *went outside* and *told* his brothers.
NRSV	And Ham, the father of Canaan, *saw the nakedness of his father*, and *told* his two brothers *outside*.
NWT	Later Ham the father of Canaan *saw his father's nakedness* and *went telling it* to his two brothers *outside*.
REB	Ham, father of Canaan, *saw his father naked* and *went out* and *told* his two brothers.

Three elements in this brief text stand out: 'nakedness', 'told', and 'outside'. If the Hebrew word *'erwah*, 'nakedness', means genitals, as many biblical passages suggest (cf. Lev. 18), this may well be important for the point the narrator is making. Five versions in table 23 successfully leave this option open (CCB, JPS, NKJV, NRSV, NWT). However, the majority of seven versions has chosen to downplay the genital aspect by stating, simply, that Ham 'saw his father naked'. These translators provide their readers with the mere vision of a male body with no clothes on it. The disadvantage is that there is no way of telling whether or not Noah's genitals are visible. In other words, the language used by seven translations is more evasive than the biblical original.

The next important element is the fact that Ham, after seeing Noah inside the tent, leaves his father and steps outside. This is successfully conveyed by all translators. Ten versions take a literal approach as they render the Hebrew adverb *bachuts* 'outside'. Two versions divide the action into two parts: 'he went out' and 'told' (NLT, REB), all of which is according to logic even though the Hebrew does not specify 'went out'. The third element is the fact that Ham goes on to share the news of what he has seen. Primarily operating in the *Hiphil* verb pattern, the Hebrew verbal root *n-g-d* denotes that information is being passed on. As all versions rightly have it, Ham literally 'told' his brothers. In a number of situations in the HB, *n-g-d* holds different aspects and nuances such as 'declare', 'announce', 'proclaim', 'broadcast', and 'report' (BDB p. 616–17; DBHE p. 475).

In Genesis 41.25, God 'communicates' a message to Pharaoh by means of a dream. In the Joseph story, his brothers, as they meet him in Egypt, 'provide him with information' in response to several questions (43.7). Joseph declares his intention of 'reporting' the latest news to Pharaoh (46.31). In Leviticus 5.1, the same verbal root *n-g-d* is used by the lawgiver to threaten with punishment any citizen who fails to 'declare' or 'report' knowledge of illegal affairs to the authorities. By means of the same verb, in Joshua 2.14, the Israelite spies sent to Jericho ask their hostess Rahab not to 'disclose' the nature of their mission to the local king. Given this wider context, it is possible that what Ham goes outside to share has an element of disclosure, i.e. he is being indiscreet. What he witnessed in private *inside* the tent, he is making public by going *outside* to spread the news.

Was Noah Castrated?

As noted earlier, several major interpretive trends are detectable in relation to the Noah/Ham episode in Genesis 9. One such hermeneutical school, which was relatively popular in the Middle Ages, argued that Ham actually castrated his father. To verify the likelihood or unlikelihood of such a hypothesis, I wish to consider what textual elements would have to be present in the Hebrew text for it to deal with a subject of this nature.

The *Oxford Dictionary* defines castration as the act whereby the testicles are removed from a male animal or man.[82] Any removal of an organ of the human body is likely to require the use of a sharp tool or instrument. The HB provides several situations in which such tools are employed for cutting operations. For example, in an emergency situation described in Exodus 4.25, Moses's wife Zipporah takes a 'flint' (Hebrew *tsor*) and cuts off her son's foreskin. Similarly, Joshua has a number of flint knives made so that all male Israelites may become circumcised (Josh. 5.2-7). The Hebrew word for 'knife' is *cherev*, which also means 'sword' or 'dagger'. At a crucial moment in the lives of Abraham

---

[82] http://oxforddictionaries.com/ (2012).

and Isaac, the unusual noun *maakheleth* plays an important part. This is what Abraham intends to use as he prepares to sacrifice his son (Gen. 22.6, 10). A likely translation of *maakheleth* seems to be 'sacrificial knife' (cf. Judg. 19.29).

In Genesis, several cutting operations are mentioned for which the tool is not specified. However, the meaning of the accompanying verbs is unmistakable. Such is the case of *bathar*, 'cut', for instance in 15.10 where Abraham sacrifices several animals, some of which are cut in two. A very frequent verb in connection with acts of cutting is *laqach*, 'take'. Following the flood experience, in 8.20, Noah 'takes' a number of animals and offers them up as burnt offerings, and in 22.13, Abraham 'takes' a ram to use it for identical purposes. To honour his commitment to hospitality, Abraham 'takes' a calf from the herd and prepares it for a feast (18.7). In 27.9, Rebekah tells Jacob to go to the herds to 'take' two kids, which are going to be served in a special meal for his father, Isaac.

In descriptions of cutting operations, the act of 'taking' does not apply exclusively to animals. The very first act of surgery in the Bible occurs in the Garden of Eden where God 'takes' one of the earthlings' sides and turns it into a woman (2.21–22). When the moment has come for Abraham to be circumcised, he 'takes' his son Ishmael and other male members of his household for them all to undergo the operation on the same day. In these cases, Abraham acts as surgeon (17.23–27; cf. 21.4). On the subject of circumcision, when adult men in the HB are circumcised, it is sometimes pointed out that they are left unfit for work for several days. Obviously there may be initial bleeding followed by pain and discomfort (Gen. 34.24–25; Josh. 5.8). In 22.12, a messenger from Y<small>HWH</small> tells Abraham not to 'raise his hand against' his son Isaac and not to 'do anything' to him. Because the sacrificial knife is already in Abraham's hand, the intervention is clearly designed to stop him from performing a lethal cutting operation.

All the aforementioned factors seem relevant when it comes to deciding whether or not Noah was castrated by Ham. First, for an act of castration, the presence of a cutting instrument would seem not only highly appropriate but indispensable. However, the text provides no such reference. Second, some allusion to the act of cutting should be expected. Again, the narrative is silent. Third, if the verb *laqach*, 'take', had been present it might conceivably have hinted at some procedure whereby Ham did something physical to his father. Even this possibility can be ruled out. Fourth, there is no hint in the text that Noah was left in a state of bleeding or great pain. Had that been the case, he would naturally have cried for help as soon as he came to, and promptly his wife or sons (Shem and Japheth) would have taken action. They might even have discovered the crime themselves if they happened to enter the tent because the puddle of blood forming around Noah's body would be noticeable. Finally, not only would Noah have been indignant but also such transgressive behaviour on Ham's part would have triggered a major conflict within the family with potential disastrous consequences.

In summary, none of these interpretations is applicable to the Hebrew text. In other words, it makes little sense to imagine the problem between Noah and Ham as having anything to do with castration.

Was Noah Raped?

For a long time, commentators and exegetes have wondered about the reason for Noah's vehement curse of his grandson Canaan in Genesis 9.25. Could it be that Ham actually took advantage of Noah's drunken state to assault his father sexually? To answer such a question, further textual analysis of the drama unfolding in Genesis 9.21–24 is required. The verbs included in 9.21 are 'he drank', 'became drunk', and 'uncovered himself', and in 9.24 Noah 'awoke' and 'knew'. As for Ham, the three verbs that describe his conduct vis-à-vis his drunken father are found in 9.22 and 9.24: 'he saw' (Hebrew *raah*), 'he told' (Hebrew root: *n-g-d*), and 'he did' (*'asah*).

With regard to sexual violence, Classical Hebrew usually expresses assaults in fairly concrete, non-euphemistic language. Two verbs are often associated with sexual aggression, namely, *'anah*, 'debase', and *'alal*, 'mistreat'. Having discussed *'anah* in the context of Genesis 34.2 (chapter 2), I now focus on *'alal* (Poel verb pattern). The DBHE translates this verb as 'maltreat', 'abuse', and 'mistreat',[83] whereas the BDB p. 759 widens the semantic field of *'alal* to include 'busy/divert oneself with' and 'deal wantonly/ruthlessly with'. These meanings seem to apply to *'alal* in 1 Samuel 6.6 and Judges 19.25 (cf. chapter 12). Moreover, in Numbers 22.29, *'alal* means 'make fun of' or 'make sport of'. If one views *'alal* from the perspective of sexual interaction between males, an intriguing passage in the first book of Samuel may shed further light on the connotations of this verb. Samuel Kader (1999: 51) has noted the appearance of *'alal* in a context of potential sexual assault. In 1 Samuel 31, the Israelite army led by King Saul is defeated by the advancing Philistines. The bloodshed is massive, and Saul himself is badly wounded and unable to flee. Rather than survive and be taken captive, Saul prefers to die. He says to his armour-bearer (1 Sam. 31.4, emphasis added):

---

[83] Spanish renderings in DBHE p. 568: *Maltratar, vejar, abusar, malparar, dejar maltrecho.*

> Draw your sword and *run me through* with it, so that these uncircumcised may not come and *run me through*, and *make sport of me*.

The phrase 'run me through' renders the Hebrew verb *daqar*, 'pierce'. One way to interpret the repetition of the verb is to take it as a pun. Saul literally prefers to be pierced by his armour-bearer's sword to being 'run through' by Philistine soldiers. One cannot be sure, but perhaps the king alludes to anal penetration. An additional hint at approaching sexual duress may be hidden in Saul's mention of the 'uncircumcised' soldiers of the victorious army where the very concept of uncircumcision draws attention to male Philistine genitals. Saul's further use of ʿalal reinforces this impression. Given the relative frequency of sexual degradation of vanquished enemies on the battlefields of antiquity (Dover 1978: 105; Boswell 1980: 75 n. 61), it is not difficult to imagine Saul's fear of becoming the object of anal penetration and the concomitant mockery and vulgar merry-making on his captors' part. The horrific fate accorded Saul's dead body a few hours later (1 Sam. 31.8-10) makes such fears seem reasonably justified. In other words, Saul may well have a rape scenario in mind. Rather than exposing himself to imminent humiliation and torture, he chooses death (1 Sam. 31.4-5).[84]

---

[84] This is conceivably one of two rare passages in the HB in which a form of male–male rape is contemplated by the king of Israel. Typically, the scenario is one of battle and defeat, and the alleged perpetrators are non-Israelites. Arguably, the other possible scriptural allusion is made in Jer. 38.19, this time through the sole use of ʿalal. A nervous King Zedekiah confesses, 'I am afraid of the Judeans who have deserted to the Chaldeans, for I might be handed over to them and they would *make sport of* me' (emphasis added). Clearly ʿalal implies some form of mistreatment or torment, be it psychological or physical. This impression is enhanced by what happens later. Faced with the onslaught of King Nebuchadrezzar of Babylon, Zedekiah tries to flee but is captured and subjected to torture (Jer. 39.5-7).

In the story of Noah and Ham, ʿanah and ʿalal are not found. Not even the multifaceted laqach, 'take', appears in the text to reveal some form of abuse on Ham's part vis-à-vis the drunken Noah. According to some commentators, the Hebrew verb ʿasah, 'he did' (Gen. 9.24), implies illicit or violent activity (Gagnon 2001: 65; cf. Stewart 2006: 98). However, in the light of the neutral or even peaceful nature of this verb in numerous other contexts (Gen. 1.7, 16, 25, 26, 31, etc.), there is little justification for such an interpretation (Hamilton 1990: 322–3).

Finally, a psychological observation with regard to Ham's behaviour seems to be in order. Normally the first impulse of someone who has just committed a criminal offence is to hide all traces of their acts. In many cases, they try to flee the scene of the crime to avoid detection. If the Ham of the biblical story were to have committed a punishable act such as penetrating Noah anally, he might have faced the death penalty (Lev. 20.13).[85] Bearing this in mind, it would not be logical for him to go out and publicize his guilt (Rashkow 1998: 94). In summary, a rape scenario in Genesis 9 is highly unlikely.

An Act of Incest?

As shown in chapter 1, biblical narrators tend to be specific when dealing with sexual activity. First, there are two primary verbs denoting sexual relations, namely, bō and shakhav. Neither is present in the Ham/Noah incident. Second, it is striking that all secondary verbs belonging to the sexual realm are absent from the text. For example,

---

[85] The assumption that Lev. 20.13 punishes anal penetration is widely held but not the only interpretation available (cf. the detailed discussion of Lev. 18.22 in this book's chapter 6).

there is no hint at any 'approaching' or 'touching' on Ham's part. Nevertheless, James Miller (2010: 24-5) finds that there are enough narrative similarities between the final part of Genesis 9 and other events in Genesis to conclude that 'this story is primarily one of incest'. Similarly, other scholars believe that Ham committed an act of homosexual incest (Milgrom 2004: 203; Carmichael 2010: 143). To verify the validity of such arguments requires a brief look at the prohibitions listed in Leviticus 18 and 20.

If the Noah/Ham incident is to be viewed as an example of male-male incest, it would establish a link to Leviticus 18.22 and 20.13 in which certain sexual acts between males are classified as illicit. It is a fact that the book of Leviticus seems to warn Israelites—at least indirectly—against having incestuous relations with their fathers (Lev. 18.7). According to Leviticus 18.6 and a string of other verses, the expression used to prohibit incest with mother, father, aunt, sister, etc., is, literally speaking, to 'uncover' (*galah*) their nakedness (*'erwah*). In the Levitical context, whose elevated literary style provides evidence of careful editing, the exact wording is often crucial (Douglas 2000: 7). In addition, the lawgiver seems to indicate that the act of uncovering someone's nakedness denotes intent and initiative.[86]

Within this framework, it is perhaps to be assumed that the mere fact of seeing someone naked may be accidental or involuntary. Moreover, the only specific case in which 'seeing' is involved is in Leviticus 20.17. The Hebrew legislator declares that no Israelite should 'take' his sister in order to 'see' her nakedness. For her part, she should not

---

[86] Time and again in Lev. 18 the noun *'erwah* appears jointly with the verb *galah*. Hence, the act of 'uncovering' the nakedness of a close relative may signify a concrete, intentional step in a general erotic sense or, possibly, the more specific sense of 'touching their genitals'.

'see' him without his clothes on (abbreviated text, emphasis added):

> And if a man *takes* his sister, a daughter of his father or a daughter of his mother, and *sees* her nakedness, and she *sees* his nakedness, both have committed an abomination.

It should be noted here that 'take' precedes and determines the situation in which 'seeing' occurs. As mentioned in chapter 2, in Classical Hebrew the verb *laqach*, 'take', frequently occurs with a male subject and a female object. In these situations, 'take' implies a formal step whereby the woman taken becomes the man's wife.[87] In other words, the moment a male 'takes' a female they become married (Brenner 1997: 93-4 n. 5). At other times, *laqach* does not have marital connotations, and the sequence is reversed. Thus, in 34.2, Shechem first 'sees' Dinah and then immediately goes on to 'take' her without further ado.

Perhaps both interpretive possibilities are present in the 'take' featured in Leviticus 20.17. In the light of the severity of the punishment—deportation—for both parties, it is plausible that the woman does not refuse to participate and that no violence is involved. In other words, a consensual relationship may be alluded to. At any rate, the verb *laqach* seems to involve intent on the man's part because he 'takes' in order to 'see', and following on from there, the woman's 'seeing' is a consequence of his move. Thus, both persons arrive at seeing each other's nakedness at the same time, i.e. some visual communication is taking place. Obviously Leviticus always finds the sight of a family member's

---

[87] Cf. the so-called sons of God who take wives in Gen. 6.2, the two young men of Sodom who are expected to take Lot's daughters (19.14), Abraham who takes a new wife (25.1), and Judah who takes a Canaanite wife (38.2).

genitals reprehensible (18.6). In the case of 20.17, however, there seem to be added complications. With regard to this particular occurrence of 'take', two hypotheses may be submitted, both of which deal with illicit situations: (1) The man tries to persuade his sister to show him her naked body; (2) the man is 'taking' his sister in the marital sense of the word, i.e. he treats her as a wife.[88]

In summary, for the HB to refer to circumstances comparable to incest, the typical procedure would be to use the verb *galah*, 'uncover', combined with the noun *ʿerwah*, 'nakedness' (Lev. 18.6-19). Also *laqach* may play a part as it oscillates between denoting the initiation of a formal, marital relationship and a simple act of will on the man's part, occasionally accompanied by the use of force—physical or institutional—towards the woman (Gen. 34.2). Given these textual facts, it is significant that both *galah* and *laqach* are absent from Genesis 9.21-22. No 'uncovering' or 'taking' is occurring. Stated another way, the text does not provide any clues for deducing that Ham approaches or touches his father's genitals. It is Noah who uncovers himself, leaving his naked body for anyone to behold (9.21).

Seeing a Naked Man

According to Miller (2010: 24), 'To gaze upon the nakedness of another is a sexual act'. Moreover, for Ham to 'enjoy his father's exposure' by gazing on it is 'a literal example of the euphemism used in Leviticus 18 for incest, to "uncover the nakedness" of the offended relative' (p. 25). Several other

---

[88] In most cases, these texts were written with the male Israelite listener or reader in mind. For the context discussed here, it is important to remember that ancient Israelites lived in extended families in which there would be not only sisters and brothers but very often half sisters and half brothers, stepsisters and stepbrothers, etc.

exegetes find that the phrase is a euphemism for having sex (Alter 1996: 40; Nissinen 1998: 52; Gagnon 2001: 66). David Stewart (2006: 98) agrees that 'seeing somebody's nakedness' has at least strong erotic connotations.

As for the Hebrew text itself, the narrative briefly states that Ham *raah*, 'saw', and nothing else. If the simple act of 'seeing' is supposed to mean 'uncovering', it would be helpful to have more textual examples from the HB to substantiate this claim. Hence, a search for such passages is required. In regard to this aspect of *raah*, there are certainly several instances in which the verb denotes erotic attraction or arousal. Thus, in Genesis 6.2, the sons of God 'see' human women and find them attractive. Similarly, Abraham is fearful that he will be killed as soon as the Egyptians 'see' Sarah's beauty (12.12). In these cases, no nakedness is involved.

On some occasions, *raah* indicates that someone directs their eyes towards a place, person, or issue over a period of time, be it long or short. For example, in Genesis 18.21, *raah* expresses a clear intent on Yhwh's part to 'see' what is going on in Sodom, i.e. to examine or look into the specific details of the matter. Sometimes *raah* means 'watch' as in 21.9 where Sarah watches Ishmael playing with Isaac. In 21.16, Hagar decides not to watch Ishmael succumbing to hunger and thirst. Again, however, there is no textual example of this applying to a situation in which someone gazes at another's naked body. In general terms, *raah* denotes the simple act of seeing at a glance. Often it means 'catch sight of' or 'discover' as in Genesis 18.2 where Abraham suddenly sees three strangers approaching his tent. Likewise, Lot sees the two messengers entering the gateway of Sodom (19.1); Hagar discovers a well of water in the middle of the desert (21.19); Abraham spots a ram caught in a thicket by its horns (22.13), and Abimelech sees by chance the tender way in which Isaac fondles Rebekah (26.8).

Classical Hebrew has other verbs operating in this semantic field, notably *navat* (*Hiphil* pattern). In addition to 'look up' and 'see', it often means 'gaze'. Thus, Abraham is invited to look (*navat*) towards heaven and count the stars (Gen. 15.5); Lot and his family fleeing Sodom are urged not to stop and spend any time 'gazing' (19.17). As Lot's wife turns into a pillar of salt, the occurrence in this context of *navat* seems to entail that she gazes at the destruction of her hometown (19.26). As he becomes aware of the burning bush in the desert, Moses moves closer (Exod. 3.2). After being told that Yhwh is present, and feeling afraid to gaze at God (*navat*, 3.6), he hides his face.

One passage in particular involving *navat* clearly illustrates how this verb may operate in the erotic sphere. The prophet Habakkuk exclaims in 2.15 (text abbreviated, emphasis added):

> Alas for you who make your neighbours drink . . .
> until they are drunk, in order to *gaze upon their nakedness*.

Perhaps this prophetic passage is of relevance for the Ham/Noah context. If Ham had been the one who made Noah drink wine in excess, he might be suspected of belonging to the category of immoral persons alluded to by Habakkuk. Likewise, if the Hebrew verb present in Genesis 9.22 had been *navat* rather than *raah*, it might have provided another potential textual link. All one finds, however, is *raah*, which is the more common and more neutral of the two verbs for 'seeing'. Genesis 9.21 makes it plain that Noah 'drank of the wine', apparently without being prompted or urged on by anyone, and subsequently stripped himself bare.[89] On this basis, the fact that Ham 'saw' the naked Noah inside the tent does not necessarily denote anything more than a quick glance. Similarly, Ham's presence in the tent may not be the result of any premeditated act on his part and may well be accidental.

For these reasons, it makes sense to conclude that the sole act of seeing someone naked is insufficient to imply sexual activity, including incestuous intent (Rashkow 1998: 91-2). The above reflections lead to the conclusion that the often-imagined sexual encounter between an aroused Ham and the naked Noah is a hypothesis not grounded in the text. Perhaps a more plausible explanation of Noah's indignation is provided by the ancient Greek historian Herodotus who wrote that, among many 'barbarian' (non-Greek) nations, for a man to be seen naked 'is an occasion of great shame' (Carmichael 2010: 143). Using this perspective for interpreting the Noah/Ham episode, Calum Carmichael (2010: 90) observes,

> Shame by its very nature comes into play only when the switch from private to public realm is made. The situation of Noah, lying naked in his tent in a drunken stupor, becomes shameful only when his son looks upon him and tells his two brothers about what he has seen.

Ham and His Brothers

As already noted, several proposals have been made over the centuries to explain the exact nature of Ham's sin.

---

[89] Cf. Lam. 4.21-22: 'But to you also the cup shall pass; you shall become drunk and strip yourself bare' (NRSV).

Particularly, scholars have tried to establish why some of his offspring were cursed for what he 'did' (Gen. 9.24). Having discarded the interpretations suggesting castration, rape, and incest as extraneous to the text, four elements in Ham's behaviour remain to be explored for a viable approach to the incident: (1) he *saw* his father's nakedness, (2) this happened *inside* Noah's tent, (3) Ham went *outside*, (4) he *spoke* to his brothers. Noah's irate response is likely to be a reaction to one or several of these elements.

If one now focuses on the steps taken by Shem and Japheth, several facts emerge. The text makes it clear that they 'took', 'put', 'walked', 'covered', 'turned away', and 'did not see' (9.23). In other words, responding to Ham's report his brothers perform four crucial acts as they (1) *keep quiet*, (2) *go in*, (3) avoid *seeing* Noah, (4) respectfully *place a cover* over his naked body. The characteristics of the two different procedures are shown in table 24.

Table 24
Behaviour of Ham and His Brothers

Ham	Shem and Japheth
saw	did not see
went out	went in
left Noah vulnerable	protected Noah
spoke	were silent
showed disrespect	showed respect
was cursed	were blessed

Table 24 highlights Ham's total lack of discretion in a family situation that is a cause of embarrassment to Noah. Ham's behaviour contrasts vividly with the discreet, elaborate efforts displayed by Shem and Japheth (Wenham 1987: 200).

In the light of these parallel sequences, the Hebrew narrator seems to be suggesting that Israelites can adopt two very different attitudes to their parents: one attitude characterized by respect and the other disrespectful. To appreciate the social and religious importance of this, it may be valuable to remember the centrality of the Ten Commandments in the HB. The situation involving Ham and his brothers appears to be connected to the fifth commandment saying, 'Honour your father and your mother'. Placed in a prominent position—before the prohibitions of murder, adultery, theft, and false witness—it first appears in Exodus 20.12 and is highlighted for a second time in Deuteronomy 5.16.

As pointed out by Cotterell and Turner (1989: 102), the wide culture gap between the ancient world that generated the biblical text and modern Western readers makes it difficult for us to know exactly what responsibilities social convention laid at the feet of a Near-Eastern son or daughter. However, the HB does provide us with some clues. Several narratives certainly demonstrate that one such responsibility was obedience. Cases in point are Isaac submitting his life to his father Abraham (Gen. 22.3-12), Abraham's sons by Ketura emigrating at his behest (25.6), Jacob and Esau taking wives acceptable to their parents (28.1-9), and Joseph obeying his father Jacob in spite of exposing himself to the violent hostility of his brothers (37.13-20).

In some passages, the focus is on the dire consequences of disobedience and disrespect. In Genesis 35.22, Reuben, Jacob's eldest son by Leah, breaks the rules by 'lying with' his father's concubine Bilhah.[90] As a result, he loses the privileges normally conferred upon the firstborn son (49.4).

---

[90] Brueggemann (1982: 284) calls this 'a political issue'. It may be interpreted as an act of rebellion against his father on Reuben's part (Alter 1996: 200). The fact that Reuben 'lies' with Jacob's concubine evokes a similar situation where Absalom stages a full-scale rebellion

For such an act, Deuteronomy 27.20 invokes a curse: 'Cursed be the one who lies down with his father's wife'. In this context, it is significant that the name of Reuben gradually fades from view in the HB (McKeown 2008: 209, 214).[91] For his part, Judah's son Onan only half-heartedly complies when told by his father to 'go in' to his sister-in-law Tamar. Onan's disobedience is punished by death (38.9–10).

Curse and Blessing

A puzzling detail in the Ham/Noah narrative has generated considerable debate among biblical scholars. Surprisingly the full weight of the curse pronounced by Noah in Genesis 9.25–27 falls not directly on his son Ham but rather on his grandson Canaan.[92] Why is Canaan cursed? The Hebrew text itself seems to provide several significant clues. Both Noah and his three sons are blessed by God in Genesis 9.1. This is the third time in Genesis in which a divine blessing is bestowed on humankind (Wenham 1987: 192). Moreover, it is true that Ham, from a technical perspective, deserves some harsh words from Noah. The book of Deuteronomy is in no doubt: 'Cursed be the one who dishonours father and mother' (Deut. 27.16). However, by sheer logic, Ham cannot be both blessed and cursed. Noah's words may have considerable authority and set a precedent (Wenham 1987: 201), but he cannot invalidate the powerful blessing pronounced previously by the deity on the entire family. In fact, God's words of blessing to Noah and his family after they leave the ark (Gen. 9.1) echo almost verbatim the

---

against his father and takes possession of David's concubines by 'going in' to them (2 Sam. 16.22).

[91] Deut. 33.6 laments the decline of the tribe of Reuben: 'May Reuben live, and not die out, even though his numbers are few.'

[92] Wenham 1987: 200; Hamilton 1990: 324; Alter 1996: 40; Rashkow 1998: 88; Jennings 2005: 86.

original commission to Adam: 'Be fruitful and multiply' (1.28; cf. Wenham 1987: 207).

Ham has got three other sons, namely, Cush, Egypt, and Put (Gen. 10.6). Since Noah's curse is addressed specifically to his grandson Canaan, only the latter is affected by what his father Ham did. It is worth noting that the narrator underlines Ham's special paternal relationship with Canaan, calling him 'the father of Canaan' no fewer than three times (9.18, 22; 10.6). This intriguing repetition may serve several purposes: (a) to indicate that Ham is very proud, or fond, of this particular son; and (b) to set the stage for the surprising cross-identification between Ham and Canaan. The latter appears in 9.25 as a 'brother' of his uncles Shem and Japheth: 'Let Canaan be cursed. The lowest of slaves shall he be to his brothers', an emphatic statement occurring three times in 9.25-27 (cf. Wenham 1987: 203). Thus, Ham's fall from grace disadvantages only one group of his descendants, not his whole family (p. 207). Given the paradigmatic force of the narratives included in Genesis (Brodie 2001: 113),[93] the story of Ham and Canaan in Genesis 9 and 10 provides a primeval justification for the eventual Israelite colonization of the territory occupied by various Canaanite peoples (Carden 2006: 32).

---

[93] In antiquity, both rabbinic commentators and early church fathers used the puzzling incident involving Noah, Ham, and Canaan to demean black people; cf. Perdue 2005: 96-7; Adamo and Eghwubare 2010: 279. In recent centuries, the text was used to justify the institution of slavery in North America (Svartvik 2006: 221-6). Until well into the twentieth century, colonialism in Africa rested on similar ideological foundations (Perdue 2005: 294-5; Adamo & Eghwubare 2010: 280). Similarly, Jacob Milgrom (2004: 201) has pointed out that the alleged immorality of Ham and his Canaanite descendants made them cursed to the point that the land they inhabited would vomit them out; cf. Lev. 18.25-28. As noted by Milgrom, attributing sexual immorality to an enemy has always been a ruse for stigmatizing them.

As Noah's grandson, Canaan is placed a generation away from the direct blessing bestowed upon his father and uncles. Furthermore, if the HB is explored from an intergenerational perspective, it will become clear that Canaan's situation is not so unheard of as many readers may think (Hamilton 1990: 325). Indeed, the curse and blessing pronounced by Noah were essentially addressed not to his sons but rather to the descendants of Shem, Ham, and Japheth (Wenham 1987: 198). Plausibly Genesis 9.25 is echoing the severe warning in Exodus 20.5 pronounced against those who behave irreverently towards their fathers and mothers (emphasis added):

> I Yhwh, your God, am a jealous God. I punish *children* for the iniquity of fathers to the third and the fourth generation.

This warning reappears in Numbers 14.18 and Deuteronomy 5.9. Thus, Genesis 9 provides an example of how the consequences of a serious act of disloyalty of a father (Ham) are transferable to his son (Canaan). The offensive nature of the transgression is highlighted in Exodus 34.7 where the Hebrew lawgiver insists on the intergenerational reach of the punishment (emphasis added):

> Yhwh . . . who visits the guilt of the fathers *upon the children and grandchildren* to the third and the fourth generation.

If a curse in the HB context is capable of haunting a given family, clan, or nation for generations,[94] a comparable, yet radically different situation arises when it comes to blessings.

---

[94] A radical departure from this principle is signalled in Ezek. 18 where the prophet announces that every Israelite should be judged on his own merit.

In fact, Israelites who commit themselves to the full observance of the commandments of Y‍HWH receive splendid promises of permanent well-being and prosperity. Shem and Japheth choose to conduct themselves with the utmost respect vis-à-vis their father. This earns them Noah's blessing in Genesis 9.26-27 (Hamilton 1990: 325). Thus, Ham's brothers qualify for the fulfilment of the promise: 'So that your days may be long in the land' (Exod. 20.12; Deut. 5.16). The two passages from the book of Exodus quoted above contain juxtapositions of curse and blessing. The blessing recorded in Exodus 20.6 is more than intergenerational. It virtually goes on forever (text abbreviated, emphasis added):

> I Y‍HWH your God . . . show unwavering love *to the thousandth generation* of those who love me and keep my commandments.

For further emphasis, the blessing is repeated and expanded in Exodus 34.6-7 (italics added):

> Y‍HWH, a God merciful and gracious, slow to anger and rich in steadfast love and faithfulness, keeping steadfast love *for the thousandth generation*.

Victor Hamilton (1990: 325) points out how the perhaps surprising curse invoked on Canaan runs parallel to the words of blessing awarded Shem. Curiously, Shem's blessing is indirect inasmuch as it is literally addressed to 'Y‍HWH, God of Shem' (9.26). This seems to indicate that Shem loyally carried out the divine commandment. In this manner, the narrator skilfully creates a remarkable textual and literary balance between the indirect curse of some (Ham and Canaan) vis-à-vis the indirect blessing of others (Shem and Japheth).

A final point is worth making in relation to Shem. The blessing he receives from his father's lips is the first intimation in the HB that the line of God's election is going through one of Noah's three sons, namely, Shem. Indeed, Shem carries forward the line of election from Seth, third son of Adam and Eve (Gen. 4.25 ff.). In practical terms, this means that the chosen people of Israel are descended from Seth, Shem, and Abraham (11.10–29).

Conclusion

In the English versions examined, no major translation errors have occurred. However, several minor inaccuracies have been detected in the language used by translators when they deal with Noah's uncovering himself and his subsequent nakedness. Some commentators have ascribed a homoerotic dimension to the story of Noah and his son Ham (Gen. 9.21–27). However, the exegesis carried out in this chapter has not documented any such inclinations on either Noah's or Ham's part. The primary sexual verbs *bō* and *shakhav* are absent, and so are the secondary verbs (cf. table 14). Other scholars have interpreted the story from one of three perspectives: incest, sexual penetration, and castration. Again, a careful analysis of the Hebrew text has demonstrated that the narrator does not make use of the specific vocabulary associated with incest or sexual assault. The same is true of the terminology denoting cutting operations.

In summary, there is little or no evidence for arguing that the biblical story deals with sex, sexual assault, or castration. According to the Hebrew text, Ham's crime consists in performing two specific acts: (1) he looks at his father's nakedness, and (2) he speaks — perhaps disrespectfully — of what he has seen. Viewed within the biblical context, Ham's sin seems to be that he dishonours his father, a transgression condemned by the legal sections of the Pentateuch (Exodus, Numbers, and Deuteronomy). In the incident narrated in Genesis 9, the intriguing cross-identification between Ham and Canaan causes the latter to receive the full weight of the curse. The intergenerational nature of the punishment illustrates several passages of the Pentateuch in which the children and grandchildren of transgressors are made liable for crimes committed by their progenitors.

There is a remarkable contrast between Ham's indiscreet behaviour, which moves Noah to indignation, and the way in which Shem and Japheth are rewarded for their approach to the situation. The latter conduct themselves with utmost discretion and respect, a fact that merits their father's blessing. Even more intergenerational than the curse, the generous nature and lasting effect of a blessing pronounced or sanctioned by YHWH is highlighted several times in the Hebrew Bible, particularly in the books of Exodus and Deuteronomy.

5

CONSECRATED

Be holy to me
For holy am I, Yhwh.

— Leviticus 20.26

Introduction

A little-known legal text in chapter 23 of the book of Deuteronomy contains several unusual words. In some versions this text is placed at Deuteronomy 23.18–19 (CCB, JPS, NJB), but most manuscripts situate it at 23.17–18. Traditionally these verses have been regarded as an allusion to so-called sacred prostitution, and even today, the sexual focus is so prevalent among exegetes that some English versions of the Bible limit themselves to mentioning, simply, 'prostitution'. The *Complete Jewish Bible* (1998) goes one step further, rendering Deuteronomy 23.17–18 in the following terms (emphasis added):

> No woman of Israel is to engage in ritual prostitution, and no man of Israel is to engage in ritual *homosexual* prostitution.
>
> Nothing earned through *heterosexual or homosexual* prostitution is to be brought into the house of Adonai your God in fulfilment of any vow, for both of these are abhorrent to Adonai your God.

The word ADONAI is the reverential reading of YHWH preferred by Jewish tradition because the name YHWH is considered too sacred to be pronounced by human lips (Browning 2009: 384). More difficult to justify is the presence in this ancient text of the modern words 'heterosexual' and 'homosexual'. Similar problems occur in several other English versions. The *21st Century King James Version* (1994) lets us know that the deity does not want any 'sodomite' among the sons of Israel. The same word is present in *The American Standard Version* (1901) and the *Amplified Version* (1987). Supposedly 'sodomite' is derived from the biblical name of Sodom. However, the word does not take on a sexual sense until the Middle Ages (cf. this book's chapter 8). Its use in an English text purportedly rendering ancient scripture is confusing.

Few modern scholars seem to be completely at ease with Deuteronomy 23.17–18. This is understandable because the text contains several unusual words. In the past exegesis has been based on the commonly held view of sacred prostitution in the land of Canaan. However, this is a major problem since no solid archaeological, historical, or cultural evidence in the form of extra-biblical sources has yet been produced (Guest 2006: 140; Stone 2006: 235). The same difficulty arises with respect to alleged homoerotic activity. Until such evidence appears, the only material available to exegetes is this two-verse passage from Deuteronomy. Below I subject it to close scrutiny, often comparing my findings with twelve English versions of the Bible.

A Mysterious Group of People

A literal translation of Deuteronomy 23.17–18, with two Hebrew words left unprocessed, might look like this:

> There shall not be a *Qedeshah* among the daughters of Israel and there shall be no *Qadesh* among the sons of Israel. You shall not bring into the house of Y<small>HWH</small>, your God, a prostitute's gift or the price of a dog.

Taking as our starting point the need to verify the exact nature of the key words of this brief passage, the first striking feature is the occurrence of the two Hebrew nouns. They are seemingly related without being identical. Who, then, are the *qedeshah* and the *qadesh*? What do these words actually mean? Why are the people of biblical Israel not supposed to present themselves as such?

From a grammatical viewpoint, these words are gendered nouns with *qedeshah* being feminine and *qadesh* masculine, and both are in the singular (the respective plurals being *qedeshōth* and *qedeshīm*). In addition, from a morphological point of view, both words contain the Hebrew consonantal root *q-d-sh*, which is related to the concept of holiness (see below). The latter aspect raises an important question: could the people alluded to have something to do with the religious sphere? Further contextual questions need addressing: why are *qedeshah* and *qadesh* followed by *zonah*, 'prostitute',[95] and *kelev*, a word that means 'dog'?

Among scholars, there is considerable debate as to the exact nature of *qedeshah*. Some believe that *qedeshah* and *zonah* are more or less identical but that *qedeshah* seems to play a role in religious contexts (Nissinen 1998: 39–40; Gagnon 2001: 102–3). However, for Ken Stone (2006: 235), there is no doubt: *qedeshah* and *zonah* are not identical. With regard to the

---

[95] Lev. 19.29 issues this command (NRSV): 'Do not profane your daughter by making her a prostitute.' The JPS proposes, 'Do not degrade your daughter and make her a harlot.'

subject of homoeroticism in the Hebrew Bible, *qedeshah* never applies to what in modern times might be called lesbianism. Below I examine the enigmatic nature of those male figures called *qadesh* (singular) and *qedeshīm* (plural), after which I examine the specific issues surrounding *qedeshah*.

QADESH: A Matter of Debate

One scholar who feels that Deuteronomy 23.17 deals with a cult-related form of male prostitution is Robert Gagnon (2001: 100–110). In an attempt to document his hypothesis, he has explored a series of sources from various cultures of the ancient Near East, including pre-biblical Mesopotamia and Syria under the Roman Empire. In both areas, some form of prostitution seems to have been attached to the temples (p. 103). Gagnon takes note of the presence of the word *qedeshīm* in other books of the Bible, specifically in Kings and Job. In the latter case (Job 36.14), the Hebrew narrator explains that the *qedeshīm* die young. This enables Gagnon to draw the conclusion that the persons in question must be prostitutes who lead miserable lives involving physical and moral debasement. Inevitably, such circumstances are detrimental to their life expectancy (2001: 103). Similarly, Gagnon observes that *qadesh* in Deuteronomy 23.17 is followed almost immediately by the word *kelev*, 'dog' (23.18). As far as Gagnon is concerned, these terms are interchangeable. In passing, he is convinced that the 'dogs' mentioned in the book of Revelation (22.15) belong to the same category (2001: 104–5). In order to reinforce his anti-homosexual stance, he argues that the searing prohibition of transvestism in Deuteronomy 22.5 is another indication of the 'abominable' character ascribed in the HB to homoerotic relationships (pp. 105, 109). He concludes that 'the existence of homosexual cult prostitutes in Judah was a recurring problem' (p. 110).

Unlike Gagnon, Martti Nissinen (1998: 40) draws attention to the fact that nowhere do the biblical texts—including Job and both 1 and 2 Kings—explain who the *qedeshīm* are or what they do. Nissinen argues that both *qadesh* and the term *kelev* (Deut. 23.18) may well be used in a derogatory sense in reference to the cultural and religious environment of Canaan, which included transvestism and eunuchs (1998: 42-3). At the same time, he abstains from drawing firm conclusions given the insufficiency of the evidence (p. 41). In Nissinen's view, the most likely explanation of the prohibitions in Deuteronomy 23.17-18 is that they reflect taboos of the ancient Near East, including taboo-protected gender roles (1998: 41-2).

For his part, Daniel Helminiak (2000: 54) points out that the word *qadesh* not only means 'holy' or 'consecrated' but also 'separate' or 'set apart'. He has noted the occurrences of this term in 1 and 2 Kings (p. 120). For the specific case of Deuteronomy 23.17, Helminiak considers the translation 'devoted' or 'dedicated ones' suitable. Indeed, the underlying biblical issues to which the term refers seem unrelated to the realm of sex. In all probability, the prohibition attached to the *qedeshīm* alludes to a specific aspect of Canaanite culture, namely, religion. Thus, the issue is idolatry (2000: 121).

Steven Greenberg (2004: 176) focuses on the transvestism forbidden and labelled in Deuteronomy 22.5 as *to'evah*, 'abomination'. He links this to Leviticus 18.22, a verse that in his view describes 'male intercourse'. Greenberg notes the occurrence of *qedeshīm* in 2 Kings 23.7. Recognizing the opacity of the concept and its likely Canaanite background (2004: 177), he concludes by emphasizing the subversive aspects inherent in transvestism since such practices threaten gender-role identity (p. 178). In his view, if the great male/female divide is at stake, male same-sex intercourse then becomes not only a personal sin but also a collective threat (p. 179).

Deryn Guest (2006: 139) proposes to render *qedeshīm* 'sanctuary women/men'. This is because the only biblical references to which readers have access reveal that these persons perform cultic duties. Guest acknowledges the efforts carried out by Nissinen to locate literary precedents in ancient Middle Eastern literature, but in her view, the evidence discussed is inconclusive. Quoting Phyllis Bird, Guest goes on to argue that the Deuteronomical text abstains from describing the phenomenon it condemns. Above all, the deliberate intention is to polemicize against Canaanite culture (p. 140).

Ken Stone (2006: 236) finds it obvious that the words *qadesh* and *qedeshīm* occur in contexts of polemics against deep-seated traditions among the Israelites. The frequent allusions in the HB to polytheism and religious pluralism testify to this. Stone rejects the traditional explanation of Canaanite religion as 'fertility cult'. He argues that the word *qadesh* does not have any sexual connotations (p. 235). Given the Hebrew root *q-d-sh*, which alludes to things 'holy' or 'sacred', it would seem to make sense to translate *qedeshīm* as 'holy persons' or 'consecrated persons' (p. 234). All that is known about them is that they may have been religious functionaries. The context of 2 Kings 23.7 seems to suggest some association between the *qedeshīm* and the women weaving for the Canaanite goddess Asherah (p. 235).

Hebrew Holiness

As mentioned, the three Hebrew consonants at the heart of the words studied are *q-d-sh* whose basic meaning is 'holy', 'consecrated', or 'set apart'. The associated verb *qadash* translates as 'to be holy' or 'to be sanctified' (Exod. 29.21). The noun *qodesh* is equivalent to 'holiness' (Exod. 15.11; 22.31). Sometimes this word acts as an adjective (Is. 56.7) while in other cases it takes the form of *qadosh* (Deut. 23.14), plural *qedoshīm* (Job 5.1). While some variations occur in vocalization, the consistent consonant morphology based on the common root *q-d-sh* provides an obvious semantic link between *qadash*, *qadosh*, *qodesh*, *qedoshīm*, *qadesh*, *qedeshah*, and *qedeshīm*.

This general context forms the backdrop to the specific words analyzed in this chapter. The nouns *qadesh*, singular (Deut. 23.17), and *qedeshīm*, plural (1 Kings 15.12), operate within this general framework. Seeing that *qadesh* occurs in Deuteronomy 23.17, for this survey, it is intriguing that the adjective *qadosh* is present in the very same text, namely, in 23.14. In order to compare the two terms and distinguish between them, I will now examine how the English versions translate the adjective *qadosh*.

Table 25
QADOSH According to the Versions

Version	Deut. 23.14
CCB	your camp must be sacred
HCSB	your encampments must be holy
JM	your camp must be sacred
JPS	let your camp be holy
NCV	the camp must be holy
NIV	your camp must be holy
NJB	your camp must therefore be a holy place
NKJV	your camp shall be holy
NLT	your camp must be holy
NRSV	your camp must be holy
NWT	your camp must prove to be holy
REB	your camp must be kept holy

The picture painted by the twelve versions in table 25 is unequivocal. All without exception define the meaning of *qadosh* as either 'holy' or, in two cases, 'sacred' (CCB, JM). The NJB turns the word into a noun saying, 'a holy place'. In all cases, *qadosh* refers to the state of hygiene in which the Israelite camp should be kept at all times in deference to the presence of Yhwh. This allows us to conclude that all versions have dealt adequately with the text.

QADESH According to the Versions

If the adjective *qadosh* in Deuteronomy 23.14 alludes to the required purity of the environment surrounding the divine presence, it would seem logical to assume that the derived noun *qadesh* in 23.17, which applies to male persons, also denotes some form of special status, including holiness. On this basis, it may be reasonably inferred that a tentative translation such as 'holy male' or 'consecrated man' would seem acceptable. While *qadesh*, singular, occurs in Deuteronomy 23, in two related cases in 1 Kings the word is in the plural. For the purpose of this survey, it is important to explore how the twelve English versions approach the three occurrences. All are shown in table 26.

Table 26
Translating QADESH and QEDESHĪM

Version	QADESH Deut. 23.17	QEDESHĪM 1 Kings 14.24	QEDESHĪM 1 Kings 15.12
CCB	consecrated homosexual	male cult prostitutes	male cult prostitutes
HCSB	cult prostitute	male shrine prostitutes	male shrine prostitutes

JM	temple-prostitute	temple-prostitutes	temple-prostitutes
JPS	cult prostitute	male prostitutes	male prostitutes
NCV	temple prostitute	male prostitutes	male prostitutes
NIV	shrine prostitute	male shrine prostitutes	male shrine prostitutes
NJB	sacred prostitute	male sacred prostitutes	male prostitutes
NKJV	perverted one	perverted persons	perverted persons
NLT	temple prostitute	male shrine prostitutes	male shrine prostitutes
NRSV	temple prostitute	male temple prostitutes	male temple prostitutes
NWT	temple prostitute	male temple prostitutes	male temple prostitutes
REB	temple prostitute	male prostitutes attached to the shrines	male prostitutes attached to the shrines

Table 26 invites several comments. First, unlike the single words *qadesh* and *qedeshīm* in the original Hebrew, most versions use two, three, or more words for their English renderings. These go all the way from the frequent 'temple prostitute' to the infrequent 'male prostitutes attached to the shrines' (REB). Second, the vast majority seem to be convinced that *qadesh* is associated with prostitution and that some temple cult is involved. Third, two versions go their own separate ways (CCB, NKJV).

A Vertical View

I now wish to read the three columns of table 26 vertically. The first column reflecting Deuteronomy 23.17 presents no fewer than five different renderings of *qadesh*, the most popular being 'temple prostitute' (JM, NCV, NLT, NRSV, NWT, REB) followed by 'cult prostitute' (HCSB, JPS). The options 'shrine prostitute' (NIV) and 'sacred prostitute' (NJB) belong in the same semantic category as the majority. However, the rendering 'consecrated homosexual' suggested by the CCB is so unusual that one wonders why it was chosen. Certainly the adjective 'consecrated' adequately reflects an important aspect of *qadesh*. However, the anachronistic insertion of the modern word 'homosexual' in this context is astonishing. Curiously, this very passage is part of a chapter for which the CCB editors provided the heading 'Act worthily as a consecrated people' (p. 211). Even though the CCB allows some space for footnotes, the glaring contradiction between the overall exhortation to be a 'consecrated people' and the specific, severe indictments of consecrated 'homosexuals' is left unexplained.

Just as surprising is the 'perverted one' introduced by the NKJV. At first sight, it appears deceptively simple, but the role it is being made to play is anything but that. Above all, there is no hint at things sacred or holy. According to the *Oxford Dictionaries*, the verb 'pervert' means to 'distort', 'corrupt', or 'lead (someone) away from what is considered natural or acceptable'. In the sexual realm, the adjective 'perverted' refers to what is 'sexually abnormal and unacceptable'.[96] Applying the latter sense to 'perverted one', one arrives at a person whose sexual conduct is 'abnormal and unacceptable', for whatever reason. However, this information does not explain the context. No one knows

---

[96] oxforddictionaries.com/definition/pervert (2012).

for certain exactly what kind of person the 'perverted one' alludes to. In addition, given a time gap of many centuries, what may have been regarded as perverted in antiquity is not necessarily seen that way in the early twenty-first century (and vice versa).

In summary, three different literary approaches to *qadesh* are present in the first column. The most popular seeks to place *qadesh* in an imaginary ancient context in which a religious and/or cultural phenomenon called temple prostitution is thought to be operating. The second approach (CCB) unhelpfully mixes biblical terminology ('consecrated') with modern sexology ('homosexual'). The third approach represented by the NKJV imports into *qadesh* semantic elements unrelated to the Hebrew *q-d-sh* root. In fact, it might be argued that 'perverted one' is almost the exact opposite of 'consecrated one'. In terms of semantic coherence, the renderings in column 1 are in agreement with each other for the most part. Options such as 'cult prostitute', 'sacred prostitute', 'shrine prostitute', and 'temple prostitute' are roughly interchangeable. The debatable 'consecrated homosexual' and 'perverted one' are exceptions.

As for the other two columns reflecting the plural *qedeshīm* in 1 Kings 14 and 15, a vertical view shows how all versions are consistent given the semantic overlap of their chosen terminology. The two columns are literally identical. Clearly their mutual proximity has enabled the translators to use identical language. Most versions rightly stress the fact that *qedeshīm* are male. However, in addition to the NKJV's 'perverted one', another curious trait emerges. While most versions speak of 'male cult prostitutes' or 'shrine prostitutes', etc.—relating *qedeshīm* to the religious sphere—two versions take a different approach. In their view, *qedeshīm* translates, simply, as 'male prostitutes' (JPS, NCV). Here all sacred connotations have disappeared to be replaced by what one might choose to call 'secular' prostitution. This happens despite a curious fact: both versions acknowledged the religious connotation of *qadesh* in column 1.

A Horizontal View

If table 26 is read horizontally, one can gauge to what degree the versions are using consistent terminology when translating *qadesh*. Two are being consistent: (a) JM whose 'temple-prostitute' appears in all three columns, (b) the problematic 'perverted one' introduced by the NKJV. Another two versions are relatively consistent. The NRSV and the NWT begin with a gender-neutral 'temple prostitute' (Deut. 23) and go on to speak of gender-specific 'male temple prostitutes' (1 Kings). In this sense, there is no contradiction between the columns even though columns 2 and 3 yield more specific gender information than column 1. This is understandable in the light of the context in Deuteronomy 23, which stresses that the subject alluded to is male ('no *son* of Israel should become a *qadesh*'). Similar procedures have been adopted, with minor variations, by the NIV and the NJB.

In many cases, however, the gap widens between *qadesh* in column 1 and *qedeshīm* in columns 2 and 3. The JPS and the NCV are in danger of severing the link almost entirely given the considerable semantic difference between the religious sounding 'cult prostitute' or 'temple prostitute' and the non-religious 'male prostitutes'. The different options suggested by the HCSB, the NLT, and the REB are on somewhat safer ground. The distance between 'cult prostitute' or 'temple prostitute' and 'male shrine prostitute' is acceptable although one wonders why the translators have wanted to introduce these variations.

In table 26, the CCB is by far the most inconsistent version. The single occurrence of 'consecrated homosexual' in Deuteronomy 23 is, from all points of view, so unusual that it hardly fits any context. As already noted, its presence in this text raises questions and provides no answers. While this version wisely refrains from using 'consecrated homosexual' elsewhere, the CCB loses out on consistency. There is no obvious connection between column 1 and the rest. That said, it is fair to point out that 'male cult prostitutes' for *qedeshīm* in 1 Kings is mainstream inasmuch as the CCB interprets the term in the same light as the majority.

In summary, it is evident that the notion of sacred prostitution preoccupies all translators, not only the CCB. It is surprising that no version in table 26 has chosen the most direct and obvious rendering for *qadesh*, which would be something like 'holy male' or 'consecrated one'. This would certainly have been justified semantically given the root meaning of *q-d-sh*.

QEDESHĪM According to the Versions

On another three occasions *qedeshīm*, the plural form of *qadesh*, plays an important role in biblical texts. A close inspection reveals considerable variations among the versions and even within the versions themselves. Table 27 provides an overview. Some options are presented in italics because they are not proper translations but belong to the category of paraphrases.

Table 27
Translating QEDESHĪM

Version	1 Kings 22.46	2 Kings 23.7	Job 36.14
CCB	male cult prostitutes	*effeminate men who dedicated themselves to prostitution*	the reprobate
HCSB	male shrine prostitutes	male shrine prostitutes	male cult prostitutes
JM	temple-prostitutes	sacred prostitutes	men debased by vice
JPS	male prostitutes	male prostitutes	the depraved
NCV	male prostitutes	male prostitutes	*their lives end in disgrace*
NIV	male shrine prostitutes	male shrine prostitutes	male prostitutes of the shrines
NJB	male sacred prostitutes	sacred male prostitutes	male prostitutes of the temple
NKJV	perverted persons	perverted persons	perverted persons
NLT	male shrine prostitutes	male shrine prostitutes	*after wasting their lives in immoral living*
NRSV	male temple prostitutes	male temple prostitutes	*their life ends in shame*
NWT	male temple prostitutes	male temple prostitutes	male temple prostitutes
REB	male prostitutes attached to the shrines	male prostitutes attached to the house of the LORD	male prostitutes

The first column in table 27 holds no major surprises. A solid majority of nine versions has opted for renderings based on the notion of sacred prostitution. However, the JPS and the NCV are exceptions as they leave out any reference to temples or shrines. The 'perverted persons' suggested by the NKJV have been commented upon above.

The second column is more unusual. The number of versions focusing on sacred prostitution has shrunk to eight. Within this majority group, the REB offers a surprise: the male prostitutes mentioned in 2 Kings do not operate in some Canaanite temple but are 'attached to the house of the LORD', i.e. to the main Israelite temple in Jerusalem. Again the JPS, NCV and NKJV provide the same minority options already mentioned. A major novelty in column 2 is introduced by the CCB. According to this version, there is nothing holy about the *qedeshīm*. Rather, they were 'men who dedicated themselves to prostitution'. In addition, readers are informed that these men were 'effeminate'. However, there is nothing in the root *q-d-sh* to indicate prostitution and there is no hint of effeminacy. In all probability, the CCB has looked to the ancient Vulgate version (ca. 400 CE), which in this verse mentions *aediculas effeminatorum*, 'the quarters of the effeminate men'. This problematic choice made by Jerome has set a precedent, which is partly replicated by the CCB. The English rendering offered by the latter is questionable for at least three reasons: (1) it does not reflect the actual nature of *qedeshīm*, (2) it imports several unsubstantiated concepts into the English text, and (3) it raises questions about the overall methodology adopted by the translators.

Even more noteworthy in table 27 is the third column. For this text from the book of Job, the translation options on offer are extremely varied. In fact, no two renderings of *qedeshīm* are identical. Intriguingly, the number of versions that centre their renderings on perceived cult prostitution has gone down to four (HCSB, NIV, NJB, NWT). In addition, this time only one version suggests, plainly, 'male prostitutes'

(REB). An entirely new approach to *qedeshīm* has emerged, including 'the reprobate' (CCB), 'the depraved' (JPS), and 'men debased by vice' (JM). For the first time in this survey, the 'perverted persons' suggested throughout by the NKJV seem to have found like-minded company.

In table 27, the most curious options for Job 36.14 are provided by the three remaining versions: 'after wasting their lives in immoral living' (NLT), 'their life ends in shame' (NRSV), and 'their lives end in disgrace' (NCV). The gap between these options and the rest of column 3 is striking. Further examination of the Hebrew text reveals that the final word of this verse in Job is *baqqedeshīm*, which literally translates as 'in the *qedeshīm*' or 'among the *qedeshīm*'. No other word is present to denote shame, disgrace, or immorality. The Vulgate is of little help here since it simply suggests *inter effeminatos*, 'among effeminate men'. Thus, it remains unclear why the NCV, NLT, and NRSV have chosen to turn a noun referring to specific persons (*qedeshīm*) into abstract concepts taken from the moral sphere. These versions are rivalled by the CCB where there is some semantic link between columns 1 and 2 but, regrettably, none between column 3 and the rest.

If table 27 is read horizontally, it soon becomes clear that a limited number of the versions represented have remained consistent. In fact, only two achieve total consistency through columns 1–3, namely, the NKJV and the NWT. Another three show minor variations (HCSB, NIV, NJB). The REB has provided an inconsistent picture of *qedeshīm*. After mentioning 'shrines' and 'the house of the Lord' in columns 1 and 2, the REB suddenly relinquishes all mention of shrines or temples in column 3 to refer to, simply, 'male prostitutes'. Similarly, the JPS, which tends to prefer 'male prostitutes', forgoes this option in Job 36, replacing it with 'the depraved'.

For its part, JM abandons the usual 'temple-prostitutes' in favour of 'men debased by vice'.[97]

Holiness or Depravity?

In the third column of table 27, the adjectives 'debased', 'depraved', 'immoral', 'perverted', and 'reprobate' operate alongside nouns such as 'shame' and 'disgrace'. Being present in a total of seven versions, such notions are obviously popular among translators for this particular occurrence of *qedeshīm*—despite the fact that the word is the same as in the texts discussed above. Once again, it should be pointed out that nowhere in the HB does *qedeshīm* necessarily have the sense of persons characterized by 'perversion' or 'moral debasement'. Such notions are remote from the meaning of the *q-d-sh* root, which basically refers to sacredness. All we know of the *qedeshīm* is that they seem to belong to some ancient religious institution and that, according to Deuteronomy 23.17, Israelite men are not allowed to join their ranks.

It is also worth noting that Classical Hebrew has other well-known terms capable of expressing moral depravity. Among the more frequent are *beliya⟨al*, 'base' or 'mean' (Deut. 15.9); used as a noun it means 'scoundrel' (1 Sam. 10.27; Judg. 19.22; Job 34.18). Moreover, *rasha⟨* means 'evil' or 'wicked' (Job 34.18; Ps. 3.7). In the books of Psalms and Proverbs, such terminology is abundant along with ⟨*awel*, 'unjust' (Ps. 71.4), *naloz*, 'perverted' (Prov. 3.32) and ⟨*ikkesh*, 'twisted' (Prov. 8.8). In summary, the HB is well provided with derogatory vocabulary. There is no need to include

---

[97] Curiously, the overall tendency towards inconsistency is not exemplified by the Vulgate, which in all three cases translates *qedeshīm* as 'effeminate men' (*effeminatos* or *effeminatorum*).

qedeshīm in that category. In fact, it is astonishing how all English versions to varying degrees have distanced themselves from the sacredness implied by the *q-d-sh* root. In several cases, they have caused it to mean almost exactly the opposite. John Boswell (1980: 99) has pointed out that part of the confusion reigning in modern translations of *qadesh* goes all the way back to the Septuagint, which employed no fewer than six different Greek terms to translate this Hebrew word.

Consecrated

One of the most striking features of these translations of *qadesh* and *qedeshīm* is the way in which the notion of prostitution is taken for granted. If so many translators adopt this approach, there has to be a specific reason that seems convincing enough to produce a solid consensus. The dictionaries provide us with an important clue. For the nouns *qadesh* (m) and *qedeshah* (f), the DBHE explains on page 650 that they reflect 'sacred prostitution'. Similarly, the BDB calls *qadesh* a 'temple-prostitute (man)' while *qedeshah* is reduced to '(woman) = *harlot*' (p. 873). This partly explains the omnipresence of prostitution in the twelve versions surveyed. Undoubtedly this aspect is reinforced by a specific circumstance, namely, the ambiguity inherent in the term *qedeshah*, 'consecrated female' or 'holy woman' (Carmichael 2010: 126), which occurs in three biblical texts. In each passage, a certain amount of doubt surrounds the concrete meaning of *qedeshah*, a noun interpreted by some exegetes as a partial synonym of *zonah*, 'prostitute' (2010: 125). Perhaps this explains the general tendency to associate even the male *qadesh* with prostitution.

Nonetheless, certain obscure details remain unaccounted for. First, one needs to ask why a woman called a *qedeshah* will sometimes be classified by modern exegetes as a 'prostitute', without qualification, and why in other cases she appears as a '*sacred* prostitute'. Table 28 lists the translations offered by the twelve versions of *qedeshah* in Deuteronomy 23.17. For comparative purposes, their renderings of *qadesh* in the same verse are shown in the right-hand column.

Table 28
Comparing QEDESHAH and QADESH

Version	QEDESHAH	QADESH
CCB	consecrated prostitute	consecrated homosexual
HCSB	cult prostitute	cult prostitute
JM	temple-prostitute	temple-prostitute
JPS	cult prostitute	cult prostitute
NCV	temple prostitute	temple prostitute
NIV	shrine prostitute	shrine prostitute
NJB	sacred prostitute	sacred prostitute
NKJV	ritual harlot	perverted one
NLT	temple prostitute	temple prostitute
NRSV	temple prostitute	temple prostitute
NWT	temple prostitute	temple prostitute
REB	temple prostitute	temple prostitute

As already mentioned, the nouns *qedeshah* and *qadesh* denote holiness due to the shared consonantal root *q-d-sh*. Read vertically, column 1 shows that this aspect is adequately reproduced by all versions as far as *qedeshah* is concerned. The presence in the English versions of adjectives such as 'consecrated' (CCB), 'sacred' (NJB), and 'ritual' (NKJV) along with the nouns 'cult' (HCSB, JPS), 'shrine' (NIV), and 'temple' (six versions), ensures a certain focus on the religious dimension. At the same time, all translators seem convinced that the *qedeshah* is to be regarded as a prostitute.

Moving to column 2, at first sight *qadesh* seems to present a similar picture, albeit with some variations. Three adjectives are there, namely, 'consecrated' (CCB), 'sacred' (NJB), and 'perverted' (NKJV). As for the nouns used, there is repetition of 'cult' (HCSB, JPS), 'shrine' (NIV), and 'temple' (six versions). Thus, eleven versions maintain the religious aspect as they move from *qedeshah* to *qadesh*. At the same time, the massive presence in ten versions of 'prostitute' reinforces this particular aspect. It reveals a direct link between the ways in which *qedeshah* and *qadesh* are viewed by the translators.

Two notable exceptions in column 2 merit critical comment. First, the NKJV abandons 'ritual harlot' in favour of 'perverted one'. Thus, it refrains from providing a noun limiting itself, simply, to joining the adjective 'perverted' with the ambiguous, gender-neutral 'one'. The NKJV has failed to create any sense of continuity or consistency between columns 1 and 2. Another unusual option is provided by the CCB. On the one hand, it is to be commended for the repeated occurrence of 'consecrated', which is clearly adequate for both *qedeshah* and *qadesh*. On the other hand, the sudden appearance in column 2 of the word 'homosexual' is confusing. The CCB is the only version to take this curious step.

The multiple references to prostitution in table 28 are significant inasmuch as they may well have a common source. Indeed, a search in earlier versions reveals that the vast majority of those represented are indebted to Jerome's Vulgate. In Deuteronomy 23.17, this famous Bible translation introduces the Latin word *meretrix*, which means 'prostitute'. This allows us to conclude that even today, five hundred years after the Reformation, many Bible translators still seem to use the Vulgate as a point of reference whenever they are unsure of the meaning of the original Hebrew. Strictly speaking there is nothing reprehensible about this method. All translators consult the works of earlier colleagues whenever they struggle with a difficult text. However, modern approaches to *qedeshah* and *qadesh* reveal that the Vulgate is regarded by many as more than a supplementary resource. It is almost being elevated to the status of canonical authority. The fact that Jerome uses *meretrix* for *qedeshah* enables modern readers to see how the biblical text was understood in the early Roman Catholic Church around the year 400 CE. However, there are no compelling reasons for jumping to the conclusion that *qedeshah* would have had exactly that meaning seven, eight, or nine centuries earlier in the land of biblical Israel.

What Does a QEDESHAH Do?

In order to complete this overview of the cultural, literary, and theological roles played by the enigmatic *qedeshah* and *qadesh* in the HB, it is time to explore the specific realm in which the female *qedeshah* operates. Using the English versions as a starting point, table 29 shows their approaches to *qedeshah* in three biblical contexts. *qedeshah*, singular, occurs in Genesis 38 and Deuteronomy 23, whereas Hosea 4.14 contains the plural form *qedeshōth*.

Table 29
Translating QEDESHAH / QEDESHŌTH

Version	Gen. 38.21–22	Deut. 23.17	Hos. 4.14
CCB	prostitute	consecrated prostitute	temple prostitutes
HCSB	cult prostitute	cult prostitute	cult prostitutes
JM	temple-prostitute	temple-prostitute	temple-prostitutes
JPS	a. cult prostitute b. prostitute	cult prostitute	prostitutes
NCV	prostitute	temple prostitute	temple prostitutes
NIV	shrine prostitute	shrine prostitute	shrine prostitutes
NJB	prostitute	sacred prostitute	sacred prostitutes
NKJV	harlot	ritual harlot	ritual harlot
NLT	shrine prostitute	temple prostitute	shrine prostitutes
NRSV	a. temple prostitute b. prostitute	temple prostitute	temple prostitutes
NWT	temple prostitute	temple prostitute	female temple prostitutes
REB	a. temple-prostitute b. (no such) prostitute	temple-prostitute	temple-prostitutes

A vertical glance at column 1 reveals that for Genesis 38.21-22, a number of different renderings of *qedeshah* are suggested: 'prostitute', 'harlot', 'cult prostitute', 'shrine prostitute', and 'temple prostitute'. Several versions provide

- 176 -

two options for the same word (JPS, NRSV, REB). What is characteristic in column 1 is the coexistence of terms for 'secular' prostitution and 'sacred' prostitution. Seven times one finds the 'secular' option 'prostitute' and 'harlot' once. Slightly more frequent are the nine renderings that may be classified as 'sacred'. Two versions make no real distinction between the sacred and secular spheres (JPS, NRSV) unlike the REB, which stresses the sacred connection. In both cases, the overall focus is clearly on prostitution.

In the second column, already commented upon in relation to table 28, all versions define *qedeshah* as a *sacred* (or similar) prostitute. The same tendency is clear in column 3 in regard to the text from Hosea 4. Here eleven versions adhere to options evoking the sacred realm. The JPS, however, hesitates to emphasize the sacred aspect limiting itself to 'prostitutes'. Despite the plural *qedeshōth* in the Hebrew, the NKJV curiously speaks of a single 'ritual harlot'.

In regard to consistency and continuity, the overall picture is far from uniform. As they insert the same term in all slots, the most successful versions are the HCSB, JM, NIV, and REB. Slightly less consistent are the NLT and NWT. Moving down the consistency scale, the next step is occupied by the NCV, NJB, NKJV, and NRSV. At the bottom are the CCB and the JPS. In all cases represented in table 29, the dominant subject continues to be prostitution. All versions seem to be under the spell of the Vulgate, which in the three passages cited offers the noun *meretrix*.

The Veiled Woman

I have commented on the disadvantages attached to the rendering 'prostitute' regarding *qedeshah* and *qadesh*, the main drawback being that this English term places the text at an unwarranted distance from the sacred realm. In order to investigate the origins of the nexus between *qedeshah* and the notion of prostitution, Genesis 38 is particularly relevant. When Jacob's son Judah, elderly and recently widowed, is on his way to a town called Einayim, he spies an anonymous woman wearing a veil sitting by the roadside. He immediately thinks she is a *zonah*, 'prostitute' (Gen. 38.15). This initial impression is confirmed as she readily accepts the commercial deal he proposes. In terms of payment, he promises to send her a kid from the flock as soon as he is able. Judah makes good his promise by sending the animal with Hirah, a Canaanite friend of his (38.1). However, the latter is unable to find the veiled woman. At this point, a subtle change occurs in the wording of the text (38.21–22):

> And [Hirah] asked the locals, 'Where is the *qedeshah* who was at Einayim by the wayside?' But they said, 'No *qedeshah* has been here'. And [Hirah] returned to Judah, and said, 'I have not found her. For the locals said, «No *qedeshah* has been here».'

In table 29, all English versions have chosen to translate *qedeshah* in this passage with a term associated with prostitution. In other words, they clearly regard and treat *zonah* and *qedeshah* as synonyms. This underlying hypothesis is difficult to support. There is no reason to exclude other interpretive avenues. What modern readers do not know is the extent to which the Hebrew narrator and his reading and listening audiences would distinguish between these terms. In addition, nobody knows the exact words pronounced by Judah at the moment he sent his friend Hirah off to meet the unknown woman at Einayim. As often happens in the book of Genesis, the narrator uses his words sparingly, reducing dialogue to a bare minimum. His style may be described as minimalist.[98]

All things considered, the situations described in Genesis 38 may well have been somewhat delicate for an older, respectable man like Judah. It cannot be excluded that he himself is the one who changes the vocabulary. Perhaps he has explicitly sent his friend and colleague to look for a *qedeshah* because having dealings with a woman of this category may have been regarded as respectable in the local community. Perhaps sending a kid to a *qedeshah* was not unusual (cf. the notion of 'sacrifice' in connection with table 30). According to Genesis 38.15-18, Judah thought he slept with a *zonah*. He may be loath to confess this because the latter belonged, in all probability, to a lower social category (Brodie 2001: 364). One of the intriguing details in the drama is precisely the fact that Hirah looks for a *qedeshah* and is told that no such woman has been seen in the area. Perhaps a specific clue is to be sought in the way women dressed. This seems to be hinted at in Genesis 38.13-15, where a veiled Tamar successfully attracts Judah's attention.[99] If a *zonah* dresses according to a particular fashion and a *qedeshah* uses a different style, the townspeople have told Hirah the truth. It is also possible that Tamar, who appears to be well-informed about where her father-in-law is going and when he is travelling, cunningly veils herself a moment

---

[98] According to Cotterell and Turner (1989: 249), the Hebrew Bible has a number of narratives that would be familiar to the intended reading public and/or listening audiences. In other words, the first generation or two of hearers would understand the context to which the story belonged, which enabled them to pick up all subtle hints and allusions. This sharing of data means the style of the text could be condensed.

[99] Kirsten Nielsen (1997: 70) argues that Tamar put on 'the prostitute's veil'. Calum Carmichael (2010: 122-33) interprets Tamar's strategy for having a child as falling within the special role of a Nazirite; cf. Num. 6.2-21.

before Judah appears on the road, and few other passers-by will have noticed her presence.

Prostitutes and Priestesses

Among the texts already discussed, only two passages discriminate between *zonah* and *qedeshah* with a relative amount of certainty: Deuteronomy 23.17–18 and Hosea 4.14. Table 30 shows the renderings of both terms in the Hosea text suggested by the twelve English versions. Given its importance for understanding the overall context, the word 'sacrifice' is highlighted.

Table 30
ZONAH and QEDESHAH in Hosea 4.14

Version	ZONAH	QEDESHAH
CCB	you yourselves go off with harlots	and *sacrifice* with temple prostitutes
HCSB	the men themselves go off with prostitutes	and make *sacrifices* with cult prostitutes
JM	the men themselves go off with harlots	and *sacrifice* with temple-prostitutes
JPS	they themselves turn aside with whores	and *sacrifice* with prostitutes
NCV	the men have sexual relations with prostitutes	and offer *sacrifices* with the temple prostitutes
NIV	the men themselves consort with harlots	and *sacrifice* with shrine prostitutes
NJB	the men themselves are wandering off with whores	and offering *sacrifice* with sacred prostitutes

NKJV	the men themselves go apart with harlots	and offer *sacrifices* with a ritual harlot
NLT	sinning with whores	and shrine prostitutes
NRSV	the men themselves go aside with whores	and *sacrifice* with temple prostitutes
NWT	with the harlots . . . they get off to themselves	with the female temple prostitutes they *sacrifice*
REB	your men resort to whores	and *sacrifice* with temple-prostitutes

In the biblical text, two different activities are being described. Hosea criticizes the men of Israel for (a) going off with a *zonah* and (b) offering sacrifice with a *qedeshah*. All versions rightly translate *zonah* as 'whore', 'harlot' or 'prostitute'. The renderings of *qedeshah* were discussed above in connection with table 29. One version (JPS) treats *zonah* and *qedeshah* as interchangeable calling them, respectively, 'whore' and 'prostitute'. That said, several specific details in table 30 are worthy of attention. First, in this passage, eleven versions recognize a certain link between *qedeshah* and the sphere of religion. This shows in the coupling of 'prostitutes' with references to 'ritual', 'temple', 'shrine', and 'cult'. Second, a remarkable detail in this text by Hosea is the way in which the prophet describes the different jobs or tasks performed by the two groups of women. Thus, a *zonah* is a woman with whom men can have some physical intimacy in private inasmuch as they 'resort' to them, 'go off' or 'go apart' with them. With a *qedeshah*, the relationship is different. This woman clearly represents a religious environment. A key idea is that the men of Israel do not approach a *qedeshah* for sexual pleasure but rather turn to her for ceremonial purposes. Her status enables her to perform sacrifices in public. Eleven versions correctly translate the Hebrew verb *zavach*, 'sacrifice', which occurs frequently in ritual contexts (DBHE p. 215). In table 30, the NLT inexplicably omits this essential detail.

Now, if a *qedeshah* performs ritual duties in Canaanite shrines, it makes sense to assume that she is trained for the job. In the context of Hosea 4.14, no prostitution seems to be involved because that specific activity is covered by a different category of women called *zonah*. Therefore, it would be relevant and desirable for the English versions to suggest a word unrelated to prostitution whenever they deal with *qedeshah*. Unfortunately, no version represented in this study has made this essential choice. However, a wider search through other versions of the Bible shows that a very small handful of translators have successfully distinguished between *zonah* and *qedeshah*. Thus, the *Common English Bible* (CEB) offers an intriguing translation of this verse in Hosea (emphasis added):

> For the men themselves visit prostitutes
> And offer sacrifices with *consecrated workers* at temples.

Here is a version which clearly acknowledges the sacred dimension implied by the Hebrew root *q-d-sh*. Not only does the CEB avoid the general tendency to associate *qedeshah* with cult prostitution, but the term 'consecrated worker' adequately describes the functions assigned to *q-d-sh* women. In this particular passage (and in Deut. 23.17), the CEB is to be commended for a high level of accuracy. Occasional parallels are found in current versions of the Bible published in languages other than English. Among Spanish versions, only the *Nueva Versión Internacional* uses the phrase *sacerdotisas del templo*, 'temple priestesses'. Again this is an adequate reference to the environment in which a *qedeshah* operates. Indeed, the *qedeshah* mentioned by Hosea is a woman who assists the men of Israel wishing to perform sacrifices to Canaanite deities. In other words, what the prophet is denouncing here is the practice of polytheism which, in biblical terms, is classified as 'idolatry'.

If this perspective is applied to Deuteronomy 23.17, a fresh translation of the text becomes possible. In the place of *qedeshah*, one may choose to insert either 'consecrated worker' or 'priestess', which changes the meaning considerably. This also has a bearing on the male *qadesh* as he is likely to belong to the category of 'consecrated workers' or 'priests'. In both cases, this new translation comfortably fits the basic meaning of the *q-d-sh* root.[100] In the HB, the word most frequently used for priests within Israelite religion is *kohen* (Lev. 1.5–17), and for obvious reasons, Deuteronomy 23.17 is not warning the Israelites against turning a son into a *kohen*.[101] Instead, the widespread practices of Canaanite religions are being prohibited, to which *qadesh* and *qedeshah* belong. Thus, the HB makes a clear distinction between *kohen*, 'priest', and *qadesh*, 'consecrated worker'. Given the absence of priestesses in Israelite religion, for the female *qedeshah*, the translation 'priestess' may be helpful. In order to avoid any confusion of terminology between the two distinct realms represented by *kohen* and *qadesh/qedeshah*, for the latter category, it would seem appropriate to use English renderings such as 'consecrated man' for *qadesh* and 'consecrated woman' for *qedeshah*. Likewise, for either term 'consecrated worker' might be suitable.

This clarification illuminates the expulsion of the *qedeshīm* from the Jerusalem temple in 2 Kings 23.7. The narrator

---

[100] Deryn Guest (2006: 140) points out that in ancient texts written in Ugaritic, a Northwest Semitic language related to Classical Hebrew, the root *q-d-sh* applies to 'a class of married, male cultic personnel, mentioned after the category of priests'.
[101] In biblical Israel, the priesthood was reserved for the male descendants of Aaron; cf. Exod. 40.12–15.

explains that they operated next door to the women whose job was to weave garments for the Canaanite goddess Asherah. In other words, this is the universe to which both *qedeshah* and *qadesh* belonged. The alleged link to prostitution is difficult to substantiate. As this section has shown, it seems far more likely that their duties included performing rituals, including sacrifices, associated with some of the religions of the non-Israelite peoples living in ancient Palestine (Helminiak 2000: 120–1; Guest 2006: 140; Stone 2006: 235–6).

The Price of a Dog

According to some exegetes, another element in the Deuteronomical text relates to the subject of homoeroticism in the HB. A literal translation of this passage may read as follows (Deut. 23.18):

> You shall not bring the pay of a whore or the price of a dog into the house of Yhwh your God in fulfilment of any vow, for both are abominable to Yhwh your God.

Most of the Hebrew terms in this text are well-known due to their presence in numerous other biblical contexts. Examples are *zonah*, 'prostitute' (Josh. 2.1), *to'evah*, 'abomination' (Gen. 43.32), and *neder*, 'vow' or 'promise' (Deut. 23.21). The same is true of *kelev*, 'dog'. In the HB, this word generally applies to the four-legged domestic animal (Exod. 22.31; Isa. 56.10). Gordon and Rendsburg (1997: 104) point out that Semitic peoples have a general aversion to dogs. However, the context provided for *kelev* in Deuteronomy 23.18 is not entirely transparent. It is remarkable that the dictionaries treat it as a special case. According to the BDB, *kelev* alludes to a male temple prostitute (p. 477) while the DBHE suggests the rendering *prostituto*, 'male prostitute' (p. 360). Gagnon

(2001: 105) widens the perspective of *kelev* to encompass 'any who engage in homosexual practice' and, even more specifically, 'an expression of particular disgust for the receptive partner in male homosexual intercourse' (p. 156).

However, other exegetes are more cautious (Nissinen 1998: 41; Guest 2006: 141). Peter Pett entertains two hypotheses: (1) that the word 'dog' refers to an animal, (2) that a male cult prostitute is meant. In any case, both are unclean in regard to the Israelite sanctuary.[102] For his part, Heacock (2011: 87 n. 154) notes that in various ancient Near Eastern societies, 'The association of *kelev* with cultic prostitution need not have a pejorative etymology'. Moreover, the detailed investigation of ancient Near Eastern documents by D. W. Thomas (1960: 424–6), in particular a series of letters written in the Akkadian language of Babylonia, raises the likely possibility that *kelev* in Deuteronomy 23 has a different meaning that has been overlooked. Thomas has found several examples in which *kelev* (Akkadian *kalbu*) is used in the specific sense of 'faithful servant' or 'devoted follower'. A concrete literary example shows a suppliant in Mesopotamia addressing the supreme deity Marduk saying, 'Like a little dog, O Marduk, I run behind thee' (p. 424). Given the influence of Akkadian on the world of the HB, Thomas finds a religious connotation for *kelev* likely. In addition, he is reminded of the temple of Astarte at Kition, Cyprus, whose temple servants were known as *kelavīm*, 'dogs' (p. 425). Similarly, Everett Fox (1995: 957 n. 19) suggests that 'dog' is 'clearly a term of derision for a pagan priest'.

More immediately transparent than *kelev* in Deuteronomy 23.18 is 'the pay of a prostitute', and this is due to two factors. First, the connection between the terms *ethnan*, 'remuneration', and *zonah*, 'prostitute', is easy to establish.

---

[102] www.angelfire.com/ultra2/pp2000ad/deuteronomy4.html (2011).

Second, the very same phrase *ethnan zonah* is found in several comparable texts of the HB (Mic. 1.7; Hos. 2.12),[103] all of which provide relevant material for interpretation. What remains to be elucidated in Deuteronomy 23.18 is *mechīr kelev*, 'the price of a dog'. Taken separately, both words occur frequently in the HB. The term *mechīr* is used in commercial transactions, for example in reference to the market price for horses (1 Kings 10.28), for a field or piece of land (1 Kings 21.2; Prov. 27.26), or for a field with oxen (2 Sam. 24.24). In a figurative sense, *mechīr* occurs in several philosophical reflections on the value of wisdom that cannot be measured in monetary terms (Job 28.15; Prov. 17.16). The difficulty with *kelev* and *mechīr* is to establish what they mean when they occur together. The combination *mechīr kelev* only appears in Deuteronomy 23.18. No other biblical context speaks of buying or selling dogs or, for that matter, of any other way in which they may generate income for their owners. Moreover, no scholarly investigation of this curious phrase seems to be available. Hence, the question remains: what exactly is meant by 'the price of a dog', and how should such a phrase be translated?

Translating 'Dog'

Often a glance at the English versions proves helpful. Their proposals for *mechīr kelev* are shown in table 31 in addition to the footnotes provided by six versions.

---

[103] For the book of Hosea, verse numbers are indicated according to the NRSV.

Table 31
Translating MECHĪR KELEV

Version	Deut. 23.18
CCB	the wages of a dog, that is, a homosexual
HCSB	a male prostitute's earnings* *Lit *a dog's*
JM	the wages of a catamite
JPS	the pay of a dog* *i.e. a male prostitute
NCV	a male prostitute's pay
NIV	the earnings of a male prostitute* *Hebrew of a dog
NJB	the earnings of a 'dog'
NKJV	the price of a dog
NLT	the earnings of a prostitute, whether a man* . . . *Hebrew a dog
NRSV	the wages of a male prostitute* *Heb a dog
NWT	the price of a dog* *Gen. 19.5; Rom. 1.27; 1 Tim. 1.10; Rev. 22.15
REB	the pay of a male prostitute

The renderings of *mechīr kelev* in table 31 may be divided into several groups according to their degrees of literalness. The first group translate the Hebrew literally by including the word 'dog': 'the price of a dog' (NKJV, NWT), 'the wages of a dog' (CCB), 'the pay of a dog' (JPS). The NJB might belong to this group even though 'dog' has been placed between single quotation marks. Literal translations such as these have an ancient precedent in the Vulgate whose rendering into Latin of *mechīr kelev* is *pretium canis*, 'the price of a dog'. The English versions in the second group do not mention 'dog' but offer explanatory footnotes that include this word. Four versions point out that 'dog' is found in the original text (HCSB, NIV, NLT, NRSV). The third group of versions omit any reference to this animal: 'the wages of a catamite' (JM), 'a male prostitute's pay' (NCV), and 'the pay of a male prostitute' (REB).

Despite the footnotes in table 31, the meaning of several elements is not obvious. Clearly the nature and context of the 'pay', 'wages', and 'earnings' remain a puzzle. The versions that provide no explanation seem preferable. At least they leave the text with the same amount of opacity as the original. In addition, few readers are likely to understand what the CCB means by saying 'the wages of a dog, that is, a homosexual'. I am mystified on two counts: (a) personally I have never encountered the unfamiliar phrase 'the wages of a dog'; and (b) I am unable to see any connection between the common ancient word *kelev*, 'dog', and the modern term 'homosexual'.

Furthermore, a large group of eight versions seem to agree that *kelev* is to be interpreted as 'male prostitute' (HCSB, JPS, NCV, NIV, NJB, NLT, NRSV, REB). If such is the case, the main problem of the text is certainly solved. In other words, these versions virtually postulate that *qadesh* and *kelev* are synonyms. This hypothesis is perhaps worth advancing if no other solution is available. However, the weakness of a suggested link between *qadesh* and sacred prostitution has been demonstrated above, and there is no compelling evidence indicating that *kelev* should be translated as 'male prostitute'. JM adds to the complexity of this passage by using the arcane phrase 'the wages of a catamite'. The *Oxford Dictionary* explains that a 'catamite' is a 'young boy kept for homosexual practices'.[104] The fact that he is 'kept' may well indicate that this youngster is a slave. If such is the case, there may be a connection with the concept of 'wages' because the boy's social status makes him liable to being sold and bought. However, JM's proposal is flawed in that the word 'catamite' alludes to Greco-Roman culture and is unattested in biblical literature.

For its part, the NWT invites a separate comment. The rendering 'the price of a dog' is certainly literal and could have been left as such. However, the NWT translators obviously felt that more explanation was needed. So in a marginal note, they provided cross-references to four biblical texts, which purportedly explain what 'dog' means. There is nothing wrong about the methodology, which can help readers to gain further insights. The NWT suggests interpreting Deuteronomy 23.18 in the light of four specific biblical passages: Genesis 19.5, Romans 1.27, 1 Timothy 1.10, and Revelation 22.15. However, a search of the first three texts suggested reveals that Genesis 19.5 is part of the story of Sodom and Gomorrah and no part of Genesis 19 alludes to dogs. In Rom. 1.27, the apostle Paul frowns upon certain male–male sexual frenzies (see chapter 14). While Rom. 1.23 suggests that these people worship images of 'four-footed animals', there is no specific mention of dogs in the entire chapter. A list of people with reprehensible vices is found in 1 Timothy 1.10, but again the word 'dogs' is absent. (The NWT's fourth cross-reference to Rev. 22.15 is discussed below.) Thus, the approach adopted by the NWT raises questions of methodology, and ideology as the suggested nexus between Deuteronomy 23 and the other texts is at best tenuous. The explanation seems to be that, within the Christian church, the passages discussed here tend to be quoted, often together, whenever the subject of homosexuality and the Bible is debated. Stated another way,

---

[104] http://oxforddictionaries.com (2012).

the cross-references inserted by the NWT for *kelev* may not be there in order to clarify the ancient meaning of the word. Rather they seem to provide a clear signal to modern readers of the NWT's position in the ongoing Bible/homosexuality controversy.

By comparison, the NWT is more subtle than the CCB. Footnotes and marginal notes are less intrusive than textual enlargement. By grafting the word 'homosexual' onto the biblical text, the CCB has openly manipulated Deuteronomy 23.18. This passage reveals that both versions apparently share the same hermeneutical principle when it comes to presenting 'homosexuality' as undesirable. As mentioned in the introduction to the present book, all Bible readers and interpreters bring assumptions to the book. The striking examples provided by the CCB and the NWT seem to confirm the following reflection by Robert Alter (1992: 131–2):

> Interpreters ineluctably betray texts by translating them . . . into their own conceptual frameworks, epistemological assumptions, and implicit ideological aims . . . No comment on a text is ever innocent . . . Every act of exegesis or even of ostensibly simple glossing is a means of intervening in the text, asserting power over it and over those who would use it.

In summary, so far table 31 has not yielded any new data that would enable exegetes to solve the conundrum of *mechīr kelev*. The obstacle to further progress is clear enough: the HB provides a single occurrence of *mechīr kelev*, which is precisely the verse in Deuteronomy 23 examined on these pages.[105]

---

[105] *The Knox Bible* (1950) proposes the rendering 'the price of a nameless sin' while the *New Life Version* (1969) translates Deut. 23.18 in

Trade, Prostitutes, and Dogs

One may wonder whether there is a conceptual parallel between the fee of a prostitute and the price of a dog. As for *ethnan*, 'pay' or 'fee', the HB uses the word on three occasions: Deuteronomy 23.18, Hosea 2.12, and Micah 1.7, and always in the combination *ethnan zonah*, 'the fee of a prostitute'. Hosea uses *ethnan zonah* as a metaphor for certain material gains obtained by Israelites participating in the religious practices of other peoples. Similarly, Micah employs *ethnan zonah* in a context of images associated with idolatry. In all cases, then, *ethnan* invariably combines with *zonah*. These examples suggest a nexus between the two prophetic passages and the verse in Deuteronomy 23, where *ethnan zonah* is preceded by a prohibition against letting any Israelite join the Canaanite groups described as *qedeshah* or *qadesh*. Concretely the actual payment of the fee may take the form of material goods such as a vineyard or a fig grove (Hos. 2.12), while its nature is left unspecified in Mic. 1.7.

However, *mechīr kelev*, 'the price of a dog', presents a different picture. Taken separately, the noun *mechīr* occurs in a number of commercial contexts. It is often counted in cash, i.e. coins of gold and silver (2 Sam. 24.24; 1 Kings 10.29). As noted, however, the main difficulty persists: no text says anything about dogs being bought or sold. From a different perspective, it is important to point out that, in biblical contexts, the word *kelev* refers to animals (Exod. 11.7; 2 Kings 9.36). Only sporadically does it apply to people, viz. to express humility (2 Sam. 9.8; 2 Kings 8.13) and in reference

---

these terms (emphasis added): 'You must not bring *the pay* of a woman who sells the use of her body or *of a man who does sex sins* into the house of the Lord your God for any promised gift.' In his paraphrased English version entitled *The Message* (1993), for *mechīr kelev* the translator Eugene Peterson creatively suggests 'the earnings of a priest-pimp'.

to insignificant persons (1 Sam. 17.43; 2 Sam. 3.8). The HB rarely uses *kelev* as an insult. A special case is the polemic context of Isaiah 56.10–11 where the prophet poetically castigates some Israelite citizens who ought to be vigilant but behave like sluggish, silent dogs. Others are described as voracious dogs. The passage provides no sexual innuendo.

As noted, the emphasis on prostitution in table 31 is massive. Clearly the translators are influenced by church tradition, including the Vulgate. For this reason, and given the joint presence of *kelev* and *zonah* in Deuteronomy 23.18, the situation depicted in table 31 is perhaps understandable. Many scholars seem to infer that if *zonah* refers to a female prostitute, *kelev* must be the male counterpart. Obviously such a possibility cannot be ruled out entirely. However, it is no more than a hypothesis and, like any other, should not be allowed to exclude alternative avenues of interpretation.

Based on the exploration carried out above, I believe that the phrase *mechīr kelev*, 'the price of a dog', will continue to be opaque, perhaps for years to come. As noted earlier, some scholars have tried to resolve the puzzle by going to Revelation 22.15 in the Second Testament, viewing the 'dogs' mentioned there as cult prostitutes (Gagnon 2001: 105; NWT). However, Thomas Hanks (2000: 255) adopts a different approach. In his analysis, the 'dogs' in Revelation refer to renegade or apostate Christians capable of betraying their brothers and sisters to the imperial authorities. Similarly, Hanks argues that the warning issued by Paul in Philippians 3.2 ('Beware of the dogs') alludes to bad missionaries who distort the Christian message (2000a: 140). For all these reasons, perhaps this is the time when biblical scholars should acknowledge that there is a limit to our comprehension of ancient texts (Groom 2003 p. *xxvi*). Little is known of the specific social, cultural, religious, and economic factors at work in Deuteronomy 23.18. Several hypotheses are available, but given the absence of comparable exegetical material in other parts of the HB, the phrase 'the price of a dog' continues to be obscure. Since paraphrases into 'current' English are likely to lead readers astray, the safest procedure is a literal translation.

Conclusion

This chapter has examined a brief biblical text in the book of Deuteronomy from which *bō* and *shakhav*, prominent Hebrew verbs in the sexual realm, are absent. The short passage in Deuteronomy 23.17–18 hinges on four concepts that are of interest because of the interpretations they have received historically: *qedeshah* (plural *qedeshōth*), 'consecrated woman'; *qadesh* (plural *qedeshīm*), 'consecrated man'; *zonah*, 'prostitute', and *kelev*, 'dog'. Traditionally, and with a significant precedent in the Latin Vulgate, these terms have been interpreted in connection with alleged cult prostitution in the land of Canaan. According to the approach adopted by the vast majority of translators, *qedeshah* and *zonah* are roughly interchangeable. A similar situation is assumed to apply to *qadesh* and *kelev*. Undoubtedly this translation method is simple and enables biblical interpreters to carry out their task without major complications, hence its popularity.

However, the discussion in this chapter has exposed the weak points inherent in the traditional procedure. Some important background issues may not have been properly understood. In Classical Hebrew, sacredness or holiness is expressed by means of the consonantal root *q-d-sh*, which forms the backbone of nouns such as *qedeshah* and *qadesh*. Consequently, translators of Deuteronomy 23 should take the fundamental significance of *q-d-sh* into account. Exegetes who choose to refer to 'consecrated persons' or 'consecrated workers' obtain two major advantages: (a) they provide readers with the core aspect of *qedeshah* and *qadesh*, words with connections to the realm of religion; and (b) they avoid entering into the hermeneutical quagmire attached to the subject of sacred prostitution, a phenomenon which may not have existed in the land of Canaan.

With regard to the puzzle posed by *mechīr kelev*, 'the price of a dog', in Deuteronomy 23.18, two hypotheses are in circulation. According to some scholars, the phrase is a derogatory allusion to sacred prostitution. Others are more cautious suggesting that *kelev* is used, perhaps metaphorically, as a reference to the domestic animal. Several factors seem to favour the latter option. First, in the HB *kelev* tends to refer to actual dogs. Second, whenever the term *mechīr*, 'price', occurs accompanied by an animal, it denotes a commercial transaction. Third, polemic use of *kelev* as a pejorative term for certain types of people is rare. Fourth, insulting language is mostly absent from the lofty, legalistic style that usually characterizes the laws of the HB, including large sections of the books of Exodus, Leviticus, Numbers, and Deuteronomy. Fifth, if one is not entirely sure of what is meant by *mechīr kelev*, the simplest and most honest procedure for translators is to choose a literal rendering such as 'the price of a dog'. The only thing certain is that the lawgiver makes it clear that the money involved is unacceptable as a donation for the temple.

Finally, the alleged homosexual prostitution, which for centuries has been at the forefront in Christian commentaries on *qadesh* and *kelev* in Deuteronomy 23.17–18, is without a solid basis in the biblical texts and contexts examined above. As for *qadesh* and *qedeshah*, Hosea 4.14 makes it seem likely that both terms refer to people performing ritual duties associated with Canaanite, i.e. non-Israelite, religion. They may possibly have priestly rank. At the heart of both words are the consonants *q-d-sh*, which indicate that some form of consecration has taken place.

6

WITH A MALE

Leviticus reveals itself as a modern religion, legislating for justice.

— Mary Douglas [106]

Introduction

In current debates on homoeroticism in the Bible, Leviticus 18.22 is widely quoted. Within the Jewish tradition, this verse is believed to prohibit homoeroticism (Alpert 1989: 62) while scholars from a wide range of backgrounds argue that Leviticus 18.22 and the parallel text in 20.13 are the only explicit references to so-called male homogenital acts in the Hebrew Bible (Heacock 2011: 89). What is more, for centuries interpreters have read Leviticus 18.22 in the light of the destruction of Sodom and Gomorrah in Genesis 19, and vice versa, whereby one text is taken to illustrate the other (Gagnon 2001: 43). Thus, the alleged ban on homoerotic relationships is taken for granted. However, the prominence assigned to Leviticus 18.22 in theological debates in recent years contrasts with the absence of references to this verse in other parts of the Bible and the writings of the early church. In addition, the alleged intertextual link with Genesis 19 is difficult to prove (cf. chapters 7, 10, & 11).

---

[106] Douglas 2000: 2.

Given these contradictions, a careful textual analysis of the original Hebrew text is required. All biblical texts are placed within a context, and the overall context of Leviticus 18.22 is the Hebrew Bible. Scholars often refer to the five books of Moses by the Greek name *Pentateuch* or the Hebrew term *Torah*. The sequence of these books is Genesis, Exodus, Leviticus, Numbers, and Deuteronomy. Strategically placed between Exodus and Numbers, the privileged third position of Leviticus makes it the centrepiece. According to Everett Fox (1995: 502), Leviticus is divided into three major sections: (a) The Sacrificial Cult, chapters 1–10; (b) Ritual Pollution and Purification, chapters 11–17; and (c) Holiness, chapters 18–27. For her part, Mary Douglas (2004: 148–51) confirms the book's basic three-part structure but groups the chapters differently: (a) chapters 1–17, (b) 18–24, and (c) 25–27. In Douglas's view, the literary structure of Leviticus is modelled intentionally on the architecture of the tabernacle (pp. 126–7, 154).

The literary genre of Leviticus is characterized by great complexity. Narratives, cultic rules, and laws are interspersed in such a manner that narratives exemplify laws, and laws follow narratives in an intricate pattern of reciprocity. Past, present, and future are intermingled and explain each other in fruitful ways. One fascinating aspect is the way in which the book takes priestly rules and transmutes some of them for use by the general populace. Dramatic examples are the dietary laws and the area of sexual taboos (Fox 1995: 503). At the same time, it is a paradox that even though the book is often in the narrative mode, it is a narrative virtually without events (Douglas 2004: 128). The language presented by Leviticus is at all times sophisticated, polished, and with poetic qualities as observed by Mary Douglas (p. 175): 'Every verse in Leviticus is another expert cut; each new facet of the diamond reflects the same crystalline structure.'

Given this situation, the book poses huge challenges to translators (Lings 2009: 233). According to Adrian Schenker (2003: 162–3), the single precepts and their systematic order in Leviticus 18 and 20 are 'rationally transparent'. He goes on to explain that this is so because

> Ancient oriental law in general and biblical law in particular follow rational principles, which means that they are logical and can be understood. Hence it is methodologically necessary for the interpretation to look in every case for an intelligible principle, although such seems at first to be lacking.

Encouraged by Schenker's argument and accepting his advice, I plan to apply several tools, particularly semantics and literary analysis, in pursuit of a bona fide approach to Leviticus 18.22. I anticipate that this, combined with examinations of twelve English versions of the Bible, will enable me to establish the 'intelligible principle' governing the role of this biblical verse in its context, endeavouring to reach some understanding within the limited space of the present book.

Restricted Bisexuality

Numerous renderings of Leviticus 18.22 exist, some of which are expressed in so-called everyday language. A representative example is Eugene Peterson's paraphrased version of the Bible called *The Message* (2002), in which Leviticus 18.22 reads as follows:

> Don't have sex with a man as one does with a woman. That is abhorrent.

Perhaps the word 'abhorrent' cannot be classified as 'everyday language', but everything else can. The phrase 'don't have sex' sounds distinctly modern, i.e. late twentieth and early twenty-first century, which matches the stated aims of the translator and the date of publication.[107] Thus, at first sight, this text appears to be precise and 'straightforward'. A closer inspection, however, leads to the discovery that it is fraught with ambiguities.

To gauge some of the complexity of Leviticus 18.22, it may be helpful to carry out an experiment. Imagine presenting these words cited from *The Message* to someone completely unfamiliar with the Bible, asking them how they interpret the text. Before venturing an answer, they are likely to request information about the context. For example, they may ask, 'To whom is this prohibition addressed? To a man or a woman?' The question is relevant because the English wording does not reveal whether the addressee is male or female or whether both genders are included. So in this hypothetical scenario, the person confronted with this text for the first time might justify their need for clarification in the following ways: if the word 'one' refers to a female, the text seems to serve two possible purposes. It may conceivably address a lesbian woman who is allowed to have sex with another woman but not with a man. Viewed from another angle, the addressee might be a bisexual woman allowed to have sex with a man as well as with a woman. However, if she chooses a male partner, there is a limitation: she should not do the same things in bed with him as when sleeping with a woman. Conversely, if the addressee, referred to as 'one', is male, the hypothetical scenario might be visualized as follows: the addressee is (a) a bisexual man given permission to have sex with a woman but not with a man, or (b) a bisexual man allowed to have sex with a woman and a man but facing restrictions when he wishes to have a male partner.

---

[107] *The Message* (1993, 1994, 1995, 1996, 2000, 2001, 2002), NavPress Publishing Group.

Some readers may dismiss this imaginary test as too theoretical or light-hearted, and some may argue that the modern word 'bisexual' is anachronistic. However, the same argument might be levelled against Eugene Peterson's phrase 'don't have sex', which belongs to contemporary English. Viewed from this perspective, 'don't have sex' and 'bisexual' are a good match as both belong to the realm of modernity. In reality, the reasoning behind the experiment carried out above is perfectly logical. Taken at face value, the English words of Leviticus 18.22 according to *The Message* fall into three parts: (1) 'Don't have sex with a man', (2) 'as one does with a woman', and (3) 'that is abhorrent'. Leaving the word 'abhorrent' for later, at this stage I am going to concentrate on (1) and (2). The fundamental part of the prohibition seems to be 'as one does with a woman'. Put differently, this part of the sentence is stated in positive terms, i.e. it is not negated; hence, it implies that it is right and proper for everyone to have sex with a woman. This phrase is connected to the preceding imperative 'don't have sex with a man' by means of the conjunction 'as', which in Standard English means 'to the degree that' or 'in the same way as'. In this manner, a comparison is established along with a caveat. Given the positive ring of 'as one does with a woman' vis-à-vis the negative connotations of 'don't have sex with a man', it might be argued that *The Message* is advocating limited bisexuality for women as well as for men and that, in both cases, sex with a woman is presented as the better, and more complete, option.

Translating Leviticus 18.22

The Bible text examined in this chapter appears in two editions that are intimately connected. The words of Leviticus 18.22 are repeated almost verbatim in Leviticus 20.13, but the latter verse is longer owing to the addendum of the death penalty.

A literal rendering of the original Hebrew text of Leviticus 18.22 and 20.13 would read approximately as follows:

> With (a) male you shall not lie (the) lyings (of a) woman. (An) abomination (is) that.

> (A) man who lies with (a) male (the) lyings (of a) woman, (the) two of them have done (an) abomination. They shall surely die. Their blood (is) upon them.

Below I focus almost exclusively on Leviticus 18.22. To become well acquainted with the passage, and to glean potential insights provided by modern Bible translators, it may be useful to examine the approaches adopted by a representative segment of contemporary English versions. Their renderings are shown in table 32.

Table 32
Translating Lev. 18.22

Version	Leviticus 18.22
CCB	Do not lie with a man as one lies with a woman
HCSB	You are not to sleep with a man as with a woman
JM	You shall not lie with a male as with a female
JPS	Do not lie with a male as one lies with a woman
NCV	You must not have sexual relations with a man as you would a woman
NIV	Do not have sexual relations with a man as one does with a woman
NJB	You will not have intercourse with a man as you would with a woman
NKJV	You shall not lie with a male as with a woman
NLT	Do not practice homosexuality, having sex with another man as with a woman

NRSV	You shall not lie with a male as with a woman
NWT	And you must not lie down with a male the same as you lie down with a woman.
REB	You must not lie with a man as with a woman

These examples reveal that the original text has not caused major problems to the translators. Apparently the lawgiver expresses himself with conciseness and authority about an issue that is not up for debate or negotiation and in no need of further clarification. Yet on closer examination, the same fundamental ambiguities incurred by *The Message* are present throughout table 32. Linked to the noun 'woman', the prepositions 'as' and 'with' establish a parallelism between what happens with a man and what goes on with a woman, except that one part is negated and the other is not. Furthermore, the ambiguous 'you' and 'one' in these English renderings do not reveal who is being addressed, for which reason the original Hebrew must be consulted. The lawgiver is, in fact, quite unambiguous: the addressee of Leviticus 18 is a male Israelite. In other words, the issue of lesbianism or female bisexuality can be ruled out. However, taken at face value, each English version is in agreement with *The Message* in suggesting three points: (a) male bisexuality is a likely target of this prohibition, (b) the prohibition only affects the male side of the equation, and (c) the restriction imposed on male–male intimacy is only partial. Whether or not the translators intended this to be the case is a different matter.

One version in table 32 stands out from the rest. By saying 'do not practise homosexuality', the NLT introduces at least two words that are nowhere to be seen in the Hebrew original: 'practise' and 'homosexuality'. Due to the contemporary tone, these words are easily understandable, but the NLT's choice raises serious questions.[108] First, Classical Hebrew has no equivalent of the word 'homosexuality'. Second, in the light of the recent arrival in world history of the term (1869), its presence is anachronistic in a text that is at least 2300 years old and, possibly, considerably older.[109] Third, 'homosexuality' is applicable to either sex, i.e. it includes lesbian relationships, which are not mentioned. If the original text were limited to 'with a male you shall not lie', and stopped there, the NLT might have a better case, but the sentence is longer. In any case, this version has amplified the beginning of the verse to such an extent that Leviticus 18.22 ceases to deal with ancient concerns and addresses current controversies.[110] Even so, and despite the precision of 'do not practise homosexuality', the NLT slips into the ambiguity incurred by other versions as it goes on to say, 'having sex with another man *as with* a woman' (emphasis added), i.e. indirectly suggesting some limited form of bisexuality.

'As With' Inserted

As noted above, the Hebrew wording is far less transparent than the familiar English phrases suggest (Alpert 1989: 64-5). Indeed, modern English translations of Leviticus 18.22

---

[108] The phrase evokes the title of Robert Gagnon's work *The Bible and Homosexual Practice* (2001).

[109] Keith Sharpe (2011: 20, 26) suggests that the book was composed 3500 years ago, but most scholars provide a later date. For instance, Mary Douglas (2000: 7) is inclined to settle on the post-exilic period around the fifth century BCE.

[110] Cotterell and Turner (1989: 52) caution against the contemporary tendency to import into the text knowledge, which is available to us but which was unavailable to ancient readers or hearers of this text, whereby the text is misrepresented. This is crucial because our current conventions 'predispose us to read predictable meanings into any given text' (p. 55). Sue Groom (2003: xvii) observes that 'what a reader gets out of a text, to a certain extent, depends upon what that reader is looking for in the text'.

are interpretive, not literal (Olyan 1994: 184). Furthermore, the original text is considerably shorter than the English renderings. Seemingly innocent key terms in the translations do not appear in the Hebrew, indicating that the translators have struggled to compensate for perceived lacunae in the biblical text (Lings 2009: 236). In transcription, the Hebrew sentence looks like this:

Weth-zakhar lō tishkav mishkevey ishshah

If Leviticus 18.22 were reduced to *weth-zakhar lō tishkav*, 'with a male you shall not lie', the meaning would be clear. However, this simple translation is not possible because the sentence continues, adding the two Hebrew words *mishkevey ishshah*, which present enormous exegetical difficulties (Jennings 2005: 205). The literal meaning is 'the lyings of a woman' or 'the lyings-down of a wife', given that *ishshah* may be rendered 'woman' or 'wife'. A hypothetical translation of *mishkevey ishshah* is 'a woman's beds' (or 'a wife's beds'). Yet table 32 has shown how English translators generally agree on the way they render *mishkevey ishshah*: 'as with a woman' (HCSB, NKJV, NLT, NRSV, REB), 'as you lie down with a woman' (NWT), 'as one lies with a woman' (CCB, JPS), 'as one does with a woman' (NIV), 'as you would with a woman' (NJB). Presumably, the NCV is meant to be read the same way as the NJB even though the preposition 'with' is absent. One version suggests 'as with a female' (JM). No version has opted for translating *ishshah* as 'wife'.

While the preposition 'as' is present in all English versions, there is no equivalent in the Hebrew text (Stewart 2006: 96). Between the words *tishkav* and *mishkevey*, one would expect the Hebrew prepositional particle *kĕ*, which means 'like' or 'as'. Grammatically it operates as a prefix by attaching itself directly to a noun or an infinitive (DBHE p. 345). In Leviticus 18.22, *kĕ* should then appear directly in front of *mishkevey* being the first syllable of the hypothetical combination *kĕ-mishkevey*. However, *kĕ* is not there. Instead, in the Hebrew text *mishkevey* is placed as the direct object of *tishkav*. In a strictly formal sense, then, it is these 'lyings' that are not to be performed (literally, 'lain' or 'lain down'). Another word worth noticing is the preposition *eth*, 'with', which occurs once in the early part of the sentence preceded by the letter *w* and linked to *zakhar*. Nonetheless, it is common for translators to repeat the English preposition 'with' in front of *ishshah*, as if *eth* appeared there for the second time. In the light of these significant differences between the biblical text and its modern English translations, a question arises: what exactly causes the translators to insert two prepositions into the phrase '*as with* a woman'?

In summary, the first half of Leviticus 18.22 is fairly transparent. There are no major obstacles to understanding the phrase 'and with a male you shall not lie'. However, problems accumulate as soon as the translators approach *mishkevey ishshah*, where the text is amplified by means of the prepositions 'as' and 'with'. It is true that in English 'with' cannot be left on its own in front of the noun 'woman' and so its insertion requires the additional presence of 'as'. It is also true that in this way the translators arrive at an expression that sounds acceptable to English ears. In fact, 'as one lies with a woman' works deceptively well. Perhaps the translators are unaware that the phrase 'as one who lies' exists in Classical Hebrew, concretely in the book of Proverbs (23.34): *kĕshokhev*, 'like one who lies down'. This compound is made up by the particle *kĕ*, 'as' or 'like', and the participle *shokhev*, with two vowel changes, derived from the verb *shakhav*, 'lie down'. By adding *eth*, the three-part sequence of *kĕ* + *shakhav* + *eth* becomes *kĕshokhev eth*, a phrase equivalent to 'as one who lies down with'. If this were present in the Hebrew original of Leviticus 18.22, the matter would have been resolved (Lings 2009: 237–8). However, given its absence, there is no linguistic justification for the common renderings offered by the English versions.

On account of the laconic, almost impenetrable nature of *mishkevey ishshah*, perhaps the translation procedure chosen by so many versions is understandable. In defence of the translators, it has to be admitted that the noun *mishkevey* derives from the verb *shakhav*, and in 18.22, it connects syntactically to *ishshah* in a so-called construct genitive. It is indeed tempting to see *mishkevey ishshah* as the second element in a symmetrical juxtaposition of 'with a male' on the one hand and 'with a woman' on the other. This probably would have been justified if the lawgiver had produced a slightly different text, establishing an obvious semantic balance between *zakhar* and *neqevah*, or between *ish* and *ishshah*, but such is not the case. Clearly a large part of the problem stems from the very strangeness of *mishkevey ishshah*.[111] Its veiled character is augmented by the fact that it features nowhere outside chapters 18 and 20 in Leviticus. In other words, no other biblical text comes to the translator's rescue in terms of providing comparable contexts with similar vocabulary, which is why caution should be observed. Only in the post-biblical Talmud, Daniel Boyarin (1995: 346-7) has noticed a few references to 'a woman's lyings', a phrase taken to connote two kinds of intercourse with a woman, namely, vaginal and anal.

In conclusion, it may be inferred that the translators have faced a difficulty in 18.22 since they have inserted the two words 'as' and 'with', which are not part of the Hebrew text. If the sentence is viewed once again in its original state, and if one takes *mishkevey* 100 percent literally, this rather odd translation of the passage may become the result: 'And

---

[111] Olyan (1994: 180) calls it 'an idiom whose meaning is not at all transparent'.

with a male you shall not lie down the lyings of a woman.' Varying the text a little, another exotic-sounding rendering is this: 'And with a male you shall not lie down a wife's beds.' The outcome is awkward in both cases.[112] Translators adhering to modern English syntax perceive a gap between *tishkav*, 'lie down', and *mishkevey*, 'lyings' or 'beds' and have used 'as with' to fill it. The problem is that the insertion of 'as with' does not really produce a strict prohibition of male to male sex, which contradicts current wisdom. It rather serves to advocate male bisexuality, albeit with restrictions. In summary, the presence of 'as with' is based on an interpretive hypothesis. There is nothing wrong with using a hypothesis when trying to translate a difficult text, but in the case of Leviticus 18.22, the logical implications of the hypothesis commonly applied have never really been examined in any detail. Apparently its elevation to the status of absolute truth has kept exegetes from seeking other avenues of interpretation.

Male/Man, Woman/Wife

To shed light on the complex structure of Leviticus 18.22, further analysis of *weth-zakhar lō tishkav mishkevey ishshah* has to be carried out. As noted, the occurrence of the verb *shakhav* in the form of *tishkav*, 'you will lie down', joined by the preposition *eth*, 'with', is a strong indicator that 'lying down with a male' belongs in the sexual realm. If this sentence were not followed in the Hebrew text by *mishkevey ishshah*, the meaning would be clear: 'do not lie down with a male person', which in modern English might be paraphrased as

---

[112] Everett Fox (1995: 497) mentions the numerous technical terms in Leviticus which are difficult to render accurately into modern English. He finds awkward language impossible to avoid (p. 498).

'male homosexuality is not allowed'.[113] However, this simple solution is blocked by several literary subtleties present in the Hebrew of Leviticus 18.22. For instance, and somewhat unusually, the prepositional phrase *weth-zakhar*, 'and with a male', receives special emphasis due to its fronted position.

Two groups of translations are distinguishable in table 32 when it comes to their use of the nouns 'male' and 'man' for *zakhar*. Where the English term 'man' appears, readers with some knowledge of Hebrew may be forgiven for assuming that the original text in this place has the common Hebrew word for 'man', which is *īsh*. It has two meanings, namely, 'man' in the biological sense and 'husband'. However, the Hebrew writer is not using *īsh* but rather the less frequent noun *zakhar*, whose basic meaning is 'male' in reference to human beings (Gen. 1.27) and animals (Lev. 3.1). On this basis, the majority of seven versions using 'man' in table 32 is being imprecise while the five versions saying 'male' must be commended for their accuracy (JM, JPS, NKJV, NRSV, NWT).

The question of whether an English version of the Bible prefers 'male' or 'man' in Leviticus 18.22 may not seem important to all readers. Yet it is worth pointing out that using one term rather than another makes a difference because it may well have a bearing on our interpretation of the text. While a boy is male from birth, and 'male' refers to any member of the male sex from underage boys to hundred-year-olds, in most cultures, he will have to wait until adulthood to be called a man. For this reason, it is fair to say that the seven versions that chose the translation 'man' fail to do the Hebrew term *zakhar* full justice. A more

---

[113] David Stewart (2006: 97) observes that, if the intent was to condemn male homosexuality, the lawgiver would not need to write more than 'You shall not lie with a male'.

precise term is in order, for which reason 'male' is preferable (Lings 2009: 235). In table 32, one version has incurred a similar problem with respect to the noun *ishshah*. Instead of rendering it literally as either 'woman' or 'wife', JM has chosen 'female'. This is inaccurate because the matching Hebrew word would be *neqevah* (Gen. 1.27).[114]

Clearly one of the difficulties inherent in Leviticus 18.22 is the coexistence in one sentence of *zakhar*, 'male', and *ishshah*, 'woman' or 'wife'. Just as *ishshah* often appears next to *ish*, 'man' (Gen. 2.24) or 'husband' (Gen. 24.16), it would seem logical for *zakhar* to be accompanied by *neqevah*, 'female', as in the creation story (Gen. 1.27). Had this been the case in Leviticus 18.22, a balance would be established between the masculine and the feminine from a syntactic, literary, and ideological point of view. However, the Hebrew lawgiver does not speak of *mishkevey neqevah*, 'the lyings of a female'. Instead one is confronted with the surprising juxtaposition of *zakhar* and *ishshah*, two nouns that do not belong in the same categories and are not normally seen together. This odd situation may again be a reminder of the importance of paying attention to unusual details. Given the polished nature of the language and the elegance of the literary structure of the whole book (Douglas 2000: 7), the very fact that *zakhar* and *ishshah* interact seems to suggest that something uncommon, or noteworthy, is happening. Perhaps by focusing intently on this textual challenge, one may eventually be able to unlock part of the mystery.

---

[114] In a few cases, *ishshah* translates as 'female' but only accompanied by *ish* in the sense of 'male'. In Genesis 7, YHWH tells Noah to enter the ark taking various birds and four-legged animals with him. For each species, a male and a female have to be selected. In one part of the text, each pair is made up by *zakhar* and *neqevah* (7.3, 9, 16). In 7.2, the narrator uses *ish* in the sense of 'a male' along with *ishshah* in the genitive form of *ishtō*, 'his (female) mate'.

In summary, two Hebrew nouns belong on the male side of the gender divide, namely, *īsh*, 'man' or 'husband', and *zakhar*, 'male'.[115] Similarly, on the female side two terms are in regular use: *ishshah*, 'woman' or 'wife', and *neqevah*, 'female'. A closer inspection of Leviticus 18 reveals that *ishshah* plays two roles throughout the text. In five verses, it translates as 'woman' (18.17–19, 22, 23), while in six verses a better rendering is 'wife' (8, 11, 14–16, 20). Thus, the sense of 'wife' is salient in the context. Obviously Classical Hebrew allows for easy coexistence of the two senses 'woman' and 'wife' as well as smooth transition between their usages (Lings 2009: 242). In a text that primarily focuses on the issue of incest (18.6–16), the word 'woman' can refer to any adult member of the female sex while 'wife' is necessarily defined in relation to a man. In the light of this information, a preliminary conclusion may be drawn. Perhaps the connotation of 'wife' that repeatedly surrounds *ishshah* in Leviticus 18 offers an unexplored clue for the intractable phrase *mishkevey ishshah*.

Lyings or Beds

Examining the word *mishkevey* on its own, one is able to establish that it is a noun in the plural. It is important to note that this plural form is a rarity. By comparison the singular noun *mishkav* is frequent in numerous books of the Bible as it generally means 'bed' (Lev. 15.4-5; 2 Sam. 4.11). At the same time, owing to its affinity with the verb *shakhav*, *mishkav* also has the sense of 'the act of lying down'. In the light of this information, the literal sense in English of the plural *mishkevey* becomes either 'lyings', 'acts of lying down', or 'beds'. The situation in Leviticus 18.22 is confusing because

---

[115] A third noun denoting 'adult human male' is *gever*; cf. Exod. 10.11; Num. 24.15; Deut. 22.5.

there is no telling exactly which 'beds' or 'acts of lying down' the lawgiver has in mind. All one can see is that *mishkevey* appears in conjunction with the noun *ishshah* because the two words are grammatically linked. This is indicated by the final syllable-*ey* in *mishkevey*, which reveals its genitive attachment to *ishshah*. The very oddity of the pairing of these two words suggests that something unusual may be intended, or that a significant point is being made (Lings 2009: 238-9).

With no immediate solution to the puzzle in sight, a possible way forward may be provided by other writings in the HB. In some cases, *mishkav*, singular, takes on an unmistakably sexual sense. This occurs from a woman's perspective in Numbers 31.18, 35, in the combination *mishkav zakhar*. The text speaks of women who have not known 'the lying/bed of a male' (cf. Judg. 21.11-12).[116] In the light of the fierce biblical restrictions on sexual expression for women outside marriage,[117] I interpret this phrase as applicable to young, betrothed, but as yet unmarried, women who have not had their first sexual experience. In practice, they have not yet celebrated their wedding night (Lings 2009: 239).[118] Thus, the singular phrase *mishkav zakhar* appears to operate in contexts associated with legitimate marriage (Milgrom 2000: 1539, 1569).

The next step is to search the HB for occurrences of the plural word *mishkevey* outside the book of Leviticus. One example is found in the book of Genesis.[119] In 49.4, the moribund

---

[116] See also comments by Olyan 1994: 184; Nissinen, 1998: 44, 98; Helminiak 2000: 59; Walsh 2001: 205; Greenberg 2004: 80; Stewart 2006: 97.

[117] Lev. 21.13-14; Num. 5.12-31; Deut. 22.13-29. See also Lipka 2006: 89, 208 and p. 205: 'Young women in biblical Israel were expected to marry as virgins'.

[118] For a discussion of Hebrew terminology related to young women of marriageable age, see Lipka 2006: 77-80.

[119] An article posted at homepage.ntlworld.com/pharseas.world/Leviticus.html (2012) claims that the word 'mishkevey' occurs

patriarch Jacob is speaking to his eldest son Reuben, characterizing a specific act committed in the past by his son in the following terms (my translation, emphasis added):

> Because you mounted your father's *sleeping places*
> Then you profaned
> My *bed* he mounted.

With these words, Jacob alludes to the irreverence shown to him when Reuben slept with Bilhah, one of Jacob's two concubines (Gen. 35.22). Stylistically it is noteworthy that Jacob begins by speaking to Reuben in the second person 'you', after which he switches to third person 'he' to address Reuben's brothers (Lings 2009: 239). If one takes a look at the two italicized nouns in this fragment, it seems perfectly normal that the word *bed* should be in the singular. Incidentally, the original does not have *mishkav* in this place but rather the noun *yatsuaʽ*, which means 'bed', 'couch', or 'sleeping mat'. As far as *sleeping places* is concerned, I have deliberately chosen this plural term to draw attention to the cryptic *mishkevey*, which appears in this position. This is indeed the same plural variant as the one found in Leviticus 18.22 (Lings 2009: 241).

In other words, in this brief poetic passage of Genesis, the Hebrew writer uses two different words. Since one is singular and the other plural, this may mean that they are not entirely interchangeable. One option could be to view the singular *yatsuaʽ* as a reference to the physical location where the sexual act took place, while the plural *mishkevey* perhaps focuses on the illicit nature of Reuben's liaison with Bilhah (Milgrom 2000: 1569; Stewart 2006: 97). Jacob's 'sleeping places', plural,

---

forty-six times in the Hebrew Bible. It is problematic that the unnamed author of an otherwise well-argued essay does not distinguish between the frequent *mishkav*, singular, and the rare *mishkevey*, plural, which occurs twice.

were his private territory invaded by a rebellious son. The BDB (p. 1012) acknowledges the significance of the plural in Genesis 49.4, calling it 'a place of copulation'. In spite of this potentially significant difference between singular and plural, the vast majority of Bible translators treat the plural noun *mishkevey* in Genesis 49.4 as if it were singular, i.e. identical to the singular *mishkav* and interchangeable with *yatsuaʿ*. Regrettably such simplification is likely to erase crucial semantic nuances (Lings 2009: 240).[120]

Thus, the scholars behind most modern translations of Leviticus 18.22 and Genesis 49.4 seem reluctant to face the special implications suggested by the plural *mishkevey*.[121] Unfortunately, the outcome contrasts with the experience of those exegetes who find that, in many cases, the most fruitful key to unlocking the mystery is located at the heart of the very difficulty causing the headache,[122] a procedure that requires patience and perseverance.[123]

---

[120] Sue Groom (2003: 62) comments, 'An essential part of lexicography is observation of the oppositions between words, the points at which they become contrasted, where it is possible to discover why one word has been used rather than another, and where they may differ in connotation and overtone.'

[121] Victor Hamilton (1995: 645 n. 6) quotes the *Gesenius Hebrew Grammar* (1910), which calls *mishkevey* 'a plural of local extension to denote localities in general' and allows for the possibility that the reference is to a double bed. Robert Alter (1996: 293) translates *mishkevey* as 'the place where your father lay'. In a footnote he explains, 'The plural form used . . . has an explicitly sexual connotation, whereas the singular *mishkav* can also mean simply the place where one sleeps.'

[122] Under the heading 'Text Linguistics', similar issues are discussed by Sue Groom (2003: 131), who regards 'text linguistics' and 'discourse analysis' as practically equivalent.

[123] Gareth Moore (2003: 65) points out that the rationale behind biblical condemnations may have been obvious to contemporaries. Given the time gap of several millennia, 'we have to guess at the explanation, as intelligently as we can, by looking around the text concerned at other texts which will illuminate for us the culture and the mentality in which the condemnation had its original home.' See also Douglas

Abomination

The final part of Leviticus 18.22 is a very short statement encompassing two words: *toʿevah hī*, literally, '(an) abomination that (is)'. Table 33 shows the renderings chosen by the English versions. Emphasis is added to words with no equivalent in the original Hebrew.

Table 33
Translating TOʿEVAH HĪ

Versions	**TOʿEVAH HĪ, Lev. 18.22**
CCB	It is an abomination.
HCSB	It is detestable.
JM	That would be loathsome.
JPS	It is an abhorrence.
NCV	That is a hateful *sin*.
NIV	That is detestable.
NJB	That is a hateful thing.
NKJV	It is an abomination.
NLT	It is a detestable *sin*.
NRSV	It is an abomination.
NWT	It is a detestable thing.
REB	That is an abomination.

Among the versions, there seems to be broad agreement on the general meaning of 'abomination' (CCB, NKJV, NRSV, REB) and 'abhorrence' (JPS), notions sometimes expressed as 'detestable thing' (NWT) or 'hateful thing' (NJB). Some

---

(2000: 123): 'Leviticus is full of phrases ambiguous to us now but which make sense if restored to an original context of oracles and retaliatory justice'; cf. Groom 2003: 136.

versions turn the noun into an adjective such as 'detestable' (HCSB, NIV) and 'loathsome' (JM). However, two versions amplify the text by adding the noun 'sin' as in 'hateful sin' (NCV) and 'detestable sin' (NLT). These renderings erroneously suggest the presence in the Hebrew text of the word for 'sin', namely, the noun *chattaath* (Gen. 18.20).

Among commentators, it is not unusual to come across a polemic argument about the noun *toʻevah*. The fact that it is often translated as 'abomination' in Leviticus 18.22 has caused some to draw the conclusion that the offence prohibited in this verse is judged more severely than the other transgressions listed in Leviticus 18 (Gagnon 2001: 83, 113). Some support for this view is offered by Weston Fields (1997: 174 n. 62), but this reasoning has little basis in the Bible. While it is true that *toʻevah* provides a label for the transgression discussed in 18.22, several translations are available. Daniel Helminiak (2000: 56–7) renders *toʻevah* as 'uncleanness' and 'taboo' (p. 64) while Hilary Lipka (2006: 253) regards the use of *toʻevah* in Leviticus 18 and 20 as an indicator of a transgression of a religious boundary. Rebecca Alpert (1989: 68) argues that the word is 'a technical term used to refer to a forbidden idolatrous act'. For his part, Martti Nissinen (1998: 39, 44) primarily views *toʻevah* in connection with illicit issues involving gender bending. To Saul Olyan (1994: 180 n. 3), *toʻevah* suggests 'the violation of a socially constructed boundary' or the 'undermining of what is conventional', viewed as established by the deity. Steven Greenberg (2004: 81) points to the fact that, in Genesis 43.32 and 46.34, *toʻevah* refers to Israelite customs that are repugnant to the Egyptians. David Stewart (2006: 83, 99) observes that *toʻevah* is widely used in the Hebrew Bible and covers a number of crimes, including unjust weights and measures (Deut. 25.16).

In other words, no scholarly consensus exists as to the exact significance of *to'evah hī* in Leviticus 18.22. However, the text itself provides several clues. It should not be overlooked that a number of disapproving terms are used at different points throughout Leviticus 18 (Lings 2009: 248). For example, in 18.17, the word *zimmah*, 'depravity', is introduced, followed in 18.23 by *tevel*, a noun referring to bestiality. Bible translators are at a loss when it comes to rendering *tevel*. Several have suggested 'perversion', including the HCSB, JPS, NIV, NKJV, NRSV, with others opting for 'a perverse act' (NLT), 'it is not natural (NCV), 'a violation of nature' (NJB, REB), and 'a violation of what is natural' (NWT). However, several scholars have pointed out that the basic meaning of *tevel* is 'confusion' or 'mixing',[124] suggesting that the most accurate rendering would perhaps be '(reprehensible) confusion'.

Furthermore, towards the end of the chapter Leviticus, 18.26 uses the heading 'abominations', in Hebrew *to'evoth* (plural of *to'evah*), to summarize all the indicted acts previously mentioned: 'The inhabitants of the land . . . committed all of these abominations' (18.27, NRSV; cf. Jordan 1997: 31). This wider sense of *to'evah* is emphasized in 18.26, 27, 29, 30 (Milgrom 2000: 1569). For this reason, it makes little sense to ascribe to *to'evah* a particular degree of repulsiveness with regard to some acts more than others (Lings 2009: 248). In Leviticus 18, the primary objective of the Hebrew lawgiver is to draw a line of purity around the family circle in order to keep its sexual life free of offensive acts. More generally, *to'evah* covers a range of abominable acts that makes the men and women of Israel stray from the way marked out for them by Y<small>HWH</small>, particularly idolatrous practices (Deut. 18.9–12; Ezek. 16.1, 22).

---

[124] Countryman 1989: 26; Olyan 1994: 200, 202; Lipka 2006: 53 n. 43, 61; Stewart 2006: 82.

Early Interpretations of Leviticus 18.22

As noted above, it is clear that contemporary English versions of the Bible have difficulties in dealing with Leviticus 18.22, particularly the enigmatic phrase *mishkevey ishshah*. I now wish to see whether this problem is recent or, perhaps, has existed for centuries. The earliest Greek translation of this verse is found in the Septuagint (ca. 200 BCE): *kai meta arsenos ou koimēthēsē koitēn gynaikos*, literally 'and with a male you shall not lie a woman's bed'. Evidently the translator has kept close to the Hebrew original, producing a Greek version that is almost word for word. The only exception is *koitēn*, 'bed', which is singular unlike the Hebrew plural *mishkevey*.

Outside the Bible, an early Hellenistic interpretation of Leviticus 18.22 is offered by Philo of Alexandria (first century CE), a Jewish philosopher writing in Greek and who is familiar with the Septuagint. Philo is convinced that the Levitical prohibition applies to pederasty, i.e. sexual relationships between 'active' adult men and 'passive' teenage boys (Nissinen 1998: 95; Moore 2003: 109). Philo is disgusted on two counts. On the one hand, he strongly dislikes the 'feminized' appearance adopted by some of the boy lovers he observes in Alexandria (Jennings 2005: 209-10), characterizing their demeanour as being 'against nature'. On the other hand, he is adamantly opposed to the 'squandering' of semen involved in anal intercourse because, in his view, male seed is meant for procreation only. This is so much the case that Philo even chastises men who knowingly marry infertile women. In his view, such unions are a form of debauchery motivated by lewdness, which goes against God (Countryman 1989: 60-1; Nissinen 1998: 96).

In the Christian tradition, by contrast, it is remarkable that the early church pays little attention to Leviticus 18.22. Not until the end of the fourth century is the verse linked explicitly to the story of Sodom and Gomorrah whereby both texts are taken as references to illicit male to male sex. This occurs in the Greek document *Apostolic Constitutions* (Carden 2004: 125).[125] The Latin Vulgate, which appears around the year 400 CE, offers this Latin rendition of Leviticus 18.22: *cum masculo non commisceberis coitu femineo*; literally 'with a male you shall not unite ('mingle') in womanish intercourse'. Reflecting the Hebrew *mishkevey ishshah*, the Latin phrase *coitu femineo* is of special interest because the noun *coitus* (*coitu*), 'collecting', 'fitting together' or 'sexual intercourse', is singular, and so is the adjective *femineus* (*femineo*), 'feminine', 'effeminate', or 'womanish'. With *femineo*, Jerome rightly focuses on the female gender but, at the same time, he has lost the sense of 'wife' also implied by the Hebrew noun *ishshah*.[126] Like the Septuagint before him, Jerome has clearly struggled to produce a suitable rendering of the arcane *mishkevey ishshah*.

In a highly polemic, anti-homoerotic context, Leviticus 18.22 is cited in the eleventh century in a work by Peter Damian (1982: 33) and in the twelfth century in the writings of Peter of Poitiers (Carden 2004: 166) and Peter Cantor (p. 182). In other words, the tendency to attribute to Leviticus 18.22 and 20.13 a strict prohibition of homoerotic relationships does not become mainstream until the Middle Ages, at least in Christian circles.[127] Like the Septuagint and Jerome, early English translators of the Bible have wrestled with *mishkevey ishshah*. Based on the Vulgate, John Wycliffe's edition (1382) suggests the following, elaborate rendering in two versions:

---

[125] www.newadvent.org/cathen/01636a.htm (2012).
[126] In Latin, the common word for 'woman' is *mulier* while 'wife' is *uxor*.
[127] Saul Olyan (1994) and Daniel Boyarin (1995) provide detailed discussions of early Jewish interpretations.

> Thou shalt not be meddled, [(or) mingled,] with a man, by lechery of a woman, for it is abomination. (Thou shalt not be mixed together with a man, like in fleshly coupling with a woman, for it is an abomination.)

Several instances of influence from the Vulgate on Wycliffe's English are traceable, notably 'meddled', 'mingled', and 'mixed' for the Latin *commisceberis* and 'lechery' or 'fleshly coupling' for *coitus*. Significantly, Wycliffe has interpreted the Latin adjective *femineo* in two ways: 'of a woman' and 'with a woman'. Intriguingly, he offers two rather different renderings of *coitu femineo*: 'by lechery of a woman' and 'like in fleshly coupling with a woman'. Understandably, the notion of 'wife' — not implied by *femineo* — is absent and, significantly, the presence of the preposition 'with' in his text sets a precedent for subsequent English versions. William Tyndale's English version of the Hebrew Pentateuch appears in 1530, producing this translation of Leviticus 18.22:

> Thou shalt not lie with mankind as with womankind, for that is abomination.

Two features are noticeable in Tyndale's wording: (a) 'mankind' and 'womankind' are presented as parallels and (b) the prepositions 'as with' appear jointly. Thus, this seems to be the historical starting point of the popular trend among today's Bible translators who deploy the prepositions 'as with' as an alleged equivalent of the Hebrew noun *mishkevey*, 'lyings' or 'beds'. Indeed, 'as with' is the preferred choice of successive English versions, including Miles Coverdale (1535), the Bishops' Bible (1568) and the King James Version (1611). The Geneva Bible (1587) has suggested the variant 'as one lies with', which remains popular with translators as shown in table 32 (CCB, JPS, NCV, NIV, NJB, NWT).

Leviticus and Tradition

Earlier in this chapter, an imaginary interpreter unfamiliar with the Bible was asked how they understood Leviticus 18.22 as presented by *The Message*. It is intriguing to discover that the improvised interpretation offered by that interpreter, based on simple logic, is nowhere to be found in commentaries produced by biblical scholars in the real world. Despite the ambiguities embedded in the phrases 'as with' and 'as one (who) lies with', no commentator today discusses bisexuality in the context of Leviticus 18.22. Instead, this verse is believed to provide a universally valid prohibition of homoerotic relationships. Clearly the hermeneutical tradition initiated by the *Apostolic Constitutions* (late fourth century) and consolidated by medieval theologians such as Peter Damian (eleventh century) has proved to be durable.

A prominent, traditionalist voice is that of Robert Gagnon (2001). His view is that, according to Leviticus, all homoerotic relationships are condemned in all circumstances. Gagnon initially leaves the word 'homosexuality' undefined (p. 25), specifying it later as 'same-sex intercourse' (p. 26). Many times he speaks of 'homosexual behaviour' (pp. 31, 35, 37-8), 'homosexual practice' (pp. 29-30, 43-4, 55-6), 'homosexual intercourse' (pp. 43, 47, 55-6) and 'same-sex intercourse' (pp. 30, 37, 40, 45, 55-6), generally without clarifying whether the term refers to an activity performed by males, females, or both. Hence, homoerotic relationships involving both sexes seem to be included. Rather late in his work, Gagnon explicitly focuses on 'same-sex male intercourse' (p. 103) and 'same-sex intercourse between males' (p. 113). However, such precision appears to be accidental, and throughout his book, the more general terminology prevails. Specifically in connection with Leviticus 18, Gagnon argues (p. 56):

> The level at which the Levitical laws stigmatize and criminalize all homosexual intercourse . . . goes far beyond anything else currently known in the ancient Near East.

In other words, Gagnon is saying that no culture in antiquity condemned homoerotic interaction as much as the Israelites did. This observation is correct—provided that Leviticus actually does stigmatize and criminalize 'all homosexual intercourse'. In Gagnon's view, Leviticus 18.22 refers to 'lying with a man as though lying with a woman' (p. 75). He takes this to mean 'to treat a man as though his masculine identity counted for nothing', i.e. 'as though he were not a man but a woman'. Apart from this reflection, Gagnon refrains from engaging in any semantic or literary analysis. His opinion seems to be based on the assumption that all exegetical issues posed by the original Hebrew text in Leviticus 18.22 have been clarified.[128]

In recent decades, however, the unwavering consensus of past generations with regard to the sinfulness of homoerotic relationships is being replaced by more cautious approaches.[129] A representative Jewish voice is that of Saul Olyan (1994). In his view, it is far from clear what specific act Leviticus 18.22 is addressing (p. 179). The language is certainly opaque (pp. 179–80), and Olyan observes that many biblical scholars seem to ignore the unique exegetical difficulties (p. 181). As a result, commentators disagree among themselves. Some argue that Leviticus prohibits the wasting of male seed in non-procreative acts (p. 198)

---

[128] Two examples of a shared exegesis are Robert Gagnon (2001: 111–20) and Rebecca Alpert (1989: 62–70). However, they differ considerably in their interpretations of the wider significance of Lev. 18.22.

[129] Gareth Moore (2003: 66–8) draws attention to the complexity of the biblical material, reminding readers that the modern concept of 'homosexual' has no equivalent in the Bible.

while others focus specifically on anal penetration. In the latter context, Olyan is prepared to consider that a special concern of Leviticus may be the impure commingling of two substances such as semen and excrement in the body of the receptive partner (p. 203). Moreover, Olyan has undertaken a wide search for parallels through the literature of the ancient Greco-Roman and Assyrian worlds. He finishes by settling for anal penetration believing that Leviticus 18.22 specifically addresses the action performed by the insertive partner (pp. 199, 204–5). At the same time, Olyan explicitly refrains from exploring other interpretive avenues suggested by the text such as incest, bestiality, and adultery (p. 183).

Similar conclusions are reached by Daniel Boyarin (1995). His approach is grounded in the Talmud literature produced in the early centuries CE by the Jewish community of Babylon. According to Boyarin, the Talmud is in no doubt that what is outlawed in Leviticus 18.22 is male–male anal intercourse. He finds a parallel in Talmudic literature where the term for male–female anal intercourse is 'penetration not according to her way' (1995: 346). At the same time, he makes it clear that non-penetrative manifestations of homoerotic intimacy are of no concern to Leviticus (pp. 336, 339). Boyarin is inclined to seek the justification of Leviticus 18.22 in the ancient Israelite aversion to cross-dressing expressed in Deuteronomy 22.5 (1995: 342). He finds an intriguing structural parallelism between these two texts, namely, 'a woman's garments' in Deuteronomy 22.5 vis-à-vis 'a woman's lyings' in Leviticus 18.22. In this context, Boyarin argues that male–male anal penetration generates a specific problem in the androcentric universe of the Pentateuch because this sexual act is tantamount to a gender role violation. When the receptive male is downgraded to the social level of a woman (1995: 341), the act violates the ancient male/female dichotomy (pp. 342–3).

Several additional clues to Leviticus 18.22 have been suggested over the years. It is often argued that the lawgiver is condemning Canaanite cult prostitution, with a possible reference to Deuteronomy 23.18. However, this argument has been challenged by many scholars. For instance, Martti Nissinen (1998: 41) has come across too much 'speculation based on circumstantial evidence', an issue discussed in the present book's chapter 5.

Continuing Debate

Despite, and perhaps because of, the many centuries gone by since its composition, the exegetical debate about Leviticus 18.22 continues unabated at the present time. The arguments adduced by Olyan, Boyarin, Gagnon, and others, keep being subjected to critical examination. Thus, Jerome Walsh (2001) begins his article on Leviticus 18.22 with a discussion of Saul Olyan's work. He finds the latter's semantic analysis convincing (p. 201) and shares his understanding of the text as a metaphor of anal penetration (p. 204). However, Walsh disagrees with the main conclusions drawn by both Olyan and Boyarin. In his view, several elements in the Levitical text reveal that the prohibition does not reflect any concern about undue mixing of male and female categories. Similarly, Walsh does not share the idea that 18.22 addresses the Israelite male who plays the 'active' role as penetrator in anal intercourse. According to Walsh, the opposite is the case, i.e. Israelite men are being warned against accepting the 'passive' or 'receptive' role (pp. 205–8). Walsh agrees with those who argue that Leviticus condemns no other form of homoerotic intimacy (p. 209).

Rabbi Steven Greenberg (2004) emphasizes the fact that Leviticus 18 is recited in synagogues every year on *Yom Kippur*, the Day of Atonement (p. 74). According to Greenberg, 18.22 expresses 'the prohibition of male homosexual relations'. However, he adds that Jewish tradition since antiquity has refused 'to read the Torah as if it meant and has always meant only one thing'. From the perspective of Orthodox Judaism, all verses in the Pentateuch are pregnant with multiple meanings, 'some on the surface, others more deeply hidden, and some yet unborn' (p. 78). In addition, asking questions is a hallmark of Jewish spirituality. This is so much the case that 'God loves it when we ask why' (p. 79). Consequently, Greenberg emphasizes that there is no reason for making assumptions in advance about the meaning of the Levitical verses. From his reflections, Greenberg concludes that 18.22 speaks about anal intercourse. Like Olyan and Boyarin, he argues that the prohibition addresses the penetrating male and that there is no allusion to any other forms of homoeroticism (2004: 81).

Theodore Jennings (2005: 208–11) shares the view expressed by Walsh, finding that the prohibition in 18.22 particularly addresses 'males who desire to be penetrated by other males', but it extends, subsequently, to 'the males who collaborate with this desire' (p. 210). However, Jennings points out that 'same-sex relationships as such are nowhere prohibited in biblical literature' (p. 207). Similarly, Keith Sharpe (2011: 18) opines that Leviticus 18.22 relates to anal penetration only. For a man to be penetrated by another man is, from a biblical perspective, 'a terrible confusion of categories'. For ancient Israelite society, this happens when men act 'as if they were women'. Such behaviour was perceived to 'undermine the very basis of the sexual hierarchy' on which the stability of the community depended (p. 19). Thus, according to Sharpe, the word abomination expresses 'revulsion at the idea of a male acting as a female' since it threatens 'the system of male domination' (p. 26). Like several other scholars, Sharpe highlights the fact that homoerotic activity per se is not being condemned (p. 18), i.e. Leviticus does not prohibit other types of male–male sexual intimacy or, for that matter, close female–female relationships (p. 26).

James Miller (2010: 53) warns against the dangers of interpreting a text like Leviticus 18.22 outside of its context. In his view, the overall aim of Leviticus 18 is to preserve family order (pp. 50, 56). An essential element seems to be the control of body fluids, specifically that of 'seed' or semen, in Hebrew *zeraʕ* (pp. 50-3). In Miller's words, 'the man's emissions hold the key to the ban on male homosexual activity' (p. 51). Miller also discusses the issue of 'infertile emission', i.e. seminal emission which does not lead to procreation, but he concludes that the infertility of certain forms of sexual intercourse does not trouble the lawgiver (p. 53). In this regard, his approach differs from those other scholars who believe that Leviticus is concerned about fomenting procreation among the Israelites in order to ensure the nation's survival. For centuries, biblical Israel was a small nation surrounded by powerful, hostile neighbours. Thus, the argument goes, to avoid the spilling of precious semen, homoerotic sex between males had to be banned.[130]

For his part, Adrian Schenker (2003: 168) opines that, according to Leviticus, the semen of the Israelites should not be deposited in the wrong vessel, and newborn babies should not be sacrificed to the wrong deity such as Molekh (Lev. 18.21) because they belonged to Yhwh. To some extent, Miller's and Schenker's arguments are supported by Jacob Milgrom (2004: 207) who argues that the common denominator of all the prohibitions in Leviticus 18 is that they 'involve the emission of semen', resulting in incest, illicit

---

[130] wizzley.com/what-does-the-bible-say-about-homosexuality-leviticus-18-22 (2012); www.whosoever.org/bible/leviticus.shtml (2012).

progeny or lack of progeny. However, if the safeguarding of procreation were the rationale throughout the chapter, Milgrom himself wonders why the lawgiver and the ancient rabbis did not condemn masturbation (p. 207) and sexual relations after the onset of menopause (p. 208).

Unresolved Issues

One of the problems posed by Leviticus 18.22 is that, from the Middle Ages onwards, its apparent simplicity has prompted biblical commentators to make sweeping generalizations. Many take it to condemn erotic same-sex relationships in general despite the fact that the HB nowhere condemns intimacy between women. Hence it is a major mistake to argue that Leviticus 18.22 prohibits 'homosexuality' (Milgrom 2004: 208). Furthermore, the original Hebrew wording of this minuscule text is so arcane that the entire verse becomes almost untranslatable. Given the unresolved nature of these questions, and in the light of the enormous importance attached to Leviticus 18.22 in recent controversies, further textual analysis is still needed.[131]

The considerable amount of exegesis and the variety of arguments presented in recent decades about Leviticus 18.22 make it clear that scholars have not reached a point of full convergence. The discussions outlined above lead to the inevitable conclusion that current interpretations are incomplete since no single approach has succeeded in convincing an overwhelming majority. In other words, it would seem that some aspects of the text remain opaque. Several factors should be highlighted. First, the frequent use

---

[131] Referring to the Hebrew Bible, Sue Groom (2003: 130) points out that 'there is much more work to be done in the lexical semantics of Classical Hebrew'.

of 'homosexuality', 'homosexual intercourse', and 'same-sex intercourse' made by Gagnon (2001) and many others is anachronistic. These modern terms refer to homoerotic interaction between men or women of equal status, a situation not contemplated by an ancient work such as Leviticus, which is specifically addressed to circumcised Israelite males entering the land of Canaan, as emphasized repeatedly in Leviticus 18.3–5, 24–30 (Milgrom 2004: 196, 208).

Second, a number of scholars take the view that male–male anal penetration is a major concern for the lawgiver. However, within this group, there is disagreement between those who argue that the penetrator is being addressed and another group focusing on the receptive partner. Whichever assertion is preferred, both fail to account for the death penalty attached to the prohibition in Leviticus 20.13. This verse clearly establishes equal punishment for the two males involved, mentioning *'both of them'*, *'they* shall be put to death' and *'their* blood is upon *them'* (NRSV, emphasis added). Third, the argument that Leviticus forbids the undue commingling of substances, in particular of semen and excrement during anal intercourse, is unconvincing if one considers the absence in the Torah of any prohibition of male–female anal intercourse. Sexological research has documented that the latter practice is fairly common in heterosexual couples (Vanggaard 1969: 106; Boyarin 1995: 346–7; Jennings 2005: 205–6). As far as Greco-Roman antiquity is concerned, Paul's letter to the Romans 1.26 seems to provide a biblical example (cf. the present book's chapter 14).

It has often been said that male–male sex is banned in Leviticus 18.22 because it does not lead to procreation. However, procreation is nowhere in focus in the immediate context (Jennings 2005: 206), with the possible exception of the intriguing sacrifice of 'seed' to Molekh mentioned in 18.21. Moreover, it has been argued that the presence of such words as 'abomination' and 'a woman's lyings' in Leviticus 18.22 suggests a parallel to Deuteronomy 22.5, where the prohibition of cross-dressing includes 'a woman's garments' as well as 'abomination' (Boyarin 1995: 342-3). However, this interpretation disregards the fact that, while Deuteronomy speaks of *īsh*, 'a man', and *ishshah*, 'a woman', the wording in Leviticus 18.22 refers specifically to *zakhar*, 'a male', and *ishshah*, an unusual combination that seems to point in a different direction.[132] Some scholars argue that the phrase *mishkevey ishshah*, 'the lyings of a woman', mirrors *mishkav zakhar*, 'the lying of a male', found in Numbers 31.17-18, 35 and Judges 21.11-12 in relation to young women experiencing their first sexual intercourse (Helminiak 2000: 59). Yet this alleged parallel fails to account for the unusual plural of 'lyings' in Leviticus 18.22 vis-à-vis the singular 'lying' (*mishkav*) of a male in Numbers and Judges, and it seems to ignore the curious juxtaposition of *zakhar* and *ishshah*. In a number of other biblical texts, one finds the more logical male/female combination of *zakhar* (Lev. 12.2) and *neqevah* (12.5), while *īsh*, 'man/husband', is congruent with *ishshah* (Deut. 24.1-5).

All hermeneutical approaches to Leviticus 18.22 have one thing in common: they agree that the lawgiver expresses condemnation. However, what exactly is being condemned is a matter of interpretation or conjecture. Table 34 shows the twelve hypotheses identified thus far.

---

[132] David T. Stewart (2006: 94) cautions, 'Readers should resist the temptation to harmonize Deuteronomy and Leviticus, or let Deuteronomy's laws trump Leviticus,' because the latter 'speaks with a different voice'.

Table 34
Hypotheses about Lev. 18.22

What/Who Is Condemned

Unrestrained bisexuality

Same-sex eroticism ('homosexuality')

Sexual intercourse between males

Sexual intercourse between Israelite males in Canaan

Anal penetration between males

The active or insertive partner in anal intercourse

The passive or receptive partner in anal intercourse

Male cult prostitution

Gender confusion (male acting as female)

Social humiliation (male treated as female)

Undue commingling of substances (semen & excrement)

Failure to ensure procreation (waste of semen)

The variety of interpretations in table 34 makes three things clear: (a) some approaches overlap; (b) other approaches contradict each other, particularly the alleged opposition between insertive and receptive male partners; and (c) none of the arguments presented thus far has succeeded to convince all exegetes. Therefore, the recurring scholarly debate about Leviticus 18.22 suggests that the social and cultural significance of this verse within its ancient context is still waiting to be uncovered. In the case of Leviticus 18.22, certain aspects of the text seem to need further scrutiny and research. Stated another way, it may be deduced that a sufficiently detailed exegetical and literary analysis continues to be missing in current literature.[133]

Incest, Part One

Like Robert Gagnon (2001), Adrian Schenker (2003: 167) argues that Leviticus 18.22 forbids 'male homosexual intercourse'. In his view, what motivates the lawgiver is a desire to safeguard procreation and keep people's sex lives away from 'a barren use' (p. 169). An additional argument adduced by Schenker is that male–male sex would 'heavily damage the peace and unity of the family' and the larger community (p. 170). This is so, in his view, because male–male sexual intercourse is not only barren but it also troubles interpersonal relationships in the extended family. He feels that sexual relations between men entail too much 'confusion', which would endanger family life 'because of their passionate character' (p. 169). Thus, Schenker interprets Leviticus 18.22 simultaneously from different perspectives, including 'homosexual intercourse between men', 'confusion' and 'dangerous passion'.

Reading the book of Leviticus from a different angle, James Miller (2010: 49, 54-6) places Leviticus 18.22 in a group of verses classified as 'non-incest'. He argues that the common phrase used to define incest throughout this section is to 'uncover the nakedness' of a close relative (pp. 49, 53), which does not occur in 18.22. According to Miller's analysis, verses 19-23 follow the incest laws to address a variety of other sexual offences, which cannot be described as incest (p. 53). Other scholars, however, have moved in the opposite direction. Among them is Jacob Milgrom (2000 & 2004)

---

[133] While many ancient texts do not have clear meanings, Peter Cotterell and Max Turner (1989: 26) wonder why biblical interpretation has so far failed to involve itself in the relevant aspects of linguistics — and even now seems almost wilfully to ignore them.

who used to take a traditional approach to Leviticus 18.22. Having been persuaded to reconsider the unusual nature of the Hebrew wording, he now accepts the possibility of regarding it as a law against male-male incest (2000: 1569; 2004: 196-7). The initiator of this recent approach, mentioned by Milgrom, is David Stewart (2006).

If Leviticus is 'the most important book in the Hebrew Bible', David Stewart (2006: 77) argues that it should come as no surprise that it is quoted extensively in the Second Testament. Stewart finds sufficient reasons to believe that a fresh interpretation of Leviticus 18.22 is needed. He observes that for a general condemnation of male-male sexual relations, the lawgiver might well have limited himself to writing 'You shall not lie with a male', without adding the obscure phrase 'the lyings of a woman' (2006: 97). According to Stewart's approach, the seemingly metaphorical addendum of *mishkevey ishshah* is best explained by linking it to the numerous warnings against incest in Leviticus 18. Indeed, incestuous liaisons are the primary concern throughout the chapter (pp. 97-9). By inserting the prohibition in 18.22, the lawgiver ensures that all incestuous relationships are banned, that is, both heterosexual and homosexual.

Prompted by David Stewart's work on incest, I have examined Leviticus 18.22 from the perspective of male-male incest (Lings 2009 & 2011). The general proscription of incest is introduced in 18.6: 'None of you shall approach any member of his own flesh to uncover nakedness'.[134] While 'flesh' means 'kin', it is significant that the lawgiver includes relatives of both sexes, i.e. Israelite men receive clear orders not to approach any next of kin, whether male or female,

---

[134] The Hebrew word for 'flesh' is *basar*, which often reflects kinship; cf. Gen. 2.23; 29.14; 37.27. This point is stressed by Loader (2004: 58, 81, 87, 91) and Greenberg (2004: 263 n. 18).

for sexual purposes. If one assumes that male–male incest is being forbidden in 18.22, this would involve fathers (18.8) and uncles (18.14) as well as brothers, brothers-in-law, sons, and sons-in-law. Implicitly, then, erotic intimacy is circumscribed to legitimate spouses, i.e. wives and concubines.[135] The regulations against incest continue until 18.17. The argument of James Miller (2010: 49) that Leviticus 18.22 is 'non-incest' because of its position between 18.21 (sacrifice to Molekh) and 18.23 (bestiality) loses its force if the parallel prohibition in Leviticus 20.13 is brought into the picture. The context of this verse differs from Leviticus 18.22 in significant ways. Most remarkably, the two preceding verses clearly speak of incest, i.e. Leviticus 20.11 and 20.12 announce the death penalty for incestuous acts. According to 20.13, the same punishment applies to males who engage in *mishkevey ishshah* (Lings 2009: 245).

Therefore, while it is impossible to speak with absolute certainty at this stage,[136] various factors seem to point in the direction of a possible location for *mishkevey ishshah* within the biblical vocabulary pertaining to incestuous relationships (Lings 2009: 245). For his part, Jacob Milgrom (2004: 196) finds grounds to conclude that 'the lyings of a woman' may well be an idiom used specifically for illicit heterosexual

---

[135] For a discussion of the social and ethical aspects of these regulations against incest, see Milgrom 2004: 202–5. Mary Douglas (2000: 237) provides a schematic overview. Confusingly, Douglas applies the non-Hebrew term 'sodomy' to Lev. 18.22 and 20.13. Milgrom (2004: 206) uses similar anachronistic language: 'Sodomy is attested in all periods'; cf. Milgrom 2000: 1552, 1565–6. The imprecise word 'sodomy' was not invented until the eleventh century CE (see chapter 8).

[136] Rebecca Alpert (1989: 67) cautions that in biblical interpretation, 'complete objectivity is unattainable'. See also Sue Groom (2003 p. *xviii*): 'A brief glance at the range of commentaries on any one chapter of a biblical book reveals a range of possible interpretations. The text is like a multi-faceted diamond which can be viewed from any number of angles.'

unions. In his view, this implies that the prohibition in Leviticus 18.22 does not cover all male–male liaisons, but only those within the limited circle of the family (p. 197). This interpretation coincides to some extent with other laws from the ancient Near East. For example, §189 of the laws of the Hittites punishes abusive sex between a man and his mother, daughter or *son* (emphasis added).[137]

Incest, Part Two

The fact that the word *mishkevey* is plural invites further reflection. It may be a reminder that the concept applies to all the relationships within Leviticus 18 in which women, or wives, are involved. Milgrom (2000: 1569) highlights this point, suggesting that male–male incest is forbidden precisely for 'the equivalent degree of forbidden heterosexual relations, namely, those enumerated in the preceding verses'. Viewed from this angle, Leviticus 18 focuses on what might be termed 'the wrong kinds of relationship' to be avoided by all Israelites. Even the ban on Molekh worship (18.21) and the bestiality clause (18.23) may be read as areas in which the wrong kinds of relationship are being practised. In v. 23, the wrong kind of partner is chosen for sex while v. 21 mentions a deity unworthy of receiving the objectionable sacrifice of 'seed'.

Prompted by the apostle Paul's condemnation of an incestuous relationship in the Christian community at Corinth,[138] Alan Cadwallader (2012: 59) has read Leviticus 18.22 in the Greek Septuagint. In this ancient version, *mishkevey ishshah*, 'the lyings of a woman', is rendered *koitēn*

---
[137] Olyan 1994: 192; Gagnon 2001: 54; Milgrom 2004: 207; Stewart 2006: 97; Lings 2009: 246; Heacock 2011: 83; cf. Ezek. 22.10-11.
[138] See 1 Cor. 5.1-13 and the discussion of 1 Cor. 6.9 in the present book's chapter 13.

gynaikos. Cadwallader takes the phrase to be a euphemistic reference to a man sleeping in another man's bed, particularly his father's, and regards it as falling under the same prohibition as the more obvious provisions against incestuous acts in Leviticus 18. In the polygamous setting described in 18.7–11, the lawgiver draws a clear distinction between 'your mother' (v. 7) and 'your father's wife' (v. 8), referring to two different women. If, for example, a man sleeps with his father's wife, he is not only violating the social boundary separating him from the woman concerned but also invading his father's privacy. In the interpretation of Cadwallader and several other scholars, Leviticus 18.8 strongly suggests that whoever sleeps with his father's wife is guilty of 'uncovering his father's nakedness', i.e. sleeping with his father.[139]

Apparently Cadwallader takes the Greek noun *gynaikos* (from *gynē*) to mean 'wife', which is legitimate inasmuch as the word may be rendered as either 'woman' or 'wife',[140] a situation echoing the semantic duality inherent in the Hebrew term *ishshah*. In support of Cadwallader's approach, it may be pointed out that the only narrative setting in the HB containing the word *mishkevey* is Reuben's transgression with his father's wife Bilhah in Genesis 35.22. In 1 Corinthians 5, Paul strongly condemns a Christian man's incestuous cohabitation with his father's wife. Both situations may well be argued to reflect the anti-incest concerns expressed about fathers and fathers' wives in Leviticus 18.8. If Cadwallader's hypothesis is accepted, it completely changes the exegetical focus for 18.22. While current scholarship primarily discusses anal sex between males, it is being suggested that this

---

[139] Cf. Countryman 1989: 35: 'It is the man's father whom he violates in incest, even though the physical act takes place with his wife.' David Stewart (2006: 98) suggests this paraphrase of Lev. 18.7: 'Don't incest your father or your mother.'

[140] Cf. Paul's reflections on marriage in 1 Cor. 7.1-2 where the two senses of *gynē* alternate.

assumed situation is of no concern to the lawgiver. Instead, he may be determined to ensure that the property rights of fathers, uncles, and other males are respected at all levels, including sexual rights. In addition, the fact that *mishkevey* is plural may indicate that several illicit liaisons are alluded to. In the given context, the various forms of heterosexual incest previously proscribed seem to be the most obvious frame of reference (Milgrom 2000: 1569; 2004: 207). Read in this context, Leviticus 18.22 becomes an emphatic addendum to the various biblical injunctions against male–female incest.

Furthermore, it is often overlooked that every time a woman/wife is mentioned in Leviticus 18.7–20, 22–23 and 20.10–14, 16–21, the word is associated with a proscription. Given the general tone of admonition and warning permeating the entire text, the multiple prohibitions surrounding *ishshah* challenge the rationale behind the approaches to *mishkevey ishshah* adopted by most translators (Lings 2009: 247). Not only do phrases such as 'as with a woman' or 'as one lies with a woman' suggest bisexuality, as noted earlier, but, even more importantly, they erroneously present sexual relations with a woman/wife as something desirable in the context of Leviticus 18.22. To conclude this discussion of the possible links to incest of *mishkevey ishshah*, it seems reasonable to add two items to the twelve already included in table 34, namely, (a) male–male incest and (b) male–female incest. In summary, the number of hypotheses adduced thus far amounts to fourteen.

Translating MISHKEVEY ISHSHAH

Having pondered the fourteen hypotheses presented in this chapter, I posit that the arguments focusing on incest are substantial and deserve to be taken seriously. However, given the numerous uncertainties surrounding *mishkevey ishshah* in Leviticus 18.22, a discussion of adequate translation options would merit an entire essay in its own right.[141] Hence, I will limit myself to offering a few tentative ideas for Bible translators to ponder. The primary purpose of these experimental proposals is not to offer ready-to-use solutions but rather to indicate that further avenues of exploration exist beyond the procedures usually adopted. In any case, the textual difficulties examined in this chapter may serve as a timely reminder to translators of the importance of being cautious when approaching an obscure text like Leviticus 18.22. For this occasion, let the following suggested interpretations be appetizers:

1. With a male, you shall not lie down the lyings-down of a woman/wife.
2. With a male, you shall not engage in a sexual relationship prohibited with a woman/wife.
3. You shall not have sex with a male by lying with a/his wife.
4. You shall not lie down with a male family member by accessing his wife's bed(s).

The first rendering is literal throughout. This 'plain' translation has several advantages: (a) it reflects the original Hebrew text verbatim, (b) it shows respect for the HB, (c) misinterpretation (*eisegesis*) based on post-biblical prejudice is avoided, and (d) curious readers are invited to become co-interpreters. The main disadvantage is the opacity of the English wording, which makes the second part of the verse virtually incomprehensible. My second suggested idea entails a dual approach, which combines

---

[141] In the experience of Rebecca Alpert (1989: 69–70), there is no easy way of coming to terms with Leviticus. This may partly explain why, according to Jacob Milgrom (2004: 6), the ethical values, rituals, and commandments of Leviticus are often misunderstood and mistranslated.

literalness with the dynamic method: literal enough to be a recognizable rendering of the Hebrew text and dynamic enough for it to be comprehensible. It must be conceded that the paraphrase 'prohibited with' is interpretive, not literal. The third proposal resembles the second in that it is partly literal, partly dynamic. Having pointed out the ambiguity embedded in the phrases 'as with a woman' and 'as one lies with a woman', it may be fruitful to consider using other prepositional phrases. One such possibility is 'by lying with a/his wife'. It highlights the fact that the forbidden act is conceptualized within the family framework and is likely to relate to incest. The fourth suggestion, which is a paraphrase, echoes the stern warnings of Leviticus 18.8 and 18.14 to respect fathers' and uncles' property rights over their wives, with similar injunctions issued in Deuteronomy 22.30 (23.1) and 27.20.

Turn It and Turn It

Following this exploration of Leviticus 18.22 and 20.13 in the light of current biblical scholarship, one thing has become clear: further research is needed before a satisfactory exegesis can be established. According to Rebecca Alpert (1989: 67), 'more creative work needs to take place in the area of interpreting the text'. A series of potentially fruitful research questions to be considered in the future include the following:

- The language associated with incest in different biblical narratives
- Ancient extra-biblical narratives in which incest occurs
- The connotation of 'wife' that repeatedly surrounds *ishshah* in Leviticus 18
- *To'evah*, 'abomination', compared with other terms of disapproval, e.g. *zimmah* ('lewdness'), *sheqets* ('repulsiveness'), *tevel* ('confusion'), etc.

- The death sentence in Leviticus 20.13 ('their blood is upon them') compared with other biblical texts featuring identical punishment
- *Shakhav*, 'lie down', used as a transitive verb in other HB passages
- Unusual juxtapositions of nouns in the HB analogous to *zakhar* ('male') and *ishshah* ('woman')
- Other nouns with semantic changes between singular and plural analogous to *mishkav* and *mishkevey*.

Before leaving the exegetical conundrum presented by Leviticus 18.22, it may be helpful to be reminded of the way in which ancient rabbis, who never relinquished the study of the HB in the original language, approached scripture. Convinced that there are 'seventy faces to the Torah' (Greenberg 2004: 20), they compared the Bible to a splendid diamond: 'Turn it and turn it again, for everything is in it' (Magonet 2004: 217). This open-mindedness enabled them to avoid any confident assertion that one's own form of exegesis is 'the only truly scientific one' (Reif 1998: 148). Steven Greenberg (2004: 78) ponders this approach, stating how rabbinic tradition has refused to read the Torah 'as if it meant and has always meant only one thing'. There must be no final reading of any verse because all verses are 'pregnant with multiple meanings'. Perhaps, then, by turning and turning Leviticus 18.22, allowing it to be looked at from seventy different angles, fresh insights will emerge into the crystalline structure of the diamond (Douglas 2004: 175).

Conclusion

In the recent past, a number of interpretations of Leviticus 18.22 have been offered. However, all arguments tend to leave some aspects unresolved. For a long time, Bible translators and commentators have thought that Leviticus

18.22 prohibits all forms of erotic expression between two men. In recent decades, it has been suggested that only anal penetration is being forbidden. However, even if this reading of the text is granted, the debate is far from over. Some exegetes feel that, from the perspective of Leviticus, the penetrator commits a crime, while others argue that the focus is on the role of the receptive or 'passive' male, i.e. the one penetrated. Neither approach resolves the fact that both participants in the sexual interaction are said to commit an 'abomination' to which the death penalty applies (20.13).

So far no satisfactory method has been devised for converting the obscure phrase 'with a male you shall not lie down the lyings-down of a woman' into good, idiomatic English. Neither the literal approach nor the dynamic method yields satisfactory results. Being too ambiguous and misleading, the familiar translation 'as with a woman' does not exhaust the full interpretive potential of the Hebrew wording. Several linguistic and literary features of Leviticus 18.22 merit more attention. This verse is likely to have been included for a specific purpose, and a detailed literary analysis of chapters 18 and 20 of the book of Leviticus appears to have provided some fresh clues. For instance, the combined presence in the Hebrew of *zakhar* ('male') and *ishshah* ('woman') is very unusual. Since the overall aim of Leviticus 18 and 20 is to ban incestuous heterosexual practices, a growing number of biblical scholars find it logical to assume that Leviticus 18.22 and 20.13 are there for similar purposes. Still, the elusive nature of the Hebrew text, particularly the arcane phrase *mishkevey ishshah*, may serve as a reminder that a considerable amount of further research is required if biblical scholars are to attain a greater degree of certainty. As it encourages exegetes to seek fresh insights into the biblical text, the ancient hermeneutical principle of 'seventy faces to the Torah' seems particularly fruitful.

PART THREE

Sodom and Gomorrah

7

SODOM IN THE BIBLE

Was not your sister Sodom a byword in your mouth
In the days of your pride
Before your own wickedness was uncovered?

—Ezekiel 16.56–57

Introduction

Shrouded in legend and steeped in tradition, the story of Sodom and Gomorrah is one of the most famous in the entire Bible. Whenever the names of these cities are mentioned, images of risqué or sinful behaviour are conjured up, often associated with homoeroticism. This interpretation is so pervasive that it is reflected in countless academic, literary, religious, and cinematic works. Historically the destruction of Sodom in Genesis 19 has been used to justify systematic persecution of people in homoerotic relationships. In fact, no other biblical text has had such sinister repercussions for so-called sexual minorities. In the penal codes of some countries today, one still finds the medieval concept of *sodomy*. It first emerged in a monastic environment in Italy in the eleventh century (cf. chapter 8). Subsequently the term was chosen by legislators to classify various sexual conducts, particularly those forms of physical intimacy that go beyond traditional vaginal coitus in heterosexual couples (Karras 2005: 134).

The reception history of the drama of Sodom and Gomorrah is so varied that a detailed study of the various stages is required.[142] The survey presented in the following chapters reveals the important hermeneutical shifts that have occurred over the centuries. No other narrative in the Bible has undergone such widely differing interpretations over a time span of at least two thousand years. Given the enormous theological resonance of the story of Sodom and Gomorrah, and in the light of its extraordinary literary complexity, several chapters of the present book are dedicated to this subject.

The Story

> Lot looked about him . . . and moved his tent as far as Sodom. (Gen. 13.10–12)
>
> The men set out from there and looked towards Sodom. (Gen. 18.16)
>
> Abraham went early in the morning . . . and looked down towards Sodom and Gomorrah. (Gen. 19.27–28)

Sodom as a biblical theme is discreetly introduced in Genesis 10.19. The narrator informs readers that the city was founded by Canaanites, i.e. persons descended from Noah's grandson Canaan, which makes Sodom a significant representative of ancient Canaanite city states (van Wolde 2012: 95). The name of Sodom occurs for the second time in 13.10–13 where

---

[142] I define *reception history* as the history of the meanings that have been imputed to mythological, literary, or historical events. Reception history traces the different ways in which texts have been interpreted, preached, used, and abused over the centuries in different cultures; cf. Browning 2009: 309.

readers are informed that the city is located in the fertile Jordan valley. The lushness of the area attracts Lot, nephew of Abraham, who 'moves his tent as far as Sodom' (13.12). In a subtle change of tone, the narrator goes on to explain that the inhabitants of Sodom and Gomorrah are 'wicked' and 'great sinners'. Genesis does not specify the nature of such wickedness and sinfulness, but the fact that the cities will be destroyed eventually is pointed out in 13.10.

Sodom is at the heart of the drama of Genesis 14. This is where the kings of Sodom and Gomorrah form a coalition with several neighbouring cities in order to rebel against foreign occupation. However, the rebel forces lose the battle. The victorious troops proceed to loot Sodom and Gomorrah and carry away the inhabitants as prisoners of war. The prisoners include Lot who at this stage has become a citizen of Sodom. As soon as Abraham receives the news, he organizes an armed expedition. In the middle of the night, he succeeds in liberating all the prisoners, including King Bera of Sodom, and taking them back. King Bera wishes to express his gratitude by offering Abraham the material possessions belonging to the people of Sodom. However, Abraham emphatically refuses (Gen. 14.23). Indirectly the narrator suggests that there is a significant difference between Abraham and Lot. While the latter seeks full integration with the Canaanites of Sodom, where he has immigrant status, Abraham keeps his distance.

The longest sequence in the story of Sodom, which is also the most dramatic and best known, unfolds in the unified narrative spanning Genesis 18 and 19 (Safren 2012: 159). A highly significant preamble is found in Genesis 17 where the formal, far-reaching covenant between YHWH and Abraham is established. At the start of Genesis 18, the deity appears incognito with two companions in front of Abraham's tent with the intention of paying him and his wife, Sarah, a visit. Spontaneously and in exemplary fashion Abraham rises to the occasion. Quickly and generously, he organizes water for the visitors to wash themselves before enjoying a succulent meal. As soon as the banquet is over, the leader of the anonymous group announces to Abraham and Sarah that they, in spite of their advanced age, are going to have a son (18.10). At this stage they realize who their interlocutor is: YHWH himself in human form. As his visitors prepare to leave, Abraham walks them part of the way. The two companions continue their journey towards Sodom. However, YHWH remains standing next to Abraham in order to explain that he is going to investigate what happens in Sodom and that the destruction of the city may well be imminent (18.22).[143] Abraham quickly intercedes on behalf of those innocent inhabitants who should not be swept away with the wicked. YHWH makes a promise: if ten righteous citizens are found in the city, it will be saved.

In the meantime, the two envoys of YHWH arrive at the gate of Sodom at sundown (19.1). Immediately they are greeted by Lot who goes out of his way to persuade them to spend the night at his house. In the process, he displays the same commitment to hospitality, typical of the Middle East, that was shown earlier by his uncle Abraham. Following some discussion, the unnamed messengers accept the invitation. They settle in at Lot's house and enjoy the evening meal that he prepares. At bedtime, all the male inhabitants of Sodom surround the house, bang on the front door, and ask Lot to

---

[143] In Gen. 18.22, most modern versions follow the Masoretic Text, which says 'Abraham remained standing before the LORD'. However, another ancient tradition reads 'YHWH remained standing before Abraham' (Brueggemann 1982: 168), which is according to the logic of the narrative. Throughout Gen. 18, the deity takes the initiative, and Abraham responds. It is the deity who grants Abraham a moment of intercession or negotiation before moving on in 18.33 (Brodie 2001: 243). A few versions rightly reflect this situation (CCB, NJB, NLT, NWT).

hand over the visitors immediately. Their stated aim is to 'know' the strangers (19.5). Lot refuses to break the laws of hospitality. At the same time, as a vulnerable immigrant, he feels pressured by such a tense situation to the point of having to make a reasonable countermove. Hence, he suggests handing over his two underage daughters in lieu of the visitors (19.8). However, the deal is rejected. The spokesmen of the city find that Lot, the foreigner, has committed an act of disobedience and immediately proceed to arrest him, while others intend to break down the door (19.9). At the very last minute, the two divine messengers take action by rescuing Lot and temporarily blinding the mob (19.11).

This dramatic incident, in which Lot has found himself in the eye of the hurricane, is evidence of the wickedness of the inhabitants of Sodom (19.13). The visitors proclaim that the city is going to be destroyed the very same night and order Lot to flee with his family without delay and take refuge in the mountains. Before leaving everything behind, Lot unsuccessfully tries to persuade his two 'sons-in-law', i.e. the young men of Sodom who are planning to marry his daughters, to come along, but they regard his warning of impending disaster as a joke (19.14). During their flight, Lot's wife pauses to look back at the spectacular destruction of her home city, instantly turning into a pillar of salt (19.26). Towards the end of the story, Lot and his two daughters settle in a hillside cave (19.30). On two occasions, the girls decide to have incestuous sexual relations with their father for the sake of having children. They achieve this by plying Lot with wine, using him as a sperm donor, and both become pregnant (19.36). Their children grow up to be founders of Moab and Ammon, two nations situated on the eastern banks of the Jordan River.

A Text in Genesis

Several scholars believe that the writers of Genesis deliberately shaped their prose to be read aloud (Fox 1995 pp. *ix–x*; Brodie 2001: 76). Nothing is known about the anonymous authors, redactors, editors, and copyists who at some stage were involved in its composition and transmission (Alter 1996 pp. *xl–xliii*), which means that the concept of individual authorship does not apply to the books of the HB as we know them (Alter 1992: 2-3). The anonymity of Classical Hebrew narrative sets it apart from the writings by different named authors, which came out of ancient Greece. Moreover, the HB spans 'nearly a millennium of literary activity' (1992: 76). Many observers admire the sophistication of the book of Genesis. Few ancient works match the Hebrew text with respect to literary craftmanship in the form of original, precise, and elegant expression (Alter 1992: 53-4, 167). Thomas Brodie (2001: 10, 34, 76) has compared the polished artistry of Genesis to the works of William Shakespeare.

On account of its condensed nature, the literary style of Genesis may be characterized as 'minimalist' in the sense of having a marked tendency to reduce the number of essential words to a minimum. The narrator usually omits any comment that is not deemed indispensable and only rarely does the text include supplementary information that might be described as 'footnotes'. Consequently, certain passages come across as laconic or even opaque to today's readers because their perceived lacunae are difficult to fill in for the untrained modern eye used to more transparent literary styles (Carden 2004: 4-5). As far as the story of Sodom is concerned, the writer skilfully juxtaposes singular and plural, first and third person, anonymity and revealed identity, knowledge and ignorance, similarities and differences as well as seriousness and laughter (Bechtel 1998b: 126).

The Sodom narrative occupies a prominent position in the middle of the book of Genesis. Readers who have the patience to investigate and meditate on the tragic destiny of Sodom will discover the multifaceted nature of the narrative. The material included in Genesis is not historiography in the modern sense. Rather, it would be more accurate to describe it as a fascinating collection of mythological episodes of special interest to the time in which the narrator lived.[144] That is, if one takes the drama of Sodom literally, it appears as a chain of events in the distant past. However, if one moves into the text with an open mind and pays attention to details, it will become clear that its purpose is really to contribute to a social, cultural, and theological debate in which literature becomes an interpretive mirror of the social reality surrounding the narrator and his people.

As mentioned above, the Sodom and Gomorrah narrative spans three chapters of Genesis. However, it should be pointed out that the division into chapters to which modern Bible readers are accustomed is a late phenomenon that was not created until the thirteenth century. Even more recent is the fragmentation into verses, which occurred in the sixteenth century (Long 2001: 113). The present book focuses primarily on Genesis 18 and 19 for two reasons: (a) these two chapters form a distinct unit of great philological, literary, and theological interest (Meir 2012: 54); and (b) over the centuries, the first section of Genesis 19 has generated more literature of all kinds than any other part of the story.

---

[144] In biblical studies, 'myth' has a technical meaning and 'covers those stories or narratives which describe the actions of the other-worldly' (Browning 2009: 260). In the context of Genesis, the creation myth should not be treated as a 'historical' account of the origin of the universe. Don Smith (2006: 7) defines a myth as 'a story about the past that is used to give meaning to the present'. A myth may use symbolic or allegorical language. Oftentimes myths are useful as they provide 'reason to the current state of things by explaining how they came to be'.

Sodom in the Hebrew Bible

Due to its prominence in Genesis, the legend of Sodom and neighbouring cities became widely discussed in the HB, particularly in the prophetic books, where the names of Sodom and Gomorrah occur twenty times. This frequency enables us to acquire an impression of the way in which the story was interpreted in the early stages of the HB, including the Babylonian exile (sixth century BCE). Historically speaking this is the first known hermeneutical tradition in relation to Sodom. The most characteristic elements will be highlighted below.

Motivated by faith and passion, the turbulent lives led by the Hebrew prophets often generate polemics. Their commitment impels them to express openly what God YHWH has put in their hearts. At times they pay a high price for their candour. The prophets address the burning religious, social and political issues of their day, and the expression of vehement protests is a key element in their messages. Time and again they are moved to indignation and condemnation of the shocking injustices they see happening around them. In some cases, they are overwhelmed by feelings of horror and utter despair.

In prophetic literature, the names of Sodom and Gomorrah are frequently introduced as a *leitmotif*, a poetical, vigorous metaphor that serves as a hermeneutical key. Whenever the name of Sodom appears, it refers to one or several of four categories of subjects: (a) destruction, desolation, ruins and sterile, desert-like landscapes; (b) selfishness and arrogance; (c) idolatry and apostasy; and (d) social injustice, oppression, and violence. A detailed survey of the prophetic discourse on Sodom is given in the tables below. Each table is a collage arranged according to subject matter. The texts listed in this section are partly my own translations, partly adapted from the NRSV.

Table 35
DESTRUCTION AND DESOLATION

Deut. 29.23	Sulphur and salt
	Its soil burned out
	Nothing sown
	Nothing sprouting.
Isa. 13.20–21	She will never be inhabited
	Or lived in for all generations
	And there the Arab will not pitch his tent
	No shepherds will make their flocks lie down there.
Jer. 49.18, 50.40	As when God overthrew
	Sodom and Gomorrah and their neighbours
	Says Y<small>HWH</small>
	No one shall live there
	No one shall settle in her.
Isa. 13.21	And there wild animals will lie down
	And its houses will be full of howling creatures.
Jer. 50.39	Therefore wild animals shall live with hyenas . . .
	And in her ostriches shall dwell.
Jer. 49.17	Everyone who passes by it will be horrified
	And will hiss because of all its disasters.
Am. 4.11	I overthrew some of you
	As when God overthrew Sodom and Gomorrah
	And you were like a brand
	Snatched out of the fire.
Zeph. 2.9	Moab herself shall become like Sodom
	And the Ammonites like Gomorrah
	A land possessed by nettles and saltpits
	And a desolate waste for ever.

Table 36
PRIDE AND ARROGANCE

Ezek. 16.56	Was not your sister Sodom
	A byword in your mouth
	In the days of your pride
	Before your own wickedness was uncovered?
Ezek. 16.49–50	This was the guilt of your sister Sodom:
	She and her daughters had pride
	Excess of bread and prosperous ease
	But they did not aid the afflicted and the poor
	They were haughty.
Isa. 13.19	And Babylon, the glory of kingdoms
	The splendour and pride of the Chaldeans
	Shall become like Sodom and Gomorrah
	When God overthrew them.
Jer. 49.14–18	Gather yourselves together
	And come against her
	And rise up for battle.
	For I am making you [Edom] least among the nations
	Despised by humankind.
	The terror you inspired
	And the pride of your heart
	Have deceived you.
	Edom shall become an object of horror
	Like the overthrow of Sodom and Gomorrah
	And their neighbours, says Y$_{HWH}$
	No one shall live there.
Jer. 50.29	Summon archers against Babylon
	Repay her according to her deeds
	Just as she has done, do to her

	For she has acted arrogantly against Y<small>HWH</small>
	The Holy One of Israel.
Jer. 50.31	I am against you, O arrogance
	Says Y<small>HWH</small>, God of hosts
	For your day has come
	The time when I will punish you.
Jer. 50.40	As when God overthrew Sodom and Gomorrah
	And their neighbours.
Zeph. 2.9–10	Therefore, as I live
	Says Y<small>HWH</small> of hosts, the God of Israel
	Moab shall become like Sodom
	And the Ammonites like Gomorrah.
	This shall be their lot in return for their pride.

Table 37
APOSTASY AND IDOLATRY

Deut. 29.22–25	The next generation, your children
	Who rise up after you
	As well as the foreigner
	Who comes from a distant country
	Will see the plagues and diseases
	With which Y$_{HWH}$ has afflicted her
	Like the destruction
	Of Sodom and Gomorrah, Admah and Zeboiim.
	All the nations will ask,
	Why did Y$_{HWH}$ do thus to this land?
	What caused the heat of this great anger?
	And they will say,
	It is because they abandoned the covenant of Y$_{HWH}$
	The God of their ancestors
	Which he made with them
	When he brought them out of the land of Egypt
	They turned and bowed down to other gods
	Worshipping them
	Gods whom they had not known.
Deut. 32.32–33	Their vine is from the vine-stock of Sodom
	From the vineyards of Gomorrah
	Their grapes are grapes of poison
	Their clusters are bitter
	Their wine is the poison of serpents
	The cruel venom of asps.
Isa. 3.8–9	For Jerusalem has stumbled and Judah has fallen
	Because their tongue and their deeds
	Are against Y$_{HWH}$

	Defying his glorious presence
	The look on their faces testifies against them
	They proclaim their sin like that of Sodom
	They have brought calamity on themselves.
Jer. 50.38	For it is a land of graven images
	And they go mad over frightful idols.
Ezek. 16.48–51	As I live, says the Lord Y$_{HWH}$
	Your sister Sodom and her daughters have not done
	As you and your daughters have done
	Samaria has not committed half your sins
	You have committed more abominations than they.

Table 38
CORRUPTION AND OPPRESSION

Jer. 23.14	And in the prophets of Jerusalem
	I have seen a horrible thing:
	They commit adultery and walk in falsehood
	They strengthen the hand of evildoers
	So that no one turns from wickedness
	All of them have become like Sodom to me
	And its inhabitants like Gomorrah.
Isa. 1.21–23	Alas, she has become a whore
	The faithful city.
	She that was full of justice
	Righteousness would dwell in her
	And now murderers.
	Your princes are rogues
	And companions of thieves.
	Everyone loves a bribe
	And chases after gifts
	They do not render judgment for the orphan
	And the widow's cause does not come before them.
Isa. 1.10	Hear the word of Y$_{HWH}$
	Rulers of Sodom
	Listen to the teaching of our God
	People of Gomorrah.
Isa. 1.15–16	Your hands are full of blood
	Wash yourselves, make yourselves clean
	Remove the evil of your doings
	From before my eyes
	Learn to do good
	Seek justice
	Rescue the oppressed
	Render judgment for the orphan
	Plead the cause of the widow.

Sodom and Polytheism

In the religious sphere the main commitment of the Israelite prophets is to monotheism, i.e. the worship of the one god Elohīm YHWH in opposition to the widespread polytheism or syncretism of neighbouring nations. Usually such practices are denounced as idolatry,[145] and occasionally they are classified as 'rebellion against God'.[146] In terms of literary style, the prophets often include strong allusions to the realm of sex. For instance, 'unfaithfulness', 'whoring', 'adultery', and 'prostitution' are blunt metaphors for polytheistic practices. The books of Jeremiah, Ezekiel, and Hosea are rich in examples.[147] Alluding to Sodom, Jeremiah lashes out at the social and political elite of his day for their 'promiscuity' (Jer. 23.14). The polemical sexual imagery employed in Ezekiel 16 describes prostitution in such graphic detail that it borders on pornography (Nissinen 1998: 47; Mein 2001: 102, 114).

Apart from sexual metaphors, it should be pointed out that the prophets take no interest in the specific physical details of the intimate lives of the ruling classes of their society. In other words, they are not out to expose the private life of anyone in particular. Instead they focus on various issues in the public domain that they find shocking. Moreover, for the subject of the present book it is significant that the sexual metaphors used by the prophetic books do not include homoerotic relationships. Instead, this literature focuses on two specific sides of the male–female sexual spectrum outside marriage, namely, prostitution and adultery.

---

[145] Deut. 32.16–17, 21, 37–38; Isa. 2.8, 18, 20; 31.7; 42.17; 48.5; 66.3; Jer. 16.18; 23.13; 50.2, 38; 51.17–18; Ezek. 14.3–7; 16.17–21, 36; 20.8, 16, 18, 24; Hos. 4.17; 8.4–6; Am. 5.26; Zeph. 1.4–5.
[146] Isa. 1.2, 23, 28; 58.1; 59.13; Jer. 5.23; 28.16; 29.32; Lam. 1.18, 20; 3.42; Ezek. 17.12, 15; 20.8, 13, 21; Hos. 7.13–14; 13.16 (14.1); Am. 2.4; Zeph. 3.11.
[147] Jer. 5.7; 13.27; 23.10, 14; Ezek. 16.15–17, 20–22, 25–38, 41, 58; 23.5, 8, 11, 14, 18–19, 30, 35, 37, 49; Hos. 1.2; 2.2, 5; 4.12–15; 5.3–4; 6.10; 7.4.

When Ezekiel in 16.50 discusses the 'abominations' committed in Sodom, the term is generic as it encompasses all the transgressions that the city has committed. In Ezekiel, the Hebrew word *to'evah*, 'abomination', refers primarily to unacceptable religious practices in the form of polytheism.[148] In terms of ethics, all Hebrew prophets highlight the importance of humility and social justice. They observe that such virtues are conspicuously absent in the top echelons of the political establishment. This situation causes them to use forceful, vehement language as they denounce the blatant ways in which the rights of the poor are trampled underfoot. Sodom is the prophets' favourite metaphor for describing excessive pride and arrogance, injustice and corruption, social insolence, and proclivity for violence and murder (cf. tables 35–38).

Hebrew Texts Mentioning Sodom

The prophetic sources include two that do not mention the name of Sodom directly, namely, Hosea and Psalms. However, the contexts are unmistakable. In the latter book, Psalm 11.6 contains a phrase reminiscent of the destruction of Sodom and Gomorrah with fire and sulphur (NRSV):

> On the wicked he will rain coals of fire and sulphur
> A scorching wind shall be the portion of their cup.

Even clearer is the context of Hosea 11.8. The prophet mentions Admah and Zeboiim, two cities destroyed along with Sodom and Gomorrah (Gen. 10.19; 19.25; Deut. 29.23). In this particular passage of Hosea, Y<small>HWH</small> is reflecting on

---

[148] Ezek. 5.9, 11; 6.9; 7.3–4, 8–9; 8.6, 9, 13, 15, 17; 9.4; 11.18, 21; 12.16; 14.6; 16.2, 22, 36, 43, 47, 50–51, 58; 18.12, 24.

his relationship with the biblical territories of Ephraim and Israel (NRSV):

> How can I give you up, Ephraim?
> How can I hand you over, O Israel?
> How can I make you like Admah?
> How can I treat you like Zeboiim?

Table 39 provides an overview of the prophetic texts in which Sodom is named explicitly or implicitly.

Table 39
Sodom in the Hebrew Bible

Texts	Allusions to Sodom
Deuteronomy	29.22–23; 32.32–33
Isaiah	1.10–17; 3.9; 13.19
Jeremiah	23.14; 49.17–18; 50.39–40
Lamentations	4.6
Ezekiel	16.46–50, 53–57
Amos	4.11
Zephaniah	2.9
Hosea	11.8 (indirect)
Psalms	11.6 (indirect)

All the texts quoted were composed in the same language, namely, Classical Hebrew. Judging from several linguistic investigations of the evolution of Biblical Hebrew it seems likely that the sources listed in table 39 appeared — whether in an oral version or in written form — some time prior to the year 500 BCE. This suggestion does not exclude the possibility of successive revisions over the centuries. From the point of view of historical linguistics, both Genesis and the prophetic books belong to the older part of the HB (Sáenz-Badillos 1993: 52).

On this basis, it does not seem far-fetched to imagine a shared linguistic heritage and cultural framework among all these writings. In the context of Sodom and Gomorrah, this factor is significant given that the persons who wrote the prophetic books were in a privileged position for interpreting the drama of Genesis 18 and 19. By comparison, modern readers studying the narrative face a considerable obstacle in the form of distance in time, space, language, and culture. In addition, a long church tradition may have led to misinterpretation and errors of translation, some of which continue to affect today's versions of the Bible. Since the issues addressed by the Hebrew prophets are idolatry, pride, social injustice, and oppression, it is indeed remarkable that today's scholarly consensus emphasizes sexual violence. If the prophetic books use sexual language as a metaphor for polytheistic practices, then the question remains: What was the sin of Sodom? What exactly caused the city to be destroyed? Over the following pages, a patient, detailed search for a plausible answer will be carried out. The first two 'witnesses' to be called are Isaiah and Ezekiel.

Isaiah and Ezekiel on Sodom

As noted, the visions of Sodom provided by the HB are rich and specific at the same time. Two prophets in particular employ Sodom as a metaphor, namely, Isaiah and Ezekiel. Some of the following scripture passages have been mentioned in the collages of tables 35–38. Below they are discussed in the light of their original contexts. The first message is taken from Isaiah 1.10–17 (cf. table 38). It is addressed to the 'rulers of Sodom' and 'people of Gomorrah'. Very soon it emerges that Isaiah has the governing establishment of Jerusalem in mind (text abbreviated, NRSV with my modifications):

> Hear the word of Y\textsc{hwh}, you rulers of Sodom.
> Listen to the teaching of our God, people of Gomorrah.
> What is to me the multitude of your sacrifices?—says Y\textsc{hwh}.
> I have had enough of burnt-offerings of rams and the fat of fed beasts.
> I do not delight in the blood of bulls or lambs, or goats.
> Your new moons and your appointed festivals my soul hates
> They have become a burden to me . . .
> When you stretch out your hands, I will hide my eyes from you.
> Even though you make many prayers, I will not listen.
> Your hands are full of blood.
> Wash yourselves, make yourselves clean
> Remove the evil of your doings from before my eyes.
> Cease to do evil, learn to do good.
> Seek justice, rescue the oppressed.
> Defend the orphan, plead for the widow.

In this passage, Isaiah associates the name of Sodom with empty, formalized religious practices performed in the midst of a crude social situation characterized by great injustice. For Isaiah, Sodom and Gomorrah are not unknown entities or faraway places. The cities are not even geographical locations but rather a situation that exists wherever injustice and violence prevail. Thus, Isaiah provides an early example of contextualized biblical interpretation applied directly to the social, political, and religious environment in which the prophet lives. In other words, such a reading strategy is not a recent invention of twentieth-century liberation theologies but has profound biblical roots. In another part of the book, Isaiah manifests a concern for all marginalized groups, including foreigners and eunuchs. Someday all of these will be invited to worship in the temple of Y̲HWH (56.3–8). The requirement for admission is to 'maintain justice and do what is right' (56.1), a clear reference to the basis of the covenant between Y̲HWH and Abraham mentioned in Genesis 18.19, i.e. within the story of Sodom and Gomorrah.

In regard to Sodom, the prophet Ezekiel has made a special contribution. His reflections on Sodom are detailed and specific. Weston Fields (1997: 171) has rightly described Ezekiel 16 as 'a remarkably expanded application of the Sodom tradition'. Parts of his discourse may, at first glance, seem opaque, but on closer inspection the prophet's interpretation turns out to be 'extraordinarily incisive'. It is no exaggeration when Fields writes of Ezekiel's observations in the following terms (1997: 183–4):

> Ezekiel . . . comes closest to the heart of the matter in his charge against the Sodomites of overbearing arrogance resulting in the mistreatment of the socially disadvantaged.

In the HB, Ezekiel excels in making use of Sodom as a metaphor. From his tragic exile in Babylon, the prophet addresses his native city Jerusalem with these critical words (16.56–57):

> Was not your sister Sodom a byword in your mouth
> In the days of your pride
> Before your own wickedness was uncovered?

In Classical Hebrew, the noun ʿir, 'city', is of feminine gender. When he speaks of the 'daughters' of different cities, Ezekiel actually refers to all their inhabitants, male and female.[149] Establishing a comparison between Jerusalem on the one hand and the neighbouring cities of Samaria and Sodom on the other, the prophet astonishingly declares in 16.46-48 that the Jerusalem he has known has been far more sinful than they (text abbreviated):

> Your elder sister is Samaria . . . and your younger sister is Sodom.
> You not only followed their ways and acted according to their abominations.
> You were more corrupt than they in all your ways.
> As I live—says God Y<small>HWH</small>—
> Your sister Sodom and her daughters have not done as you and your daughters have done.

One of the most virulent words in Ezekiel's vocabulary is 'abomination', which reflects the Hebrew noun *toʿevah*. In Ezekiel 16, it occurs no fewer than nine times.[150] In 16.52, it takes the form of the verbal root *taʿav*, 'make abominable' (*Hiphil* verb pattern) or 'cause to be an abomination' (16.25, *Piel*). As noted previously, in prophetic language the word 'abomination' refers to the practice of idolatry or polytheism. In other words, Ezekiel accuses both Jerusalem and Sodom of being idolatrous. Each abomination is not a new sin; it is rather 'the sin of the previous sentence recapitulated' (Jordan 1997: 31). In the same context, the prophet resumes his vision of the guilt incurred by Sodom (16.49-50, NRSV):

---

[149] I thank Elisabeth Cook for pointing out that this phenomenon occurs frequently in the literary traditions of the ancient Near East. See also Lam. 4.21-22 ('daughters of Edom').
[150] 16.2, 22, 36, 43, 47, 50, 51x2, 58.

> This was the sin of your sister Sodom: she and her daughters had arrogance, excess of food, and prosperous ease, but did not aid the poor and needy. They were haughty, and did abomination before me; therefore I removed them, as you have seen.

Thomas Hanks (1983: 9) has pointed to Ezekiel's status as exile in Babylon and how his frequent use of the Hebrew verb *yanah*, 'oppress', shows a clear relationship between the concepts of oppression and poverty. Thus, the prophet insists that the just person must be generous with the poor and hungry. Because the leaders of Judah disobeyed this divine requirement, they were carried into captivity (Ezek. 18.7, 12, 16; 22.29). By emphasizing the injustices faced by the poor and needy, all prophetic books make it clear that their visions of the drama of Sodom in Genesis 19 specifically focus on the outsider or resident alien who is mistreated by the locals. Weston Fields (1997: 184) summarizes Ezekiel's approach to the drama in these terms:

> He saw, therefore, that the main point of the story was a polemic against mistreatment of the *ger* ['outsider'] as exemplified by the Sodomites' mistreatment of Lot.

In summary, both Isaiah and Ezekiel use the name of Sodom for focusing on the deplorable lot of the poor and vulnerable, i.e. all who are victims of social and political injustice (Fields 1997: 178). Likewise, the above overview has shown that notions of homoeroticism are not included in the prophetic interpretations of the story of Sodom and Gomorrah. From pre-Hellenistic antiquity until the Middle Ages, three major hermeneutical shifts occurred with respect to Sodom and Gomorrah. In the present book, the relevant interpretive foci will be termed paradigms A, B, C, and D. Thus, as the first stage in a long historical chain, the prophetic hermeneutics will be called paradigm A.

Sodom in the Apocrypha

The Hellenistic era was a time of great linguistic and cultural transformations. For example, Classical Hebrew was abandoned as a vehicle of literary expression following the Babylonian exile (587–538 BCE). It was replaced by Late Hebrew, which came under the growing influence of Aramaic, the lingua franca of the ancient Near East during the time of the Persian empire and well into Roman times (Sáenz-Badillos 1993: 55). Hellenism began with the extensive conquests of Alexander the Great in the fourth century BCE. A major consequence of this process was the rise of Greek as a literary language throughout the empire.

While the HB approached the story of Sodom and Gomorrah according to paradigm A, the Hellenistic era witnessed the birth of paradigm B. It emerged in the so-called apocryphal literature.[151] Several apocryphal books are included in the Septuagint (LXX), the earliest known Greek version of the First Testament. The concrete allusions to Sodom in the Apocrypha are listed in table 40.

---

[151] Within Roman Catholicism these writings are called 'deuterocanonical' (CCB p. 887).

Table 40
Sodom in the Apocrypha

Writing	Date	Original Language
Sirach (Ecclesiasticus)	180 BCE	Late Hebrew
Wisdom of Solomon	First century BCE	Greek
3 Maccabees	1st century BCE/CE	Greek
4 Esdras	First century CE	Late Hebrew
5 Esdras	Second century CE	Latin

The apocryphal work *Sirach* (*Ben Sira*) emerged in the Hellenistic era. For centuries it was thought to be a Greek document, given the absence of any Hebrew manuscripts. However, a Late Hebrew original of *Sirach* has been discovered, which enables scholars to conclude that the well-known Greek work is really a translation (Sáenz-Badillos 1993: 127). In respect of Sodom, *Sirach* continues operating within paradigm A. The book mentions that God abhorred the pride displayed by Lot's fellow citizens in Sodom (16.8). Similarly, the apocryphal *3 Maccabees* 2.5–7 explains that the inhabitants of Sodom were devoured by fire and sulphur because of the arrogance of their actions and their vices, whose exact nature is left unspecified.[152]

For its part, *4 Esdras* refers in 2.8 to the wicked, unjust people of Assyria who do not listen to the voice of God. The author warns the Assyrians against the danger of undergoing the same destiny as Sodom and Gomorrah, i.e. being reduced to rubble. In an apocalyptic vision (5.1–7), *4 Esdras* presents a detailed picture of future suffering for the people living on

---

[152] www.biblegateway.com/passage/?search=3+Maccabees+2%3A5-7&version=CEB (2013).

the earth. At that time, truth and faith will vanish, injustice will take hold, birds will flee, and 'the sea of Sodom' (possibly an allusion to the Dead Sea) will vomit all fish onto the shore. Finally, *4 Esdras* recalls in 7.36 that Abraham interceded for Sodom.[153] The work *5 Esdras* exists only in a Latin version. However, in some manuscripts, it is included as chapters 1 and 2 of *4 Esdras*, the original of which was penned in Late Hebrew.

Another important apocryphal work is the *Book of Wisdom* (also called *Wisdom of Solomon*), which was written in Greek. It highlights the way in which Sodom and neighbouring cities today are nothing but desolate, smoking wastelands (10.6–7). The author states that the area was destroyed because of the ungodliness, unbelief, foolishness, and wickedness of the inhabitants. Up until this point, the perspective adopted by the author of Wisdom is in accordance with paradigm A. The second time Wisdom alludes to the drama of Sodom is in 19.13–17, but this time without mentioning the city by name. In the latter passage, the punishment meted out to the 'sinners' is described as a direct consequence of their 'wicked acts' and 'bitter hatred of strangers' (19.13); they refused to receive strangers and tried to make slaves of them (19.14), and because they treated the visitors with hostility, those at the door of the righteous man (Lot) 'were stricken also with the loss of sight' (19.17).

The mention of strangers is a novelty of great historical interest. For the first time in the literature of antiquity, the subject of hospitality, or the lack of it, is brought up explicitly in reference to Sodom. While Isaiah, Ezekiel, Jeremiah, and other prophetic voices have focused on the vulnerability characterizing the life of the resident alien living in Sodom

---

[153] etext.virginia.edu/toc/modeng/public/Kjv4Ezr.html (2013).

(Lot and his family),[154] Wisdom 19 changes the perspective by turning the spotlight on the messengers sent to Sodom by YHWH (Gen. 18.22; 19.1-13). The latter approach to the legend, with its noteworthy emphasis on the visitors, is going to play an increasingly significant role in the Hellenistic era and beyond. This, then, is the birthplace of paradigm B. Eventually it will completely eclipse the original paradigm A.

Obviously some parts of the Apocrypha agree in certain respects with paradigm A. At the same time, the analysis carried out here has made it clear that, in their reflections on the story of Sodom, the authors of apocryphal literature oscillate between paradigms A and B. Their discussions of Sodom do not include any subjects of a sexual nature, be it heterosexual or homoerotic (Bailey 1955: 10).[155]

Sodom in the Second Testament

The Second Testament is the foundational literature of Christianity. This collection of writings was produced in the Hellenistic variant of the Greek language known as *koiné*. Virtually all ST references to the First Testament are based on the Septuagint version whose prestige in the early church was enormous (Loader 2004: 127; Brayford 2007: 5). The uneven literary and grammatical standard of the Greek employed in different parts of the ST reveals that these writings came about in a period marked by important cultural, social, and linguistic changes. In several cases, the mother tongue of the author(s) seems to have been Aramaic or, possibly, Late Hebrew. For example, the phenomenon is

---

[154] For further details, see the present book's chapter 11.
[155] As stated in my introduction, the terms 'heterosexual' and 'homosexual' have no equivalents in ancient literature.

detectable in the quality of the Greek prose of the book of Revelation (Hanks 2000: 251).

In the pages of the ST, Sodom is mentioned nine times. In the Gospel of Matthew (11.23-24), Jesus refers to the destruction of Sodom as less serious than the fate awaiting the city of Capernaum. The latter has seen several miracles performed by Jesus with little impact on its inhabitants. According to Luke 17.29-31, the second coming of Jesus is likely to be as sudden as the moment in which Sodom was annihilated. For his part, in Rom. 9.29, Paul joins the prophetic visions of Sodom in the HB by quoting Isaiah 1.9. The author of Revelation follows the same tradition in 11.8 by using the name of Sodom as a metaphor for a city he knows well, probably Jerusalem.

The main novelty concerning Sodom and Gomorrah in the ST is the specific way in which Jesus refers to the cities as an emblem of unacceptable behaviour, particularly their failure to show hospitality to the messengers of God (Matt. 10.15; Lk. 10.12). This change of perspective on the drama of Sodom is in keeping with the approach taken approximately a century earlier by the apocryphal *Wisdom of Solomon*. In both cases, the language of composition is Greek. In other words, the Hellenistic era seems to be witnessing an important new trend away from the earlier prophetic visions of the oppressed residents of Sodom (paradigm A). The focus is shifting toward the visiting strangers (paradigm B). In summary, in the ST two coexisting visions of the sin of Sodom have been traced. A few writings (Rom. 9 and Rev. 11) remain within the prophetic tradition of the HB while several others (Matthew and Luke) follow the new trend in Hellenistic literature in which the central issue is (in) hospitality to strangers. Table 41 offers an overview of the nine ST references.

Table 41
Sodom in the Second Testament

Second Testament	Date	Original Language
Letter to the Romans	57–58 CE	Greek
Gospel of Luke	80–90 CE	Greek
Gospel of Matthew	85–90 CE	Greek
Revelation	95–100 CE	Greek
Letter of Jude	ca. 100 CE	Greek
Second Letter of Peter	ca. 125 CE	Greek

If the references to Sodom in the entire Bible are added up, the HB contains forty-one, the Apocrypha seven, and the ST nine. The total is fifty-seven biblical references. The particular approaches adopted by the letters of Jude and 2 Peter are discussed below.

Sodom in Jude

In regard to Sodom, two short letters in ST occupy a special place, namely, Jude and 2 Peter. Dating biblical literature with any precision is notoriously difficult. For the time of composition of these writings, scholars have arrived at widely diverging conclusions. Perhaps a slender majority is settling for the late first or early second century CE for Jude.[156] Most scholars agree that some of its points are

---

[156] Some examples: Thomas Hanks (2000) accepts the nominal authorship of Jude, brother of Jesus. This leads him to suggest 50–60 CE for Jude (pp. 241-2, 247, 259) and 80–90 CE for 2 Peter (pp. 217, 241, 260). Similarly, Carroll Osburn (2000: 750) argues that 'Jude could very well be dated in the '50s and very possibly be one of the earliest ST documents. This position finds backing in Richard Bauckham (1990: 177) who assumes Jude to be an early work of Palestinian

quoted and expanded in 2 Peter. Thus, Jude seems to have been composed first.[157] Some regard 2 Peter as the latest of the books in the Greek scriptures (Rogerson 1999: 126).

Whatever the actual dates, it is significant that it took a lengthy process for these two Epistles to become admitted to the Christian biblical canon.[158] By the early fourth century CE, their status was still under debate.[159] Only during the second half of that century did they gradually appear to become formally endorsed by most church authorities.[160] However, their canonical status has not been universally recognized.[161] For instance, Martin Luther regarded Jude as a secondary source and consigned it to an appendix of his German ST

Jewish Christian provenance; cf. Countryman 2006: 748–9. As for 2 Peter, Osburn (2000: 1040) indicates a first-century date in the period 75–90 CE. By contrast, Geza Vermes (2001: 110–12) regards Jude as a pseudonym used by a person unrelated to Jesus. Vermes suggests ca. 100 CE for Jude (p. 110) and 125 CE, if not later, for 2 Peter (p. 112). This view is shared by Rogerson (1999: 97, 98, 125–6), who proposes 100–110 CE for Jude and 120–140 CE for 2 Peter. Bauckham (1990: 168–9) offers a revealing chart in which the suggested dates for Jude range all the way from 54 CE to 160 CE.

[157] Ackroyd and Evans (eds.) 1970: 283; Rogerson 1999: 125; Hanks 2000: 217; Vermes 2001: 112; Gorsline 2006: 734–6.

[158] Richard Bauckham (1990: 137) observes that the church fathers had problems with Jude's explicit quotation from the extra-canonical *Book of Enoch*; cf. discussion below.

[159] In his *Church History* (sometimes called *Ecclesiastical History*), Eusebius of Caesarea [ca. 265–340] mentions several 'disputed' books including James, 2 and 3 John, Jude and 2 Peter; cf. Ackroyd and Evans (eds.) 1970: 304–05. See also A. G. Patzia 1995: 93, 95.

[160] The Eastern Church at Alexandria seems to have moved in this direction in 367. The Western Church at Rome may have taken this step in 382 and certainly in 405 CE. The North African Church synods followed suit in 393, 397 and 419. See Ackroyd and Evans (eds.) 1970: 544; Metzger and Coogan (eds.) 1993: 103–4; Patzia 1995: 159.

[161] Neither Jude nor 2 Peter was included in the *Peshitta*, the Bible used by the East-Syrian Nestorian Church; cf. Ackroyd and Evans (eds.) 1970: 365; Metzger 2001: 28; Metzger and Coogan (eds.) 1993: 104; Patzia 1995: 93, 95.

(Countryman 2006: 748). In the nineteenth century, a fresh debate on this issue flared up, particularly among Roman Catholic scholars (Bauckham 1990: 138).

To discuss the position of Jude within the biblical canon is important due to the letter's unusual take on Sodom. The religious, social, and ethical issues highlighted by other biblical writings now fade into the background as a different subject claims the attention of the author, namely, sex. The reference in Jude to Sodom is found in v. 7. This one-chapter letter is the first canonical writing to explain that the people of Sodom and Gomorrah committed 'fornication' and 'went after other flesh'. The 'other flesh' (sometimes translated as 'different flesh' or 'strange flesh') is a literary curiosity inasmuch as it alludes to sexual relations between human beings and angels from heaven (cf. v. 6). According to some scholars, this could be regarded as an allusion to Genesis 6.2–4 where the so-called sons of God took earthly wives and impregnated them (Carden 2004: 59). However, it seems more likely that Jude has found inspiration in several Jewish writings from the Hellenistic period. In fact, the letter does not focus on the text of Genesis but refers to two pseudepigraphal works: *The Assumption of Moses* (v. 9)[162] and *The Book of Enoch* (v. 14).

Jude reflects a number of issues faced by the early church, including mistaken doctrine, unacceptable teaching, and behaviour unworthy of followers of the Gospel.[163] In the context of Sodom, the impact on biblical interpretation of this modest Greek letter has been far-reaching. With the inclusion of Jude, new hermeneutical material was inserted into the ST canon. Whereas the Hebrew prophets would often resort to

---

[162] Hanks (2000: 243) mentions the *Testament of Moses*. For a detailed discussion of the so-called pseudepigrapha, see the present book's chapter 8.
[163] Jude vv. 4, 8, 10–13, 16, 18–19.

polemical metaphors from the sexual realm, Jude uses sex in a more specific, non-metaphorical sense. The scenario described in v. 7 primarily reflects concerns pertaining to the realm of 'heterosexuality'. On this basis, the Epistle of Jude (followed by 2 Peter, see below) occupies a unique position in the biblical panorama dealing with Sodom and Gomorrah. In the context of the present book, I call Jude's hermeneutical approach, which includes an important sexual aspect, paradigm C. Given the remarkable situation created by this letter, it is worth remembering that at the moment of its composition, the Christian canon had not yet become established. Many apocryphal and pseudepigraphal writings of the Hellenistic era enjoyed considerable prestige and popularity in Jewish and Christian circles alike (Nickelsburg 2003: 21, 23; Carden 2004: 43).

Translating 'Other Flesh'

To illustrate the impact of Jude on Christian hermeneutics in the context of Sodom and Gomorrah, it is instructive to verify how today's English versions of the Bible approach the issue of 'other flesh' in Jude v. 7. Their suggested solutions are shown in table 42.[164] The acting 'they' refers somewhat obliquely to the 'angels' who sinned (v. 6) and to the people of Sodom and Gomorrah.

---

[164] In this table, the Lexham English Bible (LEB) takes the place of JPS, which is limited to the Hebrew Bible.

Table 42
Translating Reference to Sodom in Jude

Version	Jude v. 7 on Sodom and Gomorrah
CCB	who prostituted themselves and were lured into unnatural unions
HCSB	committed sexual immorality and practiced perversions*
	*Lit *and went after other flesh*
JM	which similarly glutted themselves with vice and sensual perversity
LEB	indulged in sexual immorality and pursued unnatural desire*
	*Lit. 'went after other flesh'
NCV	they were full of sexual sin and people who desire sexual relations that God does not allow
NIV	gave themselves up to sexual immorality and perversion
NJB	who with the same sexual immorality pursued unnatural lusts
NKJV	having given themselves over to sexual immorality and gone after strange flesh
NLT	which were filled with immorality and every kind of sexual perversion
NRSV	which . . . indulged in sexual immorality and pursued unnatural lust*
	*Gk *went after other flesh*
NWT	after they . . . had committed fornication excessively and gone out after flesh for unnatural use*
	*Gen. 19.5, Lev. 18.22, Rom. 1.26
REB	they committed fornication and indulged in unnatural lusts

Two Greek expressions in Jude v. 7 are of interest: (a) *ekporneusasai*, 'they committed fornication'; (b) *apelthousai opisō sarkos heteras*, 'they went after other flesh'. The former phrase clearly denotes sexual activity. Two versions in table 42 have opted for a literal rendering of *ekporneusasai*, namely, 'committed fornication' (NWT, REB). The renderings of six other versions are fairly literal as they include 'sexual immorality' (HCSB, LEB, NIV, NJB, NKJV, NRSV). Slightly more distant from the Greek are 'full of sexual sin' (NCV) and 'filled with immorality' (NLT), and even less successfully, the CCB suggests 'they prostituted themselves'. The phrase 'glutted themselves with vice' (JM) takes the prize not for accuracy but for colourfulness. In summary, in all versions, Jude offers an unmistakable picture of sexual immorality at the heart of the drama of Sodom.

The other crucial element in v. 7 is the notion of 'other flesh'. As on so many other occasions in the ST, the noun *sarx*, 'flesh', here in the form of *sarkos*, signifies the human body and its instincts.[165] Curiously only one version has attempted a literal translation such as 'strange flesh' (NKJV). Just one more version, to which I return below, includes the word 'flesh' in the text (NWT). Three versions wisely supply footnotes acknowledging the presence of 'other flesh' in the Greek original (HCSB, LEB, NRSV). However, many versions turn *sarx/sarkos* into abstract nouns such as 'lust' (NJB, NRSV, REB), 'desire' (LEB), 'use' (NWT), 'relations' (NCV), and 'union' (CCB). The HCSB has paraphrased the idea of 'they went after other flesh' converting it to 'practiced perversions' (HCSB). JM speaks of 'sensual perversity' while the NIV has chosen the short option 'perversion'. Other paraphrases are 'were lured into unnatural unions' (CCB), 'pursued unnatural lust(s)' (NJB, NRSV), 'indulged in unnatural lusts'

---

[165] Cf. Rom. 7.18; 8.3–9, 12–13; 13.14; 1 Cor. 15.39, 50; 2 Cor. 10.2–3; 12.7; etc.

(REB), and 'gone out after flesh for unnatural use' (NWT). The longest paraphrase of all is offered by the NCV. If this version is to be trusted, 'going after other flesh' means to 'desire sexual relations that God does not allow'.

The Greek phrase *sarkos heteras* is an unusual combination not found elsewhere in the ST. Therefore, the notion of 'other flesh' should be approached and translated with care. Yet it is remarkable how many versions have coined specific English paraphrases that are understandable to modern readers but which may have little to do with the meaning of the original text. To take the most extreme example, the NCV's turn of phrase 'sexual relations that God does not allow' is difficult to justify. The desire for sexual relations may well be implicit in 'going after other flesh', but in the Greek text neither 'God' (*theos*) nor 'allow' (*epitrepō*) are mentioned. It would seem that such concepts are located in the eyes of the beholder, i.e. the translator. Unfortunately, 'every kind of sexual perversion' (NLT) is not much better. No single word in this English phrase has a Greek equivalent in Jude v. 7. Similar observations apply to most other translations in table 42.

In the overall context of table 42, the most striking adjective is 'unnatural' found in no fewer than six versions (CCB, LEB, NJB, NRSV, NWT, REB). From a linguistic point of view, this is highly problematic. In ST Greek, 'unnatural' is not expressed by means of *heteros* ('other'). Rather, the exact equivalent would be *para physin* ('against nature') as attested in Rom. 1.26–27 and 11.24.[166] The excessive emphasis in the versions on 'perversion' and 'unnatural' liaisons is revealing. The impression left by such renderings is that, in the minds of the translators, those who 'go after

---

[166] See chapter 14 for discussions of *para physin* in Paul's letter to the Romans.

other flesh' have homosexual inclinations. Given the Greek wording, this is indeed ironic. If one analyses the modern term 'heterosexual', it refers precisely to those who are attracted to the 'other' sex. Strictly speaking, at least from a linguistic viewpoint, this should fit the context of Jude. Yet oddly enough, many versions have (probably unwittingly) stood the logic of *sarkos heteras*, 'other flesh', on its head. The translators have caused it to mean exactly the opposite, namely, same-sex attraction.[167] As observed by Countryman (2006: 749), 'going after strange flesh' is hardly a natural idiom for same-gender intimacy.

The most telling example of this imbroglio is provided by the NWT. In a marginal note, this version suggests that 'going after other flesh' echoes three other biblical passages, namely, Genesis 19.5 (Sodom and Gomorrah), Leviticus 18.22 ('With a male you shall not lie down . . . '), and Romans 1.26. All of these are much-quoted texts in current debates on homoeroticism and the Bible. Thus, in a not-so-subtle way, the NWT has created dubious links between the letter of Jude and various other parts of the Bible, despite the fact

---

[167] Table 40 illustrates translators' reluctance to render *sarx* as 'flesh' in v. 7. The very same noun reappears in v. 8 in the phrase *sarka men miainousin*, 'they defile their flesh'. In this second case, curiously, five versions, i.e. close to 50%, feel able to use 'flesh' (HCSB, JM, NKJV, NRSV, NWT) while four versions prefer 'bodies' (CCB, NIV, NJB, REB). The NCV euphemistically speaks of those who 'make themselves filthy with sin' while the NLT paraphrases even more in 'live immoral lives'. Similarly, in v. 23 *tēs sarkos espilōmenon*, 'defiled by the flesh', *sarx* becomes 'flesh' in five versions (HCSB, JM, NIV, NKJV, NWT). Two versions prefer 'bodies' (NJB, NRSV), reduced in the CCB to 'body'. Again the NCV resorts to euphemism ('dirty from sin') to be matched by the REB's paraphrase 'contaminated with sensuality'. In other words, here is another striking example of how many modern English versions surrender to inconsistency whenever they deal with sexual issues, particularly same-sex relationships (real or perceived). Mark Jordan (1997: 36) has characterized these renderings as 'irresponsible'.

that 'other flesh' is mentioned nowhere else.[168] In addition, the NWT translators have overlooked the crucial fact that Jude is *not* quoting scripture as we know it but extra-biblical, or pseudepigraphal, literature.

Sodom as Immorality

In summary, within the Christian tradition the short, unassuming Greek letter of Jude has set a powerful precedent for reinterpreting the story of Sodom and Gomorrah. Indeed, as it deviates from all earlier biblical sources, the hermeneutical paradigm C adopted by Jude represents a clean break with the past on two levels. In the letter, there is no trace of the strong concerns for social justice that characterize the prophetic visions of Sodom in the HB (paradigm A). Similarly, the issue of inhospitality to strangers, introduced by the book of Wisdom and reinforced by the Gospels of Matthew and Luke (paradigm B), is absent. Instead, Jude focuses remarkably on the dubious morality of different unnamed circles of 'ungodly' men who stir up trouble within Christian congregations (vv. 10–18).

Expressed in highly polemic language, the sexual concerns voiced by the letter of Jude establish connections between issues afflicting the addressees in vv. 6–15 and earlier pseudepigraphal writings (cf. Countryman 2006: 751). Given the evolution of post-biblical Christian theology, which is strongly indebted to paradigms B and C with respect to Sodom and Gomorrah, it would seem that Jude's privileged position in the ST canon has contributed to the rise of a new interpretive tradition. If this is so, the fault line between a biblical and a post-biblical hermeneutics of the story of

---

[168] James Miller (2010: 97) argues that '*sarkos heteras* **cannot** be used to describe lust for the same gender' (his emphasis).

Sodom and Gomorrah runs near the very end of the ST, with Jude at its inception.[169]

As indicated above, Jude is not alone. Several points made in this letter are taken up in 2 Peter and almost quoted verbatim. In 2.6-10 the author of 2 Peter explains in relation to Sodom that the 'unrighteous' are kept 'under punishment until the day of judgement — especially those who indulge their flesh in depraved lust' (NRSV). As he mentions 'flesh' (2.10, Greek *sarx*), it becomes clear that 2 Peter shares some of the sexual assumptions about Sodom adopted by Jude based on earlier pseudepigraphal sources, i.e. paradigm C. In other respects, 2 Peter is more Hellenistic or Greek-oriented than Jude and less influenced by Jewish literature. The author of 2 Peter seems to be conscious of the problems surrounding the status of various pseudepigraphal books. While Jude clearly accepts and respects *The Assumption of Moses* and *1 Enoch*, in 2 Peter all explicit references to these works have been removed. At this stage, no biblical canon exists for the Christian church, but the almost imperceptible references in 2 Peter to the pseudepigrapha suggest that the prestige of these writings is waning.

A special concern for 2 Peter is the problem of heretical preachers and commentators. The letter's second chapter begins with a scathing attack on dangerous 'false teachers' who are about to lead some of the fledgling Christian communities astray by bringing in 'destructive opinions' (2.1-3). Their morality is called into question as they are described as 'licentious', 'greedy', 'deceptive', and 'ungodly'. This matches 2.6-10 where the men of Sodom are depicted in very similar

---

[169] It is ironic that the Christian ST includes allusions to Jewish pseudepigraphy while the Jewish canon does not. This significant difference may, at least in part, explain why Judaism and Christianity have gone their separate ways on the issue of Sodom and Gomorrah; cf. Nickelsburg 2003: 2.

terms as 'ungodly', 'licentious', 'lawless', 'unrighteous', and 'depraved' (NRSV). The author of 2 Peter warns the faith community against selfish gossipers who are 'creatures of instinct' given to gluttony, with hearts 'trained in greed' and whose eyes are 'full of adultery' (2.11-14).[170] It would seem that in 2.14, the word 'adultery' is to be taken literally and not metaphorically as in the prophetic writings of the HB.

In regard to Sodom one thing in particular is important to keep in mind. The fact that 2 Peter picks up several points made by Jude provides them with additional canonical corroboration and authority. In this manner, paradigm C becomes the basis of a Christian sexual approach to Sodom and Gomorrah. Put differently, as they debate some of the difficulties faced by the nascent Christian communities, both Jude and 2 Peter have added significantly to the complexity of the reception history of the story of Sodom. Finally, as pointed out by Michael Carden (2004: 59), in 2 Peter one finds no allusion to homoeroticism. In fact, Jude and 2 Peter do not regard homoerotic relationships as an issue. Viewed from this perspective both letters are in tune with the rest of the ST (Miller 2010: 97).

Lot in the Bible

As protagonist of Genesis 19, Lot is a major figure in the context of Sodom, but outside Genesis relatively few scriptural references to Abraham's nephew are available. The book of Deuteronomy 2.9, 19 alludes to him indirectly, calling the nations of Moab and Ammon 'children of Lot'.[171] In the light of this historical connection, YHWH

---

[170] 2 Peter 2.11-14, 17-22; 3.3-4. See also Jude vv. 4, 8, 10, 12, 16, 18-19.
[171] Arguably it would be more accurate to speak of 'the children of Lot's daughters'; cf. Gen. 19.32-38.

orders the Israelites to respect the rights of the Moabites and Ammonites, including their land. However, a far more sceptical approach to Moab and Ammon is voiced in Psalm 83.6-8. Again called 'children of Lot' (83.8), both nations are counted among the enemies of Israel along with the Edomites, Assyrians, and Philistines.

The apocryphal *Sirach* (Ecclesiasticus) dispassionately comments in 16.8 that 'the neighbours of Lot', i.e. the Sodomites, paid a high price for their arrogance. Implicitly the passage suggests that Lot's mentality was different. *The Wisdom of Solomon* (*Book of Wisdom*) mentions in 10.6 and 19.17 'a righteous man' who saved his life due to divine intervention unlike other impious inhabitants of cities in the Jordan valley. In summary, while the descendants of Lot are criticized at times, the few direct references to Abraham's nephew are neutral or even respectful in the HB and the Apocrypha alike.

In the Second Testament, Lot is mentioned four times. Three such occasions are found in the Gospel of Luke in connection with words of warning spoken by Jesus about unforeseen natural disasters (Luke 17.28-32). The overall tone of the passage is factual and instructive. In this context, Lot is presented as a positive symbol of detachment from material possessions in contrast to his wife (17.32). For its part, the letter of 2 Pet. 2.7-8 refers to Lot in respectful terms as a 'righteous' man who suffered considerably as a result of the 'licentious' lifestyle of his fellow citizens. Thomas Hanks (2000: 219) observes that some of the Greek terms used by 2 Peter describe Lot as being 'oppressed' by violence. Thus, the vocabulary chosen by 2 Peter reminds readers of Lot's immigrant, marginalized status in Sodom.

In summary, biblical references to Lot are few. A small number of comments reflect a negative attitude to his descendants in Moab and Ammon. However, the outraged comments on

Lot that are typical of contemporary academic literature are not shared by the biblical authors. In general terms, the First and Second Testaments as well as the Apocrypha regard Abraham's nephew dispassionately or with respect.

Conclusion

In this chapter, the whole Bible has been searched for early interpretations of the legend of Sodom and Gomorrah. Three major paradigms A, B, and C have been detected within the biblical framework. While each paradigm has its own characteristics, there may occasionally be some overlap between them. paradigm A is primarily represented by the prophetic books, which are important 'eyewitnesses' due to their direct access to the original Hebrew text. These interpreters associate the name of Sodom with a social, political, and theological situation characterized by polytheism and appalling injustices. The sexual metaphors employed by the prophets refer to idolatrous practices embarked upon by the Israelite community. In short, in the world of the Hebrew prophets Sodom is not a geographical location. The name symbolizes a cruel social reality, which is very much at odds with the commandments of Yhwh.

While paradigm A casts the oppressed citizens of Sodom as victims, the focus switches during the Hellenistic period to the visiting strangers (paradigm B). This change is visible in the apocryphal *Wisdom of Solomon* and the ST Gospels, all written in Greek. It coincides with the cultural and linguistic changes in the Hellenistic world whereby a clear hermeneutical shift occurs with regard to the story of Sodom and Gomorrah. As a result, the sin of the Sodomites is redefined as inhospitality.

Adding to the interpretive complexity surrounding the drama of Sodom, the Second Testament presents a third factor which has not been present in Classical Hebrew literature nor in the Apocrypha or the Gospels: problematic sexual relationships (paradigm C). The short letter of Jude suggests that the people of Sodom were 'promiscuous' and that they wanted to overstep the limit between the divine and human spheres as they lusted after 'other flesh'. This unusual phrase reveals that in Jude's vision, which is strongly connected to extra-biblical literature, heavenly beings are regarded as an object of desire. In this unique literary setting, the perceived problem of Sodom is sexual immorality. The particular vision presented by Jude is partly supported by 2 Peter, according to which Sodom was full of 'licentious' people. The repeated ST references to illicit sex in Sodom and Gomorrah have reinforced this impression. Indeed, the new combination of inhospitality and sexual transgression will have a decisive impact on biblical hermeneutics for many centuries to come.

The present chapter has shown that no biblical text referring to Sodom and Gomorrah deals specifically with homoerotic relationships. Only the letter of Jude touches upon the subject marginally within its discussion of sex between angels and human beings. To summarize the biblical approaches to Sodom, three main trends or paradigms have been identified:

1. *Paradigm A.* Location: the Hebrew Bible.
   The inhabitants of Sodom practise idolatry and commit social injustice. The victims are Lot the immigrant and his family.
2. *Paradigm B.* Location: Apocrypha and Gospels of Matthew and Luke.
   Sodom is an inhospitable place.
   The visiting messengers are identified as victims.
3. *Paradigm C.* Location: Jude and 2 Peter.
   Sodom represents debauchery.

8

SODOM YESTERDAY

*If blasphemy is the worst,
I do not know in what way sodomy is better.*

— Peter Damian [172]

Introduction

The previous chapter has shown how three different perspectives on Sodom and Gomorrah are found within the biblical corpus viewed as a whole. The following exploration documents how these paradigms A, B, and C reappear in post-biblical literature from the Hellenistic period onwards. They coexist intermittently and occasionally overlap but, as times and interpretations vary, the emphasis tends to fall on different aspects of the biblical story. Eventually one perspective will permeate Christian theology to the exclusion of all other approaches: the vision of Sodom as a place of rampant homoerotic activity subject to divine retribution (paradigm D). Warren Johansson (1990: 1229) has called the gradual expansion of the Christian obsession with homoeroticism 'the sodomy delusion'. By contrast, sexual issues play only a minor part in pre-modern Jewish literature. Here Sodom represents inhospitality, selfishness, and cruelty, with interpretations primarily based on paradigm B and, sporadically, paradigm C.

---

[172] Damian 1982: 89.

Sodom in Pseudepigraphy

As mentioned in chapter 7, the letter of Jude alludes to Sodom and Gomorrah by quoting several literary sources not included in the Bible. Often these works are called pseudepigrapha. This multifaceted collection includes *1 Enoch*, *The Assumption of Moses*, *Jubilees*, and *Testaments of the Twelve Patriarchs*. Written in Late Hebrew, Aramaic or Greek, these Jewish writings generally emerged during the second and first centuries BCE. Some pseudepigrapha were translated into other languages, including Greek, Latin, Syriac, and Ethiopian. In the Coptic tradition, some of this literature holds canonical status, particularly the books of *Enoch* and *Jubilees*.[173]

The subjects addressed by the pseudepigrapha are primarily apostasy, idolatry, and intermarriage between Jews and non-Jews. In times of crisis for the Jewish community, mixed marriages are problematic because of the concomitant risk of a diminishing number of believers (Carden 2004: 43). The issue becomes acute for isolated communities in which the pressure of the values, customs, and rites of the surrounding majority culture is relentless. In chapter 16.5-6, *Jubilees* mentions the immorality and sinfulness of Sodom whose inhabitants committed sexual transgressions. The nature of these acts is left unspecified (Hammershaimb *et al.* 1953-63: 230). The subject recurs in 20.5-6 with respect to idolatry and intermarriage (p. 238). Intriguingly, the narrator establishes a connection with Genesis 6.1-4 as he identifies the 'sons of God' with 'angels', an interpretation included several centuries later in the letter of Jude (Carden 2004: 59).

The collection entitled *Testaments of the Twelve Patriarchs* mentions Sodom several times. As in *Jubilees*, the narrator

---

[173] gbgm-umc.org/umw/bible/ethold.stm (2010).

of the *Testament of Naphtali* (3.4–5) evokes Genesis 6, using it as a warning. In his view, the biblical story seems to imply that what led to the flood was the cohabitation of the sons of God with women (Hammershaimb *et al.* 1970–76: 757). For its part, the *Testament of Benjamin* associates the name of Sodom with promiscuity in the sense of intercourse with 'loose-living' women (Hammershaimb *et al.* 1970–76: 787; Carden 2004: 59). Similar observations apply to the *Testament of Levi* (14.6), where intermarriage of Jewish men and Gentile women is emphatically rejected. Such unions are compared to the sins of Sodom and Gomorrah (Hammershaimb *et al.* 1970–76: 720). The *Testament of Asher* (7.1) warns readers against acting in the arrogant manner in which the Sodomites treated the divine messengers. Their sin was to overstep the limit between the divine and human realms (Hammershaimb *et al.* 1970–76: 769).

To summarize, in pseudepigraphy the names of Sodom and Gomorrah are used as metaphors for arrogance, apostasy, and idolatry, all of which echo concerns voiced by the Hebrew prophets. The specific problem of intermarriage is addressed in this context because it is seen as a threat to Jewish traditions. However, new concerns are debauchery and perceived irresponsible conduct vis-à-vis angels. While the pseudepigrapha initiate and provide the raw material for paradigm C, no pseudepigraphal work refers to homoeroticism (Carden 2004: 57).

Sodom in Philo and Josephus

The hermeneutical tradition begun by the pseudepigrapha was to have far-reaching consequences. In addition to its impact on the letters of Jude and 2 Peter, during this period, another set of commentaries on Sodom appeared in the works of the Hellenistic Jewish philosopher Philo (ca. 20 BCE–50

CE). Based in Alexandria, Philo addressed a substantial part of his writings to Gentile readers to whom he set out to explain the fundamentals of Judaism. Within Philo's philosophical universe, the human body with its needs and desires represents the lower, carnal part of a person. Philo classifies it as feminine while the higher, spiritual part is male (Carden 2004: 61). For instance, he is critical of any excessive intake of food and alcoholic beverages because, in his opinion, such indulgence is contrary to reason and allows sensuality to dominate (Martin 2006: 58). In Philo's view, this issue is present in the drama of Sodom. He seems to base his reflections on Sodom on various social, cultural, and sexual phenomena that he observes in his native Alexandria, and of which he emphatically disapproves (Bailey 1955: 22; Nissinen 1998: 97).

By the time Philo began his writing career, the pseudepigrapha were well-known. Their inclusion of sexual concerns in regard to Sodom meant that sexual elements became increasingly frequent in ancient literature on Genesis. In his work *De Abrahamo*, sections 134–136, Philo describes the people of Sodom as hedonists and great adulterers with unbridled sexual appetites (Philon 1966: 79). In this respect, he is in tune with paradigm C. The biblical commentaries provided by Philo, including some of his Greek terminology, are based on the Septuagint (Paget 1996: 480; Loader 2004: 12; Runia 2006: 169). In the context of Sodom, it is important to point out that the LXX version of Genesis 19.5–8 differs from the original Hebrew in several crucial aspects. For instance, the vocabulary used by the LXX suggests sexual innuendo as the inhabitants of Sodom express their desire to 'know' Lot's guests (cf. chapter 10).

In summary, Philo's distinct approach to Sodom takes inspiration from four separate sources: (1) Genesis 19 according to the LXX; (2) Ezekiel 16.49, which comments on the carefree, materialistic life of the townspeople; (3) Hellenistic pseudepigraphal literature suggesting the Sodomites were licentious and immoral; and (4) Greek philosophy, primarily Plato (Rajak 1983: 8–9; Davidson 2008: 219). Regarding Lot's guests as victims, Philo subscribes to Hellenistic perspectives on Sodom (paradigms B and C). However, he does not stop there. He goes on to argue that homoerotic activity was rife in Sodom, specifically in the form of pederasty (Carden 2004: 61). In *De vita contemplativa*, sections 59–62, Philo explains that pederasty is an undignified passion that deviates from the 'natural' course of human sexuality. With an unmistakable element of misogyny, Philo argues that pederasty causes a 'sickly femininity' to spread among the male population as it corrupts adolescent boys, leads adult men to moral and financial ruin, and leaves entire cities sterile and depopulated (Philon 1960: 41).

This particular vision of Sodom produced by Philo represents a radical departure from previous approaches. Indeed, what makes Philo unique vis-à-vis other ancient writers is the way in which he adds an explicit anti-homoerotic element to his interpretation of the story of Sodom and Gomorrah. Influenced by the form of pederasty that he observes in Alexandria, he is convinced that all same-sex physical attraction is indecent and reprehensible (Philon 1966: 79–80). Viewed over a longer time span, and in the light of his Jewish identity, it is significant to note that Philo's reflections on Sodom have largely been ignored by Jewish interpreters (Bailey 1955: 23–4). At the same time, his particular approach had a major impact on the evolution of Christian thinking during the patristic period.[174] Indeed, Philo's scathing picture of pederasty in Sodom may be considered as the historical starting point for the notion of rampant homosexual desire

---

[174] Bailey 1955: 25–6, 153; Runia 2006: 169–71; Sheridan 2006: 159; Davidson 2008: 219; Miller 2010: 61.

in Genesis 19 with which modern readers are familiar. I call this approach paradigm D.

The Jewish historian Flavius Josephus lived half a century after Philo and is likely to have known the latter's works. Josephus also addressed a non-Jewish audience, wrote in Greek and seems to have been familiar with the LXX. In his work *Jewish Antiquities* (I.200), Josephus argues that Lot was 'very friendly with the outsiders' and that the inhabitants of Sodom displayed violent sexual desires, including same-sex desire for attractive visitors (Josephus 1998a: 99). He considers same-sex intimacy to be 'unnatural' and explains, almost with pride, that it is 'abhorrent' and punishable according to Jewish law (Nissinen 1998: 94). However, unlike Philo, for whom same-sex attraction is the number one concern, Josephus also focuses on problems such as violence and xenophobia (Carden 2004: 74). For him Sodom was inhabited by hard-hearted people who practised exclusion, deportation, and assault. Thus, Josephus's interpretation of Sodom is attuned to two paradigms: the Hellenistic paradigm B (the divine visitors depicted as victims of inhospitality and violence) and paradigm D (homosexual desire; cf. Philo).

From a historical viewpoint, perhaps the most intriguing aspect of the reflections on Sodom presented by these two prominent Jewish writers of the Hellenistic era is the fact that their perspectives, particularly Philo's—not that of the Hebrew prophets—would eventually become the cornerstone of the approach adopted by the vast majority of Christian thinkers, i.e. paradigm D (Carden 2004: 77). In summary, three characteristics of Philo and Josephus should be highlighted: (a) the victims of the drama of Sodom are the visiting outsiders; (b) for Josephus the main issues are xenophobia and violence; and (c) according to Philo, the people of Sodom are motivated by pederastic lust.

Sodom in the Early Church

The literary situation in antiquity during which the biblical canon was forming was characterized by extreme diversity. On the one hand, the HB and its various Greek translations were well known, particularly the prestigious Septuagint, as well as a large number of Christian writings in the form of gospels and epistles attributed to different apostles. On the other hand, an enormous quantity of apocryphal, pseudepigraphal, Gnostic, rabbinic, and Christian literature on biblical subjects was in circulation. Undoubtedly many people who mastered the art of reading would study such books in parallel without distinguishing clearly between orthodox and unorthodox material. The majority of readers may not have felt a great need to establish such delimitations. Instead, they may well have enjoyed acquainting themselves with several or all literary genres. However, a series of theological controversies in the early centuries CE were fuelled by the multitude of religious and pseudo-religious writings available. The wide variety of approaches to the Bible created a growing need in Christianity for defining essential doctrine and orthodoxy.

This varied theological panorama explains why a well-defined approach to Sodom and Gomorrah would be welcomed in post-biblical literature. As the early church grew and evolved, the focus on the bodily existence of believers became increasingly marked. Influenced by Neo-Platonism, many Christians tended to see the universe as a battlefield in which the faithful were encouraged to choose between participating in or abstaining from the processes that sustain this material world. It was thought that only through asceticism could they be truly committed to the radical spiritual transformation heralded and promised by the second coming of Christ (Brown 1990: 482). Moreover, the ascetic movement competed with an important theological trend known as Gnosticism. While leading Christians rejected Gnostic doctrines, there is no question that Christianity as a whole absorbed some Gnostic notions such as renunciation, sexual abstention, chastity, and celibacy. Already suggested in various parts of the ST, these concepts would eventually become firmly embedded in church environments (Holloway 1999: 54–5).

From the point of view of language, it should be noted that the early church very soon lost the direct link with the First Testament in the original Hebrew. This was primarily due to the prestige of Greek as the vehicle of culture and literature and the massive presence of the Septuagint (Schulz-Flügel 1996: 643; Stemberger 1996: 572; Brayford 2007: 5). In the specific case of Sodom, there was a growing tendency toward reducing the linguistic, literary, theological, and symbolic complexity of the original to a manageable formula. The outcome was simple: Sodom was awash with illicit sexual practices, most of which were imagined to be homoerotic (paradigm D).

A wide range of church fathers and theologians from the early centuries CE have mentioned the name of Sodom in their works. In fact, the literature is so copious that for reasons of time and space only a representative selection will be mentioned here. Clement of Alexandria (d. 215 CE), who wrote in Greek, was the first major Christian theologian to endorse the approach to Sodom introduced by Philo. In his work *Paedagogus* (The Instructor), Clement specifically associates Sodom with problems such as sexual immorality and unbridled appetites, especially in the form of adultery and pederasty. In other words, his vision contains elements of paradigms C and D (Clement, book 3, chapter 8; Bailey 1955: 25).

Tertullian (d. 225), who lived in Carthage, wrote his essays and treatises in Latin.[175] On several occasions, he uses the name of Sodom as a metaphor and shows himself to be well versed in the First Testament. The most intriguing aspect of his writing is the way in which Tertullian establishes a link between Sodom and marriage (Carden 2004: 129–30). During his lifetime, celibacy was on the rise as the ideal state for committed Christians wishing to practise their religion at a deeper level. In this context, he warns readers that the final days are approaching and that those who marry and want to produce children are being thoughtless (Tertullian 1951: 17, 57). Tertullian is married, but he still maintains a critical attitude to those believers who are more concerned about married life than the life of the Spirit. He feels particularly uncomfortable with widowers who consider remarrying. He compares them with Lot's wife who halted on the road to look back and perished (Tertullian 1951: 106).[176] In summary, the vision of Sodom that pervades Tertullian's thinking is predominantly heterosexual. In this respect, his concerns are in accordance with the pseudepigrapha and paradigm C.

A great third-century scholar was Origen (ca. 185–ca. 254). He was from Alexandria and studied under the tutelage of Clement. Writing in Greek, Origen knew Hebrew and was familiar with the works of Jewish commentators. His best-known masterpiece was the *Hexapla*, a sextuple version of the First Testament, which included the original Hebrew compared with several Greek translations. From Origen's

---

[175] It is not entirely clear which version(s) of the Bible Tertullian was reading. He often seems to be quoting directly from the Greek. On several occasions, he has different Latin versions at hand (Tertullian 1951: 97, 117). Tertullian's Latin prose sometimes comes closer to the style of the original Hebrew and to the Septuagint than the Vulgate text does in later times (p. 123).

[176] Both Augustine and Jerome critiqued Tertullian's views (Tertullian 1951: 5).

viewpoint, the people of Sodom were not in the least governed by sexual appetites. To him the place was rife with injustice, and the townsmen showed no regard for hospitality (Origen 1982: 103-20; Carden 2004: 130-3). In other words, his focus on social injustice and inhospitality indicates that Origen's understanding of Sodom included elements from both biblical Testaments, i.e. he was familiar with paradigms A and B.

Sodom in the Fourth Century

In the fourth century, the trend towards associating Sodom with homoerotic relationships became increasingly visible. The approaches suggested by the pseudepigrapha (paradigm C, heterosexual) had been reinterpreted by Alexandrians Philo and Clement with a firm emphasis on pederasty. In other words, paradigm D was taking centre stage. A Christian document from the fourth century entitled *Apostolic Constitutions*, manuscripts of which survive in Greek and Latin, declares that the sin of Sodom was *contra natura* ('against nature'). In addition, for the first time in history a clear textual link is established between Sodom and the prohibition of Leviticus 18.22: 'With a male you shall not lie down . . .' (Carden 2004: 125). The author of *The Apocalypse of Paul*, an apocryphal Christian text written in Greek, observes while on a journey to the underworld a group of men who committed the crimes of Sodom and Gomorrah, 'men with men'. Their punishment consists of being permanently immersed in a river of fire, tar, and brimstone.[177] For his part, and using the fate of Sodom and

---

[177] An English translation of the Latin version of this texts reads as follows (Greek, Coptic, and Syriac manuscripts omit this paragraph): 'And I saw other men and women covered with dust, and their appearance was as blood, and they were in a pit of pitch and brimstone and borne down in a river of fire. And I asked: Who are these, Lord? And he said unto me: These are they that committed the

Lot's wife as warning exemplars, Gregory of Nyssa (fourth century) points the finger at those monks who are unable to master their passions (Carden 2004: 124–5).

According to Ambrose of Milan (340–397), Sodom illustrates a flagrant violation of the laws of hospitality. In another passage he emphasizes anarchy. At the same time, Ambrose feels that Sodom is inhabited by wicked people controlled by hedonistic instincts. In particular he is opposed to male–male sexual relationships because, in his view, they lead to selfish, aggressive attitudes, and inhospitality. Ambrose argues that when Lot's wife stops to look back at the burning city she is returning to the impure region of lust that she has just left behind. This is what causes her to perish (Jordan 1997: 34). Similarly, John Chrysostom of Antioch (347–407) explains the essence of the drama of Sodom saying that the male population 'overturned the laws of nature' and made inhospitality a characteristic of their city. For Chrysostom, sexual iniquity and self-indulgence are akin to pride. He is keen to purge monastic life of all signs of licentiousness because he fears that any tolerance of sensuality will lead to dubious practices, 'abominations' and plagues (Carden 2004: 142).

Jerome (ca. 340–420), one of the greatest figures in the early history of biblical interpretation, offers a wide range of readings. Quoting Ezekiel 16, he identifies the sin of Sodom as 'pride' amid a situation of prosperous ease. Referring to Isaiah 1 he especially notes the brazen 'arrogance' of the rulers of the city. Elsewhere Jerome mentions various allegorical or spiritual meanings associated with the name of Sodom. For instance, he reports a reading according to which Samaria and Sodom mean, respectively, 'heretics and

---

wickedness of Sodom and Gomorrah, men with men, wherefore they pay the penalty without ceasing.' The curious mention of women is not explicated. Text located 2012 at fam-faerch.dk/pseudigrapher/apocl/apcpaul.htm (v. 39).

Gentiles' (Jordan 1997: 33). Jerome's interpretation of Sodom incorporates elements from the Hebrew prophets as well as some sexual concerns found in Hellenistic literature. In other words, he combines paradigms A, B, and C and, on a few occasions, suggests vague hints of paradigm D.

In the works of Augustine of Hippo (354–430), one again finds a multifaceted vision of Sodom. For Augustine, all kinds of sexual desire are potentially sinful and believers should keep them firmly under control. In his view, the punishment meted out to Sodom was in direct proportion to the inability of the townspeople to control their sensual instincts. At the same time, he comments that the natural order was overturned which, in his universe, is an allusion to any form of sexual behaviour unrelated to procreation. In addition, Augustine reflects on the concept of sexual violation. For example, he wonders whether it is better for men to rape women than to violate other men. His answer is affirmative. So while same-sex copulation is unacceptable to him (paradigm D), what really worries Augustine is the violent eruption of disordered sexual passion in general (Jordan 1997: 35).

John Cassian (ca. 365–ca. 435) was one of the pioneers of the monastic movement. His asceticism made him concerned about all manifestations of material wealth. He warns monks not against wine but rather against indulging the pleasures of tasty food because that may lead to situations of loose living with serious moral consequences. With respect to Sodom, John Cassian's interpretation envisages the dangers inherent in unbridled sensuality (Carden 2004: 125).

Paul Orosius (ca. 383–ca. 418) took a highly significant step in a new direction. In his opinion, not only are men who practise same-sex eroticism liable to divine punishment, but also they will cause calamities to strike the whole community. Orosius refers specifically to the disasters that befell the Roman Empire that, in his view, was punished for tolerating the sins practised in Sodom (Carden 2004: 125-6). This interpretive approach reappears in new contexts at certain intervals. For example, in 538 and 544 the Roman emperor Justinian (483-565) issued decrees against sexual relationships between males. The stated motivation is that such acts provoke the wrath of God as it did in the case of Sodom and Gomorrah. Concretely Justinian feared the onslaught of major disasters within his empire, including earthquakes and outbreaks of plague (Carden 2004: 126-7).

This overview has shown that reflections on Sodom and Gomorrah vary in the early church. Several theologians are still aware of the social concerns expressed by the Hebrew prophets (paradigm A), but a clear historical trend is evident. The Hellenistic focus, according to which the victims of the sin of Sodom were the visitors, gradually becomes mainstream (paradigm B). In addition, numerous commentators interpret the biblical story from a sensual/sexual perspective (paradigm C). However, specifically for the Latin-speaking Roman church in the western Mediterranean, the biblical drama of Sodom gradually becomes an illustration of the consequences of illicit sexual practices, with an increasingly negative view of homoerotic relationships (paradigm D).

Sodomite and Sodomitic Vice

In the ancient Near East, the main languages of the early church were Greek, Syriac, and Aramaic. Of interest in this context are some Syriac writings from the eighth and ninth centuries authored by Christian theologians Theodore bar Koni and Isho'dad of Merv. In the work of the latter, one finds the noun *s'doomayootha*. It alludes to the biblical name of Sodom and means 'practices of the Sodomites'. It seems to refer primarily to hatred of foreigners, i.e. xenophobia (Carden 2004: 159). No sexual dimension seems to play a role in the version of the drama of Sodom expressed by Isho'dad, which links it to paradigm B.

In the writings of Pope Gregory the Great (ca. 540–604), the name of Sodom is repeatedly attached to a warning. In his *Moral Readings in Job,* Gregory does not specify exactly which sins he has in mind, but his vocabulary points to homoerotic liaisons described as 'crimes of the flesh' and 'perverse desires'. Clearly Gregory's vision of Sodom is influenced by paradigm D as he describes a reprehensible environment that stinks of sulphur and is characterized by unbridled passions linked to male genitals or 'loins', which have been given over to demonic control (Jordan 1997: 39; Carden 2004: 127).

Since the days of Josephus, who in the first century CE wrote his *Jewish Antiquities* in Greek (1998a), the word 'Sodomite' is used to refer to the inhabitants of the biblical city of Sodom (pp. 87–89, 95–99). Several patristic and medieval writers do the same. However, coinciding with the growing importance of Latin in the Roman church, the word 'Sodomite' increasingly appears with a moral twist in reference to illicit sex. Thus, Augustine of Hippo (354–430) argues that 'disgraceful acts against nature' are always and everywhere to be detested and punished 'as those of the Sodomites were' (Jordan 1997: 148). At other times, the word Sodomite describes a variety of undesirable personality traits in those given to materialistic lifestyles and self-indulgence (Carden 2004: 122). Over the centuries, different meanings derive from different contexts (p. 159). In his writings, Jerome (ca. 340–420) occasionally uses the term 'Sodomite' but without offering a clear definition. Gradually the word seems to allude to irregular sexual practices (Jordan 1997:

33). However, as late as the eigth century, there is evidence that the adjective 'sodomitic' does not necessarily refer to male–male intimacy. Boniface, the British missionary monk, understood sodomitic lust to involve incest, promiscuity, adultery, and 'impious unions with religious and cloistered women' (Boswell 1980: 203; Goss 1993: 95).

As pointed out by Mark Jordan (1997: 3-4), 'there is no linear progress in the genealogies of Christian moral terms'. Stated another way, the Latin term *vitium sodomiticum*, 'sodomitic vice', was not born overnight. What is clear, however, is its frequent use in scholastic texts in specific reference to homoerotic intimacy (1997: 3). In popularity, the term sodomitic vice competes in Peter Damian's work with 'the vice against nature' (1982: 27), 'the sin of the Sodomites' (p. 67), 'the plague of Gomorrah' (p. 69), 'the crime of Sodom' (p. 78) and 'unnatural vice' (p. 80). Mark Jordan (1997) has located similar terminology in the works of Alan of Lille (p. 90), Paul of Hungary (pp. 94-9), William Peraldus (pp. 110-11), Albert the Great (pp. 126-7), and Thomas Aquinas (pp. 145-6). In all such cases, it might be tempting for modern readers to translate sodomitic vice as 'homosexuality'. However, and because of the wide cultural gap between our time and the Middle Ages, it would be a mistake to make such a connection without pondering the consequences (Karras 2005: 4-9). First, dictionary definitions are insufficient because they are too often generalizations (Jordan 1997: 4). Second, each historical period attaches its own assumptions and connotations to a given word or concept.[178] Third, scholastic theologians themselves differentiated between a series of illicit sexual acts between males. Peter Damian, for

---

[178] Cf. Karras 2005: 'No medieval text was written for the purpose of providing information to historians of sexuality hundreds of years later' (p. 10). 'The past is like a puzzle, but it is a puzzle with many of the pieces missing . . . Medieval people often did not write frankly about sex' (p. 15).

instance, lists three such acts, each of which merits specific classification and quantified punishment (Damian 1982: 29, 49–50).

The Invention of Sodomy

In a letter to one of his subordinates, Pope Gregory the Great (ca. 540–604) mentions 'the crime of the Sodomite' (Böhringer 1992: 152). According to John Boswell (1980: 203–4), Gregory's letter is the first documented example of the existence of the term 'sodomy' in medieval literature, which places its origin as early as the sixth century. However, three factors make this statement untenable: (1) Gregory himself did not use this word;[179] (2) 'sodomy' occurs nowhere else in sixth-century writings; and (3) the term is inserted into Gregory's text by scribal error in a tenth-century copy, whereby 'the crime of the Sodomite' appears as 'the crime of sodomy' (Jordan 1997: 36).[180] What the presence of 'sodomy' in two tenth-century manuscript copies seems to reveal is the embryonic stage in the making of a new term.[181]

---

[179] See the complete collection of Gregory's letters, Book 10, Epistle 2, consulted 2012 at: www.kennydominican.joyeurs.com/LatinPatrology/GregoryGreatRegEpistularum.htm.

[180] The word *sodomiae*, 'of sodomy', which should have been *sodomitae*, 'of the Sodomite', occurs twice on the same page in a treatise on divorce written in Latin by Bishop Hincmar of Rheims (806–882). Hincmar is quoting a letter from Gregory the Great. In Letha Böhringer's edition of this treatise (1992), the repeated scribal error, with the letter t missing, is on p. 185. The correct spelling *sodomitae* occurs in another passage on p. 152. When Hincmar speaks of *eum peccatum sodomitanum*, 'the Sodomite sin', Boswell (1980: 204) erroneously reduces it to 'sodomy'.

[181] Intriguingly, this literary process coincides with the historical era in which celibacy is becoming mandatory for nuns, monks, and clergy at large (Karras 2005: 9, 29). Celibacy defined as 'the unmarried state' is linked to chastity, which denotes a moral obligation to abstain from sexual activity (p. 29).

In the eleventh century, the Latin word *sodomia* makes a second literary appearance. This time there is no mistake. The real birthplace of sodomy seems to be an Italian monastery with the reforming monk Peter Damian (1007–1072) performing as 'midwife'. *Sodomia* is included once in Damian's polemic work entitled *Liber Gomorrhianus*, 'The Book of Gomorrah' (Damian 1982: 89). As he wrote in Latin, it would be natural to assume that Peter's Bible quotations were taken from the Vulgate. Curiously, however, some passages cited by Peter do not belong textually to this source (Payer 1982: 23). What is certain is the relative ease with which the non-biblical term *sodomia* was coined and how it was subsequently used by a string of scholastic theologians familiar with the Vulgate (Jordan 1997: 31). Another striking feature is its longevity. In some environments and countries, the term sodomy has survived until the present day.[182]

Although he often resorts to circumlocution and polemic caricature, on the pages of the *Liber Gomorrhianus*, Peter Damian gives some idea of what he means by sodomy. Three things soon become clear: (1) some sexual activity is hinted at, (2) it takes place between males, and (3) it is to be avoided at all costs (Damian 1982: 27 ff). Peter distinguishes between four types of 'criminal wickedness', the first being solitary masturbation. Modern readers may be struck by the fact that in Peter's universe simple masturbation is counted as a crime. Initially he mentions it as an act performed by those who 'sin with themselves alone' (p. 29). Subsequently, he interprets the coitus interruptus undertaken by Onan, son of Judah (Gen. 38), as masturbation. Peter takes the fact that Onan is struck down with premature death (Gen. 38.10) as

---

[182] Mark Jordan (1997) capitalizes the word Sodomy (pp. 1–9, 29 ff.). However, some sources quoted by him do not. For Jordan, Sodomy is 'a theological category' and 'an artefact of Christian systematization' (p. 80).

clear evidence that all masturbation is a 'detestable thing' in the eyes of God (1982: 32-3).

According to Peter's classification, the second type of 'criminal wickedness' is mutual masturbation between males. This is so because whenever a man 'pollutes another in any manner whatsoever' he is undoubtedly 'to be convicted of having committed the crime of Sodom' (Damian 1982: 78). The third category is intercrural (interfemoral) sex. Fourth, Peter mentions 'the complete act against nature' (p. 29). Presumably this refers to anal penetration, which at a later stage is called 'anal fornication' (p. 52). The author emphasizes the 'ascending gradation' of these four categories to the point that those who sin by performing the complete act against nature sink deeper than the rest into 'the depths of hell's pit' (p. 29).

Peter Damian's overriding concern is the fact that sodomy as he defines it seems to be omnipresent among the clergy of his time. In the world of the *Book of Gomorrah*, Sodomites are dangerous men who live in hiding among monks, priests, and bishops and against whom everyone must be on guard. Indeed, for Peter, male–male eroticism is a 'vice against nature' which, very like an infection, 'creeps in like a cancer' (p. 27). He finds the presence of Sodomites among the sacred orders so pervasive that it is comparable to an outbreak of 'destructive plague' (pp. 39-40). Most of all, Peter finds sodomy incompatible with religious vocation. The reforming zeal underlying *Liber Gomorrhianus* produces in Peter an ardent desire to purge the entire church body of 'this shameful act' (p. 32), 'hidden poison' (p. 53), and 'filthy intercourse against the law of nature' (p. 59). He does not hesitate to describe the act he has in mind as 'worse than all other crimes' (p. 32).

Peter Damian's book is dedicated to Pope Leo IX with an appeal for action (pp. 27, 91). The requested purge is crucial because, in the author's view, he is describing a vice that 'surpasses the enormity of all vices' (p. 63). Viewed theologically, Peter is in no doubt that sodomy should be judged at least on the same level of severity as blasphemy (p. 89). Indeed, he argues that the sodomitic vice 'evicts the Holy Spirit' from the human heart while introducing the devil 'who incites to lust'. In this manner it 'separates the soul from God to join it with devils' (p. 63). In Peter's opinion, there are precedents in the writings of the church fathers showing that 'sodomists' (*sic*) are possessed by 'a diabolical spirit' (p. 60).

A number of scripture passages quoted by Damian to bolster his argument are almost exactly the same as the ones found in today's debates on Christianity and homosexuality: Genesis 19 (pp. 32, 38-9); Leviticus 20.13 (p. 33); Ephesians 5.5 (p. 35); 1 Timothy 1.10 (p. 36); Romans 1.26-27 (p. 37); Romans 1.28-32 (p. 39); 2 Peter 2.9-10, 13-14 (p. 79); 2 Peter 2.4, 6; and Jude vv. 6-7 (p. 80). Leaving aside its literary peculiarities and polemic passion, the *Book of Gomorrah* is significant as it reflects an important historical epoch in the life of the Christian church. On a relatively small number of pages, the book condenses an issue, which is to reappear over and over in the lives of successive generations. Within Roman Catholicism, Peter Damian is recognized as a saint and doctor of the church.[183] In regard to Sodom and Gomorrah, his life and work represents the culmination of a process that virtually awards canonical status to paradigm D.

Amplifying Sodomy

In the twelfth century, the French theologian Pierre le Chantre (Peter Cantor) is responsible for amplifying the

---

[183] www.newadvent.org/cathen/11764a.htm (2011).

semantic range of the concept of sodomy. In his commentary on the Bible, Pierre stretches the meaning of the word to include intimate relationships between women (Carden 2004: 164, 182). In his lifetime, however, the use of the term has not yet become pervasive. Hence, Pierre prefers the archaic sounding 'sodomitic vice' whenever he deals with homoerotic relationships. From his theological reflections, he draws the conclusion that sodomitic vice should be treated with the same severity as homicide. In fact, the reader is left with the impression that to Pierre le Chantre the sin committed by Sodomites is worse than murder (pp. 181).

Like other theologians of the Middle Ages, the great Thomas Aquinas (1224–1274) wrote in Latin. Taken as a whole, his reflections on sins related to Sodom are complex and, at times, paradoxical (Jordan 1997: 137). Thomas mentions Sodom in several of his works, including the important *Summa theologiae*. Like some of his predecessors, he employs several different terms for the concept of sodomy. For instance, in Thomas's prose one finds 'the sodomitic vice' closely linked to *luxuria* (lechery) and 'unnatural vice' (Heacock 2011: 69–70). The latter is in opposition to 'natural' vices such as adultery, promiscuity, and rape of women (sic). By letting his definition of sodomitic vice include lesbian relationships, Aquinas follows in the footsteps of Pierre le Chantre.

It would be erroneous to assume that Thomas Aquinas speaks of 'homosexuality' in the modern sense of the word. It would not fit into his categories. The term 'homosexual' simply has no direct equivalent in medieval literature (Jordan 1997: 155-6, 161; Karras 2005: 7-9). What really matters to Thomas is the problem of the so-called unnatural vices (Jordan 1997: 147, 155). In his view, the 'natural' vices are always preferable to the 'unnatural' ones (Carden 2004: 185). Almost to a higher degree than blasphemy, unnatural vices are transgressions of the cosmic order instituted by the Creator of the universe. The most worrying aspect for Aquinas is the absence of procreation because, in his thinking, this represents the true purpose of sexuality in human beings and animals alike (Jordan 1997: 146–7).

One of the great problems concerning the points made by Thomas Aquinas about Sodom is the fact that they are dispersed in different theological treatises. At the same time, they are not always interconnected, consistent, or even logically coherent. It is certainly true that for his discussions of male–male sexual relationships Thomas occasionally makes a rather biased use of Aristotle. He misreads the Greek philosopher, making him suggest a connection between male homoeroticism and such polemical concepts as bestiality and cannibalism (Jordan 1997: 149–50). In this manner, Aquinas hits two targets by presenting the sodomitic vice as unacceptable in theological terms and morally repulsive (p. 150).

In this context, a major issue in or behind virtually all theological literature produced in the Middle Ages is misogyny (Karras 2005: 15, 116–18). The horror expressed by leading thinkers of the church vis-à-vis the concept of sodomy is matched by their constant fear of effeminacy. Indeed, they violently condemn anything feminine. Above all, they feel provoked by those men who seem to surrender masculine privilege. This explains why they are revolted by any man who in 'voluntary' fashion lets himself be downgraded to act 'like a woman', most of all in the sexual realm (Jordan 1997: 57, 169).

By the thirteenth century, the anti-homoerotic interpretation of the story of Sodom and Gomorrah has become an integral part of Catholic discourse. Hence, the acceptance of the concept of sodomy by the church hierarchy is almost inevitable (Jordan 1997: 80). Obviously the very term 'sodomy' is shorter and more practical than 'sodomitic vice'. Since the time of Peter Damian and Thomas Aquinas until the present day, and in spite of its impreciseness, the medieval concept of sodomy has been the primary hermeneutical tool for Bible readers to interpret the story of Sodom and Gomorrah (Jordan 1997: 1). In other words, by the late Middle Ages virtually all traces of paradigm A (social injustice) have vanished from theological literature. In the context of Sodom, paradigms B (inhospitality to strangers) and C (sexual concerns) have coalesced into paradigm D (condemnation of homoerotic relationships). From this point on, the latter reigns supreme.

Renaissance and Reformation

Based in Florence, Dante Alighieri (1265–1321) became famous due to his masterpiece *The Divine Comedy*. In two parts of the book entitled *Inferno* (Hell) and *Purgatorio* (Purgatory), Dante mentions a group of people who are likely to be 'Sodomites'. In *Inferno*, they are constantly running for their lives lest they be caught by a cloud of fire chasing them. Among them are several well-known individuals from Dante's Florence. Intriguingly, the Sodomites are described indirectly: 'they were all clerks and great and famous scholars, defiled in the world by one and the same sin' (Dante 1971a: 197), and the author observes their fate with a certain amount of benevolence (p. 205). The same 'sinners' reappear in *Purgatorio*, but here they are identified as belonging to Sodom and Gomorrah (Dante 1971b: 339, 341). Dante leaves open the possibility that, after enduring a long, taxing purification process, they may eventually gain access to the doors of Paradise (pp. 339, 343).

However, following Dante's death, some commentators criticized the author of *The Divine Comedy* for being too 'soft' on Sodomites. Writing half a century after Dante Alighieri and, like him, from Tuscany, Giovanni Boccaccio (1313-1375) also touched on the subject of Sodom. It emerges in the second novel included in his famous *Decameron* where Boccaccio describes a journey from Paris to Rome undertaken by a French Jew named Abraham. Upon arrival, Abraham observes the lives of the pope, bishops, priests, and nuns and is astonished to find that everyone without any hesitation whatsoever is happy to indulge in sensual and carnal pleasures. Among the vices listed by Boccaccio are 'the sodomitic variant'. According to the context, he refers to erotic same-sex relationships between adults as well as intimate liaisons between adult men and teenage boys (pederasty). His language reveals that Boccaccio disapproves of what Abraham is seeing.[184]

Two landmark events in biblical studies occurred during the Renaissance. In 1482, the first printed edition of the Hebrew Pentateuch was published in Bologna, and a few years later other parts of the HB appeared. The subsequent milestone was the Greek New Testament edited by Erasmus of Rotterdam and published in Basel in 1516.[185] Such ground-breaking access to essential resources enabled the Protestant reformers to detach themselves from Catholic tradition. The availability of the Bible in Hebrew and Greek created a new situation in which Bible translations into the vernacular no longer depended on the Vulgate or the Septuagint. From this time onwards, it became customary to translate the book of Genesis directly from the Hebrew.

However, when it came to exegesis of the story of Sodom and Gomorrah, no real departure from medieval

---

[184] www.ciudadseva.com/textos/cuentos/ita/bocca/deca01.htm (2010).
[185] In Spain the *Biblia políglota complutense* (Complutensian Polyglot Bible) was published in 1520 at the initiative of Cardinal Jiménez de Cisneros.

Catholic discourse occurred. A characteristic slogan of the Reformation was the Latin phrase *sola scriptura*, 'scripture only', by which the Bible was assigned a place of honour to the detriment of church tradition.[186] In the case of Sodom, however, it is an irony of history that the exact opposite happened in the sense that the reformers willingly adopted the medieval notion of sodomy without performing any independent scriptural analysis.[187]

The medieval fusion of political and church power contributed to the longevity of sodomy as a legal concept. At a time in which governments penalized homoerotic relationships adducing biblical arguments, legislation, and biblical hermeneutics combined to such a degree that no neutral or free space remained for alternatives to be considered and publicly shared. Dissidents ran the risk of attracting negative attention including persecution for heresy, sometimes punishable by execution. At this time, in large parts of Europe, it was common to accuse heretics of practising sodomy (Vanggaard 1969: 131; Boswell 1980: 283; Karras 2005: 132). Although the concept of heresy became somewhat weakened in Reformed circles, it did not cease to exist.[188] The prevailing authoritarianism during the feudal era tended to block theological innovation. In the case of Sodom, many years would pass before fresh exegesis challenged the rigid hermeneutical assumptions imposed by church and state alike.

---

[186] Martin Luther considered the scriptures to be the sole authority for his teaching, relying on his own interpretation to the exclusion of other evidence (Long 2001: 139).

[187] An exception worth mentioning is John Calvin, who once or twice considered the hypothesis that the people of Sodom were trying to verify the identity of the unknown travellers spending the night at Lot's house (Bailey 1955: 5).

[188] In 1553 Michael Servetus was found guilty of heresy in John Calvin's Geneva and executed; cf. www.britannica.com/EBchecked/topic/535958/Michael-Servetus (2012).

Sodom According to Martin Luther

The most prominent figure among the Protestant reformers is Martin Luther (1483–1546). Luther attributes the authorship of Genesis to Moses and argues that all scripture may be divided according to two main topics: promises and threats versus benefits and punishments. Among the punishments, he feels convinced that the destruction of Sodom by fire should be preached in churches. This is so because 'the Church is never altogether pure' (Luther 1961: 225). The people of Sodom, according to Luther, became 'even worse than beasts'. They completely forgot how Abraham had delivered them in Genesis 14. They spoke harshly to Lot because he was against their sinful pride and 'lusts' (p. 226). Luther goes on to explain (p. 227),

> Not satisfied with their own wives, they desired others but made prostitutes of their own, until they finally engaged in practices which are contrary to nature and more than bestial. This is Satan's procedure after he has turned people away from God and has made them ungrateful toward Him.

Several concepts stand out in this passage, namely, 'contrary to nature' and 'Satan's procedure'. As noted, both phrases were found almost verbatim in Peter Damian's *Book of Gomorrah*. Luther goes on to argue that the messengers visiting Sodom in Genesis 19 were treated 'most outrageously' as the inhabitants attempted 'to inflict on them the most shameful disgrace that can happen to a male' (Luther 1961: 228). Reluctant to use blunt language about the sin of Sodom, Luther consistently resorts to metaphor and paraphrase. He highlights what he regards as a major contrast within the story. While the righteous Abraham is deeply concerned about the possible existence of a group of innocent citizens in the city, the townspeople actually 'live in luxury and do violence to their guests, altogether unconcerned about their own destruction' (p. 238).

Luther confesses that he does not discuss 'this awful account' with pleasure. He believes the story of Sodom was written to warn readers against sinning like the Sodomites 'through lust in conformity with their example' (p. 239). Convinced that it was the foremost citizens of Sodom who rudely and cruelly importuned Lot and his visitors at bedtime, begrudging them their sleep, Luther suspects that the people of Sodom 'were swilled with wine' because, in his view, it is well known 'what usually results from drunkenness' (p. 248). He has no doubt that the Sodomites were stirred up to attempt 'a terrible sin' and 'a horrible crime', demanding the men 'for their sensual desire' (p. 252). He suggests that they sought to kill the visitors by subjecting them to 'the utmost contumely', i.e. the worst kind of abusive and contemptuous treatment (p. 249). Without specifying the nature of the alleged crime, Luther limits himself to moralistic insinuation: 'And that in public and against innocent guests!' (p. 253). Again he shares his discomfort (p. 251):

> I for my part do not enjoy dealing with this passage, because so far the ears of the Germans are innocent of and uncontaminated by this monstrous depravity.

It is intriguing to discover that, according to Martin Luther, male–male sexual relations were unknown in Germany until Carthusian monks arrived from monasteries in Italy.[189] He asserts that 'this terrible pollution' was rife there and

---

[189] The Carthusian order was founded in the French Alps in 1084 by German-born St. Bruno of Cologne; cf. www.catholic.org/saints/saint.php?saint_id=575 (2012).

immediately takes a swipe at the pope: 'Of course, they were trained and educated in such a praise-worthy manner at Rome' (p. 252). Ironically, Luther's Roman Catholic heritage is evident in the way Catholic thinking dictates his own approach to Sodom and Gomorrah. As shown by the following paragraph (p. 255), his statements are in complete consonance with the points made in previous centuries by Peter Damian and Thomas Aquinas:

> The heinous conduct of the people of Sodom is extraordinary, inasmuch as they departed from the natural passion and longing of the male for the female, which was implanted into nature by God, and desired what is altogether contrary to nature. Whence comes this perversity? Undoubtedly from Satan.

Luther's statements demonstrate that on this issue the Reformation did not break with Catholic tradition. On the contrary, Roman Catholic and Protestant theologies were to remain virtually interchangeable for centuries as far as the interpretation of the story of Sodom and Gomorrah was concerned. In fairness, it should be noted that a sophisticated scholar like Luther was well aware of the comments on Sodom made by the Hebrew prophets. Indeed, he regularly quotes the books of Psalms, Isaiah, and Ezekiel to focus on the material wealth of the Sodomites, their arrogance and selfishness.[190] Historically speaking, however, Luther's approach to Sodom is largely post-Hellenistic and in line with medieval theology. He argues repeatedly that male–male sexual desire is 'unnatural' and that its punishment is justified. In short, Luther decidedly adheres to paradigm D.

---

[190] Luther 1961: 181, 230, 247, 249, 255.

The Triumph of Sodomy

Following the hermeneutical uniformity imposed during the Middle Ages and the Reformation on the subject of Sodom and Gomorrah, the theological landscape remained static for centuries. However, some changes occurred outside the walls of churches and monasteries as penal codes were reformed. Gradually sodomy was introduced and defined as a legal concept. From the very outset, however, the term was ill defined and applied to several different phenomena understood as unacceptable sexual behaviour.[191] In England, laws written in Latin in 1290, during the reign of Edward I, mention sodomy. A few years later, further laws produced in Norman French call for the punishment of burning alive for 'sorcerers, sorceresses, renegades, sodomists and heretics publicly convicted'.[192] Under the *Buggery Act* implemented in 1533 during the reign of Henry VIII, a sentence for sodomy could still carry the death penalty. This law remained virtually unchanged for three hundred years. Over time, sodomy was defined as sexual intercourse between two individuals in which the penis of one was inserted into the anus of the other. One party had to be male while the other might be male or female (Friends 1964: 33). Until well into the twentieth century, repressive measures continued to apply in England and Wales (1963: 33–4). In 1967 homosexual conduct was finally decriminalized, but with legal restrictions in place until 2003.[193]

---

[191] Cf. Jordan (1997: 1): 'The fearful abstraction in our use of the term is medieval, as are our prurient confusions over what the word really means.'
[192] www.acclawyers.org/wp-content/uploads/2011/05/2-Kirby-The-Sodomy-Offence-2011-JCCL-22.pdf, p. 23 (2012).
[193] news.bbc.co.uk/2/hi/uk_news/politics/3120924.stm (2003, consulted 2012).

In Spain, concepts such as usury, heresy, Judaism, and sodomy began to be lumped together in the late Middle Ages. Between 1250 and 1300 the first laws were implemented calling for the death penalty in cases of sodomy, which was sometimes defined as any sexual act not leading to procreation. In the thirteenth century the *Siete Partidas* law collection of King Alfonso X *El Sabio* ('the Wise' or 'Learned') imposed the death penalty for 'sins against nature'. *Siete Partidas* absorbed elements from the older Justinian Code (sixth century), which alluded to the purported social, political, and natural dangers caused by the 'sodomitic vice'. In the kingdom of Castile the first executions for sodomy took place around 1495. In their *Pragmática* issued in 1497, King Ferdinand and Queen Isabella hardened the sodomy laws by classifying the concept both as 'an unmentionable sin' and 'an unnatural crime', against which secular and ecclesiastical authorities were exhorted to take joint action. With the introduction of systematic torture, including for members of the clergy and nobility, records from this period in Spain show several cases in which confessions were obtained by force. In Seville, between 1560 and 1699, at least fifty persons were burned at the stake for the alleged crime of sodomy.[194]

From several European countries, the notion of sodomy was carried overseas to the colonies. Following Christopher Columbus's first voyage to the Caribbean in 1492, which he imagined was India, a number of Spanish explorers and adventurers followed suit. As they conquered the newfound territories, they imposed the medieval mindset in which they were raised. Fernanda Molina (2010) has studied the descriptions of the indigenous populations given by some Spanish conquistadores and settlers.[195] Initially Columbus

---

[194] personal.us.es/alporu/histsevilla/leyes_sodomia.htm (2012).
[195] 200.69.147.117/revistavirtual/documentos/2010/Cronicas-sodomia-Molina.pdf (2012).

and others provided an idyllic vision of the simple lifestyles of the 'Indians', but soon this was replaced by a more hostile approach, according to which the Indians practised idolatry, cannibalism, and sodomy. A major literary figure in this context was Gonzalo Fernández de Oviedo (1478–1557), who was appointed official chronicler of the Indian territories. His *Historia general y natural de las Indias* explains that 'many men and women' of the native population of the Caribbean islands and Central America were 'Sodomites', and that it was not unusual to see people wearing golden brooches depicting 'one man upon another, in that diabolical and nepharious act of Sodom' (1944: 242).[196] Fernández de Oviedo's portrayal of the Indians as idolatrous, sodomitical cannibals was hugely influential and impacted many other historians of his time,[197] despite the existence of dissenting voices.[198]

---

[196] *Y ved en qué grado se precian de tal culpa, que como suelen otras gentes ponerse algunas joyas de oro y de preciosas piedras al cuello, así en algunas partes de estas Indias traían por joyel un hombre sobre otro, en aquel diabólico y nefando acto de Sodoma, hechos de oro de relieve.*

[197] Further south, in the regions known today as Ecuador, Peru, and Bolivia, Spanish chroniclers reported having observed numerous cases of sodomy, particularly in the lowlands. Presenting the Inca civilization of the Andean highlands as superior, the Peruvian historian Inca Garcilaso de la Vega (1539–1616) defended in his work *Comentarios reales de los Incas* the 'clean' record of Inca culture by ascribing to it the same attitudes to sodomy as those held by the Spanish conquistadores, including the severe measures adopted to punish individuals caught practising the sex acts thus described (Garcilaso 1985: 146–7; Molina 2010).

[198] Among Fernández de Oviedo's opponents was Bartolomé de Las Casas (1484–1566), who for several years served as bishop of Chiapas in southern Mexico. Las Casas took a very different view of the indigenous cultures of the American colonies and vigorously opposed what he regarded as unfounded, ideologically motivated justifications of the brutal colonization process, which fomented Spanish greed and brought immense suffering on the native populations (Molina 2010). See also (2012): www.princeton.edu/~achaney/tmve/wiki100k/docs/Bartolom%C3%A9_de_las_Casas.html

According to Human Rights Watch, more than half of the world's remaining 'sodomy' laws criminalizing consensual sexual activity among adults of the same sex are relics of British colonial rule. This is true of laws in over three dozen countries from India to Uganda and from Nigeria to Papua New Guinea. Eleven former British colonies in the Caribbean also retain sodomy laws derived from a different British model than the one imposed on India in 1860.[199] In thirteen states in the USA, it was illegal, until fairly recently, for same-sex intimacy to take place in the privacy of people's homes. Some laws, like the one in Massachusetts that prescribed a five-year jail term for oral sex and twenty years in jail for anal sex, dated back to the Puritan period in the 1600s. In a landmark decision issued in 2003, the U.S. Supreme Court declared sodomy laws to be unconstitutional (Greenberg 2004: 236). In other parts of the world, a number of countries had come to recognize sodomy laws as antiquated and harmful. For example, France and Belgium abolished their laws in the 1790s; Brazil, Spain, and the Netherlands abolished theirs in the early 1800s while Denmark, Sweden, and Portugal repealed their sodomy laws in the first half of the 20th century.[200]

Sodomy in Literature

A number of examples from nineteenth-century world literature reveal that the concept of sodomy had become firmly established in social, legal, and religious contexts. An eloquent illustration appears in the monumental work

---

[199] www.hrw.org/news/2008/12/17/sodomy-laws-show-survival-colonial-injustice and southasia.oneworld.net/todaysheadlines/hrw-urges-repeal-of-oppressive-sodomy-laws.
[200] www.thetaskforce.org/issues/nondiscrimination/sodomy (2012).

In Search of Lost Time by Marcel Proust (1871–1922).[201] The fourth volume is entitled *Sodom and Gomorrah*. In this book, published shortly before the author's death, Proust speaks of a social group nominally descended from the Sodomites of the Bible. Its members behave like a secret lodge and are found in all strata of society (Proust 1987: 522). Proust reflects on the latent danger posed by present-day Sodomites wishing to create their own independent urban community, a sort of reinvention and reconstruction of the Sodom described by the book of Genesis. He finds the notion grotesque and compares it with the absurd dream of Zionists wanting to establish a Jewish state in Palestine. In this context, it is intriguing to note the ease and naturalness with which Proust employs the words 'Sodom' and 'Sodomite'. His work leaves the impression that these terms are readily understood by his readers (p. 522). At the same time, however, whenever he refers to people with homoerotic inclinations in contemporary French society, Proust clearly prefers a different terminology, namely, 'inversion' and 'invert'.

If one compares the nineteenth-century description of Sodom offered by Proust with the environment depicted by Peter Damian eight centuries earlier, a significant parallel emerges: in both cases the people alluded to belong to a kind of underground movement. However, there are striking differences too. While the Sodomites of the Middle Ages, according to Damian, primarily existed among the clergy and in monasteries, in Proust's world the same people have stepped out of the realm of the church to become integrated into the wider community at all levels.

---

[201] Also known as *Remembrance of Things Past*, the original French title is *À la recherche du temps perdu*.

In 1869—during Proust's lifetime—a major linguistic innovation took place in Europe. The Hungarian-born journalist Karl-Maria Benkert (Károly Mária Kertbeny, 1824–1882) created the neologism 'homosexual'. Within a few decades, this new term became so widely accepted that it appeared in psychoanalytical and psychiatric literature (Rosen 1993: 484). Soon it would completely eclipse and replace 'Sodomite', with the concomitant decline of 'sodomy' caused by the growing popularity of 'homosexuality'. As far as Proust is concerned, his writings show that he was familiar with the term homosexuality but found it unattractive (Proust 1987: 503). He generally applied it to the forms of homoeroticism that are known from ancient Greece and Rome (pp. 511, 514).

By the early twentieth century, the word 'sodomy' was rarely heard in allusion to homoerotic relationships. The trend has been so pronounced that even official treatises of the Roman Catholic Church, in which the concept of sodomy has been a constant since the late Middle Ages, have gradually adopted the word homosexuality due to its modern tone. However, the change of language has not substantially modified the contents. Remaining faithful to its medieval roots, today's Catholic hierarchy maintains its anti-homoerotic discourse in conformity with paradigm D.[202]

Sodom in Judaism

Due to Jewish scholars' adherence to the Classical Hebrew text, Jewish approaches to Sodom and Gomorrah differ from the characteristic sexual dimension of Christian exegesis (Carden (2004: 7, 10). Over the centuries, Jewish tradition has produced an abundant interpretive literature

---

[202] www.catholic.com/library/Homosexuality.asp

written in Late Hebrew, Aramaic, and Medieval Hebrew. A noteworthy genre is known by the name *midrash* (plural *midrashim*), which means 'exegesis' or 'interpretation'.[203] The concept applies to a series of texts by anonymous authors, the latest of which were composed in the thirteenth century (Greenberg 2004: 34). Here is a current definition:[204]

> Midrash is a tool of interpretation which assumes that every word, letter, and even stroke of the pen in the Torah has meaning. Midrash Aggadah focuses on biblical narratives, Midrash Halakhah interprets legal passages. In modern times, midrash can include any retellings, additions, or twists on Torah stories.

A general feature of midrashic literature is that it accommodates several different viewpoints. There is no necessity to arrive at some unified or 'authorized' interpretation of a given narrative or passage. Within the framework of Jewish hermeneutics, all biblical exegesis and commentary occur within a long, continuous process, which will never end (Carden 2004: 80). While readers can always be enriched by the knowledge accumulated by tradition, space is left for new insights and innovative approaches. In many cases, midrashic literature is characterized by flexibility, creativity, and adventurousness and has become a kind of entertaining appendix to biblical interpretation, which amplifies the horizon of the scriptural narrative (p. 81). At the same time, it 'competes' with academic and literary commentaries. For a long time, numerous midrashim have occupied a position of

---

[203] The word derives from *derash*, whose literal meaning is 'search' (Greenberg 2004: 33). In the context of Jewish literature, Stefan Reif (1998: 149, 152) defines *derash* as 'applied exegesis'. For Kirsten Nielsen (1997: 19) the basic exegetical principle in midrash is that 'missing information in one text can be deduced from other texts'.

[204] www.myjewishlearning.com/texts/Rabbinics/Midrash.shtml (2012).

prestige within Jewish biblical studies (Nissinen 1998: 97). In addition, they serve as much-appreciated reading material for Jewish citizens of all ages.

The midrashim invite readers to respond with their imagination to biblical stories. Given the laconic, opaque nature of the original Hebrew, it is no coincidence that the story of Sodom and Gomorrah has attracted so many midrashic writers. Within this body of writings, the two cities represent and exemplify such reprehensible phenomena as inhospitality, selfishness, and cruelty. The date of composition of the apocryphal *Genesis Rabbah* is difficult to determine accurately. Possibly the book was composed around the sixth century CE. It contains a series of comments on the biblical book of Genesis written in Late Hebrew, with some sections in Aramaic. *Genesis Rabbah* offers several midrashic sections in which Abraham is depicted as the ideal host while Lot and the people of Sodom represent inhospitality (Carden 2004: 87–9). According to the narrator of *Genesis Rabbah*, the city of Sodom had draconian laws prohibiting almsgiving to the poor. Visitors ran the risk of being robbed of all their money as well as suffering sexual humiliation (2004: 97). *Genesis Rabbah* awards considerable space to the subject of Lot and his family and suggests a certain amount of sexual tension between father and daughters (2004: 91).

Some of the subjects mentioned here appear in different variants in other writings. One famous rabbinic tale mirrors the Greek myth of Procrustes, which inverts the ethic of hospitality. Thus, the people of Sodom had a special guest room in which weary visitors might spend the night. However, when the wayfarer lay down, the locals were on hand to make sure that he fit the bed perfectly. With the necessary mechanical tools a short man would be stretched and a tall visitor would be cut to size (Greenberg 2004: 66). Another midrash describes how the wealthy Sodomites in their selfishness would harass beggars entering their city. One legend claims that whenever a beggar wandered into Sodom, the people would mark their names on certain gold coins and fake generosity by giving the beggar money. However, when he tried to buy food no local shopkeeper would sell him bread. As soon as the beggar perished of hunger, everyone would come and claim their coins (Greenberg 2004: 65).

According to one midrashic legend, a maiden (sometimes named Pelotit and thought to be a daughter of Lot) once met a poor stranger in the street. She decided to carry bread concealed in her water pitcher and take it to him each day. After several days had passed and the man had not died of starvation, the city authorities realized something unusual was happening. They spied on the beggar, and soon the maiden was discovered, arrested, and sentenced to a cruel death. She was covered from head to toe with honey and placed atop the city walls from whence there was no escape, where the wild bees came and ate her (Greenberg 2004: 65).

A typically Jewish concept is 'the yardstick of Sodom', in Hebrew *middat Sedom*. It is not midrashic but occurs primarily in legal contexts. *Middat Sedom* especially refers to ungenerous conduct between Jews. The term is relevant for specific situations in which, without reasonable justification, a Jewish citizen refuses to grant a fellow citizen a favour. For instance, someone in the community may ask a neighbour for permission to make a shortcut from their house to the public road by walking across one corner of this neighbour's property. A curt refusal of a polite request, whose implementation would entail no expenditure for the landowner, is classified as *middat Sedom* (Greenberg 2004: 71).[205]

---

[205] The *Encyclopaedia Judaica*, Vol. 15 (1971) translates *middat Sedom* 'acting in the manner of Sodom' . . . 'about a man who refuses to

To varying degrees, Jewish scholars and writers of the pre-modern age display familiarity with paradigms A, B, and C of the story of Sodom and Gomorrah. The anti-homoerotic strand (paradigm D), which is typical of the Christian tradition, is largely absent in Judaism, emerging sporadically in a tenth-century rabbinic work written in Babylonia. Subsequently it appears in a midrashic commentary edited in Italy by Menahem ben Solomon who lived in the twelfth century (Greenberg 2004: 68–9). Generally speaking, Jewish hermeneutics in relation to Sodom has remained in keeping with paradigms A and B, with occasional concerns typical of paradigm C.

In recent decades, however, paradigm D has had an impact on Jewish commentaries. Steven Greenberg (2004: 20) fears that Jewish approaches to the Pentateuch may have become 'influenced more by Western prejudices than religious leaders presume'. In the work of Jacob Milgrom (2004: 206), paradigm D has indeed made its mark: 'Sodomy is attested in all periods . . . and is most often reviled, if not proscribed. The sodomy or rape (Gen 19.5) of the Sodomites (hence its name) is a cause for their destruction.' The unquestioning certainty displayed by Milgrom leaves no room for the 'seventy' interpretations of the Torah proposed by the Jewish sages (Reif 1998: 148; Magonet 2004: 25), making Milgrom's anachronistic approach indistinguishable from that of Christian commentators. More recently, Harlan J. Wechsler (2012: 195) has reflected on traditional rabbinic readings of the sin of Sodom. He writes that, according to the Rabbis, the inhabitants of the city 'are misanthropes, unconcerned about other people, persecuting the poor, the wayfarer being a common example of the vulnerable. *Ma'aseh Sedōm*, the act

---

confer a benefit which costs him nothing.' Calling it 'the Sodomitic rule', Martti Nissinen (1998: 98) defines the concept as 'justice without charity'.

of Sodom, or, if you will, "sodomy", is the persecution of the vulnerable.' While Wechsler's definition of sodomy accords with paradigm A, the very presence of the word evokes paradigm D.

The Ambiguous World of Lot

The above survey shows how far interpretations of the story of Sodom have strayed from the world of the Hebrew Bible since the early Middle Ages. The social concerns expressed by the HB prophets were entirely displaced by the anti-homoerotic preoccupations inherent in paradigm D. The omnipresence of the latter would affect the exegesis of Genesis 19 in several ways. As for Abraham's nephew Lot, a variety of roles have been assigned to him in the post-biblical era by Jewish and Christian theologians. Part of the following overview is based on the historical research performed by Michael Carden (2004). Some positive appraisals of Lot exist. An early example is the Jewish historian Josephus who presents Lot as a noble ancestor figure. When challenged by the violent Sodomites, he responds in a reasonable fashion (2004: 74). In early Christian literature, the Greek work *1 Clement* (first century CE) argues that Lot was saved from the destruction of Sodom on account of his 'hospitality and piety' (2004: 120). Similar considerations are found in the apocryphal Coptic work *Apocalypse of Paul* (fourth century) and the fifth-century writings of Bishop Paulinus of Nola (2004: 121).

For John Chrysostom (fourth century), who was patriarch of Constantinople, Lot was a righteous man who learned a fair amount from Abraham about the importance of hospitality. Chrysostom finds it intriguing that Lot was keen to invite the two travellers to his home and that he himself prepared the evening meal. The inhabitants of Sodom are presented as licentious anarchists. By contrast, Lot acts like a physician sent to this city by the deity in order to correct the worst flaws and excesses of the townsmen. For Chrysostom, Lot is clearly a heroic figure (Carden 2004: 142-3). Similarly, Archbishop Ambrose of Milan (fourth century) regards Lot as a 'holy man' who chose to shut his house to the sinful men of Sodom and fled the city to avoid being contaminated by their 'vices' (2004: 145).

The rabbinical work *Pirke de Rabbi Eliezer* (eighth century) describes the behaviour of Lot in fairly positive terms, making him almost comparable to Abraham. While the latter passionately interceded before the deity on behalf of the righteous citizens of Sodom (Gen. 18), Lot took it upon himself to offer up his daughters in order to defend the basic virtues associated with hospitality (Carden 2004: 92). The Franciscan Nicholas of Lyra (fourteenth century) recognizes the human qualities demonstrated by Lot acting as host in Genesis 19. He reflects at length on the moment when Lot proposed to hand over his two daughters instead of the male visitors. Lyra debates whether or not such an act was justified. He concludes by saying that, at the end of the day, Lot behaved correctly because he succeeded in preventing greater disasters in the form of physical aggression aimed at the divine messengers (2004: 187-8).

A number of commentators offer mixed appraisals of Abraham's nephew as presented in Genesis 19. The Jewish philosopher Philo (first century CE) is one of the earliest exegetes to read biblical stories as allegories, a pioneering method which regularly caused him to tease out the secret or spiritual meaning of scripture (Carden 2004: 62-3). Philo's works contain some reflections on Lot. In *De ebrietate*, the writer is highly critical of Lot because this man represents, in Philo's view, misguided behaviour combined with a false idea of his own wisdom (2004: 64). Nevertheless, in

Quaestiones et solutiones in Genesim, Philo describes Lot with a certain amount of empathy. Abraham's nephew appears to be fleeing from Sodom because he is keen to escape immorality and materialism. Thus, he undertakes a journey towards 'the mountains', i.e. towards the higher spheres of peaceful contemplation above material concerns (Carden 2004: 65).

Generally speaking, pseudepigraphal and early rabbinical writings are characterized by considerable ambivalence vis-à-vis Lot and his family as the reflections oscillate between criticism and eulogy (Carden 2004: 77). The Christian scholar Origen (third century) shares some of the critical viewpoints expressed previously by early Jewish sources vis-à-vis Lot, but he still concedes that Lot was saved by virtue of his commitment to hospitality (2004: 131–2). Bishop Basil (fourth century) encourages his fellow monks to take inspiration from the example of Lot in Sodom. According to Basil's interpretation of the story, God does not abandon those who dedicate their lives to him. At the same time, however, Basil feels uncomfortable at the thought of Lot's alleged sensuality. He urges the monks under his care to remain firmly committed to celibacy and to practice chastity in all senses of the word (2004: 134–5).

Centuries later, Peter Damian (eleventh century) somewhat disapprovingly presents Lot as a person who was 'unable to spend time with Abraham far from the Sodomites' (Damian 1982: 86). However, he concedes that Lot migrated from the city at the last minute to avoid destruction. In a different context, Damian speaks respectfully of Abraham's nephew calling him 'blessed Lot' (p. 38). Finally, Martin Luther occasionally provides a benevolent picture of Lot as a pious man who offered generous hospitality to strangers (Luther 1961: 245, 249–50). The very fact that Lot was found worthy to show hospitality to angels is 'distinct proof of his sanctity and godliness' (p. 258). Furthermore, he gave thanks to God after being saved (p. 243). In Luther's view, Lot did well to resist 'the madness of his fellow citizens with sound instruction' (p. 256). However, Luther disapproves of Lot's behaviour on another count. He finds it 'a disgrace' for any parent to expose young daughters to a situation, which, in Luther's interpretation, implies prostitution, adultery, and possibly death. While Lot's loyalty toward his guests was praiseworthy, his 'extreme disloyalty toward his daughters' was nothing short of 'execrable' (pp. 257–8).

Conclusion

This chapter has outlined how theologians in post-biblical times have tended to interpret the drama of Sodom and Gomorrah. Hellenistic literature represented a departure from the prophetical writings of the HB. Written in several classical languages it displayed a growing concern for the two visitors to Sodom along with perceived sexual issues in the biblical text. Philo of Alexandria launched a major hermeneutical shift as he understood the sin of Sodom to be pederasty, a step that was fundamental for the future evolution of Christian theology. The early church accepted and developed Philo's exegesis, turning it into an all-out rejection of homoeroticism. Furthermore, the growing tendency of the early church to glorify the ascetic life came to imply abstention from all types of carnal pleasure. Increasingly, the only purpose of the sexual instinct was seen to be procreation. Some forms of marital sex as well as all erotic activity outside the framework of heterosexual marriage were classified as 'contrary to nature'.

By the eleventh century, Christian clergy were reading the Bible exclusively in Latin. The invention of the concept of sodomy represented the culmination of a long process in which the words 'Sodomite' and 'sodomitic vice' acquired sexual connotations, increasingly (but not exclusively) in reference to people with homoerotic inclinations. In the thirteenth century, 'sodomy' was admitted into the official vocabulary of the Roman Catholic Church alongside blasphemy and *luxuria* ('lechery'). The Protestant Reformation rejected a large part of church tradition as it proclaimed allegiance to the principle of *sola scriptura*, 'scripture only'. However, the anti-homoerotic ideology associated with the word sodomy was accepted unexamined by the Reformers whose churches continued to adhere to it for centuries. The longevity of sodomy as a legal concept in the penal codes of a number of countries until recent years is evidence of this.

In post-biblical times, the main hermeneutical approaches to Sodom were as follows:

- For Hellenistic literature, Sodom represented inhospitality (paradigm B) and a number of sexual dangers, for example undesirable mixed marriages (paradigm C);
- Philo was the first writer to identify Sodom with homoerotic pederasty (paradigm D);
- The growing ascetic movement within the early church associated Sodom with sensual pleasures;
- Partly due to Philo's influence, the terms 'Sodomite' and 'sodomitic vice' began to be used in the Roman church;
- The word 'sodomy' emerged between the tenth and eleventh centuries. Initially it referred to several sexual acts, including anal penetration and different forms of male–male sexual relationships. Eventually sodomy was understood to include sexual intimacy among women;

- By the late Middle Ages, Christian theology had completely absorbed paradigm D;
- The concept of sodomy was accepted unchallenged by the Reformation;
- Given the close links between church and state in many countries, sodomy became a legal term;
- From the late nineteenth century onwards, the term sodomy was gradually replaced by 'homosexuality';
- In Christian and Jewish literature on Sodom until the twentieth century, Lot is viewed as an ambiguous figure.

9

SODOM TODAY

The story of Sodom and Gomorrah is the touchstone of all emotional, religious and societal hysteria about homosexuality.

—Witi Ihimaera [206]

Introduction

The Devouring Fire (*Den fortærende ild*, 2004) by H. J. Lundager Jensen is a detailed discussion of the compositional and literary aspects of the story of Sodom and Gomorrah. It describes Genesis 18–19 as a unified literary work (pp. 466, 475), technically located on the border line between myth and legend (p. 537). Among the dramatic narratives in Genesis, for Lundager Jensen this is perhaps the most sophisticated and something of a climax. In literary and theological resonance, it is comparable to Genesis 2 and 3, with which the Sodom text has 'obvious' connections (p. 462). In Lundager Jensen's view, nonetheless, scholars' exegetical curiosity with respect to the Sodom text has been relatively modest (p. 464). While he accepts paradigm D (2004: 499, 506), he finds significant parallels between the story of Sodom and a legend told by Ovid. In the latter tale, an old married couple named Philemon and Baucis were, in spite of their extreme poverty, the only ones in their area to

---

[206] Witi Ihimaera, *Nights in the Gardens of Spain*, 1995: 107.

welcome the humbly disguised gods Zeus and Hermes into their home (2004: 504, 508). At that stage, the gods had been turned away everywhere else. On account of their generosity, Baucis and Philemon were richly rewarded and escaped the punishing flood that inundated their country.

According to Lundager Jensen (2004: 523), in the Bible a number of shared elements with Sodom are found in the narrative of Elisha and the woman from Shunem (2 Kings 4.8–17). Another significant echo of Sodom occurs in the book of Judges 19–21. Far from being an isolated incident in Genesis, the drama of Sodom borrows from and adds to a universal narrative system (p. 520). In the light of the complex reception history of Sodom and Gomorrah since antiquity, it is understandable that even today the biblical story gives rise to a whole series of interpretations and reflections. Due to the multi-faceted literary complexity addressed by Lundager Jensen's work, it contains enough elements to be representative of the diversity of approaches adopted by contemporary scholarship. In this chapter, I look at other examples of current academic literature to explore what Sodom means to modern readers. In particular, I seek to discover to what extent scholars do or do not adhere to the historical paradigms A, B, C, and D identified in previous chapters.

Gagnon: A Traditional Reading

In regard to Sodom and Gomorrah, Robert Gagnon (2001: 71) acknowledges that the story is not an ideal text 'to guide contemporary Christian sexual ethics'. At the same time, however, he is convinced that the biblical narrator is intent on eliciting 'feelings of revulsion' on the part of readers/hearers at the mere thought of the 'inherently degrading quality' of sexual relationships between males (p. 71). The analysis of the Sodom text undertaken by Gagnon includes a number of cross-references to other biblical passages, which allegedly reinforce his point. For instance, he draws a straight hermeneutical line between Genesis 19 and Leviticus 18.22, whereby one text interprets the other. Gagnon then extends the line further from Leviticus 18.22 to Ezekiel 16. Finding the concept of 'abomination' in both texts (but not in Gen. 19), he returns to the legend of Sodom and uses this word as key to his own discussion (2001: 80).

Gagnon reflects on the notion of 'homosexual rape'. In his view, this is what makes the inhospitality of Sodom so 'dastardly' (2001: 76). While he concedes that rape is an act of aggression, he is sure that 'it is usually not void of all sexual desire'. He admits that no one knows the exact nature of the message conveyed by the narrator but suggests that a reasonable conjecture seems to be that the text warns against 'a combination of homoerotic or bisexual lust' and 'an aggressive intent to dominate and humiliate strangers', which involves 'an abominable and shameful practice' (p. 77). Gagnon does not limit himself to condemning sexual aggression. Given that the main purpose of his book is to present same-sex relationships at large in a negative light (pp. 72–7, 84, 137, 438), he explicitly rejects the distinction introduced in recent decades between sexual aggression (such as rape) and loving same-sex relationships between consenting adults (p. 78). In regard to Sodom, Gagnon clearly and energetically promotes paradigm D.

Sodom as Humiliation

Over the centuries a number of commentators have hypothesized that what is described in the opening paragraphs of Genesis 19 is a group of immoral men desiring to gang rape the visiting messengers staying at the house of

Abraham's nephew Lot. The fact that Lot reacts defensively by offering his young daughters, seemingly as a substitute, is interpreted to mean that he is convinced that it is better for girls to be raped than for grown-up males. Reflections in this direction are found, for instance, in the writings of John Chrysostom, Ambrose, and Augustine (Carden 2004: 143, 146, 148). The framework for this interpretation is paradigm D.

In the 1960s, new psychosocial elements were added. In his book *Phallós* (1969),[207] psychiatrist Thorkil Vanggaard describes how the Sodomites in Genesis 19.5 were driven, not by desire, but by male aggressive instincts. Vanggaard (p. 95) quotes the authorized Danish version of the Bible of 1931: *Bring dem herud, at vi kan stille vor Lyst paa dem*, literally 'Bring them out here so that we may pacify our lust on them.' This leads him to draw the conclusion that the lust suggested is 'aggressive pleasure' derived from a 'collective violent impulse' to anal rape. The anal connection has always been viewed as 'self-evident', according to Vanggaard, who (erroneously) indicates this as the origin of the term 'sodomy' (p. 94).

Since Vanggaard's work was published a large number of academic books and articles have dealt with the subject of Sodom and Gomorrah. In many cases, the approaches adopted are so similar that they have caused a new consensus to crystallize. Above all it has been promoted by those theologians and biblical scholars who identify themselves as gay, bisexual or queer, who have been successful in exposing the serious flaws of earlier hermeneutics, particularly paradigm D. Their main conclusion is that the biblical story does not speak of homoeroticism per se because it sheds no light whatsoever on the subject of same-sex intimacy between consenting adults. Like Vanggaard, modern

---

[207] English edition by InterVarsity Press, New York (1972).

exegetes point out that the brutality displayed in the opening verses of Genesis 19 looks more like attempted gang rape.[208]

This recent argument makes a clean break with the established routines of countless generations in relation to Sodom and Gomorrah and is now widely accepted. Based on logical reasoning, the current academic consensus concludes that the real problem in Genesis 19 is not homoeroticism but gang rape, and more specifically that the men of Sodom wanted to penetrate the visitors anally. According to this hypothesis, the townsmen intended to inflict physical pain, personal humiliation, and sexual shame on the two strangers in order to neutralize them in case they were spies or intended to carry out subversive activities (cf. Vanggaard 1969: 98). Viewed from this perspective, Lot's role is that of a nervous host determined to avoid such a tremendous challenge to his self-esteem. In the light of the acute crisis at his front door, he has to move very quickly and chooses the most obvious diversionary tactic. He will let the men of Sodom do with the girls whatever they like as long as they leave the two male visitors alone. According to this interpretation, Lot is using his daughters as a sexual distraction (McKeown 2008: 107).

These recent innovative psychosocial approaches to Sodom represent an offshoot of paradigm D, which arguably might be called paradigm E. However, this latest development is firmly rooted in paradigm D and is contributing to its longevity, I continue to call it by the latter name. Since the original version (pederasty) of paradigm D was first introduced by Philo, it has survived for two thousand years and is still going strong, albeit with a somewhat changed focus. Combining elements from paradigms B and C, and

---

[208] Stone 1996: 80; Hanks 2000: 243-4; Helminiak 2000: 45-6; Brodie 2001: 243, 251; Heard 2001: 52; Goss 2002: 193-4; Carden 2004: 21; Greenberg 2004: 67; Milgrom 2004: 206; Jennings 2005: 49, 200; Lipka 2006: 44 n. 4; Boyarin 2007: 139-41; Heacock 2011: 92.

often ignoring paradigm A, paradigm D continues to be successful in virtually eclipsing all previous approaches.

Lot: Villain or Hero?

Operating within paradigm D, today's biblical scholars are highly critical of Lot's behaviour in Genesis 19. Contemporary observers are outraged by the perceived frivolousness with which he decides to hand over his underage daughters to the spokesmen of Sodom. In fact, in post-biblical literature no single figure in the story of Sodom and Gomorrah has been reviled more than Lot. According to the current consensus, readers are faced with a case of moral turpitude and complete surrender to the alleged barbaric lifestyle of the townsmen. This is so much the case that some cast Lot—more than the men of Sodom—in the role of villain. Angered by the way in which he seemingly exposes his innocent daughters to physical degradation and danger, many modern observers find Lot irresponsible, indecent, cruel, and despicable.[209] Below are a few representative quotations:

- All males were to be granted their wishes. Conflict among them could be solved by the sacrifice of females. The male protector, indeed the father, became procurer (Trible 1984: 75);
- Here we are face to face with a standard that strikes us as barbaric, to say the least ... there is nothing that can be said that will excuse the crudity of the girls to be raped instead of the men (Horner 1978: 50);
- This violent trade of women makes a contemporary reader shiver (Nissinen 1998: 46);

---

[209] Bal 1988: 92; Winter 1992: 215; Hamilton 1995: 36; Alter 1996: 85; Fields 1997: 124–5; Rashkow 1998: 100; McKeown 2008: 107; Schneider 2008: 188; Lyons 2012: 10.

- Lot's offer of his daughters to the mob is shocking to readers (Goss 2002: 193);
- The replacement of the guests by virgin daughters is, no doubt, a horrific suggestion to contemporary sensibilities (Greenberg 2004: 64);
- Lot's gesture can be seen as 'a caricatured offer of hospitality, exaggerated and grotesque' (Warner 2012: 118).

Steven Greenberg (2004: 73) adds: 'Lot revealed in the offer of his daughters to the crowd how much he had learned from his neighbours', and 'for Lot the rule of no predation between men (all men are brothers) did not exclude male predation of women'. According to Michael Carden (2004: 21, 39), 'questions gather around the character of Lot' to such an extent that he cannot be seen as a positive character in the story. Thus, Lot is 'rescued on the basis of his kinship with Abraham and not for any intrinsic merit on his part' (p. 21). This negative view is fuelled by the fact that Lot's daughters 'were offered up for rape by their father' (p. 22). Moreover, Lot appears 'weak, prevaricating and distrustful of the angels' guarantees' (p. 27). Carden concludes that Lot is 'revealed as subscribing to the same ideology as the men of Sodom' (pp. 35, 39).

The modern approach to Lot has some ancient precedents. Among the pseudepigrapha, the book of *Jubilees* (second century BCE) suggests that Lot's daughters do not take the initiative for the incestuous episodes that draw the drama of Sodom to a close. Instead, Lot himself is cast in the role of initiator (Carden 2004: 53). Furthermore, the narrator of *Jubilees* presents Abraham's nephew as a man who has assimilated the moral corruption he has observed in Sodom. At the same time, *Jubilees* finds that the people of Moab and Ammon behave very much like their ancestor (2004: 53). Generally speaking, rabbinic literature is unkind to Lot.

Frequently early Jewish writers compare him unfavourably with his uncle Abraham who remained faithful to the true religion. Lot is regarded as an apostate who sought integration with the pagans of Sodom. The negative portrait of Lot is based on Genesis 13 where he is depicted as choosing a way of life that is entirely different from that of Abraham. Both the midrashic *Genesis Rabbah* (sixth century CE) and Rashi (eleventh century) are inclined to think that for Abraham it is an advantage to part company with a relative like Lot, given the purported materialism, selfishness, and sensuality of the latter (Carden 2004: 90).

Lot as Dirty Old Man

In a psychoanalytical study of the story of Sodom inspired by the work of Sigmund Freud, Ilona Rashkow (1998) focuses on Lot. Rashkow directs her attention to the perceived behaviour of Lot the individual, particularly vis-à-vis his daughters. In her essay, Lot is portrayed as a lustful man given to the pleasures of wine (pp. 98–9, 105) and unconventional sex, including procuring, voyeurism, incest, and possibly sadism (pp. 99–100, 102). Several pointers in the language employed by Rashkow indicate that describing the perceived shady side of Lot's character forces her out of her comfort zone. Indeed, she seems to be on a virtual collision course with everything Lot does and says. She confesses to being mystified by the 'disturbing' and 'complicated' aspects of the story (pp. 98, 104). Particularly, she finds Lot's different moves quite intractable, describing them as 'strange', 'shrouded in secrecy', 'abhorrent', 'incredible', 'baffling', and 'reprehensible' (pp. 99–100).[210]

---

[210] Rashkow's exasperated reactions to Lot's perceived behaviour fit into a pattern that Ann Loades (1998: 82) has observed in several scholars.

Although she employs psychoanalysis, Ilona Rashkow does not address some significant aspects of the Sodom narrative. Personally, I would have appreciated a reflection on the likely psychological effects on Lot of late-night mob intimidation (Gen. 19.9) and the fact that he and his family are told to flee immediately, leaving behind all material possessions (19.17). This is followed by survivor trauma given Lot's narrow escape from total annihilation (Heard 2001: 57). Add to this the abrupt loss of his wife (19.26), after which he fears for his life and flees for the second time (19.30). Most of the same unsettling factors would seem to affect Lot's daughters. The classical Syrian scholar Ephrem portrayed both Lot and his daughters as survivors suffering from what today might be called post-traumatic stress disorder (Carden 2004: 137).

In addition to her strictly Freudian approach to Lot and his immediate surroundings, and like the majority of contemporary exegetes, Rashkow is indebted to a long post-biblical tradition of Bible translation and commentary: her interpretation of Lot owes more to rabbinic tradition than to the Hebrew text of Genesis 19. Indeed, she conflates biblical narrative and post-biblical commentary and midrash in the form of 'classical rabbinic literature' (1998: 100). No distinction is drawn between these categories, and all are treated as equal components in a seamless continuum. A closer look at Rashkow's sources shows that they include the pseudepigraphal book of *Jubilees* and the midrashic *Genesis Rabbah*. As noted above, *Jubilees* portrays Lot as committing incest with his daughters. He takes the initiative, not the women. In addition, *Genesis Rabbah* clearly links sexual sin with Lot and not with the city of Sodom (Carden 2004: 91). Thus, Abraham's nephew is complicit in what happens because, according to *Genesis Rabbah*, 'it is clear that Lot lusted after his daughters', a viewpoint shared by Rashi and many subsequent commentators (Rashkow 1998: 106–7; Carden 2004: 108).

Ilona Rashkow explicitly cites *Genesis Rabbah* in her discussion of Noah's curse of Canaan (1998: 93) but fails to acknowledge the same source in the context of Lot and his daughters. For readers unfamiliar with early and medieval Jewish literature, this is confusing.[211] The portrait of Lot offered by Rashkow places her essay within the exclusive framework of paradigm C.

The Ambiguity of Lot

In contemporary literature, positive or neutral appraisals of Lot are rare. Thomas Brodie (2001: 250-1) criticizes Lot's character speaking of his 'limited' hospitality and communication skills. In Brodie's analysis, Lot's actions, 'including his offering of his daughters, are suspect' because of his limited awareness, and there is considerable uncertainty about 'his accuracy and truthfulness' (2001: 250-1). In addition, Lot is perceived to be too close to the people of Sodom (p. 252). Another critical approach to Lot is taken by Doyle (1998). He speaks of Lot's 'ambiguous behaviour' and character (pp. 87, 96), the high degree of 'ignorance' on the part of Lot, and 'his lack of knowledge' (p. 97). Often Doyle sees Lot as not understanding what is going on (p. 87). Unlike Abraham, Lot 'does not know God' (p. 92).

---

[211] Leo Perdue (2005: 29) provides an explanation of the imbroglio. He notes that many Jews tend to reject biblical theology and replace it with Jewish theology, which specifically includes later corpora of texts (Mishnah, Talmud, Midrashim, Commentaries, and later Jewish thinkers). Religious Jews are required to interpret the text from the joint perspectives of Jewish tradition and modern critical methods.

While the vast majority of biblical scholars use paradigm D for their analysis of Lot and regard him as a villain, two exceptions should be mentioned here. An original picture of Lot based on sociological analysis is provided by Lyn Bechtel (1998b). She explains that Lot's proposal to hand over his two underage daughters may at first seem 'incongruent and totally inappropriate' because it does not address the concerns of the men of Sodom. They are responding to a perceived threat to their community. However, Lot is aware of this. His strategy is to 'defuse a tense situation' (p. 123). This is why he asks the crowd to treat the girls *well*, which certainly does not involve raping them (p. 124). However, the townsmen feel offended by the fact that Lot the sojourner has been trying to discern 'what is good for the community'. Just as he has tried to act as a judge, they themselves decide to judge Lot (p. 125).

For his part, Mark Sturge (2001) occupies a solitary position with respect to the current consensus on Sodom. According to Sturge, Lot is neither a villain nor an ambiguous figure but rather a hero. Abraham's nephew is described as 'a fellow saint who had to overcome extreme difficulties in his life' and was rewarded with divine grace (p. 63). In Sturge's view, Lot is aware of his responsibility to teach hospitality to the people of Sodom and persuade them to change their evil ways.[212] For Sturge, it is Lot the foreigner who utters the cry of protest against the people of Sodom, which reaches the ears of Yhwh in Genesis 18.20–21 (p. 75). Sturge's vision of the drama resembles the reflections on the poor of Sodom shared by the Hebrew prophets (paradigm A).

---

[212] In this respect, Sturge's approach to Lot is in accordance with the picture presented by the *Qur'an* (Koran; cf. Appendix 1).

Standing Sodom on Its Head

In recent decades, various liberation theologies have widened and enriched the field of biblical interpretation, including queer theology and postcolonial theology. In connection with the story of Sodom, some of the most intriguing contributions have been made by scholars who define themselves as queer, namely, Marcella Althaus-Reid (2003: 2) and Michael Carden (2004: 1, 9). Althaus-Reid has opted for a pro-Canaanite interpretation of the tale, and occasionally Carden does the same. Particularly compelling is their sense of identification and solidarity with the victims who perish in the annihilation of the city, whereby they virtually stand the conventional way of reading the narrative on its head.

With respect to the story of Sodom, Althaus-Reid (2003: 90) argues that queer theology cannot be neutral; the theologian must take sides (p. 89). She does so by defying theological tradition and siding with the biblically reviled Canaanites, arguing that the people of Canaan, Sodomites included, have 'a particular and respectable sexual culture and tradition', which characterizes them as 'a loving community' (p. 85). She suggests that the Sodomites may be seen as 'a rebellious movement against a hegemonic theodicy'. They have an 'ample understanding of sexuality and divinity' (p. 90). However, the whole story is 'saturated with violence' (p. 91–2):

> Men from Sodom against these particular visitors; a father against his own daughters, and God against almost everybody and everything, threatening to destroy people and environment alike. The issue of violence in this text is regrettable but that includes God's violence too.

Althaus-Reid finds that to accuse the Sodomites of inhospitality, as so many commentators do, is unfair. It may have been perfectly normal for visiting travellers to spend the night in the town square. Althaus-Reid suggests that the real inhospitality came from the divine messengers 'involved in a mission of policing sexuality' (p. 92). In her view, the annihilation of the city was the result of the violence and 'evil gestures' of a 'God of destruction'. In other words, the real villain in Althaus-Reid's interpretation is the deity (p. 92). She concludes her discussion of Sodom by predicting that one day 'the Sodomites must be resurrected'. God will remember them, and sexual justice will be done (p. 93).

For his part, Michael Carden (2004: 40) is acutely aware of the 'invisible victims' of Sodom, i.e. 'the people of these cities, especially their children and slaves'. He indignantly classifies the destruction of Sodom and Gomorrah as genocide, emphasizing 'the genocide at the heart of Yhwh's mighty deed' and 'the genocide wrought by the deity', which deserves 'condemnation' (p. 14). Carden notes that 'not even Abraham raises his voice for the children of Sodom and Gomorrah' and in Genesis 19, Yhwh expresses 'no regret for the mass death on Jordan's plain'. Death by fire and brimstone is swift and leaves 'no rotting corpses to accuse Yhwh and ourselves of murder' (p. 40). In other words, Carden finds that we, present-day spectators of the holocaust of Sodom, are accomplices in the crime. He is reminded of the great Syrian scholar Ephrem (ca. 306–373 CE), who portrayed Lot and his daughters as 'haunted in nightmares by the dying screams of the people of Sodom' (2004: 40-1).

While some have regarded the sudden transformation of Mrs. Lot into a pillar of salt (Gen. 19.26) as an image of inflexibility, death or even fossilization (Brodie 2001: 252), Carden interprets the event as an act of defiance (2004: 41):

> The death of Lot's wife can be read as an act of compassionate protest against Yhwh's programme of genocide. As readers, we continually look back on Sodom and, while in awe of the magnitude of the disaster, as we face no risk of being turned to salt, we, too, should stand beside Lot's wife and condemn Yhwh's crime.

Althaus-Reid and Carden are among the extremely few modern scholars who have reflected on the thorny issue of genocide and mass destruction in relation to Sodom.[213] They openly raise this question: 'From a theological perspective, is it ever possible to justify the extermination of entire communities or nations?'[214] Citing Jewish thought, Carden feels it is permissible to criticize God 'as long as it is in defence of God's creation' (2004: 14).

The Challenge of Postcolonialism

In modern theology, postcolonialism represents a radical departure from traditional Western scholarship as it actively confronts the dominant patterns of thought. As stated by R. S. Sugirtharajah (1998: 93), postcolonialism may be described as a critical reading posture aimed at unmasking the link

---

[213] For a brief discussion of medieval debates on the victims of the destruction of Sodom, see Carden 2004: 169–70, 174.

[214] In the late 1980s, Harry J. Cargas (1989: 125) observed with dismay how an insignificant number of Christian theologians had publicly repudiated the Nazi-led extermination of Jews during World War II. In general terms, Church leaders have been slow to issue half-hearted apologies for Christian acquiescence in, and lack of opposition to, the massacre. Cargas characterizes silence vis-à-vis genocide as 'truly blasphemy' (p. 17). He points out that the subject of the *Shoah* (Holocaust) is of little import in contemporary Christian theology. Even today, there are misguided efforts to missionize the Jews (pp. 119, 127).

between idea and power. According to Sugirtharajah, the movement 'caters to a variety of concerns, oppositional stances, and even contradictory positions' (p. 93). In his words, 'everything is contested, everything is contestable' (2002: 12). In particular, postcolonial enquiry aims to make Western readers aware of the constant risk of collusion with the multiple forces of oppression in the global picture (2002: 74-9).[215]

Postcolonial theology is community oriented rather than individualistic. Unlike the current Western tendency to focus on the individual in biblical narratives, postcolonialists discuss agendas and ideologies. Sugirtharajah (2002: 79) is aware that anyone who engages critically with texts knows that they are not 'innocent'. Instead they reflect the cultural, religious, political, and ideological interests and contexts out of which they emerge.[216] Postcolonial biblical criticism focuses on expansion, domination, and imperialism as central forces in defining both the biblical narratives and biblical interpretation. The HB is constantly reflecting on situations of oppression and exile as well as the hope for liberation, fulfilment, and restoration (p. 25).[217]

Furthermore, the HB pursues group-oriented political agendas involving genealogies and conflicts between families, clans, communities, tribes, and nations (cf.

---

[215] Feminist scholar Sharon Ringe (1998: 139–40) reflects on the sobering and even intimidating thought that the background of any Western analyst makes us liable to suspicion and critique on the part of postcolonial scholars.

[216] Judith McKinlay (1996: 23) mentions the interests already coded within the text.

[217] Thomas Hanks (1983: 4) has found that biblical Israel was largely a small, weak nation dominated by great empires. Frequently a local oligarchy collaborated to maintain the oppressive status quo. In Hanks's view, this explains why oppression and the resulting poverty receive so much attention in biblical literature.

Meyers 1988: 123-4). This is true of the book of Genesis. More than the mythic history of the first individual human beings, which figures prominently in Christian biblical interpretation, this is a Jewish tale discussing the origins of the people of Israel.[218] As Richard Horsley (1998: 153) has pointed out, postcolonial criticism may make it possible to discern different layers in biblical literature and how they are the products of the very emergence of, or struggle for, domination and authority. In the process, previously submerged biblical voices can enable modern colonized readers to challenge and undermine what he describes as 'the self-authorization of ancient authorities as well as their authoritarian modern colonial beneficiaries'. For his part, R. S. Sugirtharajah (2002: 75) finds that postcolonial criticism is at its best when it critiques not only the interpretation of texts but also the texts themselves.

If the Sodom narrative is read in this light, it opens up a political perspective. Thus far, very little critical commentary on the colonial or imperial politics of Gen. 18 and 19 appears to have been produced (cf. Sugirtharajah 2002: 74). Nevertheless, the allusions in Genesis to Sodom's Canaanite origins seem significant (Gen. 10.19). Sodom is an evil place (13.13) and has been cast in the role of villain along with other Canaanites to form a contrast with the righteous

---

[218] David Moody (1993: *xi*) wonders how Genesis came to be read as a record of the origin of the human race, rather than of the Jewish nation. In his view, the book is concerned to establish the origins of the people of YHWH. Genesis is intimately linked to a nation's visions and revisions of its history. It is the record of a specific culture (p. *xiii*). Thomas Brodie (2001: 100) adds that Genesis may sound like history, but is not. In fact, Genesis is unrelated to known history and cannot, therefore, be used reliably as a basis for Israel's beginnings. In another way, however, Genesis is profoundly historical. Brodie describes it as 'an artistic synthesis of history — complete with flood, famine, migration, war, and consuming fire'. In this regard, Genesis clearly helps to lay political foundations (p. 113).

Abraham, known by God (18.19), and his legitimate descendants, the Israelites. Within this framework, the story of Sodom comes to play an important early part in the long history of Israelite antagonism to the original inhabitants of the land of Canaan, having thus become the first link in a long chain of anti-Canaanite propaganda. In a not-so-subtle way, the narrative sets the tone for the Israel/Canaan conflict throughout the HB, particularly following the exodus from Egypt and subsequent Israelite invasion and occupation of Palestine.[219] While the HB consistently portrays the Canaanites—the colonized victims—in very negative terms, the people of Canaan presumably viewed the Israelites as unwelcome intruders, invaders, and oppressors.

However, modern commentators writing on Sodom tend to focus on other issues. In this sense, the story may be said to have been colonized by Christian tradition (cf. paradigm D). The question of territorial colonization as well as ethnic vilification and victimization remains, begging comparisons with similar approaches over the centuries regarding the conquest and subjugation of different nations and territories around the world.[220] A parallel might be drawn to the European domination of North America. While the European settlers represented 'civilization', the indigenous peoples were portrayed as 'savages'. The political and cultural manipulation at the heart of this process resonates in an

---

[219] As recommended by Carol Meyers (1988: 15), I deliberately refrain from using the term 'conquest'. Meyers explains that 'conquest' does not adequately represent what we now know to have been a complex and drawn-out process of immigration and settlement.

[220] Writing from a Latin American perspective, Marcella Althaus-Reid (2000: 151) has argued that it is no longer possible to justify exegetically the claim that Israel was under divine guidance in the pillage of Canaan. Althaus-Reid privileges a reading of the story from a Canaanite perspective, which partakes in the memory of the nations and cultures massacred by other nations claiming they had a God-given right.

essay by Robert Allen Warrior (1991: 287–95), who compares the situation of Native Americans with that of ancient Canaan. In both cases, the vanquished nations were reviled and stigmatized as well as systematically exterminated.

In the light of this discussion, it may be argued that if the Sodom text in Genesis is *not* analysed from a political perspective, the interpretation process remains incomplete. Indeed, the xenophobic bias of the narrative may continue to have the potential to function as a tool of oppression (Sugirtharajah 2002: 206). The first victim may well be the HB itself. The widespread antipathy against the First Testament in the Western world, particularly in Protestant circles, is only likely to be reinforced by one-dimensional interpretations of narratives in which brutality is a central ingredient. Another undesirable side effect may be the fomenting of anti-Jewish sentiment.[221]

Likewise, Michael Carden (2004: 12, 14) draws attention to the violence embedded in the fictional events described in Genesis. Over time, the story of Sodom has proved its effectiveness for victimizing homoerotic relationships to the extent that, in some circles, the narrative is still employed as a toxic proof-text. If violent narratives are left unexamined, their impact can be lethal, as noted by Carole Fontaine (1997: 94):

> Until we understand that injustice has been coded into the very text itself as it pursues the class interests of its authors and protagonists, progressive believers will be dumbfounded by the Bible's ability to support oppression.

---

[221] This risk is acknowledged by Trible 1990: 24; Loades 1998: 87; Horsley 1998: 154, and Morgan 1998: 115.

Rediscovering Biblical Sodom

Until the second half of the twentieth century, the medieval approach to the story of Sodom and Gomorrah in the form of paradigm D reigned supreme in Christian circles. In 1955, the British theologian Derrick Sherwin Bailey attempted to reinterpret the drama in his book *Homosexuality and the Western Christian Tradition*. Bailey was well aware of the reception history of Sodom and proposed to distinguish between different interpretive paradigms. In particular, Bailey drew attention to the occurrence in the Hebrew text of the verb *yada'*, 'know', in Genesis 19.5. According to Bailey, the Sodomites wanted to examine the identity of the strangers staying at Lot's house and to verify the nature of their visit (1955: 3). In the entire HB, the verbal root *yada'* and various derivatives appear 943 times. In most dictionaries, ten occurrences (in some cases twelve) are connected to the realm of sex, including Genesis 19.5. However, Bailey finds that in this specific case no sexual innuendo seems to be suggested by the narrator. It is more likely that the inhabitants of Sodom were curious and keen to inspect the credentials of the wayfarers for security reasons. Bailey points out that in the numerous allusions to Sodom within the HB there is no indication that the men of Sodom were homoerotically inclined. While it is true that Lot is prepared to hand over his two daughters to the crowd, in Bailey's view this gesture primarily reveals that Lot can think of no better solution in a desperate emergency (1955: 6).

In order to understand the fundamental issues in the story of Sodom and Gomorrah, Bailey proposes comparing the Hebrew narrative with other ancient legends in which deities interact with human beings (1955: 7). He draws a parallel to the story of the tower of Babel in Genesis 11, highlighting the wickedness and vanity of the people as the main causes of the general confusion that dispersed them. He points out that the narrative contains no allusions to sexual misbehaviour. In addition, Bailey focuses on the fact that the sexual references to Sodom found in the letters of Jude and 2 Peter are based on the pseudepigrapha and not on Genesis. Bailey is aware of the importance of Philo of Alexandria for whom Sodom was a hotbed of pederasty (p. 22). In summary, Bailey has identified various interpretive paradigms. His personal preference in regard to interpretations of Sodom is paradigm B with its emphasis on hospitality/inhospitality.

For several decades, Bailey's innovative approach has influenced biblical commentators. Among these are John McNeill (1993) who emphasizes the hospitality *leitmotif* exemplified by Abraham in Genesis 18 and Lot in Genesis 19 (pp. 44–5). McNeill observes that Jesus adopts a similar approach to the story of Sodom in Luke 10.10–12 (p. 45) and that the name of Sodom in the entire Bible represents the sins of arrogance, injustice, and inhospitality (p. 46). In summary, McNeill's analysis includes elements of paradigms A and B.

John Boswell's monumental *Christianity, Social Tolerance, and Homosexuality* was published in 1980. Boswell takes note of Bailey's insights and agrees with his argument that the story of Sodom and Gomorrah does not deal with sex. Likewise, Boswell observes that other biblical texts alluding to Sodom address different concerns (1980: 93–4). Thus, he prefers to use an interpretive framework based on an incident from ancient Rome in which a defenceless prefect, faced with a dire emergency on his doorstep, declared himself prepared to hand over his underage children to an angry crowd. The incident involved no sexual interest (p. 95). Furthermore, Boswell's readers are reminded that ancient Greek culture greatly valued the virtue of hospitality, to the extent that, in Greek religion, Zeus himself acts as protector of guests and strangers. Likewise, in the HB the book of Joshua is 'eloquent testimony to the paramount importance of hospitality' (Josh.

2 & 6). While the city of Jericho was completely destroyed, the one who was saved was Rahab the prostitute with her family because she had previously offered hospitality to the spies that Joshua sent to the city (1980: 96).

Boswell stands out among commentators because of his observations on different interpretive approaches to the story of Sodom. From the works of fellow scholars he gleans four plausible reasons for the destruction of the city, which roughly coincide with paradigms A, B, C, and D: (1) general wickedness, (2) inhospitable treatment of divine visitors, (3) a desire to have sex with angels, and (4) attempted gang rape. Without engaging in any detailed polemics, Boswell seems to argue that options (1) and (2) are the most likely in the light of the interpretations offered by the HB (p. 93). In summary, the gist of his analysis coincides with paradigms A and B.

Tradition and Innovation

Mark Jordan's *The Invention of Sodomy in Christian Theology*, published in 1997, offers a detailed literary analysis of a series of theological treatises from medieval tradition. Significantly, Jordan is able to locate the time and place of birth of the term 'sodomy' (eleventh century; cf. chapter 8). Jordan has noted that some commentaries, dictionaries of Biblical Hebrew and modern versions of the Bible translate the text of Sodom and Gomorrah irresponsibly (1997: 4, 36, 160). He concludes that 'sodomy' should not be rendered as 'homosexuality'. The two concepts belong to very different categories and have never been interchangeable (p. 161). In other words, it is a mistake to think that the story of Sodom is about same-sex pleasure—it is not (p. 162). The sin of Sodom was ingratitude, pride, and arrogance (p. 32). Like

Boswell, Jordan's approach to the story of Sodom situates him between paradigms A and B.

Several contemporary scholars partly adhere to paradigm D while also contributing independent or fresh insights. In his book *Sodom and Gomorrah* (1997), Weston Fields highlights some significant elements that interconnect three biblical narratives: the divine messengers in Sodom (Gen. 19), Joshua's spies in Jericho (Josh. 2 & 6), and the crime of Gibeah (Judg. 19 & 20). Fields agrees with the current consensus inasmuch as he is convinced that the men of Sodom have violent intentions (1997: 109, 117). At the same time he acknowledges that the prospect of gang rape does not materialize. He then ventures the hypothesis that the threatened sexual aggression is so unheard of that no collection of laws in the HB ever mentions it (p. 123). Fields suggests that perhaps Lot himself becomes the target of threats of physical violation (p. 124). It is intriguing to note that Fields distances himself from current wisdom in another respect. In his view, the punishment that falls from the sky on the people of Sodom is primarily due to the repressive steps they take against a vulnerable immigrant, namely, Lot (p. 137). Fields observes that the subject of immigration is discussed repeatedly in the HB (pp. 178–9). In other words, Fields largely interprets the story of Sodom from the perspectives of paradigms A and D.

In the realm of biblical scholarship today, the most detailed study of the biblical drama of Sodom and its reception history is provided by the work of Michael Carden. In *Sodomy: A History of a Christian Biblical Myth* (2004) he offers a historical overview of an ample collection of Christian and Jewish sources. From the outset Carden rejects the anti-gay approach for two concrete reasons. First, he finds it too narrow and too distant from the biblical material. Second, it is too heavily imbued with homophobia defined as aversion to, and fear of, intimate same-sex relationships (pp. 6, 8). Generally speaking Carden operates within the current consensus, i.e. the latest version of paradigm D, according to which he imagines the main problem in the story of Sodom to be attempted gang rape (2004: 9, 14, 21, 28-9).

Like some other scholars Carden has noted that any serious exegesis of the Hebrew text will hinge on the way in which the verb *yada'*, 'know', is perceived and translated in Genesis 19.5. He himself is prepared to accept that the word has sexual connotations (2004: 20). That said, he admits that the biblical text in Genesis 19 is fraught with gaps and 'obscurity' (p. 4). For instance, the reader is never told the exact nature of the wickedness of the city. Similarly, it is not entirely clear what the disagreement between Lot and his fellow citizens is all about. Nevertheless, Carden feels that the story of Sodom and Gomorrah describes a situation of attempted gang rape, although he concedes that rabbinic interpretations provide a different picture and that the latter tradition is to be considered as the original (p. 10).

Since antiquity Jewish and Christian traditions have gone their separate ways. However, in recent years there are signs that some Jewish exegetes are adopting the Christian consensus as far as the story of Sodom and Gomorrah is concerned. One example is Rabbi Steven Greenberg who discusses the subject in his book *Wrestling with God & Men* (2004: 64-73). On the one hand, Greenberg primarily trusts the ancient Jewish sources, including the Hebrew text in Genesis (paradigms A, B, and C). On the other hand, he refers to the issue of attempted gang rape, i.e. paradigm D, several times (pp. 67, 72-3).

Within paradigm D it is customary for biblical scholars to juxtapose the drama of Sodom with another biblical narrative, namely, the crime of Gibeah narrated in Judges

19 and 20. This interpretive framework has the advantage of enabling the exegete to highlight the literary parallels between the two stories. Specifically, apparent gaps in one story may be remedied by importing details from the other account. In this manner, one narrative is made to provide explanations of the other. However, this popular procedure is fraught with pitfalls as numerous scholars fail to acknowledge the multiple narrative and stylistic differences between Genesis 19 and Judges 19 (Bechtel 1998b: 127 n. 45), including the specific literary setting in which each text unfolds (cf. chapter 12).

The Collectiveness of Sodom

> As biblical scholars approach the Hebrew scriptures, they inadvertently allow their modern world view to determine their reading or translation of the text. They assume things about the text that it may not assume.

With these words, Lyn Bechtel (1998b: 108) draws attention to the wide cultural gap between modern readers and the First Testament. She points out that the HB is androcentric and patriarchal. Yet people's lives and issues such as women and sexuality in biblical narrative are usually interpreted from a modern perspective. This fallacy has led to justifications of the marginalization of women and the condemnation of homoerotic relationships whereby injustices against women and gay people are significantly compounded, while the biblical text is distorted and impoverished (p. 108). The main hermeneutical difficulty here is the fact that biblical society was group-oriented in contrast to the individual-orientation of the modern western world (pp. 110–11). In this regard, Bechtel coincides with postcolonial approaches. For her, the Hebrew narratives primarily hinge on groups, clans, tribes, cities, and nations while modern scholars tend to concentrate on high-profile individuals such as Abraham, Sarah, Hagar, Ishmael, Isaac, and Lot. According to Bechtel, the shift from the earlier group paradigm to individualism occurred during the Hellenistic period. Such a crucial ideological transformation had a major impact on interpretations of the story of Sodom in post-biblical times.

In keeping with Lyn Bechtel's psychosocial analysis, group-oriented societies are defined and governed by a series of rules and norms. In ancient Canaanite city-states and biblical Israel, collective security and well-being would be defined rigorously, that is, in relation to physical limits or geographical borders. Any violation of such limits was perceived as a threat. Peaceful wayfarers like the two messengers arriving at Sodom in Genesis 19 would have been regarded with suspicion by the locals, particularly at a time when a major military revolt ended in disaster, as in Genesis 14 (Bechtel 1998b: 113). Similarly, the text specifically states that Lot is a sojourner, i.e. an outsider who has been allowed to dwell in the city and enjoy limited political rights. What is true of Lot is also true of his daughters. He runs the risk of becoming an object of vigilance for the authorities especially as he seems to have bonded with travellers of unknown nationality. An additional problem arises when Lot sets out to convince his fellow townsmen of his own views on right and wrong (19.7–8). Being of marginal status, it is not Lot's place to judge (Bechtel 1998b: 114).

According to Lyn Bechtel, the story's ambiguity is a major characteristic in Genesis 19. The men of Sodom act with remarkable mistrust, fear, and uncorroborated guesswork, all of which leave readers with a wide range of unanswered questions. In actual fact, the ambiguity of the men's intention is deliberate on the narrator's part and important to discern (1998a: 28). To Bechtel, it is obvious that the Sodomites are supposed to be mature adults but they seem incapable of behaving as such (p. 24); particularly, they fail when it comes to telling good from bad (p. 35). Thus, in her analysis, the narrator highlights the importance of knowing how to deal with and accept human diversity (p. 36). Bechtel concludes that the sin of the Sodomites has nothing to do with alleged homoeroticism but rather with their psychological immaturity and failure to interact meaningfully with people expressing opinions that seem to differ from their own (pp. 29, 35). Bechtel stresses that when the story of Sodom is read from a group-oriented perspective, it broadens the interpretive horizon considerably (p. 22). She reflects on the importance of belonging to the inner circle of native citizens as distinct from those who live on the margins. It is possible that the nervousness of the Sodomites was caused by political uncertainties that had caused regional turmoil in the recent past (Gen. 14). At any rate, both they and Lot do their best to assuage the pressure on their security by facing up to potential threats. In the process, both parties go a step too far (1998a: 29).

The innovative analysis of the drama of Sodom presented by Bechtel has enriched biblical hermeneutics. She is unconvinced by the traditional anti-homoerotic approach to the story (1998a: 22, 29). Nevertheless, Bechtel leaves open the possibility of a veiled sexual threat (pp. 28–33). In her view, the Hebrew verb *yadaʿ* is likely to have sexual connotations in Genesis 19.5 as well as in 19.8. Bechtel argues that the narrator deliberately imbues the text with threatening insinuations to create a virtually impenetrable veil of ambiguities (1998a: 28). The originality of Bechtel's analysis of Sodom allows it to include elements of paradigms A (the vulnerable sojourner exposed to social injustice) and B (inhospitality towards outsiders), while paradigm C is present in Bechtel's admission of sexual innuendo in her interpretation of the verb *yadaʿ*.

Like numerous modern commentators, Bechtel makes comparisons between the story of Sodom and the drama of Gibeah in Judges 19. One weak aspect of her discussion of the Sodom text is that she limits her focus to the first eleven verses of Genesis 19 without explaining her motivation for this (1998a). However, she avoids this error elsewhere by clearly stating that this is the text under discussion (1998b: 112). On just one occasion, and in passing, Bechtel mentions the important preamble to Genesis 19, which is Genesis 18 (1998b: 113).

Can the Sodomites Know God?

'How can wicked people like the inhabitants of Sodom presume to know God?' is a question raised by Brian Doyle (1998: 88). As he observes, the steady flow of fresh academic discussions of the story of Sodom and Gomorrah is an indication that the Hebrew narrative itself contains ambiguity and that 'a number of exegetical questions remain bereft of a satisfactory and consistent answer' (p. 86). According to Doyle, until today's exegetes learn to decipher the literary agenda of the narrator, including the story's multifaceted character, the text will continue to appear fraught with secrecy, mystery, and pitfalls. Above all, Doyle is ready to let go of the 'inhospitality' argument because 'it can be so simply reduced to sexual abuse'. While many scholars are inclined to associate Sodom with 'sodomy' interpreted as anal rape, he feels 'there is support for a non-sexual interpretation of the focal verses of Genesis 19.4–11' (p. 86).

Inspired by the work of several biblical scholars, Doyle sets out to analyse two key elements in the story of Sodom, namely, the characters interacting in the drama and the narrative framework. In particular, his attention is drawn to the vocabulary used by the narrator, including an apparently deliberate emphasis on certain words. For instance, it is paramount to explore what the men of Sodom have in mind when they express their desire to 'know' the two messengers. The meaning of the verb *yada'* has to be clarified throughout the story (p. 88). Another essential subject is the point of disagreement in the conversation between Lot and his fellow townsmen. According to Doyle, these issues are far from transparent.

Focusing specifically on the role of *yada'*, Doyle observes that the verb occurs four times in the text, i.e. twice in Genesis 18 and twice in Genesis 19. The multivalent character of *yada'* enables the narrator to use the same verbal root in different contexts. Doyle is aware of the popular sexual interpretation of *yada'* in ten occurrences out of a total of 943 in the HB. In his view, however, statistical data of this nature is insufficient and needs further refinement. The fact that a number of biblical dictionaries and commentaries suggest a given translation is not necessarily valuable. To obtain a clear picture of how a given word operates, a detailed examination of its role in different contexts is required (1998: 91). Doyle finds it hard to believe that the townsmen are bent on having sex with the visitors at Lot's house when they express their desire to 'know' them. Such an imperative would be absurd because 'it comes close to aspiring to superiority to the divine will' (p. 88). Doyle is convinced that the apparent irregularities in the text are not accidental (p. 89). While Abraham is worthy to receive the blessing of God to the point of meeting YHWH face to face (Gen. 18), Lot is not. Similarly, the men of Sodom, paradigms of wickedness, are refused such access (1998: 91). They demanded to know what for them was unknowable (pp. 88, 100).

Among today's biblical scholars Brian Doyle is unusual in distancing himself from the current consensus on the subject of *yadaʿ*. For him, the odds remain stacked against a sexual interpretation of *yadaʿ* in Genesis 19.5 (1998: 91), regarding the context sufficiently ambiguous to look for non-sexual motivations behind the behaviour of the men of Sodom. Doyle finds some help in the Septuagint, which differentiates between the occurrences of *yadaʿ* in 19.5 and 19.8 by rendering the verb with two different Greek terms (p. 92). At the same time, Doyle observes that Yhwh speaks of 'knowing' Abraham in Genesis 18.19. The significance of this utterance of the deity must necessarily influence subsequent occurrences of *yadaʿ* within the text of Sodom (1998: 93). According to Doyle, what is important to the narrator is to demonstrate who can be in a 'knowing' relationship with Yhwh and who cannot (pp. 93–4).

For his final reflections on the sin of Sodom, Doyle quotes Ezekiel 16 where the concept of arrogance plays a major part. Doyle underlines his previous point that nothing seems to imply that the Sodomites are dominated by sexual impulses. The real error committed by the men of Sodom is the violence with which they go about trying to know something, or somebody, out of their reach or grasp. They are punished with temporary blindness in Genesis 19.11 because they are driven by delusion and arrogance (1998: 98). For Doyle the story presents a group of unjust oppressors who treat the socially weak and vulnerable with brutality. Such procedures leave them in a blind alley in which they will try in vain to find the door of knowledge (pp. 98–100). Assessed from the perspective of paradigms A, B, C, and D, Brian Doyle's approach to Sodom is particularly inspired by paradigms A (arrogance) and C (sexual connotations of *yadaʿ* in Gen. 19.8).

Reassessing 'Know'

The prominence of the verb *yada'* in the Sodom text has given rise to much speculation among biblical scholars over the centuries (cf. chapters 3 and 10). Since the early Middle Ages, sexual connotations have been ascribed to *yada'* in Genesis 19.5 and 19.8. In the eleventh century, this hypothesis gave rise to the concept of sodomy, which in turn contributed powerfully to the consolidation of the well-known anti-homoerotic interpretation of the biblical legend (paradigm D). Given the popularity of the sexual focus in regard to Sodom, the omnipresence of this interpretation of *yada'* is understandable. It is found in the vast majority of dictionaries, commentaries, articles, and monographs.[222] On this basis, the current consensus explains the drama of Sodom as an illustration of attempted sexual abuse. Although Sodom is no longer seen as a place inhabited by people with homoerotic inclinations, paradigm D is still the main point of reference for today's biblical scholarship.

In studying and discussing the text of Sodom, numerous exegetes concentrate almost exclusively on the passage Genesis 19.1–11.[223] This limitation leads many to conclude that *yada'* occurs on two occasions only, i.e. in Genesis 19.5 and 19.8. However, such a narrow focus misses several important clues. It is worth remembering that the division

---

[222] Representative examples are: McNeill 1993: 47; Hugenberger 1994: 272; Fox 1995: 80; Hamilton 1995: 34; Alter 1996: 85; Stone 1996: 74–5; Fields 1997: 123–5; Nissinen 1998: 46; Helminiak 2000: 44–5; Brodie 2001: 250; Gagnon 2001: 72–4; Heard 2001: 54; Carden 2004: 20–1, 26; Greenberg 2004: 64–5; Lipka 2006: 44; McKeown 2008: 107; Schneider 2008: 186; Carmichael 2010: 102, 104; Heacock 2011: 91.

[223] Trible 1984: 75; Countryman 1989: 30–1; Comstock 1993: 40–2; Scanzoni and Mollenkott 1994: 60–2; Stone 1996: 70–7, 80–3; Bechtel 1998a and 1998b; Helminiak 2000: 43–4; Greenberg 2004: 64–9; Carr 2005: 53; Guest 2005: 164, 171–4, 228; Lipka 2006: 44 n. 4; Heacock 2011: 91.

into chapters and verses of English editions of the book of Genesis did not take place until the sixteenth century (Long 2001: 172). Strictly speaking, from a literary point of view the drama of Sodom and Gomorrah comes in two parts. Part 1 begins in Genesis 10.19, continues in Genesis 13.10-13 and culminates in Genesis 14. Part 2 is initiated in Genesis 18.1 and finishes in 19.38. If this second and more famous part is taken as a whole, and there are good reasons for doing so (Meir 2012: 54), one finds *yada'* not in two instances (or four; cf. Doyle 1998: 91) but rather on six occasions, namely, 18.19, 18.21, 19.5, 19.8, 19.33 and 19.35 (cf. chapters 3 and 10).

In recent decades dissenting voices have highlighted the sophisticated ways in which the Hebrew narrator has imbued his text with considerable amounts of ambiguity (Bechtel 1998a: 28). Significantly, a few scholars have distanced themselves from the sexual interpretation of *yada'*—at least in Genesis 19.5—indicating that the real problem of Sodom should be sought elsewhere (Jordan 1997: 32, 173; Doyle 1998: 91). Ellen van Wolde (2012: 71) wonders why this occurrence of *yada'* is never analysed from a legal perspective given the overall juridical framework of the Sodom text, which is well documented (cf. Boyce 1988; Bovati 1994; Bruckner 2001). In fact, the legal aspects of *yada'* in this narrative are crucial (van Wolde 2012: 93) since the verb regularly occurs as an important link in a verbal chain describing a judicial process in the form of an enquiry. In these contexts *yada'* tends to combine with *raah*, 'see', as in Genesis 18.21 (Bovati 1994: 251; van Wolde 2012: 86; Warner 2012: 116).

Other crucial legal terms occurring in the text of Sodom and Gomorrah are *tsa'aqah* or *za'aqah*. Both mean 'outcry' or 'complaint' (Bovati 1994: 314; Bruckner 1997: 91-3; van Wolde 2012: 72, 84) and are so similar in pronunciation and usage that they occur interchangeably in the HB (Lings

2006: 147). The corresponding verbs are *tsaʿaq* and *zaʿaq*, both of which are 'technical terms for legal complaints requesting deliverance' (van Wolde 2012: 89). In summary, current academic literature is showing signs of unease with the exclusive scholarly reliance on paradigm D for understanding the story of Sodom and Gomorrah. Since further analysis of the roles of *yadaʿ* is needed, this subject is discussed in chapter 10.

Conclusion

The unwavering hermeneutical uniformity that governed Christian approaches to the story of Sodom and Gomorrah in centuries past no longer exists. At present several different approaches to the narrative are emerging. While it is still widely accepted, the traditional paradigm D now occurs in two variants. One is defended by Robert Gagnon who is convinced that Genesis 19 presents Sodom as an objectionable hotbed of homosexual practice or, as argued by some, 'homosexuality'. In recent years, however, many exegetes have found this approach irrelevant, arguing that the biblical text has nothing to say on intimate same-sex relationships but rather illustrates a situation of imminent sexual assault. On this basis, the current consensus has labelled the sin of Sodom 'attempted gang rape'. The biblical figure of Abraham's nephew Lot is widely disliked and criticized by modern scholars, particularly among those who believe that the issue in Genesis 19.5–8 is sexual violence.

Several queer scholars have raised important theological questions in regard to the troubling aspects of genocide in scripture. Interpreted as a massacre, the destruction of Sodom and Gomorrah is difficult to reconcile to the concept of a merciful deity promoting justice. For its part, postcolonial analysts have begun to challenge traditional western, Eurocentric approaches to biblical studies. From the point of view of postcolonialism, all biblical texts respond to an agenda, which may or may not be part of a wider scheme of colonization. According to this approach, the Sodom narrative may be read as a link in a series of literary justifications of the invasion and domination of the land of Canaan by the ancient Israelites. Significant parallels may be drawn to the ways in which European nations have justified their colonization of overseas territories in centuries past.

Although still in the minority, some dissenting voices in today's hermeneutical spectrum are suggesting that the popular sexual approaches to the story of Sodom have not been able to resolve all ambiguities in the Hebrew text. Some opaque aspects are awaiting elucidation. At the centre of this debate is the verb *yada'*, 'know', particularly the two occurrences in Genesis 19.5 and 19.8. A growing number of contemporary exegetes believe that in 19.5 *yada'* is unlikely to have sexual connotations. Until fairly recently the juridical framework, within which the language of the Sodom text unfolds, has been ignored. In the specific case of *yada'*, it has been demonstrated that the verb regularly plays a judicial role in connection with an official enquiry. If this is so, two enquiries take place in Genesis 18 and 19. Much further work on the issue of legal language in this text is required. Therefore, chapter 10 focuses specifically on the possible meanings of *yada'* in the drama of Sodom. A detailed analysis of this pivotal verb is indispensable for answering the question of whether or not some degree of homoeroticism is present in the biblical text.

10

TRANSLATING SODOM

Each document in the Old Testament has a style of its own. Each book ought to speak its own message in its own way, even in a translation.

—The Complete Bible [224]

Introduction

The most famous section of the story of Sodom and Gomorrah is Genesis 19.1–11. In the light of many centuries of commentary and interpretation, it would be logical to assume that all textual problems have been sufficiently analysed and discussed. However, the Hebrew text contains a number of overlooked details. The overall sophistication of the biblical narrative shows in the form of several significant phrases, including 'from boy to old man' and 'from small to great'. Viewed together, they provide an intriguing picture of the mob laying siege to Lot's front door and the kind of intimidation to which Lot is subjected (cf. chapter 11). In chapter 1, I have explained how the book of Genesis tends to use *bō* ('come', 'go' or 'arrive') and *shakhav* ('lie down') for describing sexually charged situations. Because their presence contributes decisively to the drama throughout

---

[224] www.questia.com/read/82396727/the-complete-bible-an-american-translation.

Genesis 19, a detailed analysis of the roles of both verbs is carried out below.

As noted in the preceding chapters, paradigm D is the gateway currently used for entering the text of Sodom and Gomorrah to the detriment of other approaches. In particular, most interpreters limit themselves to apply an alleged sexual perspective to *yadaʿ* ('know') in two occurrences of this verb. However, the fact that *yadaʿ* appears six times in the story invites a more comprehensive methodology. Therefore, this chapter discusses the important literary and legal functions carried out by *yadaʿ* in the Sodom narrative followed by an overview of how *yadaʿ* has been translated in the past, including the Greek Septuagint. The six occurrences of *yadaʿ* provide an illustrative example of the art of Significant Repetition. The renderings of *yadaʿ* offered by twelve contemporary English versions of the Bible are explored and compared.

Any Homoeroticism in Sodom?

With respect to homoeroticism, one verse of the Hebrew text in Genesis 18–19 seems to use ambiguous language, namely, 19.5. This is where the men of Sodom call out to Lot (emphasis added): 'Where are the men who have *come to you* tonight?' Since 'come to' often has sexual connotations in Genesis, the Sodomites in theory might be seen to insinuate to Lot that his visitors have just had sex with him. The innuendo is perhaps subtly accentuated by the close proximity of *shakhav* in 19.4, 'before they lay down' (Peleg 2012: 133, 137). If this hypothesis is valid, it would have several implications: (1) Lot is supposed to have homoerotic inclinations, (2) this is common knowledge in Sodom, and (3) the townsmen consider Lot's house to be something like a brothel.

The HB offers an intriguing parallel in the story of Rahab, a Canaanite woman living in Jericho (Josh. 2.1–21). Described as a *zonah*, 'prostitute', she receives the visit of two Israelite spies sent out by Joshua. However, the arrival of these strangers has not gone unnoticed. Soon the local king's men appear at her front door ordering Rahab to 'bring out the men who have *come to* you, who *entered* your house' (NRSV, emphasis added). Undoubtedly the repeated occurrences of *bō* and *el* add spice to the conversation, emphasizing the innuendo. According to Frank Anthony Spina (2005: 54), this is part of the story's 'penchant for suggestive and teasing language'. The fact that the two Israelite men have come to a prostitute and entered a brothel may indeed be a double entendre. In Spina's words, 'a verb that is innocuous in one setting may be provocative in another' (p. 54). In the story, there is no evidence that Rahab and the spies actually have sex, and this does not seem to be included in the remit given by Joshua. However, the word play involving *bō* and *el* in this passage is likely to have been easily understood and enjoyed by ancient Israelite audiences.

Returning to Lot in Sodom, I wish to discuss whether or not a similar double entendre is likely to be present in Genesis 19.5. I start by examining how the twelve English versions have interpreted *shakhav* and *bō* and *el* in this context. Their renderings of *shakhav* are shown in table 43.

Table 43
Translating SHAKHAV in Gen. 19.4

Version	SHAKHAV in English (emphasis added)
CCB	They had not yet *gone to bed*
HCSB	Before they *went to bed*
JM	They had not *lain down to rest*
JPS	They had not yet *lain down*
NCV	Before *bedtime*
NIV	Before they had *gone to bed*
NJB	They had not *gone to bed*
NKJV	Now before they *lay down*
NLT	But before they *retired for the night*
NRSV	But before they *lay down*
NWT	Before they could *lie down*
REB	Before they had *lain down to sleep*

Table 43 shows some variation of style among the versions. Their renderings go all the way from the very literal 'lay down' (NRSV) to the free paraphrase 'bedtime' (NCV). While many versions focus on the actual time of the event in the form of 'gone/went to bed' (CCB, HCSB, NIV, NJB), 'lain down to rest' (JM) or 'lain down to sleep' (REB), others follow the example of the Hebrew text by focusing on the simple act of 'lying down' (JPS, NKJV, NWT). The NCV offers the euphemism 'retired for the night'. These various options adequately reflect the situation of an evening meal just finished and people starting to think of going to bed. Table 44 reflects renderings of *bō* and *el*.

Table 44
Translating BŌ & EL in Gen. 19.5

Version	BŌ & EL in English (emphasis added)
CCB	Where are the men who *arrived here* tonight?
HCSB	Where are the men who *came to* you tonight?
JM	Where are the men who *came to visit* you to-night?
JPS	Where are the men who *came to* you tonight?
NCV	Where are the two men who *came to* you tonight?
NIV	Where are the men who *came to* you tonight?
NJB	Where are the men who *came to* you tonight?
NKJV	Where are the men who *came to* you tonight?
NLT	Where are the men who *came to spend the night with* you?
NRSV	Where are the men who *came to* you tonight?
NWT	Where are the men who *came in to* you tonight?
REB	Where are the men who *came to* you tonight?

Once again, this is a situation of near-consensus with very few variations in the way the versions perceive *bō* and *el* in Genesis 19.5. By far the most popular rendering is the straightforward 'came to you', which is suggested by eight versions. More neutral paraphrases are 'arrived here' (CCB) and 'came to visit' (JM). The two remaining options are 'came to spend the night with you' (NLT) and 'came in to you' (NWT), both of which are ambiguous and lend themselves to being perceived as innuendo.

Thus, the presence of *bō* and *el* in 19.5, preceded by *shakhav* in 19.4, leads to a question: how likely is the narrator to let these verbs suggest sexual activity? If a few English versions are to be taken at face value, their renderings in tables 43 and 44 might be seen as pointing in that direction. However, I find a sexual scenario unlikely for a variety of reasons. First, *shakhav* basically means 'lie down' and is perfectly suited for the moment when people go to bed. Second, for *shakhav* to denote sexual intercourse it combines with a preposition, usually *eth* or ʿ*im*, as occurs later in the story (Gen. 19.32, 33). Both prepositions are absent from 19.4–5. Third, the only unmistakable reference to male–male sexual intercourse in the HB, which involves *shakhav* and *eth*, is in Leviticus 18.22 and 20.13, but the wording is highly unusual (cf. chapter 6). Fourth, in the vast majority of cases, the combination of *bō* and *el* does not denote sex but indicates movement from A to B, with *el* attaching to the point of arrival. Such is the case of nine occurrences in the Sodom narrative.[225] Fifth, 'come to' somebody often means 'approach' as in Genesis 7.9 where all the animals 'came to Noah' in the ark. Sixth, unlike Rahab in Jericho and a disguised Tamar at the roadside (38.15), nothing in the text suggests that Lot is a prostitute, and nowhere in the Bible and beyond is Lot described as such. Seventh, the remit of the divine envoys to Sodom does not include having sex with anyone. They are there to investigate the nature of the 'outcry' coming from the city (18.20–21; 19.13).

For all such reasons, the people of Sodom are unlikely to be referring to sex, particularly homoeroticism, as they use *bō* and *el* in Genesis 19.5. Their concern is of a different nature. The townsmen are stating in plain language that they know two strangers have come to town and that they are staying at Lot's house.

---

[225] Gen. 19.1, 3, 8, 9, 10, 22, 23, 33, 34.

All the People

Who are the people who show up at Lot's front door when it is nearly bedtime? How many are there and what do they look like? The twelve English versions are not very helpful on this despite the various clues provided by the narrator. Several elements describing the late-night mob are present in the story, beginning with three elements in Genesis 19.4 (emphasis added):

> The *men* of the city, the *men* of Sodom surrounded the house, from *boy* to *old man*, *all the people*.

The first information given here makes it clear that this event is for men. Presumably the women are not supposed to leave their homes at this late hour, and the same is true of small children. The second and third pieces of information provide further details as the Hebrew narrator highlights the massive dimensions of the crowd converging on Lot's house. 'All the people' is unmistakable and so is the phrase *minnaʿar weʿad-zaqēn*, which literally means 'from boy and to old man'. In other words, in just one sentence readers are told that the populace is all male, that every man in town is there, and that men of all age groups are represented, including unmarried adolescents and aged grandfathers (cf. Jer. 42.1, 8). Prima facie this should not pose a major problem for English translators. Table 45 shows their renderings of *minnaʿar weʿad-zaqēn* in Genesis 19.4.

Table 45
Translating 'From Boy to Old Man'

Version	From Boy to Old Man
CCB	young and old
HCSB	both young and old
JM	young and old
JPS	young and old
NCV	both young and old
NIV	both young and old
NJB	both young and old
NKJV	both old and young
NLT	young and old
NRSV	both young and old
NWT	from boy to old man
REB	both young and old

Perhaps the most striking thing about table 45 is the fact that only one version has taken a literal approach, namely, the NWT. All other versions have opted for paraphrases. Six versions say 'both young and old' (HCSB, NCV, NIV, NJB, NRSV, REB), while four reduce the phrase to 'young and old' (CCB, JM, JPS, NLT). The NKJV reverses the word order to 'both old and young'. Renderings such as 'both young and old' and 'young and old' adequately reflect the age dimension, but they cause readers to lose sight of the gender aspect. The Hebrew wording chosen by the narrator makes it clear that only the men of Sodom are present. If the women and young girls of the city had attended this event, the detailed description of the mob is likely to have been different as shown by other HB texts.[226] In addition, 'young and old' is less graphic than the 'from/to' turn of phrase in the Hebrew. By contrast, the NWT's choice is both gender specific and encompasses the entire age spectrum. Given the androcentric nature of public life in ancient Palestine, 'from boy to old man' is adequate. Being literal need not be an obstacle to clarity and accuracy. On the contrary, in this case it is an advantage.

An additional element in the narrator's description of the populace assembled in front of Lot's house appears in Genesis 19.11. This is where the divine visitors strike the men of Sodom with temporary blindness. The text reveals that the crowd includes people who are 'small', others who are 'great' and, it may be inferred, the full range of persons between these extremes. The Hebrew phrase is *miqqatōn weʿad-gadōl*, literally 'from small to great'. Table 46 reflects the approaches adopted by the twelve English versions in Genesis 19.11.

Table 46
Translating 'From Small to Great'

Version	'From Small to Great'
CCB	from the smallest to the largest
HCSB	both young and old
JM	young and old alike
JPS	young and old
NCV	both young and old
NIV	young and old

---

[226] When the HB describes mixed groups, the narrators explicitly mention the men and the women; cf. Josh. 6.21; Esth. 3.13; Jer. 44.15, 19–20, 24.

NJB	one and all
NKJV	both small and great
NLT	young and old
NRSV	both small and great
NWT	from the least to the greatest
REB	both young and old

The most striking impression left by table 46 is that no version is entirely literal. Fairly close is 'both small and great' (NKJV, NRSV) followed by 'from the least to the greatest' (NWT) and 'from the smallest to the largest' (CCB). However, in most cases no new information is provided. Instead, the phrase already introduced in 19.4 is repeated almost verbatim. Again one finds 'both young and old' (HCSB, NCV, REB) and 'young and old' (JPS, NIV, NLT). A variation occurs in 'young and old alike' (JM), and the NJB has the paraphrase 'one and all'. Thus, at least seven versions out of twelve seem to postulate that *minna'ar we'ad-zaqēn* overlaps entirely with *miqqatōn we'ad-gadōl*. However, while the two phrases may not be very far apart semantically and grammatically, they are not identical. The fact is that, in this tense drama, many versions have become repetitious where the Hebrew text provides variation in the form of fresh information. In this sense, the translators have simplified the text, reducing to mechanical repetition what in the Hebrew of 19.11 is a sophisticated addendum.[227]

The CCB does well to keep the 'from/to' sequence intact but introduces a new emphasis. As this version focuses on the physical dimensions of the assembled men by juxtaposing 'smallest' with 'largest', it seems to me that such graphic

---

[227] This detail seems to have escaped Weston Fields (1997: 77). While he rightly emphasizes that 'the entire population of Sodom' is there, he sees the two Hebrew idioms discussed above as 'semantically equivalent', which in my view makes little sense.

imagery changes the style and nature of the text. The adult, almost sociological style of the Hebrew prose is lost when the CCB opts for an approach that resembles that of a fairy tale. The notion of 'small' versus 'large' men is easily understood and certainly makes the phrase accessible to youthful audiences but, regrettably, it fails to convey the social implications of *miqqatōn weʿad-gadōl*. By contrast, the NWT's solution is well crafted. Without being entirely literal in the grammatical sense, the NWT accurately highlights the sociological aspect of this crowd by saying 'from the least to the greatest'.

Indeed, in 19.4, the narrator makes it clear that all age groups are represented ('from boy to old man'), and in 19.11 he elaborates. In the phrase *miqqatōn weʿad-gadōl*, the adjective *qatōn* literally means 'small'. It frequently appears in the HB in the sense of 'insignificant' or 'lowly' (Isa. 60.22; Jer. 49.15; Ob. 1.2). Likewise, the other word *gadōl*, usually translated as 'great', often means 'important', 'distinguished' or 'powerful' (Exod. 11.3; Esth. 9.4; Job 1.3). A striking parallel is found in the book of Jeremiah 42.1, where the prophet is approached by a large crowd of people described as 'all the people, from small to great'. In this case, the 'great' or powerful members of the community are mentioned by name (Johanan and Jezaniah). A virtually identical picture is presented in Jeremiah 42.8.

On this basis, it would seem that Genesis 19.11 is not providing a repeated observation on the age composition of the crowd. Rather, through the use of such adjectives as 'small' and 'great', all social classes are included, from the humblest slave at the bottom of the hierarchy via all the intermediate strata to the ruling élite. This information is crucial. Indirectly readers and hearers are being told that the king himself is present. As previously noted, the king of Sodom is called Bera (Gen. 14). Clearly the city is not a democracy in any modern sense, and in a hierarchical society no ordinary citizen can stage a riot on the spur of the moment. On the contrary, the phrase 'from the small to the great' seems to imply that the king is in charge. It takes an order from the ruler to organize an event on this scale and as late as bedtime. Therefore, in all probability, King Bera has commanded all male citizens of Sodom to leave the comfort of their homes and turn out. From a literary point of view, it is intriguing that the Hebrew narrator has chosen to let him remain unnamed in Genesis 19, a move that causes the 'men of Sodom' to speak with one voice.

To Come Upon Two Women

Once the destruction of Sodom and Gomorrah is a thing of the recent past, *bō* reappears in Genesis 19.31. According to some versions, what one of Lot's daughters says is sexually loaded. Here is a literal translation with emphasis added:

> There is not a man on earth to *come upon* us according to the manner of all the earth.

The translation 'come' represents *bō*, but in the Hebrew the verb is not joined by the frequent preposition *el*, 'to'. Instead one finds the preposition *ʿal*, which means 'upon' or, occasionally, 'towards' or 'beside'. This combination of *bō* and *ʿal* is unusual. Consequently, the narrator is not simply saying 'come to us'. Lot's elder daughter seems to be expressing that in this remote mountain region the chance appearance of a man who might want to become betrothed to them in the customary way is highly unlikely. The only other example of *bō* combining with *ʿal* in Genesis is in 34.25–27. Here it takes on an aggressive sense inasmuch as Jacob's irate sons violently 'come upon' the unsuspecting inhabitants of the city of Shechem. Outside Genesis, in Deuteronomy 25.5

the *bō* and *ʿal* combination denotes the special relationship between a man and a woman called levirate marriage (Fields 1997: 132). Applying this to Genesis 19.31, it might be argued that Lot's daughters are commenting on the fact that no surviving brothers exist of the young men in Sodom to whom they were betrothed (cf. 19.12, 14). The narrator has made it clear that all the people of Sodom perished (19.25).

Table 47 shows the ways in which the twelve English versions have interpreted *bō* and *ʿal* in Genesis 19.31.

Table 47
Translating BŌ & ʿAL in Gen. 19.31

Version	BŌ & ʿAL in English (emphasis added)
CCB	there is not a man in the country to *lie with* us
HCSB	there is no man in the land to *sleep with* us
JM	there is not a man on earth left to *marry* us
JPS	there is not a man on earth to *consort with* us
NCV	there are no men around here *for us to marry*
NIV	there is no man around here to *give us children*
NJB	there is no one here to *marry* us
NKJV	there is no man on the earth to *come in to* us
NLT	there are no men left anywhere . . . so *we can't get married*
NRSV	there is not a man on earth to *come in to* us
NWT	there is not a man in the land to *have relations with* us
REB	there is not a man in the country to *come to* us

Table 47 reveals a fair amount of discrepancy among the translators as they deal with the infrequent combination of *bō* and *ʿal* and the possibly special meaning involved. Strikingly, not a single rendering is entirely literal. Three versions have attempted some degree of literalness with 'come in to us' (NKJV, NRSV) and 'come to us' (REB). However, these options are deceptively simple and would be better suited for *bō* and *el*. JM and the JPS have chosen the problematic 'marry us'. Whenever a man in the HB marries a woman, the typical verbs are *laqach*, 'take' (Gen. 6.2) and *yadaʿ*, 'know' (4.1). The only connection between *bō* and *ʿal* and marriage in the HB is the aforementioned reference to levirate marriage (cf. Deut. 25.5), which may or may not be present in Genesis 19.31. More tentative, and probably less problematic, are 'consort with us' (JPS) and 'have relations with us' (NWT), although neither can be termed as literal.

Three versions in table 47 have tried other options but with limited success. The HCSB suggests 'sleep with us'. While too specific for an opaque context such as this, this rendering would have been adequate if the Hebrew sentence had contained any of the verbs *yashēn* ('sleep'), *bō* and *el* or *shakhav* and *ʿim*. The CCB's 'lie with us' clearly reflects a hypothetical *shakhav* which, unfortunately, is not present in the original text. 'Give us children' is a highly creative option introduced by the NIV. The paraphrase might well make sense in a situation in which two girls dream of having children. The trouble with the NIV's rendering is that the word 'children' is not even hinted at in the Hebrew text.

Two versions completely invert the grammatical order of the sentence under discussion. In the renderings offered by the NCV and the NLT, the grammatical agent is not the desirable wayfaring stranger mentioned in the original text. Rather, these versions make the girls say 'for us to marry' (NCV) and 'so we can't get married' (NLT). The use of 'marry' is very specific and does not do justice to the much less precise *bō* and *ʿal* combination, except if levirate marriage is intended. Usually the notion of marriage would require the occurrence of a different verb such as *yadaʿ* (cf. 19.8).

Surprisingly, one straightforward option is not included in table 47. If one considers that the Hebrew preposition *'al* generally means 'upon' or 'towards', *bō* and *'al* may well be translated as 'come upon' or 'come across'. In fact, this translation is commendable for two reasons. First, it is literal and accurately reflects the original text. Second, given the occasional meaning of 'come upon' and 'come across' as 'meet or find by chance' (OD), this seems to be a perfect match for the situation described by Lot's daughters.

Come, Lie Down, and Know

Despite the active presence of the verb in Genesis 19, with eight occurrences, few scholars have paid attention to *shakhav*, 'lie down'. As noted above, on a single occasion *shakhav* simply means 'go to bed' (19.4). In most other cases, however, particularly when *shakhav* combines with prepositions such as *eth* or *'im*, the connotation is 'have sex'. It has been seen above how *shakhav* plays a major part in the final incident of the story of Sodom when Lot's daughters decide to use their aging father as a sperm donor (Gen. 19.32, 34). The verb appears seven times in rapid sequence. Of these occurrences, five are openly sexual and two implicitly so. Below is an English translation of the Hebrew text in which Lot's daughters carry out their ruse. The seven occurrences of *shakhav* are emphasized (text abbreviated):

> 'Let us give our father wine to drink and we will *lie down* with him so that we can give life to seed by our father'. And that night . . . the elder went in and *lay down* with her father who did not know in her *lying down* or in her getting up. The next day the elder said to the younger, 'Last night I *lay down* with my father. Tonight let us give him wine again . . . and you go in, *lie down* with him . . .'

> And also that evening they gave wine to their father . . . and the younger *lay down* with him. And he did not know in her *lying down* or in her getting up.

One of the most intriguing textual details in this sexual incident is the way in which *shakhav* interacts twice, in 19.33, 35, with *yadaʿ* ('he did not know'). To this situation I return below. In Genesis 19.4, the Hebrew narrator explains that the drama of Sodom unfolds a moment before bedtime, i.e. the time for 'lying down' (*shakhav*). In 19.5 the men of Sodom announce their desire to 'know' (*yadaʿ*) the two visitors who have 'come' (*bō*) to Lot's house. In other words, the three verbs *shakhav*, *bō* and *yadaʿ* interact. On account of their joint presence and the overall sophistication of the Hebrew text, it is to be assumed that the narrator uses these verbs for different purposes. The passage reads as follows (19.4–5; emphasis added):

> And before they *lay down*, the men of the city, the men of Sodom, from boy to old man, all the people to the last man, surrounded the house. And they called to Lot, 'Where are the men who have *come* to you tonight? Bring them out to us and let us *know* them'.

Table 48 shows the approaches taken by the twelve English versions vis-à-vis *shakhav*, *bō* and *yadaʿ* in Genesis 19.4–5.

Table 48
Translating SHAKHAV, BŌ and YADAʿ

Version	SHAKHAV 19.4	BŌ 19.5	YADAʿ 19.5
CCB	go to bed	arrive here	have sex with
HCSB	go to bed	come to you	have sex with
JM	lie down to rest	come to visit you	rape
JPS	lie down	come to you	be intimate with
NCV	bedtime	come to you	have sexual relations w.
NIV	go to bed	come to you	have sex with
NJB	go to bed	come to you	have intercourse with
NKJV	lie down	come to you	know carnally
NLT	retire for the night	come to spend the night with you	have sex with
NRSV	lie down	come to you	know
NWT	lie down	come in to you	have intercourse with
REB	lie down to sleep	come to you	have intercourse with

According to table 48, all versions translate *shakhav* correctly in Genesis 19.4. The most literal option is 'lie down' (JPS, NKJV, NRSV, NWT) followed by 'lie down to rest' (JM) and 'lie down to sleep' (REB). Slightly less literal are 'go to bed' (CCB, HCSB, NIV, NJB) and 'retire for the night' (NLT). The NCV has turned the verb into the noun 'bedtime'. Despite the frequent sexual connotations of *shakhav* elsewhere, no version has included this aspect in their translation as they focus on the root meaning of the verb. All approaches seem perfectly suited to the context. A similar picture emerges in the case of *bō*. While it may often take on a sexual role in Genesis, the most likely interpretation of the verb in this verse indicates the act of arriving or coming. The only truly ambiguous rendering is suggested by the NLT, 'the men who came to spend the night with you'. At least to a modern readership the phrase 'spend the night with you' is not devoid of innuendo. In short, for both *shakhav* and *bō* most versions have remained fairly literal and successfully so.

When one turns to *yada'* in table 48, the situation changes considerably. The NRSV provides the only completely literal option saying 'know'. The NKJV significantly amplifies the meaning of *yada'*, transforming it into 'know carnally', which places the phrase squarely in the realm of sex. The remaining versions offer even longer, sexually charged paraphrases such as 'have intercourse with' (NJB, NWT, REB), 'be intimate with' (JPS), 'have sexual relations with' (NCV), and 'have sex with' (CCB, HCSB, NIV, NLT). In a category of its very own is 'rape' (JM).

It is curious that, in the case of *yada'*, only one version has taken a literal approach. The contrast between the third column and the previous two columns is glaring. In the main, the twelve versions render *bō* and *shakhav* literally. However, this commendable approach changes as soon as they turn to *yada'*. Inexplicably, the vast majority of translators have opted for paraphrase. What is more, in the process they have turned *yada'* into a synonym of *shakhav* taken in the sexual sense. JM goes to the extreme of associating *yada'* with violence as if it were interchangeable with *'anah*, 'humiliate'. From the point of view of linguistic and literary analysis, a sexual approach to *yada'* is highly problematic, as will be seen below.

Their procedure in Genesis 19.5 reveals that numerous Bible translators of today fail to distinguish between the root meanings of certain verbs. Essentially they have made *yada'* and *shakhav* interchangeable. In English, as in any other language, there is a considerable distance between concepts such as 'know', 'lie down', and 'rape' (Hamilton 1995: 34). Classical Hebrew is no exception. It is worrying that only one English version in table 48 has remained faithful to the basic meaning of *yada⁽* whereas the vast majority succumb to the temptation of producing an inaccurate paraphrase clearly influenced by paradigm D.

YADA⁽ in Sodom

The case of *yada⁽* is particularly illustrative of the problems involved in the differences between 'formal' (literal) and 'dynamic' (free) translations. It may be helpful to remember how the narrator uses *yada⁽* to give structure to Genesis 18–19 (cf. chapter 3). Thus, table 49 provides a reminder of the occurrences of *yada⁽* in the Hebrew text (cf. tables 15 & 16).

Table 49
YADA⁽ in the Hebrew Text of Sodom

Verse	Hebrew	Person	Meaning
18.19	yeda⁽etīw	1st singular	I have known him
18.21	eda⁽ā	1st singular	Let me know
19.5	ned⁽ā	1st plural	Let us know
19.8	yad⁽ū	3rd plural	They have known
19.33	yada⁽	3rd singular	He knew
19.35	yada⁽	3rd singular	He knew

From a literary point of view, the six occurrences of *yada⁽* form a chain. They may be represented in order of appearance as A-Ax-Ax-A-A-A, a sequence shown in table 50. The letter A refers to *yada⁽* in the simple *Qal* verbal pattern and the combination Ax alludes to the so-called Cohortative aspect, which is an emphatic extension of *Qal* used in the first person (Weingreen 1959: 88).

Table 50
YADA' in the Verbal Paradigm

Verse	Mode	Sequence
18.19	*Qal*	A
18.21	Cohortative	Ax
19.5	Cohortative	Ax
19.8	*Qal*	A
19.33	*Qal*	A
19.35	*Qal*	A

'Know' in the Septuagint

In antiquity, Greek became an important vehicle of culture and communication in vast areas of the empire of Alexander the Great. The Jewish communities of the diaspora enthusiastically acclaimed the first Greek version of the First Testament known as *Septuagint* (LXX). Similarly, from the very beginning of the early Christian church this work occupied a privileged position to the detriment of the original HB. While the Second Testament was coming into formation, the LXX literally was the official Christian Bible.

Among the books included in the LXX, Genesis seems to have been among the very first to be translated (Caird 1980: 36; Metzger 2001: 16). Generally speaking, the Greek text remains faithful to the Hebrew original known today as the Masoretic Text (MT). However, in some passages the LXX translator has found it difficult to reproduce the subtle word plays present in the Hebrew prose. An emblematic case is found in the opening chapters of Genesis, particularly in connection with the creation of the first human being. The literary style of the LXX diverges from the spirit of the original (Loader 2004: 33-4). While the Hebrew text highlights mythological and philosophical aspects, the tone of the Greek prose several times hints at sexual relationships (pp. 41-2).

In numerous cases, the LXX translator follows formal or literal criteria, a method in keeping with the translation ideals commonly advocated in antiquity. At other times, however, this ideal is sidelined in favour of a 'flexible' procedure. The Greek renderings of *yada‛* in the story of Sodom are shown in table 51.

Table 51
'Know' in Sodom According to the LXX

Verse	Greek	Meaning	Sequence
18.19	*oida*	know	A
18.21	*gignōskō*	know, perceive	B
19.5	*syngignomai*	get together with	C
19.8	*gignōskō*	know, perceive	B
19.33	*oida*	know	A
19.35	*oida*	know	A

The way in which the Septuagint translator approached this verb reveals that he faced some difficulty. Where the Hebrew narrator utilized the same verbal root *y-d-‛* six times, the LXX has introduced three different Greek verbs, namely, *oida*, *gignōskō*, and *syngignomai*. From a literary point of view, these different Greek options for *yada‛* form a 'circular' chain which may be presented as A-B-C-B-A-A. Within this group *oida* predominates with three slots followed by two occurrences of *gignōskō*, while *syngignomai* appears only once.

Comparing table 51 with the two preceding tables, the nexus between the Cohortatives of *yada'* established by the original narrator in 18.21 and 19.5 has disappeared in the LXX. An analogous situation is observable between the simple pattern (*Qal*) of the verb in 18.19 and 19.8. In other words, while these connections are grammatically evident in the Hebrew text, no such allusion is made in the Greek version. The only element shared by *gignōskō* and *syngignomai* is -*gigno*-, two syllables used as building blocks in the morphology of both verbs.

The LXX establishes a clear link between 18.19 and 19.33. At least it is obvious that the same verb is present in both contexts. However, it is surprising that the LXX has chosen *oida* in two situations that have fairly little in common. In 18.19, Y<small>HWH</small> refers to his covenant with Abraham. When the verb reappears in 19.33 and 19.35, it describes Lot's lack of awareness caused by an excessive intake of wine. At the same time, the repeated presence of *gignōskō* between 18.21 and 19.8 in the LXX posits a special link, or even a certain shared identity, between the two occurrences. This is a clear discrepancy from the Hebrew original where there is a grammatical difference between the Cohortative in 18.21 and the *Qal* mode of *yada'* in 19.8. These approaches to *yada'* show that the LXX differs in several significant ways from the Masoretic text. Above all, the presence of the three Greek verbs *oida*, *gignōskō*, and *syngignomai* used to translate a single Hebrew verb, reveals a certain penchant for the free or 'dynamic' translation method.

To Know in the Greek Sense

The LXX is regarded as the most ancient literary witness to the original HB due to its proximity in time and space (Groom 2003: 75). Perhaps the single most peculiar detail in the way in which the LXX has translated *yada'* in the text of Sodom and Gomorrah, is the solitary position of *syngignomai* in Genesis 19.5. Two observations should be made. First, the basic and most frequent meaning of this Greek verbal compound is 'to be with' or 'meet with' somebody, for instance, to have a conversation. Second, in classical Greek literature the verb is used more widely, including the area of sexual euphemisms. A number of examples of the latter are found in the works of Herodotus, Plato, and Xenophon (Mather & Hewitt 1962: 498; Heacock 2011: 91-2 n. 177). There *syngignomai* tends to mean 'have carnal intercourse' with somebody, particularly in reference to a man's relationship with a woman.[228] For the subject of this chapter, the Greek connection is of vital importance. These famous writers lived during the fifth and fourth centuries BCE: Herodotus 484-425, Xenophon 431-354, and Plato 428-347 BCE. The literary prestige of the *Iliad*, the *Anabasis* and the *Symposium*, among other renowned works, was such that their authors' styles influenced all subsequent literary production in ancient Greece and the entire Hellenistic world. The LXX was translated into Greek between the third and second centuries BCE, by which time the literary tradition created by the great Classics was firmly established.

In a few cases, the verb *gignōskō* becomes a sexual euphemism comparable to *syngignomai*. Examples are found in the writings of Heraclides Ponticus and Menander, both of whom lived in the fourth century BCE (Liddell & Scott,

---

[228] Liddell and Scott, *A Greek-English Lexicon*, 1940, consulted 2010 in: www.perseus.tufts.edu/hopper/resolveform?type=start&lookup=suggignomai&lang=greek.

1940; Rösel 1994: 102). Undoubtedly, this fact has influenced the way in which some translators interpret the occurrence of *gignōskō* in 19.8 vis-à-vis Lot's daughters who have not 'known' a man or husband. Thus, while it appeared within a well-established literary tradition, in which various writers used sexual euphemisms, the LXX itself came to occupy a privileged position in the early centuries of Christianity, from where its own style had an impact on later translations. In other words, it seems natural to conclude that this pivotal Greek version set an important precedent for the interpretation of the story of Sodom and Gomorrah. In fact, the approach to *yada'* adopted by the LXX has been partially imitated by a number of versions of the Bible produced in recent centuries (cf. tables 56 & 57).

In the light of this exploration, a specific hypothesis may be formulated. The popular tendency to ascribe a sexual dimension to the verb 'know', allegedly based on the Bible, is not rooted in the HB. It seems far more likely that it derives directly from the LXX and indirectly from the classical literature of ancient Greece. I therefore propose to rebaptize the familiar phrase 'to know in the biblical sense'. Adapted to the historical and literary evidence, it becomes 'to know in the Greek sense'.

'Know' in the Vulgate

> It was the Vulgate, and not the Hebrew or the Greek texts, that proved decisive for the construction of the category of Sodomy (Jordan 1997: 31 n. 6).

While Greek maintained its privileged position in the Byzantine Empire, Latin gradually became the official language of the Roman church. For several centuries, a large number of Latin translations of the LXX and the Second

Testament were in circulation but none included every book in the Bible (Metzger 2001: 30). The Vulgate, Jerome's complete version of the Bible, appeared around the year 400 CE, i.e. approximately 600 years after the LXX. At first, Jerome had intended to translate the LXX because his Greek was good unlike his virtually non-existent Hebrew. However, as time went by he realized that many LXX manuscripts had errors. He then changed his mind and began to learn Hebrew in order to understand and translate the HB directly from the original sources (Metzger 2001: 33-34). In spite of initial opposition by Augustine of Hippo and various church communities (Hargreaves 1993: 73), the Vulgate was gradually preferred by Latin-speaking Christian circles (Long 2001: 7-8).

In the case of the LXX, as already discussed, the Greek translator approached the Hebrew verb *yada'* in the text of Genesis 18-19 by offering three different renderings. Jerome chose a somewhat similar procedure with three different interpretations of *yada'*, namely, *scio* ('know' in the sense of 'be knowledgeable'), *cognosco* ('know' in the sense of 'become acquainted with'), and *senso* ('feel' or 'perceive'). Table 52 reflects the presence of these verbs in Jerome's Latin text.

Table 52
'Know' in Sodom According to the Vulgate

Verse	Verbs	Meaning	Sequence
18.19	*scio*	be knowledgeable	A
18.21	*scio*		A
19.5	*cognosco*	become acquainted	B
19.8	*cognosco*		B
19.33	*senso*	feel, perceive	C
19.35	*senso*		C

Table 52 displays the elegance of Jerome's literary systematization. He has arranged his three verbs in duplicate making them form an A-A-B-B-C-C pattern. Compared with the former A-B-C-B-A-A sequence adopted by the LXX (table 51), this is a decisive innovation. In other words, Jerome has kept his independence vis-à-vis the prestigious LXX. However, remembering the clear interconnection in the MT of the six occurrences of *yadaʿ*, the difficulties attached to the method adopted by Jerome soon emerge. For instance, in the Latin text, there is no obvious link between *yadaʿ* in 18.19 (*scio*) and 19.8 (*cognosco*). Similarly, the grammatical nexus between the Hebrew original's two Cohortatives 'let me know' in 18.21 (*scio*) and 'let us know' in 19.5 (*cognosco*) is missing. Finally, Jerome's suggestion that Lot did not 'feel' what was going on in 19.33 and 35 deprives his readers of the opportunity to establish any connection between this passage and previous occurrences of *yadaʿ*.

With regard to Jerome's use of *cognosco* in 19.5 and 19.8, it should be pointed out that in classical Roman literature, this verb is sometimes used as a sexual euphemism. Such connotations are noticeable in the works of several important Latin writers (Adams 1982: 190), including Julius Caesar (100–44 BCE), Catullus (ca. 84–54 BCE), and Ovid (43 BCE–17 CE). Thus, in addition to 'to know in the Greek sense', it is also justifiable to speak of 'to know in the Latin sense'.

Two Classical Versions

This brief look at the two most influential versions of the Bible in the history of Christianity has detected three major problems in regard to the story of Sodom and Gomorrah. Since antiquity, translators have faced difficulties whenever they deal with *yadaʿ* in this text. The ambiguity surrounding the knowing requested by the men of Sodom in Genesis 19.5

is augmented in the LXX by the Greek verb *syngignomai*, a difficulty which in turn is compounded by *cognosco* in Jerome's Latin Vulgate. Furthermore, *syngignomai* and *cognosco* have sexual connotations in the respective classical literatures of ancient Greece and Rome. Once their presence in different versions of the Bible was consolidated, the impact of these sexual euphemisms on subsequent generations of Bible interpreters has been inevitable. Undoubtedly, the precedents set by the LXX and the Vulgate have been decisive and continue to be so in the twenty-first century.

Using the data explored in this chapter, table 53 compares the Hebrew text (MT) with the two ancient versions in order to contrast their approaches to *yada'*.

Table 53
'Know' According to the MT and Two Classical Versions

Verse	MT	LXX	Vulgate
18.19	A	A	A
18.21	Ax	B	A
19.5	Ax	C	B
19.8	A	B	B
19.33	A	A	C
19.35	A	A	C

First, in table 53, it is striking that the basic pattern woven by *yada'* in the HB, including the so-called Cohortative (Ax), is not imitated by the LXX and the Vulgate. Second, both versions introduce three different renderings for a single Hebrew word. Third, the two approaches differ. The gap between the LXX and the Vulgate vis-à-vis *yada'* in this text may be taken to mean that some aspects of this verb are opaque, or have not been clarified. Obviously, in both versions the translators have proceeded on a case-by-case basis while failing to grasp the overall function of *yada'* in the entire text. The vocabulary reveals that no attention has been paid to the Cohortative, which establishes a significant grammatical and semantic link between Genesis 18.21 and 19.5. Indeed, the most remarkable literary detail is found in 19.5 where both the LXX and Jerome have tried to liberate themselves from any ambiguity by interpreting *yada'* from a sexual perspective. At the very least, they have left such a possibility open. In all probability, this is the historical starting point of a new hermeneutics for the story of Sodom and Gomorrah, which departed radically from the concerns expressed by the Hebrew prophets. Over time, the LXX and the Vulgate have been utilized to confirm the validity of Christianity's hostility to homoeroticism (paradigm D).

'Know' According to Martin Luther

> Luther's great achievement as a translator is to have broken with the pernicious influence of the classical languages (Flood 2001: 48).

At the time of the Protestant Reformation, Martin Luther's German Bible, published in 1545, was a major innovation. Due to its plain language and the recently invented art of printing, his version of the Bible quickly became a huge success. Luther's education took place in an era when the only versions of the Bible in German were overly literal translations of the Septuagint and the Vulgate (Flood 2001: 49). People without academic training found them almost incomprehensible. Luther reacted by becoming an ardent advocate of the general reading public's right to access the biblical writings presented in everyday language. Luther's project was favoured by the publication of the Hebrew Bible (MT) in 1488 and the Greek

New Testament in 1516. With the biblical texts available in the original languages, Bible translators no longer had to make do with the LXX or the Vulgate.

As documented in several chapters of the present book, the Hebrew verb *yada⁽* is pivotal in the story of Sodom and Gomorrah. Table 54 examines Luther's German renderings.

Table 54
'Know' in Sodom According to Luther

Verse	Verbs	Meaning	Sequence
18.19	*wissen*	have knowledge about	A
18.21	*wissen*		A
19.5	*erkennen*	recognize, perceive	B
19.8	*erkennen*		B
19.33	*gewahr werden*	realize, notice	C
19.35	*gewahr werden*		C

The first thing one notices in table 54 is that Luther's version does not reflect the literary A-Ax-Ax-A-A-A pattern of *yada⁽* in the original Hebrew text (MT), as might be expected from a reformer who strongly believes in the slogan *sola scriptura* ('scripture only'). Second, it seems strange that Luther does not rely on the Septuagint, which contains the earliest surviving translation of Genesis. Third, and surprisingly, Luther adopts the very same A-A-B-B-C-C sequence that Jerome established in the Vulgate, which in his lifetime was practically the official Bible of the Catholic Church.

In table 54, Luther's renderings of *yada⁽* form three units with no links between them. The use of the German verb *erkennen* in 19.5 and 19.8 would seem to be correct from all points of view.

However, it is worth noting that in German *erkennen* may be used as a sexual euphemism,[229] and this is the sense applied by numerous scholars to these two verses of the Sodom story (Brinkschröder 2006: 189). Therefore, Luther's use of *erkennen* in Genesis 19.5 and 19.8 reveals that his interpretation of Sodom is indebted to paradigm D. Where Luther deviates slightly from Jerome's approach is in 19.33 and 19.35. His translation *gewahr werden*, 'realize', appears to be semantically closer to the meaning of Hebrew *yada'* than the Latin *senso*, 'feel'.

'Know' in the King James Version

In England, John Wycliffe (fourteenth century) produced his vernacular English version of the Bible based on the Vulgate. More than a century later, William Tyndale (1494–1536) translated the recently published Hebrew and Greek manuscripts into English. *The Geneva Bible* (sixteenth century) was the work of a group of British Protestants living in exile in Switzerland. It circulated widely and was frequently quoted in contemporary literature, including the works of William Shakespeare (Long 2001: 175, 196; Metzger 2001: 66). The most important English version of the Bible of all time dates from the seventeenth century. Owing to the active participation of James I in the official translation process (Long 2001: 189), it was called *The Authorized Version* or *The King James Version* (KJV). All forty-seven translators belonged to the Church of England. Once published in 1611, the KJV was very well received by users in other Christian denominations. Even today, the KJV occupies a privileged position in many quarters in the face of a steady flow of new versions.

Among the enduring virtues of the KJV are its literary elegance and poetic expressiveness. Table 55 shows the

---

[229] Cf. the dictionary *Brockhaus Wahrig Deutsches Wörterbuch* (1981: 562).

approach to the verb *yada'* in the text of Sodom adopted by the KJV translators.

Table 55
'Know' in Sodom According to the KJV

Verse	English	Sequence
18.19	*Known*	A
18.21	I will *know*	A
19.5	that we may *know*	A
19.8	*Known*	A
19.33	*Perceive*	B
19.35	*Perceive*	B

If the KJV is compared to the LXX and the Vulgate, it becomes clear that this veteran version of the English-speaking world is closer to the biblical original than its early forerunners. Rather successfully, the KJV limits itself to the use of the two English verbs *know* and *perceive*, both of which belong to the semantic field of *yada'*, producing a literary A-A-A-A-B-B sequence. Intriguingly, such commendable consistency does not accord with the KJV translators' stated intentions. They explicitly resist the idea of consistent use of the same word in the English translation where the same word appears in the Hebrew source text (Long 2001: 199): 'Why should we be in bondage to them if we may be free?' This contradiction between the stated aims of the KJV and their textual implementation invites comparison with the alleged policies of numerous modern versions that use 'dynamic' criteria. The latter often claim to be meticulously accurate but tend to rewrite or paraphrase rather than translate the biblical text. An illustrative example is precisely *yada'* in the story of Sodom, for which some contemporary versions of the Bible arrive at no fewer than five different renderings (A-B-C-D-E-E; cf. table 57).

'Know' in Today's English Versions

Having discussed significant historical precedents, it is time to see how modern English translators approach *yada⁽* in the text of Sodom. They are shown in table 56.

Table 56
YADA⁽ in Gen. 18–19 According to English Versions

Versions	18.19	18.21	19.5	19.8	19.33, 35
CCB	choose	know	have sex with	virgins	know
HCSB	choose* *Lit know*	find out	have sex with	have sexual relations	know
JM	choose	find out	rape	virgins	know
JPS	single out	take note	be intimate w.	know	know
NCV	choose	know	have sexual relations with	sleep with	know
NIV	choose	know	have sex with	sleep with	be aware
NJB	single out	know	have intercourse with	virgins	be aware
NKJV	know	know	know carnally	know	know
NLT	single out	know	have sex with	virgin daughters	be aware
NRSV	choose* *Heb know*	know	know	know	know
NWT	become acquainted	get to know	have intercourse with	have intercourse	know
REB	single out	know	have intercourse with	virgins	know

If table 56 is read vertically, the original Hebrew phrase in Genesis 18.19 is *yeda⁽etīw*, 'I have known him'. By far the most popular rendering is 'I have chosen him' (CCB, HCSB,

JM, NCV, NIV, NRSV) followed by 'I have singled him out' (JPS, NJB, NLT, REB), and 'I have become acquainted with him' (NWT). One version sticks to the root meaning 'know' in 'I have known him' (NKJV). Two versions acknowledge this aspect in footnotes (HCSB, NRSV). In the second vertical column (18.21), there is less diversity. In addition to eight cases of 'know', one encounters 'find out' (HCSB, JM), 'take note' (JPS) and 'get to know' (NWT).

Undoubtedly, the meaning of *yada'* in 19.5 is the subject of considerable scholarly debate. The preferred interpretations are clearly sexual. Table 56 contains paraphrases such as 'have sex with' (CCB, HCSB, NIV, NLT), 'have sexual relations with' (NCV), 'have intercourse with' (NJB, NWT, REB), 'know carnally' (NKJV), and 'be intimate with' (JPS). JM suggests 'rape', and only the NRSV has the literal option 'know'. The fourth vertical column reflects the translations of *yada'* with regard to Lot's daughters in Genesis 19.8 who 'have not known'. Only three versions use the literal 'known' (JPS, NKJV, NRSV) while the rest go for sexual paraphrases: 'slept with a man' (NCV, NIV), 'had sexual relations' (HCSB), and 'had intercourse' (NWT). Curiously, the five remaining versions convert the entire verbal phrase into a noun as they speak of daughters who are 'virgins' (CCB, JM, NJB, NLT, REB). Thus, all the translators seem to agree that Lot is affirming the physical purity of his two young daughters. The final vertical column holds no surprises. All versions accurately interpret *yada'* in 19.33 and 35 as either 'know' or 'be aware'.

Unknowing Versions

In this text the English versions raise several exegetical problems. In 18.19 the frequent paraphrases 'I have chosen him' and 'I have singled him out' are imprecise. First, 'choose' is semantically quite a long way from 'know' (Warner 2012: 114 n. 5). Second, there are other comparable contexts in the HB in which the versions translate *yada'* accurately as 'know' (Deut. 34.10; 2 Sam. 7.20). Third, there is quite a semantic gap between 'I have singled him out' (JPS) and 'I have become acquainted with him' (NWT). Fourth, Classical Hebrew already has a specific verb meaning 'choose', namely, *bachar*. This verb plays a major part in the 'preface' to the story of Sodom in Genesis 13.11. Here Lot is invited by his uncle Abraham to 'choose' between several options and decides to settle in the Jordan valley near Sodom. Likewise, in Exodus 18.25 Moses 'chooses' capable Israelites to administer justice to the people. In other words, *bachar* applies to both people and objects.

Directly comparable to Genesis 18.19 are some verses in the Pentateuch in which Yhwh chooses human beings by means of *bachar*. A number of examples are found in the book of Deuteronomy, including 'he chose their descendants' (Deut. 4.37), 'he has chosen you to be his people' (7.6), and 'Yhwh your God has chosen him' (18.5). In these specific cases, virtually all English versions coincide in saying 'choose', 'chose', and 'chosen'. Therefore, if the narrator had intended to speak of choice in Genesis 18.19, it would have been natural for him to use *bachar*. The occurrence of *yada'* in this passage seems to denote a different nuance. Remembering the notion of Significant Repetition highlighted by several modern exegetes, I will now test the popular option of 'chosen' by applying it to the other occurrences of *yada'* in Genesis 18 and 19. Already in 18.21 it becomes clear that 'choose' does not match *yada'* at all. Similarly, it makes little sense to think that the men of Sodom want to 'choose' Lot's guests in 19.5. In 19.8, the situation is somewhat different. It might not seem unreasonable to say that Lot's daughters have not yet 'chosen' the men they are going to marry. However, it is improbable that the girls are free to choose because, in their culture, fathers or parents choose partners for their children (24.2-4; 28.1-2). In Lot's case, according to 19.14 this has been done some time ago. Finally, the prose of 19.33 and 35 would seem rather odd if a translator were to say that Lot did not 'choose' when the girls entered his bed.

The reason so many versions suggest 'chosen' for *yada'* in Genesis 18.19 is found in the dictionaries of biblical Hebrew, including the DBHE (p. 307). However, this rendering does not seem ideal for the reasons given above. It is inconsistent to make *yada'* interchangeable with *bachar* in one case and not elsewhere. Obviously *yada'* and *bachar* are used in different contexts in the HB.[230] Similar considerations apply to 'take notice of' and 'regard' proposed for Genesis 18.19 by the BDB (p. 394). It would seem more fruitful to explore different ways to interpret *yada'* on its own terms. With respect to *yada'* in Genesis 19.5, the numerous sexual renderings in table 56 are out of place. It should not be forgotten that the Hebrew narrator generally, including in the text of Sodom and Gomorrah, uses *shakhav* for denoting sexual action (19.32 ff). Even more difficult to accept in 19.5 is the presence of 'rape' (JM). In no language are 'rape' and 'know' interchangeable. Moreover, for rape, rape-like scenarios or unauthorized sexual intercourse Classical Hebrew uses *'anah*, 'humiliate' (cf. Gen. 34.2).

In the case of Genesis 19.8, at least two exegetical problems are apparent. First, five versions translate the Hebrew phrase 'known a man' into 'are virgins' or similar (CCB, JM, NJB, NLT, REB). Second, the remaining seven versions translate the noun *ish* as 'man'. This option is at best incomplete because it leaves out an important aspect of *ish*, namely,

---

[230] As pointed out by Amira Meir (2012: 53), *bachar* appears in Neh. 9.7: 'You are YHWH God who *chose* Abram . . . and gave him the name Abraham' (emphasis added).

'husband' (Gen. 30.15; Num. 5.20). The text makes it clear that the girls are betrothed to two young men living in Sodom (19.14). In summary, for 19.8, it would seem reasonable to translate *yada‹* and *īsh* as 'they have not known a husband', an option regrettably absent from table 56. Again, the most likely explanation is that English Bible translators are so used to reading this passage from a sexual perspective that they routinely ignore other exegetical possibilities for *yada‹* and *īsh*. Admittedly, the Hebrew dictionaries are a contributing factor (BDB p. 394; DBHE p. 307).

It is unfortunate that so many translators fail to use 'know' in the text of Sodom and Gomorrah. If they had taken a more literal approach, it would have been much easier for readers to establish correlations between Genesis 19 and, for instance, Genesis 3, 4, 9, 18 and 38–39. In Genesis 3.7, where the first human couple become aware of their nudity, the Hebrew text explains that they 'knew' they were naked. In this case *yada‹* denotes the idea of acquiring fresh awareness. The process they experience makes them 'knowledgeable' in the sense of causing them to develop psychologically. When Lot does not 'know', his drunken state deprives him of awareness and possibly legal responsibility (19.33). Exactly the same thing happens in 9.21 when Noah's generous intake of wine leaves him unconscious, naked, and exposed to Ham's impertinent gaze. Only after his drunken stupor is over is Noah able to 'know' what his son has done (9.24). In the latter situations, 'knowledge' is incompatible with excessive consumption of alcohol.

On five occasions, the book of Genesis speaks of persons who do not 'know' in sexually charged contexts. There the verbs *bō* and *shakhav* interact with a negated *yada‹*. Lot does *not* 'know' during the sexual intercourse initiated by his daughters (19.33, 35), and Judah does *not* 'know' the veiled woman with whom he has sex (38.16). For his part, Potiphar has stopped 'knowing' the daily affairs of his house, trusting entirely in Joseph's managerial skills (39.6), a fact Joseph highlights when he is cornered by the official's wife who wants to be intimate with him (39.8).

Choose, Find Out, or Rape?

If one returns to table 56 to analyse it horizontally, several surprising facts emerge. First, only the NKJV and the NRSV manage to align themselves to a large extent with the HB, exceptions being 18.19 (NRSV) and 19.5 (NKJV). Second, every other version offers dubious solutions. The most problematic are those with a strong sexual focus for *yada*ʿ in 19.5 and 19.8 (HCSB, NCV, NIV, NWT), where the verb is turned into a synonym of *shakhav*. The main difficulty of this approach is that the sexual option is inapplicable to the remaining slots in table 56. For instance, in 18.19, where Yhwh speaks of his relationship with Abraham, the hypothetical presence of 'I have had sexual relations' or 'I have slept with him' would be outrageous, and it would be just as absurd in 19.33 and 35 to maintain that Lot 'did not have sex' during the night-time events inside the mountain cave.

In summary, it is important to emphasize that, in several cases, the options chosen by the versions differ so widely among themselves that they must be considered incompatible. In Hebrew as well as in English, it makes no sense to affirm that 'choose', 'be aware', and 'sleep with' are interchangeable. In addition, they cannot all adequately represent the concept of knowing, let alone in the same story. JM, for instance, presents five different verbs or phrases, namely, 'choose', 'find out', 'rape', 'are virgins' and 'know'. Readers with no knowledge of Hebrew might assume that five different terms are found in the original text. They have no way of realizing that just one Hebrew verb is being rendered in such disparate ways. The same readers are likely to think that 'virgins' refers back to a Hebrew noun, which in theory could be *bethulah*, 'maiden' (Gen. 24.16). Only 'find out' (18.21) and 'know' (19.33) may be described as semantically associated with *yadaʿ*.

Undoubtedly, the most striking option introduced by JM is 'rape' in Genesis 19.5. Again the issue of incompatibility must be highlighted. 'Rape' is inappropriate for all other slots in table 56. It would be preposterous to affirm that the deity has 'raped' Abraham, that he wants to go down to Sodom to 'rape' (18.21), or that Lot's daughters have not 'raped' a husband (19.8). The suggestion that Lot did not 'rape' in 19.33 and 19.35 would be just as ludicrous. As mentioned before, the absurdity created by JM is compounded by the fact that sexual transgression or violence is usually expressed in Hebrew by means of the verb *ʿanah*, 'humiliate' (*Piel* verb pattern).

In short, the overall impression left by table 56 is that the translators—with extremely few exceptions—have been unaware of the incoherencies they have inserted into the text of Genesis 18 and 19. In linguistics, such untenable procedures are sometimes described as 'illegitimate identity transfer'. It occurs when two or several words are assumed to have the same meaning when this is not the case (Cotterell & Turner 1989: 122; Groom 2003: 62). In the Sodom text, particularly in 19.5 and 19.8, this phenomenon is seen repeatedly as numerous translators are being influenced by church tradition to ascribe the same meaning to *bō*, *shakhav*, and *yadaʿ*. There is little awareness that, within the HB, each verb has its proper meaning and role. In lexicography it is important to define words in opposition to each other, i.e. their meanings should be contrasted in order to achieve a clear definition of the semantic field in which each word operates (Groom 2003: 62).

YADAʿ in Twelve Versions

Table 57 provides a comparative overview of the presence of *yadaʿ* in the original Hebrew text (MT) of Sodom and Gomorrah followed by the procedures adopted by the twelve English versions. In MT, the letter A represents the six occurrences of *yadaʿ*. In the English versions, A refers to the first translation (18.19) while the letters B-C-D-E allude to other options that differ from A.

Table 57
YADAʿ in Twelve Versions (Genesis 18–19)

Genesis →	18.19	18.21	19.5	19.8	19.33	19.35
MT	A	A	A	A	A	A
Versions ↓						
CCB	A	B	C	D	B	B
HCSB	A	B	C	C	D	D
JM	A	B	C	D	E	E
JPS	A	B	C	D	D	D
NCV	A	B	C	D	E	E
NIV	A	B	C	D	E	E
NJB	A	B	C	D	E	E
NKJV	A	A	B	A	A	A
NLT	A	B	C	D	E	E
NRSV	A	B	B	B	B	B
NWT	A	B	C	C	D	D
REB	A	B	C	D	B	B

A glance at table 57 immediately makes it clear that not a single version of the Bible has achieved full concordance with the Hebrew original (MT). Two versions come close as they limit themselves to two options for translating *yadaʿ* (NKJV, NRSV). However, five versions include four different renderings (CCB, HCSB, JPS, NWT, REB). The remaining five versions have extended the meaning of *yadaʿ* to cover an even wider area for which no fewer than five terms have been deployed (JM, NCV, NIV, NJB, NLT). Evidently, there is a strong tendency among Bible translators to resort to paraphrase for most occurrences of *yada'* in the story of Sodom and Gomorrah with the concomitant mistranslations.

In summary, the diversity of criteria for translating *yada'* in the Sodom text is difficult to justify. Ultimately, readers of most versions are faced with an English text whose meaning, atmosphere, and scope are placed at a considerable distance from the original narrative. The conclusion is inevitable: most translators have been heavily influenced by a powerful tradition, which has made it acceptable to modify the nature and essence of *yada'*. The most popular translation method is the so-called dynamic approach according to which the translator deals with the occurrences of a key term on a case-by-case basis. This causes them to miss the literary points made by the narrator as he uses the same term repeatedly. As discussed in preceding chapters, this phenomenon has important ancient precedents in the LXX and the Vulgate. No version follows them slavishly, but several imitate their example as they diversify their own approaches to *yada'*. To understand the prevalence of paradigm D in the procedures adopted by modern English versions to the text of Sodom and Gomorrah, it is essential to consider the exegesis begun during the Hellenistic and patristic eras (cf. Groom 2003: 65).

Conclusion

The Hebrew narrator describes the populace assembled in front of Lot's house in some detail, providing information on the age groups and social classes represented. The latter aspect of the story is lost in most English versions, which focus entirely on the men's age and provide repetition where the original offers variation. The opening verses of Genesis 19 contain the verbs *shakhav*, 'lie down, and *bō*, 'go in' or 'arrive', but there is no sign of innuendo. Towards the end of Genesis 19, the sexual action is carried out through *shakhav* as Lot's daughters execute the incestuous project that will enable them to have children (19.32–35). The English translators generally render *shakhav* accurately. Also *bō* is present but without playing a sexual role except for an ambiguous occurrence of this verb in 19.31 where *bō* unusually combines with the preposition ʿ*al*, 'upon'. In this passage, most versions are insecure and fail to reproduce the ambiguity in the original text.

The anonymous narrator of Genesis 18 and 19 is undoubtedly a highly educated, sophisticated writer. At all times, the Hebrew prose reveals the secure hand of a person familiar with poetic expression and an extraordinary ability to deploy a minimum of words, including at the height of dramatic tension. With six occurrences in the narrative, the pivotal verb in the Sodom text is *yadaʿ*, 'know', making Significant Repetition an important ingredient. By highlighting *yadaʿ,* the narrator achieves a considerable stylistic advantage. In practice, the verb becomes the literary axis whose repeated presence adds continuity and constancy to the story amid the growing turbulence of exceedingly dramatic events. In other words, the intermittent occurrences of *yadaʿ* provide unity in the midst of diversity, enabling readers to realize the extent to which the various narrative sequences are interconnected.

The key verses for the popular sexual interpretation of Sodom (paradigm D) are 19.5 and 19.8. There are historical reasons for this. The ancient translator of the Greek LXX version introduced three options for *yadaʿ*, of which *syngignomai* in 19.5 often has sexual connotations in classical Greek literature. Similar considerations apply with respect to the Latin verb *cognosco* used centuries later by Jerome for his Vulgate version. In the Christian world, the LXX and the Vulgate completely eclipsed the original Hebrew text. The precedents they established for translating the story of Sodom and Gomorrah have influenced the ways in which subsequent generations of Bible translators perceive the Hebrew verb *yada'*, including Martin Luther's German renderings, which run parallel to the A-A-B-B-C-C pattern established by the Vulgate.

In addition, a number of current English versions prefer 'free' or 'dynamic' approaches to translation to the extent of proposing no fewer than five different renderings of *yada'*, suggesting a varied A-B-C-D-E-E pattern. This procedure has important disadvantages. First, the basic notion of 'knowing' is absent in many cases. Second, the 'dynamic' method often produces unfortunate renderings that are so far apart semantically that they become totally incompatible. Third, the great variety of English options prevents readers from recognizing the literary interconnectedness of the six verses in which *yada'* occurs. In other words, where the original narrative emphasizes repetition, the versions tend to go in the opposite direction offering variation.

11

THE VICTIM OF SODOM

You shall not mistreat or oppress a foreigner
For you were foreigners in the land of Egypt.

—Exodus 22.21

Introduction

While Abraham is the protagonist of Genesis 18, Lot is in the eye of the hurricane throughout chapter 19. In addition to the significant verb *yada'*, his role in the story is crucial for understanding the plot. Over the centuries, Lot's actions and words have been analysed by biblical interpreters and many different and frequently contradictory conclusions have been drawn from the verses in which he plays a part. To a great extent, the widely differing views on Lot are the result of the laconic style of the Hebrew text, which leaves readers wondering about Lot's way of thinking, motivations and moral stature. Commentators have raised questions regarding the fact that he lives in Sodom. Much discussion centres upon Lot's approach to hospitality, the way he treats his daughters, and his relationship to Abraham. Additional issues are his position as head of a household and his status as a resident alien in the city of Sodom. As previously noted, post-biblical commentaries on Lot may roughly be divided into three camps: (a) Lot the Hero, (b) Lot the Ambivalent, and (c) Lot the Villain.

In the light of such diversity, this chapter explores the intriguing complexities surrounding Lot's situation in Sodom. Thomas Brodie (2001: 106) cautions that 'until psychological analysis is open to the full dimensions of all that is positive in human existence it will not be able to deal adequately with Genesis'. Taking Brodie's advice, this chapter focuses on Lot's motivations for acting the way he does in Genesis 19. Since he and his family escape annihilation, Lot is clearly among the few 'righteous' or innocent citizens suggested by Abraham's intercession before YHWH in Genesis 18. In previous chapters, I have discussed four interpretive paradigms in connection with the drama of Sodom. The framework I use below is paradigm A (i.e. arrogance, injustice, violence) because it connects the narrative with other parts of Genesis, the book of Exodus and the Hebrew prophets. The latter depict the resident poor—not the visitors—as victims of social injustice (Is. 1.10-17; Ezek. 16.49-50). Abraham's nephew is indeed a marginalized outsider in the city of Sodom.

Lot's Uncle

Placed in the very middle, the Sodom narrative is the centrepiece of the Abraham cycle, which spans Genesis 12-25. Its prominent location has given it paradigmatic force along with other symbolic stories such as the flood (Gen. 6-8) and the tower of Babel (Gen. 11). Undoubtedly, the Sodom text is highly significant in the life of Abraham of Mesopotamia who receives a divine prompting to migrate with his wife Sarah and nephew Lot to the land of Canaan (12.1-7; 20.13; 24.7). Thus, from the very beginning of the story, the narrator suggests that the life of Lot is to be interpreted in association with that of his uncle and aunt (Peleg 2012: 143). The contrast between Abraham and

Lot, both of whom live as sojourners in the land of Canaan, merits close attention (Doyle 1998: 89).

The life of Abraham is a classical example of an outsider who faithfully practises his own religion and traditions (12.8; 13.18), and who prefers not to adapt more than is strictly necessary to an alien social and cultural environment (14.22-23). Yhwh sustains Abraham through many difficulties by renewing his promises to him.[231] Abraham is often troubled by uncertainty, fear, and famine, but his faith provides him with a constant anchor.[232] Even when he upsets the pharaoh of Egypt (12.18-19) and subsequently does the same to the king of the Philistines (20.8-10), no harm befalls him. On the contrary, he becomes very prosperous.[233] In spite of his permanent outsider status, Abraham admirably manages to live in peace and harmony with his Canaanite neighbours. Virtually everywhere he goes, Abraham is respected and treated with deference.[234] On several occasions, the Canaanites who know him express awareness of the special relationship between Abraham and Yhwh (14.19-20; 21.22).

The overall picture that Genesis draws of Abraham shows a man who remains true to his calling, sometimes against overwhelming odds. He may occasionally lapse into doubt and anxiety, but rather than detract from his moral stature, this adds a very human dimension to his portrait. He is not a perfect saint, but rather a fallible person of flesh and blood with strengths and weaknesses. Above all, he has been 'known' by God to become the father of a nation in which all nations shall be blessed (18.19). In this respect, Abraham's wife Sarah is crucial. She is favoured by Yhwh and becomes

---

[231] 12.7; 13.14-17; 15.1, 4-7, 18-21; 17.1-8, 19; 22.17-18.
[232] 12.7-8; 13.4, 18; 15.6; 17.23-27; 20.17; 21.33; 22.14; 24.7.
[233] 12.5, 16; 13.2, 6; 14.23; 20.14, 16; 23.6, 14-16; 24.1, 10; 25.6.
[234] 14.18-21; 20.14-16; 21.22-23; 23.5-6, 11.

party to the covenant (17.16).[235] For his faithfulness, Abraham receives palpable blessings. The Genesis account of Abraham illustrates how the one who walks with YHWH and lives by his commandments is blessed, enjoys peace and prosperity, and is treated with respect. Having left everything behind in Mesopotamia, Abraham is richly rewarded throughout his life in Canaan. He lives among the Canaanites but is adamant not to let Isaac marry a local woman (24.2-4). Instead Abraham obtains a wife for his son from among his relatives in northern Mesopotamia, namely, Rebekah (Gen. 24). In short, Abraham does 'what is good in YHWH's eyes'. Not only does he become rich and successful in material terms, but also following Sarah's death, Abraham fathers six sons by Keturah, his second wife (25.1-6). In total, Abraham sires eight named sons (16.15; 21.3; 25.2). His old age is characterized by further blessings. When his life is ending, the presence of his sons Ishmael and Isaac enables Abraham to enjoy a peaceful death and the assurance of being buried next to Sarah (15.15; 25.8-10; cf. Brodie 2001: 280-1).[236] On account of his numerous descendants, Abraham's name will live on for many generations.

Abraham's Nephew

Most of what is known about the life of Lot relates directly to the story of Sodom and Gomorrah. While his devotion to YHWH ensures Abraham's safety in dangerous situations and

---

[235] Only those descended from Abraham and Sarah are considered part of the insider group (Spina 2005: 4). Indeed, Sarah is a major figure who will become the ancestress of royalty (Teubal 1984: 29). During her periods of marital exile in the harems of two kings, she enjoys divine protection (Gen. 12.17; 20.2-7); cf. van Dijk-Hemmes 1993: 232-3.

[236] Similar blessings are bestowed upon Isaac (35.29) and Jacob (49.29-33; 50.1-13).

provides him with material blessings, life takes a different turn for Lot who first appears in Genesis 11 and 12. When separation from his aunt and uncle becomes inevitable, Lot chooses to settle near Sodom, attracted by the fertility and lush vegetation of the area (13.10–12). He seems unaware of, or undeterred by, the sinister reputation of this city to which the narrator alludes in 13.13. Given that the people of Sodom are Canaanites (10.19), their 'evil' ways may well be associated with polytheism, usually termed 'idolatry', the overarching concern throughout the HB.[237]

With regard to Abraham, Lot represents a younger generation which seeks integration with the local community (Gen. 14.12). However, in the narrative his numerous misfortunes suggest that Lot's chosen road is a mistake. His concern for material prosperity and integration eventually contributes to his downfall (Brodie 2001: 213). While living near his uncle, Lot is wealthy (13.5). After he becomes a resident of Sodom, things change, and he and his household are carried into captivity (Gen. 14.12). Despite his kinship with Abraham, who rescues the whole city (14.14–16), Lot apparently does not rise to any respectable social position in Sodom. His foreign background leads the townsmen to regard him with suspicion (19.9). The problem worsens when Lot invites two wayfaring strangers into his home. At this point an intractable conflict erupts between Lot and the spokesmen of the city. It leads to a scuffle and the subsequent abrupt flight of Lot and his family.

Lot's life after parting company with Abraham can be viewed as a process of gradual decline. Lot has gone down the road of full integration with the Canaanites of Sodom, taking all

---

[237] The phrase 'To do what is evil in the sight of YHWH' denotes idolatry; cf. Judg. 6.1; 10.6; 13.1; 1 Kings 11.6; 13.33; 14.22–24; 15.26, 34; 16.7, 19, 25, 30; 22.52; 2 Kings 3.2; 8.18.

the steps necessary for becoming a permanent resident, including marrying a local woman (von Rad 1972: 217). His daughters are born there and become betrothed to local men, a clear indication of Lot's belief in intermarriage (19.14). He feels that he has acquired full community membership and achieved some form of insider status, which enables him to address the townsmen as 'my brothers' (19.7). Perhaps he also feels secure because of his links with Abraham. Yet all Lot's efforts at integration fail, and everything goes wrong. The longer he resides in Sodom, the more disasters befall him, including sharing the city's fate when King Bera loses the war and many inhabitants are taken captive (14.11–16). As Michael Carden (2004: 16) points out, 'This plunder and depopulation foreshadows Sodom's final fate of devastation and mass death'. When Sodom and other cities of the plain are destroyed by fire from heaven, Lot and his family lose all their material possessions. On both occasions, Abraham comes to his kinsman's rescue, ensuring, respectively, his liberty and survival (Gen. 14.11–16; 18.32; 19.29).[238]

In Genesis 19, Lot is portrayed as having difficulty accepting the messengers' repeated promptings to flee the city. Just as he finds it impossible to convince his sons-in-law of the urgent need to escape, Lot is unable to persuade himself to leave his house (19.16). Brian Doyle (1998: 96) finds that his very lingering in Sodom is a sign of how much Lot is at home there while Thomas Brodie (2001: 252) argues that Lot is afraid to leave the city for the open country. Michael Carden (2004: 18) suggests that his inability to persuade his sons-in-law to flee may have undermined Lot's own resolve. Unlike Abraham, he fails to heed the voice of Yhwh (Gen. 19.15–22).

---

[238] Wenham 1994: 43, 59; Lundbom 1998: 141; Carden 2004: 21.

Significantly, Lot has no sons. In addition, he experiences being taken captive; his fellow townsmen distrust him; he feels coerced to the point of giving up his children as a pledge (Pirson 2012: 205); he and his house are assaulted; his material goods go up in smoke; he fails to ensure the future married lives of his two unnamed daughters, and his wife perishes. After losing virtually everything, his story finishes on a dishonourable note. His dislocation and subsequent taking refuge in a mountain cave, as recommended by the messengers, carry no blessing or reward other than survival. When Lot finally does produce two sons, it is only because of the cunning stratagem of his daughters. He himself is not aware of it, playing only the part of passive inseminator. Thus, his male offspring are illegitimate.[239] Through them he becomes the less than glorious ancestor of two neighbouring nations, namely Ammon and Moab, with whom the Israelites will have conflicts and skirmishes for centuries.[240]

A Problematic Marriage

Sarah is mentioned by name throughout the Abraham cycle in connection with her husband (Gen. 11.29–23.19). In contrast, Lot's wife appears very late in her husband's story, being mentioned three times only (19.15, 16, 26). There is no reference to her when Lot leaves Mesopotamia with his uncle and aunt (12.4–5), and the moment of Lot's wedding and the identity of his wife are not disclosed. The fact that

---

[239] Lot's daughters are independent-minded. They procure offspring for themselves, not for their father (19.32, 34), and Moab and Ben-Ammi are named by their mothers (19.37–38).
[240] Still, the fact that he is Abraham's kinsman has caused YHWH to assign a special territory to Lot's descendants; cf. Deut. 2.9, 19. See also Holloway 1999: 51.

she is unnamed suggests she is a Canaanite,[241] possibly from Sodom, which makes her undesirable from a patriarchal perspective.[242] Because they disapprove of intermarriage with Canaanites, Abraham, Isaac, and Jacob all marry named Mesopotamian women.[243] Their covenant with YHWH is understood to exclude Canaanites and only applies to their own legitimate offspring engendered by a woman of the appropriate category. The fact that no son is born to Lot may be an indirect way of saying that his marriage does not enjoy divine approval. The contrast to the eight sons fathered by Abraham is striking (16.15; 21.2; 25.2). This significant difference between uncle and nephew highlights the extent to which one patriarch is richly blessed and the other only very modestly. In a patriarchy, having a son is paramount. The outsider status awarded by the HB to Lot's descendants seems to confirm the exogamous nature of his marriage (Teubal 1984: 58). In this sense, the Sodom story is political insofar as it contains a clear warning against intermarriage.[244]

Furthermore, several subtle features in the story reveal details about Lot's wife. Unlike Sarah, she leaves the meal preparations to her husband (19.3), which is a very unusual situation for most cultures in antiquity (von Rad 1972: 206; Meyers 1988: 145–7). Tragically, she ignores the messengers' warning as the family escapes the overthrow of Sodom. She makes a halt to look back and turns into a pillar of salt

---

[241] Similarly, Jacob's son Judah marries a nameless Canaanite woman (Gen. 38.2).
[242] According to the *Targum Neofiti*, Lot's wife was a native of Sodom (Carden 2004: 105).
[243] Esau's marriages to local 'Hittite' women meet with his parents' disapproval (26.34–35). As soon as he realizes his mistake, he tries to set the record straight by taking an additional wife of more respectable stock, namely, Mahalath daughter of Ishmael (28.8–9).
[244] Conflicting biblical attitudes to intermarriage exist (Meyers 1988: 71). Sometimes it is condoned (Moses and David) and at other times condemned (Exod. 34.11–16; Deut. 7.3–5).

(19.26). Both Mrs Lot and the townsmen pay a high price for their lack of discernment and receptiveness. Likewise, the meals to which Abraham and Lot treat their divine visitors are not of the same standard. Whereas Abraham is able to present his guests with an exquisite banquet (18.6-8), the food prepared at Lot's house is rather basic (19.3).[245] Moreover, Abraham has a considerable number of female and male slaves,[246] while this is only true of Lot's earlier days (12.5; 13.5-7). This may be another subtle indicator that Lot's prosperity is a thing of the past and that his life in Sodom has been reduced to modest proportions.

The above comparison between Abraham and Lot highlights one of the narrator's main points. Lot's unsuccessful attempt at integration becomes an important lesson for ancient Israelite readers and listeners. While Lot himself is not depicted as 'evil', the very fact that he settles in a city described as such makes him considerably less righteous than his uncle. At the crucial moment of the messengers' visit to his house, Lot experiences first-hand a fatal clash between the hospitality norms that he shares with Abraham and the oppressive policies governing Sodom. Indeed, the two lifestyles are irreconcilable. Lot cannot have it both ways. In other words, this story contains a dire warning to biblical Israel: *do not mingle with the Canaanites and do not intermarry. It will surely lead to disaster.*[247] Thus, Lot comes to embody the grave mistake of an apostate, a person who abandons the covenant of Yhwh to adopt non-Israelite ways (Carden 2004:

---

[245] In Weston Fields's view (1997: 41 n. 41), this narrative detail serves to maintain Abraham's place of prominence. However, Lyn Bechtel (1998a: 25 n. 5) observes that the text does not suggest that the meal prepared by Lot was ungenerous.

[246] 12.5, 16; 14.14-15; 17.13, 23, 27; 20.14; 24.2.

[247] Explicit warnings against intermarriage abound; cf. 24.3; 26.34-35; 27.46; 28.1, 6-9. The drama of Dinah and Shechem in Gen. 34 may be read in the same light (Carmichael 2010: 61).

86). In this regard, Lot's life illustrates one of the strongest concerns of the HB. Deuteronomy 7.3-4 addresses the issue succinctly:

> You shall not intermarry with them, giving your daughters to their sons or taking their daughters for your sons, for they would turn away your children from following me, to serve other gods. Then the anger of Y<small>HWH</small> would be kindled against you and destroy you promptly.

Read in this light, Genesis offers a complex portrait of Lot, which contains several didactic and doctrinal strands. In the narrator's view, whoever follows in Lot's footsteps does so at his own peril. Anyone in Lot's situation distances himself from Y<small>HWH</small>, exposing himself to different forms of hardship. He may become a loser not only in material terms, but also with respect to personal dignity and integrity. In addition, he renounces the patriarchal quest to secure an honourable mention for his name in the annals of posterity. The last days of Lot's life—including the moment of his death—are unaccounted for, which may be another way of indicating that he died in isolation and obscurity.

As the Good in Your Eyes, Part One

As shown in previous chapters, most contemporary commentators take a negative view of Lot. This is based on a crucial passage in the drama of Sodom, namely, Genesis 19.8-9. Historically, these verses have lent themselves to misinterpretation. As he argues with the townsmen about his hosting duties, Lot proposes a deal, suggesting the possibility of handing over his two underage daughters. A literal translation of his words may read as follows:

> Look here, I have got two daughters who have not
> known a husband. Now, let me bring them out to
> you, and do to them as the good in your eyes.

Once again it should be emphasized that the biblical phrase 'to know a man' may just as well be translated as 'to know a husband' whenever the grammatical subject is a young woman. For two unmarried girls such as Lot's daughters, this seems the more likely interpretation. Furthermore, and taken in a strictly literal sense, the phrase 'do to them as the good in your eyes' invites the people of Sodom to treat the girls well. However, most exegetes have gone in a different direction. Given the popular sexual approach to the verb *yadaʿ*, they believe Lot is inviting the men of Sodom to take their pleasure with the girls by raping them.[248] Dissenting voices are few. One of these is Lyn Bechtel who argues that asking someone to behave according to the 'good' in their eyes does not usually imply sexual violence (1998b: 122).

Accepting Bechtel's point, I wish to explore the way Lot's words in Genesis 19.8 have been translated since antiquity, the obvious starting points being the Septuagint and the Vulgate. In the LXX, one finds these Greek words: *kai chrēsasthe autais katha an areskē umin.*[249] A literal English translation would be 'And *make use of* them as you please' (emphasis added). Superficially this rendering of the original Hebrew may appear to be adequate. However, in the Greek translation Lot's tone of voice has changed. In the original Hebrew, he expresses himself in neutral terms. The LXX

---

[248] Fox 1995: 81; Hamilton 1995: 35; Vasey 1995: 125; Alter 1996: 85; Fields 1997: 124; Nissinen 1998: 46; Helminiak 2000: 45; Carden 2004: 20; Greenberg 2004: 64; Boyarin 2007: 139; McKeown 2008: 107; Schneider 2008: 188; Heacock 2011: 91-92.

[249] According to studybible.info/interlinear/Genesis%2019 (2010), another variant of the Greek text says *kai chrasthe autais katha an areskoi.*

rendering, particularly 'make use of', is much less ambiguous and more brutal. If a man is invited to make use of a young woman, for many readers this has sexual connotations. Add to this a certain amount of force. In classical Greek literature, there are indeed passages featuring the verb *chraomai*, 'use' or 'make use of', in which it applies to men relating sexually to women. Examples are found in the works of Demosthenes, Herodotus, Isocrates, and Xenophon.[250] To conclude, the sexual approach to Genesis 19.8 adopted by the LXX has established an important historical precedent. Viewed in this way, Lot is perceived as trying to bribe the inhabitants and authorities of Sodom.

The other important ancient version of the Bible is the Vulgate. As he translates the phrase 'do to them as the good in your eyes' into Latin, Jerome provides readers with a major surprise. In Genesis 19.8 one finds *et abutimini eis sicut placuerit vobis*. A literal English translation would be 'and *abuse* them as you please' (emphasis added). Compared with the Septuagint, Jerome's rendering goes a significant step further as it leaves wide open the possibility of sexual violence. This is indeed remarkable in the history of Bible translation as this may well be the first time that a version adopts an approach to the drama of Sodom based on an unmistakable combination of violence and sex. While the language of the LXX offers innuendo, the Vulgate turns up the heat by introducing the term *abutimini*, 'abuse'. In other words, from the 'use' suggested by his Greek predecessor, Jerome has moved onto 'abuse' and thereby distanced himself considerably from the Hebrew text (MT).

To what extent is Jerome's rendering justified? The expression 'do as is good in your eyes' or 'do the good in your eyes'

---

[250] www.perseus.tufts.edu/hopper/resolveform?type=exact&lookup=xraomai&lang=greek (2010).

occurs fairly frequently in the HB. Speaking about Hagar, Abraham tells Sarah, 'Do to her the good in your eyes' (Gen. 16.6). After this conversation a frustrated Sarah *mistreats* her servant harshly. In Hebrew the action is expressed through the verb ʿ*anah* (Piel). The latter reflects the abuse which, it should be noted, is absent from Genesis 19.8. By contrast, in many other cases the phrase 'the good in your eyes' denotes trust and loyalty, as when King Abimelech tells Abraham, 'My land is before you. Settle where is good in your eyes' (20.15). In Judges 10.15, the people of Israel humbly pray to YHWH for help saying, 'Do to us all the good in your eyes'. Pleading before King David, Jonathan's son Mephibosheth declares, 'Do the good in your eyes' (2 Sam. 19.27).

In summary, there are no compelling linguistic reasons for Jerome to translate 'do to them as the good in your eyes' with words that encourage people to behave harshly or violently. In the MT, Lot is not asking the people of Sodom to rape his daughters. Judging from his language, he may well be saying the exact opposite. The very fact that he proposes such a deal may be interpreted as an act of loyalty on his part. His situation is extremely delicate. On the one hand, he feels obliged to entertain visitors according to the ancient hospitality norms. On this he is unwilling to compromise (19.8). On the other hand, he has to remain on good terms with the people and authorities of his place of residence. As noted in chapter 10, the fact that every man in town is present on this occasion is emphasized twice in the text (19.4 & 19.11). In the tension of the moment, Lot makes a significant concession, offering to hand over his underage children as a form of pledge.[251]

---

[251] John Boswell (1980: 95) draws a parallel to a Latin text penned by Ammianus Marcellinus (fourth century CE). According to the latter, a Roman prefect named Tertullus once faced a violent riot by the common people who felt doomed by the looming prospect of starvation. As a large crowd packed the square in front of his house,

Returning to the Vulgate, and taking into account the moderate nature of the three renderings of *yada'* presented by this version (cf. table 52), in Genesis 19.8, it is surprising to encounter such vehement language as 'abuse them'. Jerome's categorical paraphrase of Lot's diplomatic words cancels any ambiguity, leaving readers with a situation laden with debauchery and sexual aggressiveness.

In table 58, the original Hebrew (MT) is compared with the Septuagint and Vulgate renderings of Genesis 19.8. All are accompanied by a literal English translation.

Table 58
From 'Good' to 'Abuse': Two Interpretations

Sources	Text and Translation
MT	*wa'asū lahen kattōv be'ēnēkhem*
	and do to them as the good in your eyes
LXX	*kai chrēsasthe autais katha an areskē umin*
	and make use of them as you please
Vulgate	*et abutimini eis sicut placuerit vobis*
	and abuse them as you please

Table 58 illustrates the historically ascending scale of the text fragment from Genesis 19.8 under scrutiny. While the MT

Tertullus feared for his life. He invited those present to consider that attacking him and his defenceless family would not avert the catastrophe, if it were to occur. He tearfully held out his young children to the populace, saying, 'Here they are in your power.' This dramatic gesture had an appeasing effect on the crowd. For the full story, see Ammianus Marcellinus 1950: 521–2.

offers a neutral or diplomatic wording, which adequately underscores Lot's tricky situation, over the centuries the same phrase has been understood in terms that are increasingly sexual and violent. The Septuagint and Vulgate renderings have cemented this process. In the latter case, a dramatic semantic deviation from the original has occurred. From 'do good' in the MT, Jerome has gone to the opposite end of the spectrum with 'abuse'.

As the Good in Your Eyes, Part Two

Below I examine the approach to Genesis 19.8 taken by twelve English versions to see whether they follow the original MT or take an approach closer to their famous predecessors. The English translations of 'as the good in your eyes' are shown in table 59.

Table 59
As the Good in Your Eyes

Versions	Translations
CCB	you may do with them as you please
HCSB	you can do whatever you want* to them
	*Lit: what is good in your eyes
JM	you can do as you please with them
JPS	you may do to them as you please
NCV	you may do anything you want with them
NIV	you can do what you like with them
NJB	for you to treat as you please

NKJV	you may do to them as you wish
NLT	you can do with them as you wish
NRSV	do to them as you please
NWT	do to them as is good in your eyes
REB	you can do what you like with them

For this discussion, I divide Lot's words into two parts: (1) 'do to them' and (2) 'as the good in your eyes'. First, the versions reproduce Lot's imperative 'do to them' in four ways: 'you may/can do to/with them' (CCB, JM, JPS, NCV, NIV, NKJV, NLT, REB), 'do to them' (NRSV, NWT), 'for you to treat' (NJB), and, in the case of HCSB, 'you can do . . . to them' with a footnote attached ('what is good in your eyes'). All these options are recognizable renderings of the Hebrew text. For the second part of Lot's phrase, some variety occurs. The NWT takes a literal approach saying 'as is good in your eyes'. As for the rest, the most popular option is 'as you please' (CCB, JM, JPS, NJB, NRSV) followed by 'as you wish' (NKVJ, NLT), 'what you like' (NIV, REB), 'whatever you want' (HCSB) and 'anything you want' (NCV). All versions adequately reflect Lot's state of mind as he says to the men of Sodom that the way in which they are going to treat the two girls is entirely up to them. It is encouraging that no version has followed the Septuagint by suggesting 'make use of' and very fortunate that none has introduced the notion of 'abuse' suggested by the Vulgate.

In this passage, all versions have adopted simple language. On this basis, one might conclude that the text under discussion has been clarified from the point of view of modern English versions. However, if the immediate context is included, some translations still present considerable complications. While the notion of abuse may be absent from table 59, one version in particular has adopted it for a different verse. In table 48, JM spoke of 'rape' with regard to *yada‛* in Genesis 19.5 where the men of Sodom want to 'know' the visitors. It seems that JM has been influenced by the concept of sexual abuse introduced by the Vulgate in 19.8 and transferred it to another verse in the immediate context. For JM, the fact that Jerome used *abutimini* has somehow legitimized the presence of strong language in the surrounding text.

Given the multiple sexual renderings of *yada‛* in 19.5 and 19.8 highlighted in my discussion of table 56, and the ambiguity inherent in the phrase 'as the good in your eyes', it is apparent that most versions share an underlying assumption of threatened sexual abuse which, as noted, is buttressed by the LXX and, specifically, the Vulgate. From this overview, one concludes that the striking historical tendency of translators and commentators to explain the plot of Sodom and Gomorrah from a sexual perspective (paradigm D) is based on three pillars:

(1) The overall importance of the Septuagint and the Vulgate for the evolution of Christian biblical scholarship;
(2) The ambiguous renderings in both ancient versions of *yada‛* in Genesis 19.5 and 19.8;
(3) The brutal directness of the wording in Genesis 19.8 in Greek ('make use of them') and the hard-hitting Latin ('abuse them').

These facts directly influence modern perceptions of Lot and his part in the plot of Genesis 19. To this day, and in the light of paradigm D, Lot is usually seen as a despicable figure whose efforts in Genesis 19 are morally suspect. However, the earliest approach to the narrative is provided by the Hebrew prophets who describe the oppressed of

Sodom as the resident poor, including widows, orphans and foreigners. This is the essence of paradigm A. Viewed within this framework, the victims of Sodom are Lot the foreigner and his family. Because of the flawed nature of paradigm D, I turn now to a textual search within Genesis and several other books of the HB for links to paradigm A. My working hypothesis is if the prophets could discuss Genesis 18-19 from a non-sexual perspective, there must be textual elements in the narrative that enabled them to interpret it as a reflection of their own social, political, and religious contexts.

Women and Children in the Buffer Zone

With a focus on what is perhaps the most enigmatic part of the story of Sodom, namely, Lot's offer of his daughters to the townsmen, most modern readers find the logic underlying Genesis 19.8 difficult to grasp. It seems incomprehensible that Lot spontaneously offers to hand over his children to the spokesmen of Sodom. However, I suggest that the HB itself provides sufficient material for a plausible explanation. The abrupt moment of tense uncertainty faced by Lot's daughters is a poignant illustration of the situation of women and children in patriarchal times. Genesis contains a series of incidents in which children are totally subject to the will of their fathers. A famous, extraordinary episode involving father and child—in this case a son—is Abraham's binding of Isaac (22.1-14). Abraham is asked by Yhwh to give up his son, whom he loves (22.2), and hand him back to the same God who brought about his miraculous birth (18.10, 14; 21.1-7).[252] Just like Lot, Abraham believes strongly in

---

[252] George Caird (1980: 94) reflects on important details *not* provided by the biblical story, such as the reason for God's command to sacrifice Isaac and what went through Abraham's mind. Thomas Brodie (2001: 105) takes the view that the real problem in Abraham's case

adhering to what he considers to be his moral and religious duty (22.3-10). Both men demonstrate their willingness to relinquish their most prized possessions on the altar of a higher ideal. In both cases, there is divine intervention at the crucial moment (19.10-11; 22.10-13).[253]

With respect to women, Genesis offers three instances in which the personal integrity and comfort of wives are in jeopardy. Owing to security concerns related to his unprotected status (12.10; 20.1), Abraham literally turns his wife Sarah into a goodwill ambassador. Thus, on two different occasions Abraham averts danger to his own life by handing over Sarah to a local king, passing her off as his sister (12.11-16; 20.1-7).[254] For similar reasons, Isaac makes his wife Rebekah pose as his sister, thus exposing her to potential sexual harassment and the risk of involuntary adultery (26.7-11). In each case, the move is successful initially, but both Abraham and Isaac are reprimanded by the kings once the latter realize they have been deceived (12.18-20; 20.9-13; 26.9-10).[255]

---

is not that he may want to eliminate his son. Rather, his love for Isaac means that he clings to him (Gen. 22.2). See also the significant commandment found twice in the book of Exodus (22.29; 34.20): 'The firstborn of your sons you shall give to me'. For an anthropological interpretation of the binding of Isaac, see Delaney 1998: 129-49.

[253] The tragic story of Jephthah's daughter (Judg. 11.30-39) echoes the binding of Isaac. However, in Judg. 11 no divine intervention occurs.

[254] Fokkelien van Dijk-Hemmes (1993: 228) argues that Abram has judged the situation in Egypt correctly (Gen. 12.11-13). This is an allusion to Exod. 1.16 and 1.22 where the pharaoh will repeat Abram's words twice almost literally (1993: 228). For his part, Weston Fields (1997: 38 n. 32) reads the incident involving Sarah and King Abimelech (Gen. 20) in a similar light. Abraham fears that the mistreatment of a defenceless sojourner, which had disastrous consequences in Sodom, may be re-enacted at Gerar.

[255] Savina Teubal (1984: 68) argues that both Sarah and Rebekah participated in significant reciprocations with the kings to establish political alliances.

The story of Jacob in Genesis provides further material for reflection on the subject of children and wives deployed as human 'lightning conductors' in a situation of great insecurity. One of the most nerve-wracking moments of Jacob's life occurs when he, his family and servants are on their way from Paddan-aram to the land of Canaan (31.18). As they approach an area in which his twin brother Esau operates with a small army (32.6; 33.1), Jacob remembers well how he wronged his brother when they were young (Gen. 27). Haunted by a sense of guilt and aware of a possible desire for revenge on Esau's part, he fears for his life (32.7, 11). Jacob takes two steps in an attempt to appease his brother. Following a night of anguished prayer and wrestling with a divine envoy (32.9-13, 24-30), he decides to send a generous present to Esau ahead of the main party (32.13-21).[256] Subsequently, he takes the unusual step of placing his wives and children in front of all his servants and cattle (33.1-2). As Esau and his men draw closer, Jacob makes the final arrangements (NRSV):

> He put the maids with their children in front, then Leah with her children, and Rachel and Joseph last of all. He himself went on ahead of them, bowing himself to the ground seven times, until he came near his brother.

Jacob's prayers are answered. The potentially volatile reunion of the two estranged brothers is devoid of all hostility and resentment. Instead the encounter is deeply moving and characterized by affection, mutual respect and generosity (33.3-4, 8-16).[257] Jacob's precautions have proved

---

[256] According to Thomas Brodie (2001: 321), Jacob's arrangements follow the pattern of a court ceremonial, in which a vassal presents gifts of homage.
[257] Jacob's preventive open-handedness is matched by princely generosity on Esau's part. For Robert Alter (1992: 67, 206), the

valid and effective. After the brothers' initial embrace, the first thing that Esau notices is the presence of the women and children. He asks (33.5-7):

> 'Who are these with you?' Jacob said, 'The children whom God has graciously given your servant'. Then the maids drew near, they and their children, and bowed down; Leah likewise and her children drew near and bowed down; and finally Joseph and Rachel drew near, and they bowed down.

The way in which Jacob uses his wives and children may not be an exact parallel to the hostage-like situations in which Sarah, Rebekah, and Lot's daughters temporarily find themselves. Nevertheless, there are significant similarities in other respects. In all of these situations, the men in charge are in deep trouble. They either are under extreme pressure (Lot) or fear for their lives (Abraham, Isaac, and Jacob).[258] In each case, the women and/or children are pivotal for defusing the tension. Paradoxically their vulnerability serves as a shield. The cultural complexity of this material lends itself to being studied from a number of literary, historical, anthropological, and psychological angles (Brodie 2001: 25, 27-9, 106).

---

complex encounter is one of the great climaxes of the patriarchal narratives. According to Brodie (2001: 322), the reunion clearly enjoys YHWH's blessing.

[258] Victor Hamilton (1995: 58) has found a number of similarities in theme and vocabulary between these chapters. The most obvious parallel is the vulnerable female. Lot will turn over his daughters, and Abraham will surrender his wife. In both cases, the motive is the protection of the male. Central to both stories is the predicament of a resident alien (19.8-9; 20.1-2).

Lot's Dilemma

From Lot's perspective, the only solution to the sudden emergency on his doorstep is to propose a compromise. There is no point in putting up a fight. He and his male visitors are vastly outnumbered by the townsmen. To avoid further friction, the single privileged space left for Lot to navigate is his status as husband, father, and head of a household (19.3, 8, 12, 15–16). This enables him to present the authorities of Sodom with a significant token of his loyalty. Two vulnerable members of his family may serve as a pledge for the duration of the travellers' visit. The daughters seem to be his only children (19.8, 12, 14–16, 30–38). They are also his most prized possessions in monetary terms (Graetz 1993: 306). As regards their legal status, the two girls are literally under his care until they are 'taken' by their future husbands, from which moment they come under the jurisdiction of the latter. In other words, Lot is free to deal with his daughters as he likes until the day they marry, i.e. 'know' a man/husband.

Other parts of the HB speak of transactions involving security or pledges. Deuteronomy 24.10–11 stipulates the way in which a loan involving a pledge should be implemented (emphasis added):

> When you make any kind of loan to your neighbor, you shall not go into his house to claim what he is offering as a pledge. *You must wait outside, while the person to whom you are making the loan brings out to you what he is offering as a pledge.*

This passage partly echoes Lot's words in Genesis 19.8: 'Let me bring them out to you'. In biblical Israel, pledges could be an object such as a millstone (Deut. 24.6), a necessary garment (Exod. 22.26; Deut. 24.12; Job 22.6) or a donkey or an ox (Job 24.3). That people, including children, could be enslaved is attested in numerous passages of the HB.[259] According to Leviticus 25.39, people who became desperately poor sometimes opted for selling themselves as slaves as a means of survival. Second Kings 4.1-7 tells the story of a poor widow who faces the sad prospect of losing her two children because a hard-hearted creditor insists on selling them. In other words, the idea of using children as a pledge would not be unheard of in this ancient culture characterized by strict social norms and financial hierarchies.

With regard to Lot's daughters, they are likely to be well-known locally. In effect, they are betrothed to two young men of Sodom (19.12, 14). Given the narrator's insistence that all male citizens are present (19.4, 11), this would necessarily include these 'sons-in-law'. Readers have seen how Lot addresses his fellow citizens as 'brothers' (19.7).[260] Just as he demands being allowed to treat his guests with dignity and respect, Lot expects the men of Sodom to do the same with his daughters. However, his precarious position forces him to be deferential. Hence, his words are circumspect: 'Do to them what is good in your eyes'. If this interpretation is valid, Lot feels entitled to propose a deal in which his daughters become objects of barter. He is well aware that his refusal to grant the townsmen's request must be matched or outweighed by a generous concession on his part. Therefore, if the men of Sodom will let him carry out his hosting duties and responsibilities according to patriarchal tradition, Lot is willing to hand over his daughters to the city's spokesmen as a counterbalance. If these girls are his

---

[259] Gen. 12.5, 16; 15.3; 16.1; 17.12-13; 21.10; Exod. 2.23; Lev. 25.39-55; Deut. 24.7; etc.

[260] According to Gerhard von Rad (1972: 218), the address 'my brothers' does not necessarily denote a friendly attitude. It may rather be a claim to legal equality as a necessary precondition for Lot to strike a deal with the men of Sodom.

only children, this is indeed a significant gesture, which demonstrates how seriously he regards the situation. From his perspective, the offer is a display of loyalty, goodwill, and trust. It presupposes reciprocity.

If Genesis 19 is analysed as an existential drama within the biblical framework, the situation of Lot's daughters looks considerably like the predicament of widows and orphans to which reference is made in Exodus 22. The poignant fate of these social groups is precisely that they have no adult male relative to support them, which leaves them at the mercy of their community. Thus, if Lot's young daughters are forced to leave the security of their home, albeit momentarily, they become as exposed as widows and orphans. They are no longer 'under the shelter of their father's roof', and they have not yet 'known' their future husbands to whom they would otherwise be attached.[261] The abnormality of this legal void places them in limbo. In short, once they are turned into hostages, the girls are unprotected.

As his proposed deal is rejected, Lot's delicate position is instantly aggravated. He is literally on the verge of being arrested and prosecuted (19.9; cf. van Wolde 2012: 94). Again such a scenario puts his daughters at risk, because they would be without any male protection. Either way they are plunged into an orphaned state. Similarly, if her husband goes to prison Lot's wife is technically a widow for an unknown period of time. Hence, the 'outcry' of Sodom, mentioned three times in the story (18.20–21; 19.13), is likely to have its origin in more than one voice. Several voices blend to reach the ears of Yhwh in a single lament: the cry of Lot, the mistreated foreigner; the cry of Lot's wife; and the

---

[261] Athalya Brenner (1993: 206) mentions women who are married to or live under the legal protection of a male. The latter situation typically refers to daughters.

cry of his children, caught unawares in the abortive quid pro quo suggested by a besieged father subjected to impromptu judicial procedures.

There is another shared aspect between Lot's daughters in Genesis 19 and Jacob's wives and children in Genesis 33. The fact that these weaker members of the family are being pushed to the front of events serves, in psychological terms, as a dramatic gesture by which the father and/or husband declare their innocence and goodwill in the face of overwhelming odds. In other words, this unusual and very specific use of wives and/or children becomes a statement vis-à-vis the potential aggressors or transgressors. What Jacob and Lot are both saying may be thus expressed: 'My intentions are entirely peaceful. I am as vulnerable as these children. I ask you to trust me.'

Loyalty and Non-Aggression

Other parts of Genesis shed further light on the situation of sojourners in biblical Israel. In Genesis 14 Abraham interacts with King Melchizedek of Salem, who is a priest (14.18). There seems to be some unspecified agreement between the two men, according to which Melchizedek blesses Abraham (14.19–20) and receives a tithe in return (14.20). Whereas the nature of this agreement is not spelled out, the relationship between the two men is evidently based on respect and perhaps mutual admiration. This, then, is an example of the peaceful coexistence of Abraham the foreigner and the Canaanites.[262] Another example is given in Genesis 20, where Abraham spends some time in the land of Gerar (20.1). Once the thorny affair of Sarah's marital status has been resolved

---

[262] This includes the Philistines. For Abraham they are essentially a peaceful presence (Brodie 2001: 116).

(20.14–17), King Abimelech treats Abraham generously and invites him to settle permanently in his territory (20.15).

Even more specific information on the relationship between Abraham and the Canaanites is provided in 21.22. On this occasion, Abimelech demands a formal treaty with Abraham (21.22–24, NRSV, emphasis added):

> At that time Abimelech, with Phicol the commander of his army, said to Abraham, 'God is with you in all that you do; now therefore swear to me here by God that *you will not deal falsely with me* or with my offspring or with my posterity, but as *I have dealt loyally with you*, you will deal with me and with the land where *you reside as an alien*'. And Abraham said, 'I swear it'.[263]

This is the first occasion in the Bible in which a formal treaty between a ruler and a resident alien is recorded. The terms of the agreement are clear. It hinges on two interlocking concepts, namely, loyalty and the promise to refrain from treason. There is reciprocity since Abraham the foreigner is expected to act with the same respect and consideration that he has enjoyed from Abimelech. Thomas Brodie (2001: 258) argues that, to Abraham's great surprise, Abimelech and his servants all fear God (cf. Gen. 20.11), which makes them the antithesis of Sodom. The clause 'not deal falsely with me' is significant.[264] It echoes the fact that rulers and governments at all times have been concerned with immigrants and the potential security risk they pose. What is agreed upon, then, is perhaps best described as a pact of non-aggression.[265] As

---

[263] See also 21.31–32, where it is confirmed that Abraham and Abimelech 'swore an oath' and 'made a covenant'.
[264] The Hebrew *im-tishqor-lī* literally translates 'if you will deceive me'.
[265] When Abraham swears that he will not 'deal falsely' (*tishqor*) with Abimelech, he is offering what linguists call a 'performative

soon as this treaty is in place, Abraham feels empowered to raise a grievance with Abimelech regarding a well that he has dug and subsequently lost (21.25-31). The complaint is dealt with successfully, which enables Abraham to live in the land of the Philistines for many years (21.34).

Driven by a famine (26.1, 6) and following in the footsteps of his father, Abraham's son Isaac also goes to sojourn in Gerar, where he makes the acquaintance of King Abimelech (26.8-11, 16). After several years, Isaac has prospered, causing the Philistines to envy him (26.12-14). So Abimelech asks him to leave (26.16). Isaac complies but remains initially within the king's jurisdiction (26.17-22), after which he settles in Beersheba (26.23-25). Later, Abimelech realizes the need to establish a treaty with Isaac. Accompanied by his top advisers, he visits Isaac, and says (26.28-29, NRSV, emphasis added):

> We see plainly that the LORD has been with you; so we say, let there be an oath between you and us, and let us make a covenant with you so that *you will do us no harm*, just as *we have not touched you* and have done to you nothing but good and *have sent you away in peace*.

Isaac's recent status as resident alien among the Philistines is an important factor (26.3). After Isaac has left their country, the rulers evidently feel uneasy about having caused his departure, to the point of fearing some form of retaliation, and are keen to seek reassurance. Isaac is surprised to see them (26.27), but accepts their proposal. Again, the solemn agreement between the two parties is entered upon through an exchange of oaths (26.31). The pact emphasizes

---

utterance'. Through the act of enunciation, this ratifies a pact of mutual non-aggression (Alter 1992: 138-9).

non-aggression, which for the king is paramount. The parallel with the life of Abraham is unmistakable. Isaac may have been born in Canaan, but to immigrant parents. Father and son share the condition of *gēr* ('sojourner') and are subjected to similar pressures.[266]

This recurring theme in Genesis shows that sojourners in ancient Canaan were regarded as a security risk. A frequent way of dealing with the situation was to establish formal, solemn agreements confirmed by oath, by which rulers and immigrants committed themselves to live in harmony and respect without recourse to treason or violence. The fact that no such agreement is mentioned in Genesis 19 may indicate that Lot has no legal rights. His precarious status is highlighted by the townsmen in 19.9: 'This one came here as a sojourner, and he wants to play the judge.'

A Resident Alien

With at least eighty-one occurrences in the Hebrew Bible, a common Hebrew verb is *gūr*. It means 'sojourn' or 'reside as an outsider' and is a relatively frequent player in the Abraham story; cf. 17.8: *wenāthatī lekhā eth erets megurekhā*, 'and I give you the land in which you sojourn'.[267] In a threatening tone, the men of Sodom remind each other of Lot's status: *hāechād bā-lagūr*, 'this one came to sojourn' (19.9). The corresponding noun is *gēr*, a 'resident alien', 'sojourner'

---

[266] For Robert Alter (1992: 146), biblical stories are never merely didactic. A careful examination of the sister-bride incidents involving Abraham and Sarah, and Isaac and Rebekah enables us to see that, instead of simple repetition for emphasis, each version is worked out to achieve different thematic ends. Thus, significant variation in seeming repetition is itself a distinctive feature of the Bible's narrative art.

[267] Other occurrences are 12.10; 20.1; 21.23, 34; cf. Jacob in 32.4.

or 'immigrant', which is even more frequent than the verb.[268] The Abraham cycle contains two occurrences of this noun in reference to Abraham (15.13; 23.4). Since *gēr* clearly applies to Lot's status in Sodom, it is of interest to ascertain the situation and living conditions of sojourners in biblical Israel. In the light of the wealth of material on the subject, a fairly clear picture can be established.[269]

In some passages, the term *gēr* is used factually or poetically.[270] Other texts describe the legal requirements that are in place for those foreigners who want to become integrated into Israel.[271] In a number of passages, resident aliens are mentioned as a distinct category and, in some areas, special statutes apply to this group.[272] Repeatedly, the Israelites are encouraged to accept foreigners in their midst,[273] the general trend in the Hebrew scriptures being toward acceptance and integration. This is borne out by frequent pronouncements saying that the same law is to be observed by native Israelites and resident aliens alike.[274]

---

[268] According to Larry Mitchel (1984: 14), the noun *gēr* occurs 93 times in the HB.

[269] As Weston Fields observes (1997: 21 n. 36), the sheer volume of references to them in the Hebrew Bible and the variety of laws applying to the *gēr* demonstrate what a central social issue foreigners and outsiders were. The recurrence of this theme demonstrates its importance (p. 185). There is no question that sojourners were a very significant fact of life in both pre-monarchic and monarchic Israel (p. 21).

[270] Gen. 15.13; 23.4; Exod. 2.22; 18.3; Lev. 25.23; 2 Sam. 1.13; 1 Chr. 22.2; 29.15; etc.

[271] Exod. 12.48–49; Num. 9.14; 15.14–16.

[272] Lev. 25.35, 45–47, 50, 53; Deut. 14.21; 16.11, 14; 26.11; 28.43; 29.11; 31.12; Josh. 8.33, 35; etc.

[273] Lev. 19.34; Exod. 22.21; Deut. 10.19; 23.7–8.

[274] Exod. 12.19, 49; 20.10; 23.12; Lev. 16.29; 17.8, 10, 12–13, 15; 18.26; 20.2; 22.18; 24.16; etc.

On closer inspection, however, it becomes obvious that foreigners are often classified as a socially vulnerable group. Thus, they partake in the specific financial and material arrangements set up for the benefit of the poor.[275] In effect, it is striking that sojourners are sometimes mentioned on a par with disadvantaged groups such as widows and orphans, particularly in Deuteronomy.[276] In other words, it is their lot to eke out a living at the bottom of the social pyramid. That their situation is generally not to be envied is highlighted in a number of passages in which native Israelites are clearly instructed not to 'oppress' the foreigners living among them.[277] On this basis, Lot's interaction with the men of Sodom acquires a new poignancy. As noted, he evidently feels integrated enough to call them *achay*, 'my brothers' (19.7). By suggesting equality between him and the townsmen, he is literally claiming insider status, a position which automatically carries a strong element of security in group-oriented societies (Bechtel 1998a: 25, 30). By contrast, the locals place him squarely in the category of outsider (*gēr*, 19.9).[278] Because he resists the pressure and tries to strike a compromise, they respond by proceeding to arrest him. As they say to Lot, 'we will deal *worse* with you' (emphasis

---

[275] Lev. 19.10; 23.22; Deut. 10.18; 14.28-29; 24.19-21; 26.12-13; Job 31.32; Ps. 146.9.

[276] Exod. 22.21-22; Deut. 10.18; 14.29; 16.11, 14; 24.17-21; 26.12-13; Ps. 146.9. As noted by Elizabeth Stuart (1998: 58), the resident aliens and other economically vulnerable groups—the poor, widows, and orphans—were recognized to be in the position that Israel was in Egypt. Deut. 23.15-16 also demands protection of runaway slaves and the provision of acceptable living conditions for them (Hanks 1983: 8).

[277] Exod. 22.21 ; 23.9; Lev. 19.33; Deut. 24.14; 27.19; Ps. 94.6; Jer. 7.6 ; 22.3; Ezek. 22.7, 29; etc. Jonathan Magonet (2004: 140) comments that the repeated biblical emphasis implies that concern for the outsider was not an automatic matter.

[278] Bechtel 1998b: 114, 125. According to Weston Fields (1997: 90 n. 9), a *gēr* could be living inside a city, but sociologically remain outside of the local society.

added), the bailiffs of Sodom underline that this treatment was not present in their proposed interrogation of the two visitors (19.5).

Sodom as a Legal Treatise

Until fairly recently, few scholars have paid attention to the legal nature of the text of Sodom and Gomorrah (Boyce 1988: 50-1). Nevertheless, the text is replete with terminology pertaining to the sphere of laws, lawyers, and the judiciary. The prose of Sodom may be characterized as legal narrative, in which some of the more technical points made by the Covenant Code of the book of Exodus, for example, are fleshed out in dramatic form. The juridical aspects that permeate the narrative contribute powerfully to the creation of a coherent plot (Bruckner 2001: 20-1). Many relevant terms and phrases have been mentioned intermittently in the preceding pages.

For his part, Pietro Bovati (1994: 188, 241, 244) has examined a number of judicial terms in the Sodom text, including 'outcry' (allegation or complaint, 18.20), 'know' (investigation, 18.21), 'guilty' and 'not guilty' (18.23), 'judge', and 'justice' (18.25). That the divine messengers have collected enough evidence is clear from the firm sentence pronounced in 19.13: 'For we are about to destroy this place, because the *outcry* against its people has become great before Yhwh' (emphasis added). Verbs such as 'know' (investigate) and 'judge' imply, among other things, the capacity to distinguish between good and evil (Bovati 1994: 185). Significantly, the criminal events causing the outcry in Sodom take place in the deep darkness of night (19.4-11) while the justice meted out by Yhwh in the form of punishment and/or salvation is executed at dawn (19.15, 23–25).[279]

James Bruckner (2001: 88–107) has studied the sequence of legal processes in the Hebrew narrative. The juridical terminology is evident throughout, including Abraham's defence of the innocent citizens of Sodom (Gen. 18.23-32); the enquiry undertaken by Yhwh to 'know' first-hand the facts that have led to the outcry (18.20-21); the irreconcilable gap between the interpretation of the situation expressed by the men of Sodom and the one offered by Lot (19.6-9); the final verdict on Sodom pronounced by the representatives of Yhwh (19.13); the acquittal of Lot and his family (19.15); and the devastating punishment of the guilty that occurs in 19.24-25. For Bruckner (2001: 157), the composition of the text is so succinct that readers are forced to make up their own minds about the events described. In that sense, the narrator invites readers to become members of the jury.

Table 60 lists the vocabulary that is either readily identifiable or likely to have some measure of legal or judicial connotations. While several terms appear repeatedly in the text, they are included just once in table 60 when their meaning is constant. Only when a term represents several nuances that may vary according to context, with 'know' as a primary example, it is reproduced twice.

---

[279] Cf. Bovati 1994: 367-8; Fields 1997: 107-9; Bruckner 2001: 107.

Table 60
Legal/Judicial Language of Genesis 18–19

Verse	Expression	Interpretation
18.14	Anything too difficult for Y<small>HWH</small>?	The highest court of justice
18.19	I have known him	I have established my covenant
18.19	Doing righteousness and justice	Observing the covenant
18.20	Outcry	Complaint, allegation
18.20	Sin, transgression	Criminal offence
18.21	I must go down and see	Inspection, investigation
	Whether they have done	Has a criminal act been committed?
	That has come to me	Been brought before me
	Let me know	Let me investigate
18.23	Abraham came near	Presenting himself before the judge
	The righteous and the wicked	The innocent and the guilty
18.23	Remove, wipe out	Punish, execute sentence
18.24	Forgive	Acquit
18.25	Slay the righteous and the wicked	Miscarriage of justice
	Put to death	Execute death sentence
	The Judge of all the earth	The supreme court of appeal
	Deal justly	Apply justice correctly
18.28	Destroy	Execute death sentence
19.1	The gateway of Sodom	Place for adjudicating legal disputes
19.4	The men of the city, all the people	Every male citizen, élite included
19.5	Bring them out to us	Extradition order
	Let us know them	Interrogation, investigation

19.7	(Do not) act wickedly	*Break the rules, commit an offence*
19.8	Not known a husband	*Unmarried*
19.9	Come near	*You are under arrest*
	Sojourner	*Person with limited rights*
	Play the judge	*Act with unwarranted authority*
	Deal worse with you	*Treat more harshly*
	They pressed hard against Lot	*Proceeding to arrest him*
	Break down the door	*Violation of domicile*
19.11	The small and the great	*Everyone, city authorities included*
19.12	Sons-in-law	*Sons-in-law-to-be*
19.14	Who were taking his daughters	*Planning to marry*
19.16	YHWH being merciful to him	*Generous treatment*
19.19	Found favour with you	*Acquittal*
19.21	Grant a favour	*Generous treatment*
19.31	After the manner of all the earth	*In the legally sanctioned way*
19.33	He did not know	*He was not legally responsible*

Within the legalistic pattern of the Hebrew text, several significant repetitions are discernible. The powerful markers offered by *yada'* (six occurrences), 'outcry' (three occurrences) and *nagash*, 'draw near' (three occurrences) stand out. Other notable cases included in table 60 are 'practise justice' (18.19, 25); 'sin' (crime) and 'iniquity' (18.20; 19.15); 'whether they have *done*' (18.21) vis-à-vis 'do not *do*' (19.9); 'the righteous/innocent and the wicked/guilty' (18.23, 25); 'the judge' (18.25; 19.9); 'punish', 'put to death', 'destroy', 'wipe out', and 'annihilate' (18.23, 24, 25, 28, 31, 32; 19.13, 14, 15, 21, 25); 'forgive' (18.24, 26); as well as 'be merciful' and 'grant a favour' (19.16, 19, 21). The numerous allusions to the death sentence underline the seriousness with which the narrator regards the sin of Sodom. To oppress the poor and vulnerable is not only despicable and morally reprehensible, but also it undermines social stability to the extent of causing a nation's downfall.

Outcry

Among the terms pertaining to procedural law the word *tsaʿaqah* (*zaʿaqah*), 'protest' or 'outcry', occurs three times in the Sodom text (Gen. 18.20, 21; 19.13). In the HB, there is an intimate connection between this word and the oppression suffered by the socially vulnerable, especially immigrants. Specifically, the noun evokes passages from the book of Exodus where a bitter complaint is uttered by the enslaved Israelites in Egypt who repeatedly 'cry out' (*tsaʿaq*) to YHWH (Exod. 2.23-25; 3.7-9).[280] In the story of Sodom, it is precisely the outcry arising from the city which causes YHWH to intervene. According to the Hebrew prophets, the victims of Sodom are oppressed and marginalized citizens (cf. chapter 7). The one person who matches these characteristics is Lot the resident alien (Gen. 14.12; 19.9).

Genesis 19 dramatizes a clash between two opposing sets of cultural norms. Lot instinctively respects the ancient laws of hospitality that he learned from his uncle (19.1-3, 6-8; cf. 18.1-8), but his decision to invite two strangers into his home arouses suspicion among his neighbours and generates a conflict of interests. The spokesmen of Sodom question Lot's legal status and do not grant him any rights of autonomy (19.9). The authorities intimidate him by having the men of the city surround his house at night and order him to

---

[280] José Ramírez-Kidd (2009: 47) observes that *tsaʿaq*, 'cry out', denotes appeal to a higher lawcourt. Weston Fields (1997: 92 n. 13) takes the noun *tsaʿaqah* to be allusive to the Sodom story in several parts of the HB, including the books of Exodus and Jeremiah.

relinquish all efforts at hospitality (19.4–5).[281] However, for Lot backtracking would be shameful according to the ancient code of honour governing his behaviour (19.7–8). Faced with massive mob pressure, he is keen to strike a deal. As shown above, to prove his loyalty to the locals he takes the extreme step of offering members of his family as a pledge (19.8). However, and despite the debt of gratitude the city of Sodom owes his uncle Abraham (14.14–16), Lot falls victim to suspicion, interference, intimidation, contempt, failed negotiation offers, attempted arrest, and imminent break-in.

The exposed situation of Lot and his family illustrates the precarious living conditions of immigrants in biblical times. Exodus 22.21–24 emphasizes that the vulnerability of the poor and marginalized is a special concern to YHWH (text abbreviated, emphasis added):

> You shall not wrong or oppress a resident alien, for you were aliens in the land of Egypt . . . If you do abuse him, and when he *cries out* to me, I will surely heed his *outcry*, and my anger shall burn.

This image of red-hot divine anger evokes the destructive fire falling on Sodom and Gomorrah out of the heavens of God (Gen. 19.24). Thus, the narrative provides a literary reflection of an acute legal and social problem, making Lot and his family prototypes of the lives of thousands of migrants and refugees in the ancient world. In this connection, the interpretation of the story of Sodom provided by the prophet Ezekiel in Ezekiel 16.48–50 is precise, as pointed out by Weston Fields (1997: 184):

---

[281] Every male citizen is there. Since the narrator highlights this fact twice (19.4, 11), King Bera must be included (cf. Gen. 14). For Sodom, this is a time of crisis in the light of the recent military disaster described in Gen. 14.

> [Ezekiel] saw, therefore, that the main point of the story was a polemic against mistreatment of the *gēr* as exemplified by the Sodomites' mistreatment of Lot.

The strong biblical emphasis on the vulnerability of foreigners reveals a concern for the issue of xenophobia, which may well have been acute at various points in the history of biblical Israel. It was indeed a fact of life in pre-monarchic and, especially, monarchic Israel (Fields 1997: 21). In Lyn Bechtel's view (1998a: 127), the narrator 'challenges these xenophobic and isolationist tendencies by projecting them onto the men of Sodom'. In this sense, the story advocates openness to outsiders, peaceful coexistence, and negotiations with surrounding nations as the way forward for the community.[282] Indirectly the story of Sodom places a spirit of cooperation in the very roots of Israel, because eventually this will be a nation of outsiders.

Come Forward or Stand Back?

The Hebrew verb *nagash* primarily means 'draw near' or 'come forward'. It occurs three times in two verses of the story of Sodom, once in 18.23 and twice in 19.9. In the context of litigation, *nagash* has procedural value denoting 'appear before the judge' (Bruckner 2001: 96). Abraham famously appears before the judge, assuming the role of counsel for

---

[282] As observed by Weston Fields (1997: 150), the book of Ruth demonstrates the desirable way for Israelites to treat outsiders by showing how Ruth the Moabitess is accepted by Boaz and the women of Bethlehem. Given that the name of Moab is found in both narratives, Fields calls the book of Ruth 'the reworking of the Sodom story in a positive vein', which does not just discuss the treatment of the *gēr* as a social issue but is 'widely related in a higher and broader sense to national salvation' (p. 179).

the defence, in 18.23-32 (Bovati 1994: 218-20; Bruckner 2001: 148-51). This is in accordance with the description of Yhwh as 'judge of all the earth' in 18.25. Similar meanings of *nagash* are found in Exodus 24.14, Deuteronomy 25.1, and Joshua 14.6.[283] In Genesis 19.9 the spokesmen of Sodom reject Lot's improvised offer of a compromise. Specifically, they criticize him for trying to 'play the judge'. Leaving no room for negotiation, they immediately order him to 'come forward' or 'draw near' (Warner 2012: 117), which in the context seems to mean 'you are under arrest'. Lot is disobedient and does not draw near, so the men of Sodom move towards him. They press hard against the man and unsuccessfully try to break down the door.

In all cases, *nagash* denotes forward movement, particularly for judgment (Bechtel 1998b: 124-5).[284] However, the role of this verb in Genesis 18 and 19 needs further clarification. The approaches adopted by the twelve English versions are shown in table 61. Paraphrases of *nagash* are in italics.

---

[283] On some occasions a special favour is being requested, as in Gen. 43.19 and 44.18.
[284] Ellen van Wolde (2012: 94) rightly observes that the men of Sodom tell Lot to 'draw near'. Confusingly she also allows the same phrase to be translated 'Stand back!' (p. 96).

Table 61
Translating NAGASH

Version	Gen. 18.23	Gen. 19.9 (a)	Gen. 19.9 (b)
CCB	go forward	*Get out of the way!*	draw near
HCSB	step forward	*Get out of the way!*	come up
JM	go nearer	*Out of the way!*	mob
JPS	come forward	*Stand back!*	move forward
NCV	approach	*Move out of the way!*	be ready to
NIV	approach	*Get out of our way!*	move forward
NJB	step forward	*Stand back!*	move forward
NKJV	come near	*Stand back!*	come near
NLT	approach	*Stand back!*	*lunge* toward
NRSV	come near	*Stand back!*	come near
NWT	approach	*Stand back there!*	get near
REB	draw near	*Out of our way!*	crowded *in on* Lot

Table 61 shows that most versions render *nagash* adequately on two occasions. The most accurate options are offered in 18.23 while 19.9b includes a few paraphrases. A minority is inconsistent between columns 1 and 3, notably 'go nearer' vs. 'mob' (JM), 'approach' vs. 'lunge toward' (NLT), and 'draw near' vs. 'crowd in on' (REB). However, the greatest surprise is found in 19.9a. The whole second column is a striking example of generalized error. All translators disregard the basic meaning of *nagash* as they suggest 'get out of the way' or 'stand back'. Astonishingly, they are saying exactly the opposite of what the Hebrew narrator has written. If the verb usually denotes forward movement or drawing near, it cannot also mean 'stand back'. Few verbs are able to contain such semantic contradiction. Perhaps the worst renderings in table 61 are produced by versions that propose three different options, as in 'approach', 'move out of the way', and 'be ready to' (NCV) and 'go nearer', 'out of the way', and 'mob' (JM).

The almost uniform approach to *nagash* in 19.9a revealed by table 61 is probably no coincidence. It suggests a common source consulted by the translators. Indeed, they reproduce almost verbatim an error committed long ago by the LXX translator. For his Greek text, he chose the rendering *aposta*, which means 'step aside'. This approach was perpetuated centuries later by Jerome who used the Latin word *recede*, 'stand back'. With such prestigious precedents, a curious early tradition became established whereby it was deemed legitimate to ascribe two completely different meanings to one verb, even within the same verse. This illogical procedure on the translators' part is replicated in, and supported by, several dictionaries of biblical Hebrew (BDB pp. 620–1; DBHE p. 478).

In summary, what is missing from table 61 is a consistent approach to *nagash* in all three columns. Simple options such as 'move forward' or 'come near' would be adequate throughout and in conformity with narrative logic. The importance of the common mistranslation of *nagash* in 19.9a should not be underestimated. For centuries it has added further confusion to the blurred picture of Sodom brought about by successive post-biblical interpretive approaches, particularly paradigm D.

Conclusion

Lot the foreigner and his family are the victims of the sin of Sodom. Lot's life contrasts with that of his uncle Abraham. While the latter is blessed in many different ways, Lot's life deteriorates from the moment he decides to settle near Sodom. He is likely to have married a local woman. Two daughters are born to him and no sons. Despite his efforts, he never becomes fully integrated. While offering hospitality to two visiting strangers, conflicts of interest erupt between Lot and the city. The locals want the travellers to be handed over for interrogation, but he refuses to comply and proposes a compromise. As a vulnerable immigrant, he is aware that he must offer a token of his loyalty. If the men of the city will allow him to perform his hosting duties, he is prepared to give them his children as a pledge. While such a deal is unheard of in modern times, it reflects cultural patterns of antiquity, particularly the exposed situation of women, children, and poor people, of which the HB provides numerous examples.

When the story of Sodom is interpreted according to paradigm A, the juridical nature of the language of Genesis 18 and 19 becomes prominent. In fact, the text is replete with legal and judicial terminology. In addition to *yada'* (know), some key terms are *tsa'aqah* or *za'aqah* (outcry, complaint or allegation) and *nagash* (come forward). An extraordinary translation problem exists in Genesis 19.9. Here the English versions treat two occurrences of *nagash* as if this were a case of two distinct verbs with contradictory meanings. In one instance, the majority rightly says 'move forward' (19.9b), but in the other case (19.9a), all versions erroneously make *nagash* mean 'step aside' or 'stand back'. In this manner, the narrative logic is distorted. There are ancient Greek and Latin precedents for this translation error in the LXX and the Vulgate, respectively.

When paradigm A is applied to Genesis 19, Lot's behaviour is seen to conform to ancient biblical logic. In this highly sophisticated narrative, part of the overall message seems to be that Lot's decline represents the fate of the apostate or renegade who abandons the ways of YHWH (as opposed to the faithful Abraham). The story contains important warnings to the people of Israel. The repeated occurrences of the word 'outcry' connect the text of Sodom to the Covenant Code of Exodus 22 in which Israelites are warned against mistreating the foreigner and other marginalized groups in their midst. They are reminded that they were foreigners in the land of Egypt and that, if they commit injustice, the anger of YHWH will flare up. Thus, the tragic destiny of Sodom serves as a potent mirror for Israelites to test the ways in which they themselves treat the socially vulnerable and oppressed.

PART FOUR

Politics, Polemics, and Passions

12

THE OUTRAGE AT GIBEAH

Texts always speak to each other.

— Umberto Eco [285]

Introduction

Chapters 12, 13, and 14 have two essential things in common: (a) all deal with polemical situations in which some unusual or illicit form of sexual action takes place, and (b) the texts discussed are widely quoted in current discussions of homoeroticism in the Bible. While chapters 13 and 14 explore issues raised in the Second Testament by a few letters attributed to the Christian missionary Paul, this chapter focuses on a tense political drama that unfolds in the Hebrew Bible, specifically in the book of Judges.

Some readers of the present chapter may wonder how the dramatic tale of the sexual assault on a young woman can have anything to say about homoerotic relationships. The answer is simple: the original text of Judges 19 and 20 has some features in common with the story of Sodom and Gomorrah in Genesis. Given this fact, numerous exegetes and commentators interpret the outrage in the city of Gibeah in

---

[285] Umberto Eco, *Mouse or Rat?*, 2003: 114; cf. Carden 2004: 4: 'Texts echo and allude to each other.'

the light of events at Sodom and vice versa.[286] Some versions of the Bible do the same by providing cross-references (CCB, NWT). In this manner, two narratives—despite significant differences—have been interlocked and analysed as if they were written for the same purpose (Lings 2008: 27-8). The tradition for this common procedure is long. At certain times in history, the story of Gibeah has been quoted in conjunction with Sodom for the purpose of stigmatizing intimate same-sex relationships.[287] This is achieved by associating homoeroticism with violent, criminal behaviour (Guest 2006: 182).

In order to understand how this connection came about, a detailed study of the Hebrew text in Judges 19 and 20 is required. This is undertaken below. It will soon become apparent that the original narrative is a sophisticated literary composition from the hands of a highly skilled writer. Technically the story is laid out as a report on a crime committed in Gibeah against an unnamed woman from Bethlehem. However, many allusions and indirect references in the text indicate that, read allegorically, the victim described is David who repeatedly in his youth became the target of persecution and attempted murder. The fact that the setting is Gibeah is no coincidence: this was Saul's birthplace and where he set up headquarters after becoming king of Israel. In some parts of the HB the city is known as 'Gibeah of Saul' (see below).

---

[286] Fox 1995: 81; Nissinen 1998: 50; Helminiak 2000: 47; Goss 2002: 196-7; Carden 2004: 14-41; Greenberg 2004: 67; Lundager Jensen 2004: 523; Jennings 2005: 206; Carden 2006: 37-8; Boyarin 2007: 140-1; Heacock 2011: 93.

[287] A representative voice among modern scholars is Robert Gagnon (2001: 432). In his view, this is one of 21 anti-gay Bible texts.

The Story

The tale of Gibeah begins in Judges 19 with an anonymous Levite, i.e. a member of the tribe of Levi, which has priestly responsibilities. He lives in the northern region of Ephraim and marries an unnamed girl from Bethlehem of Judah in the south. The young woman is described as a *pilegesh*, an unusual term about which scholars are not in complete agreement (Hugenberger 1994: 106-7). Some translate it as 'concubine', but in modern languages this word usually suggests an informal relationship in which the woman is regarded as a man's lover. This does not necessarily match the ancient Israelite context. It may be more appropriate to classify a *pilegesh* as a woman whose marital arrangement follows a less rigid or less formalized procedure than ordinary marriage contracts.[288] For such reasons, I prefer not to translate the Hebrew term *pilegesh*. The importance of the word in Judges 19 may indicate that the Levite's marriage to the girl was decided upon and carried out in a short time span, i.e. without the traditional betrothal period, which tended to last years. At the same time, a *pilegesh* may have had slave status. For instance, such was the case when a father ceded his daughter to a creditor as the final instalment of a debt. In other situations, when the owner of a female slave is a married woman, the latter can choose to give her slave to her husband as a *pilegesh*. This is what Rachel, Jacob's wife, does with her handmaid Bilhah (Gen. 30.4).

---

[288] Fewell 1992: 75; Exum 1993: 177; Schneider 2000: 128-9; Thatcher 2002: 128. In ancient Athens, the equivalent was *pallakis* (*pallaké*, *pallax*), and *pilegesh* may be a Hebrew adaptation. In philology, such phenomena occur frequently (Groom 2003: 65). According to Sarah Pomeroy (1975: 91), some Athenian men lived with concubines in unions resembling marriage, i.e. the woman was considered her husband's property in much the same way as an 'official' wife. However, the children of concubines had limited rights (p. 91). Crimes committed against a concubine drew the same penalties as offences against a wife (p. 86).

At the very beginning of the story told in Judges 19, the newly arranged marriage (19.1) is interrupted as the *pilegesh* leaves the Levite's house and travels by herself to her parental home in Bethlehem (19.2). The narrator classifies this manifestation of female independence as an act of infidelity by saying, literally, *wattizneh ʿalaw*, 'she was unfaithful to him' (cf. Brenner 1997: 150). Several months later, the Levite and his male servant set out to find her and bring her back to Ephraim. The *pilegesh* and her father offer the Levite a warm welcome and hospitality. The girl's father treats his son-in-law lavishly and goes out of his way to make his guest stay for as long as possible. Once the Levite, the *pilegesh* and the servant boy undertake the journey back to Ephraim, it is getting late. After just a few hours on the road, they have to find somewhere safe to spend the night. The Canaanite town of Jebus is located nearby, but the Levite rejects the idea of going there (19.11). He prefers to continue on to Gibeah because the people there are Israelites belonging to the tribe of Benjamin. The travellers arrive at sunset (19.14). However, the inhabitants ignore the small group of wayfarers sitting in the town square waiting for someone to invite them into their home for the night. Finally an elderly man, an incomer from Ephraim, appears on the scene. He takes them in and treats them to a meal.

After a while, the pleasant atmosphere inside the house is interrupted by a group of men assembling in the street. Described as *beney-beliyyaʿal* ('sons of worthlessness'), they start pounding on the door and demand to 'know' the man who just arrived, i.e. the Levite. The host goes out to them, dismisses their demand as 'wicked', and tries to reason with them. However, the scoundrels refuse to negotiate. Given their obstinate and threatening attitude, the host makes a counteroffer: he will not let them speak to the Levite, but they may have his own daughter and the *pilegesh* for sexual amusement. However, his efforts are unsuccessful as the locals are bent on having their way.[289] As for the Levite himself, he is acutely aware that the few men inside the house would be unwise to engage in a fight with the gang outside. Very quickly, he makes up his mind. He seizes the *pilegesh*, pushes her through the front door, and leaves her to fend for herself. Immediately the pressure on the Levite stops as she becomes the focus of attention. The narrator lets us know that they 'know' her and 'entertain themselves' with her all night long until daybreak. When they finally let her go, the violated *pilegesh* falls down at the door of the Ephraimite's house where her master and husband is staying, placing her hands on the threshold.

The Levite is the first person in the house to get up. As he prepares to leave and opens the door, he finds the seemingly lifeless body of the *pilegesh*, puts her on the donkey, and sets out for his home. Upon arrival he takes a knife, cuts the woman's body into twelve pieces and sends them throughout the territory of Israel with a report of the crime. Subsequently a wave of indignation against Gibeah and the tribe of Benjamin sweeps across Israel. Within a few days, thousands of Israelite men assemble at Mizpah to discuss what to do (20.1). Here the Levite delivers a minimal report of his bitter experience of spending the night at Gibeah. He explains that the 'lords of Gibeah' threatened to kill him and 'humiliated' his *pilegesh* to death (20.5). The assembly agrees that the culprits should be executed. However, the city of Gibeah and the tribe of Benjamin refuse to cooperate (20.13). As a consequence, civil war erupts (Judg. 20 & 21). The hostilities continue for days and finish shortly before the complete extermination of the Benjaminites (21.6). Paradoxically, the other tribes help the surviving members of the tribe to obtain wives by unorthodox and cruel means (Judg. 21.14, 23).

---

[289] The description of this event is elliptical. Some key elements for its interpretation occur later in the text.

Gibeah Yesterday

The historian Josephus (first century CE) was the author of an extensive commentary on the drama of Gibeah. It was included in his famous work *Jewish Antiquities* (V.136-49). In the panorama painted by Josephus, the *pilegesh* from Bethlehem takes centre stage. The Levite loves her tenderly and passionately, but she does not return his feelings. In Josephus's interpretation, the young men of Gibeah, who see the strangers in the public square, find the girl very attractive. They decide to do something about it and soon form a large group in front of the Ephraimite's house. They want the *pilegesh* to be handed over to them (Fields 1997: 63 n. 20; Carden 2004: 76). They are unmoved by the objections and counteroffers presented by the host. According to Josephus, they break down the front door without delay, invade the house and seize the *pilegesh* to take her outside (Josephus 1998b: 223-9).

In traditional Jewish literature, Gibeah is rarely mentioned. For Rashi (eleventh century), the word 'know' in Judges 19.22 is to be taken in a sexual sense. According to his commentary, the Levite and the *pilegesh* have not signed any formal marriage contract. For his part, Ramban (Nahmanides, thirteenth century) argues that the relationship between the two is different from conventional marriage in the sense that there has not been a period of betrothal. Unlike the official nature of marriage, taking a concubine is a private arrangement (Carden 2004: 84, 112). Ramban feels that the *pilegesh* is at least partially to blame for what happens to her because she was a 'harlot' and she herself decided to leave the Levite's house and return to Bethlehem. Ramban thinks that the rogues of Gibeah did not leave the girl dead but that they let her go at dawn (2004: 112).

In the history of Christian theology, few reflections on the Gibeah story have been recorded. Athanasius of Alexandria (fourth century CE) interprets the text as an allegory of the struggles that theologians had to go through in his day (Carden 2004: 155). For Ambrose (fourth century), it is vital to highlight the importance of chastity. Ambrose notes a considerable age gap between the Levite and the *pilegesh*. He agrees with Josephus that the riffraff of Gibeah are keen to be intimate with the young woman from the start. Throughout his reflection on the story, Ambrose shows great respect for Josephus.

For medieval Christianity, the book of Judges ceases to be of interest beyond the story of Samson in chapter 16 (Carden 2004: 160). A rare exception is Nicholas of Lyra (1270–1349) whose biblical commentary discusses the drama of Judges 19 and 20. Nicholas stresses several connections between Gibeah and Sodom. Since he mostly uses the Latin Vulgate, it is intriguing that he also quotes the Hebrew text and that he has studied Josephus. For Lyra, Gibeah is a place terrorized by a mafia. In the city it is forbidden to show any form of hospitality to wayfaring strangers. Nicholas seems to think that in Judges 19.22 the Levite is threatened with murder and anal penetration. For the latter transgression, Lyra uses the Latin phrase *carnali concubito et nephario* ('carnal and nepharious intercourse'). In his view, the threats have a single purpose, namely, to force the Levite to hand over his *pilegesh* (Carden 2004: 190–1).

A Text of Terror

Until the second half of the twentieth century, Christian scholars had awarded Gibeah scarce attention. This situation changed gradually owing to the rise of feminism combined with a profound revision of sexual taboos, including rape. A growing number of commentators now reflect on the drama of Gibeah, frequently coupling their discussions with references to the story of Sodom and Gomorrah. Although many modern readers find the events described in Judges 19 and 20 unpalatable, this story of a nameless young woman who suffered brutality at the hands of a gang of strangers is often regarded as a report from the scene of a real crime. Today's scholars perceive the protagonists as individuals of flesh and blood with distinct personalities. This feature is especially true of the Levite and the old Ephraimite who has settled in Gibeah. As later discussion will show, both men are the target of much indignation as they are accused of inflicting a cruel death on the *pilegesh* from Bethlehem.

In 1984, Phyllis Trible published *Texts of Terror* with the subtitle 'Literary-Feminist Readings of Biblical Narratives'. In this work, Trible presents her analysis of four stories from the HB. The appropriateness of the term 'text of terror' has made it popular in biblical studies (Goss 1993: 89–91 & 2002: 206, 210; Guest 2005: 174 & 2006: 188). In the third chapter of her book, Trible studies the drama of Gibeah, focusing particularly on the hair-raising ordeal faced by the *pilegesh*. For Trible, the text exemplifies above all a moment in which the legendary hospitality of the Middle East is breached and how this results in an orgy of violence (1984: 71, 76, 83). In Judges 19.19, Trible suspects a certain falsehood in the language used by the Levite. She guesses that he is offering the *pilegesh* as bait to the old Ephraimite hoping that the thought of having sex with her will persuade him to invite the travellers into his home (1984: 72). Trible acknowledges the ambiguity of 'know' in Judges 19.22. However, the context leads her to conclude that this occurrence of *yada'* reveals the violent, sexual intentions of the aggressors (1984: 73–4). For Trible, the interaction between the Ephraimite and the mob at the front door means that the host readily accepts sacrificing the virtue of the two young women under his care. Acting as procurer and granting the wicked men 'licence to rape' (p. 74), he literally gives the girls away. At the same time, Trible observes that the host himself does not volunteer to take the place of his male guest (p. 75).

According to Trible, what follows is a non sequitur (1984: 76-7). While it is true that the description of the night scene in the street is neither pornographic nor sensationalist, the narrator 'cares little' about the suffering of the *pilegesh*. Trible notes that the Levite hurries to push her outside in order to save his own skin, i.e. the woman is betrayed by her own master. Nobody within the house comes to her rescue. Trible argues that *yada'* in 19.25 loses all ambiguity and means 'rape' (p. 77). Finding his behaviour throughout the story 'perverse' and 'despicable', in her view the main culprit of the night-time horror in Gibeah is the Levite because he has acted with 'manipulation and force' (pp. 77-8). He is a coward incapable of showing compassion or remorse (p. 79). Upon his return to the hill country of Ephraim, the Levite 'takes the knife' (19.29). For Trible, it is 'provocative' that the narrative echoes a line from the binding of Isaac where Abraham prepares to sacrifice his son by 'taking the knife' (Gen. 22.10). In the Gibeah story, the battered body of the *pilegesh* is brutalized even further when it is dismembered by her husband, who may well be the real murderer (p. 80). As he summons the tribes of Israel to assemble at Mizpah, Trible argues that his version of the event at Gibeah is not to be believed (1984: 82). In her view, the story has a certain complexity and literary artfulness (p. 78), but the ambiguities surrounding the Levite seem to indicate that the male narrator is protecting his male protagonist (p. 80).

Gibeah after Trible

The polemical analysis of the outrage at Gibeah offered by Phyllis Trible has had a major impact on biblical studies. Mieke Bal (1988: 186) finds the story the most 'uncanny' in the book of Judges and perhaps in the entire Bible. While she derives no pleasure from discussing it, she adds that extreme violence can only be mastered if the underlying mechanisms are understood (p. 119). Bal speaks of 'homosexual rape' as an expression of social disorder (p. 92). For her, several parts of the Gibeah story may be described as a form of 'sadistic discourse' (p. 119) in which the excessive amount of sacrifice leaves the impression that the whole episode is to be seen as a ritual (p. 121). Like Trible, Bal feels that the primary murder suspect is the Levite (pp. 119–20, 126, 190). Judging by his actions, Bal draws the conclusion that the man seeks and creates situations of violence. When the unruly mob finally releases the *pilegesh* (Judg. 19.25), she is no longer a woman or wife in the ordinary sense of the word because her death has begun (pp. 123). At the same time, Bal is aware that, in any gender-motivated analysis, including her own, the ideological and socio-cultural background of the exegete plays a major part (pp. 236–7). Therefore, she warns modern readers against the temptation of 'cheap indignation motivated by anachronistic ethnocentrism' (p. 159).

Cheryl Exum (1993: 177) confesses initially that she proposes to 'over-interpret' the drama of Gibeah. Her intention is to break open 'the text's phallocentric ideology' whose encoded messages 'control women and keep them in their place'. Exum feels that the narrator is not consciously misogynistic. Rather, the story has 'a gender-motivated subtext' driven by 'male fear of female sexuality' (p. 181), the overall agenda being androcentric (p. 182). Given its brutality and scenes of sexual abuse, if this biblical material were to be portrayed by contemporary cinema, many would label it pornographic (p. 196). According to Exum, the story of the *pilegesh* in Gibeah is a form of 'literary rape' (pp. 200–1), and significantly, her analysis is entitled 'Raped by the Pen'. In her view, the Levite is threatened with rape (p. 182), but apparently, the male narrator's androcentric ideology makes this 'too threatening to narrate' (p. 183). With respect to the Levite's summary of the night-time drama (Judg. 20.4-7), Exum finds it 'strange' because he describes himself as the primary victim of the tragedy (1993: 185-6). In her view, the Levite is 'base', 'irresolute', 'stubborn', 'callous', and 'a disreputable character' (p. 186). Moreover, she criticizes the narrator himself for his apparent 'lingering guilt' and 'discomfort' about the treatment meted out to the young woman (pp. 187-8).

If the protagonist of Judges 19 and 20 is a Levite, he has priestly responsibilities. However, Tammi Schneider (2000: 247) finds that he does not live up to any expectations of decency. On the contrary, readers are left wondering about the deeper motivations behind his behaviour. Schneider is suspicious of the morals displayed by the old host and his male guest because both remain safe and secure while they force two young women to face sexual abuse (pp. 261, 263). She finds that many commentaries do not address the underlying issues, apparently because the whole episode is so painful (p. 262). Finding him insensitive and irresponsible, Schneider asserts that 'the text indicts the Levite man' (p. 263). While the question of who was ultimately responsible for the death of the *pilegesh* is left unresolved on the narrator's part, it may well have been the Levite (pp. 264, 267). In Schneider's view, it is part of the irony of the story that an entire nation was called to war by a murder suspect (p. 267).

A critical view of Phyllis Trible's analysis of Judges 19 is adopted by Koala Jones-Warsaw (1993). Writing from a womanist perspective,[290] she finds Trible's approach

---

[290] According to Leo Perdue (2005: 166), 'womanist' biblical interpretation responds to the needs of African-American women who read the Bible differently than their white, privileged sisters. The socio-cultural location of African-American women is shaped by a long history of struggle against slavery, racism, and male dominance.

'one-dimensional' and incomplete for women of colour who experience multiple forms of victimization (p. 172). Jones-Warsaw fears that 'the very ideology Trible tries to avoid, she ends up reinforcing' because Trible's polemical statements function 'to anger the reader toward the men', leading to a thought pattern which ignores the interrelatedness of the fates of men and women in the story (p. 180). By reducing the narrative to the victimization of women, Trible's 'white middle-class' perspective fails to account adequately for the complexity of the problems addressed by the narrator. In Jones-Warsaw's view, the overall purpose of the story told in Judges 19 and 20 is not to expose horrors suffered by individuals but rather to favour the institution of kingship (pp. 181–3).

Gibeah, Sodom, and Jericho

Numerous modern commentators combine their analysis of Sodom and Gomorrah with a study of Gibeah. Michael Carden, who does this in some detail, finds the similarities between these biblical texts 'remarkable' (2004: 7), noting that it has become customary to discuss the two stories jointly. However, while Sodom has had a huge impact as the 'foundational myth of Christian homophobia', Gibeah has not played a part in such debates until fairly recently (p. 8). Acknowledging the parallel themes and dramatic tensions, Carden uses the two stories 'to let each shed light on the other' (p. 15). In Carden's analysis, the drama of Gibeah is 'a disaster story'. It opens by describing a marital break-up (p. 22) and evolves into 'a horror story set in a nightmare men's world' (p. 24) in which the dominant motif is rape (p. 28). When the time comes for seeking shelter for the night, the Levite treats his young wife as expendable merchandise. For Carden, there is no doubt about the complicity of the Levite and the old Ephraimite in the injustice that takes place (p.

36). He draws attention to the servant boy mentioned several times in the story (Judg. 19.3, 9, 11-13, 19). By the time the Levite leaves Gibeah in 19.28, the boy seems to play no part. This curious detail causes Carden to speculate that perhaps the old host insisted the young man should remain with him in exchange for the *pilegesh*. While he would have preferred the woman, there is no point in thinking about that now in the light of all that has happened (p. 26).

In Carden's view, what unites the tales of Sodom and Gibeah is the theme of rape of defenceless aliens (pp. 28-9). For him both texts are set in a phallocentric Mediterranean culture in which male superiority is paramount, and female subordination is 'crucial for male honour' (pp. 29-30). With respect to male-male sexual relationships, it is perfectly acceptable to be a penetrator while the one penetrated is stigmatized (pp. 30, 32). The 'passivity' of the latter is considered shameful and classifies him on a level with women and foreigners, i.e. homosexual rape diminishes the victim's honour and status. In some situations in antiquity it was used as a form of punishment (p. 31). The Gibeah story reflects this indirectly as the Levite's self-esteem and social status are lowered the moment his wife is raped (pp. 30, 37). Carden grants that his interpretation of the plot relies on the meaning he ascribes to the verb *yada'*, 'know', in Judges 19.22. He has no doubt that it is to be taken in a sexual sense (p. 26). On a different matter, Carden is aware of several literary hints in the text that predispose the reader against King Saul and everything he represents (p. 44).

Another scholar who has looked closely at Sodom as well as Gibeah is Weston Fields (1997). He includes a third story in his analysis of the drama, namely, the two Israelite spies visiting the Canaanite city of Jericho (Joshua 2). Fields has found several recurring themes or motifs common to all three narratives (1997: 19). At the same time he is aware of the distinctive characteristics of each text (p. 17). According to Fields, a specific motif is 'the stranger in (*sic*) your gates' (pp. 27–53). In Classical Hebrew, the word *gēr* typically corresponds to someone 'without full civic rights' (p. 27), translatable as 'sojourner' (p. 30) or 'outsider', i.e. an Israelite living among a tribe other than his own (p. 32). Further motifs shared by these stories are travellers appearing unexpectedly, hospitality, inimical townspeople, night spelling danger, sexual harassment of strangers, and cities destroyed by fire (p. 23).

For Fields, a number of literary details in the Gibeah story hark back to events at Sodom, indicating that Judges 19 is dependent upon the narrative in Genesis (1997: 47). Various philological and stylistic issues from Genesis 19 reappear with slight modifications in Gibeah (p. 62). For instance, the lack of hospitality combined with hostility occurring in both texts makes the low moral level of Gibeah, an Israelite city, comparable to the Canaanites of Sodom (p. 72). In Gibeah, the crime committed is not only gang rape but also the adulterous assault on a married woman (p. 125 n. 24). According to Fields, the Gibeah text is ambiguous, leaving readers wondering exactly who pushed the *pilegesh* out of the door at the critical moment. From a purely grammatical point of view, it may have been the Levite or the elderly host, but the Hebrew wording of the passage seems to imply that it was the Levite (p. 66). In Fields's view, what outrages the Israelites assembled at Mizpah is, above all, the fact that the people of Gibeah disregarded elementary norms of hospitality vis-à-vis fellow Israelites (1997: 63). Finally, it is crucial to highlight the political motivation for the tale's composition. It carries severely anti-Benjaminite polemic (pp. 47–8), which indicates, in Fields's view, that the story would never have been told 'had not the narrator wanted to make a statement about Gibeah and the Benjaminites' (p. 71).

Gibeah as Politics

Marc Zvi Brettler (2002: 83) finds the current focus on rape in Judges 19 unconvincing because it 'does not go far enough'. He warns that, by limiting themselves to be impacted by the mob terror erupting in the streets of Gibeah, modern readers run the risk of missing several essential clues. The Hebrew text contains a whole series of studied or fanciful elements, which reveal that this is not a historical text in any traditional sense, i.e. the narrator is not describing events he has seen. Instead, he creates them (pp. 82, 84). The drama of Gibeah is not even historical fiction but rather didactic literature. Specifically, Judges 19 is 'a learned, polemical text, arguing against the kingship of Saul' (p. 90). In Brettler's view, although there is not 'very strong coherence' in the book of Judges (p. 104), it is still constructed as a book with an introduction and a conclusion (p. 109). The overall purpose is political inasmuch as events are connected to political issues in ancient Israel (p. 105). In the case of the outrage at Gibeah, the text is strongly biased against Saul and has a marked pro-Davidic political message (p. 115). For Brettler, the dismemberment of the body of a young woman symbolically represents the disintegration of the Israelite federation of tribes in the pre-monarchic era. The macabre incident echoes the narrator's recurring lament: 'In those days there was no king in Israel' (Judg. 17.6; 18.1; 19.1; 21.25). Indirectly the key message of the Gibeah story seems to be that Saul would be incapable of reinstating unity among the people of Israel (2002: 91).

The name of Gibeah occurs in the HB 52 times, namely, in the book of Judges (24), the two books of Samuel (19), the book of Joshua (3), Hosea (3), the two books of Chronicles (2), and Isaiah (1). First and foremost, Gibeah is repeatedly presented as the place where Saul was born and raised and where he set up his base once the prophet Samuel had proclaimed him king of Israel.²⁹¹ This is so much the case that, on several occasions, the HB uses the composite name 'Gibeah of Saul'.²⁹² A curious aspect of the drama spanning Judges 19 and 20 is the fact that Saul is not mentioned by name. Instead, Gibeah and the tribe of Benjamin are cast as co-protagonists. Evidently the Hebrew narrator has mastered the art of coded writing. The numerous literary allusions and indirect references in the text are likely to have been perfectly comprehensible to the audience for whom the story was composed.

Yairah Amit (1999: 342, 348–9) recognizes the political aspects of Judges 19 and interprets the plot as a virulent political diatribe against Saul, Gibeah, and the tribe of Benjamin, as does Tammi Schneider (2000: 169, 246, 249). Similarly, I have studied the plot and detected a number of inter-textual allusions in the story, which reinforce the impression of a political agenda (Lings 2007: 203). To denigrate an enemy for alleged sexual atrocities is a well-known tactic in politics and warfare. The impressive literary skills of the Hebrew narrator are reflected in the consternation his fictional account is capable of producing in many modern readers (2007: 204).

'Know' According to the Translators

Tammi Schneider (2000: 262) argues that the Hebrew of Judges 19 is 'rather straightforward' and 'there are no philological issues to discuss'. I beg to differ. In the Gibeah text, several problems have not been sufficiently examined, particularly the role of the verb *yada'*. As with the case of Sodom, most scholars are convinced that *yada'* is

---

[291] 1 Sam. 10.26; 14.2, 16; 22.6; 23.19; 26.1.
[292] 1 Sam. 11.4; 15.34; 2 Sam. 21.6; Isa. 10.29.

sexually charged.[293] However, the complexity of the context makes it important to reflect on *yada‛* in Judges 19.22 and 19.25 because its non-sexual connotations are crucial for understanding the plot (Lings 2008: 29). It particularly affects the way one perceives the Levite's behaviour.

A literal translation of the two passages containing *yada‛* would be (emphasis added): 'Make the man who has entered your house come out and we will *know* him' (19.22), and 'they *knew* her' (19.25). Table 62 shows the approaches to *yada‛* taken by the twelve English versions.

Table 62
Translating 'Know' in Judges 19

Version	YADA‛ 19.22	YADA‛ 19.25
MT	know	they knew her
CCB	amuse ourselves with	violated
HCSB	have sex with	raped*
		*Lit *knew*
JM	rape	[violated]
JPS	be intimate with	raped
NCV	have sexual relations with	forced her to have sexual relations
NIV	have sex with	raped
NJB	have intercourse with	had intercourse with
NKJV	know carnally	knew
NLT	have sex with	abused
NRSV	have intercourse with	wantonly raped
NWT	have intercourse with	began to have intercourse with
REB	have intercourse with	raped

---

[293] Stone 1996: 75; Fields 1997: 81; Nissinen 1998: 49–50; Schneider 2000: 260; Gagnon 2001: 73–4; Carden 2004: 26; Heacock 2011: 91.

On the basis of the two occurrences of *yada'*, the Hebrew narrator (MT) creates continuity and interconnectedness between Judges 19.22 and 19.25, making it a case of significant repetition. However, table 62 documents that no version is entirely literal. With 'know' and 'knew', the NKJV comes fairly close, but in 19.22, the text is amplified with the adverb 'carnally'. The only other version to acknowledge the presence of 'know' is the HCSB, which does so in a footnote, but only in 19.25. Specifically, in the first column, with respect to *yada'*, the most popular rendering is 'have intercourse with' (NJB, NRSV, NWT, REB) followed by 'have sex with' (HCSB, NIV, NLT). The remaining options occur just once: 'have sexual relations with' (NCV), 'amuse ourselves with' (CCB), 'be intimate with' (JPS), and 'rape' (JM).

Read vertically, the first column reveals that the basic cognitive and social aspects of knowing at the heart of *yada'* are virtually absent. For the vast majority of translators, *yada'* in 19.22 expresses physical intimacy or sexual intercourse. However, this causes the verb to be stretched semantically, probably overstretched, given the tension between 'amuse ourselves with', 'be intimate with', and 'have sexual relations with'. Only JM explicitly equates *yada'* with sexual violence, by its use of the word 'rape'. It is also worth noting that in this verse of the MT, there is no trace of the language of sex normally used in the HB, namely, *bō* and *el* or *shakhav* and *eth*. The apparent self-assuredness with which the translators proceed in spite of these facts suggests the existence of a long exegetical tradition.

In the second column, several facts should be highlighted with regard to *yada'*. First, in 19.25, only the NKJV conveys the root meaning of 'know'. Second, two versions retain 'have intercourse with' (NJB, NWT). Third, the frequency of 'rape' has increased considerably from one to four (HCSB,

JPS, NIV, REB), while the NRSV inserts an element of scandal by saying 'wantonly raped'. Analogous options are 'violated' (CCB), 'abused' (NLT), and 'forced to have sexual relations' (NCV). In 19.25, JM only provides 'violated'. This is a reduction vis-à-vis the Hebrew text, which includes the two verbs *yadaʿ* ('know') and *ʿalal* ('make sport of'; cf. discussion below).

The literary coherence between *yadaʿ* in Judges 19.22 and 19.25, which is obvious in the Hebrew text, has clearly been lost in translation. Once again, most translators confusingly ascribe to *yadaʿ* the semantic contents of *bō* and *shakhav*. In addition, while the narrator achieves an almost mechanical effect by repeating *yadaʿ*, most versions neglect this aspect and use two different terms leading to stylistic variation. This is apparent as soon as table 62 is read horizontally. For instance, there is an abrupt leap from 'amuse ourselves with' to 'violate' (CCB), from 'be intimate with' to 'rape' (JPS), and from 'have intercourse with' to 'wantonly rape' (NRSV).

In summary, the above brief exercise has highlighted four major translation issues in relation to *yadaʿ*: (1) the considerable confusion among translators regarding the verb's semantic field; (2) the widespread tendency to endow *yadaʿ* with concepts belonging to other Hebrew verbs such as *bō*, *shakhav* and *ʿanah*; (3) confirmation that today's English versions follow 'free' or 'dynamic' translation procedures, which allow plenty of freedom for paraphrase and subjectivity; and (4) a remarkable change of style, especially a higher emotional pitch when violent events are narrated. The latter phenomenon is especially noticeable in 19.25 where *yadaʿ* operates in a literary context saturated with tension and brutality.

Sexual Violence in Gibeah and Beyond

Given the problems detected above, there are good reasons for emphasizing once again the non-sexual nature of *yada'*. Furthermore, the literary refinement inherent in various Hebrew wordplays reflects the hand of an expert narrator fully aware of composition techniques. His choice of vocabulary is in no way accidental. Thus, the execution of the violence that takes place is efficiently controlled by means of two specific verbs well suited for the purpose, namely, *'anah* and *'alal*. Their presence in the text makes it possible to determine the nature of the sexual assault.

The verb *'anah* is deployed in some parts of the HB to describe seduction, sexual assault, or rape-like scenarios. On account of its primary meaning of 'oppress' or 'humiliate' (Hanks 1984: 16–17), sexual aggression is regarded as an act of humiliation. In Genesis 34.2, for instance, Shechem saw Jacob's daughter Dinah and took her, lay with her and 'humiliated' or 'debased' her. There is no mention of *yada'*. Similarly, in 2 Samuel 13 David's beautiful daughter Tamar is assaulted sexually. Again *yada'* is absent while *'anah* occurs twice (13.12, 14). In the Gibeah narrative, *'anah* appears on two occasions, producing another case of Significant Repetition (19.24; 20.5). In 19.23–24, the elderly Ephraimite host is desperately trying to protect the Levite from the threat of being murdered (cf. 20.5). In an impromptu show of solidarity with the small group of travellers staying at his house, he proposes to hand over his own unmarried daughter so that she may give the *pilegesh* company. Adamant that the scoundrels shall not come near the Levite, the host offers them compensation in the form of 'humiliation' (*'anah*) of the two women. The occurrence of this strong word may be taken to indicate two concerns on the Ephraimite's part: (a) the perceived need to make an offer that will be taken seriously in the circumstances, and (b) to remind the rogues outside of the fate of women survivors of rape who are literally debased and reduced to spending the rest of their lives in virtual anonymity and segregated from their communities (2 Sam. 13.20; 16.20-22; 20.3).

According to the dictionaries, the meaning of ʿalal, the other verb in Judges 19.25, is 'maltreat', 'abuse', and 'mistreat' (DBHE),[294] whereas the BDB p. 759 widens the semantic field to include 'busy/divert oneself with' and 'deal wantonly/ ruthlessly with'. In Numbers 22.29, ʿalal seems to mean 'make fun of' or 'make sport of' (cf. chapter 4). In the drama of Gibeah, the presence of ʿalal in 19.25 may imply that the *pilegesh* has been placed at the centre of a rowdy party held in the middle of the street. In fact, ʿalal may arguably be taken to denote that she is the focal point of lewd games and competitions. This would not be surprising given the lateness of the hour and the unflattering description of the gang of locals in 19.22 as *beney-beliyyaʿal*, often translated as 'sons of worthlessness' or 'good-for-nothings'. Wine is not mentioned in the text, but since these excesses lasted all night, ancient readers and listeners may well have imagined generous supplies of alcoholic beverages.

'Know' in a Violent Setting

As noted above, it is important to pay attention to the role of *yadaʿ* in this text. There are no compelling linguistic reasons for making *yadaʿ* interchangeable with ʿanah or ʿalal. In fact, doing so is a semantic error. Only in this verse, and nowhere else in the HB, does *yadaʿ* play an active part in what appears to be a full-blown rape scene. After all, the nature of *yadaʿ* is cognitive. In addition to certain technical functions in legal

---

[294] Spanish renderings in the DBHE p. 568: *Maltratar, vejar, abusar, malparar, dejar maltrecho*.

settings, it usually reflects some aspect of knowing such as acquaintance, acknowledgement or awareness, even when it appears in episodes characterized by sexual tension (cf. Gen. 19.33; 38.16) or, as here, by turbulence and brutality. Leaving aside the sinister context, and recalling the sophisticated literary qualities of the Hebrew text, the narrator is likely to have inserted *yada'* deliberately.

With respect to 19.22, where the Levite is wanted for 'knowing', in many parts of the world, it is customary for locals to express their desire to be introduced to a stranger who has just arrived. Moreover, according to the social hierarchy in male-dominated cultures, people will habitually begin social interaction by speaking to a woman's husband even if their ultimate focus is on her.[295] From the perspective of the *pilegesh*, the Levite is not only her husband (Hebrew *īsh*, Judg. 20.4) but also her 'master' or 'lord' (*adōn*), as stated in Judges 19.26–27.[296] While it is true that the villains at the front door have vicious things in mind, this aspect is not conveyed euphemistically through *yada'*. Instead, the narrator is explicit. First, he calls the mob *beney-beliyya'al*, 'sons of worthlessness'. Second, the very fact that they appear late at night and pound insistently on the front door indicates their sinister intentions and that danger is lurking (Fields 1997: 108, 110–12).

In 19.25, the narrator specifies that these local men 'knew' the *pilegesh*. Given the crude brutality unleashed at that moment, such simple language sounds like understatement. Again, this is likely to be deliberate. Deployed in the basic sense of 'acquainting oneself with', the presence of this neutral verb

---

[295] Cf. Gen. 18.9–15 where the deity speaks to Abraham *about* Sarah rather than *to* her. As pointed out by Tammi Schneider (2008: 32), the phrase 'No, you did laugh' (18.15), which is addressed directly to Sarah, may well have been uttered not by YHWH but by Abraham.
[296] In Gen. 18.12, Sarah uses the same term in reference to Abraham.

amid such turmoil creates an extraordinary, arresting effect. Indeed, *yadaʽ* forms a very effective contrast to the savageness that invades the scene in the form of *ʽanah* and *ʽalal*. The matter-of-fact manner in which it is said that they 'knew' her, i.e. acquainted themselves with her, provides a realistic glimpse of the scene. One can imagine the scoundrels joking among themselves about how much fun it is to 'get to know' the young woman. In this subtle way, the narrator makes it clear that the gang at the front door is not really interested in the Levite or the host's unmarried daughter. They only want the visiting woman.

In other words, while *yadaʽ* is direct speech in 19.22, where the object is the Levite ('we will know *him*'), the indirect speech in 19.25 ('they knew *her*') draws attention to the one the rogues really want to meet, namely, the *pilegesh*. In other words, in 19.22 the *beney-beliyyaʽal* intend to threaten the Levite to force him to hand over his young wife. Initially they follow social convention, demanding to 'know' the visitor but, once they see the young woman alone and defenceless in front of them, they completely forget about everything else. That this is the basis of the plot emerges from the concise report submitted by the Levite to the assembly of the Israelite tribes in Judges 20.5. He limits himself to focus on two crucial details: (1) in Gibeah he was threatened with murder and (2) his *pilegesh* was violated and died.

To Humiliate a Woman

For translators, the Judges 19.24–25 passage is a challenge because three crucial verbs appear in rapid succession: *ʽanah*, *yadaʽ* and *ʽalal*. While the meaning of *yadaʽ* has already been discussed in connection with table 62, it is important to analyse the way in which the other two verbs interact for a clearer appreciation of the plot. In the Hebrew text, each verb adds a special overtone to the terror scene unfolding in the streets of Gibeah. Since it occurs both in 19.24 and 20.5, the more prominent of the two is ʿanah. Table 63 shows the way in which the twelve English versions approach this verb.

Table 63
Translating ʿANAH

Version	ʿANAH 19.24	ʿANAH 20.5
MT	**humiliate them**	**humiliated** (her)
CCB	ravish *her*	abused
HCSB	use them	raped
JM	ravish them	ravished
JPS	have your pleasure of them	ravished
NCV	0	forced . . . to have sexual relations
NIV	use them	raped
NJB	ill-treat *her*	had intercourse with
NKJV	humble them	ravished
NLT	abuse them	raped
NRSV	ravish them	raped
NWT	rape them	raped
REB	abuse them	raped

According to the MT, in 19.24 the old Ephraimite proposes to hand over both the *pilegesh* and his young, nubile daughter (Hebrew *bethulah*) to the men at the front door. The word *otham*, 'them', implies that the host seems to have permission to strike a deal that includes both women. Obviously the incident takes place within a cultural framework characterized by patriarchal or androcentric structures where the woman either belongs to her father or to her husband. If this scenario seems shocking to modern readers, it should not be forgotten that the HB did not invent patriarchy but is a product of an ancient patriarchal culture (Fontaine 1997: 93).

Curiously, in the first column of table 63 two English versions (CCB, NJB) reduce the text, making the old man mention only 'her', i.e. his daughter. In this manner, they distance themselves from the MT. As both versions are Roman Catholic, this is surprising because Jerome's famous Latin Vulgate—the official Catholic Bible until the 1960s—coincides with the MT saying *eas*, 'them'. By focusing only on the host's daughter and leaving out the *pilegesh*, the CCB and the NJB have distorted this part of the plot.

Bearing in mind that the basic meaning of ʿ*anah* is 'oppress', 'humiliate' or 'debase', the initial impression of table 63 is that these renderings are only partially represented. Indeed, considerable diversity exists. In the first vertical column corresponding to 19.24, no fewer than six renderings of ʿ*anah* are on offer: 'ravish' (CCB, JM, NRSV), 'use' (HCSB, NIV), 'abuse' (NLT, REB), 'have your pleasure of' (JPS), 'ill-treat' (NJB), 'humble' (NKJV), and 'rape' (NWT). The NCV omits any specific reference to ʿ*anah* in this column. The most accurate rendering would seem to be the NKJV's 'humble' in the light of the marginalization that befalls an Israelite woman who has been subjected to sexual assault. Less precise are 'ravish', 'abuse', and 'ill-treat' because they focus entirely on the actual physical act and do not take into account the concomitant social degradation of the victim. Similarly, 'have your pleasure of' and 'use' are somewhat bland for this context—quite apart from the fact that 'use' in Hebrew is written ʿ*asah*, not ʿ*anah*.

The second column refers to ʿ*anah* in 20.5. Here the picture presented by the versions changes to some extent. Five renderings are suggested, of which the most popular by far is 'raped' (HCSB, NIV, NLT, NRSV, NWT, REB). It is followed by 'ravished' (JM, JPS, NKJV), 'abused' (CCB), 'had intercourse with' (NJB) and 'forced to have sexual relations' (NCV). The last two options were not proposed for 19.24 while the other three are reappearances. In all cases, however, the emphasis falls on the use of force and sexual violence and the important aspect of oppression or humiliation is absent.

Read horizontally, table 63 further illuminates the methodology adopted by English translators. Intriguingly, in only two cases do the versions provide the same rendering of ʿanah in 19.24 and 20.5, namely, 'ravish' (JM) and 'rape' (NWT). All other versions have opted for variation. In most cases, there is no major contradiction between their choices with the exception of the NJB, whose two renderings are virtually incompatible. In no case can 'ill-treat' be said to be interchangeable with 'have intercourse with', and vice versa. The phrase 'have intercourse with' is neutral and belongs, in modern English, to the realm of sex, while 'ill-treat' denotes abuse in any context, sexual or otherwise. The main impression gained from a horizontal reading of table 63 is inconsistency. Unlike the original Hebrew text, most English versions do not enable curious Bible readers to detect the significant repetition of ʿanah.

Having Fun at Someone's Expense

The other verb ʿalal occurs once in this story, namely, in Judges 19.25, which makes its specific meaning more difficult to determine. As noted above, ʿalal is normally used in the sense of 'busy/divert oneself with', 'deal wantonly/ruthlessly with', and 'make fun/sport of'. Given the numerous subtle allusions in Judges 19–21 to the two books of Samuel (cf. table 69), the appearance of ʿalal in 1 Samuel

31.4 just before King Saul commits suicide may shed light on the meaning of the verb in Judges 19.25 and the plight of the *pilegesh*. Table 64 shows the ways in which the English versions deal with these two occurrences of ʿalal.

Table 64
Translating ʿALAL

Version	ʿALAL Judg. 19.25	ʿALAL 1 Sam. 31.4
MT	**Made sport of** (her)	**Make sport of** (me)
CCB	maltreated	make fun of
HCSB	abused	torture
JM	[violated]	make a fool of
JPS	abused	make sport of
NCV	abused	make fun of
NIV	abused	abuse
NJB	raped	make fun of
NKJV	abused	abuse
NLT	taking turns raping	taunt and torture
NRSV	abused	make sport of
NWT	kept on abusing	deal abusively with
REB	abused	make sport of

In the first column, the most popular rendering of ʿalal is 'abused' (HCSB, JPS, NCV, NIV, NKJV, NRSV, REB). The NWT intensifies the concept suggesting 'kept on abusing'. Further proposals are 'raped' (NJB), 'taking turns raping', (NLT) and 'maltreated' (CCB). JM's 'violated' does not directly reflect ʿalal but is a conflated paraphrase of the two verbs yadaʿ and ʿalal. The fact that eight versions have chosen 'abuse' for ʿalal calls for reflection. According to the *OD*, one of the definitions of 'abuse' is 'treat with cruelty or violence, especially regularly or repeatedly'. An example offered is 'riders who abuse their horses'. Another nuance of 'abuse' is 'assault someone sexually', especially a woman or child. At first sight, then, it would seem that 'abuse' corresponds rather accurately to the bitter experience of the *pilegesh* in Judges 19.24. However, the *OD* specifies the definition saying 'especially regularly or repeatedly'. It is of course plausible that the young woman was assaulted sexually several times during the night since the perpetrators only let her go at dawn. On the other hand, the plight of the *pilegesh* does not match that of children abused by their parents because such abuse may take place over an extended period of time. Hence, 'abuse' does not seem to be an ideal translation for ʿ*alal* in a text fraught with ambiguity, tension, and drama.

The CCB's suggested 'maltreated' is not exactly wrong but seems rather bland for the context. The NJB and the NLT say 'rape', a term which would be better suited for ʿ*anah*. Furthermore, if 'maltreat', 'abuse', and 'rape' are taken together, they may overlap to a minor degree without being interchangeable. In other words, the versions appear to take a rather dim view of ʿ*alal*. They are aware that the verb denotes something unpleasant but unsure of the precise nuance. The contradictions among the options in the first column may not be overwhelming, inasmuch as all refer to a scenario of violence, but these renderings show that the exact nature of what the narrator is describing eludes the translators.

Perhaps an examination of the second column in table 64 will offer further clues to the meaning of ʿ*alal*. In this case, a group of three versions has opted for 'make fun of' (CCB, NCV, NJB) while another three have chosen 'make sport of' (JPS, NRSV, REB). Adopted by only two versions (NIV, NKJV), 'abuse' has lost terrain and is paraphrased just once as 'deal abusively with' (NWT). Further renderings are 'make a fool of' (JM) and 'torture' (HCSB) along with 'taunt and torture' (NLT). None is conspicuously wrong. The least precise is 'abuse' while the amplification 'taunt and torture' is probably the most colourful. The majority succeed fairly adequately in conveying a sense of making fun or sport at someone's expense.

The main problem in table 64 is the inconsistency when a horizontal reading is carried out. A few versions succeed in being consistent, namely, the NIV and the NKVJ ('abuse') and, to a considerable extent, the NWT with two closely related options. However, several others offer very little semantic overlap between their two renderings of ʿalal. For instance, there is a substantial gap between 'abuse' and 'make fun/sport of' as proposed by a number of versions, and very little connection between 'take turns raping' and 'taunt and torture' (NLT).

To complete this exercise, one needs to ask how well the versions manage to reflect the combined presence of two verbs of violence or abuse in Judges 19 and 20, namely, ʿanah and ʿalal. This becomes apparent if some of the material of tables 59 and 60 is juxtaposed as shown in table 65.

Table 65
Translating Two Verbs of Violence

Version	ʿANAH 19.24	ʿANAH 20.5	ʿALAL 19.25
MT	**humiliate them**	**humiliated** (her)	**made sport of** (her)
CCB	ravish *her*	abused	maltreated
HCSB	use them	raped	abused
JM	ravish them	ravished	[violated]
JPS	have your pleasure of them	ravished	abused
NCV	0	forced [. . .] to have sexual relations	abused
NIV	use them	raped	abuse
NJB	ill-treat *her*	had intercourse w.	raped
NKJV	humble them	ravished	abused
NLT	abuse them	raped	taking turns raping
NRSV	ravish them	raped	abused
NWT	rape them	raped	kept on abusing
REB	abuse them	raped	abused

A horizontal reading of table 65 reveals that, where the Hebrew text features two verbs, a picture of complete consistency is offered by one English version only, namely, the NWT. In JM's rendering of Judges 19.25, ʿalal is absent as it has been conflated with yadaʿ into 'violated', while the NCV has omitted any reference to ʿanah in 19.24. Furthermore, it is significant that the borderline between ʿanah and ʿalal is blurred in most versions, with very little semantic distinction or precision. In other words, where the MT is consistent, no fewer than eleven English versions (representing 92 per cent) have ignored this important literary detail, replacing it with considerable diversity. Once again it becomes clear that most modern translators have serious difficulty in dealing adequately with situations of sex and sexual violence in the Bible.

The Good in Your Eyes

Elsewhere I have discussed how Lot in Genesis 19.8 speaks to the men of Sodom, offering to hand over his daughters and adding, 'Do to them as the good in your eyes' (cf. table 59). While the situation is difficult for modern minds to gauge and understand, one thing is clear: nothing in his utterance indicates that Lot intended his daughters to suffer any harm. In Judges 19.24-25, the situation is different in several respects. First, the narrator omits the short Hebrew preposition *kĕ*, 'as', included in Genesis 19.8 ('as the good'). Second, the words 'Do with them the good in your eyes', uttered by the old Ephraimite, are preceded by a highly significant verb, namely, *ʿanah* ('humiliate'). In other words, the narrator of Judges 19 is reworking the theme from Genesis 19 to make a different point. Unlike Lot in Sodom, in the Gibeah text the Ephraimite is not trying to keep two girls out of harm's way. Instead, the local 'sons of worthlessness' are, to all effects and purposes, being invited to carry out a sexual assault.

Furthermore, in Judges 19 it is significant that part of the conversation between the Ephraimite and the dubious townsmen at the door is eliminated. With just a few words to ponder, readers are barely allowed to sense the tension in the air: 'The men did not want to listen to him' (19.25). How the English translators interpret the phrase 'do with them the good in your eyes' is shown in table 66.

Table 66
'The Good in Your Eyes' (Judges 19.24)

Version	Renderings
MT	**the good in your eyes**
CCB	what seems good to you
HCSB	whatever you want*
	*Lit what is good in your eyes
JM	what you like
JPS	what you like
NCV	anything you want
NIV	whatever you wish
NJB	what you please
NKJV	as you please
NLT	whatever you like
NRSV	whatever you want
NWT	what is good in your eyes
REB	what you please

Table 66 demonstrates that, in this passage, no major differences have arisen among the versions. The most precise, or literal, rendering is 'what is good in your eyes' (NWT). In this regard, it is followed by 'what seems good to you' (CCB). The only other version to include the adjective 'good' in a footnote is HCSB. The remaining versions have all opted for paraphrases: 'what you like' (JM, JPS), 'what you please' (NJB, REB), 'whatever you want' (HCSB, NRSV), 'whatever you like' (NLT), 'whatever you wish' (NIV), 'anything you want' (NCV), and 'as you please' (NKJV).

While none is entirely literal, most of these options come close to being adequate. There is no contradiction between the versions and the overall tenor of the Hebrew wording, which is dominated by the sinister overtones sounded by the presence of ʿ*anah* in 19.24.

Differences between Gibeah and Sodom

Above I have noted the strong tendency among modern commentators to interpret the crime story of Gibeah in the same light as the Sodom narrative in Genesis. The method has obvious advantages. Above all, it enables scholars to point out literary analogies, which in turn make it possible to fill apparent gaps in one story with details from the other. Nonetheless, the procedure is deceptive because it encourages interpreters of the Bible to ignore a number of literary, contextual, and political elements that are specific to each text. Table 67 reflects some significant differences between the two narratives.

Table 67
Differences between Gibeah and Sodom

ELEMENTS	GIBEAH Judg. 19–20	SODOM Gen. 18–19
Travellers	19.3: two men	18.2: three men
	19.15: 2 men & 1 woman	19.1: two men
Social rank	Levite, wife, servant	Divine messengers
Ethnic groups	Levi, Ephraim, Judah,	18: Foreign (Abraham & Sarah)
	Jebusites, Benjamin	19: Canaanite, Ammon, Moab
Host	19.3–9: father-in-law	18: Abraham, a foreigner
	19.16: a fellow Israelite	19: Lot, a foreigner
Host and guest	From the same area	No shared place of origin
Travellers	Carry food provisions	Arrive empty-handed
Host's wife	19.4: not mentioned	18: Sarah
	19.21: not mentioned	19.15, 26: Lot's wife
Host's children	19.1–4: a daughter	18.10: promise of a son
	19.24: a daughter	19.8: two daughters
Persons mentioned	All nameless	Abraham, Sarah, Lot
Places	Benjamin, Bethlehem,	18: Mamre, Sodom
	Ephraim, Gibeah, Jabesh,	19: Sodom, the Plain, Zoar, mountains
	Jebus, Mizpah, Ramah	
Tribes of Israel	Benjamin, Ephraim,	0
	Judah, Levi	
Crowd	Rogues	All male citizens
Purpose	Sex with young woman	Interrogation
Method	Death threat	Mass intimidation
Defensive move	Sexual bait (two women)	Pledge (two children)

Proposed deal	'Humiliate them'	'Treat them well'
Victims	19.22, 25 & 20.5: visitors	Residents (Lot & family)
Host attacked	No	Yes
Form of violence	19.22, 25: threat & assault	19.9: attempted arrest, break-in
Duration	All night	A few minutes
Divine intervention	No	Yes
Victim	Dies	Is rescued
Host's fate	Not mentioned	Lot and daughters survive
Eyewitnesses	The Levite (one)	Messengers (two)
Punishment	Destructive war	Natural disaster
City's destiny	Reconstruction	Permanent ruins
Life continues	Judg. 21: forced marriages	18: miraculous pregnancy
		19: incest through trickery
Occurrences of yada'	Two	Six
Cohortatives of yada'	0	Two
Verbs of aggression	19.24; 20.5: 'anah	19.9: 'Deal worse with you'
	19.25: 'alal	'They pressed hard against Lot'
Transformation	19.29: dismemberment	19.26: pillar of salt
Subjects (selection)	Crime, tribal conflicts, anti-Benjamin sentiment, revenge and punishment, feud of Saul and David	Two foreigners: Abraham and Lot, intercession, oppression of sojourner, punishment, origin of Moab & Ammon

Literary Allusions

Every story in the HB is located within a literary framework. The allusions interspersed in the language used by narrators reveal the nature of the text, as pointed out by Robert Alter (1992: 107):

> Nothing confirms the literary character of biblical narrative and biblical poetry more strikingly than their constant, resourceful, and necessary recourse to allusion.

The drama of Gibeah is set in the book of Judges and preceded by a narrative covering chapters 17 and 18, which introduces a series of noteworthy details. I refer to this story as Micah-Dan because of its protagonists. Micah is a rich man living in the north, while Dan is one of the twelve tribes of Israel. As in Judges 19.1, in 17.1, the hill country of Ephraim is mentioned, and again a Levite plays a central part. Table 68 reflects the textual allusions between Micah-Dan and the tale of Gibeah.

Table 68
Micah-Dan and Gibeah

Chapters ELEMENTS	Judges 17–18 MICAH-DAN	Judges 19–21 GIBEAH
Ephraim	17.1, 8; 18.2, 13	19.1, 16, 18
Bethlehem	17.7–9	19.1–2, 18
Dan	18	20.1
Levite	17.7–13	19
	18.3–6, 15–20, 27, 30	20.1–11

Sanctuaries	17.5; 18.14–20, 30–31	19.18; 20.1, 23, 26–28; 21.4
Y<small>HWH</small> consulted	18.5–6	20.18, 23, 27; 21.2–3
'There was no king'	17.6; 18.1	19.1; 21.25
Genocide	18.27	20.37; 21.10

The textual elements in table 68 show the close links between the two stories. For instance, the phrase 'there was no king in Israel' is a refrain throughout. Thus, both narratives seem to describe a period prior to the life and death of the despot Abimelech, son of Gideon (Judg. 9), and before Samuel proclaims Saul king of the Israelites (1 Sam. 10.24).

In addition, the drama of Gibeah contains repeated literary allusions to the book of Genesis (Alter 1992: 112). Such references include the danger faced by a vulnerable traveller accompanied by a beautiful wife (Gen. 12.12; 20.1-13; 26.7); the danger faced by a young woman away from home (34.2); the sanctuary at Bethel (12.8; 28.19); hospitality vs. inhospitality (18 & 19); taking the knife of sacrifice (22.10); fierce punishment visited on a community in which sexual transgression has taken place (34.25); and the leadership of Judah, ancestor of David (37.26-27; 44.14-18; 49.8-9). Numerous pointers in the text of Gibeah also evoke passages from the books of Joshua, 1 Samuel and 2 Samuel. Table 69 reflects the most noteworthy intertextual connections.

Table 69
Literary Allusions in Judges 19–21

HB TEXTS	THEMES	JUDGES 19–21
Gen. 12.12; 20.1–13; 26.7	Danger: man and wife travelling	19.12, 22–26; 20.5
Gen. 12.8; 28.19	The Bethel sanctuary	20.18
Gen. 18.2–8; 19.1–3	Hospitality	19.3–4, 17–21
Gen. 19.5	Locals demanding to know	19.22
Gen. 19.7–8	Host negotiating	19.23–24
Gen. 19.9	Locals threatening	19.22, 25; 20.5
Gen. 19.26	Wife perishing away from home	19.25; 20.5
Gen. 22.10	Taking 'the knife'	19.29
Gen. 34.2	Humiliating a young woman	19.25; 20.5
Gen. 34.25	Bloody revenge	20.9 ff.
Gen. 44.14–18; 49.10	Leadership of Judah (David)	20.18
Josh. 18.1; 22.9, 12	Shrine at Shiloh	21.19
Judg. 1.1–10, 16–19	Leadership of Judah (David)	20.18
Judg. 1.21	Jebus	19.11
1 Samuel (12 refs.)	'Gibeah of Saul'	19: Gibeah (5 refs.)
1 Sam. 8.5	Israel without a king	19.1; 21.25
1 Sam. 10.17	Mizpah	20.1
1 Sam. 11.1–11	Jabesh-gilead	21.8–14
1 Sam. 11.7	Dismembering oxen	19.29
1 Sam. 11.7	Summoning the tribes of Israel	19.29
1 Sam. 18.11; 19.10	Saul trying to kill David	19.22, 25; 20.5
1 Sam. 31.4	Horror imagined by Saul (ʻalal)	19.25
2 Sam. 2–4	Protracted war (David and Saul)	20.11–48
2 Sam. 20.1–22	Hostilities (David & Benjamin)	20.11–48

The story of the outrage at Gibeah contains further evidence of being a work of literary fiction. For instance, in real life a priest is not permitted to defile himself by touching a corpse (Lev. 21.1-4). Yet in Judges 19.29, the Levite personally dismembers the body of the *pilegesh* and sends off the pieces. Moreover, it is hardly conceivable that an anonymous Levite from the remote hill country of Ephraim would be capable of summoning all the tribes of Israel (Judg. 20.1). By comparison, when King Saul tries to do the same, his royal status provides him with the necessary authority. Yet he feels the need to add coercion in the form of a virulent threat to anyone who does not comply (1 Sam 11.7).

Furthermore, to execute a death sentence, ancient HB law requires the testimony of two or three eyewitnesses as expressed in Deuteronomy 17.6 (NRSV):

> On the evidence of two or three witnesses the death sentence shall be executed; a person must not be put to death on the evidence of only one witness.

Yet in Judges 20.5, the only eyewitness to give evidence is the nameless Levite. Based on his testimony alone, the entire Israelite community pronounces a death sentence on the alleged culprits of Gibeah (20.13) and declares war on the tribe of Benjamin. Finally, the inflated numbers of men killed on the battlefield are another sign of literary fiction (Judg. 20.21, 25, 35), but the fact that so many modern readers are moved by the story told in Judges 19 and 20 attests to its literary qualities. This text reflects the hand of a brilliant narrator who has produced a fascinating coded account of one of the most embittered feuds between two ancient Israelites, namely, Saul and David.

Conclusion

The drama of Gibeah in Judges 19 and 20 has a sinister plot and a scandalous ending. In church history and rabbinical tradition, the story has received scant attention. However, in recent decades, a growing number of biblical commentators have focused on this text, which some feminist scholars have called a 'text of terror'. Simultaneously, it has become customary to read the tale of Gibeah in parallel with the legend of Sodom and Gomorrah, mainly due to the relative similarity of the hospitality *leitmotif*, which is prominent in both narratives. These perceived connections lead many exegetes to include this story in the ongoing debate on biblical texts dealing with homoeroticism.

In a highly suggestive move, not without ironic or sinister overtones, the Hebrew narrator uses *yadaʿ* in the basic sense of 'become acquainted with' or 'meet'. The verb occurs twice in the Gibeah text. From a linguistic and semantic point of view, there is no justification for the widespread tendency to ascribe sexual content to *yadaʿ*. When this happens, translators tend to lose sight of the verb's cognitive, social, and legal aspects. Even when it occurs in the midst of a tumultuous incident, *yadaʿ* still means 'know'. Significantly, the sexual and violent side of the drama is described by means of other verbs such as *ʿanah* and *ʿalal*. While *ʿanah* means 'humiliate', 'debase' or 'oppress', *ʿalal* corresponds to 'maltreat', 'mock', or 'make sport of'. The approaches adopted by almost all English versions betray considerable inconsistency. Their frequently incoherent methods fail to bring readers closer to the Hebrew text and offer a blurry picture of a complex plot.

Interpreted in its biblical context and translated with careful attention to detail, the story unfolding in Judges 19 and 20 does not reflect any form of homoeroticism. Instead, a series of textual clues showcase an artful literary procedure whereby the narrator introduces a number of allusions to the books of Genesis and 1 Samuel, among others. The inspiration provided by Genesis is not limited to the story of Sodom and Gomorrah but includes a series of situations in the lives of Abraham and his descendants. The abundance of subtle references to 1 Samuel indicates the political purpose of the drama of Gibeah. Using sophisticated allegories, the narrator presents a scathing picture of the kingship of Saul, his native city Gibeah and the tribe of Benjamin. The polemical, coded message would have been readily understood by ancient readers and listeners. Viewed from this perspective, the story is clearly biased in favour of David of Bethlehem who was persecuted by Saul and, like the tragic literary figure of the young *pilegesh*, also belonged to the tribe of Judah.

13

SOFTIES AND MALE-LIERS

What Paul once wrote has subsequently been perceived as the word of God.

— Martti Nissinen [297]

Introduction

In relation to current Christian debates on homoeroticism in the Bible, several important texts found in the Second Testament (ST) are dealt with over the following three chapters. Given that Jesus nowhere condemns homoerotic relationships, the four Gospels and the book of Acts have received little attention in such debates until fairly recently.[298] Instead, most exegetes and biblical commentators have devoted extensive analysis to three letters commonly attributed to Paul (5-67 CE), namely, Romans, 1 Corinthians, and 1 Timothy.[299] Composed in the Hellenistic Koiné variant of Greek, Paul's letters or Epistles to a string of fledgling Christian communities around the northern rim of the

---

[297] Nissinen 1998: 103.
[298] A growing number of scholars are focusing on the four Gospels and Acts. See Goss and West (eds.) 2000: 185-226; Hanks 2000: 3-79; Jennings 2003: 13-210; Guest, Goss, West and Bohache (eds.) 2006: 487-581; Martin 2006: 91-109; Sharpe 2011: 68-76, 95-125, 170-200.
[299] Brooten 1996: 189-302; Nissinen 1998: 108-18; Kader 1999: 60-87; Hanks 2000: 80-109; Helminiak 2000: 75-115; Gagnon 2001: 229-339; Moore 2003: 86-113; Alison 2006: 123-40; Hanks 2006: 582-605; Martin 2006: 37-64; Sharpe 2011: 44-67.

Mediterranean basin have been scrutinized for generations. Undoubtedly, Paul's thinking has played a major part in the making of Christian theology. Biblical scholar Robert Gagnon (2001: 434) regards Paul as one of the most important authors of the ST, 'if not *the* most important' (his emphasis). In other words, for Gagnon, the apostle is crucial for defining the essence of Christianity, including Christian approaches to intimate same-sex relationships.

The sheer number of writings attributed to him in the ST certainly places Paul of Tarsus in a prominent position. In addition, each Pauline text is complex enough to merit in-depth analysis. However, with regard to the realm of sex, as observed by David Carr (2003: 54), it should be remembered that Paul's sexual universe is Hellenistic, which in many respects places it at a considerable distance from its biblical predecessors:

> Paul's sexual system and the rules of other New Testament writings are profoundly different from both the Hebrew Bible and any contemporary positions.

Thus, the terminology employed by the apostle is hardly comparable to the Hebrew terms discussed in chapter 2, most of which describe sexual intercourse in 'plain' language, e.g. 'go in to' or 'lie down with'. By contrast, few Greek words in the ST refer directly to sexual intercourse. When mentioned, and particularly in the writings of Paul, sexual matters tend to be framed in negative terms. Typical examples are 'desire' or 'lust' (*epithymia*; cf. Matt. 5.28), 'adultery' (*moicheia*; cf. Matt. 15.19) and 'irresponsible sex' (*porneia*; cf. 1 Cor. 6.18). Two letters of Paul present the notion of 'burning' as a metaphor for a strong sex drive. In 1 Corinthians 7.9, Christian men are advised to marry in order to assuage their sexual urges rather than 'burn' (*pyroō*) and, in Romans 1.27, an unidentified group of pagan men is described as having become 'inflamed' (*ekkaiō*) in lust for each other.

Paul's Vices

The Greek terms to be discussed in this chapter occur within, or next to, so-called vice lists, which were popular in Hellenistic literature (Helminiak 2000: 112).[300] The ST provides several examples, two of which are reproduced below (NRSV). One is from the Gospel of Mark (7.21-22) and the other from the book of Revelation (21.8):

> (1) For it is from within, from the human heart, that evil intentions come: fornication, theft, murder, adultery, avarice, wickedness, deceit, licentiousness, envy, slander, pride, folly.

> (2) But as for the cowardly, the faithless, the polluted, the murderers, the fornicators, the sorcerers, the idolaters, and all liars, their place will be in the lake that burns with fire and sulphur . . .

In Paul's letters similar catalogues abound, including Romans 1.29-31, 1 Corinthians 5.10-11, 2 Corinthians 12.20-21, Galatians 5.19-21, and Ephesians 5.3-5. The present chapter specifically discusses two Pauline passages purportedly dealing with homoeroticism, namely, 1 Corinthians 6.9 and 1 Timothy 1.10. While biblical historians agree that 1 Corinthians was written by Paul (Ashworth 2006 p. xiv), 1 Timothy is assumed to have been composed by a different author, probably one of his disciples or colleagues.

---

[300] According to Robert Goss (2002: 198), Paul's contemporary Philo of Alexandria uses lists of vices over a hundred times in his writings.

A likely date seems to be the year 85 CE (Hanks 2000: 167), i.e. about twenty years after Paul's death.

In the passage from 1 Corinthians 6, two groups of people, described as *malakoi* and *arsenokoitai*, are of particular interest for the subject of the present book. To appreciate these terms in their immediate contexts, a preliminary translation of Paul's Greek prose is offered below. Because of their specific vocabulary, the following English versions of both Pauline texts have been selected to provide a clear focus on the key issues (emphasis added):

> 1 Cor. 6.9 according to *The Easy-to-Read Version* (2006)
>
> Surely you know that people who do wrong will not get to enjoy God's kingdom. Don't be fooled. These are the people who will not get to enjoy his kingdom: those who sin sexually, those who worship idols, those who commit adultery, *men who let other men use them for sex or who have sex with other men*, those who steal, those who are greedy, those who drink too much, those who abuse others with insults, and those who cheat. Or do you not know that the unrighteous will not inherit the kingdom of God?
>
> 1 Tim. 1.8–10 according to *The Worldwide English New Testament* (1998)
>
> The law . . . was made for those who use sex in the wrong way and for *men who have sex with other men*. It was made for those who steal people, for those who tell lies, for those who make a promise that is not true, and for any other thing that is not right.

The suggested 'men who let other men use them for sex' in 1 Corinthians 6.9 corresponds to the Greek plural noun *malakoi*, and 'men who have sex with other men' is, according to these versions, the translation of *arsenokoitai*. While the latter term is present in both 1 Corinthians and 1 Timothy, *malakoi* only occurs in 1 Corinthians 6.9. The numerous issues surrounding Paul's use of both words are discussed below.

Softies

One scholar who agrees with the approaches to *malakoi* and *arsenokoitai* adopted by the versions quoted above is Robert Gagnon (2001: 303 n. 83). His own translations of these Greek terms are 'effeminate males who play the sexual role of females' (*malakoi*) and 'males who take other males to bed' (*arsenokoitai*). Gagnon's renderings also accord with other English versions of the Bible such as the NAB, NIV, NJB, NLT, and NRSV (2001: 303-4). For his interpretation of *malakoi*, Gagnon seeks support in the first-century works of Philo of Alexandria, a Jewish philosopher writing in Greek for a Gentile (non-Jewish) audience. In Gagnon's view, Philo discusses 'homosexual behaviour', particularly that of 'passive homosexual partners who cultivate feminine features' (2001: 308). His fierce disapproval of effeminacy in males makes Philo declare that such individuals deserve to be killed by law-abiding citizens (2001: 309). According to Gagnon, Paul fully shares Philo's strong dislike of effeminate men. While Paul's term *malakoi* refers to people, two related abstract nouns in Philo's works are *malakia* and *malakotēs* (both meaning 'softness'). Gagnon argues that these words describe 'the whole feminizing process of receptive male partners in homosexual intercourse', implying that Paul's *malakoi* reflects the same thing (p. 309). Thus, Gagnon places Philo, a rich Jewish philosopher, and Paul, a poor Christian missionary, within the same powerful misogynous current that was noticeable in Hellenistic philosophy since the days of Plato (424–347 BCE), particularly in his works *Timaeus* and *Laws*.[301]

Unlike Gagnon, Gareth Moore (2003: 106) reminds his readers that, when it comes to *malakoi* and *arsenokoitai*, 'there is no commonly accepted translation of either'. He goes on to wonder why so many scholars regard *malakoi* and *arsenokoitai* as a pair given that the vice list in 1 Corinthians in which they are included does not seem to be constructed out of pairs (p. 108). The overall emphasis of the context is on injustice, i.e. doing wrong to another. In other words, what unites the ten terms included in Paul's list is their reference to people acting unjustly (p. 111). Moore is highly sceptical about the popular tendency to attach homoerotic overtones to *malakoi* and *arsenokoitai*. He points out that lesbian, gay, and bisexual Christians feel violence is done to them as they are being lumped together with idolaters, drunkards, adulterers, and murderers (pp. 111–12).

As for the plural noun *malakoi*, Daniel Helminiak (2000: 108) points out that this is a very common Greek word (singular *malakos*). In certain contexts, it may mean 'effeminate', but without being linked to people's sexuality. Thus, there is no reason to assume that *malakoi* alludes specifically to homosexual men. In Helminiak's view, a far more accurate translation of *malakos* is 'self-indulgent' (p. 109). For his part, Thomas Hanks (2000: 107) posits that *malakoi* and *arsenokoitai* should be interpreted in connection with the primary Pauline

---

[301] www.philosophicalmisadventures.com/?p=30 (2012). It is worth mentioning that, in his *Metaphysics* and *Economics*, Aristotle (384–322 BCE) depicted women negatively as the weaker sex while presenting maleness in positive terms. A substantial number of church fathers and medieval theologians adhered to this approach which, in some quarters, persists until the present day (Cranny-Francis, Waring, Stavropoulos & Kirkby 2003: 2).

concern in 1 Corinthians 5–7, namely, *adikia*, which is to be understood as 'oppression and injustice'. In regard to the literal meaning of *malakos*, Hanks points out it is 'soft'. While it is true that occasionally the word was used in the literature of Greco-Roman antiquity as a metaphor for effeminate men, Hanks clarifies (p. 108),

> In ancient times an 'effeminate' male could be someone who spent excessive time in the company of women and in frequent sexual relations with them.

In other words, the assumed effeminacy inherent in *malakos* has nothing to do with homoeroticism (cf. Goss 2002: 199). In fact, in some classical sources the opposite may be the case inasmuch as male–male love was regarded as more 'manly' than male–female intimacy. Men who fell in love with women demonstrated *malakia*, 'softness' (Martin 2006: 46). Another intriguing detail worth noting is that, for centuries of church history, *malakoi* has been interpreted, quite erroneously, as a condemnation of masturbation (Hanks 2000: 108). Focusing on the issue of slavery in the Roman Empire, J. Albert Harrill (2006: 131–2) interprets the 'softness' suggested by *malakoi* as a specific reference to 'youthful effeminacy, prized by slave dealers', sometimes achieved by artificial means.

Dale Martin (2006: 43–7) finds *malakos* easy to define due to an abundance of evidence from ancient sources. The word may refer to the softness of expensive clothing, the delicacy of gourmet food and the gentleness of a light breeze. In the human sphere, *malakos* alludes to laziness, physical weakness, decadence, or cowardice, all of which are associated with feminine behaviour. This connection was taken for granted because women were regarded as fearful, weak and tender with soft bodies and flaccid, porous flesh.

In terms of the rank misogyny that characterized ancient philosophy, several early English versions of the Bible were correct to translate *malakoi* as 'effeminate' (pp. 44, 47). Whereas a man who allowed himself to be penetrated—by either a man or a woman—could, in theory, be labelled a *malakos*, to limit the meaning of the word to this specific situation is, in Martin's words, 'simply wrong'. In fact, a perfectly good Greek word existed that seems to have had that narrower, sexual meaning: *kinaidos* (p. 44; cf. Brooten 1996: 6, 24).

According to the comprehensive Greek dictionary of Liddell and Scott (L&S, 1940), *kinaidos* translates as 'catamite', an archaic English term coined in the late sixteenth century.[302] Taken from Latin, 'catamite' is defined by the *OD* as 'a boy kept for homosexual practices'. The term may have been associated with Ganymede, a handsome young prince abducted by Zeus from the city of Troy and carried to the Olympus, where he became cupbearer of the gods.[303] At any rate, *kinaidos* is a frequent term in classical Greek literature, with 43 occurrences recorded by L&S. It is used by Plato, Aeschines, Strabo, Epictetus, Plutarch, and other well-known writers. In no text is *malakos* equated with *kinaidos* (Martin 2006: 204 n. 22). Instead, the 872 literary references in L&S to *malakos* address the entire complex of softness, weakness, and femininity outlined above. Frequently men condemned other men by calling them *malakoi* in the sense of 'softies' or 'sissies'.

Early Translations of *Malakoi*

One of the earliest translations of 1 Corinthians is provided by the Vulgate. For his rendering of *malakoi*, the Latin term

---

[302] L & S consulted at www.perseus.tufts.edu/hopper/ (2012).
[303] www.windows2universe.org/mythology/ganymede.html (2012).

chosen by Jerome was *molles*, the plural form of *mollis*. According to the dictionaries, the literal meaning of this adjective is 'soft', 'pliant', 'flexible' or 'supple'. All entries adequately match the Greek *malakos*. In other words, Jerome's noun *molles* may be rendered as 'soft ones'. Early English versions of the Bible were based on the Vulgate, including that of John Wycliffe (Long 2001: 85–6). In his version of the ST from 1388, Wycliffe renders *molles* in 1 Corinthians 6.9 as 'lechouris ayen kynde'. In the modernized spelling of Terence P. Noble's edition, this expression is transliterated to 'lechers against kind'.[304]

At first sight, the presence of 'lechers', i.e. 'lecherous men', is surprising since the word has no obvious connection with the 'soft ones' implied by Jerome's *molles*. Hence, a further search for additional meanings attached to the adjective *mollis* is required. Some Latin dictionaries suggest 'mild', 'easy', 'tender', and 'gentle'.[305] Applied to persons, further suggestions are 'effeminate', 'womanish', 'unmanly', 'feeble', and 'weak', not to mention 'cowardly' and 'untrustworthy'.[306] While most of these terms may be said to belong to the realm of undesirable character traits, at least from the point of view of Roman culture, there still is quite a leap to Wycliffe's 'lechers'. It is intriguing that Wycliffe and his team of translators should adopt a sexual approach to *molles*. Exactly when this hermeneutical shift took place is far from clear, but it may have occurred at some point during the early Middle Ages.

Curiously, late medieval English translations do not follow the 'lechers' example set by Wycliffe. Rather, due to the

---

[304] www.ibiblio.org/tnoble/download/Wycliffe%20NT%20individual%20books/11-1-Corinthians.pdf (2012).
[305] www.archives.nd.edu/cgi-bin/lookup.pl?stem=m&ending=s (2012).
[306] latinlexicon.org/definition.php?p1=1010127; www.latin-dictionary.net/q/latin/mollis.html (2012).

availability of the recently published Greek ST, they bypass the Latin to engage with the Greek (Long 2001: 139–40). Returning to Paul's original text in 1 Corinthians 6.9, they interpret *malakoi* by terms that denote general weakness of character or degeneracy. Thus, William Tyndale's version of 1526 renders *malakoi* as 'weaklings', which is later adopted by Miles Coverdale (1535) and the Bishops' Bible (1568). However, the Geneva Bible, published in 1560, surprisingly presents *malakoi* as 'wantons'. According to the *OD*, 'wanton' taken as an adjective connotes 'deliberate' (of a cruel or violent action) or, applied in archaic English to a woman, 'sexually immodest or promiscuous'. Used as a noun, 'wanton' signifies 'a sexually immodest or promiscuous woman'. In one sense, the Geneva Bible's shift away from the 'weaklings' of its predecessors represents a return to the sexual realm of the 'lechers' suggested by Wycliffe. However, if 'wantons' normally alludes to women, as the *OD* indicates, this definition does not fit Paul's *malakoi*, which refers to a group of male persons. Therefore, either the *OD* definition of 'wanton' is incomplete or the Geneva translators have made a serious mistake by focusing on the wrong gender. The puzzle is partly solved by the translators themselves in a footnote where they explain 'wanton' as 'immoral or unchaste, lewd', presumably without special reference to the female sex.

Toward the end of the sixteenth century, the preferred translation of *malakoi* changed to 'effeminate', as manifested by the Roman Catholic Douay-Rheims version (1582) and the King James Version (1611). Curiously, the Douay-Rheims translators used the Latin text of the Vulgate whereas the KJV team based their work on the original Greek. For their English text, the KJV translators were expected to follow the Bishops' Bible (Long 2001: 193). In actual fact, however, the case of 1 Corinthians 6.9 makes it clear that they consulted a number of different available versions, including Douay-Rheims. The idea of rendering *malakoi* as 'the effeminate' was to remain popular for several centuries as evidenced by the American Standard Version of 1901 (cf. Martin 2006: 44).

Translating *Malakoi* Today

> Generations of translators and interpreters have inevitably and sometimes clumsily obscured Paul's meaning . . . uncritically accepted ways of translating Paul mislead today's reader and introduce a mystifying complexity into scholarship on Paul (Ashworth 2006, Preface).

Table 70 presents the English renderings of two occurrences of *malakoi* in the Second Testament as offered by twelve modern versions of the Bible.[307] For comparative purposes, one occurrence is the singular *malakos* in Matthew 11 (first column), which refers to clothing. The second column reflects the plural *malakoi* in 1 Corinthians 6.

Table 70
Translating *malakos* and *malakoi*

Version	*Malakos* Matt. 11.8	*Malakoi* 1 Cor. 6.9
Literal	Soft	Soft ones
CCB	fine (clothes)	[homosexuals of any kind]
HCSB	soft (clothes)	[anyone practising homosexuality]* *Lit *passive homosexual partners*
JM	soft (raiment)	catamites

---

[307] In this chapter, the Lexham English Bible (LEB) takes the place of JPS, which is limited to the Hebrew Bible.

LEB	soft (clothing)	passive homosexual partners
NCV	fine (clothes)	those who are male prostitutes
NIV	fine (clothes)	male prostitutes
NJB	fine (clothes)	the self-indulgent
NKJV	soft (garments)	homosexuals*
		*That is, catamites
NLT	expensive (clothes)	male prostitutes
NRSV	soft (robes)	male prostitutes
NWT	soft (garments)	men kept for unnatural purposes
REB	fine (clothes)	[sexual pervert]

A vertical reading of table 70 shows that most versions agree to render *malakos* as 'soft' or 'fine' in respect of the garments mentioned by Jesus in Matthew 11. Only the NLT suggests 'expensive', which may be relevant since fine clothing is likely to cost more than that which is plain or coarsely woven. The translations of *malakos* offer near-unanimity and are supported by current dictionaries, including the FFM (2005: 252) and Danker (2009: 221), which propose 'soft' and 'delicate'. By contrast, the plural noun *malakoi* in 1 Corinthians 6.9 gives rise to a variety of approaches. A vertical reading of the second column of table 70 reveals the most popular option, adopted by four versions, to be 'male prostitutes' (NCV, NIV, NLT, NRSV). All other versions choose their own terms: 'catamites' (JM), 'passive homosexual partners' (LEB), 'homosexuals' (NKJV), 'men kept for unnatural purposes' (NWT), and 'the self-indulgent' (NJB). In a footnote, the NKJV narrows the meaning of 'homosexuals' to 'catamites'.

A special group in table 70 is made up by three versions whose renderings of *malakoi* are placed in square brackets because of their unusual nature. These versions do not offer a separate translation of *malakoi* but conflate it with *arsenokoitai*.

Joining the two together, as if they were a single category, they come up with 'homosexuals of any kind' (CCB), 'anyone practising homosexuality' (HCSB) and 'sexual pervert' (REB). However, the HCSB acknowledges in a footnote the presence in the Greek text of two different terms, offering for *malakoi* the more specific 'passive homosexual partners', inexplicably characterizing this rendering as 'literal'. I will return to the problems posed by these versions after discussing *arsenokoitai*.

According to Alan Cadwallader (2012: 50), the primary meaning of *malakos* is 'impressionable, that is, capable of giving way under touch'. However, the wide range of options suggested for *malakoi* in table 70 is striking. Unlike the situation of the singular *malakos* in the ST, no English version has taken a strictly literal approach to the plural. Another missed option, pointed out as feasible by Dale Martin (2006: 44-7), would be 'the effeminate', if 'effeminacy' is defined more broadly than it is today. Only the NJB's 'the self-indulgent', without being entirely literal, comes relatively close to the basic meaning of the word. The 'catamite' suggested by JM and in a footnote by the NKJV would have been appropriate had Paul been referring to *kinaidos*, but he is not. Sexual connotations are unlikely to be implied by Paul's *malakoi*, and therefore *kinaidos* and *malakos* are not interchangeable.

The popular option 'male prostitutes', suggested by four versions in table 70 (NCV, NIV, NLT, NRSV), invites a critical comment. Before listing *malakoi* and *arsenokoitai* in 1 Corinthians 6.9, Paul introduces other plural nouns, including the significant *pornoi*. The singular of *pornoi* is *pornos*. The L&S Greek dictionary offers several different renderings of *pornos*: 'catamite', 'sodomite', and 'idolater'. However, L&S specifies that in the ST, which is Paul's context, *pornos* usually translates as 'fornicator'. This rendering is supported by Danker (2009: 294). Yet some older dictionaries and sources suggest that *pornos* often means 'male prostitute' (Berg 1885: 664). Even if the latter rendering is accepted for *pornos* and *pornoi*, it still makes little sense to ascribe the same meaning to *malakos* and *malakoi*. In the vice catalogue of 1 Corinthians 6.9, *pornoi* heads the list and is followed by idolaters, adulterers, and *malakoi*, in that order. Therefore, it is to be assumed that each term covers a specific semantic field.

The NWT's highly euphemistic paraphrase 'men kept for unnatural purposes' misrepresents the basic meaning of *malakoi*. In Paul's Greek prose, 'unnatural' would be *para physin* (cf. Rom. 1.26; 11.24), which is not part of 1 Corinthians 6.9. Furthermore, the modern word 'homosexual' used by several versions does not belong in table 70 for two reasons: (a) its insertion into a text from antiquity is anachronistic; and (b) 'homosexual' encompasses lesbian women, who are definitely not alluded to in this verse (Moore 2003: 108). All of these versions have placed *malakoi* under considerable semantic strain as the word is supposed to cover meanings stretching all the way from a moral category ('the self-indulgent') via interpersonal relationships ('passive homosexual partners') to the social sphere ('male prostitutes').

From Softness to Male Prostitution

A horizontal reading of table 70 exposes the astonishingly wide gap between the two columns. The only version that achieves a moderate degree of coherence is the NJB with 'fine' for *malakos* and 'the self-indulgent' for *malakoi* (cf. Helminiak 2000: 109). However, no fewer than eleven versions, i.e. 92 per cent, are glaringly inconsistent. Some move from 'expensive', 'fine', and 'soft' to 'male prostitutes' while the NWT's two renderings stretch all the way from 'soft' to 'men kept for unnatural purposes'.

Historically speaking, table 70 reveals another curious shift for renderings of *malakoi*. The words 'weaklings' and 'the effeminate' used in past centuries are universally rejected and replaced by a term that denotes a particular sexual action or orientation. Apart from 'the self-indulgent' (NJB), every rendering in the second column is sexually charged. As Dale Martin (2006: 44) argues, no real historical or philological evidence has been marshalled to support these shifts in translation. In fact, all the historical and philological evidence is on the side of some of the earlier versions (Tyndale, Douay-Rheims and KJV). The popular 'homosexuality' rendering of *malakoi* during the last fifty years has resulted, not from the findings of historical scholarship, but from shifts in sexual ideology. The only historical precedents, both of which are difficult to substantiate in the Greek text, are the 'lechers' and 'wantons' introduced by Wycliffe and the Geneva Bible, respectively.

The Greek dictionary of F. W. Danker (2009) is consulted by many translators of the ST.[308] One of Danker's options for *malakos* regarded as a noun is 'one who is passive in a same-sex relationship' (p. 221). Such an authoritative reference explains why analogous notions appear in current English versions of the Bible. Similarly, the FFM (2005: 252)

---

[308] The 2009 concise edition summarizes Danker's work, *A Greek-English Lexicon of the New Testament and Other Early Christian Literature. Third Edition*, University of Chicago Press, 2000. The Lexicon was based on previous English editions by William F. Arndt and F. Wilbur Gingerich and the 1979 edition by F. W. Gingerich and F. W. Danker, in addition to Walter Bauer's *Griechisch-deutsches Wörterbuch zu den Schriften des Neuen Testaments und der übrigen urchristlichen Literatur*, sixth edition 1988 by K. Aland and B. Aland, with V. Reichmann. According to Kim Haines-Eitzen (2001), the BDAG (Bauer, Danker, Arndt, Gingerich) is the major lexical tool for New Testament Greek studies.

indicates that in a figurative sense *malakos* may be taken to depict men who are 'effeminate' or 'unmanly'. Even more specifically, the FFM refers directly to 1 Corinthians 6.9 arguing that Paul's term *malakos/malakoi* reflects 'a man or boy who submits his body to homosexual lewdness'. According to the FFM, adequate English renderings are 'catamite' and 'homosexual pervert'. In other words, the FFM clearly regards *malakos* as a synonym of *kinaidos*, which is not present in Paul's text. These sources are supported by the four options provided by the grammatical analysis of Zerwick and Grosvenor (1988: 508): 'soft', 'effeminate', 'catamite', 'homosexual'. With these reference tools, it is understandable that today's translators of the Bible reproduce the well-established, anti-homoerotic exegesis with which most Bible readers are familiar. In other words, the Greek dictionaries and Bible commentaries currently in circulation seem to be part of the problem rather than its solution.

In the dictionary of Liddell and Scott (1940), the primary translation of *malakos* is 'soft'. Significantly, and in contrast to the very specific translation 'passive homosexual partners' offered above by the LEB and the HCSB (supported by Danker and the FFM), the many examples of *malakos* listed by L&S in relation to persons do not refer to sexual matters. Renderings based on classical Greek literary usage include 'mild', 'tender', 'delicate', and 'gentle'. Occasionally the term acquires derogatory nuances such as 'feeble', 'morally weak', and 'cowardly'. In the moral sphere discussed by Paul, the latter categories seem to match *malakoi* in 1 Corinthians 6.9.

Male-Liers

For current discussions of homoeroticism in the Bible, the other significant Pauline term in 1 Corinthians 6.9 is the plural *arsenokoitai*, whose singular form is *arsenokoitēs*. Being a compound formed by the noun *arsēn*, 'male', and the participle *koitē*, 'lying', the plural literally translates as 'male-liers', 'those lying with males' or 'liers with males' ('liers' in the sense of 'those who lie down', not to be confused with 'liars', i.e. persons who tell lies). However, the translation effort is complicated by the fact that, in the ST, *koitē* is generally used as a term for 'bed' (Lk. 11.7) and, in the plural, in reference to casual or illicit sexual affairs as in Romans 13.13 (Danker 2009: 204; FFM p. 233). Add to this the fact that *arsenokoitai* is a neologism coined by Paul (Gagnon 2001: 312-13). All these factors should be borne in mind when a realistic translation of this rare term is sought.

Robert Gagnon (2001: 111 n. 178) believes *arsenokoitai* refers to 'men who functioned as the active partner in same-sex intercourse', where *malakoi* denotes the passive partner. He translates *arsenokoitai* as 'males who take other males to bed' (p. 303). Citing early rabbinic sources, Gagnon imagines *arsenokoitēs* to be Paul's equivalent of the Hebrew phrase *mishkav zakhur*, 'the lying of/with a male' (p. 111 n. 178). Furthermore, Gagnon is convinced that *arsenokoitēs* reflects the prohibition in Leviticus 18.22 ('With a male you shall not lie down the lyings of a woman'). This is so because in the Septuagint version of this verse, the Greek noun *arsēn* occurs as well as *koitē* (2001: 315). Thus, Gagnon is confident that Paul used the phrase provided by the LXX to invent the unusual Greek word *arsenokoitēs*, making it mean 'lying with a male'. By extension, Gagnon interprets *arsenokoitēs* as 'a man who lies with a male' or 'a man who goes to bed with a male' (p. 111 n. 178). He summarizes his discussion of the juxtaposition of *malakoi* and *arsenokoitai* in 1 Corinthians 6.9 with these words (p. 316):

> Given such a pairing, our identification of *malakoi* with passive homosexual partners confirms the

supposition that the term *arsenokoitai* refers to the active partners in homosexual intercourse.

His elaborate arguments on *arsenokoitai* show that Gagnon is convinced that Paul, like several other Hellenistic writers (cf. Philo), fully shares his own disapproval of erotic intimacy between same-sex partners (2001: 326–31).

In opposition to Gagnon, Daniel Helminiak (2000) emphasizes a number of factors that raise uncertainty about the actual meaning of *malakoi* and *arsenokoitai* in 1 Corinthians 6.9. Finding it impossible to establish what these words really denote, he rejects as 'dishonest and unfair' any attempt to use them to condemn persons with homoerotic inclinations (p. 107). In particular, the unusual Pauline compound *arsenokoitai* is difficult to explain. While its two elements are *arseno-*, 'male', and *koitē*, 'bed', 'bedroom' or 'lying', the specific meaning is unclear. Helminiak compares *arsenokoitai* with the English term 'lady killer', which to native speakers is an accepted reference to a man who knows how to charm ladies. However, if the term is taken at face value, a non-native learner of English might misunderstand it thinking it means 'lady who kills' or 'killer of ladies' (p. 109).[309] Similarly, *arsenokoitēs* may be interpreted as 'male who lies down' or 'one who lies down with males'. What modern readers do not know is whether or not the term had a specific usage in first-century Greek (p. 112). After discussing various options, Helminiak concludes

---

[309] In private correspondence (2012), Stephen Barton has suggested a comparison of 'bed-male' with 'couch potato', a current English metaphor for a lazy person, which may not be readily understandable a few hundred years from now. Dale Martin (2006: 39) uses another analogy, pointing out that the actual meaning of the English verb 'understand' cannot be explained by dividing it into 'under' and 'stand'. Viewed separately, the literal meaning of both words has nothing to do with the cognitive process of understanding.

that *arsenokoitai* seems to allude to some kind of abusive sex (p. 113), particularly 'exploitative, lewd and wanton sex between men' (p. 115).

In his discussion of *arsenokoitai*, Thomas Hanks (2000: 108) observes that the modern tendency to translate *arsenokoitai* as 'homosexuals' is 'totally mistaken' and even 'ludicrous' (p. 172). He points out that the Greek term has nothing to do with the contemporary concept of sexual orientation and certainly does not refer to lesbian women (who, according to Brooten 1996: 5, would be called *tribas*). For a literal rendering of *arsenokoitai*, Hanks suggests 'bed-males'. In Romans 13.13 it should be noted that Paul's use of the word 'beds' has negative overtones (2000: 172). The most likely interpretation of *arsenokoitai* in 1 Corinthians 6.9 and 1 Timothy 1.10 seems to be, in Hanks' view, 'males who engaged in exploitative, abusive, and oppressive sexual practices, be it with women, other males, or youths' (p. 108).

To understand *arsenokoitai*, J. Albert Harrill (2006) finds it important to pay attention to the term's position in 1 Timothy 1.10 where *arsenokoitai* appears sandwiched between *pornoi* and *andrapodistai*. For *pornoi* Harrill suggests 'fornicators' (p. 131) while offering three inter-related translations of *andrapodistai*, namely, 'slave dealers', 'slave traders' (pp. 119–22) and 'kidnappers' (pp. 122–4). These renderings are supported by several dictionaries and commentaries such as Danker (2009: 30), FFM (p. 53) and Zerwick and Grosvenor (1988: 628). In the Roman Empire, slave dealers had a bad reputation due to their well-organized kidnappings of young, free-born men and women for the purpose of prostitution (Harrill 2006: 121–36).[310] Given this context of sexual immorality coupled with economic exploitation and

---

[310] The book of Deuteronomy (24.7) also has harsh words for kidnappers and slave dealers.

abuse, Harrill argues that *arsenokoitai* should be translated as 'sexual exploiters' (pp. 131, 133).

Having searched Hellenistic literature for clues to the rare noun *arsenokoitai*, Dale Martin (2006: 40-3) takes a similar view. If the word were to be traced to a narrative, the context might provide scholars with useful hints for a viable interpretation. Unfortunately, however, *arsenokoitai* only appears scattered over a few poetic passages, including vice lists and oracles, which severely limits the scope for exegesis. One of the earliest appearances of the word's verbal form *arsenokoitein* occurs in the Sibylline Oracles (Book II). Little is known about the origin of this apocryphal Greek work, and although its date is uncertain, there is little to suggest it is dependent on Paul. The text provides an independent use of *arsenokoitein* in a paragraph listing acts of economic injustice and exploitation, including accepting gifts derived from unjust deeds, betraying confidential information, and oppression of the poor. Readers are exhorted to make provision for those in need, including orphans and widows, and to refuse to commit any kind of injustice. Nothing in the context suggests that a specific sexual act is being referred to. Martin's argument is supported by the fact that a list of sexual sins occurs elsewhere in the Sibylline Oracles, which is where a reference to male–male sex might be expected. The ancient author condemns abortion, exposure of infants, 'defiling the flesh by licentiousness', and 'loosing the girdle of the maid for secret intercourse'.[311] If the prohibition against *arsenokoitein* was used to condemn same-sex intimacy, one would expect the term to occur here, rather than among the terms condemning exploitation (2006: 40-1).

---

[311] For a complete English translation, see www.sacred-texts.com/cla/sib/sib04.htm (2012).

A similar case studied by Dale Martin (2006: 41) exists in the second-century *Acts of John*, where *arsenokoitēs* appears in the middle of a vice list referring to the rich men of Ephesus: 'So also the poisoner, sorcerer, robber, swindler, and *arsenokoitēs*, the thief and all of his band . . .' In summary, the only thing that is certain about Paul's use of the noun *arsenokoitai* is that no previous occurrences in Hellenistic literature have been found, and that none of the post-biblical evidence is conclusive.[312]

Early Translations of *Arsenokoitai*

The literal meaning being 'male-liers' or 'liers with males', i.e. 'those who lie with males', it is interesting to see how early versions of the Bible approached *arsenokoitai*. For his Latin translation of 1 Corinthians 6.9 (positioned as 6.10 in the Vulgate), Jerome suggested *masculorum concubitores*, 'those who lie with men'; a rendering recurring in 1 Timothy 1.10. In John Wycliffe's fourteenth-century version of both passages, the Latin phrase becomes 'they that do lechery with men'. In theory, the pronoun 'they' is comprehensive enough to encompass women. Wycliffe clearly uses stronger language than Jerome in that 'do lechery with' is morally charged where 'lie with' is more factual, indicating male sleeping partners. Working from the Greek, William Tyndale (1526) produces in 1 Corinthians the archaic sounding phrase 'abusers of themselves with mankind'. In 1 Timothy, the wording is equally harsh: 'Them that defile themselves with mankind'. Tyndale's strong language indicates that he shares Wycliffe's moral disapproval of perceived male–male eroticism. Miles Coverdale's Bible (1535) follows Tyndale

---

[312] Given the scarcity and imprecision of the literary material available, the debate about the meaning of *arsenokoitai* is far from over. See Robert Gagnon 2001: 317–36 and Jeramy Townsley at www.bridges-across.org/ba/jt_add3.htm (2012).

verbatim, saying 'abusers of themselves with mankind' and 'they that defile themselves with mankind'.[313] The same is true of the Bishops' Bible (1568). In all these cases, 'them that' and 'abusers' are ambiguous, at least for modern readers, as they may be taken to include women.

However, the Geneva Bible (1560) innovatively introduces *arsenokoitai* as 'buggerers' in both 1 Corinthians 6.9 and 1 Timothy 1.10. A footnote clarifies that this term refers to 'someone who engages in anal copulation (especially a male who engages in anal copulation with another male)'. According to the *OD*, the modern variant 'bugger' is used (1) in reference to 'a person, typically a man, for whom one feels pity or respect'; (2) 'an annoyingly awkward thing'; and (3) in a derogatory sense, 'a person who commits buggery'. The latter term refers to anal intercourse. In the Geneva version, the occurrence of 'buggerers' seems to reveal a certain penchant for popular language, while such is not the true of the Roman Catholic Douay-Rheims version (1582), which offers 'liers with mankind' (1 Cor. 6.9) and 'them who defile themselves with mankind' (1 Tim. 1.10). As is to be expected, the Douay-Rheims translators have followed the Vulgate in 1 Corinthians. However, in 1 Timothy, it is astonishing that they have aligned themselves with William Tyndale, given that the latter was persecuted, arrested, convicted of heresy, and burned at the stake in 1536 (Metzger 2001: 59–60).

For its part, the King James Version (1611) offers 'abusers of themselves with mankind' and 'them that defile themselves with mankind'. This is an obvious example of the extent to which the KJV translators are indebted, not only to the Bishops' Bible, but also to William Tyndale. In fact, despite the enormous difficulties he faced throughout his adult life, the quality of the English Bible produced by Tyndale and

---

[313] Throughout this period, 'mankind' generally refers to the male sex.

his associates became not only vindicated over time but influenced successive generations of translators.[314] Bruce Metzger (2001: 60) comments on Tyndale's work:

> Its simplicity and directness mark the work as a truly great achievement in literature, apart from its epoch-making religious importance. It became, in fact, a foundation for all subsequent efforts of revision, so much so that 80 percent or more of the English Bible down through the Revised Version [1885] has been estimated to be his in those portions of the Bible on which he had worked with such skill and devotion.

Undoubtedly Jerome, Wycliffe, Tyndale, the Geneva Bible, and the KJV, among others, have set powerful precedents for interpretations of Paul's *arsenokoitai* in 1 Corinthians 6.9 and 1 Timothy 1.10. All give the impression that the apostle refers to men practising immoral male–male sex, possibly in the form of anal intercourse.

Translating *Arsenokoitai* Today

Table 71 shows the approaches taken by twelve modern English versions of the Bible to the two occurrences of *arsenokoitai* in the ST.

---

[314] George Steiner (1992: 366) calls Tyndale 'the greatest of English Bible translators', while Robert Alter (1996 p. *xxv*) speaks of 'the great model of Tyndale' and 'there is a great deal to be said for the general procedure of Tyndale and the King James Version' (p. *xxx*).

Table 71
Translating *arsenokoitai*

Version	*Arsenokoitai* 1 Cor. 6.9	*Arsenokoitai* 1 Tim. 1.10
Literal	**Male-Liers**	**Male-Liers**
CCB	[homosexuals of any kind]	those who indulge in homosexuality
HCSB	[anyone practising homosexuality]* *Lit *active homosexual partners*	homosexuals
JM	sodomites	sodomites
LEB	dominant homosexual partners	homosexuals
NCV	men who have sexual relations with other men	people who have sexual relations with people of the same sex
NIV	homosexual offenders	perverts
NJB	sodomites	homosexuals
NKJV	sodomites	sodomites
NLT	those who practise homosexuality	people who practise homosexuality
NRSV	sodomites	sodomites
NWT	men who lie with men	men who lie with males
REB	[sexual pervert]	perverts

A vertical reading of table 71 shows that, in the first column, 'sodomites' is adopted by four versions (JM, NJB, NKJV, NRSV) while all other versions offer varying renderings. Short paraphrases are 'homosexual offenders' (NIV) and 'dominant homosexual partners' (LEB). Longer paraphrases are 'those who practise homosexuality' (NLT), 'men who lie with men' (NWT), and 'men who have sexual relations with other men' (NCV). Three options are placed in square brackets because they do not provide a separate translation of *arsenokoitai* but conflate it with *malakoi*. Having turned the two terms into a single category, they come up with 'homosexuals of any kind' (CCB), 'anyone practising homosexuality' (HCSB), and 'sexual pervert' (REB). In a footnote, the HCSB acknowledges that a literal translation of *arsenokoitai* viewed in isolation would have to be different. Strangely, the HCSB suggests that literalness in this case equals 'active homosexual partners'.

The second column also offers some variety. Three versions have opted for 'sodomites' (JM, NKJV, NRSV) with another three suggesting 'homosexuals' (HCSB, LEB, NJB). Two versions have chosen 'perverts' (NIV, REB). The rest render *arsenokoitai* with paraphrases: 'those who indulge in homosexuality' (CCB), 'people who have sexual relations with people of the same sex' (NCV), 'people who practise homosexuality' (NLT), and 'men who lie with males' (NWT). This overview shows that only one version in table 71 has offered the literal translation 'men who lie with men/males', and the alleged literal option suggested by the HCSB's footnote is a highly subjective paraphrase.

A major problem detected in table 71 is the widespread use of anachronistic language, coupled with the unwarranted tendency to ascribe to the rare Greek term *arsenokoitai* a generic meaning corresponding to the common modern word 'homosexuals'. For this reason, a brief reflection on the language of homoeroticism in ancient Greece is required. Unlike Biblical Hebrew, which has no specific terminology for homoerotic relationships, the classical art, and literature of Greece bristle with erotic episodes and allusions. In antiquity sexual expression often followed well-defined rules. One set of such rules was established by hierarchical social structures, according to which same-sex relationships between males conformed to a pattern known as *paiderastia* ('pederasty', lit. 'love of boys'). Typically, this involved an adult male and a teenage boy. The adult, 'active' man was termed *erastēs* (also *paiderastēs* or *philetor*), which translates as 'lover' or 'admirer'. His younger, 'passive' partner was known as 'beloved', i.e. *erōmenos* (Brooten 1996: 6; McCleary 2004: 211).[315] The other type of relationship would be between two equal partners, of which there is some literary evidence. Also in these cases *erastēs* and *erōmenos* would frequently be used.[316]

Paul's contemporary, Philo of Alexandria, was familiar with Greek sexual terminology. In addition to the terms discussed above, he often calls the passive partner in a pederastic relationship *androgynos*, 'man-woman' (Nissinen 1998: 95). Tables 70 and 71 have revealed that many English-speaking Bible translators consider *malakoi* and *arsenokoitai* to be a pair although they are unlikely to be (Moore 2003: 108; Cadwallader 2012: 51). This leads these versions into the error of taking *malakos* to be a synonym of *erōmenos* (*androgynos*, *kinaidos*) while *arsenokoites* is assumed to be interchangeable with *erastēs* (*philetor*, *paiderastēs*).

Inconsistent Translators

A horizontal reading of table 71 reveals considerable semantic distance between the two columns. Only three versions have achieved absolute consistency with 'sodomites', namely, JM, NKJV, and NRSV. However, their choice is problematic for two reasons: (a) Paul never uses the term 'sodomite' and (b) *arsenokoitai* has nothing to do with the story of Sodom and Gomorrah (Cadwallader 2012: 54). The word 'sodomites' is found in Josephus' first-century

---

[315] See www.studentpulse.com/articles/175/examining-greek-pederastic-relationships (2012).
[316] Considerable fluidity in relationships seems to have been allowed, at least in the city of Athens (Boswell 1980: 28 n. 52). See also Jeramy Townsley's essay at www.bridges-across.org/ba/jt_add3.htm (2012).

work *Jewish Antiquities*. Written in Greek ca. 94 CE, in the sense of 'men of Sodom' (Josephus 1998a: 87–89, 95–99), and in fourth-century patristic literature composed in Latin, it begins to take on a sexual sense.[317] However, 'sodomite' does not connote 'male person practising homoerotic sex' until the Middle Ages (cf. chapter 8). Therefore, in modern translations of a biblical text composed in first-century Greek, the presence of 'sodomite' is misleading.

Furthermore, no other version in table 71 is entirely consistent. In column 1 the NWT translates *arsenokoitai* as 'men who lie with men', which in column 2 becomes 'men who lie with males'. The subtle change from 'men' to 'males' is worth highlighting as 'men' refers to adults only while the spectrum suggested by 'males' includes boys. The NIV goes from 'homosexual offenders' to 'perverts', a curious move for several reasons. First, the Greek text has no word equalling the modern term 'homosexual'. Second, 'offender' corresponds in ST Greek to *parabatēs*, 'transgressor' (Rom. 2.25; cf. Danker 2009: 266) or *anomos*, 'lawless' (1 Tim. 1.9; cf. Danker 2009: 35; FFM p. 57), both of which are absent here. Third, the change from 'homosexual offenders' to 'perverts' is unbalanced since the latter covers a different semantic area. Indeed, the *OD* defines 'pervert' as 'a person whose sexual behaviour is regarded as abnormal and unacceptable'. In other words, a pervert may well be heterosexual. Thus, neither translation of *arsenokoitai* in the NIV is convincing, quite apart from this version's lack of consistency.

In the LEB, the presence of the very specific 'dominant homosexual partners' in column 1 is striking vis-à-vis the generic 'homosexuals' in column 2. In both cases the anachronistic use of 'homosexual' is problematic because this modern word encompasses both sexes, i.e. it includes

---

[317] Examples are found in some letters of Jerome; cf. chapter 8.

women—a group not alluded to by *arsenokoitai*. The operation performed by the NCV between columns 1 and 2 presents further complications. From the paraphrase 'men who have sexual relations with other men', the NCV moves to 'people who have sexual relations with people of the same sex'. In the process, a major reinterpretation is taking place. While the word 'men' in the King James Bible sometimes refers to people of both genders (cf. John 12.32), in modern English this is no longer the case. Therefore, the NCV's move from 'men' to 'people' is a radical one. While the NCV's Paul in 1 Corinthians 6.9 is presented as condemning homoerotic relationships between males, in 1 Timothy 1.10 *all* intimate same-sex relationships are ruled out. Clearly both translations are paraphrases with little justification in the original Greek. The NLT augments the error. In both columns, this version simultaneously addresses both gay men and lesbian women as it speaks of '*those* who practise homosexuality' and '*people* who practise homosexuality' (emphasis added).

The final group to be commented upon here consists of the three versions whose options in column 1 are placed between square brackets. With 'sexual perverts' and 'perverts', the REB is being fairly consistent, although one might wonder why 'sexual' is added in one case and not in the other. The CCB exceeds the limits of standard translation procedures in several ways. First, in column 1 'homosexuals of any kind' is meant to cover both *malakoi* and *arsenokoitai*. Second, the terms 'homosexuals' and 'homosexuality' belong to modernity, not to the Hellenistic era. Third, and despite their absence from the original Greek, women are clearly included in both columns. Similar objections may be raised vis-à-vis the HCSB, which commits the additional error of telling readers that *arsenokoitai* 'literally' means 'active homosexual partners'.

Once again, one of the primary reasons why the translators take very one-sided approaches to *arsenokoitai* in Paul's letter to the Corinthians is to be found, not only in early Bible versions, but also in current dictionaries of ST Greek. For instance, Danker (2009: 55) suggests the renderings 'pederast', 'sodomite' or 'a male who engages as dominant entity in same-sex activity'. The FFM (2005: 76) explains *arsenokoitēs* as 'an adult male who practises sexual intercourse with another adult male or a boy', adding specific terms such as 'homosexual', 'sodomite', and 'pederast'. A similar approach is adopted by Zerwick and Grosvenor (1988: 508) who suggest 'sodomite' and 'homosexual'. In the case of *arsenokoitēs*, L&S (1940) is only partly to blame as it translates the word not with a noun but with the participle 'lying with men', which is presumably (and problematically) applicable to a grammatical subject of either gender.

Paul's Concerns

> Paul and the gospel writers certainly wanted to be assimilated into the Roman world (Goss 2002: 116).

Many scholars have assumed that Paul's terms *malakoi* and *arsenokoitai* form a pair. However, as this chapter argues, the assumption seems to be unfounded and certainly makes little sense in 1 Timothy 1.10 where *malakoi* is absent. Holly Hearon (2006: 613-14) draws attention to the fact that the vice list in 1 Corinthians 6.9-10 is framed by several significant arguments unrelated to homoeroticism. The chapter begins with Paul's harsh words for those Christians who take recourse to lawsuits to settle trivial disputes with fellow believers (6.1-8; cf. Moore 2003: 110). Immediately after listing the vices, Paul exhorts his readers to look after their bodies and minds and goes on to critique men who visit prostitutes (6.12-20). Hearon (2006:

613) takes *malakoi* to mean 'the morally weak' and associates it with decadence (p. 614). The infrequent *arsenokoitai*, which occurs in Hellenistic, extra-biblical literature in conjunction with economic exploitation, may have to do with pimping. If Hearon's point is accepted, the occurrence of *malakoi* in 1 Corinthians 6.9 may be due to the frontier-like situation of early Christianity in the Roman Empire. The ST writers emphasize that the threat of persecution was ever-present.[318] Given this panorama, Paul may have been stressing that in the community of the faithful there was no room for spineless *malakoi*, i.e. 'softies'. To be a Christian required firm commitment and endurance (Eph. 6.10–17).

Alan Cadwallader (2012: 49) stresses that, in the Greco-Roman world, vice lists had rhetorical functions. He emphasizes the rhetorical importance of Paul's vice list taken as a whole 'beyond the forensic meaning of any one of the items' (p. 56), pointing out that the list in 1 Corinthians 6.9 is positioned within a literary unity, namely, 1 Corinthians 5 and 6. In chapter 5 Paul strongly objects to an incestuous relationship that has been reported to him because 'an intense moral taboo governs incest in ancient societies' and, not least, because 'the taboos about incest were directly related to issues of male honour and property holdings' (2012: 57). This is made clear in Paul's agitated response to the Corinthians in 1 Corinthians 5.1–2 where his focus is 'not on the woman-wife but on the dishonour to a father' (p. 57). Cadwallader concludes that, from Paul's perspective, an *arsenokoitēs* is a male acting 'dishonourably and violently in a sexual intrusion upon the body of another' (p. 60).

Other scholars have argued that Paul's *arsenokoitai* was coined by joining together two words from the Septuagint

---

[318] Matt. 5.11–12, 44; Acts 13.50; 14.1–6, 19; 1 Cor. 4.12; 2 Cor. 11.23–26; 12.10.

version of Leviticus 18.22 and 20.13: *arsēn*, 'male', and *koitē*, 'lying' (Gagnon 2001: 315). While there may be some linguistic basis for this hypothesis, the argument is weakened by the opacity of the cited passages (cf. chapter 6). Furthermore, even if *arsenokoitai* could be proved to have been modelled on Leviticus 18.22, this does not explain why Paul should single out this particular injunction and leave out hundreds of others from the books of Exodus, Leviticus, Numbers, and Deuteronomy. Elsewhere Paul is adamant in instructing Christian converts with a Jewish background that keeping the Torah is irrelevant because the laws of Moses are superseded by the liberating mission of Jesus Christ (Cadwallader 2012: 61). This is so much the case that, in his letter to the Galatians, Paul forcefully argues against the tradition of circumcision because this would imply loyalty to the Torah and contradict the central message of the Christian Gospel (Gal. 5.1–6; cf. Bohache 2000: 230).

In addition, the isolated occurrences of *arsenokoitai* in first-century literature make it an unlikely candidate for a crusade against same-sex eroticism. Had this been Paul's concern, he could easily have marshalled more suitable terminology from the Greek classics. His letters are addressed to congregations in the Roman Empire in which some members are slaves, or former slaves. Thomas Hanks (2000: 211–12) has documented that a large number of first-generation Christians mentioned in the ST were unmarried. Whether or not some were also engaged in same-sex relationships, or had been at some point, is unknown, but within the overall framework of Greco-Roman culture this would not be unusual (cf. Matt. 8.5–13; Hanks 2000: 14–15). Moreover, same-sex eroticism was respected at the highest levels of society. Hadrian, the third of the so-called Five Good Emperors of Rome, started his rule in 117 CE, i.e. fifty years after the death of Paul. Hadrian's public relationship with his young male lover Antinous ended abruptly when the latter died accidentally in the year 120 CE. The grieving emperor responded by founding a city, Antinoopolis, and having multiple statues of Antinous erected around the empire. Several Roman poets wrote elegies in Antinous's honour (Vanggaard 1969: 117), and a number of Greek cities arranged commemorative festivals named after him.[319]

Given this cultural backdrop, as well as the vulnerable minority position of the Christian movement in the religious sphere, for Paul to be intent on purging the recently founded communities of Gentile converts with homoerotic inclinations would seem both hazardous and illogical. Paul was not seeking to make his mission more complicated than it already was. Above all, the early Christian missionaries were keen to spread the good news of Jesus Christ, whose message does not include condemnation of intimate same-sex relationships. Paul even takes pride in his Roman citizenship (Acts 16.37; 22.25–28), which on one occasion motivates him to protest against an unfair trial by appealing to the emperor (25.10–12). It is often forgotten that Christian aversion to homoeroticism does not become mainstream until after Christianity is awarded official status in the Roman Empire in the year 380.

The book of Acts, in whose second half Paul plays a prominent role, describes the heated debates that took place in the early Christian community following the death and resurrection of Jesus. A major issue was who could, or should, receive the Gospel message. With the apostles preaching in numerous languages, Acts 2 bears witness to the discovery of the universality of Christianity. This point is reinforced in Acts 10, where Peter is astonished to learn that

---

[319] www.britishmuseum.org/explore/themes/leaders_and_rulers/hadrian/ (2012).

Gentiles are of equal worth to God vis-à-vis believers with a Jewish background, and that the purity laws of Leviticus no longer apply. The assembly held in Jerusalem, where Paul is present (Acts 15), adopts a resolution saying that Christians should abstain from irresponsible sexual activity, from all things associated with idolatry (including sacrificial meals) and from eating food made from strangled animals and blood (15.20, 29). Implicitly, the resolution backs Paul's firm position on the undesirability of circumcision (Rom. 2.25–29; Gal. 5.2–6).

The Greek term *porneia*, 'unchastity' or 'irresponsible sex', is frequently used in the ST, including the letters of Paul.[320] Significantly, the concept is mentioned in Acts 15.29, which connects the passage with 1 Corinthians and 1 Timothy. In both instances, the vice list includes the noun *pornoi*, 'the unchaste' or 'sexually irresponsible'. By order of appearance, the sequences are as follows for (a) 1 Corinthians 6.9 and (b) 1 Timothy 1.10 (my translation):

> (a) *pornoi, eidōlolatrai, moichoi, malakoi, arsenokoitai, kleptai, pleonektai* . . .
> the unchaste, idolaters, adulterers, softies, male-liers, thieves, swindlers . . .
>
> (b) *pornois, arsenokoitais, andrapodistais, pseustais, epiorkois* . . .
> the sexually irresponsible, male-liers, kidnappers, liars, perjurers . . .

In both passages *arsenokoitai* precedes Greek nouns relating to the sphere of economic and social immorality. While an unambiguous English translation of the term eludes modern

---

[320] Matt. 5.32; 19.9; Mk. 7.21; 1 Cor. 5.1; 6.13; 7.2; 2 Cor. 12.21; Gal. 5.19; Eph. 5.3; etc.

scholars, the proximity of *arsenokoitai* to *kleptai*, 'thieves', and *andrapodistai*, 'kidnappers' or 'slave-dealers', respectively, appears to confirm the point made by J. Albert Harrill (2006: 131, 133) that sexual and/or economic exploitation may be in focus. In any case, enough elements in the ST draw attention to this aspect, which should be borne in mind whenever Paul's use of the rare term *arsenokoitai* is discussed.

Conclusion

The apostle Paul is often portrayed as misogynous and anti-gay. However, this chapter has demonstrated that certain parts of his Greek letters, which purportedly deal with homoeroticism, are of little relevance for contemporary debates. The common practice of lumping together the two terms *malakoi* and *arsenokoitai* in 1 Corinthians 6.9 has no precedent in Hellenistic literature. While the meaning of *malakoi* is fairly easy to establish due to frequent occurrences in ancient writings, the exegesis of *arsenokoitai* (also found in 1 Tim. 1.10) is difficult because scholars have located extremely few cases of this word in Hellenistic literature. The word is unlikely to allude to men involved in homoerotic relationships in general given that the usual Greek terms for two male lovers are *erastēs* and *erōmenos*, among others. Instead, a more credible alternative is to view *arsenokoitai* as a specific reference to men who practise abusive sex or commit economic exploitation, including theft and kidnapping young people of either sex into sexual slavery.

The twelve English versions of the Bible examined in this chapter frequently misinterpret Paul's Greek original and mistranslate key terms accordingly. Some are capable of transforming the ancient nouns *malakoi* and *arsenokoitai* into 'people who practise homosexuality', which is anachronistic. The modern concept of homosexuality is alien to a text composed two thousand years ago. In a number of instances, the procedures utilized by English Bible translators are clearly inadequate in terms of literary analysis and excessively influenced by current ideological concerns. They seem to rely heavily on earlier translations of the Bible, including the Latin Vulgate, and their choices are frequently supported by important dictionaries of Second Testament Greek, including Danker (2000, 2009) and the FFM (2005), but sometimes contradicted by comprehensive dictionaries of ancient Greek such as Liddell and Scott (1940). This chapter has provided yet another example of how, in the field of Bible translation, a long, anti-homoerotic church tradition often overrides linguistic and literary criteria.

14

BEYOND NATURE

There is therefore now no condemnation for those who are in Christ Jesus.

—Romans 8.1 (NRSV)

Introduction

In relation to current Christian debates on homoeroticism in the Bible, perhaps the most important text of all is found in chapter 1 of Paul's letter to the Romans. Of the seven Second Testament letters undoubtedly written by Paul himself, Romans (58 CE) is thought to be the last. It has had a greater impact on the evolution of Christian theology than any other biblical book, having powerfully influenced, among others, Augustine of Hippo, Martin Luther, John Wesley, and Karl Barth. Located in the ST immediately after the book of Acts, this particular letter has been the focus of a vast amount of scholarly study, particularly since the Reformation (Hanks 2000: 81).

The passage Romans 1.26–27 is of special interest for the subject homoeroticism. According to Eugene Peterson's paraphrased version known as *The Message* (1993), the text reads as follows:

> Refusing to know God, they soon didn't know how to be human either—women didn't know how

to be women, men didn't know how to be men. Sexually confused, they abused and defiled one another, women with women, men with men—all lust, no love. And then they paid for it, oh, how they paid for it—emptied of God and love, godless and loveless wretches.

For today's readers this text is readily understandable. Although the accuracy of terms such as 'sexually confused', 'abused and defiled', 'godless', 'loveless', and 'wretches' is more than debatable, the overall hermeneutics governing this English rendering is widely accepted. Many scholars take this text to be an injunction against same-sex eroticism, a viewpoint also advocated by the *Worldwide English New Testament* (1969):

> That is why God left them to do the wrong things they wanted to do. Their women left the right way for women and did things that are wrong for women to do. Their men also left the right way with women. They wanted to have sex with one another. They did wrong things with other men. Their own bodies were punished because of the wrong things they did.

While these two renderings of Paul's text may come across as straightforward, their apparent simplicity and transparency are deceptive. As this chapter is about to demonstrate, the literary context in which these verses are placed is among the most complex in the entire Bible. Below some of Paul's Greek vocabulary is examined along with the approaches adopted by a number of biblical commentators and translators.

Interpreting Romans 1

Calum Carmichael (2010: 173) speaks of 'Paul's condemnation of lesbian and homosexual behaviour' in Romans 1.26–27. Taking this point a step further, Robert Gagnon (2001: 229) declares: 'with good reason, Romans 1.24–27 is commonly seen as the central text for the issue of homosexual conduct on which Christians must base their moral doctrine'. He calls Paul's reflections 'the most substantial and explicit discussion of the issue in the Bible'. In Gagnon's interpretation, Romans 1 makes a statement 'not only about same-sex intercourse among men but also about lesbianism' (p. 229). Gagnon repeatedly argues that Paul clearly rejects 'homosexual practice' (p. 230 ff.), including in those relationships 'where mutual choice and gratification on the part of both partners was involved' (p. 124). Thus, in Paul's writings, 'same-sex intercourse comes under the heading of "depraved sexuality" that is to be "laid aside" along with other vices' (p. 244). In Gagnon's view, all variants of same-sex eroticism function in Paul's universe as 'a particularly poignant example of human enslavement to passions and of God's just judgment' (p. 254). Hence, it would be 'erroneous' to posit that contemporary Christians should cease judging homosexual Christians (p. 243).

Thomas Hanks (2000: 81) takes a different view of Romans 1. He points out that the widespread tendency among today's Christian commentators to present the letter as a condemnation of same-sex relationships has fateful historical precedents. In the thirteenth century, Thomas Aquinas misinterpreted Romans 1 by emphasizing Paul's focus on 'unnatural acts' in 1.26–27. Thus, Aquinas provided the principal biblical justification for the massive Nazi persecution of people with homoerotic inclinations in the 1930s and early 1940s (Hanks 2000: 81). In fact, the Nazis started to round up gay people soon after assuming power in 1933 (p. 89). Furthermore, Hanks finds that Romans 1, the most controversial chapter of the entire letter, is very often misunderstood. He highly recommends reading the letter 'in reverse', i.e. starting at chapter 16 and finishing at chapter 1. In this manner, Paul's theological perspective and concerns become much clearer (p. 94). For instance, by the end of Romans (15.7-13) Paul calls for an inclusive, tolerant Christian community (Hanks 2000: 93). Throughout the letter, Paul is concerned with the situation of the oppressed and poor in the Roman Empire (p. 83). He emphasizes God's justice as liberating justice (p. 84).

Unlike Gagnon, Hanks finds no allusion to lesbian relationships in Romans 1.26, where Paul speaks of females. Instead, Hanks takes this passage as a reference to Gentile women who offered themselves to men for anal sex (2000: 90). This is certainly how the text was interpreted during the first four centuries of the Christian church, with literary examples in the writings of Clement of Alexandria (ca. 150-ca. 215 CE) and Augustine of Hippo (354-430 CE). Hanks goes on to explain that 'not until John Chrysostom (ca. 400 CE) does anyone (mis)interpret Romans 1.26 as referring to relations between two women' (2000: 90). Thus, it is logical to conclude that no text in the Hebrew Bible and the ST contains any prohibition of physical intimacy between women (p. 90). As for the references to male–male sex in Romans 1.27, Hanks is inclined to think that Paul is indebted to Leviticus 18.22 and 20.13. Having spoken in Romans 1.26 of females who offer themselves to males for anal sex, Paul turns to males in Romans 1.27, where he, in Hanks's view, simply extends what is usually thought to be the Levitical prohibition of male–male anal sex (2000: 91). At the same time, Hanks cautions that 'Paul does not aim any cannons at persons with a homosexual orientation.' This is so because 'sexual practices that do no harm to one's neighbour are not condemned in the Bible, including Romans' (p. 94).

Elsewhere (2006: 585) Hanks posits that many analyses adduced in recent years are superficial because they often fail to take into account the wider context of Romans 1, which is the entire letter.

For his part, Gareth Moore (2003 : 86) argues that Paul paints 'a very unflattering picture of Gentile society'. He adds that, to the untrained eye, in Romans 1.26–27 Paul seems to condemn homosexual practice between both women and men (p. 87). However, it is legitimate to suppose that the women in 1.26 commit their 'unnatural' acts with men, not with women (p. 98). In addition, it is intriguing to note that the apostle does not use the typical language associated with sin. Such language only occurs towards the end of the chapter. In other words, Moore argues that Paul does not present same-sex practices (between males) as 'sinful', which is a theological concept. Instead, he calls them 'shameful and dishonourable', which places them in the social realm (p. 90). Thus, in Paul's world the sinful and the shameful remain different concepts (p. 91). Moore concludes this part of his reflection by saying: 'There is no reason at all on biblical grounds for inferring that Paul's description of same-sex practices as shameful implies that they are also sinful' (p. 92). When it comes to Paul's use of the word 'passion' (Greek *pathē*), to be subject to passions is always dishonourable (p. 93). The modern debate among Christians about the admissibility of intimate same-sex relationships between consenting adults is incongruous with Hellenistic antiquity. Moore reminds readers that pederasty was a prominent part of sexual expression (p. 94).

According to Daniel Helminiak (2000: 75), Romans 1 has been misunderstood. In Paul's universe, same-sex intimacy is subject to social disapproval without being ethically wrong (p. 77). The central word in this passage is clearly *physis*, 'nature'. For Paul, the nature of something was its particular character or kind. Some people are Jews 'by nature' (Gal. 2.15) while Gentiles in Romans 2.27 are described as 'uncircumcised by nature' (2000: 78). In Paul's view, Gentiles are capable of following their conscience and doing 'by nature' what is right, an expression translated by Helminiak as 'instinctively'. In 1 Corinthians 11.14, Paul asks whether it is not 'nature' itself that teaches men to avoid wearing long hair (2000: 78). The latter example shows that, in Paul's vocabulary, the term *physis* often refers to culture and custom. Therefore, something is 'natural' when it is as people expect it to be. To act unnaturally, by analogy, is to do something surprising or out of character. The term *para physin*, 'against nature', may often be rendered as 'unexpectedly' or 'in an unusual way' (p. 79). Helminiak points out that, in Romans 11.24, even God acts *para physin* through Christ by 'unnaturally' grafting the wild branch of the Gentiles into the cultivated olive tree that is the Jews. God is certainly not bound by social or cultural strictures. Therefore, 'unnatural' here means 'atypical' (2000: 82). With respect to sexual activity, *para physin*, 'unnatural', was used in Stoic philosophy to denote non-procreative sex. Similarly, sex for procreation was called *kata physin*, 'according to nature' (p. 83). However, Paul was not concerned about procreation. Rather, in Helminiak's view, the issue seems to be purity in the sense suggested by Leviticus 18.22 (p. 93).

Past vs. Present, Part One

The scholarly debate summarized above makes it clear that, to attain a clear understanding of the key message of Romans 1, a number of issues have to be addressed. From a literary perspective, Romans 1 may be divided into three parts: (1) vv. 1–15, introduction; (2) vv. 16–17, a theological statement; and (3) vv. 18–32, a fierce critique of idolatry and idolaters. Paul's complex literary style includes applying different time frames sequentially. He begins by giving a brief outline of God's promises to humanity in which his Greek verbs are held in the past tense (Rom. 1.1-6). For the following section the apostle switches to the present tense to address his readers in Rome directly (1.7-17). The present tense continues in 1.18-20, but this section completely departs from the subject matter presented in the preceding verses by focusing on 'ungodliness and wickedness'. From 1.21, the past tense predominates as Paul retrospectively discusses situations and events affecting pagans or idolaters and their excesses. The chapter finishes in the present tense to lash out at 'foolish, faithless, heartless, ruthless' idolaters who continually practise vices and wickedness (1.30-31). The latter passage leads directly into Paul's challenge to the judgmental reader in Romans 2, where the present tense predominates.

For the verbs employed in the much-debated text of Romans 1.26-27, a temporal aspect called aorist places the action in the past. The key verbs are *paredōken*, 'he handed over', *metēllaxan*, 'they exchanged', and *exekauthēsan*, 'they burned'. Attached to these primary verbs are secondary, dependent clauses formed by means of participles, including *aphentes*, 'abandoning', *katergazomenoi*, 'committing', and *apolambanontes*, 'receiving'. Below I explore the extent to which a similar verbal structure is provided, or not, by early versions of the Bible: the Vulgate (ca. 400 CE) and two English renditions of this Latin text from 1388 and 1582, respectively. Jerome's translation into Latin of Romans 1.26-27 reads as follows (key verbs and participles highlighted):

> Propterea *tradidit* illos Deus in passiones ignominiae; nam feminae eorum *inmutaverunt* naturalem usum in eum usum qui est contra naturam. Similiter autem et masculi *relicto* naturali usu feminae *exarserunt* in desideriis suis in invicem, masculi in

masculos turpitudinem *operantes* et mercedem quam oportuit erroris sui in semet ipsis *recipientes*.

Compared to Paul's three Greek verbs in the past tense, Jerome accurately offers three Latin renditions: *tradidit* ('he gave up'), *inmutaverunt* ('they exchanged'), and *exarserunt* ('they burned'). Like the original, the Vulgate lists three participles: *relicto*, 'having abandoned', *operantes*, 'working', and *recipientes*, 'receiving'. Adapted to modern English spelling, John Wycliffe's version from 1388 of this Vulgate text reads as follows (spelling modernized, emphasis added):

> Therefore God *betook* them into passions of shame. For the women of them *changed* the natural use into that use that is against kind. Also the men *forsook* the natural use of woman, and *burned* in their desires together, and men into men *wrought* filthhood, and *received* into themselves the meed that behooved of their error.

Aside from the archaic nature of his vocabulary, where 'betook' means 'led' and 'meed' equals 'reward' or 'fair share', this passage shows that Wycliffe's English verbs rather faithfully reproduce the Latin. The principal verbs are held in the past tense (betook, changed, burned) while the two participles *operantes* and *recipientes* are converted to English past tense (wrought, received). The Latin *relicto naturali usu feminae*, literally 'having abandoned the natural use of woman', has adequately been transformed into 'the men forsook the natural use of woman', past tense. The translation procedure is transparent throughout.

Based on the same passage in the Vulgate, the Roman Catholic Douay-Rheims version (D-R, 1582) produced the following English text (spelling modernized, emphasis added):

> For this cause God *delivered* them up to shameful affections. For their women *have changed* the natural use into that use which is against nature. And in like manner, the men also, *leaving* the natural use of the women, *have burned* in their lusts one towards another, men with men *working* that which is filthy, and *receiving* in themselves the recompense which was due to their error.

Evidently the verbal aspects conveyed through the use of participles (leaving, working, and receiving) are rendered adequately in the D-R. Compared to the older version by Wycliffe, however, some intriguing changes have occurred in the temporal aspect of the key verbs. The first English verb is 'delivered', past tense, which corresponds to the Latin *tradidit*. Given that Paul is referring to past events, a similar approach to the second and third Latin perfect verbs *inmutaverunt*, 'they changed' and *exarserunt*, 'they burned', would make good sense. However, despite the obvious syntactic and temporal parallelism in the Latin text between *tradidit*, *inmutaverunt*, and *exarserunt*, the D-R translators have applied a different perspective to the latter verbs, removing them from the distant past and bringing them close to the time of writing by saying 'have changed' (the women) and 'have burned' (the men).

Several factors appear to complicate the translation process. For instance, the Latin perfect form *tradidit* may be rendered into English in two ways: (a) 'delivered', past tense; or (b) 'has delivered', perfect tense. Viewed from this angle, it cannot be excluded that Jerome's other Latin verbs in the past tense are to be interpreted as English perfect tense, reinforcing the exegesis of the D-R version vis-à-vis that of Wycliffe. However, the sequence of the key verbs in the D-R is gave-have changed-have burned, which may be presented as past-perfect-perfect. Thus, the D-R is being more inconsistent than Wycliffe and Jerome, oscillating more than they between past and perfect (not to mention the somewhat surprising move from present to past in 'which <u>is</u> against nature' vs. 'which <u>was</u> due to their error'). This temporal fluctuation introduced by the D-R is problematic vis-à-vis the Greek and Latin texts, where the three actions occur simultaneously. The significant change of temporal focus between 'delivered' and 'have changed' causes D-R readers to believe that God delivered some time in the distant past, while people supposedly have changed and burned fairly recently.

Early English versions of the Bible translating straight from the Greek have avoided the problems incurred by the D-R with respect to the verbs. William Tyndale's version from 1526 is reproduced here (spelling modernized, emphasis added):

> For this cause God *gave* them up unto shameful lusts. For even their women *did change* the natural use unto the unnatural. And likewise also the men *left* the natural use of the woman and *brent* in their lusts one on another. And man with man *wrought* filthiness and *received* in themselves the reward of their error as it was according.

In the three primary verbs, Tyndale has preserved the past tense to match the Greek forms while all participles have been converted to past tense (left, wrought, received). The verb 'brent' is an older variant of 'burned'. The influence of Tyndale's English text shows in the virtually identical approaches adopted by subsequent versions, including Miles Coverdale (1535), the Geneva Bible (1560), and the Bishops' Bible (1568). The King James Version (1611), however, signals a more literalist respect for the verbal structure of the Greek text (emphasis added):

> For this cause God *gave* them up unto vile affections: for even their women *did change* the natural use into that which is against nature: And likewise also the men, *leaving* the natural use of the woman, *burned* in their lust one toward another; men with men *working* that which is unseemly, and *receiving* in themselves that recompense of their error which was meet.

Like Paul's original, the KJV lists three primary verbs in the past tense (gave, did change, burned) and three participles (leaving, working, receiving).

Past vs. Present, Part Two

The translations of Romans 1.26–27 offered by twelve modern English versions of the Bible are listed below. All are quoted in extenso to explore how the English translators respond to the verbal syntax of the Greek text, specifically the three key verbs and the three associated participles (emphasis added):

> CCB
> Because of that, God *gave* them up to shameful passions: their women *exchanged* natural sexual relations for unnatural ones. Similarly, the men, *giving up* natural sexual relations with women, *were lustful* of each other, they *did*, men with men, shameful things, *bringing* upon themselves the punishment they deserve for their wickedness.

HCSB
This is why God *delivered* them over to degrading passions. For even their females *exchanged* natural sexual relations* for <u>unnatural</u> ones. The males in the same way also *left* natural relations* with females and *were inflamed* in their lust for one another. Males *committed* shameless acts with males and *received* in their own persons** the appropriate penalty of their error.
* Lit *natural use*. **Or *in themselves*.

JM
That is why God *has given* them up to vile passions; their women *have exchanged* the natural function of sex for what is unnatural, and in the same way the males *have abandoned* the natural use of women and *flamed out* in lust for one another, men *perpetrating* shameless acts with their own sex and *getting* in their own persons the due recompense of their perversity.

LEB
Because of this, God *gave* them over to degrading passions, for their females *exchanged* the natural relations for those contrary to nature, and likewise also the males, *abandoning* the natural relations with the female, *were inflamed* in their desire toward one another, males with males *committing* the shameless deed, and *receiving* in themselves the penalty that was necessary for their error.

NCV
Because people did those things, God *left* them and *let* them do the shameful things they wanted to do. Women *stopped* having natural sex and

started having sex with other women. In the same way, men *stopped having* natural sex and *began wanting* each other. Men *did* shameful things with other men, and in their bodies they *received* the punishment for those wrongs.

NIV
Because of this, God *gave* them over to shameful lusts. Even their women *exchanged* natural sexual relations for unnatural ones. In the same way the men also *abandoned* natural relations with women and *were inflamed* with lust for one another. Men *committed* shameful acts with other men, and *received* in themselves the due penalty for their error.

NJB
That is why God *abandoned* them to degrading passions: why their women *have exchanged* natural intercourse for unnatural practices; and the men, in a similar fashion, too, *giving up* normal relations with women, *are consumed* with passion for each other, men *doing* shameful things with men and *receiving* in themselves due reward for their perversion.

NKJV
For this reason God *gave* them up to vile passions. For even their women *exchanged* the natural use for what is against nature. Likewise also the men, *leaving* the natural use of the woman, *burned* in their lust for one another, men with men *committing* what is shameful, and *receiving* in themselves the penalty of their error which was due.

NLT
That is why God *abandoned* them to their shameful desires. Even the women *turned against* the natural way to have sex and instead indulged in sex with each other. And the men, *instead of having* normal sexual relations with women, *burned* with lust for each other. Men *did* shameful things with other men, and as a result of this sin, they *suffered* within themselves the penalty they deserved.

NRSV
For this reason God *gave* them up to degrading passions. Their women *exchanged* natural intercourse for unnatural, and in the same way also the men, *giving up* natural intercourse with women, *were consumed* with passion for one another. Men *committed* shameless acts with men and *received* in their own persons the due penalty for their error.

NWT
That is why God *gave* them up to disgraceful sexual appetites, for both their females *changed* the natural use of themselves into one contrary to nature; and likewise even the males *left* the natural use of the female and *became violently inflamed* in their lust toward one another, males with males, *working* what is obscene and *receiving* in themselves the full recompense, which was due for their error.

REB
As a result God *has given* them up to shameful passions. Among them women *have exchanged* natural intercourse for unnatural, and men too,

giving up natural relations with women, *burn* with lust for one another; males *behave* indecently with males, and *are paid* in their own persons the fitting wage of such perversion.

Among these versions, two (LEB, NKJV) have remained true to Paul's verbal pattern of three key verbs in the past tense plus three participles. Slightly less literal, but still recognizably in tune with the Greek syntax, two have turned one participle into a verb in the past tense, namely, the CCB ('did') and the NWT ('left'). The NLT does the same to two participles ('did' and 'suffered') as does the NRSV ('committed' and 'received'). Two versions (HCSB, NIV) have converted all three participles to the past tense. One version (JM) has chosen the English perfect for the three key verbs: 'has given', 'have exchanged', 'have . . . flamed out', applying the same form to one participle ('have abandoned') but preserving the participles 'perpetrating' and 'getting'.

The remaining three versions offer major departures from the approaches just described. The NCV begins by splitting its translation of the single Greek verb *paredōken* ('he handed over') in two by saying 'God *left* them and *let* them' (emphasis added). Similarly, this version transforms *metēllaxan* ('they exchanged') into a two-step action in the form of 'women *stopped* having natural sex and *started* having . . .' The NCV resorts to further paraphrase where the participle *aphentes* ('abandoning') becomes 'men *stopped having* natural sex', while the verb *exekauthēsan* ('they burned') is rephrased as '*began wanting* each other'. A curious case of paraphrase is provided by the NJB. While the three participles are all in their expected places, the situation of the key verbs in the NJB is different from other versions. Initially, *paredōken* is adequately rendered as 'abandoned', past tense, to be followed by the English perfect 'have exchanged' reflecting *metēllaxan*. In the third case, however, the NJB has transformed the past tense of the Greek *exekauthēsan*, 'they burned', into English present tense in '*are* consumed with passion' (emphasis added). In other words, the verbal sequence in the NJB is past tense-perfect-present tense. Similarly, the REB treats the Greek key verbs according to a mixed procedure: 'has given', 'have exchanged', and 'burn', i.e. perfect-perfect-present tense. Only one participle, 'giving up', is retained while the other two are converted to present tense: 'behave' and 'are paid'.

Past vs. Present, Part Three

Understanding the temporal aspect of the verbs in Romans 1.26-27 is crucial for evaluating the views on homoeroticism that Paul appears to be expressing. As noted, the three Greek key verbs are all held in the past tense (aorist) indicating distant events. If these verbs are translated accordingly, readers receive correct information: Paul is referring to one or several sources or incidents, with which he assumes his Roman audience to be familiar (see below). Most English versions respect the verbal structure of the Greek text by placing the referred events in the past where they belong: *paredōken*, 'gave them up'; *metēllaxan*, 'exchanged'; *exekauthēsan*, 'burned'; etc.

However, three versions have moved the action away from the past and connected it to the present. First, James Moffatt (JM) has chosen the English perfect for the key verbs rather than the past tense. By saying 'has given', 'have exchanged', 'have . . . flamed out', JM virtually brings the referred actions up to date, suggesting that they have occurred in recent times and are relevant for the lives of contemporary believers. In other words, JM invites readers to ponder what manifestations of homoeroticism they may have observed in their own communities and interpret them in the light of the polemic arguments uttered in Romans 1. JM's perfect tense seems to include a subtle invitation to regard all persons with homoerotic inclinations as pagans or idolaters. For its part, the REB appears to share this view and even to reinforce it. Two key verbs are expressed by means of the English perfect 'has given' and 'have exchanged', which places the actions in the very recent past. However, the REB goes a step further as it unexpectedly lets the third verb 'burn' occur in the present tense. By this move, which is grammatically incorrect, the translators provide a strong hint that the issue discussed or alluded to by Paul is ongoing, i.e. there are people out there today who are consumed with homoerotic passion and behave outrageously.

Equally troubling as the REB is the procedure adopted by the NJB. Where the original Greek throughout has the aorist forms of *paredōken*, *metēllaxan*, and *exekauthēsan*, the NJB has opted for temporal variation beginning with the past tense ('he abandoned'), going on to the perfect ('have exchanged'), and finishing with the present tense ('are consumed with passion'). Here is a sliding time scale moving across a wide spectrum all the way from the distant past via the recent past to the present moment. Given the immediate context, particularly the vitriolic vice list in Romans 1.28–32, the NJB is encouraging readers to make connections: such people are wicked, insolent, and rebellious and deserve to die. Understandably, no other version except the REB has dared to join the NJB for this ideological move. It is puzzling that both have seen fit to render *exekauthēsan*, an aorist form meaning 'they burned', as the present tense 'are consumed' and 'burn'. If the verb were to refer to the present time, the form would not be *exekauthēsan* but rather *ekkaiousi(n)*, 'they burn', a hypothetical variant not found in the Second Testament. Therefore, the present tense offered by both the REB and the NJB in Romans 1.27 betrays disregard for Greek grammar.

In different parts of this book, I have pointed out how some mistranslations in the English versions can be traced directly to commonly used biblical dictionaries, many of which were produced at a time in which homoerotic relationships were illegal and certainly frowned upon as immoral in most countries. However, the apparent ease with which the NJB and the REB have replaced the original text's past tense *exekauthēsan* with the present tense 'they burn' and 'are consumed with passion' has nothing to do with dictionaries. It seems more likely that a hermeneutical bias is at play. This serves as a reminder that English versions, in the words of Mark Jordan (1997: 36), 'tend to become particularly irresponsible when translating terms having to do with same-sex copulation'.

Idolatrous Females

For some time it has been argued that Romans 1.26 is the one biblical text that condemns homoerotic love between women (Brooten 1996: 249, 253; Gagnon 2001: 145, 229). However, such has not always been the case. An early Christian writer named Anastasios dismissed the claim that Romans 1.26 was a reference to lesbianism. In his view, the women mentioned 'offer themselves to men' (Brooten 1996: 337). More specifically, Clement of Alexandria speaks of how the women were 'roommates with indulgence' and practised anal intercourse with men, sexually misusing 'the passage made for excrement' (Alison 2006: 133), a viewpoint shared by Augustine of Hippo (Brooten 1996: 353).

For these reasons, Romans 1.26 merits a detailed discussion. In table 72, I examine what the twelve English versions say about the women mentioned in Romans 1. They are literally described as *thēleiai autōn*, 'the females of them', i.e. 'their females' (emphasis added).

Table 72
Translating 'Their Females'

Version	*Thēleiai autōn*, Rom. 1.26
CCB	*Their women* exchanged natural sexual relations . . .
HCSB	*Their females* exchanged natural sexual relations* . . . [*Lit *natural use.*]
JM	*Their women* have exchanged the natural function of sex . . .
LEB	*Their females* exchanged the natural relations . . .
NCV	*Women* stopped having natural sex . . .
NIV	*Their women* exchanged natural sexual relations . . .
NJB	*Their women* have exchanged natural intercourse . . .
NKJV	*Their women* exchanged the natural use . . .
NLT	*The women* turned against the natural way . . .
NRSV	*Their women* exchanged natural intercourse . . .
NWT	*Their females* changed the natural use of themselves . . .
REB	*Among them women* have exchanged natural intercourse . . .

In this verse, nine versions speak of 'women' vs. three versions mentioning 'females' (HCSB, LEB, NWT). From a literal point of view, the minority group is correct since 'females' is the English equivalent of the Greek term *thēleiai* (derived from the singular adjective *thēlus*, 'female'). The definition of 'female' is wider than 'woman' inasmuch as the concept includes young women and girls who are as yet unmarried. The usual Greek word for 'woman' is *gynē*, which sometimes connotes 'adult woman of the female sex' and, at other times, 'wife'. For instance in 1 Corinthians 7, Paul plays on both senses of *gynē*, using it in 7.1 in the sense of 'woman' ('It is well for a man not to touch a woman') and, in 7.2, letting it mean 'wife' ('each man should have his own wife'). Therefore, the fact that Paul uses *thēlus*, 'female', rather than *gynē* in Romans 1.26 may suggest that he is talking about both married and unmarried women who participated in the pagan ceremonies or orgies referred to in the immediate context. Another issue centres on the possessive marker *autōn*, 'of them', which provides the sense of 'their' females. Nine versions accurately render *autōn* as 'their'. As pointed out by Bernadette Brooten (1996: 240-1), 'their females' is a reference to the wives and daughters of the Gentiles. The presence of *autōn* signals that these women did not act independently or in isolation but belonged to the Gentile males described in 1.27. In other words, the sexual interaction implied by Paul's language in 1.26 was a group activity in which men played a part. Viewed from this perspective, a rendering like the NLT's '*the* women' is less precise than the majority since it erroneously suggests female independence. Similarly, the REB presents an inaccurate picture with 'among them women', as if only certain women behaved in this fashion. The Greek word for 'among' is absent (cf. *par' hymin*, 'among you', Col. 4.16).

The verb *metēllaxan*, 'they exchanged', seems to have caused few problems to the translators. Nine versions offer a straightforward rendering while the NWT has opted for the related 'changed', and the NCV colloquially suggests 'stopped having'. The NLT's non-literal 'turned against' is the only phrase to hint at abruptness, rebelliousness, or force on the part of the unnamed women, for which there is no direct warrant in Paul's wording.

Another important element in the Greek text is *tēn physikēn chrēsin*, 'the natural use'. The technical, almost crude, nature of the word *chrēsis*, 'use', in relation to sex indicates that the apostle refers to a specific physical act, probably vaginal intercourse. Curiously, only four versions adequately reproduce the tone of Paul's language: 'use' (NKJV, NWT), 'function' (JM) and 'way' (NLT). The majority of eight have chosen a non-literal approach: 'sex' (JM, NCV); 'sexual relations' (CCB, HCSB, NIV);'intercourse' (NJB,

NRSV, REB); and 'relations' (LEB). Compared with Paul's mechanical-sounding *chrēsis* these renderings come across as commonplace and euphemistic. They might be adequate if the scenes described by the apostle were person-to-person relationships, but what characterizes Romans 1.26-27 is the impersonal, unusual activity of a group of people engaging in orgies. The recurrence of *chrēsis* in 1.27 emphasizes that conventional vaginal intercourse is replaced by something else, and as noted above, anal penetration is a likely candidate.

In summary, while some commentators have argued that Romans 1.26 condemns same-sex eroticism between women, a rigorous analysis of the text and its early reception history do not confirm this assertion. A growing number of scholars are finding sufficient reasons to conclude that 'there is no reference to lesbianism in Holy Scripture' (Alison 2006: 125).

Natural vs. Unnatural

With respect to the women who acted *para physin*, 'contrary to nature', Bernadette Brooten (1996: 2) explains that, according to ancient gender hierarchies, women should never be active.[321] Similarly, free, adult male citizens ought never to be passive. If anyone transgressed these boundaries, society deemed their behaviour to be *para physin*. Furthermore, the literature of antiquity provides examples of women dressing up as satyrs with large phalluses so that they could be penetrators, thus inverting accustomed gender roles (Alison 2006: 133).

---

[321] For discussions of the meaning of *para physin* in Romans, see Boswell 1980: 110-12; Brooten 1996: 241-54; Nissinen 1998: 105-7; Hanks 2000: 92 and 2006: 587; Martin 2006: 54-60. On the use of *para physin* in Philo and Josephus, contemporaries of Paul, see Brooten 1996: 245, 247-8 and Nissinen 1998: 93-5.

The different semantic connotations of the ancient term *physis* and the modern word 'nature' should be noted. Related to 'physics' and 'physical', it is true that the Greek words *physis* and *physikos* roughly correspond to 'nature' and 'natural', respectively. However, Paul's understanding of the concept of nature exceeds common usage in the twenty-first century. The Greek terms often denote what is instinctive and, in other cases, what is conventional or according to tradition or common sense. The letter to the Romans provides several examples, including Gentiles who 'instinctively' do what the law requires (2.14). Elsewhere this group is described as uncircumcised 'by nature', i.e. 'from birth' or 'according to their tradition' (2.27).

As noted above (**Past vs. Present, Part 1**), in the Vulgate the 'natural use' of the women mentioned in Romans 1.26 is *naturalem usum* and the Greek *para physin* is rendered as *contra naturam*, 'against nature'. Consistent with this wording, in 1.27 'the natural use of woman' becomes *naturali usu feminae*, and 'their error' is expressed as *erroris sui*. In this passage, Jerome's approach is clearly literal. The relevant phrases from John Wycliffe's translation of Jerome's text makes it easy to locate 'the natural use', 'against kind', and 'error'. The *OD* explains that 'kind' in Old English is related to 'kin', the original sense being 'nature, the natural order', in addition to 'innate character, form, or condition'. Thus, Wycliffe's 'against kind' is an archaic, but adequate, rendering of *contra naturam*.

With few exceptions, subsequent English translations have engaged directly with Paul's Greek text. In William Tyndale's version from 1526, the phrases discussed here are rendered as 'the natural use', 'the unnatural', and 'error'. A few changes are detectable in Tyndale's wording vis-à-vis that of Wycliffe, the most notable being 'unnatural' replacing 'against kind'. In all verbs Tyndale has preserved the past tense to match the Greek aorist. Essentially, Miles Coverdale's version (1535) is modelled on Tyndale's English text. Historically speaking, the Geneva Bible (1560) is the first to render Paul's *para physin* as 'against nature'. It is seconded by the Bishops' Bible (1568) and the King James Version (1611).

A number of different renderings of *para physin* in 1.26 are offered by contemporary scholars. Some representative examples are 'against nature' (Zerwick & Grosvenor 1988: 460), 'unnatural' (Brooten 1996: 2; Nissinen 1998: 104), 'contrary to nature' (Brooten 1996: 2; Gagnon 2001: 160), 'atypical' (Helminiak 2000: 86), 'in excess of nature' (Hanks 2006: 588), and 'in excess of what is natural' (Martin 2006: 57). As pointed out by Moore (2003: 95), the Greek preposition *para* in *para physin* does not always mean 'against' but often translates as 'beyond', a sense retained in the English adjective 'paranormal'. This reasoning has literary antecedents in an early Christian translation into Latin suggesting the rendering *extra naturam*, where *extra* means 'outside' or 'beyond' (Brooten 1996: 241 n. 74). Supported by Dale Martin (2006: 54, 57, 59, 207 n. 11), who regards it a more exact translation than other common proposals, I myself have preferred 'beyond nature'.

Translating *Para Physin*

Whichever option is preferred, it is striking that *para physin* occurs twice in Romans. In 1.26 it applies to the sexual behaviour of a group of idolatrous women. This is in keeping with the views expressed by Greek philosophers of Paul's era, according to which all non-procreative sexual acts were categorized as 'unnatural' (Hanks 2006: 592).[322] Intriguingly, *para physin* reappears in 11.24 where God acts 'contrary to

---

[322] However, as observed by Dale Martin (2006: 59), Paul's case is different inasmuch as he, in general, 'shows no concerns for procreation whatsoever'; cf. 1 Cor. 7.

nature'. From a Jewish point of view, it is surprising that Gentile believers are able to join the Christian movement without having to undergo traditional conversion rites such as circumcision. Paul employs a metaphor borrowed from the cultivation of olive trees. For him Judaism represents the 'cultivated' tree and the Gentiles belong to a 'wild' tree. Addressing the Gentile converts in 11.24, the verse reads as follows (NRSV, emphasis added):

> For if you have been cut from what is *by nature* a wild olive tree and grafted, *contrary to nature*, into a cultivated olive tree, how much more will these *natural* branches be grafted back into their own olive tree.

Here, 'contrary to nature' clearly renders *para physin* to denote the extraordinary character of the new conversion procedures introduced by the Christian movement. The two significant occurrences of *para physin* in Romans are compared and contrasted in table 73 through the approaches adopted by the twelve English versions.

Table 73
Translating *para physin* in Romans

Version	*Para physin* 1.26	*Para physin* 11.24
CCB	unnatural	in spite of being a different species
HCSB	unnatural	against nature
JM	unnatural	contrary to nature
LEB	contrary to nature	contrary to nature
NCV	having sex with other women	not natural
NIV	unnatural	contrary to nature
NJB	unnatural	unnaturally

NKJV	against nature	contrary to nature
NLT	indulged in sex with each other	contrary to nature
NRSV	unnatural	contrary to nature
NWT	contrary to nature	contrary to nature
REB	unnatural	against nature

While the first column in table 73 reflects the case of a group of women who surrendered their bodies to a certain kind of 'use', the second column refers to an act of God. Nine versions deal reasonably well with the two occurrences of *para physin*, offering renderings that in no case become mutually exclusive. However, three versions are stuck in major difficulties (CCB, NCV, NLT). The NCV says, 'Women stopped having natural sex and started having sex *with other women*' (emphasis added). This paraphrase raises a series of questions. First, the preposition 'with' (*syn*), the pronoun 'other' (*heteros*), and the noun 'woman' (singular *gynē*, pl. *gynaika*) are not present in the Greek original. Second, the NCV induces unsuspecting readers to believe that Paul refers to lesbian sex. Third, the NCV excludes any other potential reading of *para physin*. Fourth, 'having sex with other women' in 1.26 is not only out of step with the Greek original but would also be completely incompatible with the context of 11.24.

A similar serious obstacle to consistency has been erected by the NLT's 'indulged in sex with each other'. This happens despite the fact that the Greek has neither 'indulge' (*entryphaō*) nor 'each other' (*allēlōn*). Thus, the translators of the NCV and the NLT clearly adhere to a single interpretation of *para physin*, having settled for the least likely option available, which under no circumstances is applicable to 11.24. The CCB finds itself in the reverse situation. While 'unnatural' is acceptable for 1.26 and would be for 11.24, the same cannot be said of 'in spite of being a different species' (second column), which does not fit the context of 1.26 at all.

Idolatrous Males

In addition to *physikos*, 'natural', and *chrēsis*, 'use', an important Greek word in Romans 1.27 is the noun *planē*, 'error', which summarizes the conduct of the idolatrous *arsenes*, 'males', mentioned in this verse. As proposed by the twelve versions, the English renderings of *arsenes* and *tēs planēs autōn*, 'their error', are shown in table 74 (emphasis added).

Table 74
Translating 'Males' & 'Their Error' in Rom. 1.27

Version	Greek: *tēs planēs autōn*
CCB	the *men* . . . the punishment they deserve for their *wickedness*
HCSB	the *males* . . . received the appropriate penalty of their *error*
JM	the *males/men* . . . getting the due recompense of their *perversity*
LEB	the *males* . . . the penalty that was necessary for their *error*
NCV	*men* . . . received the punishment for those *wrongs*
NIV	the *men* . . . received the due penalty for their *error*
NJB	the *men* . . . receiving . . . the due reward for their *perversion*
NKJV	the *men* . . . receiving the penalty of their *error* which was due
NLT	as a result of this *sin*, the *men* suffered . . . the penalty they deserved
NRSV	the *men* . . . received the due penalty for their *error*
NWT	*males* . . . receiving the full recompense . . . due for their *error*
REB	*men/males* . . . are paid the fitting wage of such *perversion*

Using the same procedure as with the idolatrous females discussed earlier, where 'females' were turned into 'women', seven versions have changed the meaning of *arsenes*, 'males', to 'men'. This move is problematic since the Greek word for 'men' is *andres* (singular *anēr*), which applies to adult males. Sometimes *anēr* is used in the sense of 'husband' (Rom. 7.2; 1 Cor. 7.2-3). By contrast, 'males' connotes all members of the male sex, including boys. In other words, the possibility that the Greek text contains an allusion to pederasty cannot be ruled out. Two versions use 'males' and 'men' interchangeably (JM, REB). The more accurate rendering 'males' is offered by a small minority of three (HCSB, LEB, NWT), all of which were equally correct and consistent in the case of the females in 1.26.

The other significant word in table 74 is *planē*, 'error'. The Greek verb corresponding to *planē* is *planaō*, whose basic meaning is 'wander' or 'stray'. By extension it is used in the sense of 'go astray' or 'be mistaken'. In some contexts, *planaō* is a transitive verb meaning 'cause to wander', which often takes on the sense of 'lead astray', 'mislead' or 'deceive'. For the noun *planē*, the comprehensive dictionary of Liddell and Scott (1940) lists the following definitions: (a) 'wandering', 'roaming', and (b) 'discursive treatment'. As a metaphor the word is used to denote going astray, illusion, irregularity, deceit, and imposture. In Romans 1.27 *planē* seems to be used in the metaphorical sense to make a factual observation: those males went astray, i.e. behaved in mistaken ways.

By translating *planē* as 'error', six English versions successfully make this point clear (HCSB, LEB, NIV, NKJV, NWT, NRSV). The NCV's suggested 'wrongs' falls into a related category, even though it would often be a better match for a Greek noun such as *adikia* ('injustice', 'wrongfulness', or 'wrongdoing'). However, five other versions have approached the Greek text differently. The

CCB renders *planē* as 'wickedness'. Now, in English 'error' or 'illusion' are not interchangeable with 'wickedness' and the latter word seems an inappropriate choice for *planē*. This becomes even clearer if Paul's text is searched for 'wickedness'. The concept appears in several forms in Romans 1, including *adikia* ('injustice') in 1.18, which reappears in 1.29 together with *ponēria* ('baseness', 'malice') and *kakia* ('wickedness'). A similar problematic situation surrounds the word 'sin' proposed by the NLT. The Greek equivalent would be *hamartia*, which occurs repeatedly in other parts of the Epistle (5.12–13, 20–21; 6.1–2, 6–7). While Paul clearly differentiates between 'error' and 'sin' in Romans, the NLT regrettably fails to do so.

The three remaining versions have rendered *planē* as 'perversion' (JM, NJB) and 'perversity' (REB). To take 'perversion' first, the *OD* offers two definitions: (1) *the alteration of something from its original course, meaning or state to a distortion or corruption of what was first intended*; (2) *sexual behaviour or desire that is considered abnormal or unacceptable*. In the light of the overall context, it cannot be ruled out that some of the ideas inherent in 'perversion', particularly the *OD*'s option 1, are present in Paul's mind (cf. the verb 'exchanged') or, perhaps, in the mind of the Jewish Teacher whom he is quoting or critiquing (see below). However, the word actually used is *planē*, which in itself does not connote the unacceptable sexual behaviour or desire implied by option 2. In addition, Paul's general vocabulary has no specific equivalent of 'perversion'. Rather, in the realm of sex he repeatedly warns against *porneia*, which translates as 'unchastity' or 'irresponsible sexual conduct' (2 Cor. 12.21; Gal. 5.19; Eph. 5.3). Curiously, *porneia* is not included in the vice list spanning Romans 1.29–31. Instead, the word plays a central role in Paul's first letter to the Corinthians, chapter 5, which precedes his forceful argument against having intercourse with prostitutes (1 Cor. 6.15–20).

Returning to the English versions, only the REB translates *planē* as 'perversity'. Regarding this term, the *OD* offers three entries: (1) *a deliberate desire to behave in an unreasonable or unacceptable way*, (2) *the quality of being contrary to accepted standards or practice*, and (3) *the quality of being sexually perverted*. In this particular case, entry 2 fits the context very well given that the described behaviour in Romans 1.27 is *para physin*, which indeed means 'contrary to accepted standards or practice'. However, entries 1 and 3 are difficult to accommodate in this text. Furthermore, a closer inspection of the three versions proposing 'perversion' and 'perversity' for the noun *planē* reveals an important inconsistency. The verb corresponding to *planē* is *planaō*, which basically means 'wander'. Often it is used figuratively in the sense of 'go astray' or 'be mistaken'. Employed as a transitive verb it translates as 'cause to wander', i.e. 'mislead' or 'deceive'. Using the plural imperative of *planaō*, in 1 Corinthians 6.9 and 15.33, Paul literally says to the Corinthians *mē planasthe*, 'do not be deceived'. This is accurately translated as 'Make no mistake' (NJB, REB) and 'Make no mistake about it' (JM). No hint at perversity here. Thus, while these versions are proceeding correctly vis-à-vis *planaō* in Corinthians, their renderings in that letter provide no link to the 'perversion' or 'perversity' inadequately ascribed to *planē* in Romans 1.27.

The choices made by JM, the NJB, and the REB are likely to be inspired by various commentaries and dictionaries. The grammatical commentary of Zerwick and Grosvenor (1988: 460) translates *planē* as 'a going astray' or 'perversion'. Adding moral censure, the commentary by C. E. B. Cranfield (1975: 126-7) twice mentions 'sexual perversion' in relation to 1.27. Similarly, the FFM page 314 offers 'completely wrong behaviour' and 'perversion'. However, other options are available to biblical scholars, translators included. Danker's Greek Lexicon (2009: 285) suggests 'deviation', 'error', and 'deceit' (FFM p. 314), and other New Testament dictionaries add these definitions of *planē*:

mental straying; error, wrong opinion relative to morals or religion; error which shows itself in action.[323]

In summary, in JM, the NBJ, and the REB, there seems to be a clear link between their use of the nouns 'perversion' and 'perversity' on the one hand and their conversion into present tense of Paul's past verbal tenses on the other, which were discussed above. In this context, 'perversion' and 'perversity' anachronistically and polemically insert an issue into the text that Paul does not discuss, i.e. the contemporary debate on same-sex relationships in Christian contexts.

Text and Context

This overview has demonstrated that many Bible translators rely on church tradition more than linguistics and literary analysis as regards the two verses 1.26–27. They seem unaware that this brief text is part of an intricate literary pattern whose hermeneutical clues have not always been obvious. It is intriguing to discover signs in the Second Testament that within a relatively short time span of Paul's death in the year 67 CE, some parts of his writings were not entirely clear to Christian readers. The Epistle known as 2 Peter may have been composed around 80–90 CE (Hanks 2000: 217) or perhaps as late as 120–140 CE (Rogerson 1999: 97, 98; cf. chapter 7). In a direct reference to Paul's letters, the author of 2 Peter issues a warning in 3.15–16 (NRSV):

> There are some things in them hard to understand, which the ignorant and unstable twist to their own destruction, as they do the other scriptures.

---

[323] www.biblestudytools.com/search/?q=plane&s=References&rc=LEX&rc2=LEX+GRK (2012).

The wealth of academic writings on Romans produced in recent years testifies that some of Paul's points are still a matter of debate. In order to grasp the logic of the narrative framework in which the 1.26-27 passage is placed, a textual analysis of Romans 1 is attempted below. The first significant detail to highlight is that the letter is addressed to the nascent Christian community in the imperial city of Rome (Rom. 1.7). Some members are Jewish converts but the vast majority are former Gentiles, i.e. people with non-Jewish backgrounds, including many slaves (Hanks 2000: 82). This becomes evident in Romans 16, where Paul sends personal greetings to 28 individual members of the community. Six are Jews while the majority of 22 bear non-Jewish names such as Phoebe, Prisca, Ampliatus, and Urbanus (Hanks 2006: 604-5). The apostle clearly engages in dialogue with both groups, first addressing the Jewish Christians directly (Rom. 3.1-2; 4.1; 7.1) and later the Gentile converts (11.13).

With respect to Romans 1.18-32, it is customary to regard this section of the letter as a cluster of moral judgments expressing Paul's views on homoeroticism. In particular, some scholars take the verses 1.26-27 as a reference to the prohibitions in Leviticus 18.22 and 20.13.[324] However, on closer inspection, it would seem that several textual factors are being overlooked. First, the purity concerns regulated by Leviticus are addressed to Israelite males and appear to be of little relevance for understanding the conduct of the Gentile females mentioned in Romans 1.26. Second, the Levitical injunctions presuppose male circumcision (Gen. 17.10-14; Josh. 5.2-8), a practice debated by Paul in Romans 2.25-3.2 and strongly opposed elsewhere (Gal. 3.23-29; 5.2-14). Third, key words in Romans 1.26-27 such as 'passion', 'nature', and 'error' are absent from Leviticus 18 and 20. Fourth, Paul is usually rather precise

---

[324] Brooten 1996: 282-3; Nissinen 1998: 106; Helminiak 2000: 93; Gagnon 2001: 122; Hanks 2006: 594.

when quoting the First Testament (Septuagint), of which Romans provides numerous examples.[325]

Moreover, Paul is proud to call himself 'apostle to the Gentiles' (Rom. 11.13; 15.16). Even if a man of his educational standing really meant to use the opening chapter of this letter to polemicize against those who practise polytheism, it would appear insensitive, not to say crude, to use such virulent language with a death sentence attached: 'those who practise such things deserve to die' (1.32). Therefore, what has the appearance of an anti-Gentile diatribe in 1.18-32 may in reality be there for other reasons. The fact that this section is positioned early in the letter suggests that Paul wants to deal with the issue urgently. Clearly the apostle is well aware of his style and vocabulary as stated in 3.5: 'I speak in a human way'; 6.19: 'I am speaking in human terms because of the weakness of your flesh' (NRSV: 'because of your natural limitations'); and 15.15: 'I have written to you rather boldly'. Furthermore, how Paul really feels about Gentiles is lovingly expressed throughout the letter.[326] Repeatedly he teaches readers to be patient with other members of the community and avoid being judgmental (12.3-18; 14.1-19). In 15.5-21, he urges the Roman Christians to create an inclusive church for Jewish and Gentile Christians alike and not be led astray by those who misinterpret Paul's teachings (16.17-19).

Paul and Wisdom

An important question remains with respect to the unnamed people in Romans 1.26-27: to whom is Paul referring? In the light of the overall sophistication of the letter to the

---

[325] Rom. 3.10-20; 4.3, 6-12, 17-23; 8.36; 9.6-17, 25-29, 33; 10.5-8, 11-13; 11.2-4, 8-10; etc.
[326] Cf. 1.13-14; 2.13-16, 28-29; 3.28-30; 9.30; 10.12-13; 11.11-25; 15.9-21, 26-27; 16.26.

Romans, this controversial passage may respond to a specific literary background for which Paul offers some clues in the preceding verses: despite knowing the Creator (1.20–21), they *emōranthēsan*, 'became foolish' (v. 22), exchanging the glory of God for 'images resembling a mortal human being or birds or four-footed animals or reptiles' (v. 23). Along with such idolatrous practices, they took up impure pursuits leading to physical degradation (vv. 24–25). As a consequence, they fell into 'shameful passions'. In Romans 1.26, the Greek text says *dia touto paredōken autous ho theos eis pathē atimias*, literally 'through this God gave them up into passions of dishonour' (Martin 2006: 54, 56). In the ST, the prevailing view of passion is negative (Zerwick & Grosvenor 1988: 460), and Paul is no exception. According to Dale Martin (2006: 59), 'Paul never has a positive word to say about sexual passion or desire' because 'passion is characteristic of Gentiles and must be avoided completely by Christians'.

As pointed out by James Alison (2006: 131-2), Romans 1.18–32 strongly echoes parts of an earlier, prestigious work, namely, the apocryphal *Book of Wisdom* (cf. Helminiak 2000: 84). Douglas Campbell (2009: 360) agrees:

> The principal resonances take place between Romans 1.18–32 and Wisdom 11–16, but the connections are by no means limited to these two stretches of text.

Also known as *The Wisdom of Solomon*, this Hellenistic work was written in Greek, apparently in Alexandria. The exact time of publication is unknown but it seems to have appeared in the first century BCE or early first century CE (Browning 2009: 227), which makes Wisdom one of the last books to be included in the Septuagint. Table 75 provides an overview of some passages with thematic overlaps between Romans 1 and Wisdom, some of the main concepts being 'ungodliness', 'idolatry', and 'error' (NRSV, citations from Wisdom italicized).

Table 75
The Book of Wisdom in Romans 1

Ro 1.18	For the wrath of God is revealed . . . against all ungodliness and wickedness of those who . . . suppress the truth
W 11.15	*In return for their foolish and wicked thoughts . . . you sent upon them a multitude of irrational creatures to punish them*
W 14.9	*For equally hateful to God are the ungodly and their ungodliness*
Ro 1.19	For what can be known about God is plain to them
W 12.27	*they saw and recognized as the true God the one whom they had before refused to know*
Ro 1.20	his eternal power and divine nature . . . have been understood and seen
W 13.5	*For from the greatness and beauty of created things comes a corresponding perception of their creator*
Ro 1.21	they became futile in their thinking, and their senseless minds were darkened
W 12.23	*those who lived unrighteously, in a life of folly*
W 13.1	*they were unable from the good things that are seen to know the one who exists*
W 17.2	*they . . . lay as captives of darkness and prisoners of long nights*
Ro 1.22	Claiming to be wise, they became fools
W 13.1	*all people who were ignorant of God were foolish by nature*
W 13.9	*if they had the power to know so much that they could investigate the world, how did they fail to find the Lord of these things?*
W 15.11	*they failed to know the one who formed them*
Ro 1.23	they exchanged the glory of the immortal God for images resembling a mortal human being or birds or four-footed animals or reptiles
W 12.24	*accepting as God those animals that even their enemies despised*
W 13.10	*miserable, with their hopes set on dead things, are those who give the name 'gods' to the work of human hands . . . and likeness of animals*

W 14.21	*people, in bondage to misfortune or to royal authority, bestowed on objects of stone or wood the name that ought not to be shared*
W 15.18	*they worship even the most hateful animals*
Ro 1.24	Therefore God gave them up in their lusts of their hearts
W 14.12	*For the idea of making idols was the beginning of fornication, and the invention of them was the corruption of life*
Ro 1.25	they worshipped and served the creature rather than the Creator
W 13.1	*nor did they recognize the artisan while paying heed to his works*
Ro 1.26	God gave them up to degrading passions
W 14.24	*they no longer keep either their lives or marriages pure but . . . grieve one another by adultery*
W 14.26	*confusion over what is good . . . defiling of souls, sexual perversion,[327] disorder in marriages, adultery, and debauchery*
Ro 1.27	Men committed shameless acts with men
W 14.23	*For whether they . . . celebrate secret mysteries, or hold frenzied revels with strange customs*
Ro 1.27	Men . . . received in their own persons the due penalty for their error
W 12.24	*they went far astray on the paths of error*
W 12.27	*Therefore the utmost condemnation came upon them*
W 14.22	*Then it was not enough for them to err about the knowledge of God*
W 14.31	*the just penalty for those who sin*
Ro 1.28	And since they did not see fit to acknowledge God, God gave them up to a debased mind and to things that should not be done
W 14.27	*For the worship of idols not to be named is the beginning and cause and end of every evil*
W 14.30	*they thought wrongly about God in devoting themselves to idols*

---

[327] 'Sexual perversion' is a dubious translation of the Greek *geneseōs enallagē*. The CCB and the NJB render this as 'sins against nature'. Other translations are 'changing of kind' (KJV), 'changing of birth' (Bishops' Bible) and 'changing of nature' (Douay-Rheims). The latter

Ro 1.29	They were filled with every kind of wickedness, evil, covetousness, malice . . . murder, strife, deceit
W 14.22	*living in great strife due to ignorance, they call such great evils peace*
W 14.24	*they . . . treacherously kill each other*
W 14.25	*all is a raging riot of blood and murder, theft and deceit, corruption . . .*
Ro 1.30	slanderers, God-haters, insolent, haughty, boastful, inventors of evil, rebellious towards parents
W 14.29	*they swear wicked oaths and expect to suffer no harm*
W 14.30	*in deceit they swore unrighteously through contempt for holiness*
Ro 1.31	foolish, faithless, heartless, ruthless
W 14.25	*faithlessness, tumult, perjury*
Ro 1.32	Those who practise such things deserve to die
W 12.20	*you punished . . . those deserving of death*

The author of Wisdom has dedicated a sizeable part of his material to theological reflections on the books of Genesis (e.g. Wis. 10.13-14) and Exodus (e.g. Wis. 10.15-20), meditating repeatedly on the futility of Egyptian idolatry versus the steadfast love of God for his people Israel (e.g. Wis. 11). While he clearly finds the work important, the fact that Paul does not cite Wisdom verbatim seems to suggest that he does not regard it as scripture but expects his Jewish readers in Rome to be familiar with the above subjects.[328] Furthermore, his use of the past tense in Romans 1.21-29 ('they knew God', 'they became fools', 'God gave them up')

---

three come close to the Greek original inasmuch as *geneseōs enallagē* literally means 'changing of origin'. Whatever was meant by Wisdom in this case is unclear, but it should be noted that the words 'sin' (*hamartia*) and *para physin*, 'beyond nature', are absent from Wis. 14. Clearly, the renderings suggested by the CCB, NJB, and NRSV are interpretive, not text-based.

[328] In the letter to the Ephesians, some of the vices listed by Paul in Romans 1 recur (Eph. 4.17-19). However, Ephesians seems to have been written by a colleague or disciple of Paul around 80-90 CE (Hanks 2000: 127), i.e. several decades after Paul's death in 67 CE.

appears to be another indication that the apostle is referring to a well-known literary source.[329] In summary, Paul's style in Romans 1 may be characterized as a sophisticated mix of personal greetings, theological reflections, scriptural, and mythological allusions and, towards the end of the chapter, a rhetorical climax in the form of a polemical vice list.[330]

Passions and Idolatry

While the book of Wisdom offers several hermeneutical clues for the second half of Romans 1, the exploration carried out above does not fully explicate what happens in Romans 1.26–27. It is true that Wisdom 14.12 mentions idolatry as 'the beginning of fornication' and 14.26 speaks of 'disorder in marriages, adultery and debauchery', all of which may well be alluded to in Paul's letter. However, with the possible exception of Wisdom 14.23 ('frenzied revels with strange customs'), no passage in this work refers specifically to the unusual sexual activity described in 1.26–27. Therefore, the sexual passions unfolding here may reflect specific religious practices in the Hellenistic era. It is important to keep in mind that both Wisdom and Paul's letter to the Romans were written at a time in which Greek and Roman deities were widely worshipped in the Mediterranean region, making polytheism, or idolatry, a routine part of everyday life (Alison 2006: 131).

---

[329] As expressed by Dale Martin (2006: 53), 'Paul apparently presupposes a Jewish mythological narrative about the origins of idolatry,' and 'Paul's own logic assumes a mythological structure . . .' (p. 55).

[330] Douglas Campbell (2009: 509) observes that Paul frequently quotes writings and engages with debaters without identifying them by name, of which 1 Corinthians offers several examples (1 Cor. 1.11–12; 3.3–4; 6.12–13; 8.1–8). The analysis of J. A. Harrill (2006: 18) suggests that Paul's use of first person 'I' and the word 'slave' in Romans follows rhetorical conventions governing Greco-Roman literature, including 'Paul, a slave of Jesus Christ' (Rom. 1.1) and 'I am a slave' (7.25).

Whereas Wisdom was composed in Alexandria, Paul seems to have written his letter in the Greek city of Corinth where numerous temples existed. Moreover, in his day 420 different temples are reported to have been functioning in Rome itself (Kader 1999: 73). Established cults were dedicated to prominent goddesses such as Cybele and Aphrodite. According to James Alison (2006: 133), Paul's language in Romans 1.27 may be a reference to the cult of Cybele, which had a strong cross-dressing element:

> The rites involved orgiastic frenzies in which men allowed themselves to be penetrated, and which culminated in some of those in the frenzy castrating themselves, and becoming eunuchs, and thus priests of Cybele.

Sometimes these eunuch priests were called *galli* (lit. 'roosters' or 'men from Gaul'). Alison continues (2006: 134):

> Paul's listeners would not have needed any explanation of this sort of thing: it was a regularly occurring part of the public life of the Mediterranean world at the time. What it meant for *galli* to receive in their persons the due penalty for their error might refer to the castration, or to their general weirdness of demeanour and appearance, but Paul's readers would have picked up the sort of thing he meant. Because, as any self-respecting Jew could tell you: this was just the sort of idiotic thing that Gentiles got up to as a result of their idolatry.

With respect to the *galli*, whose ancient homeland was Anatolia in Asia Minor (McCleary 2004: 239), it was unique in Greek religion for Cybele to have a transgendered or eunuch mendicant priesthood. Often her cults included rites dedicated to a divine Phrygian castrated shepherd-consort named Attis (p. 33).[331] According to Halvor Moxnes (2003: 79), the *galli* performed 'special functions at festivals, in particular in processions'. The act of self-castration would take place in connection with the main spring festival. Not having a fixed organization, they were 'wandering groups, with song and music. They carried with them a picture of the goddess, gave oracles, and begged.' Regarding a penalty (*antimisthia*) linked to castration, the subject reappears in Galatians 5.10–12 where Paul expresses vehement disapproval of the false preachers operating among the newly converted Christians in the province of Galatia (northern highlands of Asia Minor). He concludes his observations to the Galatians in no uncertain terms (NRSV): 'I wish those who unsettle you would castrate themselves!'

Another ancient phenomenon, frowned upon by many of the apostle's contemporaries, and to which Paul may be alluding in Romans 1, is recorded in the work of Roman historian Livy (Titus Livius Patavinus, 59 BCE–17 CE). Livy wrote a popular 142-volume history of Rome, which included an account of the so-called Bacchanalia.[332] This orgiastic religious festival dedicated to Bacchus, the Roman god of wine, was eventually regarded as so scandalous that the Senate banned it in 186 BCE. It may seem odd that the Romans, normally prepared to endorse the worship of any god or goddess, objected so strenuously to the Bacchanalia:

> The fact is that almost everything associated with the sect ran counter to traditional Roman values. Ceremonies took place at night . . . and indeed

---

[331] www.theoi.com/Phrygios/Attis.html (2012). For a detailed discussion of Greco-Roman goddess cults, with which Paul is likely to have been familiar, see J. Townsley, *Paul, the Goddess Religions and Queers*, at www.jeramyt.org/papers/paulcybl.html (2012).
[332] See www.fordham.edu/halsall/ancient/livy39.asp (2012).

> initiates did make a vow of secrecy. Unrelated men and women dined, drank, and partied together. Women dressed in special costumes ran unguarded outside at night. One commentator felt that the men who participated were behaving 'like women' and were therefore unfit to serve in the army or government . . . It certainly began as an all woman cult but we have no idea of the gender balance at the end nor do we have any way of telling whether the charges of fraud and murder were legitimate or how serious was the threat to the state posed by the Bacchanalia.[333]

According to Livy, the Senate took the charges very seriously and ordered more than half of the membership of this sect to be executed. Following this turmoil, a senatorial decree made it virtually impossible for men to attend Bacchanalia thereafter (Pomeroy 1975: 217). Given the notoriety in Rome of these events, it should not be ruled out that Paul has this in mind in Romans 1.32 as he refers to those who deserve to die for 'practising such things' (cf. Wis. 12.20, 27; 14.9–10, 28–30).

Paul's Addressees

Several scholars have reached the conclusion that Paul's discourse in Romans 1.18–32 is a rhetorical trap intended to catch self-righteous Jewish converts off guard. According to Dale Martin (2006: 54), Paul entices his Jewish hearer 'to nod in agreement with this traditional Jewish indictment of Gentile corruption'. Similarly, Thomas Hanks (2006: 586) invites exegetes to pay attention to the remarkable build-up leading into Romans 2 where the trap is sprung. James

---

[333] www.womenintheancientworld.com/bacchanalia.htm (2012).

Alison (2006: 135) emphasizes that the argument of Romans 1 is incomplete without the sting occurring in 2.1, and 1.18-32 is Paul's way of ensuring full support from the Jewish part of his audience. The apostle knows what it takes and then goes on to criticize this fault-finding attitude: 'for in passing judgment on another you condemn yourself' (2.1). Moreover, Alison reminds modern Bible readers that the original text of Romans was written 'in scarcely punctuated continuous Greek prose', i.e. without the familiar verse and chapter numbers (p. 127). He emphasizes that the current chapter 2 begins with the word 'therefore', for which reason Romans 2 should be included in any analysis of 1.18-32 (p. 130).

The complex rhetorical structure of the Greek text yields additional clues to Paul's intentions. From a stylistic point of view, it is intriguing to note what happens to Paul's addressees between Romans 1.1 and 2.1. Initially, starting in 1.6, readers are addressed in the second person plural as *hymeis*, 'you', which continues until 1.15. The non-specific 'they' dominates throughout 1.18-32, and the 'you' of direct speech does not reappear until 2.1: 'Therefore *you* have no excuse, whoever *you* are' (emphasis added). However, an extraordinary feature emerges here: this 'you' no longer corresponds to the second person plural *hymeis* but rather to *sy* (2.3), 'you' or 'thou', second person singular, and *seauton*, 'yourself' or 'thyself' (2.1). In other words, the focus has changed from the entire group in Rome addressed in 1.6 to just one person in 2.1.

The presence of the adverb *dio*, 'therefore', clearly links Romans 2 to the previous argument, i.e. 1.18-32. The singular *sy* and *seauton* and their derivative forms continue in the text until 2.5, at which point Paul takes issue with his interlocutor's 'hard and impenitent heart', warning him that his attitude will be held against him 'on the day of wrath'. This leads the apostle to remind the person addressed that 'God shows no partiality' (2.11) and that 'God, through Jesus Christ, will judge the secret thoughts of all' (2.16). Subsequently, in 2.17-23, Paul provides more details about this unnamed addressee who is 'instructed in the law' (2.18), 'a teacher of children' (2.20), and a preacher (2.21). In 2.24 the plural 'you' (*hymeis*) reappears in the inserted quotation 'The name of God is blasphemed among the Gentiles because of you', which seems to be Paul's adaptation of Isaiah 52.5 (Cranfield 1975: 171). Finally, the second person singular reappears in 2.25 in the verbs *prassēs* ('you may be practising') and *ēs* ('you may be') accompanied by the possessive pronoun *sou*, 'your' or 'thy', to finalize in 2.27 with *se* ('you' or 'thee') in 'those who are physically uncircumcised but keep the law will condemn *you*' (emphasis added).

On account of this singular 'you' or 'thou' in Romans 2, Douglas Campell (2009) has approached the opening chapters of the Epistle from a fresh perspective. He suggests that a major section of Romans 1-3 may be interpreted as part of a polemic exchange between Paul and an unnamed Jewish preacher in Rome, with whom Paul strongly disagrees. Thus, Campbell argues that the apostle's own views are stated in Romans 1.16-17, where the Christian Gospel is proclaimed to be for 'everyone who has faith' (2009: 543). This is followed by a very different sequence (1.18-32) of scathing observations on pagan worship and immorality, which are introduced for a sophisticated rhetorical exercise. According to this interpretation, the apostle draws on two sources: (a) the apocryphal book of Wisdom and (b) the writings or sayings of Paul's unnamed opponent in Rome, to whom Campbell refers as 'the Teacher' (pp. 345, 528-30). The rhetorical trap set up by Paul in 1.18-32 is aimed specifically at this Teacher who is 'a guide to the blind' (2.19). Paul sternly rebukes his interlocutor, saying, 'You, then, that teach others, will you not teach yourself?' (2.21). Campbell concludes that, in Romans 1.18-32, Paul does not speak in his own voice but in that of the Teacher (2009: 529). The argument of 1.18-32 is, in fact, 'the fullest presentation of the Teacher's position that we receive from the hand of Paul' (p. 542).

From a theological perspective, Douglas Campbell's analysis would seem to be in harmony with the gist of the letter to the Romans. If this approach is accepted, it explains why Paul's admonishment of the presumed Teacher is placed early in the letter. It is possible that the apostle, aware of the tensions affecting the Roman Christians, has wanted to confront this thorny issue head-on. With that difficulty 'out of the way', he is able to dedicate the rest of the letter to the many urgent theological questions in need of clarification. Towards the end of the Epistle, Paul no longer has to address the Teacher personally but acknowledges to the whole community that he is aware of the possible impact of his words: 'I have written to you rather boldly' (15.15). Perhaps still with the Teacher in mind, he then urges the Roman converts to 'keep an eye on those who cause dissensions and offences, in opposition to the teaching that you have learned' (16.17). The teaching mentioned here clearly refers to the Gospel of Christ Jesus that the Roman community received from Paul himself (1.3-6, 14-17; 15.17-19). Thus, taken as a whole, Paul's letter to the Romans has three addressees all of whom belong to the Christian community in Rome: the Jewish converts, the unnamed Teacher, and the Gentile converts.

Conclusion

Paul's letter to the Romans is regarded as a very important document for Christian theology. In particular, the two verses 1.26–27 have been hotly debated in recent decades with respect to homoerotic relationships. Whereas early Christian interpreters took this passage to condemn anal sex, medieval theologians went further attributing to Paul a blanket condemnation of same-sex intimacy, an approach that is still adopted by a number of modern commentators and translators. However, the literary complexities surrounding Romans 1.26–27 are numerous and explain why a growing number of scholars are questioning traditional hermeneutics. It is of vital importance to consider that this section of the letter may not represent Paul's own views. Instead, there are signs in the text that the apostle is quoting statements made by an unnamed, false teacher in Rome whom the apostle forcefully rebukes in Romans 2.

In relation to the subject of homoeroticism, one thing seems clear: the Greek text of Romans 1.26–27 does not address person-to-person relationships in the form of friendship, affection, bonding, caring, love, and commitment. Instead, certain group activities are discussed. A detailed analysis of the context shows that the main focus is on sexual excesses wrought by idolatrous practices. The polemic reflections in 1.18–32 are clearly inspired by the book of Wisdom and, additionally, seem to allude to scandalous events in the past associated with the Roman cults of deities such as Cybele and Bacchus.

In their dealings with Romans 1.26–27, several English versions of the Bible reveal a biased attitude. The commentaries and dictionaries upon which the translators rely often supply them with moralistic and outdated options that have no linguistic or literary basis. Whereas Paul has placed the events described in the past by using the Greek aorist for his key verbs, some modern versions unduly replace the past tense with the English perfect and, in a few cases, the present tense. This creates the unfounded impression that Paul is addressing today's concerns and debates in Christian churches about intimate same-sex relationships. A problematic concept in Romans, which is often misunderstood, is *para physin*. While 'against nature' or 'beyond nature' are literal renderings, in ancient literature the phrase often meant 'contrary to accepted standards', 'unusual', and 'atypical'. Another word in Paul's text, which has created some confusion among translators, is *planē*, 'error'. Without being grounded in the Greek text, several versions have rendered it as 'perversity' or 'perversion'.

In summary, the relatively frequent mistranslations of Romans 1.26–27 tend to remove the text from the ancient context, transplanting it into modernity and presenting the versions concerned as unfaithful to the intentions expressed elsewhere by the apostle. If the verses 1.18–32 are to be taken as an indirect citation of the views of his unnamed opponent in Rome, it is a bitter irony of history that they have been attributed to Paul himself, turning the apostle into a fierce critic of sexual activity between members of the same sex and making him contradict his own Gospel message. In actual fact, and given his primary concerns in Romans, it seems far more likely that Paul distances himself from one or several recently converted zealots with Jewish backgrounds who spend too much time quoting the book of Wisdom to condemn idolatry, including certain orgies occurring in Roman temples.

Paul's letter to the Romans shows an author proud of being apostle to the Gentiles, a group to which he often refers with love and respect. Fundamentally, these issues are highlighted: the importance of not passing judgment on anyone, the irrelevance of circumcision, and the centrality of sound Christian doctrine, all of which are essential for creating an inclusive church. More than anything, Paul wishes to communicate the astonishing message of salvation made available 'unnaturally' to all humanity, Jews and Gentiles alike, through the life, death, and resurrection of Jesus Christ.

PART FIVE

The Language of Love

15

LOVE LOST IN TRANSLATION

See, I am making all things new.

—Revelation 21.5

Introduction

Previous chapters of this book have focused on a series of texts that are quoted in current debates on homoeroticism and the Bible. However, the linguistic and literary exploration undertaken thus far has made it clear that most of the texts examined have little or nothing to say about same-sex eroticism in the ancient world. Only two passages in the Bible refer unequivocally to sexual activity between members of the same sex, namely, Leviticus 18.22 (20.13) and Romans 1.27, but both are restricted in terms of wording and context to focus on certain forms of sexual interaction between males in specific situations (cf. chapters 6 and 14). No biblical text condemns homoeroticism between women, and the same is true of loving relationships between males.

Even more importantly, many debaters have failed to realize that very few persons who regard themselves as lesbian, gay or bisexual identify with the biblical texts discussed in chapters 4–14 of this book. Readers who are drawn to homoerotic intimacy do not see their personalities or orientations reflected in the inhabitants of Sodom and Gomorrah or among the consecrated workers of

Deuteronomy 23, let alone the Gentile women and men participating in the frenzied orgies mentioned in the opening pages of Paul's letter to the Romans. And yet translators and biblical scholars have frequently referred believers with homoerotic inclinations to these parts of the Bible, with which the latter groups feel no affinity. This constitutes a serious problem of mistaken identity (Goss 2002: 210).

The well-known Christian obsession with sexual matters goes back to the patristic era and the Middle Ages, not the Bible. Put differently, traditional church opposition to homoeroticism cannot be characterized as biblical. According to Jesus in Mark 12.30-31, where he quotes Leviticus 19.18 and Deuteronomy 6.5, there is no greater command than these: 'You shall love the Lord your God with all your heart . . . and your neighbour as yourself.' Thus, the common Christian insistence on sexual orthodoxy in the form of heteronormativity is, in theological terms, out of step with scripture, as observed by Elizabeth Stuart (2003: 109):

> In public discourse on sexuality the western Churches currently give every impression of wanting to produce heterosexual desire rather than desire for God.

At the core of both biblical Testaments lies a message of salvation. Biblical theology recognizes the exodus—not the creation—as the central First Testament doctrine, which is comparable to the cross in the Second Testament (Hanks 1983: 4). The epic of the awesome liberation from bondage of the Israelite people narrated in the book of Exodus strikes a chord with lesbian, gay, bisexual, and transgender people, as argued by Rebecca Alpert (2006: 61): 'The themes, actors and values present in Exodus have much to say to the translesbigay community'. Adopting a similar approach, Mona West (2000: 72) regards Exodus as a story of transformation and coming out. With respect to the ST, its fundamental goal is not to encourage sectarian puritanism or sexual orthodoxy but to proclaim the good news of universal access to salvation (Jn. 3.16). Thomas Hanks (2000b: 192) argues that everyone can experience authentic freedom through faith in the Liberator God who became incarnate in Jesus, the poor carpenter from Nazareth.

In the preceding chapters of this book, much attention has been given to the language of sex in the Bible. However, if justice is to be done to a complex subject like homoeroticism in biblical times, a discussion of the language of love is equally important. Human sexuality cannot, and should not, be reduced to physical activity or sexual practices but encompasses a number of important psychic components, including attraction, affection, friendship, bonding, love, caring, and commitment. Without pretending to be exhaustive, this chapter takes up some essential aspects of the terminology of love in both biblical Testaments. It begins by outlining the most common terms of endearment in the Hebrew Bible followed by a study of two narratives in which same-sex affection plays a major part. Subsequently, a similar procedure is embarked upon to explore the Second Testament. Twelve English versions of the Bible are examined for comparative purposes.

Love in the First Testament

Biblical Hebrew has several terms for expressing love and affection. In poetic language, notably in the book of Psalms, the noun *chesed*, 'loyalty' or 'love' occurs repeatedly: 'According to your steadfast love remember me' (25.7) and 'all the paths of Y<small>HWH</small> are steadfast love and faithfulness' (25.10). The refrain of Psalm 136 is 'for his steadfast love endures for ever'. For the present study, the most significant term is the common verb *ahav*, 'to love', which occurs 205 times in the HB (Mitchel 1984: 7) while the corresponding noun *ahavah* occurs 40 times (p. 26). The usage of *ahav* covers a wide range of semantic fields, including religion: love of God and the divine laws (Exod. 20.6; Deut. 5.10; 6.5; 11.13) and the way in which God loves people (Isa. 48.14; Jer. 31.3; Hos. 14.4). In the social sphere, all Israelites are encouraged to love their neighbour (Lev. 19.18) as well as the stranger (Deut. 10.19). On a more personal level, the HB uses *ahav* to depict how parents feel about their children: Abraham loves his son Isaac (Gen. 22.2), and Isaac is very fond of his firstborn son Esau while Rebekah loves Jacob (25.28). For his part, Jacob loves Joseph more than his other children (37.3).

When it comes to love with an erotic component, no book in the HB excels more in such terminology than the Song of Songs. In this lyrical, passionate poem, romantic love is called *dōd* (1.2; 7.12), a word which is also used by the female protagonist as an appellative for her lover, *dōdī*, 'my beloved' (1.13-14; 2.3). The male counterpart responds by calling her *raʿeyathī*, 'my darling' (1.9, 15; 2.2; 4.1) and frequently uses the word *achothī*, 'my sister', as a term of endearment (4.9-10, 12; 5.1) In addition to these specific terms, the common words for love, *ahav* (verb) and *ahavah* (noun), occur throughout the Song (1.4, 7; 2.5; 3.1-5, 10; etc.). Similarly, they are frequent in narrative prose. For example, it is said of King Solomon that he loved (*ahav*) many foreign women (1 Kings 11.1), i.e. the numerous wives in his harem were from different countries.

Of special interest to the present study are the biblical stories in which *ahav* describes a person loving or falling in love with a particular woman or man. A famous passage in Genesis 29.18 and 29.20 explains that Jacob loves Rachel. The fact that he is less fond of her sister Leah (29.30) is hardly surprising in view of the way in which their father Laban tricked Jacob into marrying Leah (29.23). Initially readers are not told how the two sisters feel about the situation but their rivalry soon comes to the surface (30.1-24). In the book of Samuel, a man named Elkanah also has two wives: Penninah and Hannah. Although she is childless, Elkanah loves Hannah (1 Sam. 1.5, 8). David's son Amnon loves his half-sister Tamar (2 Sam. 13.4), and in Judges 14.16, Samson's Philistine wife importunes her husband to make him explain the riddle he propounded to her fellow countrymen: 'You really hate me, you don't love me' (JPS).

When King Saul's younger daughter Michal falls in love with David she is allowed to marry him (1 Sam. 18.20, 28). David's feelings for her are not revealed, but he is evidently pleased to become the king's son-in-law (18.26-27). At a later stage, following a lengthy, forced separation, and soon after David's investiture as king, he orders Michal to be retrieved from her second husband Paltiel and brought into his household (2 Sam. 3.13-16). While it may be seen as an act of love, there are grounds for interpreting this as a political move.[334] At any rate, the resumption of Michal and David's relationship brings her no happiness (6.16-23). This may partly be due to the fact that, unlike the time of their honeymoon, Michal has ceased to be David's only wife. In the intervening years, he has set up a harem (3.2-5; 5.13-16). In addition, Michal has had to leave Paltiel behind, a man who evidently loves her (3.16).

Ruth and Naomi

Frank Anthony Spina (2005) has produced a study of remarkable outsiders in biblical narratives and the ways

---

[334] David has succeeded Saul as king of Israel. Having Saul's daughter Michal in his harem adds legitimacy to David's position vis-à-vis those who opposed his rise to the kingship; cf. 2 Sam. 2.8-10; 3.12-13.

in which they become blessed and are awarded the role of protagonists. Among the male outsiders are Naaman the Syrian officer (2 Kings 5) and Jonah who reluctantly becomes a prophet to outsiders. As told in the book of Jonah (3.1–10), the latter story is highly significant in its positive portrait of the pagans of Nineveh. Some biblical outsiders are female, including the Samaritan woman at the well (Jn. 4.1–42) as well as Tamar (Gen. 38) and Rahab (Josh. 2), both Canaanites. The book of Ruth portrays a young woman from Moab who is accepted into the Israelite community of Bethlehem. Kirsten Nielsen (1997: 1) characterizes this work as 'a literary masterpiece' and 'one of the best-structured books in the Old Testament' (p. 2).[335]

For discussions in Christian circles of same-sex relationships in the Bible, the book of Ruth is of particular relevance. Being the only text that addresses intimacy between two women, it is surprising that Ruth takes up so little space in recent academic literature explicitly dedicated to the subject of homoeroticism in the Bible.[336] Written in Classical Hebrew, the story contains the passionate declaration of loyalty and lifelong commitment spoken by a Moabite woman named Ruth to Naomi, an Israelite woman from Bethlehem (1.16–17, NRSV):

> Where you go, I will go; where you lodge, I will lodge; Your people shall be my people, and your

---

[335] Cf. Calum Carmichael (2010: 46): 'The art and sophistication that have gone into its composition are striking, and the details deserve fullest attention.'

[336] Bernadette Brooten's *Love Between Women* (1996) fails to mention the book of Ruth and a similar absence is noticeable in Martti Nissinen's *Homoeroticism in the Biblical World* (1998). Robert Gagnon's *The Bible and Homosexual Practice* (2001: 154) awards the story two lines in a footnote. A little more generous are Comstock 1993: 35; Stuart 1995: 126–7; Kader 1999: 104–7; Helminiak 2000: 126–7; Goss 2002: 99–100; Greenberg 2004: 105; Guest 2005: 140, 226–7. Actual discussions of the text occur in Duncan 2000: 92–102; Jennings 2005: 227–34; West 2006: 190–4, and Hügel 2009: 439–462.

God, my God. Where you die, I will die; there I will be buried.

This scene occurs after both Ruth and Naomi have lost their husbands (1.3–5). The narrator makes it clear that Ruth *clings to* Naomi (1.14), the Hebrew phrase being *dovqah bah*, 'she clung to her'. The expression echoes Genesis 2.24 where a man leaves his father and mother and commits himself to his wife by clinging to her, in Hebrew *davaq beishtō* (Stuart 1995: 127; Sharpe 2011: 155). In other words, as Ruth relinquishes her family ties, her commitment to Naomi is of the same strength and durability as a marital bond (Nielsen 1997: 48). At first Naomi tells Ruth to remain with her people (1.15), which would be the sensible thing to do, but Ruth's decision to go to Bethlehem with her widowed mother-in-law is not negotiable, and Naomi then concedes (1.18).[337]

For the narrator, Ruth seems to personify Prov. 18.24 where the text describes an *ohēv*, 'lover' or 'dear friend', as someone who 'sticks closer than one's nearest kin' (NRSV). In this passage 'sticks closer' renders the Hebrew participle *davēq*, from the verb *davaq*, 'cling'. The people of Bethlehem find Ruth's devotion to Naomi admirable. In 2.11, this is respectfully highlighted by Boaz, a wealthy landowner, during his first conversation with Ruth (NRSV):

> All that you have done for your mother-in-law since the death of your husband has been fully told me, and how you left your father and mother and your native land and came to a people that you did not know before.

---

[337] Weston Fields (1997: 30) regards Ruth's pact with Naomi as comparable to the oath of allegiance to David sworn in 2 Sam. 15.21 by a foreigner named Ittai.

For Robert Alter (1992: 51), Boaz's words resonate with Genesis 12.1 where Abraham is called to emigrate:

> There is a strong echo here, as surely anyone in the ancient audience would have recognized, of God's first, imperative words to Abraham that inaugurate the patriarchal tales . . . The identical verbal-thematic cluster, land-birthplace-father, stands out in both texts.[338]

Translating Ruth's Commitment

In this narrative, two significant Hebrew verbs describe Ruth's feelings for Naomi: *davaq*, 'cling' (1.14), and *ahav*, 'love' (4.15). To take the latter first, it expresses the same intensity of feeling as Jacob loving Rachel (Gen. 29.18). Virtually all English versions of the Bible adequately translate *ahav* in both passages. In the case of *davaq*, a slightly different picture emerges. Genesis 2.24 stipulates that marriage takes place when a man 'clings' or 'cleaves' to the woman who becomes his wife. In such cases, *davaq* is accompanied by the preposition *bĕ*, which often means 'in' but here translates as 'to'. In several biblical contexts, the verb depicts strong commitment or feeling: in Genesis 34.3, Shechem's soul is said to 'cling' to Dinah daughter of Jacob, and King Solomon 'clings' to his numerous foreign wives despite their devotion to a variety of gods (1 Kings 11.2). At

---

[338] Similarly, Kirsten Nielsen (1997: 1) argues that the book's purpose is to demonstrate that God himself has chosen her, 'just as in his time he had chosen the patriarchs'. Thus, Ruth's story becomes a reinterpretation of how God elected the patriarchs (p. 28). The portrayal of Ruth's departure from Moab echoes that of Abram when he left his land, his family, and his father's house (p. 16). But where Abram leaves trusting in God's promise, Ruth leaves her native land without the assurance of any such promise (p. 49).

times, *davaq* denotes sudden misfortune as when Gehazi, servant of the prophet Elisha, is punished for his greed with a skin disease 'clinging' to him for the rest of his life (2 Kings 5.27). In summary, *davaq* is an intense verb describing feelings or situations out of the ordinary. In the light of Ruth's solemn declaration of lifelong loyalty to Naomi (1.16-17), the narrator's use of *davaq* (1.14) is comparable to the marital commitment recorded in Genesis 2.24.

Table 76 shows how the twelve English versions of the Bible have rendered *davaq* and *bĕ* in Genesis 2 and Ruth 1 (emphasis added).

Table 76
Translating DAVAQ, 'Cling'

Version	Gen. 2.24: A man to a woman	Ruth 1.14: A woman to a woman
CCB	is *attached to* his wife	Ruth *clung to* her
HCSB	*bonds with* his wife	Ruth *clung to* her
JM	*cleaves to* his wife	Ruth *clung to* her
JPS	*clings to* his wife	Ruth *clung to* her
NCV	be *united with* his wife	Ruth *held on to* her *tightly*
NIV	is *united to* his wife	Ruth *clung to* her
NJB	becomes *attached to* his wife	Ruth *stayed with* her
NKJV	be *joined to* his wife	Ruth *clung to* her
NLT	is *joined to* his wife	Ruth *clung tightly to* Naomi
NRSV	*clings to* his wife	Ruth *clung to* her
NWT	he must *stick to* his vife	she *stuck with* her
REB	*attaches himself to* his wife	Ruth *clung to* her

Taken vertically, there are no contradictions between the renderings offered in the first column, i.e. all are virtually interchangeable. The most popular option is 'attaches himself to', or similar (CCB, NJB, REB). These options adequately reflect the degree of commitment associated with a marital bond. If the second column is read vertically, a majority of eight versions say 'clung to her', other expressions being 'she clung tightly to Naomi' (NLT), 'held on to her tightly' (NCV), 'stuck with her' (NWT), and 'stayed with her' (NJB). In terms of accuracy, 'clung to her' and 'stuck with her' adequately reflect Ruth's decision. The adverb 'tightly' offered by the NCV and the NLT add an element of intensity and dogged determination to Ruth's clinging to Naomi.

In column 2, the NJB's 'stayed with her' is less colourful than the rest. There is nothing egregiously wrong with the phrase, but three observations seem pertinent: (1) it is a rather pale reflection of the dogged determination or firm commitment involved in *davaq* combined with the preposition *bĕ*; (2) few translators would want to say 'stay with his wife' in the context of Genesis 2.24; and (3) for the verb to mean 'stay with' or 'keep near to' somebody, *davaq* is usually joined by another preposition, namely, *'im*, 'with'. The narrative provides an example in 2.8 where Boaz by means of *davaq* and *'im* tells Ruth to 'stay with' or 'keep close to' his young women as she goes gleaning in the field. In addition, Classical Hebrew has other ways of expressing 'stay with', e.g. Genesis 18.22 where YHWH 'remains standing before', i.e. stays with Abraham for a while to enable the latter to intercede for the innocent citizens of Sodom (Brueggemann 1982: 168).

When the two columns in table 76 are read horizontally, it becomes clear that only two versions consistently translate *davaq* as 'cling to' (JPS, NRSV) while the NWT twice offers 'stick with'. Several options in column 1 might be used for

Ruth's commitment to Naomi, particularly 'attached to' (CCB, NJB, REB), while 'united to/with' (NCV, NIV) and 'joined to' (NKJV, NLT) are perhaps less obvious choices. Conversely, in column 2 the suggestion that Ruth 'clung' to Naomi would work well for the context of column 1. However, the intensifying adverb 'tightly' introduced by two versions (NCV, NLT) would be out of place in Genesis 2.24. As noted above, the NJB's 'stayed with her' only suits one context. This brief overview has shown that many translators do not describe the two situations in identical terms, despite their textual similarities and the remarkable presence of *davaq* and *bě* in both. By drawing an intertextual parallel to Genesis 2, the narrator clearly regards *davaq* as the adequate term for Ruth's commitment to Naomi. However, as often happens in biblical translation, most versions have opted for variation where the Hebrew texts are consistent, thus depriving today's English readers of significant repetitions and resonances.

A Blessed Relationship

Naomi enjoys Ruth's company, affectionately calling the young woman *bittī*, 'my daughter' (2.2, 22; 3.18).[339] That their relationship is mutual and for life is emphasized in 2.20 and 3.2, where Naomi refers to Boaz as 'a relative of *ours*, one of *our* nearest kin' and '*our* kinsman Boaz' (emphasis added). Throughout the story, the narrator draws attention to these women and their special relationship, turning the male figures into helpers (Boaz, Obed) or background figures (the deceased husbands and their distant male relatives in Bethlehem). Naomi subtly and cleverly arranges Ruth's

---

[339] For his part, Boaz cordially addresses Ruth as 'my daughter' (2.8; 3.10), suggesting an age gap; cf. 'you have not gone after one of the young men' (3.10).

marriage to Boaz according to the so-called levirate system whereby Boaz, a kinsman of Ruth's deceased husband, replaces the latter (cf. Deut. 25.5-6). In this manner, Naomi is able to achieve economic security for both women (Ruth 3.1), and the birth of Ruth's son Obed signals that they will be taken care of in their old age (4.15). As noted by Phyllis Trible (1984: 85), the child restores life to Naomi rather than perpetuates the name of her deceased husband Elimelech.

A native of the reviled nation of Moab,[340] Ruth traces her ancestry back to one of Lot's daughters (Gen. 19.37), all of which makes her an outsider in the Israelite context (Spina 2005: 120-1). As pointed out by Calum Carmichael (2010: 128), the narrator compares Ruth to Tamar, the Canaanite woman whose strength of character ensured the survival and continuity of Judah's family tree (Gen. 38.13-27; Ruth 4.12). Like Tamar, Ruth the foreigner inscribes her name in the history of Israel by becoming an ancestress of King David (Ruth 4.21-22). Robert Alter (1992: 52) finds that this 'sets Ruth up as a founding mother, in symmetrical correspondence to Abraham the founding father'. Both she and he came from a foreign country to settle in the Promised Land and both took up the destiny of the covenanted people. Thus, this Moabitess places herself 'in the category of some of the most prominent and significant women of Israel's history' (Spina 2005: 134).

In the narrative, it is precisely due to her dedication to Naomi of Bethlehem that Ruth is given a warm welcome by her new community (2.12; 3.10). They regard her commitment as blessed by YHWH (2.12; 4.14).[341] The close bond between the two women is such that, when Ruth gives birth to Obed, the

---

[340] Num. 25.1-3; Deut. 23.3-6; Judg. 3.12-14.
[341] As pointed out by Kirsten Nielsen (1997: 30), the numerous times YHWH is mentioned in the narrative create an awareness of his never-failing presence.

townswomen celebrate the event, exclaiming: '*Naomi* has had a baby!' (4.17, emphasis added). In 4.15, they address Naomi directly, saying (NRSV, emphasis added):

> He [Obed] shall be to you a restorer of life and a nourisher of your old age; for your daughter-in-law who *loves* you, who is *more to you than seven sons*, has borne him.

This statement of approval has two striking biblical parallels. One is the occurrence of *ahav*, 'loves', the verb that describes Jacob's feelings for Rachel in Genesis 29.18. The resonance of this passage is suggested in Ruth 4.11 where allusion is made to Jacob ('Israel'), Rachel, and Leah. Another intriguing element in the text cited above is the laudatory phrase 'more to you than seven sons'. This echoes a passage in 1 Samuel 1.8 where Elkanah speaks words of appreciation to Hannah, his beloved, childless wife: 'Am I not more to you than ten sons?' Moreover, while her firstborn son Samuel is still a baby, a grateful Hannah dedicates him to service at the sanctuary of Yhwh in Shiloh, saying that 'the barren has borne seven' (1 Sam. 2.5).

Mona West (2006: 190–4) has studied the book of Ruth from the point of view of survival and the meaning of the word 'family'. In an ancient world characterized by male power and privilege, the situation of two childless women was precarious. As widows, Ruth and Naomi were exposed to penury and relegated to the bottom of the social hierarchy (Exod. 22.22; Spina 2005: 123). Nonetheless, instead of staying behind to search for a suitable Moabite husband, Ruth chose to cleave to Naomi, a poverty-stricken foreign woman. In the process she left everything behind: familiar surroundings, family, friends, personal history, language, and traditions. In a male-dominated culture, Ruth was an example of self-determination as she courageously named and affirmed her relationship to Naomi in the face of seemingly insurmountable odds (1.16-17). Following the recent tragic loss of their husbands, Ruth and Naomi creatively made a new start by establishing an unusual kind of family unit, which somehow fitted the description of 'one flesh' normally depicting the marital union of a man and a woman (Gen. 2.24). According to West (2006: 193), the joint strategies for survival adopted by Ruth and Naomi in Bethlehem are paralleled today by the efforts of thousands of couples around the world whose relationships do not respond to the norms of the heterosexual majority. Ruth, Naomi, and Boaz provide modern readers with a biblical precedent of how a creative new family structure is established.

Celena Duncan (2000: 92) has meditated on the story of Ruth from a personal perspective: 'In the spirit of rabbinic tradition, I read the book of Ruth as a bisexual midrash.'[342] She points out that many lesbian couples around the world have repeated Ruth's words of commitment to Naomi in rituals blessing their unions (p. 94). Duncan wonders why Christians are so unwilling to believe that all sexuality is as varied and diverse as the rest of God's creation. In her view, biodiversity and sexual diversity are God's created norms (p. 93). Ruth undoubtedly was surprised to find herself being drawn to the love of another woman with whom she would form a bond stronger than her family ties with Moab. Duncan reflects on the inadequacy of labels (p. 102):

> Were Ruth and Naomi close in-laws, or friends, or sexual intimates? Labelling their relationship is to limit and diminish what they had.

For Duncan, there is no point in speculating about the exact nature of the affection that united Naomi and Ruth. A better

---

[342] For a lesbian midrash of Ruth, see Rebecca Alpert 1996.

way to view the relationship is to acknowledge its unique strength (p. 100). These women dared to let go of long-held biases in favour of what God was revealing to them (p. 101).

David and Jonathan

The story of David and Jonathan has received considerable scholarly attention in recent years.[343] Situated in the two books of Samuel, this is the only text in the HB depicting love between two men not related to each other. It unfolds amid the rise to political stardom of David, a young shepherd boy from Bethlehem. Against all odds, he is selected by the prophet Samuel (1 Sam. 16.10-13) to become successor of King Saul, whose residence is at Gibeah of Benjamin (1 Sam. 10.26). On account of his youthful good looks combined with outstanding musical skills and military prowess, David becomes immensely popular (Gordon & Rendsburg 1997: 187). The common people love him (18.16) and so do all of Saul's courtiers (18.22), Saul himself (16.21) and his son Jonathan (18.1). Saul's daughter Michal falls in love (18.20) and is allowed to marry David (18.27-28).

Focusing specifically on the story of David and Jonathan, Theodore Jennings (2005: 29) interprets it as a complex relationship involving issues of personal loyalty, commitment, love, and sexual intimacy. Adopting a radically different approach, Robert Gagnon (2001: 147) argues that Jonathan's love for David is portrayed 'as part of a much larger love affair of the people of Israel with David'. Through their covenant, Jonathan virtually adopts David into the royal family, making the two relate 'as brothers, not as a

---

[343] See Comstock 1993: 82-90, 128-9; Stuart 1995: 132-6; Nissinen 1998: 53-6; Kader 1999: 107-18; Helminiak 2000: 123-5; Greenberg 2004: 99-105; Jennings 2005: 25-36; Stone 2006: 205-8; Heacock 2011: 7-55; Sharpe 2011: 141-6.

romantic couple'. Their alliance may be 'deeply personal, but nonetheless political' (pp. 148). Gagnon repeatedly stresses the political nature of this relationship (pp. 149–52), arguing that the language of love in the Hebrew text is typical of covenant-treaties in the ancient Near East (p. 148). He finds 'nothing inherently homosexual' in the way Jonathan and David interact, including the emotional farewell scene in which they kiss each other (p. 152). In Gagnon's view, the narrator is silent 'about any sexual activity' between the two young men (p. 153). He concludes that their relationship is close but 'completely asexual' (p. 154).

A more recent study by Anthony Heacock (2011: 8) expresses agreement with some of the points made by Gagnon. Particularly, Heacock finds it unlikely that 'a straight man' (sic) like Jonathan can be 'swayed to homosexual desire' solely by David's physical beauty. He finds important political, theological, and social connotations in the Hebrew vocabulary used in the narrative, which includes 'covenant' and 'oath' (p. 9). All these aspects are present when Jonathan freely accepts that 'it is God's will for David to become king' to the point of being ready to serve 'as a vehicle for its implementation' (p. 10). Heacock argues that David and Jonathan's alliance appears to be founded 'more on theologically sanctioned obligations than amity', finding the bond comparable to the relationship between God and Israel (p. 11). He explains that the feelings of the two young men are 'subsumed under the diplomatic aspect of an alliance that demonstrates a complex fusion of friendship and politics' (p. 13). Understood in this light, Jonathan's dedication to David 'serves the interests of the transference of kingship from Saul to David' (p. 14).[344]

---

[344] For an overview of recent debates on the complex nature of David and Jonathan's relationship, and a series of personal reflections on the same, see Heacock 2011: 10–55, 135–50.

For his part, Martti Nissinen (1998: 55) finds it possible to understand David's and Jonathan's love as an intimate camaraderie of two young soldiers with no sexual involvement. There is no indication in the text that David and Jonathan slept together, and both had wives and fathered children (p. 56). Above all, for Nissinen, the equality of the two men's relationship is striking (p. 55). At the same time, however, he concedes that a homoerotic interpretation of the story is conceivable. He bases this argument on the text, which reports how Jonathan loved David 'as himself'. Without being explicit, the narrative leaves the possible homoerotic associations 'to the reader's imagination'. Still, Nissinen cautions that modern readers may be conditioned to see homoeroticism in the story more easily than did the ancients (p. 56), a reminder of the massive process of 'sexualization' that took place in the Western world during the nineteenth and twentieth centuries (Heacock 2011: 48, 65). In this context, Theodore Jennings (2005: 34) points to the profound difference between the way in which homoerotic relationships were depicted in antiquity and their representations in the late modern period. However, he draws the conclusion that essential parts of the story of David and Jonathan may be regarded as an early anticipation of the modern ideal of equal life partners bound together by mutual love (p. 35).

Saul's Love for David

The Hebrew verb *ahav*, 'love', plays a major part in the narrative featuring Saul, Jonathan and David as protagonists. As Saul becomes increasingly depressed, David is brought in to provide musical therapy by playing the lyre (1 Sam. 16.16–23). Initially Saul is delighted to have him around and *loves* him greatly (16.21). This happy state of affairs continues until the day in which the women of Israel, in a public celebration of David's victory over Goliath the Philistine giant, perform a musical highlighting David's bravery and presenting him as a greater warrior than Saul. Smarting from wounded pride, King Saul becomes jealous, and their relationship badly deteriorates to the point that Saul tries to kill David (18.11; 19.10–11). In other words, his love for David is short-lived.

With respect to the verb *ahav*, it has presented few challenges to the twelve English versions of the Bible. All rightly render *ahav* as 'loved' in reference to Saul's daughter Michal falling in love with David (1 Sam. 18.20, 28), and they are similarly successful in depicting the strength of Jonathan's attraction to David in 18.1, 3. However, despite the presence of *ahav*, Saul's initial feelings for David are approached in somewhat different terms. Table 77 shows twelve English renderings of *wayyeehavēhū měōd*, 'and he loved him greatly', in 1 Samuel 16.21.

Table 77
Saul Loved Him Greatly

Version	*Wayyeehavēhū měōd*, 1 Sam. 16.21
CCB	Saul grew very fond of David
HCSB	Saul admired him greatly
JM	Saul loved him
JPS	Saul took a strong liking to him
NCV	Saul liked David
NIV	Saul liked him very much
NJB	Saul became very fond of him
NKJV	he loved him greatly
NLT	Saul loved David very much
NRSV	Saul loved him greatly
NWT	he got to loving him very much
REB	Saul loved him dearly

The versions represented in table 77 may be grouped according to their degrees of literalness. Five versions take a literal approach to the Hebrew text with options such as 'Saul loved him greatly/dearly' (NRSV, REB), 'he loved him greatly' (NKJV), 'he got to loving him very much' (NWT), and 'Saul loved David very much' (NLT). Using 'loved', but omitting 'greatly', is JM's 'Saul loved him'. Still recognizably literal are 'Saul grew very fond of David' (CCB) and 'Saul became very fond of him' (NJB). Bordering on paraphrase are 'Saul took a strong liking to him' (JPS), 'Saul liked him very much' (NIV), 'Saul liked David' (NCV) and 'Saul admired him greatly' (HCSB).

The less literal versions in table 77 have a problem in common. While the narrator uses *ahav* for Saul's feelings as well as for Jonathan and Michal loving David, creating a form of literary balance between father, son, and daughter, these versions lose the balance by failing to adopt the same approaches to *ahav* in all passages. Clearly no English translator would suggest that Michal in 1 Samuel 18.20 and 28 'took a strong liking' to David or, simply, 'liked him'. Moreover, compared with the force inherent in 'loved', the weaker 'liked' does not explain why Saul initially was so taken by David that he would bestow unusual favours upon the young man, including making him his armour-bearer (16.21), offering him his personal armour for the battle with Goliath (17.38) and appointing him commander-in-chief of the army (18.5). The English verb 'admired', introduced by the HCSB, is not interchangeable with 'loved'. It would be out of place for 18.1–3, where it would be meaningless to suggest that Jonathan 'admired David as his own soul'. In addition, Classical Hebrew expresses the concept of admiration more precisely with the verbal root *h-l-l*, which in the *Piel* verb pattern means 'praise'. For instance, in 2 Samuel 14.25 readers are told that David's son Absalom was widely lĕhallēl, 'praised' (NRSV, NWT) or 'admired' (JPS, REB), on account of his extraordinary beauty.

You Were Dear to Me

Wherever Jonathan's love for David is mentioned, virtually all English versions adequately render *ahav* as 'love'.[345] This is a rare example of precise translation across the board. However, some variation is found in their approaches to David's feelings for Jonathan. Following Jonathan's sudden death on the battlefield, a grief-stricken David exclaims (2 Sam. 1.26):

> I am distressed for you, my brother Jonathan;
> very pleasant were you to me;
> your love to me was wonderful,
> surpassing the love of women.

In this elegy, 'my brother' is a term of endearment (Stuart 1995: 136) comparable to the use of 'my sister' in the Song of Songs (4.9-10; 5.1-2). Subsequently David says *naʿamtā lī mĕōd*, which literally means 'you were very pleasant (or attractive) to me'. This verb *naʿam* belongs to the realm of poetry, occurring in the Song of Songs 7.6: 'how beautiful you are'; Ps. 141.6: 'my words were pleasant'; Prov. 2.10: 'knowledge will delight you', 9.17: 'bread eaten furtively is pleasant'; and 24.25: 'they will have delight'; and Ezekiel 32.19: 'Whom do you surpass in beauty?' Table 78 shows the versions' approaches to David's statement *naʿamtā lī mĕōd*.

---

[345] 1 Sam. 18.1, 3; 20.17; 2 Sam. 1.26 (x 2).

Table 78
David's Feelings for Jonathan

Version	*Naʿamtā lī mĕōd*, 2 Sam. 1.26
CCB	how dear you have been to me
HCSB	you were such a friend to me
JM	you were my dear delight
JPS	you were most dear to me
NCV	I enjoyed your friendship so much
NIV	you were very dear to me
NJB	very dear you were to me
NKJV	you have been very pleasant to me
NLT	Oh, how much I loved you
NRSV	greatly beloved were you to me
NWT	very pleasant were you to me
REB	you were most dear to me

Clearly the most popular option in table 78 is 'you were dear to me', a phrase adopted with minor variations by five versions (CCB, JPS, NIV, NJB, REB). JM adds poetic tenderness with 'you were my dear delight' while two versions prefer the more matter-of-fact 'you were very pleasant to me' (NKJV, NWT). Two versions emphasize the aspect of love (NLT, NRSV) and two classify David's emotional words as a reference to friendship (HCSB, NCV). Regarding love, it is surprising that the NLT and the NRSV should translate *naʿamtā* in this way. In view of the context, and taken in isolation, the NRSV's statement 'greatly beloved were you to me' is probably true, but it seems odd to introduce the idea of love at this point because it appears in the very next sentence. The noun *ahavah*, 'love', occurs twice in the form of *ahavathkhā*, 'your love', and *ahavath nashīm*, 'the love of women'. Even more surprising is the NLT's paraphrase 'oh, how much *I* loved you', which turns the speaker (David) into grammatical subject while in the Hebrew sentence it is Jonathan: '*you* were very dear to me'.

Similarly, it may be argued that the two versions suggesting that David is speaking of his 'friendship' with Jonathan are being imprecise. The HCSB's 'you were such a friend to me' implies the presence in the original of the noun 'friend', in Hebrew *ra(eh*, another option being *ohēv*, 'lover' or 'dear friend'. These words do not occur here, but *ra(eh* is found later in the story when David's friend Hushai appears on the scene in 2 Samuel 15.37 and 16.16-17. As for the NCV's rendering 'I enjoyed your friendship so much', it changes the grammatical subject from 'you' to 'I'. In addition, it presupposes the existence in the text of a phrase depicting the notion of friendship, for which the Hebrew equivalent would be the verb *ra(ah*, 'keep company with' or 'make friends with' (Prov. 13.20).

Faithful Love

Following the deaths of Saul and Jonathan on the battlefield, David uses the endearing term *neehavīm*, 'beloved' or 'lovable', to recall how both men loved him (2 Sam. 1.23). As noted, however, the most intense love affair experienced by David while serving Saul is neither with the king nor with his daughter Michal but with Saul's eldest son. In 1 Samuel 18.1-3, Jonathan takes the initiative (NRSV, emphasis added):

> When David had finished speaking to Saul, the soul of Jonathan was bound to the soul of David, and Jonathan *loved* him as his own soul . . . Then Jonathan *made a covenant* with David, because

he *loved* him as his own soul. Jonathan stripped himself of the robe that he was wearing, and gave it to David, and his armour, and even his sword and his bow and his belt.

This short passage contains a number of remarkable details. First, Jonathan feels powerfully attracted to David to the point of falling in love. As in the story of Ruth and Naomi, the narrator of 1 Samuel uses poetic language to highlight the fact that 'Jonathan loved David as his own soul' (1 Sam. 18.1-3; 20.17) and 'took great delight' in him (19.1). Second, Jonathan makes a covenant with David, i.e. he formally commits himself to the latter. Third, Jonathan, the heir apparent, surprisingly and publicly displays unconditional loyalty as he hands over to David his royal status symbols: robe, armour, sword, bow, and belt. Thus, Jonathan's gesture is more than generous. In reality, he is saying to David: 'All that is mine belongs to you.' As noted by Comstock (1993: 84-5), ancient covenants were hierarchical, i.e. they presupposed a relationship of superiority/inferiority. Yet Jonathan's pact with David builds on equality and mutuality (Nissinen 1998: 55-6).

While Jonathan is still alive, the strength of his feelings is highlighted on several occasions as in 1 Samuel 20.4: 'Whatever you say, I will do for you.' In 20.14-17, Jonathan speaks to David (emphasis added):

> 'If I am still alive, show me the faithful *love* of Y<small>HWH</small>; but if I die, never cut off your faithful *love* from my house' . . . Thus Jonathan *made a covenant* with the house of David, saying, 'May Y<small>HWH</small> seek out the enemies of David.' Jonathan made David swear again by his *love* for him; for he *loved* him as he loved his own life.

Throughout this relationship, it is significant that Jonathan invokes the divine name when his covenant with David is ratified: 'Yhwh is between you and me for ever' (1 Sam. 20.23). As they enter into a lifelong commitment, they agree to let it encompass their descendants. In 1 Samuel 20.42 Jonathan says,

> Both of us have sworn in the name of Yhwh, saying, 'Yhwh shall for ever be between me and you, and between my descendants and your descendants.'

The high-profile bond between David and Jonathan does not go unnoticed. Jonathan, whose name means 'Yhwh has given', faces the vehement opposition of a jealous Saul who cannot understand why his son places friendship above family loyalty and career opportunities. In a fit of rage, Saul grossly insults and physically attacks Jonathan (1 Sam. 20.30–34). Despite such adversity, Jonathan renounces all birthright privileges to establish with David an intimate relationship that promises no political gain for him personally.

Both David and Jonathan were married (1 Sam. 19.11; 2 Sam. 3.2; 4.4). Would it be appropriate to say that they were gay or bisexual in the modern sense? In 1 Samuel 20.30, Saul's virulent outburst against Jonathan certainly suggests an erotic liaison between the two young men as the king uses such stinging expressions as 'your own shame', 'your mother's nakedness' and 'you son of a perverse, rebellious woman' (Helminiak 2000: 123). Theodore Jennings (2005: 34) believes that an erotic reading of the story 'makes the saga far more intelligible than readings that deny this dimension of the text'. For her part, Elizabeth Stuart (1995: 136) grants that the particular friendship between Jonathan and David was 'passionate, intense and physically expressed' (cf. 1 Sam.

20.41), but otherwise she finds rigid distinctions between so-called sexual and non-sexual relationships unhelpful. Following a reflection on sex as an ingredient in political alliances and the prominence of same-sex intimacy between married men in ancient Greece, Ken Stone (2006: 208) argues that the biblical material does not make it possible to reach a definitive conclusion about the nature of the bond between David and Jonathan.

Perhaps there is no need to resolve this uncertainty. Some questions that modern readers tend to ask are left unanswered by the biblical narrator, and for ancient readers or hearers, such questions may not have seemed relevant (Nissinen 1998: 56). Concluding his exploration of the story, Anthony Heacock (2011: 150) believes that David and Jonathan were, 'in their own unique way, friends and lovers'. He continues,

> Such an assertion purposely says nothing about sex. For those on a relentless quest to 'prove' their case one way or another, my only advice is we do not know, we never will and, quite frankly, it is none of our business!

In other words, what endures is the literary legacy of a remarkable, lifelong same-sex friendship established as a covenant before Yhwh and described in the language of love.

Love in the Second Testament

The ST offers numerous reflections on the subject of love, the primary Greek noun being *agapē* with the corresponding verb *agapaō*. In the writings included in the ST, *agapē* occurs in a variety of contexts to denote 'love' in the sense of attachment, devotion and commitment: the love of God for humanity, the love of human beings for God, parental love, love of neighbour, love of enemies, love as a characteristic of the Christian community, love as a sign of loyalty, marital love, and strong interpersonal relationships based on love. With regard to the love of God, John 3.16 summarizes the essence of the Gospel message (NRSV, emphasis added):

> For God so *loved* the world that he gave his only Son, so that everyone who believes in him may not perish but may have eternal life.

In this verse, the Greek verb for 'loved' is *ēgapēsen*, a past-tense form of *agapaō*, which connotes 'love as based on evaluation and choice, a matter of will and action' (FFM p. 30). The Gospel of John states in 3.35 and 5.20 how the Father loves the Son (cf. 10.17; 15.9). The same verb *agapaō* occurs in another famous passage where Jesus sums up the greatest commandments of the Hebrew Bible on which 'all the law and the prophets' hang, according to Matt. 22.37-39 (NRSV, emphasis added):

> He said to him, 'You shall *love* the Lord your God with all your heart, and with all your soul, and with all your mind.' This is the greatest and first commandment. And a second is like it: 'You shall *love* your neighbour as yourself.'

Jesus is quoting Deuteronomy 6.5 and Leviticus 19.18, the latter being echoed by Paul in Romans 13.9 and Galatians 5.14. Jesus's command to love (*agapaō*) enemies and pray for persecutors occurs in Matthew 5.44 and Luke 6.27-28. One of the best-known passages in the letters of Paul is 1 Corinthians 13 where the apostle meditates on the pivotal importance of love. The chapter begins and finishes with these verses (NRSV, emphasis added):

> If I speak in the tongues of mortals and of angels, but do not have *love*, I am a noisy gong or a clanging cymbal . . . And now faith, hope, and *love* abide, these three; and the greatest of these is *love*.

Paul's highly poetic prose focuses on love among Christians, a concept that includes patience, kindness, simplicity (13.4), truthfulness (13.6), and endurance (13.7-8). Again, the central term is *agapē*, and the same root is present in Jesus's exhortations to his disciples to love (*agapaō*) each other as he has loved them (Jn. 13.34-35; 15.9-10, 12; cf. Rom. 12.9; 13.8). Often *agapaō* denotes attachment, e.g. in John 3.19 where Jesus refers to people who do evil as those who 'love darkness rather than light'. In a positive sense, he speaks of the ones who are devoted to him: 'If you love me, you will keep my commandments' (14.15). Jesus does not mention marital love, but the concept occurs in Paul's letter to the Ephesians (5.25): 'Husbands, love your wives.'

In the Gospel of Mark, Jesus is approached by a rich young man who desires to know what it takes to inherit eternal life (Mk. 10.21). During this dialogue the Gospel writer notes that 'Jesus, looking at him, *loved* him', using the same verb (*ēgapēsen*) that reflects the love of God for the whole world in John 3.16. Most English versions adequately say 'Jesus loved him'. A few expand the phrase: 'he felt love for him' (NWT), 'he was filled with love for him' (NJB), and 'Jesus felt genuine love for him' (NLT). Why the NLT has felt the need to insert 'genuine' is unclear. Most notably, the REB has taken a different approach from the rest, omitting the word 'loved' and producing a paraphrase: 'his heart warmed to him'.

Another Greek verb often used in the ST to express affection is *phileō*, which may be rendered 'like', 'feel affection for' or 'have a high regard for' (Danker 2009: 372; FFM p. 399). This verb occurs in John 11.3 where Mary and Martha send a message to Jesus, saying, 'He whom you love is ill'. In John 16.27, Jesus tells his disciples that, because they have loved him, the Father loves them; and Paul sends greetings to those who love him 'in the faith' (Titus 3.15). In Matthew 10.37, Jesus cautions his followers against valuing (*phileō*) parents or children to the point of forsaking him: 'Whoever loves father and mother . . . and son or daughter more than me is not worthy of me.' Similarly, he warns against undue attachment to worldly affairs: 'Those who love their life lose it' (Jn. 12.25). Among friends, *phileō* sometimes means 'greet with a kiss' (Mk. 14.44-45; Lk. 22.47), the corresponding noun being *philēma* (Lk. 7.45; 22.48).

Related nouns are *philos* and *philia*. Often *philos* translates as 'friend'; cf. *philos tou kaisaros*, 'a friend of the emperor' (Jn. 19.12). While it may overlap with *agapē* in some cases, *philia* usually connotes 'friendship' or 'affection': 'Do you not know that friendship with the world is enmity with God?' (James 4.4). The same root is present in the noun *philadelphia*, 'sibling love', a combination of *philia* and the root *adelph*—occurring in *adelphē*, 'sister', and *adelphos*, 'brother'. In Romans 12.10, Paul encourages Christians to treat one another with *philadelphia*. Some English versions translate this as 'brotherly love' (HCSB, LEB, NKJV, NWT) and 'love for the brotherhood' (JM), while others prefer 'mutual affection' (NRSV, REB), 'genuine affection' (NLT) and 'mutual respect' (CCB).

Physical Intimacy

A number of ST passages depict affection between individuals. The third letter of John greets the recipients as *agapēte*, 'beloved' (3 John 2, 5, 11). In Mk. 1.11, a voice from heaven expresses a paternal form of love, saying to Jesus, 'You are my Son, the Beloved' (*agapētos*). Similarly, Paul addresses one of his letters to a certain disciple as *Timotheō, agapētō teknō*, 'Timothy, beloved child' (2 Tim. 1.2). In all cases, the participle *agapētos* relates to the verb *agapaō* and the noun *agapē*.

As noted earlier, both *agapē* and *philia* are commonly used in the ST in connection with 'love', including close same-sex relationships. For translators, problems tend to arise in some crucial passages where physical intimacy is involved. In the highly significant Last Supper scene narrated in John 13, the narrator provides several items of information with respect to the seating arrangement. Greek verbs such as *anakeimenos* (13.23) and *anapesōn* (13.25) indicate that participants are not 'sitting' around the common table in any modern sense but 'reclining' and 'leaning back', i.e. positioned on couches as was the custom in Greco-Roman times.[346] The disciple referred to as *hon ēgapa ho Iēsous*, 'whom Jesus loved', enjoys the privilege of lying at Jesus's right hand and is able to rest his head on the master's chest. Two words meaning 'breast', 'chest', or 'bosom' are used, namely, *kolpos* (Jn. 13.23) and *stēthos* (13.25).[347]

Commenting on this setting, Thomas Hanks (2000: 63) observes, 'Modern translations create more space between Jesus and the Beloved Disciple than indicated by the Greek text'. In order to gauge the extent of this perceived gap between the original and today's English versions of the Bible, table 79 explores their renderings of *kolpos* and *stēthos*.

---

[346] The custom of reclining on couches was often associated with wealth and social status; cf. blogs.getty.edu/iris/reclining-and-dining-and-drinking-in-ancient-rome/ (2012).

[347] Sometimes *kolpos* alludes to the fold of a garment beginning at the chest and forming a kind of pocket (Danker 2009: 204; cf. Lk. 6.38), while *stēthos* refers to the thorax (Lk. 18.13).

The two Greek prepositions *en* and *epi* both mean 'on', with the latter sometimes adopting the sense of 'before' and 'near' (FFM p. 162).

Table 79
Translating 'On Jesus' Chest' in John 13

Version	*en tō kolpō*, 13.23	*epi to stēthos*, 13.25
CCB	reclining near Jesus	reclining near Jesus
HCSB	reclining close beside Jesus	leaned back against Jesus
JM	reclining on his breast	leant back on the breast of Jesus
LEB	reclining close beside* Jesus *Lit 'in the bosom of'	leaned back accordingly against Jesus's chest
NCV	sitting* next to Jesus *Lit 'lying'	leaned closer to Jesus
NIV	reclining next to him	leaning back against Jesus
NJB	reclining next to Jesus	leaning back close to Jesus' chest
NKJV	leaning on Jesus' bosom	leaning back on Jesus's breast
NLT	sitting next to Jesus	leaned over to Jesus
NRSV	reclining next to him	reclining next to Jesus
NWT	reclining in front of J's bosom	leaned back upon the breast of J.
REB	reclining close beside Jesus	leaned back close to Jesus

If these versions are placed on a sliding scale to assess their degree of literalness, or lack of it, in John 13.23 only two versions have taken the Greek text literally: 'reclining on his breast' (JM) and 'leaning on Jesus' bosom' (NKJV). The preposition *en* is correctly rendered 'on'. A larger group introduces a slight distance between master and disciple by replacing 'on' with 'near', or similar: 'reclining near Jesus'

(CCB), 'next to Jesus' (NJB), 'next to him' (NIV, NRSV), and 'close beside Jesus' (HCSB, LEB, REB). In a footnote, the LEB acknowledges that a literal rendering would be 'in the bosom of Jesus'. For its part, the NWT has rightly included the noun 'bosom', but the original intimacy suggested by 'in' or 'on' has been replaced by the more neutral sounding 'in front of'. Furthermore, nine versions have aptly translated *anakeimenos* as 'reclining' and the NKJV as 'leaning'. However, the NCV and the NLT have modernized (and weakened) their English texts presenting the Beloved Disciple as, simply, 'sitting next to Jesus'. The NCV admits in a footnote that 'lying' would be more literal.

As for 13.25, the verb *anapesōn* is adequately rendered 'leaned' in ten cases and 'reclined' in two (CCB, NRSV). In the second column no version is saying explicitly that Jesus and his disciples are 'sitting', but the implication clearly remains in two cases (NCV, NLT). A group of five has acknowledged the presence of the word *stēthos*, calling it either 'breast' (JM, NKJV, NWT) or 'chest' (LEB, NJB). The HCSB and the NIV aptly suggest a certain intimacy between master and disciple by saying 'against Jesus' but failing to specify his chest. In respect of *epi*, very few versions render this preposition as 'on' (JM, NKJV) or 'upon' (NWT). Again many have opted for introducing a physical distance: 'closer to Jesus' (NCV), 'over to' (NLT), 'close to' (REB), 'near' (CCB) and 'next to Jesus' (NRSV). Finally, the rendering offered by the NJB juxtaposes 'close to' and 'chest', going part of the way towards suggesting nearness: 'leaning back close to Jesus' chest'.

This brief overview reveals that Hanks's statement, cited above, is accurate. Many English translators clearly find the physical intimacy of the two men depicted by the Greek text of John 13 to be 'too close for comfort'. Rather than expose their readers to the cultural insight that in antiquity male–male closeness was respectable, they have preferred to amend the text by creating some space in their English versions between a master and a trusted disciple sharing a meal. While two versions have used the verb 'sitting' for this purpose, several others achieve a similar effect by moving away from concrete terminology such as 'breast', 'chest', and 'bosom' and using more abstract paraphrases, a procedure also applied by the majority to the common Greek prepositions *en* and *epi*.

The Beloved Disciple

The suggestion that Jesus had a beloved female companion occurs in some Gnostic writings, including the *Gospel of Mary* in which this person is identified as Mary Magdalene (Nissinen 1998: 119). In recent years, this hypothesis has received considerable attention due to its role in Dan Brown's best-selling novel *The Da Vinci Code*. However, the Second Testament points in a different direction. The Gospel of John refers frequently to a follower of Jesus as 'the one whom Jesus loved' and, according to the Greek text, this follower was male. Given the intimacy conjured up by the phrase, some commentators have read the relationship between Jesus and the Beloved Disciple as 'a rare instance of homoerotic desire' (Goss 2006: 560). Several have suggested the two are lovers,[348] while others see them engaged in a pederastic relationship along the lines of the Greco-Roman *erastēs*, 'mature lover', and his *erōmenos*, the beloved younger male (Goss 2002: 120). If such is the case, it would fit in with educational settings in the Hellenistic era where teachers often had a favourite male student.

---

[348] Goss 2002: 16, 114, 119, 133–4, 164, 210.

Whatever modern terms are chosen to define the relationship between Jesus and the disciple in question, they can only be tentative because the relatively few details provided by the biblical narrative correspond to a culture separated from our own by two millennia. According to church tradition, the disciple is John the Evangelist, son of Zebedee and one of the twelve apostles (Nissinen 1998: 121; Hanks 2000: 64). However, the historical evidence is 'late, slender, and equivocal' and such attribution is 'almost certainly mistaken' (Jennings 2003: 43).[349] The Second Testament itself refers to the Beloved Disciple in John 11 where the Gospel writer identifies him as Lazarus of Bethany,[350] brother of Martha and Mary. Bethany is mentioned in all four Gospels as a place frequently visited by Jesus.[351] In a message that his sisters send to Jesus they refer to Lazarus as 'he whom you love' (Jn. 11.3). In addition, the people gathered in front of the tomb to mourn Lazarus's death comment to each other when Jesus weeps: 'See how he loved him' (11.36). These and other details mark out this follower as the most likely candidate for the Beloved Disciple (Goss 2000: 209).

Mentioned by name thirteen times in John 11 and 12, Lazarus becomes a prominent figure among Jesus's companions following his miraculous resurrection (Goss 2006: 561).[352] As he leaves the open grave, the narrator refers to him as 'the dead man' who came out (11.44) and subsequently as 'Lazarus, whom he had raised from the dead' (12.1, 9, 17).

---

[349] web.campbell.edu/faculty/vandergriffk/John.html (2012) offers a detailed discussion of the arguments surrounding the identity of the Beloved Disciple and the reasons why a scholarly consensus is difficult to attain. See also Jennings 2003: 41–54.
[350] 'Lazarus' is the Greek ST adaptation of the Hebrew name Eliezer, which is known from the Hebrew Bible (cf. Abraham's servant Eliezer in Gen. 15.2). Lk. 16.19–25 mentions another Lazarus unrelated to the young man from Bethany.
[351] Matt. 21.17; 26.6; Mk. 11.1, 11–12; 14.3; Lk. 19.29; 24.50; Jn. 11.1, 18.
[352] Jn. 11.44–45; 12.1–2, 9–11, 17–19.

From John 13 onwards, the name of Lazarus disappears from the text to be replaced by references to the Beloved Disciple, a term occurring nineteen times in different variants.[353] I interpret this as a deliberate choice on the part of the narrator who no longer wishes to draw attention to Lazarus as an individual with a sensational history. From John 13, the mood of the Gospel story changes as the emphasis falls on the final stages of Jesus's ministry, including his imminent arrest, torture, and death. In this context, the narrator focuses on what the Beloved Disciple represents to Jesus, namely, a very special person who supports the master, and in whose company the latter finds solace and rest. During this crucial phase, the disciple in question is present on a number of significant occasions.[354] In 18.15-16, it is possible that 'another disciple' is the same person, given that the narrator refers to someone like him as 'the other disciple, the one whom Jesus loved' (20.2) and subsequently abbreviates the reference to 'the other disciple' (20.3-8). On each occasion, this disciple speaks and acts in Simon Peter's company, which confirms that these two men were especially close to Jesus. Keith Sharpe (2011: 96) has noted that Simon Peter and his fellow disciples appear untroubled by the great intimacy between Jesus and the Beloved Disciple suggested by John's Gospel. On several occasions, Peter recognizes the special quality of this relationship (13.24; 21.20-21).

Meditating on the prominence of the Beloved Disciple in the Fourth Gospel, Robert Goss (2006: 561) finds that he is fully devoted to Jesus, faithful to him, and courageously remains with the master until the end, including in his death vigil at the foot of the cross. The Beloved Disciple is indeed the only male follower there (19.26; cf. Sharpe 2011: 96). Jesus expresses special tenderness for him and looks

---

[353] Jn. 11.3, 5, 36; 13.23-25; 18.15-16; 19.26-27, 35; 20.2-9; 21.2, 7, 20, 21-24.
[354] Jn. 13.23-30; 19.25-27; 20.1-10; 21.4-14, 20-24.

upon the Beloved Disciple as his replacement within his family, entrusting his mother to the disciple's care and vice versa (19.26-27). Furthermore, when she wishes to share the sensational news of the empty tomb, Mary Magdalene goes straight to Simon Peter and 'the disciple whom Jesus loved'. The fact that the latter reaches the tomb first, outrunning Simon Peter (20.4-5), and sees the linen wrappings lying there (20.8), powerfully connects him with the previous resurrection story in John 11. Having experienced a miracle performed by Jesus in his own flesh, he becomes the first believer in the risen Christ (20.8) and is first to recognize the master standing on the beach (21.7).

Thus, the resurrection theme in John's Gospel establishes a significant nexus between Lazarus and the Beloved Disciple, suggesting they are the same person. In John 5.25 Jesus declares, 'The dead will hear the voice of the son of God, and those who hear will live' (NRSV). He continues, 'All who are in their graves will hear his voice and will come out' (5.28-29). This prediction comes true in John 11.43 where Jesus, standing in front of Lazarus's grave, tells the latter to 'come out'. Towards the end of the Gospel (21.21), Simon Peter wonders whether the Beloved Disciple will die or not: 'Lord, what about him?' Since Lazarus has been raised from the dead, some disciples believe that he may not have to die again (21.20-23). For several of those listening to Jesus's ambiguous answer to Peter, it seems to confirm this hypothesis: 'If it is my will that he remain until I come, what is that to you?' (21.22-23). The person reporting this dialogue is the Beloved Disciple himself (21.24), who also recalls that he was an eyewitness to the crucifixion of Jesus (19.35). Repeatedly in John's Gospel, to which Lazarus may have contributed important parts, if not all, there is a clear link between the verbs 'hear', 'see', 'love', and 'live'.[355] Identity issues apart, from a theological viewpoint the gospel writer suggests to the attentive reader that what it takes to be regarded as a beloved disciple of Jesus is to listen to his voice, follow in his footsteps and remain faithful to him until the end.

Translating the Beloved Disciple

I now turn to the twelve English versions of the Bible to examine their approaches to the concept of love in connection with the Beloved Disciple. In John 11, where Lazarus is introduced, the Greek text contains both *phileō* (Jn. 11.3, 36) and *agapaō* (11.5). In the latter case, *agapaō* refers to Jesus's close relationship with Martha and Mary of Bethany as well as their brother Lazarus. Table 80 shows the English renderings adopted by the versions, with a few minority options italicized.

Table 80
Jesus Loving Lazarus (John 11)

Version	11.3 *phileō*	11.5 *agapaō*	11.36 *phileō*
CCB	the one you love	J. loved . . . Lazarus	how he loved him
HCSB	the one you love	J. loved . . . Lazarus	how He loved him
JM	he whom you love	J. loved . . . Lazarus	how he loved him
LEB	the one . . . you love	J. loved . . . Lazarus	how he loved him
NCV	the one you love	J. loved . . . Lazarus	how much he loved him

---

[355] Jn. 3.15–16; 5.24–29; 8.47; 9.35–41; 10.3–4, 16–17, 27; 11.25–26; 12.25, 35–36, 46–47; etc.

NIV	the one you love	J. loved . . . Lazarus	how he loved him
NJB	*the man* you love	J. loved . . . Lazarus	how much he loved him
NKJV	he whom you love	J. loved . . . Lazarus	how much He loved him
NLT	your *dear friend*	J. loved . . . Lazarus	how much he loved him
NRSV	he whom you love	J. loved . . . Lazarus	how he loved him
NWT	the one *for whom you have affection*	J. loved . . . Lazarus	*what affection he used to have for him*
REB	your *friend*	he loved . . . Lazarus	how dearly he *must have* loved him

In the first column (11.3), nine versions agree to translate *phileō* as 'love'. Only the NWT has chosen to say 'have affection for' while the NLT and the REB focus on friendship. Viewed in isolation, all the options on offer may be regarded as adequate for the context where Jesus is being told about someone for whom he cares. The nine versions saying 'love' emphasize the strength of feeling on Jesus's part while the REB simply speaks of 'your friend'. The notion of friendship is accurate inasmuch as this is one of the nuances included in *phileō* and the corresponding noun *philia*. Along similar lines, the adjective 'dear' in NLT's 'your dear friend' adds tenderness, approximating it to 'love'. Undoubtedly, the most unusual rendering in the first column is the NWT's 'the one for whom you have affection'. From a formal viewpoint, the NWT is proceeding correctly given the affinity between 'have affection for' and *phileō*. Stylistically speaking, however, it might be argued that the NWT's phrase is excessively formal or even stilted. The NJB provides another noteworthy detail in the first column where this version has chosen to highlight the maleness of the Beloved Disciple by saying 'the *man* you love' (emphasis added). Strictly speaking, the Greek noun *anēr*, 'man', is not there, but it is true that the Greek text speaks of *ide hon phileis*, 'the one you love', with the pronoun *hon* referring to a male person.

By contrast, the second column is uniform throughout in the sense that all versions have translated *agapaō* adequately, resorting to 'love' to describe Jesus's feelings for the three siblings Martha, Mary, and Lazarus. In the third column of table 80, eleven versions render *phileō* as 'love' while the NWT again opts for 'have affection for', which is semantically correct. However, this version's turn of phrase 'See, what affection he used to have for him!' comes across as awkward in a situation where a fairly plain statement is made by bystanders observing Jesus's tears.

The main surprise provided by table 80 emerges when the table is read horizontally. It is striking that no fewer than nine versions have translated both *phileō* and *agapaō* as 'loved' throughout, erasing any semantic distinction between them. Stated another way, the two verbs are presented as interchangeable amid a generalized trend toward uniformity. The NLT and the REB have taken a small step toward literalness in 11.3 where they use 'friend', but otherwise they fail to differentiate between the two verbs. The overall uniformity of the English renderings in table 80 contrasts with the variety suggested by the Greek text, particularly the nuances inherent in *phileō* and *agapaō*. Connoting friendship and affection, *phileō* might be translated as 'care about' or 'be fond of', while 'love' is a good match for *agapaō*, which describes relationships characterized by durability and commitment.

In other parts of John's Gospel, where the narrator speaks of 'the one Jesus loved' or 'the disciple whom he loved', most English versions have produced accurate renderings. A close inspection, however, reveals the presence of a few unusual translations. In John 13.23, where other versions plainly speak of 'the disciple Jesus loved', the NWT is convoluted, saying, 'one of his disciples, and Jesus loved him'. The greatest surprise is provided by the CCB in 19.26, where the narrator explains that Jesus from the cross 'saw his mother and the disciple whom he loved standing beside her' (NRSV). Strangely, the CCB reduces this significant scene to 'Jesus saw the Mother, and the disciple', without providing any information about the latter.[356]

Given the overall sophistication of John's Gospel (Ashton 1998: 259), the fact that the Greek verbs *agapaō* and *phileō* interact is no coincidence. Between chapters 11 and 21 of this Gospel, where the phrases 'the one Jesus loved' and 'the disciple whom Jesus loved' occur repeatedly, *phileō* and *agapaō* alternate. Three occurrences of *phileō* (11.3, 36; 20.2) are interwoven with five appearances of *agapaō* (11.5; 13.23; 19.26; 21.7, 20), establishing a refined literary pattern. In summary, the joint presence of these verbs in the Fourth Gospel provides a significant cross-identification between Lazarus and the Beloved Disciple. In most cases, unfortunately, this link is lost in translation.

Simon Peter's Commitment

Following Jesus's death and resurrection, he appears to a group of disciples on the shore of the Sea of Tiberias (Jn. 21.1-22). In the light of their recent separation, Jesus gently but insistently asks Simon Peter to commit himself anew. Here is my own literal translation of the passage 21.15-17:

> After they had eaten, Jesus said to Simon Peter,
> `Simon, son of John, do you love me more than

---

[356] Clearly the absence of 'whom Jesus loved' in 19.26 is an oversight because the CCB includes this detail in other passages.

these?' He said, `Yes, Lord. You know that I am fond of you.' Jesus said to him, `Feed my lambs.'

He said to him the second time, `Simon, son of John, do you love me?' Peter said, `Yes, Lord. You know that I am fond of you.' Jesus said to him, `Take care of my sheep.'

Then he asked Peter the third time, `Simon son of John, are you fond of me?' Peter was hurt because Jesus asked him the third time, 'Are you fond of me?' So he said to him, `Lord, you know all things. You are aware that I am fond of you.' Jesus said to him, `Feed my sheep.'

Appearing intertwined in this text, the creative tension between the two verbs *agapaō* and *phileō* plays an essential part in the conversation. Their positions in the Greek original are shown in table 81 (emphasis added).

Table 81
Simon Peter Loving Jesus (Greek)

John	Jesus Asking	Peter Responding
21.15	*agapas* me pleon toutōn	ou oidas hoti *philō* se
21.16	*agapas* me	ou oidas hoti *philō* se
21.17	(*phileis* me)	
	phileis me	panta ou oidas, ou ginōskeis hoti *philō* se

In the form of *agapas*, 'you love', *agapaō* occurs twice (21.15, 16) and *phileō* appears four times (*phileis* and *philō*) in this dialogue. In table 81, one occurrence of the phrase *phileis me*, 'do you care for me?' (21.17), is placed in parenthesis because it is not part of the conversation but rather a comment inserted by the narrator to reflect Peter's feelings in reaction to Jesus's repeated question. A literal English translation of table 81 is presented in table 82.

Table 82
Translating Simon Peter Loving Jesus

John	Jesus Asking	Peter Responding
21.15	Do you *love* me more than these?	You know I *am fond of* you
21.16	Do you *love* me?	You know I *am fond of* you
21.17	*Are* you *fond of* me?	You know all things, you are aware that I *am fond of* you

The curious juxtaposition of *agapaō* and *phileō* is likely to be intended to make important psychological and theological points. Initially Jesus seems to challenge Simon Peter by using *agapaō*, which is the stronger verb due to its connotations of attachment and commitment as in John 13.35 (NRSV): 'By this everyone will know that you are my disciples, if you have love for one another'. Understood in this light, Jesus's question to Peter may be paraphrased as 'Are you more devoted to me than the other disciples?' The fact that Peter, somewhat surprisingly, chooses not to answer with *agapaō* reveals that he understands Jesus's question but feels cornered. Remembering all too well the sequel to John 13.35, where he spontaneously, and in front of his fellow disciples, promised to lay down his life for his master (Jn. 13.37), Peter is painfully aware of his failure to live up to that commitment. When his faithfulness was put to the test, he did not act according to his promise but denied knowing Jesus three times in one night (Jn. 18.17, 25–27). Therefore, Peter cannot truthfully reply to Jesus's question with a resounding yes. Feeling unworthy to use *agapaō*, he resorts to the more modest and matter-of-fact *phileō*.

By repeating the question in 21.16, but leaving out the second part *pleon toutōn*, 'more than these', Jesus makes a subtle move in Simon Peter's direction inviting him again to consider the implications of *agapaō*, literally offering him a second chance. Another way of framing Jesus's question is this: 'Can I still depend on you?' Again Peter is candid enough to answer in accordance with reality by means of *phileō*, i.e. he acknowledges not having behaved like more than a friend. Following this manifestation of honesty, Jesus rewards him by making another significant move in his direction. Switching to *phileō*, he asks a third question that Peter is certain to answer without hesitation: 'Do you love me as a friend?' (21.17). Jesus's unexpected insistence painfully reminds Peter of the recent past, but the questions are not meant as a punishment. Rather the purpose of the dialogue appears to be threefold: (a) to cancel out the moral defeat into which Peter's past denials of Jesus have plunged him, (b) to clarify the current status of the relationship between master and disciple, and (c) to grant Peter a new opportunity for service. Therefore, following each question and answer, Jesus tells the apostle to 'feed my sheep'.

Love Lost in Translation

Viewed from a translator's perspective, one may again ask how a modern English version of the Bible can adequately handle the subtleties inherent in the joint presence of *agapaō* and *phileō* in John 21. Is the English language capable of reflecting the different shades of meaning suggested by these verbs? Below my literal translation from table 82 is juxtaposed with three English versions, two of which represent the majority of eleven versions (HCSB, NRSV). For the sake of saving space, I have decided to leave out nine versions because their approaches coincide. In table 83 the word 'love' translates *agapaō*, and all italicized renderings refer to *phileō*.

Table 83
Translating *agapaō* and *phileō* in John 21.15–17

Version		Jesus Asking	Peter Responding
Literal	1	Do you love me more than these?	You know I *am fond of* you
	2	Do you love me?	You know I *am fond of* you
	3	*Are* you *fond of* me?	. . . that I *am fond of* you
HCSB	1	Do you love* Me more than these?	You know that I *love* You
	2	Do you love Me?	You know that I *love* You
	3	Do you love Me?	You know that I *love* You
		*Two synonyms are translated *love* in this conversation	
NRSV	1	Do you love me more than these?	You know that I *love* you
	2	Do you love me?	You know that I *love* you
	3	Do you love me?	You know that I *love* you
NWT	1	Do you love me more than these?	You know I *have affection for* you
	2	Do you love me?	. . . I *have affection for* you
	3	Do you *have affection for* me?	You are aware that I *have affection for* you

As they did with respect to John 11 (cf. table 80), table 83 shows that most English translators, represented by the HCSB and the NRSV, have resolved the conundrum of *agapaō* and *phileō* by relinquishing any attempt at making distinctions. No fewer than eleven versions render both Greek verbs as 'love'. While using 'love' throughout, the HCSB translators have provided a footnote to point out that they regard the two Greek verbs as 'synonyms'. Thus, table 83 documents that only the NWT has made an effort to reproduce the richness inherent in the Greek text. To Jesus's question 'Do you love me?' the NWT rightly lets Simon Peter reply 'I have affection for you', a phrase probably not considered stylistically elegant by everyone but which enables the NWT to differentiate between *agapaō* and *phileō*. The NWT's rendering of *phileō* is capable of highlighting Simon Peter's struggle as he is reminded of past failures. At the same time, attention is drawn to Jesus's merciful forgiveness and continued trust in him.

Thus, if 'love' is reserved for *agapaō* it is perfectly possible to render *phileō* with different terms such as 'I care for you' or, as suggested in table 82, 'I am fond of you.' A few other English versions of the Bible have remained faithful to the Greek text. The *J. B. Phillips New Testament* (1962) lets Peter answer Jesus's question by saying 'You know that *I am your friend*', and the *Worldwide English New Testament* (1996) adopts a similar approach: 'You know that *I like* you' (21.15–16) and 'You know that *I love you as a close friend*' (21.17, emphasis added).

In past centuries, *agapaō* and *phileō* have been perceived differently by a variety of translators around the world. For his Latin Vulgate, Jerome translated *agapaō* in this passage as *diligo*, 'I have a special regard for', while *phileō* is rendered *amo*, 'I love'. Curiously, Jerome has stood the logic of the Greek on its head, interpreting *phileō* as the stronger verb and *agapaō* as the weaker. Given this historical precedent, it is perhaps understandable that many modern English translators of the Bible feel confused and have given up on differentiating between *agapaō* and *phileō*. In addition, they follow the lead of a series of early English versions, including those of Wycliffe and Tyndale, the Bishops' Bible, the Geneva Bible, and the King James Version, all of which translate both verbs as 'love'.

In summary, it is regrettable that only one English version of the Bible has adopted convincing approaches to *agapaō* and *phileō* in John 21. It is true that there is nothing conspicuously wrong about the majority's homogenization of the two verbs because 'love' does reflect some aspects of both, and the story is still understandable. However, in the translation process they have deprived readers of some of the psychological and theological implications of the exchange between Jesus and Simon Peter, brilliantly suggested in the Greek original by the juxtaposition of *agapaō* and *phileō*. The common simplification of this text, which leads to the inappropriate use of 'love' in Peter's answers, has at least three side effects: (a) Jesus appears to be torturing or teasing Peter by mechanically repeating the same question, which is not the case;[357] (b) the disciple's words are presented as being on a par with his master's, which they are not; and (c) Jesus's forgiveness of Peter and renewed trust in him is minimized. Viewed from this perspective, the deeper facets of love discussed by the narrator have been lost in translation.

However, the imprecision of so many versions of the Bible cannot conceal the wider significance of the incident on the seashore. Placed towards the end of the book attributed to John the Evangelist, the interaction finishes where Jesus twice repeats his original invitation to Simon Peter: 'Follow me' (Jn. 21.19, 22; cf. 1.40-43). A possible interpretation of this passage is to see the Gospel writer proclaiming that in God's service there is room for losers who honestly acknowledge their failures. Put differently, past wrongdoings are no obstacle to following Jesus. In Greek terms, while the commitment of imperfect human beings to Jesus may be limited to *philia*, this is graciously surpassed by his *agapē*.

---

[357] Some readers may think Jesus is saying, 'Do you *really* love me?' (Martin 2006: 100). This interpretation erroneously suggests insecurity and hurt on Jesus's part.

Conclusion

To a greater extent than any of the biblical texts discussed in chapters 4–14, the stories explored in this chapter contain aspects that are relevant for discussions about homoeroticism in scripture. In these narratives from the Hebrew Bible and the Second Testament, the language reflects relationships between members of the same sex based on strong affection combined with lifelong bonding and commitment. In this regard they resemble today's intimate relationships between lesbian and gay partners. However, from a social and cultural perspective, the situations described in the biblical narratives do not entirely match modern contexts. In antiquity the notion of power in the form of social hierarchy was ever-present and influenced the ways in which affection, including erotic attraction and sexual intimacy, was expressed. Such is the setting in which King Saul and his son Jonathan both 'loved' David, a shepherd boy. Between Ruth and Naomi, there was an age gap, which awarded more authority to the older woman, and the intimacy between Jesus and the Beloved Disciple echoed close teacher-student relationships known from Greco-Roman culture.

In similar fashion, today's cultural ideal of committed relationships based on mutuality between two equal partners is not directly transferable to the biblical world. Where these stories from the Bible do resemble modern situations is in their descriptions of individuals exercising choice. Indeed, Ruth literally rebels against social convention and common sense by opting to follow her conscience and honour her feelings for Naomi. In several remarkable ways, Jonathan does the same by renouncing royal privilege and committing himself to David, and the Beloved Disciple courageously chooses to share Jesus's turbulent life, remaining by his side during the crucifixion and beyond, a time when many other disciples have fled.

Once again, the twelve English versions of the Bible analysed have demonstrated how they occasionally slip into imprecision. In the story of Ruth and Naomi, some fail to show the strength of Ruth's commitment, which is equal to a marital bond. Similarly, some translators minimize King Saul's initial feeling of 'love' for David, converting it to 'fondness' or 'liking'. In John 13, the narrator emphasizes the closeness between Jesus and the Beloved Disciple by letting the latter rest his head on the master's chest. However, many translators amend the text by positioning the disciple 'next to' or 'near' Jesus, in some cases making him 'sit'. This is anachronistic given the couches on which dinner guests would be reclining in Hellenistic times. Another significant case in point is the dialogue between Jesus and Simon Peter in John 21 where most translators fail to differentiate between *agapaō* and *phileō*, the two Greek verbs for 'love'. Instead of highlighting the psychological and theological points suggested by Jesus's questions and Peter's answers, most English versions simplify and homogenize the text by rendering these Greek verbs as if they were interchangeable.

The exploration of the language of love undertaken in this chapter has shown that biblical narrators use the relevant terminology with ease, whether they are referring to love within the family, in opposite-sex couples or in same-sex relationships. It is striking that some English versions of the Bible have difficulty in translating the Hebrew or Greek terms accurately, preferring watered-down renderings when affection between members of the same sex is expressed. Stated another way, today's English translators are more inhibited than the biblical writers when they focus on love, particularly love between males. In the process, the versions fail to relay to their readers some of the creative tension inherent in the original stories and, unfortunately, are liable to miss highly significant points suggested by the narrators. While love is the essence of the biblical message, important aspects of it have been lost in translation.

CONCLUSION

My journey has just begun.

—Howard R. Macy [358]

Over the centuries, many believers have been given an erroneous impression of scripture with respect to same-sex relationships. This book has shown that contemporary biblical interpretation in Christian circles is based on a number of assumptions that go back to the Middle Ages and the church fathers—not to the biblical sources in the original languages. In addition, there is no solid, scholarly consensus about the exact meaning of each biblical text commonly believed to focus on homoeroticism. On the contrary, despite years of academic research and debate, opinions are remarkably divided.

Highlighting the vocabulary and special characteristics of the original texts, chapters 1–14 of the present book have explored passages in the Hebrew scriptures and the Second Testament. Two aspects of each text have been discussed: (1) what the text seems to be saying within its cultural, historical, and literary context; and (2) the ways in which the text has been translated by twelve modern English versions of the Bible. Early translations of scripture such as the Greek Septuagint and the Latin Vulgate have been (and still are) hugely influential in Christian theology, particularly biblical hermeneutics, and several translation errors in these

---

[358] Howard R. Macy, 'Learning to Read the Psalms', 2006: 114.

prestigious ancient works continue to be imitated by today's English versions of the Bible.

In the vast majority of the texts examined, unresolved issues of exegesis and translation have been detected. All versions proceed accurately in some passages, but no single version is totally free of error. Thus, a version may render a given text adequately into modern English and subsequently mistranslate another. A major part of the problem lies in the dictionaries of Hebrew and Greek available to today's translators. Numerous renderings suggested by these dictionaries reflect a deep-seated anti-homoerotic bias rooted in church tradition and extra-biblical literature. Once it has been absorbed into English versions of the Bible, this bias is relayed to readers, giving rise to multiple controversies that are alien to the essence of the Christian Gospel.

Another aspect is the widespread preference given to free or dynamic approaches to Bible translation, which leave plenty of room for paraphrase, while literal approaches are rare. Excessive liberties taken by translators have led to distortion of the scriptural message. The main translation issues discussed in the present book are summarized in table 84.

Table 84
Translation Issues in Twelve Versions

Chapter	Issues	Versions
1	'Rib' rather than 'side' (Genesis 2)	All
2	Confused approaches to sexual language in Genesis	Eight
3	Inaccurate approaches to 'knowing' in Genesis	Eleven
4	Unclear picture of Noah's nakedness	Eight

5	Mistranslating *qadesh* and *qedeshah* (Deut. 23)	All
6	Mistranslating 'the lyings of a woman' (Lev. 18)	All
7	Mistranslating 'other flesh' (Jude v. 7)	Ten
8, 9	(No translation issues.)	-
10	Distorting 'know' in Genesis 18–19	Eleven
11	Mistranslating *nagash*, 'come forward' (Gen. 19.9)	All
12	Mistranslating 'know' and 'humiliate' (Judg. 19)	Eleven
13	Mistranslating *malakoi* and *arsenokoitai* (1 Cor. 6)	All
14	Mistranslating *para physin* (Romans 1)	Three
14	Mistranslating *planē* (Romans 1)	Six
15	Confused approaches to *agapaō* and *phileō* (John)	Eleven

Several major conclusions may be drawn from this study: (1) most texts discussed in chapters 4–14 deal with issues unrelated to the subject of homoeroticism; (2) the real crime of the people of Sodom and Gomorrah was idolatry, injustice, and violence against a marginalized group, as interpreted by the Hebrew prophets; (3) no text in the entire Bible condemns homoerotic relationships between women; and (4) only two of the ten passages examined seem to oppose male–male sexual intimacy: Leviticus 18.22 (20.13) and Romans 1.27. As demonstrated in chapters 6 and 14, careful analysis of the original texts shows that the intent of the Levitical lawgiver is limited to a specific context described with the opaque phrase *mishkevey ishshah*, 'the lyings of a woman'. The diatribe against 'shameful passions', which Paul launches in Romans 1, does not contemplate intimate relationships between male adults but is part of a wider polemic against idolatrous, orgiastic practices. For Paul, an important intertextual connection is the book of Wisdom, and additionally, it is possible that the apostle is quoting judgmental, anti-Gentile sayings or writings of a zealous

Christian teacher in Rome with a Jewish background, with whom he strongly disagreed. Ironically, these quotations were subsequently taken to be Paul's own position (chapter 14).

Furthermore, the widespread tendency among biblical scholars to focus on biblical texts assumed to condemn close same-sex relationships has led most interpreters to ignore other passages and stories that point in the opposite direction. As shown in chapter 15, both the Hebrew Bible and the Second Testament contain narratives describing lifelong relationships characterized by affection and commitment between women and between men.

In summary, this book has documented a considerable gap between the latest biblical research on the one hand and current dictionaries and English versions of the Bible on the other. In particular, the reliance of translators on outdated material, some of which goes back to the church fathers and the Middle Ages, is at the heart of the current unease with homoerotic relationships in many Christian circles. Instead of giving today's readers a realistic impression of the relevant Bible texts, most versions are perpetuating centuries of bias based on flawed biblical interpretation. Therefore, a fresh, analytical approach to Bible translation is urgently needed with respect to all the texts discussed in this book. This book has demonstrated the usefulness of an exegetical framework based on linguistics and literary analysis. Translators, editors, educators, and biblical scholars in general are encouraged to focus on these objectives:

- To undertake a rigorous linguistic, semantic, and literary analysis of the relevant biblical texts
- To produce biblical dictionaries and commentaries based on recent exegetical insights

- To offer interdisciplinary training to biblical scholars, particularly translators
- To offer courses on cultural anthropology, sexology, linguistics, and literary analysis to students and academic staff in theology and biblical studies.

If and when these initiatives are implemented, Bible readers in general are likely to gain a deeper understanding of the richness and complexity of scripture, and Christian churches will become better equipped to appreciate and celebrate variations in human sexuality. As shown by this book, the seemingly endless and sterile debates on homoeroticism are out of step with the primary concerns of the Bible. Both testaments urge believers to be sensitive to fellow human beings in need, proclaiming the good news of God's favour to a wounded world (Isa. 61.1–2; Lk. 4.18–19).

APPENDICES

APPENDIX 1

Sodom in Islam

The *Qur'an* (Koran) was written in Arabic and is likely to have been compiled in the seventh century CE. It appeared on the religious scene in the Middle East at a time when Christian interpretations of Sodom increasingly focused on the perceived evils of homoeroticism (Duran 1993: 182). Traditional Islamic terminology does not include the word sodomy. Instead, it refers to persons with homoerotic inclinations under the Arabic name of *qaum Lut*, 'Lot's people', sometimes abbreviated to *Luti*. This is so because, in Islamic tradition, homoeroticism is inextricably linked to the drama of Sodom and Gomorrah (p. 182).

In the Qur'an, Lot's story is mentioned five times. He himself is venerated as a major prophet (Duran 1993: 182). While the association between Sodom and homoeroticism is understandable from a historical point of view, in the Islamic context, it may seem ironic that Lot's name came to play a part in the terminology. In the Qur'anic version of Sodom, Lot represents the voice of reason and decency as he preaches to the townsmen. He distances himself from all behaviour based on same-sex attraction and emphatically criticizes the locals (1993: 181–2). Below is an extract from Sura VII in which Lot tries to persuade the Sodomites to change their ways:[359]

---

[359] sunnahonline.com/library/stories-of-the-prophets/297-story-of-prophet-lut (2012); www.fordham.edu/halsall/pwh/quran-homo.asp (2012).

> 79. And he turned away from them and said, 'O my people! I did preach to you the message of my Lord, and I gave you good advice; but ye love not sincere advisers.'
>
> 80. And Lot, when he said to his people, 'Do ye approach an abomination which no one in all the world ever anticipated you in?
>
> 81. Verily, ye approach men with lust rather than women—nay, ye are a people who exceed.'
>
> 82. But his people's answer only was to say, 'Turn them out of your village, verily, they are a people who pretend to purity.'

The hostility to homoeroticism in the Qur'anic dialogues between Lot and the people of Sodom demonstrates that the Islamic approach to Sodom runs parallel to Christianity's paradigm D. Both depict the people of Sodom as overly homoerotic. The Prophet Muhammad is reported to have said, 'Doomed by God is he who does what Lot's people did' and 'If you find anyone doing as Lot's people did, kill the one who does it, and the one to whom it is done.' He even went so far as to curse effeminate men and masculine women and ordered his followers to 'turn them out of your houses'. This ruling on homosexual persons was generally adopted by his successors. In Islamic thought, Muhammad is considered to be the *Uswa Hassanah* (the perfect example).[360] Hence, the majority of Muslims today still consider harsh treatment of people with homoerotic inclinations to be perfectly justified.[361]

---

[360] www.islamic-dictionary.com/index.php?word=uswah (2012)
[361] www.skeptive.com/sources/107824/source_urls/264540 (2012).

Shariah law is extracted from both the Qur'an and subsequent laws and jurisprudence, and many Muslims regard *shariah* as the laws of Allah. In this context, homoeroticism is not only a sin but a punishable crime against God. The fact that women are included suggests that the Islamic injunction against lesbian relationships considerably predates that of Christianity, which did not become explicit until the twelfth-century writings of Pierre le Chantre (cf. chapter 8). On the other hand, while the Qur'an — unlike medieval Christianity — expressly permits sex for pleasure's sake and even encourages erotic intimacy, it teaches that the underlying purpose of sexual activity is procreation (Duran 1993: 182-3). In the latter respect Islam fully coincides with pre-modern Christian theology.

Historically speaking, Islamic interpretations of homoerotic relationships have varied considerably over the centuries. Medieval Spanish and Persian (Iranian) literature attests to the honoured place awarded to same-sex eroticism, particularly between males. According to John Boswell (1980: 197), Spain produced outstanding Islamic jurists and theologians. During this time, many wrote poetry with homoerotic overtones. A well-known author is eleventh-century King al-Mutamid of Seville (p. 196). However, according to Duran (1993: 185), the homoerotic poetry of Muslim Spain was dwarfed by the rich literature that flourished in medieval Persia. Unlike Boswell, Duran argues that 'in Andalusian poetry, homosexuality is comparatively rare. Prose literature too scarcely relates any homosexual anecdotes, whereas they abound in Persian writings.'

In recent decades, Islamic interpretations of the Qur'an have appeared in which the sins of 'Lot's people' are not described as homoeroticism but rather as greed and lack of moderation. Such is the case of the French children's book *Si le Coran m'était conté* ('If the Qur'an was explained to me'), by Youssef Seddik, which caused controversy in traditionalist Muslim circles in France and Tunisia following its publication in 1989 (Hügel 2009: 219).

Other sources:
sharia-law.info (2012); www.cfr.org/religion/islam-governing-under-sharia/p8034 (2011); www.bbc.co.uk/religion/religions/islam/beliefs/sharia_1.shtml (2012).

APPENDIX 2

Knowing in Babylonia

> One would have thought the etymological fallacy—that word sense is determined by original meaning—was a sufficiently dead horse in educated theological circles to spare it the humiliation of further flogging.[362]

This sobering advice is well worth remembering whenever the history of certain words within interrelated languages is being discussed. Such is the case with *yada'* in Hebrew, which belongs to the Northwest Semitic branch, and its cognates in Akkadian, an ancient northeast Semitic language (Sáenz-Badillos 1993: 10). The considerable geographical and chronological divide between Hebrew and Akkadian must be reckoned with. At the same time, however, and given a number of significant similarities, a possible historical and cultural backdrop in Akkadian for the technical aspects of Hebrew *yada'* seems plausible.

As noted in chapter 10, modern interpretations of *yada'* are primarily indebted to the terms for knowing in classical Greek literature, which were adopted by the Septuagint. Other relevant sources are classical Latin literature and the Vulgate. While the familiar expression 'to know in the biblical sense' should be rephrased as 'to know in the Greek sense', it is regrettable that very little attention has been paid

---
[362] Cotterell and Turner 1989: 113–14.

to pre-biblical traditions when considering the technical roles played by *yada(* in legal contexts (Huffmon 1966: 31–7). Biblical Israel emerged in a world in which various highly developed legal systems existed (Meyers 1988: 154), and ancient precedents are documented in Semitic languages spoken outside Palestine, notably the Akkadian of Babylonia (or Mesopotamia).[363]

The famous law collection of King Hammurabi is thought to have originated about 1700 BCE.[364] Its prestige in its own day is attested by the large number of clay tablet copies that have been preserved and excavated (André-Salvini 2003: 50, 56). Written in Akkadian, this collection of statutes is a distant and early precursor of laws included in the Hebrew Bible. The frequent contacts between Mesopotamia and Palestine/Canaan in antiquity suggest that Hammurabi's legal precepts became widely known and imitated so that certain Akkadian phrases and terms were absorbed into other languages (André-Salvini 2003: 54), especially as Akkadian was the lingua franca of the Middle and Near East for centuries.[365] In the case of Biblical Hebrew, several hundred words and

---

[363] The biblical name is Babylon. In today's academic literature, 'Babylonia' is commonly used.

[364] According to Savina Teubal (1984: 82), Hammurabi's work was not state law 'but rather regulations that Hammurabi was making an effort to enforce. That these regulations often proposed to revise ancient tradition can be appreciated when they are compared to the laws of rulers like Ur-Nammu and Lipit-Ishtar, who preceded Hammurabi. They were also intended to unify and reform the city-states of which Hammurabi became sovereign.' Driver and Miles (Vol. I, 1952: 45) concur in the sense that Hammurabi's work is more like 'a series of amendments and restatements of parts of the law in force when he wrote'. Likewise, 'whatever the Laws are, they are not a code in the modern sense of the term' (p. 48). It is more accurate to describe this literary monument as 'a work of art' (p. 49).

[365] According to Angel Sáenz-Badillos (1993: 9), Akkadian was the lingua franca in the second millennium BCE. It was replaced by Aramaic in the sixth century BCE (p. 12).

phrases are thought to be of Akkadian origin (Sáenz-Badillos 1993: 13, 75).

Bernhard Anderson (1978: 134) observes that many of the case laws in the so-called Covenant Code (Ex. 20.3–23.19) are 'similar in form, and to a great degree in content, to the law codes of the Babylonians, Hurrians, and Assyrians. The same is true of the code of Deuteronomy 12–26.' David Wright (2003: 13–14) agrees, particularly with respect to the Covenant Code in the book of Exodus. Some scholars discuss the hypothesis of various common early sources in the ancient Near East.[366] There are, however, significant differences too: 'Israel's law is characterized by a humane spirit, a high ethical emphasis, and a pervading religious fervour, which make it unique' (Anderson 1978: 135).

Of special significance for the book of Genesis is the fact that several parts of the Abraham story indicate a connection with the traditions of Mesopotamia, including laws and customs.[367] Read in this light, the application of *yadaʿ* to the

---

[366] Driver and Miles (Vol. I, 1952) find it justified to speak of 'the existence of a common Mesopotamian law in the third millennium BCE; for the principles underlying them all are in a general sense the same' (p. 11). No legislator writes in a vacuum but, rather, 'every lawgiver uses existing material' (p. 15). See also Gordon and Rendsburg (1997: 76): 'The oldest known law code is that of Urnammu (in Sumerian). That earlier Sumerian law codes existed is quite probable.' Sumerian terminology certainly survived in Akkadian legal phraseology (Driver & Miles, Vol. I, 1952: 13), which reflected the fact that even after Sumerian ceased to be a spoken language, it was venerated and studied for centuries as a classical language (Gordon & Rendsburg 1997: 68). For further allusions in the Hebrew Bible to non-Hebrew texts of ancient Near Eastern origin, see Alter 1992: 51.

[367] For instance, Sarah, Rachel, and Leah give their maids to their husbands for the purpose of producing children, as attested in Gen. 16.3, 30.3 and 30.9. Bernhard Anderson (1978: 30–1) has noted that this procedure is documented in early Hurrian literature excavated in the city of Nuzi (about 1500–1370 BCE). According to Chilperic

legal status of a young woman appears to make good sense. Hammurabi's document has an important segment on family law that extends all the way from Section 127 to 194 (André-Salvini 2003: 35). In several cases, the Akkadian word *edû(m)* or *idû(m)*, 'know', is part of the definition of a man's relationship with a woman.[368] For example, Sections 155 and 156 speak of the two forms of punishment to which a man is liable if he unduly interferes with his son's upcoming marriage by seducing the bride. One sanction applies if the man has sex with the young woman *before* she is 'known' by his son the bridegroom. In this case, she is still technically unmarried. The other punishment comes into effect if he is caught having sexual intercourse with the girl *after* the formal 'knowing' has taken place, because he is committing an act of adultery. These laws draw a clear distinction between the legal aspect of 'knowing', which conveys the sense of formalizing the marriage contract, and the physical act of sexual intercourse, which Hammurabi describes as 'lying in her bosom' (or 'lying on her breasts').[369]

Below I examine the legal material to which King Hammurabi lends his name with a particular focus on the concept of knowing. I have looked for clues to any technical role(s) for 'knowing' in Akkadian in regard to the institution of marriage. I was interested to see whether it complemented or offset the usage of other words and phrases connected with the sexual sphere. To help with the technicalities of

---

Edwards (1906: 50), 'All of this is in strict conformity with §§ 144–146 of the Code [of Hammurabi]'.

[368] For a discussion of this term, see Jenni and Westermann, Vol. 2 (1997: 509, 512).

[369] Every word in Hammurabi's document has been selected with great care; cf. Driver and Miles (I, 1952: 49): 'The terminology is well chosen and used with unerring skill and accuracy. The right word is used, each clause is pregnant with meaning, and there is no verbiage (p. 49) . . . The draftsmanship is excellent; it is concise and clearly expressed' (p. 57).

ancient Akkadian vocabulary and grammar, I have enlisted the works of several translators and commentators.[370] For each section, I have tried to produce renderings that are as literal as possible. Emphasis has been added to the term(s) that are relevant to issues debated elsewhere in this book, notably in chapters 2, 3, and 10.

§ 128
If a man has *taken* a wife and has not drawn up *a contract* for her, that woman is not a wife.

This section highlights the importance of written contracts for marriages to be legally binding.[371] Driver and Miles (II: 51) explain in a footnote that 'taken a wife' also translates as 'has married a wife'. It illustrates the role of the word 'take' as the husband's prerogative. Indeed, 'take' [*aḥāzum*] is very common in such contexts, as shown in §§ 144-148, 159, 161-163, 166-167, 175-176. Frequently the verb means 'marry' from the man's perspective and includes all stages of the process, including the connotation of marital consummation (Driver & Miles, I: 246). The complementary term is 'give' [*nadānum*], which corresponds to the girl's father or agent; cf. §§ 160, 183-184.[372] The Hebrew equivalents are *laqach*, 'take' (Gen. 19.14; 25.1), and *nathan*, 'give' (Gen. 16.3; 29.19).

As for the marriage contract, the depositions were made before witnesses (Cook 1903: 61; Roth 1989: 20-2). In ancient Babylonia marriage would require the woman to move in with the husband. Thus, the laws speak of her 'entering' a

---

[370] Johns 1903; Scheil 1904; Edwards 1906; King 1910; Driver and Miles, Vol. II, 1955; Roth 1997; André-Salvini 2003.
[371] S. A. Cook (1903: 81) renders the phrase 'drawn up a contract' as 'has not laid down her bonds'. For a detailed discussion of marriage agreements in Neo-Babylonian times, see Roth 1989.
[372] Cook (1903: 78-82) also points to the importance of marriage contracts in ancient Egypt.

man's house (Driver & Miles, I: 246).³⁷³ Cohabitation may well have been a common marital arrangement in Babylonia (p. 246). Perhaps this is why § 128 emphasizes that, to enjoy full legal status, a married woman needed to be in possession of a written contract (p. 247).

> § 129
> If a married lady is caught lying with another male, they shall bind them and cast them into the water.

The issue addressed by § 129 is adultery, for which both parties are liable to the death penalty. As in Biblical Hebrew, 'lie with' seems to be an unambiguous description of sexual intercourse. The phrase recurs in §§ 131–132.

> § 130
> If a man has gagged *a married lady*, who has *not known a male and is dwelling in her father's house*, and has then *lain in her bosom* and they catch him, that man shall be put to death.

For 'married lady', Chilperic Edwards (1906: 21) proposes 'the wife of another man'. L. W. King (1910) is more explicit: 'the wife (betrothed or child wife) of another man'. This indicates that in the laws of Hammurabi the term seems to apply to two situations: (1) a woman who is party to a consummated marriage contract; (2) a girl who has not yet signed any such contract (or rather, whose father has not yet taken this step on her behalf), but who is betrothed

---

³⁷³ The authors caution that, in some cases, the entering does not necessarily imply formal marriage. In any event, it is for a Babylonian man to marry a woman, not the other way around. For a literary echo in the Hebrew Bible, see the book of Ruth 4.11 where the witnesses speak to Boaz of 'the woman who is entering your house'.

or inchoately married.[374] In § 129, the former situation is described and in § 130 the latter. This is how I interpret 'has not known a male' and the fact that the girl still lives at her father's house. The Akkadian word for 'known' used here is *idû(m)*, an early cognate of Hebrew *yada'*. The phrase parallels the role of *yada'* to describe the status of Lot's daughters in Genesis 19.8.[375]

In other words, the girl in § 130 is betrothed to a man with whom she has not yet formalized her relationship, that is, the official 'knowing' has not yet taken place let alone the ensuing consummation through 'lying'. The Hammurabi document describes a betrothed girl as a 'wife', which places the relationship between her father and her fiancé in the category of 'in-law' as stated in §§ 159–161. In the Sodom story, this parallels Lot's two 'sons-in-law' (Gen. 19.14–15). As for the sex act, it may be viewed from the woman's perspective or from that of the man. A woman 'lies with' a male (§ 129), while a man 'lies in her bosom'; cf. §§ 130, 155–158.

§ 154
If a man *knows* his daughter, they shall expel that man from the city.

This section is a good example of how cognates cannot automatically be assumed to play identical roles. While knowing in Hebrew tends to be expressed through *yada'*, the situation in Old Babylonian literature appears to be more complex due to the existence of two verbs associated with the concept of knowing. Adding a twist to the marital-sexual panorama, in the laws of Hammurabi the verb highlighted

---

[374] For a detailed discussion, see Driver and Miles I: 248–50, 299, 322–3.
[375] S. A. Cook (1903: 91) has observed another biblical parallel in Deut. 22.23.

in § 154 is not *idû(m)* but *lamādu*.[376] The latter means 'become aware', 'understand', 'learn a craft', 'study', and 'become knowledgeable'.[377] For this legal context, it is crucial to note that *lamādu* also has a technical meaning, namely, to 'recognize a legal claim or obligation', particularly when the subject is male, while the subject of *idû(m)* tends to be female.

Most translators are inclined to take *lamādu* in a sexual sense, as is often the case with *yada'* in the Hebrew Bible.[378] Thus, Driver and Miles (II: 61) suggest for § 154 'if a man (carnally) knows his daughter', making 'knowing' and 'lying with' interchangeable.[379] However, there are several reasons for proceeding with caution. First, given the precision with which Hammurabi's draftsmen have chiselled out his monumental legacy, it must be assumed that every word has been inserted exactly where it belongs (Driver & Miles I: 57). Second, if knowing and lying with someone are indistinguishable it becomes difficult to appreciate that a Babylonian marriage ceremony entailed not one but two significant rituals. One was the legally binding act of 'knowing' a person contractually and in the presence of witnesses, and the other being the physical consummation of the new relationship through sexual intercourse, for which a different verb, namely, 'lying with/lying in her bosom', applied. Third, the example of a woman's adultery shows

---

[376] I thank David Wright for bringing this to my attention.
[377] Cf. the Assyrian dictionary of A. Leo Oppenheim (1973). Like numerous other dictionaries, however, this work fails to make the necessary distinction between legal terminology in respect of marriage and the language referring to sexual relations.
[378] In her translation, Béatrice André-Salvini (2003: 49–50) treats 'knowing' and 'lying with' as synonyms. There are precedents in Scheil (1904: 29); Driver and Miles, Vol. I (1952: 246); Vol. II (1955: 61), and Roth (1997: 110).
[379] By contrast, C. H. W. Johns (1903: 31) and Chilperic Edwards (1906) remain neutral, and accurate, as they speak of 'knowing'.

that in legal terms the sex act is to be distinguished from the concept of knowing. As noted, the laws consistently describe such adultery as 'lying with another male'; cf. §§ 129, 131-132.

According to the common translations just discussed, what is punished with banishment in § 154 is any sexual act, i.e. incest, between father and daughter. However, careful examination of other parts of the laws reveals the weakness of this approach. In no other section is anyone punished for the act of knowing; cf. §§ 155-156, and in all cases of adultery and incest, it is the act of lying with someone that gives grounds for judicial procedures; cf. §§ 129-132, 155-158. Moreover, in several cases 'lying with' is juxtaposed to 'knowing', indicating that they refer to different situations; cf. §§ 130, 155-156.

Initially the use of 'know' in § 154 seems opaque but several avenues of interpretation are possible. If this section is compared to a related problem described in § 157, it is striking that a son who embarks on an incestuous relationship with his mother is punished by death rather than banishment. The mother too suffers the same fate. Here the term 'know' is not used but rather 'lie in her bosom'. In other words, actual incest is a far more serious issue than the knowing mentioned in § 154. Therefore, if the latter case depicts a father who commits incest with his daughter, as some translators insist, it is odd that he should be treated more leniently than the mother and son mentioned above. After all, banishment is a lighter sentence than execution by drowning.

Given these legal circumstances, it seems appropriate to consider alternative readings of 'know' in § 154. Nowhere else in the code is this concept associated with any illicit act. On the contrary, it appears to be the legal requirement before the physical consummation of a marriage can take place. Thus, it makes more sense to focus on the object of the man's attempted knowing, namely, the fact that he takes his own daughter to wife. This perspective becomes clearer if 'know' is read as a technical term for marriage. In other words, § 154 sets out to inhibit any intent of arranging marriage between father and daughter. This must be viewed in the light of § 128, which establishes that in Babylonia no marriage is considered legally valid unless a formal contract has been concluded.

Some material in the laws of Hammurabi sheds further light on this issue. Several sections allude to men disappearing from their communities, leaving their families without maintenance. In such cases the deserted wife may be free to move in with another man; cf. §§ 134-136. Since the woman usually brings her children with her, a relationship of stepfather and stepchildren may ensue in the new household. It is not unrealistic to imagine that the new paterfamilias finds a stepdaughter attractive and wants her to become his wife. Plausibly § 154 has this situation in mind.[380] Also, if the man becomes a widower the latter arrangement may seem alluring.

Several other procedures discussed in this Babylonian law collection may lead to young girls and stepfathers living under the same roof. One such procedure is divorce, which is described in §§ 137-141.[381] A different situation, which may have been a Babylonian peculiarity, has to do with the

---

[380] In the HB, Lev. 18.17 legislates against marrying a woman and her daughter. The biblical punishment is severe, i.e. the death penalty (20.14).

[381] To be legally binding, the dissolution of a consummated marriage had to be stated in writing; cf. Cook 1903: 123. For the dissolution of inchoate marriages a mere declaration seems to have sufficed; cf. Driver and Miles I: 290.

special conditions applying to marriages involving certain classes of women described as 'priestesses' and 'lay sisters'; cf. §§ 144-147. An additional social factor to be reckoned with is slavery whereby a man acquires a concubine. Many different family configurations may be the outcome; cf. §§ 141, 144-147, 158, 170-171, 175-177. Finally, children may enter the household through adoption; cf. §§ 185-191.[382] In summary, the primary aim of § 154 may well be to discourage a father from planning to change his relationship with a daughter (stepdaughter, adopted daughter, etc.) by making her his wife.

§ 155
If a man has chosen a bride for his son and his son has *known* her, (and if) thereafter he himself *lies in her bosom* and they catch him, they shall bind that man and cast him into the water.

§ 156
If a man has chosen a bride for his son and his son has not *known* her, and he himself *lies in her bosom*, he shall pay her half a maneh of silver.

These two sections demonstrate the varying degrees of severity with which the offence is rated when a man seduces his new daughter-in-law. In § 156, the marriage contract has not yet been entered into. The son may be in the process of 'taking' the girl, but the 'knowing', i.e. the wedding, has not yet materialized. So the transgression can be redeemed by paying a sum of money to the girl and setting her free. This is in recognition of the fact that seduction has rendered her less 'saleable' (Edwards 1906: 49). In § 155, however, the transgression is more serious as the marriage ceremony

---

[382] Driver and Miles (I: 262) regard the admission of a future daughter-in-law into the house as a form of adoption; cf. §§ 155-156.

has already been officiated. In this case, the father-in-law is committing an act of adultery, for which he receives a death sentence; cf. § 129.[383]

Table 85 provides an overview of Akkadian terminology associated with marriage and sex as reflected in the laws of Hammurabi.

Table 85
Marriage and Sex in the Laws of Hammurabi

Gender	Term/Phrase	Interpretation	Sections
Woman	Not *known* a male	Not yet formally married	130
	Know	Marry	130
	Enter a man's house	Cohabit with	133–136
	Lie with	Have sex with	129, 131–132
Man	*Know*	Sign marriage contract	154–156
	Take	Marry	128, 144–146, 148, 159, 161–162, 166–167, 172, 175–176
	Lie in her bosom	Have sex with	130, 155–157 (+ 158)
Woman's Father	*Give* daughter to man	Formally agree to her marriage	160, 183–184

Conclusion

This brief exploration of the laws of Hammurabi has shown that ancient Babylonia had a well-established technical terminology in relation to marriage. There is a gender divide, which may reflect the unequal social positions of women and men. The formal part of the wedding ceremony is described as 'knowing'. In this respect, the Akkadian language distinguishes between *idû(m)* (female subject) and *lamādu* (male subject), while sexual situations are made explicit

---
[383] This reading is shared by Paul Koschaker (1917: 143).

through the expression *lie with* (female subject) or *lie in her bosom* (male subject). A considerable overlap exists between the marriage institutions of ancient Babylonia and biblical Israel. The terminology employed in both cultures indicates that marriage would often be preceded by a prolonged period of betrothal, or inchoate marriage. Linguistically, as well as from a cultural and historical point of view, there are good reasons for suggesting significant parallels between the world in which the laws of Hammurabi came into being and the allusions to marital and pre-marital arrangements in the book of Genesis, including the stories of Adam and Eve (Gen. 4.1, 17) and Sodom and Gomorrah (19.8, 12, 14).

GLOSSARIES

HEBREW GLOSSARY

TERM	TRANSLATION
achay	my brothers
achothī	my sister
adam	earthling, groundling, human being
adamah	earth, ground
adōn	master, lord
adonāy	my lord
ahav	love (verb)
ahavah	love (noun)
akhal	eat
amar	say
anashīm	men, husbands
asham	guilt
ashēm	guilty
ʿal	upon, towards
ʿalal	make sport of, mistreat
ʿalaʿ	rib
ʿalmah	young woman
ʿanah	debase, humiliate, oppress
ʿarummīm	naked
ʿasah	do, make
ʿawel	unjust
bachar	choose
bachūts	outside
banah	build
basar	flesh; family circle, kinship
bathar	cut
bĕ	in

beliya'al	base, mean, worthless
beney-beliyya'al	sons of worthlessness, scoundrels
běthōkh ahalō	inside his tent
bethulah	maiden
betsalmenū	in our image
bittī	my daughter
bō	go in, enter, come, arrive
chattaath	sin
Chawwah	Eve
chayyah	live
chazaq	seize
cherev	knife, dagger, sword
chesed	loyalty, steadfast love
daqar	pierce
davaq	join, cling/cleave to
da'at	knowledge
derash	search, applied exegesis
dōdī	my beloved
el	to
elohīm	gods
Elohīm	God
erets	land
eth	with
ethnan	remuneration, pay, fee
etsel	beside, next to
'erwah	nakedness
'ezer	deliverer, sustainer, helper
gadōl	great, big, important, powerful
galah	uncover, disclose
gēr	sojourner, resident alien, immigrant
ha-adam	the earthling, the groundling
hāechād	this one
har	hill, mountain
hayah	to be
hī	that

īsh	man, husband
ishshah	woman, wife
ʿikkesh	twisted
ʿim	with
ʿīr	town, city
kĕ	like, as
kelev	dog
kenegdō	opposite him, alongside him, beside him
laqach	take
maakheleth	sacrificial knife
maʿaseh Sedōm	the act of Sodom
mechīr	price
mĕōd	much, greatly
middat Sedom	the yardstick/norm of Sodom
midrash	interpretation
mishkav	bed, act of lying down
mishkav zakhur	the lying of a male
mishkevey ishshah	beds/lyings of a woman/wife
nagash	draw near, come forward
nagaʿ	touch
naloz	perverted
nashim	women, wives
nathan	give
navat	gaze
naʿam	be pleasant, be wonderful
naʿar	boy
naʿaseh	let us make
neder	vow, promise
neehavīm	beloved, lovable
neqevah	female
nevalah	folly
n-g-d	tell, report
ohel	tent
ohēv	lover, dear friend
pilegesh	wife of secondary rank

qadash	to be holy/sanctified
qadesh	consecrated man
qadosh	holy, sacred
qal	simple
qarav	approach, come near
qatōn	small, insignificant, lowly
qedeshah	consecrated woman
qedeshīm	consecrated workers
qodesh	holiness
qūm	get up, rise
raah	see
rashaʿ	evil, wicked
raʿeh	friend
raʿeyathī	my darling
ruach	breath, wind, spirit
shakhav	lie down
shem	name
sheqets	repulsiveness
tama	defile
taʿav	cause to be an abomination
teshuqah	desire, urge, lust
tevel	confusion, undue mixing
thawekh	middle, centre
toʿevah	abomination
tsachaq	laugh
tsaʿaq	cry out, complain
tsaʿaqah	outcry, complaint, protest, allegation
tselaʿ	side
tsor	flint
wayyivrā	and he created
wayyōmær	and he said
yad	hand
yadayim	two hands, both hands
yadaʿ	know, be aware of, enquire, acknowledge
yanah	oppress

yashēn	sleep
yatsuaʿ	bed, couch, sleeping mat
zakhar	male
zakhar uneqevah	male and female
zanah	act adulterously, prostitute oneself
zaqēn	old man
zavach	sacrifice
zaʿaq	cry out, complain
zaʿaqah	outcry, complaint, protest, allegation
zerah	seed
zimmah	depravity
zonah	prostitute, whore

GREEK GLOSSARY

TERM	TRANSLATION
adelphē	sister
adelphos	brother
adikia	injustice, wrongdoing
anakeimenos	reclining
andrapodistai	slave dealers, slave traders, kidnappers
agapaō	love, be devoted to
agapē	committed, enduring love
agapētos	beloved
allēlōn	each other
anapesōn	leaned
androgynos	man-woman
anēr	man
anomos	lawless
antimisthia	penalty
apelthousai	they went
aphentes	abandoning
apolambanontes	receiving
aposta	step aside
arsenokoitai	male-liers, those lying with males, bed-males
arsenos	male
atimia	dishonour
autōn	of them, their
biblia	books
chraomai	use, make use of
chrēsis	use
dia touto	through this

dio	therefore
ēgapēsen	he loved
ekkaiō	inflame
ekkaiousi(n)	they burn, they are inflamed
ekporneusasai	they committed fornication
emōranthēsan	they became foolish
entryphaō	indulge
epi	on, over
epithymia	desire, lust
epitrepō	allow
erastēs	(mature) lover, admirer
erōmenos	beloved (younger male)
ēs	you may be
espilōmenon	defiled
Eua	Eve
exekauthēsan	they burned
geneseōs enallagē	changing of origin
gignōskō	know, perceive
gynē	woman, wife
hamartia	sin
heteros	other
hymeis	you (plural)
ide hon phileis	the one you love
kakia	wickedness
kata physin	according to nature
katergazomenoi	committing
kinaidos	effeminate man, passive sexual partner
kleptai	thieves
koinē	common
koitē	bed
kolpos	breast, chest, bosom
malakia	softness
malakoi	soft ones, softies
malakos	soft
malakotēs	softness

mē planasthe	make no mistake, do not be deceived
metēllaxan	they exchanged
miainousin	they defile
moicheia	adultery
oida	know
opisō	after
paiderastēs	lover of boys
paiderastia	love of boys, pederasty
pallakis (pallax)	wife of secondary rank
panta ou oidas	you know all things
para	against, beyond
para	among
parabatēs	transgressor
para physin	against/beyond nature
paredōken	he handed over
pathē	passion
philadelphia	sibling love
philēma	kiss
phileō	like, feel affection for, have a high regard for
philetor	(mature) lover
philia	friendship, affection
philos	friend
physikēn chrēsin	natural use
physikos	natural
physis	nature, custom
planaō	wander, stray, deceive, mislead
planē	error, going astray
pleon toutōn	more than these
pleura	side
ponēria	baseness, malice
porneia	unchastity, irresponsible sexual conduct
pornoi	the unchaste, the sexually irresponsible
pornos	unchaste, sexually irresponsible person
prassēs	you may be practising
pyroō	burn
sarkos heteras	other flesh

sarx	flesh
stethos	thorax
sy	thou, you (singular)
syngignomai	get together with
teknon	child
thēleiai autōn	their females
thēlus	female
theos	God
tribas	woman practising homoerotic sex
zoē	life

LATIN GLOSSARY

abutimini	abuse
aediculas effeminatorum	quarters of the effeminate men
biblia	Bible
cognosco	know, be(come) acquainted with
coitus	collecting, fitting together
coitus interruptus	sexual intercourse purposely interrupted
concubitores	those who lie down
contra naturam	against nature
costam, costis	side, rib
effeminatus	effeminate
erroris sui	their error
exarserunt	they burned
extra naturam	outside/beyond nature
femina	woman
femineus	womanlike
galli	roosters; men from Gaul
inmutaverunt	they exchanged
inter effeminatos	among effeminate men
liber	book
luxuria	lechery
masculorum	of men
meretrix	prostitute
molles	soft ones
mollis	soft
mulier	woman

naturali usu feminae	the natural use of woman
operantes	committing
peccatum sodomitanum	the Sodomite sin
pretium canis	the price of a dog
recede	stand back
recipientes	receiving
relicto	having given up
scio	know, be knowledgeable
senso	feel, perceive
sodomia	sodomy
sola scriptura	scripture only
tradidit	he gave them up
tribas	woman practising homoerotic sex
uxor	wife
vitium sodomiticum	the sodomitic vice

BIBLIOGRAPHY

ACKROYD, P. R., and C. F. Evans (eds.)
1970   *The Cambridge History of the Bible. Volume 1: From the Beginnings to Jerome.*
At The University Press, Cambridge.

ADAMO, David Tuesday, and Erivwierho Francis Eghwubare
2010   'The African Wife of Abraham: An African Reading of Genesis 16:1–16 and 21:8–21', in:
Brenner, Lee & Yee (eds.), pp. 275–292.

ADAMS, J. N.
1982   *The Latin Sexual Vocabulary.*
Duckworth, London.

ALISON, James
2001   *Faith Beyond Resentment: Fragments Catholic and Gay.*
Darton, Longman & Todd, London.
2003   *On Being Liked.*
Darton, Longman & Todd, London.
2006   *Undergoing God: Dispatches from the scene of a break-in.*
Darton, Longman & Todd, London.

ALONSO Schökel, Luis
1994   *Diccionario bíblico hebreo-español.*
Editorial Trotta, Madrid.

ALPERT, Rebecca T.
1989   'In God's Image: Coming to Terms with Leviticus', in:
Balka & Rose (eds.), pp. 61–70.
1996   'Finding Our Past: A Lesbian Interpretation of the Book of Ruth', in:
Kates & Reimer (eds.), pp. 91–96.

2000	'Do Justice, Love Mercy, Walk Humbly: Reflections on Micah and Gay Ethics', in: Goss & West (eds.), pp. 170–182.
2006	'Exodus', in: Guest, Goss, West & Bohache (eds.), pp. 61–76.

ALTER, Robert

1992	*The World of Biblical Literature.* SPCK, London.
1996	*Genesis: Translation and Commentary.* W. W. Norton and Company, New York.

ALTHAUS-REID, Marcella

2000	*Indecent Theology: Theological perversions in sex, gender, and politics.* Routledge, London.
2003	*The Queer God.* Routledge, London.

AMIT, Yairah

1999	*The Book of Judges: The Art of Editing.* Translated by Jonathan Chipman. Brill, Leiden.
2010	'The Case of Judah and Tamar in the Contemporary Israeli Context: A Relevant Interpolation', in: Brenner, Lee & Yee (eds.), pp. 213–220.

AMMIANUS Marcellinus

1950	*Ammianus Marcellinus, I.* With an English Translation by John C. Rolfe in Three Volumes. William Heinemann Ltd, London.

ANDERSON, Bernhard W.

1978	*The Living World of the Old Testament. Third Edition.* Longman, London.

ANDRÉ-Salvini, Béatrice
2003   *Le code de Hammurabi.*
        Louvre, Distribution Seuil, Paris.

ASHTON, John
1998   'John and the Johannine Literature: The Woman at the Well', in:
        Barton (ed.), pp. 259–275.

ASHWORTH, Timothy
2006   *Paul's Necessary Sin: The Experience of Liberation.*
        Ashgate Publishing Limited, Aldershot.

BACH, Alice
1999   'Rereading the Body Politic. Women and Violence in Judges 21', in:
        Bach (ed.), pp. 389–401.

BACH, Alice (ed.)
1999   *Women in the Hebrew Bible: A Reader.*
        Routledge, New York & London.

BAGEMIHL, Bruce
1999   *Biological Exuberance: Animal Homosexuality and Natural Diversity.*
        Profile Books, London.

BAILEY, Derrick Sherwin
1955   *Homosexuality in the Western Christian Tradition.*
        Longmans, Green & Co., London.

BAL, Mieke
1988   *Death and Dissymmetry: The Politics of Coherence in the Book of Judges.*
        The University of Chicago Press, Chicago.

BALKA, Christie, and Andy Rose (eds.)
1989   *Twice Blessed: On Being Lesbian or Gay and Jewish.*
        Beacon Press, Boston.

BARTON, John (ed.)
1998 *The Cambridge Companion to Biblical Interpretation.*
Cambridge University Press, Cambridge.

BAUCKHAM, Richard
1990 *Jude and the Relatives of Jesus in the Early Church.*
T & T Clark, Edinburgh.

BECHTEL, Lyn
1993 'Rethinking the Interpretation of Genesis 2.4b–3.24', in:
Brenner (ed.), pp. 77–117.
1998a 'Boundary Issues in Genesis 19.1–38', in:
Washington, Graham & Thimmes (eds.), pp. 22–40.
1998b 'A Feminist Reading of Genesis 19:1–11', in:
Brenner (ed.), pp. 108–128.

BERG, C.
1885 *Græsk-Dansk Ordbog til Skolebrug.*
Gyldendalske Boghandels Forlag, Copenhagen.

BESEN, Wayne R.
2003 *Anything But Straight: Unmasking the Scandals and Lies Behind the Ex-Gay Myth.*
Harrington Park Press, New York.

BLEDSTEIN, Adrien Janis
1993 'Are Women Cursed in Genesis 3.16?', in:
Brenner (ed.), pp. 142–145.

BOEHRINGER, Letha (ed.)
1992 *Hinkmar von Reims: De divortio Lotharii Regis et Theutbergae Reginae.*
Hannover, Hahnsche Buchhandlung.

BOHACHE, Thomas
2000 'To Cut or Not to Cut: Is Compulsory Heterosexuality a Prerequisite for

　　　　　Christianity?', in:
　　　　　Goss & West (eds.), pp. 227–239.
2006　　'Matthew', in:
　　　　　Guest, Goss, West & Bohache (eds.), pp. 487–516.
BOSWELL, John
1980　　*Christianity, Social Tolerance, and Homosexuality.*
　　　　　The University of Chicago Press, Chicago.
BOTTERWERK, G. Johannes, and
1986　　*Theological Dictionary of the Old Testament. Volume V.*
　　　　　Translated by David E. Green.
　　　　　William B. Eerdmans, Grand Rapids.
BOVATI, Pietro
1994　　*Re-Establishing Justice: Legal Terms, Concepts, and Procedures in the Hebrew Bible.*
　　　　　Translated by Michael J. Smith.
　　　　　Sheffield Academic Press, Sheffield.
BOYARIN, Daniel
1995　　'Are There Any Jews in the History of Sexuality?', in:
　　　　　Journal of the History of Sexuality, Vol. 5, No. 3, pp. 333–355.
2007　　'Against Rabbinic Sexuality: Textual Reasoning and the Jewish Theology of Sex', in:
　　　　　Loughlin (ed.), pp. 131–146.
BOYCE, Richard N.
1988　　*The Cry to God in the Old Testament.*
　　　　　Scholars Press, Atlanta.
BRAWLEY, Robert L. (ed.)
1996　　*Biblical Ethics & Homosexuality: Listening to Scripture.*
　　　　　Westminster John Knox Press, Louisville, KY.

BRAYFORD, Susan
2007	*Genesis. Septuagint Commentary Series.*
	Brill, Leiden.
BRENNER, Athalya
1993	'Female Social Behaviour: Two Descriptive Patterns within the »Birth of the Hero« Paradigm', in:
	Brenner (ed.), *A Feminist Companion to Genesis*, pp. 204–221.
1997	*The Intercourse of Knowledge: On Gendering Desire and 'Sexuality' in the Hebrew Bible.*
	Brill, Leiden.
BRENNER, Athalya (ed.)
1993	*A Feminist Companion to Genesis.*
	Sheffield Academic Press, Sheffield.
1993	*A Feminist Companion to Judges.*
	Sheffield Academic Press, Sheffield.
1998	*A Feminist Companion to Genesis. Second Series.*
	Sheffield Academic Press, Sheffield.
BRENNER, Athalya, and Carole Fontaine (eds.)
1997	*A Feminist Companion to Reading the Bible: Approaches, Methods, and Strategies.*
	Sheffield Academic Press, Sheffield.
BRENNER, Athalya, Archie Chi Chung Lee & Gale A. Yee (eds.)
2010	*Genesis: Texts & Contexts.*
	Fortress Press, Minneapolis.
BRETTLER, Marc Zvi
2002	*The Book of Judges.*
	Routledge, London.
BRINKSCHROEDER, Michael
2006	*Sodom als Symptom: Gleichgeschlechtliche Sexualität im christlichen Imaginären – eine*

religionsgeschichtliche Anamnese.
Walter de Gruyter GmbH, Berlin.

BROCKHAUS Wahrig

1981 *Brockhaus Wahrig Deutsches Wörterbuch in sechs Bänden. Zweiter Band BU – FZ.*
F. A. Brockhaus Wiesbaden & Deutsche Verlags-Anstalt, Stuttgart.

BRODIE, Thomas L.

2001 *Genesis as Dialogue: A Literary, Historical, and Theological Commentary.*
Oxford University Press, New York.

BROOTEN, Bernadette J.

1996 *Love Between Women: Early Christian Responses to Female Homoeroticism.*
The University of Chicago Press, Chicago & London.

BROWN, Peter

1990 'Bodies and Minds: Sexuality and Renunciation in Early Christianity', in:
Halperin, Winkler & Zeitlin (eds.), pp. 479–493.

BROWN, F., S. R. Driver & C. A. Briggs

2010 *The Brown-Driver-Briggs Hebrew and English Lexicon.*
Reprinted from the 1906 edition originally published by Houghton, Mifflin and Company, Boston. Thirteenth Printing.
Hendrickson Publishers, Peabody, Massachusetts.

BROWNING, W. R. F.

2009 *A Dictionary of the Bible. Second Edition.*
Oxford University Press, Oxford.

BRUCKNER, James K.
2001   *Implied Law in the Abraham Narrative: A Literary and Theological Analysis.*
Sheffield Academic Press, London.

BRUEGGEMANN, Walter
1982   *Genesis.*
John Knox Press, Atlanta.
1997   *Theology of the Old Testament: Testimony, Dispute, Advocacy.*
Fortress Press, Minneapolis.

BUCKLEY, Paul, & Stephen W. Angell (eds.)
2006   *The Quaker Bible Reader.*
Earlham School of Religion Publications, Richmond, IN.

CADWALLADER, Alan
2012   'Keeping Lists or Embracing Freedom: 1 Corinthians 6.9–10 in Context', in:
Wright (ed.), pp. 47–67.

CAIRD, George B.
1980   *The Language and Imagery of the Bible.*
Duckworth, London.

CAMPBELL, Douglas
2009   *The Deliverance of God: An Apocalyptic Rereading of Justification in Paul.*
Eerdmans Publishing Co., Grand Rapids.

CARDEN, Michael
2004   *Sodomy: A History of a Christian Biblical Myth.*
Equinox, London.
2006   'Genesis/Bereshit', in:
Guest, Goss, West & Bohache (eds.), pp. 21–60.

CARGAS, Harry James
1989   *Reflections of a Post-Auschwitz Christian.*
            Wayne State University Press, Detroit.
CARMICHAEL, Calum
2010   *Sex & Religion in the Bible.*
            Yale University Press, New Haven & London.
CARR, David M.
2003   *The Erotic Word: Sexuality, Spirituality, and the Bible.*
            Oxford University Press, New York.
CLEMENT of Alexandria
            The Instructor.
            www.ccel.org
COMSTOCK, Gary David
1993   *Gay Theology without Apology.*
            The Pilgrim Press, Cleveland.
COOK, S. A.
1903   *The Laws of Moses and the Code of Hammurabi.*
            Adam & Charles Black, London.
CORNWALL, Susannah
2009   '»State of Mind« versus »Concrete Set of Facts«: The Contrasting of Transgender and Intersex in Church Documents on Intersexuality', in: *Theology & Sexuality*, Volume 15.1, pp. 7–28.
COTTERELL, Peter, & Max Turner
1989   *Linguistics & Biblical Interpretation.*
            InterVarsity Press, Downers Grove.
COUNTRYMAN, L. William
1989   *Dirt, Greed and Sex.*
            SCM Press Ltd. (Reissued 1996.)
2006   'Jude', in:
            Guest, Goss, West & Bohache (eds.), pp. 747–752.

CRANFIELD, C. E. B.
1975 *A Critical and Exegetical Commentary on the Epistle to the Romans, I.*
T. & T. Clark Limited, Edinburgh

CRANNNY- Francis, Anne, & Wendy Waring, Pam Stavropoulos, Joan Kirkby
2003 *Gender Studies: Terms and Debates.*
Palgrave MacMillan, Basingstoke.

CREANGĂ, Ovidiu (ed.)
2010 *Men and Masculinity in the Hebrew Bible and Beyond.*
Sheffield Phoenix Press, Sheffield.

DAMIAN, Peter (Petrus Damianus)
1982 *Book of Gomorrah: An Eleventh-Century Treatise against Clerical Homosexual Practices.*
Translated by Pierre J. Payer.
Wilfrid Laurier University Press, Waterloo ON.

DANKER, Frederick William, with Kathryn Krug
2009 *The Concise Greek-English Lexicon of the New Testament.*
The University of Chicago Press, Chicago.

DANTE Alighieri
1971a *The Divine Comedy. 1: Inferno.*
Italian text with translation and comment by John D. Sinclair.
Oxford University Press, Oxford.
1971b *The Divine Comedy. 2: Purgatorio.*
Italian text with translation and comment by John D. Sinclair.
Oxford University Press, Oxford.

DAVIDSON, James
2008 *The Greeks & Greek Love: A Radical Reappraisal of Homosexuality in Ancient Greece.*
Phoenix, London.

DELANEY, Carol
1998 'Abraham and the Seeds of Patriarchy', in:
Brenner (ed.), pp. 129–149.

DOUGLAS, Mary
2000 *Leviticus as Literature.*
Oxford University Press, Oxford.
2004 *Jacob's Tears: The Priestly Work of Reconciliation.*
Oxford University Press, Oxford.

DOVER, Kenneth
1978 *Greek Homosexuality.*
Duckworth, London.

DOYLE, Brian
1998 'The Sin of Sodom: yada, yada, yada?', in:
Theology & Sexuality, No. 9, September, pp. 84–100.

DRIVER, G. R., & John C. Miles (eds.)
1952 *The Babylonian Laws. Edited with Translation and Commentary.*
Volume I: Legal Commentary.
At the Clarendon Press, Oxford.
1955 *Volume II: Transliterated Text, Translation, Philological Notes, Glossary.*
At the Clarendon Press, Oxford.

DUNCAN, Celena M.
2000 'The Book of Ruth: On Boundaries, Love, and Truth', in:
Goss & West (eds.), pp. 92–102.

DURAN, Khalid
1993 'Homosexuality and Islam', in:
Swidler (ed.), pp. 181–197.

DYNES, Wayne R. (ed.)
1990 *Encyclopedia of Homosexuality.*
St. James Press, London.

ECO, Umberto
2003 *Mouse or Rat? Translation as Negotiation.*
Phoenix, London.

EDWARDS, Chilperic
1906 *The Oldest Laws in the World.*
Watts & Co., London.

ENCYCLOPAEDIA Judaica
1971 *Encyclopaedia Judaica, Vol. 15.*
Keter Publishing House, Jerusalem.

EXUM, Cheryl
1993 *Fragmented Women: Feminist (Sub)versions of Biblical Narratives.*
Trinity Press International, Valley Forge.

FERNÁNDEZ de Oviedo, Gonzalo
1944 *Historia general y natural de las Indias. Tomo I.*
Editorial Guaranía, Asunción del Paraguay.

FEWELL, Danna Nolan
1992 'Judges', in:
Newsom & Ringe (eds.), pp. 67–77.

FIELDS, Weston W.
1997 *Sodom and Gomorrah: History and Motif in Biblical Narrative.*
Sheffield Academic Press, Sheffield.

FLOOD, John L.
2001 'Martin Luther's Bible Translation in its German and European Context', in:
Griffiths (ed.), pp. 45–70.

FONTAINE, Carole R.
1997 'The Abusive Bible: On the Use of Feminist Method in Pastoral Contexts', in : Brenner & Fontaine (eds.), pp. 84–113.

FOX, Everett
1995 *The Five Books of Moses: Genesis, Exodus, Leviticus, Numbers, and Deuteronomy.*
Schocken Books, New York.

FRIBERG, Timothy, Barbara Friberg & Neva F. Miller
2005 *Analytical Lexicon of the Greek New Testament.*
Trafford Publishing & Amazon.co.uk, Ltd, Marston Gate.

FRIENDS, A Group of
1964 *Towards a Quaker View of Sex. Revised Edition.*
Quaker Home Service, London.

GACA, Kathy L.
2003 *The Making of Fornication: Eros, Ethics, and Political Reform in Greek Philosophy and Early Christianity.*
University of California Press, Berkeley — Los Angeles — London.

GAGNON, Robert A. J.
2001 *The Bible and Homosexual Practice: Texts and Hermeneutics.*
Abingdon Press, Nashville.

GARCÍA-Estébanez, Emilio
1992 *¿Es cristiano ser mujer? La condición servil de la mujer según la Biblia y la Iglesia.*
Siglo XXI de España Editores, Madrid.

GARCILASO de la Vega, Inca
1985 *Comentarios reales de los Incas. Tomo I. Segunda edición.*
Fundación Biblioteca Ayacucho, Caracas.

GORDON, Cyrus H., & Gary A. Rendsburg
1997   *The Bible and the Ancient Near East. Fourth Edition.*
        W. W. Norton & Company, New York.

GORSLINE, Robin Hawley
2006   '1 and 2 Peter', in:
        Guest, Goss, West & Bohache (eds.), pp. 724-736.

GOSS, Robert E.
1993   *Jesus Acted Up: A Gay and Lesbian Manifesto.*
        Harper SanFrancisco.
2002   *Queering Christ: Beyond Jesus Acted Up.*
        The Pilgrim Press, Cleveland.
2006   'John', in:
        Guest, Goss, West & Bohache (eds.), pp. 548-565.

GOSS, Robert E., & Mona West (eds.)
2000   *Take Back the Word: A queer reading of the Bible.*
        The Pilgrim Press, Cleveland.

GRAETZ, Naomi
1993   'Dinah the Daughter', in:
        Brenner (ed.), pp. 306-317.

GREEN, Tony, Brenda Harrison & Jeremy Innes
1996   *Not for Turning: An Enquiry into the Ex-Gay Movement.*
        Published by the authors (UK).

GREENBERG, Steven
2004   *Wrestling with God & Men: Homosexuality in the Jewish Tradition.*
        The University of Wisconsin Press, Madison.

GRELOT, Pierre
2006   *The Language of Symbolism: Biblical Theology, Semantics, and Exegesis.*
        Hendrickson Publishers, Peabody, Massachusetts.

GRIFFITHS, Richard (ed.)
2001   *The Bible in the Renaissance: Essays on Biblical Commentary and Translation in the Fifteenth and Sixteenth Centuries.*
         Ashgate Publishing Limited, Aldershot.

GROOM, Susan Anne
2003   *Linguistic Analysis of Biblical Hebrew.*
         Paternoster Press, Carlisle.

GUEST, Deryn
2006   'Deuteronomy', in:
         Guest, Goss, West & Bohache (eds.), pp. 122–143.
2006   'Judges', in:
         Guest, Goss, West & Bohache (eds.), pp. 167–189.
2007   *When Deborah met Jael: Lesbian Biblical Hermeneutics.*
         SCM Books, London.

GUEST, Deryn, Robert Goss, Mona West and Thomas Bohache (eds.)
2006   *The Queer Bible Commentary.*
         SCM Books, London.

HADDOX, Susan E.
2010   'Favoured Sons and Subordinate Masculinities', in:
         Creangă (ed.), pp. 2–19.

HAINES-Eitzen, Kim
2001   '*A Greek-English Lexicon of the New Testament and Early Christian Literature, Third Edition* (BDAG)', reviewed 2012 at:
         scholar.lib.vt.edu/ejournals/ElAnt/V6N1/haines.html

HALPERIN, David M., John J. Winkler and Froma I. Zeitlin (eds.)
1990   *Before Sexuality: The Construction of Erotic Experience in the Ancient Greek World.*
         Princeton University Press, Princeton NJ.

HAMILTON, Victor P.
1990   *The Book of Genesis. Chapters 1–17.*
1995   *The Book of Genesis. Chapters 18–50.*
William B. Eerdmans, Grand Rapids.

HAMMERSHAIMB, Erling
1957   *Genesis: En sproglig analyse.*
G. E. C. Gad, Copenhagen.

HAMMERSHAIMB, Erling *et al.*
1953–63   *De gammeltestamentlige pseudepigrafer.*
G. E. C. Gad, Copenhagen.

HANKS, Thomas D.
1983   *God So Loved the Third World: The Biblical Vocabulary of Oppression.*
Orbis Books, New York.
2000   *The Subversive Gospel: A New Testament Commentary of Liberation.*
The Pilgrim Press, Cleveland.
2000b   'Matthew and Mary of Magdala: Good News for Sex Workers', in:
Goss & West (eds.), pp. 185–195.
2006   'Romans', in:
Guest, Goss, West & Bohache (eds.), pp. 582–605.

HARGREAVES, Cecil
1993   *A Translator's Freedom: Modern English Bibles and Their Language.*
Sheffield Academic Press, Sheffield.

HARRILL, J. Albert
2006   *Slaves in the New Testament: Literary, Social, and Moral Dimensions.*
Fortress Press, Minneapolis.

HEACOCK, Anthony
2011   *Jonathan Loved David: Manly Love in the Bible and the Hermeneutics of Sex.*
        Sheffield Phoenix Press, Sheffield.
HELMINIAK, Daniel A.
2000   *What the Bible Really Says About Homosexuality. Millennium Edition.*
        Alamo Square Press, New Mexico.
HOLLOWAY, Richard
1999   *Godless Morality: Keeping Religion out of Ethics.*
        Canongate, Edinburgh.
HORNER, Tom
1978   *Jonathan Loved David: Homosexuality in Biblical Times.*
        The Westminster Press, Philadelphia.
HORSLEY, Richard A.
1998   'Submerged Biblical Histories and Imperial Biblical Studies', in:
        Sugirtharajah (ed.), pp. 152–173.
HUEGEL, Karin
2009   *Homoerotik und Hebräische Bibel.*
        Diplomica Verlag, Hamburg.
HUFFMON, Herbert B.
1966   'The Treaty Background of Hebrew YADA', in:
        Bulletin of the American Schools of Oriental Research, Jerusalem & Baghdad, No. 181, pp. 31–37.
HUFFMON, Herbert B., and Simon B. Parker
1966   'A Further Note on the Treaty Background of Hebrew YADA', in:
        Bulletin of the American Schools of Oriental Research, Jerusalem & Baghdad, No. 184, pp. 36–38.

HUGENBERGER, Gordon Paul
1994   *Marriage as a Covenant: A study of biblical law and ethics governing marriage developed from the perspective of Malachi.*
        E. J. Brill, Leiden-New York-Köln.

HUNT, Mary E.
1992   *Fierce Tenderness: A Feminist Theology of Friendship.*
        The Crossroad Publishing Company, New York.

IHIMAERA, Witi
1995   *Nights in the Gardens of Spain.*
        Reed Publishing (NZ) Ltd, Auckland.

ISHERWOOD, Lisa
2006   *The Power of Erotic Celibacy: Queering Heterosexuality.*
        Continuum, London.

ISHERWOOD, Lisa (ed.)
2000   *The Good News of the Body: Sexual Theology and Feminism.*
        Continuum, London.
2008   *Patriarchs, Prophets and Other Villains.*
        Equinox, London.

ISHERWOOD, Lisa, and Dorothea McEwan (eds.)
1996   *An A to Z of Feminist Theology.*
        Sheffield Academic Press, Sheffield.

ISHERWOOD, Lisa, and Elizabeth Stuart
1998   *Introducing Body Theology.*
        Sheffield Academic Press, Sheffield.

ISHERWOOD, Lisa, and Rosemary Radford Ruether (eds.)
2009   *Weep Not For Your Children: Essays on Religion and Violence.*
        Equinox, London.

JASPER, David
1998   'Literary readings of the Bible', in:
            Barton (ed.), pp. 21–34.
JENNI, Ernst, & Claus Westermann
1997   *Theological Dictionary of the Old Testament.*
            Translated by Mark E. Bridle.
            Hendrickson Publishers, Peabody.
JENNINGS, Theodore W., Jr.
2003   *The Man Jesus Loved: Homoerotic Narratives from the New Testament.*
            Pilgrim Press, Cleveland.
2005   *Jacob's Wound: Homoerotic Narrative in the Literature of Ancient Israel.*
            Continuum, New York & London.
JENSEN, Hans Jørgen Lundager
            See LUNDAGER Jensen, Hans Jørgen
JOHANSSON, Warren
1990   'Sodom and Gomorrah', in:
            Dynes (ed.), pp. 1228–1230.
JOHNS, C. H. W.
1903   *The Oldest Code of Laws in the World.*
            T & T Clark, Edinburgh.
JOHNSTON, Sarah Iles
1990   *Hekate Soteira: A Study of Hekate's Roles in the Chaldean Oracles and Related Literature.*
            Scholars Press, Atlanta.
JOHNSTONE, William
1998   'Biblical Study and Linguistics', in:
            Barton (ed.), pp. 129–142.

JONES-Warsaw, Koala
1993   'Toward a Womanist Hermeneutic: A Reading of Judges 19–21', in:
        Brenner (ed.), pp. 172–186.
JORDAN, Mark D.
1997   *The Invention of Sodomy in Christian Theology.*
        The University of Chicago Press, Chicago.
2000   *The Silence of Sodom: Homosexuality in Modern Catholicism.*
        The University of Chicago Press, Chicago.
JOSEPHUS
1998a   *Jewish Antiquities. Books I–III.*
        With an English Translation by H. St. J. Thackeray.
1998b   *Jewish Antiquities. Books IV–VI.*
        With an English Translation by H. St. J. Thackeray & R. Marcus.
        Harvard University Press, Cambridge, Mass., & London.
KADER, Samuel
1999   *Openly Gay, Openly Christian: How the Bible Really is Gay Friendly.*
        Leyland Publications, San Francisco.
KARRAS, Ruth Mazo
2005   *Sexuality in Medieval Europe: Doing unto Others.*
        Routledge, Abingdon.
KATES, Judith A., and Gail Twesky Reimer (eds.)
1996   *Reading Ruth: Contemporary Women Reclaim a Sacred Story.*
        Ballantine Books, New York.
KING, Christopher
2000   'A Love as Fierce as Death: Reclaiming the Song of Songs for Queer Lovers', in:
        Goss & West (eds.), pp. 126–142.

KING, L. W.
1910   *The Code of Hammurabi.* Edited by Richard Hooker 1996.
        Retrieved from the World Wide Web, February 2007.

KINNAMAN, David, and Gabe Lyons
2007   *UnChristian: What a New Generation Really Thinks about Christianity.*
        Baker Books, Grand Rapids.

KORSAK, Mary Phil
1993   *At the Start: Genesis Made New.*
        Doubleday, New York.

KOSCHAKER, Paul
1917   *Rechtsvergleichende Studien zur Gesetzgebung Hammurapis.*
        Verlag von Veit & Comp., Leipzig.

KRAUS, C. Norman
2011   *On Being Human: Sexual Orientation and the Image of God.*
        Cascade Books, Eugene, Oregon.

LETELLIER, Robert I.
1995   *Day in Mamre, Night in Sodom: Abraham and Lot in Genesis 18–19.*
        Brill, Leiden.

LIDDELL, Henry George, and Robert Scott
1940   *A Greek-English Lexicon. Revised and augmented throughout by Sir Henry Stuart Jones with the assistance of Roderick McKenzie.*
        Clarendon Press, Oxford.

LINGS, Kjeld Renato
2006   *Restoring Sodom: Towards a Non-sexual Approach.*
        Unpublished PhD Thesis. University of Exeter, UK.

2007	'Culture Clash in Sodom: Patriarchal Tales of Heroes, Villains, and Manipulation', in: Isherwood (ed.), pp. 183-207.
2008	'Removing the Sexual Cobweb: To »Know« in a Text of Terror', in: Isherwood & Ruether (eds.), pp. 26-53.
2009	'The »Lyings« of a Woman: Male-Male Incest in Leviticus 18.22?', in: *Theology & Sexuality*, Volume 15.2, pp. 231-50, Equinox, London.
2011	*Biblia y homosexualidad: ¿Se equivocaron los traductores?* Universidad Bíblica Latinoamericana, San José, Costa Rica.

LIPKA, Hilary B.
2006	*Sexual Transgression in the Hebrew Bible.* Sheffield Phoenix Press, Sheffield.

LIPTON, Diana (ed.)
2012	*Universalism and Particularism at Sodom and Gomorrah: Essays in Memory of Ron Pirson.* Society of Biblical Literature, Atlanta.

LOADER, William
2004	*The Septuagint, Sexuality, and the New Testament: Case Studies of the Impact of the LXX in Philo and the New Testament.* William B. Eerdmans, Grand Rapids.

LOADES, Ann
1998	'Feminist Interpretation', in: Barton (ed.), pp. 81-94.

LOADES, Ann (ed.)
1990	*Feminist Theology: A Reader.* SPCK, London.

LONG, Lynne
2001   *Translating the Bible: From the 7th to the 17th Century.*
              Ashgate, Aldershot.

LONG, Ronald E.
2006   'Introduction', in:
              Guest, Goss, West & Bohache (eds.)

LOUGHLIN, Gerard (ed.)
2007   *Queer Theology: Rethinking the Western Body.*
              Blackwell Publishing Ltd, Oxford.

LUNDAGER Jensen, Hans Jørgen
2004   *Den fortærende ild: Strukturelle analyser af narrative og rituelle tekster i Det Gamle Testamente.*
              2. udgave.
              Aarhus Universitetsforlag, Aarhus.

LUTHER, Martin
1961   *Luther's Works, Volume 3: Lectures on Genesis Chapters 15–50.*
              Edited by Jaroslav Pelikan. Translated by George V. Schick.
              Concordia Publishing House, Saint Louis.

LYONS, William John
2012   'The Eternal Liminality of Lot: Paying the Price of Opposing the Particular in the Sodom Narrative', in:
              Lipton (ed.), pp. 3–23.

McCARSON, Bonnie
2002   'He/She: Jung's Concepts of the Archetypal Masculine and Feminine', in:
              www.suite101.com (2011)

McCLEARY, Rollan
2004   *A Special Illumination: Authority, Inspiration and Heresy in Gay Spirituality.*
              Equinox Publishing Ltd, London.

McGRATH, Alister E.
1998   *Historical Theology: An Introduction to the History of Christian Thought.*
       Blackwell Publishing, Oxford.
McGUCKIN, John Anthony (ed.)
2006   *The SCM Press A–Z of Origen.*
       SCM Press, London.
McKEOWN, James
2008   *Genesis.*
       William B. Eerdmans, Grand Rapids.
McKINLAY, Judith
2009   'Biblical Exegesis', in:
       Isherwood & McEwan (eds.), pp. 21-23.
McNEILL, John J.
1993   *The Church and the Homosexual. Fourth Edition.*
       Beacon Press, Boston.
1996   *Taking a Chance on God. Second Edition.*
       Beacon Press, Boston.
MACY, Howard R.
2006   'Learning to Read the Psalms', in:
       Buckley & Angell (eds.), pp. 105-115.
MAGONET, Jonathan (ed.)
1993   *Jewish Explorations of Sexuality.*
       Berghahn Books, Providence.
2004   *A Rabbi Reads the Bible. Second Edition.*
       SCM, London.
MALUL, Meir
2002   *Knowledge, Control and Sex: Studies in Biblical Thought, Culture and Worldview.*
       Archaeological Center Publications, Jaffa.

MARTIN, Dale B.
2006   *Sex and the Single Saviour: Gender and Sexuality in Biblical Interpretation.*
        Westminster John Knox Press, Louisville.
MATHER, Maurice W., and Joseph William Hewitt
1962   *Xenophon's Anabasis. Books I–IV.*
        University of Oklahoma Press, Norman.
MEIN, Andrew
2001   *Ezekiel and the Ethics of Exile.*
        Oxford University Press, Oxford.
MEIR, Amira
2012   'Why Did God Choose Abraham? Responses from Medieval Jewish Commentators', in: Lipton (ed.), pp. 53–68.
METZGER, Bruce M.
2001   *The Bible in Translation: Ancient and English Versions.*
        Baker Academics, Grand Rapids.
METZGER, Bruce M., and Michael D. Coogan (eds.)
1993   *The Oxford Companion to the Bible.*
        Oxford University Press, Oxford and New York.
MEYERS, Carol
1988   *Discovering Eve: Ancient Israelite Women in Context.*
        Oxford University Press, Oxford & New York.
1993   'Gender Roles and Genesis 3.16 Revisited', in: Brenner (ed.), pp. 118–141.
MILGROM, Jacob
2000   *Leviticus 17–22: A New Translation with Introduction and Commentary.*
        The Anchor Bible, Doubleday, New York.
2004   *Leviticus: A Book of Ritual and Ethics.*
        Fortress Press, Minneapolis.

MILLER, James E.
2010   *Raw Material: Studies in Biblical Sexuality. Second Edition.*
            www.othersheep.org (2012).

MILNE, Pamela J.
1993   'The Patriarchal Stamp of Scripture: The Implications of Structuralist Analyses for Feminist Hermeneutics', in: Brenner (ed.), pp. 146-172.

MITCHEL, Larry A.
1984   *A Student's Vocabulary for Biblical Hebrew and Aramaic.*
            Zondervan, Grand Rapids.

MOLINA, Fernanda
2010   'Crónicas de la sodomía. Representaciones de la sexualidad indígena a través de la literatura colonial', in:
            http://200.69.147.117/revistavirtual/, Número 6, septiembre.
            Programa Nacional de Bibliografía Colonial, Biblioteca Nacional, Buenos Aires.

MONTI, Joseph
1995   *Arguing about Sex: The Rhetoric of Christian Sexual Morality.*
            State University of New York Press, Albany.

MOORE, Gareth
2003   *A Question of Truth: Christianity and Homosexuality.*
            Continuum, London.

MOXNES, Halvor
2003   *Putting Jesus in His Place: A Radical Vision of Household and Kingdom.*

Westminster John Knox Press, Louisville & London.

NEWSOM, Carol A., and Sharon H. Ringe
1992   *The Women's Bible Commentary.*
        SPCK, London, & John Knox Press, Louisville.

NICKELSBURG, George W. E.
2003   *Ancient Judaism and Christian Origins: Diversity, Continuity, and Transformation.*
        Fortress Press, Minneapolis.

NIDITCH, Susan
1997   *Oral World and Written Word: Orality and Literacy in Ancient Israel.*
        SPCK, London.

NIELSEN, Kirsten
1997   *Ruth.* Translated by Edward Broadbridge.
        SCM Press Ltd, London.

NISSINEN, Martti
1998   *Homosexuality in the Biblical World: A Historical Perspective.*
        Translated by Kirsi Stjerna.
        Fortress Press, Minneapolis.

OLYAN, Saul
1994   'And with a Male You Shall Not Lie the Lying Down of a Woman. On the Meaning and Significance of Lev. 18:22 and 20:13', in:
        Journal of the History of Sexuality, Vol. 5, pp. 179–206.

OPPENHEIM, A. Leo (ed.)
1973   *The Assyrian Dictionary of the Oriental Institute of the University of Chicago. Vol. 9 L.*
        The Oriental Institute, Chicago & J. J. Augustin Verlagsbuchhandlung, Glückstadt.

ORIGEN
1982 *Homilies on Genesis and Exodus.* Translated by Ronald E. Heine.
Fathers of the Church, Volume 71.
http://books.google.com

OSBURN, Carroll D.
2000 'Jude, Letter of', in:
Eerdmans Dictionary of the Bible pp. 750-751.
2000 'Peter, Second Letter of', in:
Eerdmans Dictionary of the Bible, pp. 1039-1041.

PAGET, J. N. B. Carleton
1996 'The Christian Exegesis of the Old Testament in the Alexandrian Tradition', in:
Sæbø (ed.), pp. 478-542.

PARDES, Ilana
1993 'Beyond Genesis 3: The Politics of Maternal Naming', in:
Brenner (ed.), pp. 173-193.

PATZIA, A. G.
1995 *The Making of the New Testament: Origin, Collection, Text and Canon.*
Apollos InterVarsity, Leicester/Downers Grove.

PELEG, Yaron
2005 'Love at First Sight? David, Jonathan, and the Biblical Politics of Gender', in:
Journal for the Study of the Old Testament, Volume 30.2, December, pp. 171-189.

PELEG, Yitzhak (Itzik)
2012 'Was Lot a Good Host? Was Lot Saved from Sodom as a Reward for His Hospitality?', in:
Lipton (ed.), pp. 129-156.

PERDUE, Leo G.
2005   *Reconstructing Old Testament Theology: After the Collapse of History.*
        Fortress Press, Minneapolis.

PERKINS, Benjamin
2000   'Coming Out, Lazarus's and Ours: Queer Reflections of a Psychospiritual, Political Journey', in:
        Goss & West (eds.), pp. 196–205.

PETT, Peter
2000   *Deuteronomy.*
        www.angelfire.com (2012).

PHILON d'Alexandrie
1960   *Le traité de la Vie Contemplative de Philon d'Alexandrie.*
        Introduction, traduction et notes par Pierre Geoltrain.
        Librairie d'Amérique et d'Orient, Paris.
1966   *De Abrahamo.*
        Introduction, traduction et notes par Jean Gorez.
        Éditions du Cerf, Paris.

PIRSON, Ron
2012   'Does Lot Know about *yada*?', in:
        Lipton (ed.), pp. 203–213.

POMEROY, Sarah B.
1975   *Goddesses, Whores, Wives, & Slaves: Women in Classical Antiquity.*
        Pimlico, London.

PROUST, Marcel
1987   *A la recherche du temps perdu: Le côté de Guermantes. Sodome et Gomorrhe.*
        Éditions Robert Laffont, Paris.

PROVAN, Iain
1998   'The Historical Books of the Old Testament', in: Barton (ed.), pp. 198-211.

RAD, Gerhard von
1972   *Genesis: A Commentary. Revised Edition.* SCM Press Ltd, London.

RAJAK, Tessa
1983   *Josephus : The Historian and His Society.* Duckworth, London.

RAMÍREZ-Kidd, José E.
2009   *Para comprender el Antiguo Testamento.* Universidad Bíblica Latinoamericana, San José, Costa Rica.

RASHKOW, Ilona
1998   'Daddy-Dearest and the »Invisible Spirit of Wine«', in: Brenner (ed.), pp. 82-107.

REIF, Stefan C.
1998   'Aspects of the Jewish Contribution to Biblical Interpretation', in: Barton (ed.), pp. 143-159.

RENDTORFF, Rolf, and Robert A. Kugler (eds.)
2003   *The Book of Leviticus: Composition and Reception.* Brill, Leiden & Boston.

ROESEL, Martin
1994   *Übersetzung als Vollendung der Auslegung.* De Gruyter, Berlin.

ROGERSON, J. W.
1999   *An Introduction to the Bible.* Penguin Books, London.

ROSEN, Wilhelm von
1993 *Månens kulør: Studier i dansk bøssehistorie 1628–1912.*
Rhodos, Copenhagen.
ROTH, Martha T.
1989 *Babylonian Marriage Agreements 7th–3rd Centuries B.C.*
Neukirchener Verlag, Neukirchen-Vluyn.
1997 *Law Collections from Mesopotamia and Asia Minor. Second Edition.*
Vandenhoeck & Ruprecht, Göttingen.
SAEBØ, Magne (ed.)
1996 *Hebrew Bible / Old Testament: The History of Its Interpretation. Vol. I.*
Vandenhoeck & Ruprecht, Göttingen.
SÁENZ-Badillos, Ángel
1993 *History of the Hebrew Language.*
Cambridge University Press, Cambridge.
SAFREN, Jonathan D.
2012 'Hospitality Compared: Abraham and Lot as Hosts', in:
Lipton (ed.), pp. 157–178.
SCANZONI, Letha Dawson, & Virginia Ramey Mollenkott.
1994 *Is the Homosexual my Neighbor? A Positive Christian Response. Revised and Updated.*
HarperSanFrancisco.
SCHEIL, V.
1904 *La loi de Hammourabi (vers 2000 av. J.C.).*
Ernest Leroux, Éditeur, Paris.
SCHENKER, Adrian
2003 'What Connects the Incest Prohibitions with the Other Prohibitions Listed in Leviticus

18 and 20?', in:
Rendtorff & Kugler (eds.), pp. 162–185.
SCHNEIDER, Tammi J.
2000 *Judges.*
Berit Olam. Studies in Hebrew Narrative and Poetry.
The Liturgical Press, Collegeville.
2008 *Mothers of Promise: Women in the Book of Genesis.*
Baker Academic, Grand Rapids.
SCHOTTROFF, Luise
1993 'The Creation Narrative: Genesis 1.1–2.4a', in:
Brenner (ed.), pp. 173–193.
SCHULZ-Fluegel, Eva
1996 'The Latin Old Testament Tradition', in:
Saebø (ed.), pp. 642–662.
SEDDIK, Youssef
1989 *Si le Coran m'était conté.*
Éditeur Alef, Paris.
SHARON, Diane M.
1998 'The Doom of Paradise: Literary Patterns in Accounts of Paradise and Morality in the Hebrew Bible and the Ancient Near East', in:
Brenner (ed.), pp. 53–80.
SHARPE, Keith
2011 *The Gay Gospels: Good News for Lesbian, Gay, Bisexual, and Transgendered People.*
Circle Books, Winchester (UK) & Washington (USA).
SHERIDAN, Mark
2006 'Old Testament', in:
McGuckin (ed.), pp. 159–162.

SIMKINS, Ronald A.
1998 'Gender Construction in the Yahwist Creation Myth', in:
Brenner (ed.), pp. 32–52.

SMITH, Don
2006 'Seeking Meaning in Creation', in:
Buckley & Angell (eds.), pp. 3–29.

SPINA, Frank Anthony
2005 *The Faith of the Outsider: Exclusion and Inclusion in the Biblical Story.*
William B. Eerdmans, Grand Rapids.

STEINER, George
1992 *After Babel: Aspects of Language and Translation. Second Edition.*
Oxford University Press, Oxford & New York.

STEMBERGER, Günter
1996 'Exegetical Contacts Between Christians and Jews in the Roman Empire', in:
Saebø (ed.), pp. 569–586.

STEWART, David T.
2006 'Leviticus', in:
Guest, Goss, West & Bohache (eds.), pp. 77–104.

STONE, Ken
1996 *Sex, Honor and Power in the Deuteronomistic History.*
Sheffield Academic Press, Sheffield.
2000 'The Garden of Eden and the Heterosexual Contract', in:
Goss & West (eds.), pp. 57–70.
2006 '1 and 2 Kings', in:
Guest, Goss, West & Bohache (eds.), pp. 222–250.

STUART, Elizabeth
1995 *Just Good Friends: Towards a Lesbian and Gay Theology of Relationships.*
Mowbray, London.
1998 'A Difficult Relationship: Christianity and the Body', in:
Isherwood & Stuart, pp. 52–77.
2003 *Gay and Lesbian Theologies: Repetitions with Critical Difference.*
Ashgate Publishing Limited, Aldershot.

STUART, Elizabeth, and Adrian Thatcher
1997 *People of Passion: What the churches teach about sex.*
Mowbray, London.

STURGE, Mark
2001 'Don't Dis Me if You Don't Know Me', in:
Black Theology in Britain, 4.1, November.

SUGIRTHARAJAH, R. S.
2002 *Postcolonial Criticism and Biblical Interpretation.*
Oxford University Press, Oxford.

SUGIRTHARAJAH, R. S. (ed.)
1991 *Voices from the Margin: Interpreting the Bible in the Third World.*
SPCK, London.
1998 *The Postcolonial Bible.*
Sheffield Academic Press, Sheffield.

SVARTVIK, Jesper
2006 *Bibeltolkningens bakgator: Synen på judar, slavar och homosexuella i historia och nutid.*
Verbum Förlag, Stockholm.

SWIDLER, Arlene (ed.)
1993 *Homosexuality and World Religions.*
Trinity Press International, Valley Forge, Pennsylvania.

TERRIEN, Samuel
1985   *Till the Heart Sings: A Biblical Theology of Manhood and Womanhood.*
        William B. Eerdmans, Grand Rapids.

TERTULLIAN
1951   *To His Wife: An Exhortation to Chastity, Monogamy.*
        Translated and Annotated by William P. Le Saint.
        The Newman Press, Westminster, Maryland.

TEUBAL, Savina J.
1984   *Sarah the Priestess: The First Matriarch of Genesis.*
        Swallow Press & Ohio University Press, Athens.
1993   'Sarah and Hagar: Matriarchs and Visionaries', in:
        Brenner (ed.), pp. 235–250.

THATCHER, Adrian
1999   *Marriage after Modernity: Christian Marriage in Postmodern Times.*
        Sheffield Academic Press, Sheffield.
2002   *Living Together & Christian Ethics.*
        Cambridge University Press, Cambridge.

THOMAS, David Winton
1960   '*Kelebh* »Dog«: Its Origin and Some Usages of It in the Old Testament', in:
        Vetus Testamentum Vol. 10, Fasc. 4, October, pp. 410–427.

THOMAS, Robert L.
2000   *How to Choose a Bible Version: An Introductory Guide to English Translations.*
        Christian Focus Publications, Fearn, Ross-shire.

THUESEN, Peter J.
1999 *In Discordance with the Scriptures: American Protestant Battles over Translating the Bible.*
Oxford University Press, New York.

TRIBLE, Phyllis
1984 *Texts of Terror: Literary-feminist readings of biblical narratives.*
SCM Press Ltd, London.
1990 'Feminist Hermeneutics and Biblical Studies', in: Loades (ed.), pp. 23–29.

UNAMUNO, Miguel de
1931 *La agonía del cristianismo.*
Compañía Ibero-Americana de Publicaciones (S. A.), Madrid.

VANGGAARD, Thorkil
1969 *Phallós.*
Gyldendal, Copenhagen.
1972 *Phallos: A Symbol and Its History in the Male World.*
International Universities Press, New York.

VASEY, Michael
1995 *Strangers and Friends: A new exploration of homosexuality and the Bible.*
Hodder & Stoughton, London.

VERMES, Geza
2001 *The Changing Faces of Jesus.*
Penguin Books, London.

WALSH, Jerome T.
2001 'Leviticus 18:22 and 20:13: Who Is Doing What to Whom?', in:
Journal of Biblical Literature, Vol. 120, No. 2, pp. 201–209.

WARNER, Megan
2012 'Keeping the way of Yhwh: Righteousness and Justice in Genesis 18–19', in:
Lipton (ed.), pp. 113–126.

WARRIOR, Robert Allen
1991 'A Native American Perspective: Canaanites, Cowboys, and Indians', in:
Sugirtharajah (ed.), pp. 287–295.

WASHINGTON, Harold C., Susan L. Graham and Pamela Thimmes (eds.)
1998 *Escaping Eden: New Feminist Perspectives on the Bible.*
Sheffield Academic Press, Sheffield.

WECHSLER, Harlan J.
2012 'Beyond Particularity and Universality: Reflections on Shadal's Commentary to Genesis 18–19', in:
Lipton (ed.), pp. 191–202.

WEINGREEN, J.
1959 *A Practical Grammar for Classical Hebrew. Second Edition.*
Oxford University Press, Oxford & New York.

WENHAM, Gordon
1987 *World Bible Commentary, Vol. I: Genesis 1–15.*
Word Books, Waco.
1994 *World Bible Commentary, Vol. II: Genesis 16–50.*
Word Books, Waco.

WEST, Mona
2006 'Ruth', in:
Guest, Goss, West & Bohache (eds.), pp. 190–194.

WHITE, Mel
2010   *What the Bible Says – and Doesn't Say – About Homosexuality.*
        www.soulforce.org (2010)

WHITELAM, Keith W.
1998   'The Social World of the Bible', in:
        Barton (ed.), pp. 35-49.

WINTER, Miriam Therese
1992   *Woman Witness: A Feminist Lectionary and Psalter.*
        CollinsDove, North Blackburn, Victoria.

WOLDE, Ellen van
2012   'Outcry, Knowledge and Judgment in Genesis 18-19', in:
        Lipton (ed.), pp. 71-100.

WRIGHT, David P.
2003   'The Laws of Hammurabi as a Source for the Covenant Collection (Exodus 20:23-23:19)', in:
        Maarav, Vol. 10, pp. 11-88.

WRIGHT, Nigel (ed.)
2012   *Five Uneasy Pieces: Essays on Scripture and Sexuality. Second Printing.*
        ATF Theology, Hindmarsh, SA.

ZERWICK, Max, and Mary Grosvenor
1988   *A Grammatical Analysis of the Greek New Testament. Revised Edition.*
        Editrice Pontificio Istituto Biblico, Rome.

INDEX

SCRIPTURE REFERENCE INDEX

FIRST TESTAMENT

Genesis

1–4	4, 82	2.21	5, 13, 33, 35, 37, 55
1	4, 16, 21, 97		
1.1	8	2.21-22	30-31, 33, 35, 42, 136
1.2	7, 11		
1.7	140	2.21-24	36
1.16	140	2.22	9, 30
1.25	140	2.23	12, 24, 36-37
1.25-27	18	2.24	5, 18, 37-38, 42, 83-85, 100, 208, 575-579, 582
1.26	7, 25, 140		
1.26-27	26, 28-29, 42		
1.26-29	21-23	2.25	9, 39
1.27	4, 15, 21, 24-25, 207-208	3	*xxxv*, 7, 12, 17, 40-41, 393
1.28	15, 85, 150	3.1-7	128
1.29	22	3.3	13
1.31	15, 140	3.5	11, 82
2–3	325	3.7	9, 82, 128, 393
2	4, 5, 16-17, 34, 41, 579, 618	3.11	129
		3.16	11, 15, 40
2.4	20	3.17-19	41, 128
2.5	14	3.20	12, 38
2.8	14	3.21	41, 129
2.9	82	3.22	82
2.15	14, 127	3.23-24	83
2.17	10, 13, 82	4	12, 40, 87, 393
2.18	7, 15, 36, 83	4.1	12, 37, 57, 82-87, 102, 109, 117, 371, 641
2.18-20	41		
2.19	5		
		4.2	86

- 699 -

4.6-7	8	9.1	149
4.7	11	9.4	37
4.16	87	9.18	127, 150
4.17	9, 57, 84-86, 102, 641	9.18-27	*xliv*
		9.20	127
4.17-24	87	9.20-22	123
4.18	85	9.21	128-132, 138, 143, 145, 393
4.19-22	85		
4.25	86-87, 114, 117, 153	9.21-22	127, 143
		9.21-24	138
4.26	85	9.21-27	153
5	38, 87	9.22	125-129, 133, 138, 145, 150
5.2	3		
5.3	85	9.23	129, 147
5.21-22	87	9.24	125, 138, 140, 147, 393
5.28-30	87		
5.29	127	9.25	137, 150
6—8	401	9.25-27	129, 149, 151
6	4, 284	9.26	152
6.1-4	46, 283	9.26-27	129, 150, 152
6.2	55-57, 144, 371	10	87
6.2-4	270	10.6	127, 150
6.4	48, 53, 55-58, 61	10.19	242, 256, 340, 355, 404
6.8-9	127		
6.9-10	127	11	343, 401, 404
6.13	45	11.4-8	9
6.14-16	127	11.10-29	153
6.18, 45	127	11.29—23.19	406
6.19-20	127	11.29	57
7.2-3	208	12—25	401
7.7	45, 127	12—15	94
7.9	363	12	94, 404
7.13	127	12.1	93, 576
7.15	45	12.1-7	401
7.16	208	12.3	88, 94
8.16	127	12.4-5	406
8.18	127	12.5	408
8.20	9, 136	12.7	93-94
9—10	150	12.8	402, 481-482
9	126, 135, 140-141, 151, 154, 393	12.10	418
		12.11-13	418

12.11–16	418	16.15	403, 407
12.12	144, 481–482	17 – 19	94
12.17	403	17	93–94, 243
12.18–19	402	17.1	93–94
12.18–20	418	17.5–7	94
13	94, 332	17.8	427
13.5	404	17.10–14	94, 551
13.5–7	408	17.16	403
13.10	243	17.17	96
13.10–12	242, 404	17.23	70, 73
13.10–13	242, 355	17.23–27	136
13.11	391	18 – 19	82, 92–93, 243, 247, 258, 325, 340, 344, 351–352, 357, 359, 376, 382, 391, 395, 398, 400, 417, 432–433, 437, 478, 481, 619
13.12	243		
13.13	340, 404		
13.14	93		
13.18	402		
14	91, 94, 98, 243, 306, 349–350, 355, 368, 424		
		18	91, 94, 97, 320, 352, 393, 401, 478–479
14.11–16	405		
14.12	404, 434		
14.14–16	404, 435	18.1	93–94, 355
14.18	424	18.1–8	434
14.19–20	402, 424	18.2	144, 478
14.20	424	18.2–8	482
14.22–23	402	18.6–8	408
14.23	243	18.7	73, 136
15	93–94, 97	18.9–15	466
15.1	93–94	18.10	244, 417, 478
15.2	601	18.12	96, 466
15.5	145	18.14	417, 432
15.10	136	18.15	466
15.13	68, 93, 428	18.16	91, 242
15.15	45, 145, 403	18.17	96
16.2	48, 53, 55–56, 58, 61	18.17–21	94–95
		18.19	82, 88, 91–94, 99, 101–102, 117, 260, 341, 353, 355, 376–379, 382–384, 386, 388–392, 394, 396, 402, 432–433
16.2–4	46, 57		
16.3	59, 70, 77, 633		
16.4	48, 53, 55–56, 58, 61		
16.6	68, 412		

18.20	97, 214, 430, 432–434	19.4–11	351, 430
18.20–21	97, 335, 363, 423, 431	19.5	91–92, 97–99, 103, 111, 118–119, 189, 245, 275, 318, 328, 343, 347, 350, 353–357, 359–360, 362-363, 373–380, 382–392, 394–396, 398, 416, 430, 432, 482
18.21	91–92, 94–95, 98–99, 111, 117–118, 144, 355, 376–379, 382–386, 388–391, 395–396, 430, 432–434		
18.22	244, 266, 578	19.5–8	285, 356
18.23	430, 432–433, 436, 438	19.6–8	434
		19.6–9	431
18.23–32	94, 431, 437	19.7	405, 422, 429, 433
18.24	432–433	19.7–8	349, 435, 482
18.25	430, 432–433, 437	19.8	57, 84, 91–92, 99–102, 117, 119, 245, 350, 353–355, 357, 371, 376–379, 381–384, 386–396, 398, 410–417, 421, 433, 435, 475, 478, 635, 641
18.26	433		
18.28	432–433		
18.31	433		
18.32	405, 433		
18.33	244		
19	91, 97–98, 105, 195, 241, 247, 262, 278, 285, 287, 300, 306, 320, 327, 329–330, 333, 337, 346–349, 356, 359, 369, 393, 398, 401, 405, 416, 423–424, 427, 441, 475, 478-479	19.8–9	409
		19.9	245, 333, 404, 423, 427, 429, 433–434, 436–440, 479, 482, 619
		19.10–11	418
		19.11	98, 245, 353, 366–368, 412, 422, 433
19.1	144, 244, 432, 434, 478	19.12	100, 370, 421–422, 433, 641
19.1–3	434, 482		
19.1–11	354, 358	19.13	245, 363, 423, 430–431, 433–434
19.1–13	266		
19.3	407–408, 421	19.14	55, 100–102, 245, 370, 392–393, 405, 422, 433, 633
19.4	49, 98, 103, 359, 361, 364–365, 367–368, 372–374, 412, 422, 432		
		19.14–15	635
		19.14–16	421
19.4–5	363, 373, 435	19.15	406, 431, 433, 478

19.15–16	421	20.6	66, 77
19.15–22	405	20.7	97
19.16	72, 405–406, 433	20.8–10	402
19.17	145, 333	20.9–13	418
19.19	433	20.11	425
19.21	433	20.13	401
19.23–25	431	20.14–17	425
19.24	435	20.15	412, 425
19.24–25	431	20.17	94
19.25	256, 370, 433	21 – 22	94
19.26	50, 145, 245, 333, 337, 406, 408, 478–479, 482	21	94
		21.1–7	417
		21.2	407
19.27–28	242	21.3	403
19.29	405	21.4	136
19.30	245, 333	21.9	144
19.30–38	421	21.16	144
19.31	50, 369–371, 433	21.18	72
19.32	49–50, 53, 103, 363, 372, 392	21.19	144
		21.22	402, 425
19.32–35	49–50, 52, 398	21.22–24	425
19.32–38	278	21.25–31	426
19.33	49, 52–53, 91–92, 103–104, 355, 363, 373, 376–379, 382–384, 386–390, 392–396, 433, 466	21.31–32	425
		21.34	426
		22	94
		22.1–14	417
		22.2	417, 572
19.34	50, 52–53, 372	22.3–10	418
19.35	52–53, 91–92, 103–104, 355, 373, 376–379, 382–384, 386–390, 392–396	22.3–12	148
		22.6	136
		22.9	45
		22.10	73, 136, 453, 481–482
19.36	245		
19.37	580	22.10–13	418
19.37–38	98, 105	22.12	136
19.38	355	22.13	136, 144
20.1	418, 424	23.4	428
20.1–2	420	23.16	102
20.1–7	418	24	94, 403
20.1–13	481–482	24.2–4	392, 403
20.4	66, 77	24.3	408

24.3–4	101	29	46
24.4	100	29.5	108
24.7	401	29.14	37
24.15–16	99	29.18	572, 576, 581
24.16	57, 84, 208, 395	29.18–21	57, 100
24.30	45	29.19	633
25.1	57, 633	29.20	56, 572
25.1–6	403	29.21	46, 48, 53, 55–58
25.2	403, 407	29.22	46, 102
25.6	148	29.23	47–48, 53, 56, 61, 77, 102, 572
25.8–10	403		
25.12–18	87	29.30	47–48, 53, 56, 61, 102, 572
25.28	572		
26.1	67, 426	30.1–24	573
26.3	426	30.3	48, 53
26.6	426	30.3–4	47
26.7	67, 481–482	30.4	48, 53, 56
26.7–11	418	30.9	70
26.8	67, 77, 145	30.14–16	52
26.8–11	426	30.15	52–53, 66, 100, 393
26.9–10	418		
26.9–11	67	30.15–16	70, 74
26.10	49, 52–53, 74	30.16	48, 52–53, 55, 58, 61
26.12–14	426		
26.16	426	31.18	419
26.17–22	426	32.4	427
26.23–25	426	32.6	419
26.27	426	32.7	419
26.28–29	426	32.9–13	419
26.31	426	32.11	419
26.34–35	407–408	32.13–21	419
27	419	32.24–30	419
27.9	136	33	424
27.46	408	33.1	419
28.1	408	33.1–2	419
28.1–2	392	33.3–4	419
28.1–9	148	33.5–7	420
28.2	101	33.8–16	419
28.8–9	407	34	67, 69, 71, 83
28.14	88	34.2	51–53, 65, 67–68, 70, 73–74, 77, 138,
28.19	481–482		

	142–143, 392, 464, 481–482	38.16	44, 48, 53, 61, 74, 106, 109, 112, 116, 118, 393, 466
34.3	576		
34.4	68	38.16–18	48, 57, 61
34.5	76	38.18	48, 53, 61, 74
34.7	51–53, 65–66, 74	38.21–22	176, 178
34.13	76	38.24	74–75, 77
34.21	101	38.26	106–109, 111–113, 116, 118
34.24–25	136		
34.25	481–482	39	104, 111
34.25–27	369	39.6	110–112, 116, 118, 394
34.27	76		
34.31	75	39.7	52–53, 66, 74, 104, 116
35.22	52–53, 148, 211, 233		
		39.7–14	50
35.29	403	39.8	104, 110–112, 116, 118, 394
37.3	572		
37.13–20	148	39.10	52–53, 62–63, 66, 74, 77, 116
37.26–27	481		
37.27	37	39.12	52–53, 66, 74, 116
38 – 39	82, 99, 109, 112, 115–116, 118, 393	39.14	52–53, 64–67, 74, 77
38	108–109, 178–179, 298, 574	39.17	67, 77
		41.25	134
38.1	178	41.45	101
38.2	47–48, 53, 56, 61, 108	42.21	75
		43.7	134
38.6	108	43.19	437
38.8	47–48, 53, 55–58, 61	43.32	184, 214
		44.14–18	481
38.9	48, 53, 61	44.18	482
38.9–10	47, 149	46.31	134
38.10	298	46.34	214
38.11	109	47.30	49
38.11–14	109	49.4	148, 210, 212
38.12	48	49.8–9	481
38.13–15	179	49.10	482
38.13–27	580	49.29–33	403
38.15	75, 178, 363	50.1–13	403
38.15–18	179		

Exodus

1.11–12	68
1.16	418
1.22	418
2.22	428
2.23	422
2.23–25	434
3.2	145
3.6	145
3.7–9	434
4.25	135
10.11	209
11.3	368
11.7	191
12.19	428
15.11	160
16.3	37
18.3	428
18.25	391
20.3–23.19	631
20.5	151
20.6	152, 572
20.10	428
20.12	148, 152
20.26	123, 125
22	423, 441
22.21	400
22.21–22	429
22.21–24	68, 435
22.22	581
22.26	421
22.29	418
22.31	160, 184
23.9	429
23.12	428
24.14	437
25.10	32
25.10–15	32
25.12	30–31, 33
25.12–15	32
26.20	30
26.26	30
29.21	160
33.12	88
33.17	88
33.20–23	96
34.6–7	152
34.7	151
34.11–16	407
34.20	418
40.12–15	183

Leviticus

1–17	196
1–10	196
1.5–17	183
3.1	207
5.1	134
6.3	37
6.10	37
11–17	196
11.44	76
12.2	227
12.5	227
15.4–5	209
16.29	428
17.8	428
17.10	428
17.15	428
18–27	196
18–24	196
18	105, 125, 134, 141, 143, 197, 205, 214–215, 222, 224, 230, 232–233, 236, 238, 551, 619
18.3–5	226
18.6	18, 37, 143
18.6–7	125, 141

18.6–16	209	20.13	140–141, 195, 199–200, 217, 226, 231, 236–238, 300, 363, 516, 524, 551, 569, 619
18.6–19	143		
18.7	124, 233		
18.7–11	233		
18.7–20	234		
18.8	209, 231, 233, 236	20.14	638
18.11	209	20.16–21	234
18.14	231, 236	20.17	141–143
18.14–16	209	20.20–21	125
18.17	215, 231	20.26	155
18.17–19	209	21.1–4	483
18.19–23	229	21.9	75
18.20	209	21.13–14	210
18.21	224, 227, 231–232	23.22	429
18.22	*xxxi, xlii*, 49, 126, 141, 159, 195–209, 211–238, 275, 291, 363, 502, 516, 524, 526, 551, 569, 619	25 — 27	196
		25.23	428
		25.35	428
		25.39	422
		25.39–55	422
18.22–23	234		
18.23	49, 209, 215, 231–232	**Numbers**	
18.24–30	226		
18.25–28	150	5.12–31	210
18.26	215	5.19–20	100
18.27	215	5.20	393
18.29	215	6.2–21	179
18.30	215	9.14	428
19.10	429	14.18	151
19.15	98	15.14–16	428
19.18	570, 572, 594	19.20	76–77
19.29	157	22.29	138, 465
19.33	429	24.15	209
19.34	428	25.1	75
20	105, 141, 197, 205, 214, 238, 551	25.1–3	580
		31.17	102
20.1–3	50	31.17–18	227
20.10–14	234	31.18	102, 210
20.11	125, 231	31.35	210, 227
20.12	109, 231		

Deuteronomy

1.17	98
1.39	39
2.9	278
2.19	278
4.37	391
5.9	151
5.10	572
5.16	148, 152
6.5	570, 572, 594
7.3-4	409
7.3-5	407
7.6	391
10.18	429
10.19	572
11.13	572
12 – 26	631
14.21	428
15.9	171
17.6	483
18.5	391
18.9-12	215
21.23	76
22.5	158–159, 221, 227
22.13-29	210
22.20-21	83
22.20-24	71
22.23	635
22.28-29	69, 73
22.30	236
23	570, 619
23.1	236
23.3-6	580
23.14	160–162
23.15-16	429
23.17	158–159, 161–162, 164, 171, 173, 175–176, 182–183
23.17-18	155–156, 159, 180, 193–194
23.18	158–159, 184–187, 189–192, 194, 222
23.18-19	155
23.21	184
24.1-5	227
24.6	421
24.7	504
24.10-11	421
24.12	421
24.14	429
25.1	437
25.5	369, 371
25.5-6	580
25.5-10	47
25.16	214
27.16	149
27.20	149, 236
29.22-23	257
29.22-25	252
29.23	249, 256
32.16-17	255
32.32-33	252, 257
33.6	149
33.9	104
34.10	88, 391

Joshua

2	344–346, 457, 574
2.1	184
2.1-21	360
2.14	135
5.2-7	135
5.2-8	551
5.8	136
6	344–346
6.21	366
14.6	437

18.1	482	19—20	346, 348, 445–446, 451–452, 455–456, 460, 473, 478, 483–484
22.9	482		
22.12	482		
Judges		19	348, 351, 447, 455, 458–460, 480, 482, 619
1.1–10	482		
1.16–19	482	19.1	448, 459, 480–482
1.21	482	19.1–2	480
3.12–14	580	19.1–4	478
6.1	404	19.2	448
9	481	19.3	457, 478
9.2	37	19.3–4	482
10.6	404	19.3–9	478
10.15	412	19.4	478
11.30–39	418	19.9	457
11.39	99	19.11	448, 482
13.1	404	19.11–13	457
14.16	573	19.12	482
16	451	19.14	448
17—18	480	19.15	478
17.1	480	19.16	478, 480
17.5	481	19.17–21	482
17.6	459, 481	19.18	480–481
17.7–9	480	19.19	452, 457
17.7–13	480	19.21	478
17.8	480	19.22	171, 450–452, 457, 461–463, 465–467, 479, 482
18	480		
18.1	459, 481		
18.2	480	19.22–26	482
18.3–6	480	19.23	51
18.5–6	481	19.23–24	464, 482
18.13	480	19.24	464, 468–470, 472, 474, 476–479
18.14–20	481		
18.15–20	480	19.24–25	467, 475
18.27	480–481	19.25	138, 453–454, 461–463, 465–467, 470–471, 474–475, 479, 482
18.30	480		
18.30–31	481		
19—21	326, 470, 480, 482		
		19.26–27	466

- 709 -

19.28	457	1.15	575
19.29	136, 453, 479, 482–483	1.16–17	574, 577, 582
		1.18	575
20 – 21	449	2.2	579
20.1	449, 480–483	2.8	578
20.1–11	480	2.11	575
20.4	466	2.12	580
20.4–7	455	2.20	579
20.5	449, 464, 467–470, 474, 479, 482–483	2.22	579
		3.1	580
20.6	51	3.2	579
20.9	482	3.10	580
20.11–48	482	3.18	579
20.12–13	83	4.9–11	102
20.13	449, 483	4.11	581
20.18	481–482	4.12	580
20.21	483	4.14	580
20.23	481	4.15	576, 580–581
20.25	483	4.17	581
20.26–28	481	4.21–22	580
20.27	481		
20.35	483		
20.37	481	**1 Samuel**	
21	479		
21.2–3	481	1	482
21.4	481	1.2	113
21.6	449	1.5	573
21.8–14	482	1.5–17	113
21.10	481	1.7	114
21.11	102	1.8	573, 581
21.11–12	210, 227	1.9–12	114
21.12	102	1.10–11	114
21.14	449	1.11	113
21.19	482	1.15–16	114
21.23	449	1.15–18	114
21.25	459, 481–482	1.19	114
		1.19–20	114
Ruth		2.5	581
		6.6	138
1.3–5	575	8.5	482
1.14	575–577	9.2	115

10.17	482	31.4–5	139
10.24	481	31.8–10	139
10.26	583		
10.27	171		
11.1–11	482	**2 Samuel**	
11.4	460		
11.7	482–483	1.23	590
15.34	460	1.26	588–589
16.10–13	583	2–4	482
16.12	115	2.8–10	573
16.16-23	585	3.2	592
16.21	583, 585–587	3.2–5	573
17.38	587	3.8	192
17.43	192	3.12–13	573
18.1	583, 586	3.13–16	573
18.1–3	587, 590–591	3.16	573
18.3	586	4.4	592
18.5	587	4.11	209
18.11	482, 586	5.13–16	573
18.16	583	6.16–23	573
18.20	573, 583, 586–587	7.20	88, 391
18.22	583	9.8	191
18.26–27	573	10.4	41
18.27–28	583	10.5	41
18.28	573, 586–587	11.12	41
19.1	591	13	69
19.10	482	13.4	573
19.10–11	586	13.11	72
19.11	592	13.12	69, 464
20.4	591	13.13–17	69
20.12–16	90	13.14	69, 464
20.14–17	591	13.20	69, 465
20.17	591	13.28–29	69
20.23	90, 592	14.25	587
20.30	592	15.16	69
20.30–34	592	15.21	575
20.41	593	15.37	590
20.42	90, 102, 592	16.13	30–32
23.18	102	16.16–17	590
31	138	16.20–22	465
31.4	138, 471, 482	16.21–22	69

16.22	149	8.13	191
19.27	412	8.18	404
20.1–22	482	9.36	191
20.3	69, 465	23.7	159–160, 168, 183
24.24	186, 191		

1 Chronicles

22.2	428
29.15	428

1 Kings

1.1	114
1.2	115
1.3–4	115
1.4	114
1.6	115
1.15	115
2.17	115
2.21	115
2.22	115
10.28	186
10.29	191
11.1	572
11.2	576
11.6	404
13.33	404
14.22–24	404
14.24	162
15.12	161–162
15.26	404
16.7	404
21.2	186
22.46	168
22.52	404

Nehemiah

9.7	392

Esther

3.13	366
9.4	368

Job

1.3	368
1.21	41
3.19	98
5.1	161
22.6	421
24.3	422
24.7	40
28.15	186
31.32	429
34.18	171
36.14	158, 168, 170

2 Kings

3.2	404
4.1–7	422
4.8–17	326
5	574
5.27	577

Psalms

3.7	171

11.6	256–257	4.9–10	572, 588
25.7	571	4.12	572
25.10	571	5.1	572
71.4	171	5.1–2	588
83.6–8	279	7.6	588
83.8	279	7.12	572
94.6	429		
136	571		
141.6	588	**Isaiah**	
144.3	93		
146.9	429	1.2	255
		1.9	267
		1.10	254
Proverbs		1.10–17	257–259, 401
		1.15–16	254
2.10	588	1.21–23	254
3.32	171	2.8	255
8.8	171	3.8–9	252
9.17	588	3.9	257
13.20	590	7.14	*xlii*
17.16	186	10.29	460
18.24	575	13.19	250, 257
23.34	204	13.20–21	249
24.25	588	13.21	249
27.26	186	20.2–4	40
		48.14	572
		52.5	562
Song of Songs		56.1	260
		56.3–8	260
1.2	572	56.7	160
1.4	572	56.10	184
1.7	572	56.10–11	192
1.9	572	60.22	368
1.13–14	572	61.1–2	621
1.15	572		
2.2	572		
2.3	572	**Jeremiah**	
2.5	572		
3.1–5	572	1.5	88
3.10	572	3.1	75
4.1	572	5.7	255

7.6	429	16.6–7	41
9.24	88	16.22	41, 215
22.3	429	16.25	261
22.15–16	79, 89	16.46–48	261
23.14	254–255, 257	16.46–50	257
31.3	572	16.48–50	435
38.19	77	16.48–51	253
39.5–7	139	16.49	285
42.1	364, 368	16.49–50	250, 261, 401
42.8	364, 368	16.50	256
44.15	366	16.52	261
44.19–20	366	16.53–57	257
44.24	366	16.56	250
49.14–18	250	16.56–57	241, 260
49.15	368	16.62	88
49.17	249	18	151
49.17–18	257	18.7	262
49.18	249	18.12	262
50.29	250	18.16	262
50.31	251	22.7	429
50.38	253	22.29	262
50.39	249	32.19	588
50.39–40	257		
50.40	249, 251		

Daniel

7.5	30

Lamentations

1.18	255
1.20	255
3.42	255
4.6	257
4.21–22	261

Hosea

2.12	186, 191
2.20	88, 101
4.14	176–177, 180, 182, 194
7.5	30
8	90
8.2	89
8.4	90
11.8	256–257
14.4	572

Ezekiel

5.9	256
16	255, 260–261, 292, 353
16.1	215

Amos

3.2	88
4.11	249, 257

Obadiah

1.2	368

Jonah

3.1–10	574

Micah

1.7	186, 191

Habakkuk

2.15	145

Zephaniah

2.9	249, 257
2.9–10	251

SECOND TESTAMENT

Matthew

1.22	*xlii*
1.24	101
5.11–12	515
5.28	487
5.44	594
8.5–13	516
10.15	267
10.37	596
11.8	496–497
11.23–24	267
15.19	487
21.17	601
22.37–39	594
26.6	601

Mark

1.11	596
7.21–22	488
10.2–12	5
10.21	595
11.1	601
12.30–31	570
14.44–45	596

Luke

1.34	99
4.18–19	621
6.27–28	594
6.38	597
7.45	596
10.10–12	344

10.12	267	13.23–30	602
11.7	502	13.24	602
16.19–25	601	13.25	597–599
17.28–32	279	13.34–35	595
17.29–31	267	13.35	609
17.32	279	13.37	609
18.13	597	14.15	595
22.47	596	15.9	594
22.48	596	15.9–10	595
		15.12	595
		16.27	596
John		18.15–16	602
		18.17	609
1.40–43	613	18.25–27	609
3.15–16	604	19.12	596
3.16	571, 594–595	19.26	607
3.19	595	19.26–27	603
3.35	594	19.35	603
4.1–42	574	20.2	602, 607
5.20	594	20.3–8	602
5.25	594, 603	20.4–5	603
5.28–29	603	20.8	603
10.10	17	21	610, 613, 615
10.17	594	21.1–22	607
11–12	601	21.7	603, 607
11	601, 603–604	21.15	608–609
11.3	596, 601, 604–607	21.15–16	612
11.5	604–605, 607	21.15–17	607–609, 611
11.36	601, 604–605, 607	21.16	608–610
11.43	603	21.17	608–610, 612
11.44	601	21.19	613
11.44–45	601	21.20	607
12.1	601	21.20–21	602
12.9	601	21.20–23	603
12.17	601	21.21	603
12.25	596	21.22	613
12.32	513	21.22–23	603
13	597–599, 602, 615	21.24	603
13.23	597–599, 606–607		
13.23–25	599		

Acts

2	517
10	517
13.50	515
15	518
15.20	518
15.29	518
16.37	517
22.25–28	517
25.10–12	517

Romans

1–3	562
1	524–526, 537–538, 548, 551, 553, 557, 559, 570, 619
1.1	557, 561
1.1–6	527
1.1–15	526
1.3–6	563
1.6	561
1.7	551
1.7–17	527
1.14–17	563
1.15	561
1.16–17	526, 562
1.18	548, 554
1.18–20	527
1.18–32	526, 551–553, 560–565
1.19	554
1.20	554
1.20–21	553
1.21	527, 554
1.21–29	556
1.22	553–554
1.23	189, 553–554
1.24	555
1.24–25	553
1.24–27	523
1.25	555
1.26	226, 275, 499, 524, 538–547, 551, 553, 555
1.26–27	274, 300, 521–523, 525, 527, 531–536, 541, 550–552, 557, 564–565
1.27	189, 487, 524, 537, 540–542, 546–547, 549, 555, 558, 569, 619
1.28	555
1.28–32	300, 537
1.29	549, 556
1.29–31	488, 548
1.30	556
1.30–31	527
1.31	556
1.32	552, 556, 560
2	527, 560–562, 564
2.1	561
2.3	561
2.5	561
2.11	562
2.14	542
2.16	562
2.17–23	562
2.18	562
2.19	562
2.20	562
2.21	562–563
2.24	562
2.25	512, 562
2.25–3.2	551
2.25–29	518
2.27	526, 542, 562
3.1–2	551
3.5	552

3.10–20	552	5–7	492
4.1	551	5–6	515
5.12	*xxxv*	5	233, 548
5.12–13	548	5.1–2	515
5.20–21	548	5.1–13	232
6.1–2	548	5.10–11	488
6.6–7	548	6	18, 619
6.19	552	6.1–8	514
7.1	551	6.9	488–515, 518–519, 549
7.2	547		
7.18	273	6.9–10	514
7.25	557	6.10	506
8.1	521	6.12–13	557
9	267	6.12–20	514
9.29	267	6.15–20	548
11.13	551–552	6.16	38
11.14	38	6.18	487
11.24	274, 499, 526, 543–545	7	539
		7.1	539
12.3–18	552	7.1–2	233
12.9	595	7.2	539
12.10	596	7.2–3	547
13.8	595	7.9	487
13.9	594	8.1–8	557
13.13	502	11.8–9	6
14.1–19	552	11.14	526
15.5–21	552	13	594
15.7–13	524	13.4	595
15.15	552, 563	13.6	595
15.16	552	13.7–8	595
15.17–19	563	15.33	549
16	524, 551		
16.17	563		
16.17–19	552	**2 Corinthians**	
		11.3	39
1 Corinthians		12.20–21	488
		12.21	548
1.11–12	557		
3.3–4	557		
4.12	515		

Galatians

2.15	526
3.23–29	551
5.1–6	516
5.2–6	518
5.2–14	551
5.10–12	559
5.14	594
5.19	548
5.19–21	488

Ephesians

4.17–19	556
5.3	548
5.3–5	488
5.5	300
5.25	595
6.10–17	515

Philippians

3.2	192

Colossians

4.16	540

1 Timothy

1	486
1.8–10	489
1.9	512
1.10	189, 300, 488, 504–514, 518–519

2 Timothy

1.2	597

Titus

3.15	596

James

4.4	596

2 Peter

2.1–3	277
2.4	300
2.6	300
2.6–10	277
2.7–8	279
2.9–10	300
2.10	277
2.11–14	278
2.13–14	300
2.14	278
2.17–22	278
3.3–4	278
3.15–16	550

3 John (verses)

2	596
5	596
11	596

Jude (verses)

4	270, 278
6	270–271
6–7	300
6–15	276
7	270–274, 619
8	270, 278
10	278
10–13	270
10–18	276
12	278
16	270, 278
18–19	270, 278

Revelation

11	267
11.8	267
21.5	569
21.8	488
22.15	158, 189, 192

APOCRYPHA AND PSEUDEPIGRAPHA

3 Maccabees
264

4 Esdras
264–265

5 Esdras
264–265

Assumption of Moses
270, 277, 283

Enoch, Book of
269–270, 277, 283

Jubilees, Book of
283, 331, 333

Sirach (Ecclesiasticus)
264, 279

Testament of Asher
284

Testament of Benjamin
284

Testament of Levi
284

Testament of Moses
270

Testament of Naphtali
284

Testaments of the Twelve Patriarchs
283

Wisdom, Book of (Wisdom of Solomon)
264–267, 276, 279–280, 553–558, 562, 564-565, 619

EARLY CHRISTIAN & JEWISH SOURCES

1 Clement
319

Acts of John
506

Apocalypse of Paul
291, 319

Apostolic Constitutions
217, 219, 291

Genesis Rabbah
316, 332–334

Gospel of Mary
600

Pirke de Rabbi Eliezer
320

Targum Neofiti
407

OTHER SOURCES

Hammurabi, Laws of
630–641

Hittite Laws
90, 232

Qur'an, The
335, 625–628

Sibylline Oracles
505

NAME INDEX

Aaron, 183
Abel, 86–87, 117
Abimelech (of Gerar), 66–67, 75, 145, 412, 418, 425–26
Abimelech (son of Gideon), 481
Abishag, 114–15
Abraham (Abram), 45–46, 58, 70, 73, 88, 90, 93–97, 99, 101, 106, 117, 135–36, 142, 144–45, 148, 153, 242–44, 260, 265, 278–80, 285, 306, 316, 319–21, 328, 331–35, 337, 341, 344, 349, 352–53, 356, 379, 391–92, 394–95, 400–408, 412, 417–18, 420, 424–28, 431–32, 435–36, 440–41, 453, 466, 478–79, 485, 572, 576, 578, 580, 601, 631
Absalom, 69, 148, 587
Achilles, *xxx*
Adam, *xxi, xxxv*, 4, 7, 9, 12–14, 17, 24, 33–34, 36, 38, 41–42, 82, 84–87, 114, 117, 128–29, 150, 153, 641
Admah, 252, 256–57
Adonijah, 115
Africa, 150, 269
Alexander the Great, *xxxiii*, 263, 377
Alexandria, *xxxiii*, 216, 269, 285–86, 289–90, 553, 558
American Standard Version, 156, 496

Ammon, 104–05, 245, 249, 251, 278–79, 331, 406, 478–79
Amnon, 69, 573
Amplified Version, 156
Anatolia, 558
Ancient Near East, 57, 93, 158–59, 185, 220, 232, 261, 263, 294, 584, 631
Antinoopolis, 517
Antinous, 516–17
Aphrodite, 558
Asherah, 160, 184
Asia Minor, 558–59
Astarte, 185
Assyria, 221, 264
Athens, 447, 511
Attis, 559

Babel, 343, 401
Babylonia, 101, 185, 318, 629–30, 633–34, 638, 640–41
Bacchanalia, 559–60
Bacchus, 559, 564
Basel, 304
Baucis and Philemon, 325–26
Beersheba, 426
Belgium, 312
Beloved Disciple, the, 597, 599–605, 607, 614–15
Ben-Ammi, 104
Benjamin (tribe), 448–49, 458, 460, 478–79, 482–83, 485, 583
Bera, King, 98, 243, 368–69, 405, 435

Bethany, 601, 604
Bethel, 481–82
Bethlehem, 436, 446–48, 450, 452, 478, 480, 485, 574–75, 579–80, 582–83
Bilhah, 47, 51, 148, 211, 233, 447
Bishops Bible, 218, 495, 507, 530, 543, 555, 612
Boaz, 436, 575–76, 578–80, 582, 634
Bolivia, 311
Bologna, 304
Book of Gomorrah, 298–300, 306
Bruno of Cologne, 307

Cain, 8, 11–12, 82, 85–87, 117
Canaan (son of Ham), 123, 127, 129, 133, 137, 149–52, 154, 242, 334
Canaan (Palestine), 105, 156, 159, 193–94, 226, 228, 336, 341–42, 357, 401–3, 419, 427, 630
Caribbean, 310–12
Castile, 310
Central America, 311
Christianity, xxxiv, xlii, xlv, 13, 18, 42, 266, 277, 288–89, 300, 381, 383, 385, 451, 487, 515, 517, 626–27
Columbus, Christopher, 310
Common English Bible, 182
Complete Bible, 358
Complete Jewish Bible, 155
Corinth, 232, 558
Covenant Code, 430, 441, 631
Cybele, 558, 564
Cyprus, 185

Dan, 480, 600

David, 68–69, 88, 90, 114–15, 149, 407, 412, 446, 464, 479, 481–83, 485, 573, 575, 580, 583–93, 614–15
Dead Sea, 265
Denmark, 312
Dinah, 51, 65–73, 75–76, 83, 142, 408, 464, 576
Douay-Rheims Version, 495–96, 500, 507, 528, 555

Easy-to-Read Version, 489
Ecuador, 311
Eden, Garden of, 5, 7, 10, 13–14, 16, 30, 37, 39–40, 83, 128, 136
Edom, 250, 261, 279
Edward I, 309
Egypt, 49, 68, 82, 110, 124, 134, 140, 150, 214, 252, 341, 400, 402, 418, 429, 434–35, 441, 556, 633
Einayim, 48, 178
Eliezer, 99–100, 320, 601
Elimelech, 580
Elisha, 326, 577
Elkanah, 114, 573, 581
Elohīm, xxi, 11, 20–23, 25, 41, 255
Encyclopaedia Judaica, 317
England, 309, 387
Enkidu, xxx
Ephraim, 257, 447–48, 453, 478, 480, 483
Esau, 148, 407, 419–20, 572
Europe, 305, 310, 314, 357
Eve, xxi, xxxv, 7, 9–10, 12–14, 17, 39, 41–42, 84–87, 114, 117, 128–29, 153, 641

Ferdinand, King, 310
France, 312, 628

Ganymede, 493
Gehazi, 577
Geneva Bible, 218, 387, 495, 500, 507–8, 530, 543, 612
Gerar, 67, 75, 418, 424, 426
Germany, *xxvi*, 307
Gesenius Hebrew Grammar, 212
Gibeah, *xliv*, 346–47, 351, 445–54, 456–60, 464–65, 467–68, 475, 477–78, 480–85, 583
Gideon, 481
Gilgamesh, *xxx*
Goliath, 585, 587
Greece, *xxx*, 246, 314, 380–81, 384, 510, 593

Hadrian, 516
Hagar, 46, 58–59, 68, 70, 72, 144, 349, 412
Ham, 123–29, 132–35, 137–38, 140–1, 143–54
Hamor, 25
Hannah, 113–14, 573, 581
Hekate, 26
Henry VIII, 309
Hermes, 326
Hirah, 178–79
Human Rights Watch, 312

India, 312
Isaac, 67, 73, 75, 96, 100, 136, 144–45, 148, 349, 403, 407, 417–18, 420, 426–27, 453, 572
Isabella, Queen, 310
Ishmael, 70, 72–73, 136, 144, 349, 403, 407
Islam, 625–28
Israel (Jacob), 581
Israel (people), 14, 20, 41, 68, 73, 75, 88, 94, 101, 105, 115, 139, 153, 155–57, 166, 175, 181–83, 210, 215, 224, 251, 257, 279, 339–41, 349, 408, 412, 421, 424, 428–29, 436, 441, 446, 449, 453, 459–60, 478, 480–3, 556, 573, 580, 583–85, 630–1, 641
Italy, 241, 307, 318
Ittai, 575

Jabesh-gilead, 478, 482
Jacob, 46–47, 49, 51–52, 56–57, 65, 67, 70, 73, 76, 136, 148, 178, 211, 369, 403, 407, 419–20, 424, 427, 447, 464, 572, 576, 581
James I, 387
Janus, 25–26
Japheth, 127, 129, 137, 147, 150–52, 154
J. B. Phillips New Testament, 612
Jehoiachim, 89
Jephthah's daughter, 99, 418
Jebus, 448, 478, 482
Jericho, 135, 345–46, 360, 363, 456–57
Jerusalem, 27, 69, 169, 183, 252, 254, 259–61, 267, 518
Jesus Christ, *xxxiii*, 5, 99, 267–69, 279, 344, 486, 497, 516–17, 521, 557, 562–63, 566, 570–71, 594–615
Jezaniah, 368
Johanan, 368
John (son of Zebedee), 601
Jonathan, 10, 412, 429, 583–93, 614
Jordan, 105, 245
Joseph (son of Jacob), 49–50, 62, 64–67, 75, 82, 104, 110–11,

116, 124, 134, 148, 394, 419–20, 572
Joseph (husband of Mary), 101
Joshua, 135, 345, 360
Joshua (Rabbi), 33
Josiah, 89
Judah (son of Jacob), 47–48, 57, 61, 69, 74–75, 82, 106–9, 111, 115, 118, 142, 149, 178–80, 298, 393, 407, 481–82, 580
Judah (tribe/territory), 89, 158, 252, 262, 447, 478, 482, 485
Judaism, *xxxv–xxxvi*, 42, 223, 277, 285, 310, 314, 318, 544
Jude (brother of Jesus), 268
Judea, *xxxiii*, 139

Keturah, 403
King James Version, 218, 387–88, 495, 500, 507–8, 513, 530–31, 543, 555, 612
Knox Bible, 190

Laban, 46, 57, 572
Lamech, 127
Lazarus (Luke 16), 601
Lazarus of Bethany, 601–7
Leah, 47, 51–52, 56, 66–67, 70, 73, 148, 419–20, 572, 581, 631
Levi, 75, 284, 447, 478
Lot, 49–50, 72, 97–101, 103–5, 118, 144–45, 242–45, 262, 264–66, 278–81, 285–87, 305–7, 316–17, 319–22, 324, 328–35, 337, 343–44, 346–47, 349–50, 352, 356, 358–60, 363–64, 366, 370, 372–73, 379, 383, 390–95, 397, 400–417, 420–24, 427–29, 431, 433–38, 440–41, 475, 478–79, 625–27, 635

Lot's daughters, 49–50, 99–101, 103–4, 106, 117–18, 126, 142, 245, 278, 316, 320, 322, 328–37, 343, 349, 369–70, 372, 381, 389–91, 393, 395, 398, 400, 405–06, 409–10, 412, 417, 420–24, 433, 440, 475, 478–79, 540, 580, 635
Lot's wife, 145, 245, 290, 292, 337–38, 406–7, 423, 478

Mahalath, 407
Mamre, 478
Marduk, 185
Martha, 596, 601, 604, 606
Mary (mother of Jesus), 99, 101, 603, 607
Mary Magdalene, 600, 603
Mary of Bethany, 596, 601, 604, 606
Massachusetts, 312
Mediterranean, *xxxiii*, 294, 457, 487, 557–58
Melchizedek, 424
Mephibosheth, 412
Mesopotamia, 158, 185, 401, 403, 406, 630–31
Methuselah, 87
Mexico, 311
Micah (Judges 17–18), 480–81
Michal, 573, 583, 586–87, 590
Middle Ages, *xxxviii*, *xlvi*, 10, 19, 34, 126, 135, 156, 217, 225, 262, 296, 301–3, 309–10, 313–14, 319, 324, 354, 494, 512, 570, 617, 620
Mizpah, 449, 453, 458, 478, 482
Moab, 104–5, 245, 249, 251, 278–79, 331, 406, 436, 478–79, 574, 576, 580, 582
Molekh, 224, 227, 231–232

Moses, 88, 90, 135, 145, 306, 391, 407, 516

Naaman, 574
Naomi, 573–82, 591, 614–15
Nazareth, 571
Nebuchadrezzar, 139
New Life Version, 190
Nigeria, 312
Nineveh, 574
Noah, *xliv*, 45, 87, 123–32, 134–38, 140–1, 143, 145–47, 149–54, 208, 242, 334, 363, 393, 618
North America, 150, 341
Nueva Versión Internacional, 182

Obed, 579–81
Onan, 47, 55, 57, 149, 298

Palestine, 12, 67, 184, 313, 341, 366, 630
Paltiel, 573
Papua New Guinea, 312
Paris, 304
Patroclus, *xxx*
Paul, *xxxv, xliv*, 6, 18–19, 38–39, 189, 192, 226, 232–33, 267, 274, 445, 486–91, 495–96, 498–99, 501–6, 508, 511, 513–19, 521–29, 531, 535–37, 539–45, 548–53, 556–66, 570, 594–97, 619–20
Pelotit, 317
Penninah, 573
Pentateuch, 19, 37, 83, 125, 154, 196, 218, 221, 223, 304, 318, 391
Persia, 263, 627
Peru, 311
Peshitta, 269

Pharaoh, 49, 134, 402, 418
Philemon and Baucis, 325–26
Portugal, 312
Potiphar, 49, 110–11, 393
Potiphar's wife, 50, 62, 64–67, 104, 110
Procrustes, 316
Promised Land, 580

Rachel, 46–47, 52, 56–57, 66, 73, 419–20, 447, 572, 576, 581, 631
Rahab, 135, 345, 360, 363, 574
Ramah, 478
Rebekah, 67, 99–100, 136, 145, 403, 418, 420, 427, 572
Reuben (son of Jacob), 51-52, 73, 148–49, 211, 233
Reuben (tribe), 149
Revised Version, 508
Rome (city), 269, 304, 308, 527, 551, 556, 558–65, 620
Rome (empire), *xxxiii–xxxiv*, 158, 294, 314, 344, 384, 492, 504, 515–17, 524

Samaria, 253, 261, 292
Samson, 451, 573
Samuel, 114, 459, 481, 581, 583
Sarah (Sarai), 46, 58–59, 68, 70, 96, 106, 144, 243–44, 349, 401–3, 406–7, 412, 418, 420, 424, 427, 466, 478, 631
Saul, 115, 138–39, 446, 457, 459–60, 471, 479, 481–83, 485, 573, 583–87, 590, 592, 614–15
Septuagint (LXX), *xxxiv–xxxv*, 6, 18, 33, 38–39, 42, 172, 216–17, 232, 263, 266, 285, 287–90, 304, 353, 359,

377–86, 388, 397–99, 410–11, 413–16, 439–40, 502, 515, 552–53, 617, 629
Servetus, Michael, 305
Seth, 86–87, 117, 153
Seville, 310, 627
Shechem (city), 67, 75, 369, 408
Shechem (son of Hamor), 51, 65–70, 72–73, 76, 83, 142, 464, 576
Shelah, 47–48, 109
Shem, 127, 129, 137, 147, 150–54
Shiloh, 482, 581
Shoah (Holocaust), 332
Shunem, 326
Simeon, 75
Sodom, *xxxvi*, 49–50, 72, 91, 93–95, 97–98, 100, 103–4, 111, 117–19, 142, 144–45, 156, 241–48, 250, 253, 255–68, 270, 272–73, 276–96, 299, 301–08, 311, 313–14, 316–27, 329–38, 340–360, 363–70, 372–73, 376, 378, 382–83, 386–89, 391, 393, 395, 397–98, 400–1, 404–5, 407–12, 415–17, 421–23, 425, 427–32, 434–37, 439–41, 446, 451, 456–58, 460, 475, 477–78, 512, 578, 625–26, 635
Sodom and Gomorrah, *xxxvii–xxxviii, xliii–xliv*, 50, 82, 91–93, 96–97, 103, 105–6, 111, 117–18, 126, 189, 195, 217, 239, 241–43, 247–52, 254, 256, 258–60, 262–64, 267, 270–72, 275–78, 280–84, 286, 288, 291–92, 294, 298–300, 302–4, 308–9, 313–14, 316, 318, 322, 325–26, 328–30, 337, 343–47, 351, 355–56,

358–59, 369, 380–81, 383, 385–86, 392–93, 396–97, 399, 403, 416, 430, 435, 445, 452, 456, 484–85, 511, 569, 619, 625, 641
Solomon, 115, 572, 576
Spain, 304, 310, 312, 325, 627
Sweden, 312
Switzerland, 387
Syria, 158

Tamar (Gen. 38), 47–48, 55, 57, 61, 69, 74–75, 82, 106–9, 111, 115, 118, 149, 179, 363, 574, 580
Tamar (daughter of David), 68–69, 464, 473
Ten Commandments, *xxxvii*, 148
Tertullus, 412–13
The Da Vinci Code, 600
The Message, 191, 197–99, 201, 219, 521
Tiberias, Sea of, 607
Timnah, 48
Torah, 196, 223, 226, 237–38, 315, 318, 516
Troy, 493
Twenty-First Century King James Version, 156

Uganda, 312
United States, *xxxvii*, 312

Vulgate, 6, 34, 38–39, 42, 169–71, 175, 177, 188, 192–93, 217–18, 290, 298, 304, 381–82, 384–88, 397, 399, 410–11, 413–16, 440, 451, 469, 493–95, 506–7, 520, 527–28, 542, 612, 617, 629

Wales, 309
Worldwide English New Testament, 489, 522, 612

Y<small>HWH</small>, 20, 41, 45-46, 85, 88-90, 93-99, 101, 111, 113-14, 117, 125, 136, 144-45, 151-52, 155-57, 162, 184, 208, 215, 224, 243-44, 248-56, 259-61, 266, 278, 280, 335, 337-38, 340, 352-53, 379, 391-92, 394, 401-9, 412, 417, 420, 423, 430-35, 437, 441, 466, 481, 571, 578, 580-1, 591-93

Zeboiim, 252, 256-57
Zedekiah, 139
Zeus, 326, 344, 493
Zilpah, 70
Zipporah, 135
Zoar, 478

AUTHOR INDEX

Classical Authors

Aeschines, 493
Aristotle, 302, 491
Demosthenes, 411
Epictetus, 493
Heraclides Ponticus, 380
Herodotus, 146, 380, 411
Homer, *xliii*
Isocrates, 411
Josephus, 284, 287, 295, 319, 450–51, 511–12, 541
Julius Caesar, 383
Livy, 559–60
Menander, 380
Ovid, 325, 383
Philo, 18, 216, 284–87, 289, 291, 320–23, 329, 344, 488, 490, 503, 511, 541
Plato, 17, 286, 380, 491, 493
Plutarch, 493
Strabo, 493
Xenophon, 380, 411

Later Authors

Alfonso X *El Sabio*, 310
Alighieri, Dante, 303–4
Ambrose of Milan, 292, 320
Ammianus Marcellinus, 412–13
Aquinas, Thomas, 6, 296, 301–3, 308, 523
Athanasius of Alexandria, 451

Augustine of Hippo, 6, 293, 295, 382, 521, 524, 538

Bahya ben Asher, 93
Basil, 321
Boccaccio, Giovanni, 304
Boniface, 296

Calvin, John, 6, 305
Casas, Bartolomé de Las, 311
Cisneros, Francisco Jiménez de, 304
Clement of Alexandria, 289, 524, 538
Coverdale, Miles, 218, 495, 506, 530, 542

Damian, Peter, 217, 219, 282, 296, 298–300, 303, 306, 308, 313, 321
Dante Alighieri, 303–4

Ephrem the Syrian, 333, 337
Erasmus of Rotterdam, 304
Eusebius, 269

Fernández de Oviedo, Gonzalo, 311

Garcilaso de la Vega, *El Inca*, 311
Gregory of Nyssa, 292
Gregory the Great, 295, 297

Hincmar of Rheims, 297

Isho'dad of Merv, 294

Jerome, 34, 39, 169, 175, 217, 222, 290, 292–93, 295, 382–87, 398, 411–14, 416, 439, 469, 494, 506, 508, 512, 527–30, 542, 612
John Cassian, 293
John Chrysostom, 6, 292, 319, 328, 524
Justinian, 294, 310

Las Casas, Bartolomé de, 311
Luther, Martin, *xl*, 6, 269, 305–8, 321–22, 385–87, 399, 521

Maimonides, *xxxix*
Menahem ben Solomon, 318
Muhammad, 626

Nahmanides, 124, 450
Nicholas of Lyra, 320, 451

Origen, 290–91, 321

Paulinus of Nola, 319
Paulus Orosius, 293
Peter Cantor, 217, 300–301, 627
Peter Damian, 217, 219, 282, 296, 298–300, 303, 306, 308, 313, 321
Peter of Poitiers, 217
Pierre le Chantre, 217, 300–301, 627

Ramban, 124, 450
Rashi, *xxxix*, 124, 332–33, 450

Samuel bar Nahman (Ramban), 33–34
Servetus, Michael (Miguel Servet), 305
Shakespeare, William, 246, 387

Shlomo Yitzhaki (Rashi), *xxxix*, 124, 332–33, 450

Tertullian, 84, 100, 290
Theodore bar Koni, 294
Thomas Aquinas, 6, 296, 301–3, 308, 523
Tyndale, William, 218, 387, 495, 500, 506–8, 530, 542, 612

Wyclif(fe), John, 217–18, 387, 494–95, 500, 506, 508, 528–30, 542, 612

Modern Authors

Ackroyd, P. R., 269
Adamo, David Tuesday, 150
Adams, J. N., 383
Alison, James, 486, 538, 541, 553, 557–58, 561
Alonso Schökel, Luis, 658
Alpert, Rebecca T., 195, 202, 214, 220, 231, 235–36, 570, 582
Alter, Robert, 7–8, 19, 24, 28, 45–46, 57, 67–68, 82, 91, 97, 125–26, 132, 144, 148–49, 190, 212, 246, 330, 354, 410, 419, 426–27, 480–81, 508, 576, 580, 631
Althaus-Reid, Marcella, 336–38, 341
Amit, Yairah, 47, 460
Anderson, Bernhard W., 631

André-Salvini, Béatrice, 630, 632–33, 636
Ashton, John, 607
Ashworth, Timothy, 488, 496

Bal, Mieke, 453–54
Barth, Karl, 15, 521
Benkert, Karl-Maria, *xxvi*, 314
Bledstein, Adrien Janis, 11
Boehringer, Letha, 297
Bohache, Thomas, 486, 516
Boswell, John, 81, 139, 172, 296–97, 305, 344–46, 412, 511, 541, 627
Botterwerk, G. Johannes, 82
Bovati, Pietro, 95, 355, 430–31, 437
Boyarin, Daniel, 205, 217, 221–23, 226–27, 329, 410, 446
Boyce, Richard N., 355, 430
Brayford, Susan, 266, 289
Brenner, Athalya, 45, 49–50, 66, 80, 125, 142, 423, 448
Brettler, Marc Zvi, 459
Briggs, C. A., 34
Brinkschroeder, Michael, 387
Brodie, Thomas L., 8, 19, 40, 45, 83, 95, 125–28, 150, 179, 244, 246, 329, 334, 337, 340, 354, 401, 403–5, 417, 419–20, 424–25
Brooten, Bernadette J., 486, 493, 504, 511, 538, 540–41, 543, 551, 574
Brown, Dan, 600
Brown, Peter, *xxxi*, *xxxv*, 288
Browning, W. R. F., 20, 41, 82, 156, 242, 247, 553
Bruckner, James K., 93, 95, 355, 430–31, 436–37

Brueggemann, Walter, 19–20, 148, 244, 578
Buber, Martin, 11, 90

Cadwallader, Alan, 232–33, 498, 511, 515–16
Caird, George B., 377, 417
Calvin, John, 6, 305
Campbell, Douglas, 553, 557, 562–63
Carden, Michael, 17, 25, 30, 73, 81, 126, 150, 217, 246, 270–71, 278, 283–87, 290–95, 301, 314–16, 319–21, 328–29, 331–34, 336–38, 342, 346–47, 354, 405, 407–8, 410, 445–46, 450–51, 456–57, 461
Cargas, Harry James, 338
Carmichael, Calum, 25, 73, 84–86, 141, 146, 172, 179, 354, 408, 523, 574, 580
Carr, David M., 15–16, 30, 39, 83, 354, 487
Chouraqui, André, 91
Comstock, Gary David, 354, 574, 583, 591
Coogan, Michael D., 269
Cook, S. A., 261, 633, 635, 638
Cornwall, Susannah, 26
Cotterell, Peter, *xxxviii*, *xxxix*, 38, 67, 92, 148, 179, 202, 229, 395, 629
Countryman, L. William, 127, 215–16, 233, 269–70, 275–76, 354
Cranfield, C. E. B., 549, 562
Cranny-Francis, Anne, 491

Danker, Frederick W., 497, 499–502, 504, 512, 514, 520, 549, 596–97

Davidson, James, 286
Delaney, Carol, 418
Dijk-Hemmes, Fokkelien van, 403, 418
Douglas, Mary, 125, 141, 195-96, 202, 208, 212, 231, 237, 553, 557, 562-63
Dover, Kenneth, 139
Doyle, Brian, 81, 334, 351-53, 355, 402, 405
Driver, G. R., 34, 101, 630-36, 638-39
Duncan, Celena M., 574, 582
Duran, Khalid, 625, 627

Eco, Umberto, 445
Edwards, Chilperic, 632-34, 636, 639
Eghwubare, Erivwierho Francis, 150
Evans, C. F., 269
Exum, Cheryl, 447, 454-55

Fewell, Donna Nolan, 447
Fields, Weston W., 68, 100, 115, 126, 214, 260, 262, 330, 346, 354, 367, 370, 408, 410, 418, 428-29, 431, 434-36, 450, 457-58, 461, 466, 575
Flood, John L., 385
Fontaine, Carole R., 342, 469
Fox, Everett, 7, 20, 30, 41, 46, 82, 91, 185, 196, 206, 246, 354, 410, 446
Freud, Sigmund, 332
Friends, A Group of, 309

Gaca, Kathy L., *xxxi*
Gagnon, Robert A. J., 3, 5, 33, 81-82, 125-27, 140, 144, 157-59, 184, 192, 195, 202, 214, 219-20, 222, 226, 229, 232, 326-27, 354, 356, 446, 461, 486-87, 490-91, 502-3, 506, 516, 523-24, 538, 543, 551, 574, 583-84
García-Estébanez, Emilio, 6
Goethe, Johann Wolfgang von, *xl*
Gordon, Cyrus H., 8, 46, 81, 97, 124-25, 184, 583, 631
Gorsline, Robin Hawley, 269
Goss, Robert E., 296, 329, 331, 446, 452, 486, 488, 492, 514, 570, 574, 600-602
Graetz, Naomi, 421
Green, Tony, 671
Greenberg, Steven, 25, 30, 124, 126, 159, 210, 214, 222-23, 230, 237, 312, 315-18, 329, 331, 347, 354, 410, 446, 574, 583
Grelot, Pierre, 21, 36
Groom, Susan Anne, 20, 91, 96, 192, 202, 212-13, 225, 231, 380, 395, 397, 447
Grosvenor, Mary, 501, 504, 514, 543, 549, 553
Guest, Deryn, 156, 160, 183-85, 354, 446, 452, 486, 574

Haddox, Susan E., *xxix*
Haines-Eitzen, Kim, 500
Hamilton, Victor P., 11, 30, 34, 36-37, 41, 49, 57, 66, 82, 95, 97, 126, 140, 149, 151-52, 212, 330, 354, 376, 410
Hammershaimb, Erling, 82, 283-84
Hanks, Thomas D., 68, 125, 192, 262, 267-70, 279, 329, 339, 429, 464, 486, 489, 491-92,

504, 516, 521, 523–25, 541, 543, 550–51, 556, 560, 570–71, 597, 599, 601
Hargreaves, Cecil, 382
Harrill, J. Albert, 492, 504–5, 519, 557
Harrison, Brenda, 671
Heacock, Anthony, 81–82, 185, 195, 232, 301, 329, 354, 380, 410, 446, 461, 583–85, 593
Heard, Christopher R., 329, 333, 354
Helminiak, Daniel A., 81, 159, 184, 210, 214, 227, 329, 354, 410, 446, 486, 488, 491, 499, 503, 525–26, 543, 551, 553, 574, 583, 592
Hewitt, Joseph W., 380
Holloway, Richard, 289, 406
Horner, Tom, 330
Horsley, Richard A., 340, 342
Huegel, Karin, 628
Huffmon, Herbert B., 89–90, 630
Hugenberger, Gordon Paul, 38, 81, 83–85, 102, 354, 447

Ihimaera, Witi, 325
Innes, Jeremy, 671
Isherwood, Lisa, 675

Jasper, David, *xxxviii*, *xliii*
Jenni, Ernst, 82, 632
Jennings, Theodore W., 126, 149, 203, 216, 223, 226, 329, 446, 486, 574, 583, 585, 592, 601
Jensen, Hans Jørgen Lundager, 325–26, 446
Johansson, Warren, 282
Johns, C. H. W., 633, 636
Johnston, Sarah Iles, 26

Johnstone, William, 93
Jones-Warsaw, Koala, 455–56
Jordan, Mark D., *xxix*, *xxx*, *xxxiv*, *xxxviii*, *xlv*, 215, 261, 275, 292–93, 295–98, 301–3, 309, 345–46, 355, 381, 538
Jung, C. G., 26

Kader, Samuel, 138, 486, 558, 574, 583
Karras, Ruth Mazo, 241, 296–97, 301–2, 305
Kertbeny, Károly Mária, *xxvi*, 314
Kinnaman, David, *xxxvii*
King, L. W., 634
Kirkby, Joan, 491
Korsak, Mary Phil, 13, 23, 25, 29–30, 36, 90–91, 93, 127, 132
Koschaker, Paul, 640
Kraus, C. Norman, 4

Liddell, Henry G., 380, 493, 501, 520, 547
Lings, K. Renato, *xxx*, 197, 203–4, 208–12, 215, 230–32, 234, 355, 446, 460–61
Lipka, Hilary B., *xxix*, 49, 66, 68, 70, 73–75, 127, 210, 214–15, 329, 354
Loader, William, 18, 25, 38, 230, 266, 285, 378
Loades, Ann, 332, 342
Long, Lynne, *xxxiv*, *xl*, *xlii*, 247, 305, 355, 382, 387–88, 494–95
Long, Ronald E., *xxx*
Lundager Jensen, Hans Jørgen, 325–26, 446
Lyons, Gabe, *xxxvii*
Lyons, William John, 330

Macy, Howard R., 617
Magonet, Jonathan, *xxxv*, 10, 40–41, 83, 90, 237, 318, 429
Malul, Meir, 80
Martin, Dale B., 492, 498, 500, 503, 505–6, 543, 553, 557, 560
Mather, Maurice W., 380
McCarson, Bonnie, 26
McCleary, Rollan, 511, 558
McGrath, Alister E., 681
McKeown, James, 23, 30, 87, 149, 329–30, 354, 410
McKinlay, Judith, 339
McNeill, John J., 81, 344, 354
Mein, Andrew, 255
Meir, Amira, 80, 93, 247, 355, 392
Metzger, Bruce M., *xxxiv, xxxvi*, 269, 377, 382, 387, 507–8
Meyers, Carol, 6, 12, 99, 340–41, 407, 630
Miles, John C., 101, 630–36, 638–39
Milgrom, Jacob, 123, 141, 150, 210–11, 215, 224–26, 229–32, 234–35, 318, 329
Miller, James E., *xxxii, xlv*, 24, 129, 141, 224, 229, 231, 276
Milne, Pamela J., 6
Mitchel, Larry A., 80, 428, 572
Molina, Fernanda, 310–11
Mollenkott, Virginia Ramey, 354
Monti, Joseph, *xxv*
Moore, Gareth, 16–17, 212, 216, 220, 486, 491, 499, 511, 514, 525, 543
Moxnes, Halvor, 559

Nickelsburg, George W. E., 271, 277

Nielsen, Kirsten, 179, 315, 574–76, 580
Nissinen, Martti, *xxvi, xxvii*, 4, 38, 81–82, 125, 144, 157, 159–60, 185, 210, 214, 216, 222, 255, 285, 287, 316, 318, 330, 354, 410, 446, 461, 486, 511, 541, 543, 551, 574, 583, 585, 591, 593, 600–601

Olyan, Saul, 203, 205, 210, 214–15, 217, 220–23, 232
Oppenheim, A. Leo, 636
Osburn, Carroll D., 268–69

Paget, J. N. B. Carleton, 285
Pardes, Ilana, 12
Parker, Simon B., 90
Patzia, A. G., 269
Peleg, Yaron, 90, 359, 401
Perdue, Leo G., 150, 334, 455
Peterson, Eugene, 191, 197, 199, 521
Pett, Peter, 185
Pirson, Ron, 81, 406
Pomeroy, Sarah B., 447, 560
Proust, Marcel, 313–14
Provan, Iain, 90

Rad, Gerhard von, 422
Rajak, Tessa, 286
Ramírez-Kidd, José E., 434
Rashkow, Ilona N., 124, 126, 140, 146, 149, 330, 332–34
Reif, Stefan C., 237, 315, 318
Rendsburg, Gary A., 8, 125, 184, 583, 631
Ringe, Sharon H., 339
Ringgren, Helmer, 82
Roesel, Martin, 381
Rogerson, J. W., 269, 550

Rosen, Wilhelm von, 314
Rosenzweig, Franz, 90
Roth, Martha T., 633, 636

Sáenz-Badillos, Ángel, *xxv, xxxiii, xxxix*, 258, 263–64, 629–31
Safren, Jonathan D., 243
Scanzoni, Letha Dawson, 354
Scheil, V., 633, 636
Schenker, Adrian, 197, 224, 229
Schneider, Tammi J., 41, 330, 354, 410, 447, 455, 460–61, 466
Schottroff, Luise, 11
Schulz-Flügel, Eva, 289
Scott, Robert, 380, 493, 501, 520, 547
Seddik, Youssef, 628
Sharon, Diane M., 13, 339
Sharpe, Keith, 202, 223, 486, 575, 583, 602
Sheridan, Mark, 286
Simkins, Ronald A., 14
Smith, Don, 247
Spina, Frank Anthony, 96, 109, 360, 403, 573, 580–81
Stavropoulos, Pam, 491
Steiner, George, 508
Stemberger, Günter, 289
Stewart, David T., 126–27, 140, 144, 203, 207, 210–11, 214–15, 227, 230, 232–33
Stone, Ken, 4, 15, 82, 156–57, 160, 184, 329, 354, 461, 583, 593
Stuart, Elizabeth, *xxxi, xxxv, xxxvii*, 6, 429, 570, 574–75, 583, 588, 592
Sturge, Mark, 335
Sugirtharajah, R. S., 338–40, 342

Svartvik, Jesper, 6, 80, 150
Swidler, Arlene, 691

Terrien, Samuel, 9, 30, 33, 39
Teubal, Savina J., 403, 407, 418, 630
Thatcher, Adrian, *xxxv*, 6, 83, 90, 100–101, 447
Thomas, David Winton, 185
Thomas, Robert L., *xli, xlii–xliii*
Thuesen, Peter J., *xlii*
Townsley, Jeramy, 506, 511, 559
Trible, Phyllis, 330, 342, 354, 452–56, 580
Turner, Max, *xxxviii, xxxix*, 38, 67, 92, 148, 179, 202, 229, 395, 629

Unamuno, Miguel de, 80

Vanggaard, Thorkil, *xxx*, 226, 305, 328–29, 517
Vasey, Michael, 14, 410
Vermes, Geza, 269

Walsh, Jerome T., 210, 222–23
Waring, Wendy, *xxix*, 491
Warner, Megan, 331, 355, 391, 437
Warrior, Robert Allen, 342
Wechsler, Harlan J., 106, 318–19
Weingreen, J., 21, 92–93, 95, 377
Wenham, Gordon, 10, 18, 37, 40, 46, 68, 97, 124, 131, 147, 149–51, 405
West, Mona, 486, 570, 574, 581–82
Westermann, Claus, 82, 632
Whitelam, Keith W., *xliii*
Winter, Miriam Therese, 330

Wolde, Ellen van, 93, 111, 242, 355–56, 423, 437
Wright, David P., 631, 636

Zerwick, Max, 501, 504, 514, 543, 549, 553